CLYMER®

MERCURY

OUTBOARD SHOP MANUAL
3-275 HP • 1990-1993

The World's Finest Publisher of Mechanical How-To Manuals

INTERTEC PUBLISHING

P.O. Box 12901, Overland Park, Kansas 66282-2901

Copyright ©1993 Intertec Publishing

FIRST EDITION
First Printing July, 1993
Second Printing October, 1995
Third Printing June, 1999
Fourth Printing July, 2001

Printed in U.S.A.

CLYMER and colophon are registered trademarks of Intertec Publishing.

ISBN: 0-89287-568-2

Library of Congress: 92-74933

Tools shown in Chapter Two courtesy of Thorsen Tool, Dallas, Texas. Test equipment shown in Chapter Two courtesy of Dixson, Inc., Grand Junction, Colorado.

COVER: Photo courtesy of Sea Ray Boats, Inc., a Brunswick company.

PRODUCTION: Shirley Renicker.

The following books and guides are published by Intertec Publishing.

CLYMER SHOP MANUALS
Boat Motors and Drives
Motorcycles and ATVs
Snowmobiles
Personal Watercraft

ABOS/INTERTEC/CLYMER BLUE BOOKS AND TRADE-IN GUIDES
Recreational Vehicles
Outdoor Power Equipment
Agricultural Tractors
Lawn and Garden Tractors
Motorcycles and ATVs
Snowmobiles and Personal Watercraft
Boats and Motors

AIRCRAFT BLUEBOOK-PRICE DIGEST
Airplanes
Helicopters

AC-U-KWIK DIRECTORIES
The Corporate Pilot's Airport/FBO Directory
International Manager's Edition
Jet Book

I&T SHOP SERVICE MANUALS
Tractors

INTERTEC SERVICE MANUALS
Snowmobiles
Outdoor Power Equipment
Personal Watercraft
Gasoline and Diesel Engines
Recreational Vehicles
Boat Motors and Drives
Motorcycles
Lawn and Garden Tractors

Contents

CHAPTER FIVE
TIMING, SYNCHRONIZING AND ADJUSTING **113**

CHAPTER SIX
FUEL SYSTEM **157**

CHAPTER SEVEN
IGNITION AND ELECTRICAL SYSTEMS. **236**

CHAPTER EIGHT
POWER HEAD. **269**

CHATPER NINE
LOWER UNIT GEAR HOUSING. **388**

Quick Reference Data

TUNE-UP SPECIFICATIONS (3 AND 3.3 HP)

Cylinders	1
Bore	1.85 in.
Stroke	1.69 in.
Displacement	4.6 cu. in.
Fuel:oil ratio	50:1
Idle speed (in gear)	900-1000 rpm
Full throttle speed	4500-5500
Compression pressure	90 psi min.
Firing order	Single cylinder
Ignition type	
3 hp	Magneto breaker point
3.3 hp	Capacitor discharge (CDI)
Spark plug	NGK BPR6HS or
	Champion RL87YC
Spark plug gap	0.040 in.
Breaker point gap	0.012-0.016 in.
Ignition timing	Not adjustable
Gearcase capacity	3 oz. (88.7 mL)

TUNE-UP SPECIFICATIONS (4 AND 5 HP)

Cylinders	1
Bore	2.165 in.
Stroke	1.693 in.
Displacement	6.2 cu. in.
Fuel:oil ratio	50:1
Idle speed (in gear)	850 rpm
Full throttle speed	4500-5500 rpm
Compression pressure	90 psi min.
Firing order	Single cylinder
Ignition type	Capacitor discharge (CDI)
Spark plug	NGK BP7HS-10 or
	Champion L82YC
Spark plug gap	0.040 in.
Idle timing	5° BTDC
Maximum timing advance	28°-32° BTDC
Gearcase capacity	6.6 oz. (195.2 mL)

TUNE-UP SPECIFICATIONS (8, 9.9 AND 15 HP)

Cylinders	2
Bore	
8, 9.9 hp	2.125 in.
15 hp	2.375 in.
Stroke	1.77 in.
Displacement	
8, 9.9 hp	12.8 cu. in.
15 hp	16.0 cu. in.
Fuel:oil ratio	50:1

(continued)

TUNE-UP SPECIFICATIONS (8, 9.9 AND 15 HP) (continued)

Idle speed (in forward gear)	
8, 9.9 hp	600-700 rpm[1]
15 hp	700-800[1]
Full throttle speed	
8 hp	4500-5000 rpm
9.9, 15 hp	5000-6000 rpm
Ignition type	Capacitor discharge (CDI)
Firing order	Alternate
Spark plug	
Standard ignition coils	
8 hp	Champion L82YC
9.9, 15 hp	NGK BP8HS-15
Spark plug gap	
8 hp	0.040 in.
9.9, 15 hp	0.060 in.
High energy ignition coils	NGK BUHW (surface gap)
Spark plug gap	Not adjustable
Idle timing	6° BTDC
Maximum timing advance	36° BTDC
Gear case capacity	6.5 oz. (192.2 mL)

1. On models without an idle speed adjustment screw, the carburetors are factory calibrated to maintain idle speed of 600-700 rpm in forward gear.

TUNE-UP SPECIFICATIONS (20 AND 25 HP)

Cylinders	2
Bore	2.56 in.
Stroke	2.38 in.
Displacement	24.4 cu. in.
Fuel:oil ratio[1]	50:1
Idle speed (in forward gear)	700-800 rpm
Full throttle speed	
20 hp	4500-5500
25 hp	5000-6000
Ignition type	Capacitor discharge (CDI)
Firing order	Alternate
Spark plug	NGK BUHW or Champion L76V
Spark plug gap	Not adjustable
Pickup timing	0°-2° BTDC
Full throttle timing	25° BTDC
Gearcase capacity	7.6 oz. (225 mL)

1. Some models may be equipped with an optional oil injection system.

TUNE-UP SPECIFICATIONS (40 HP)

Cylinders	Inline 4
Bore	2.565 in.
Stroke	2.125 in.
Displacement	43.9 cu. in.
Fuel:oil ratio[1]	50:1
Idle speed (in forward gear)	600-700 rpm

(continued)

TUNE-UP SPECIFICATIONS (40 HP) (continued)

Full throttle speed	5000-5500 rpm
Ignition type	Capacitor discharge (CDI)
Firing order	1-3-2-4
Spark plug	NGK BUHW-2
Spark plug gap	Surface gap
Primary pickup timing	2° ATDC-2° BTDC
Idle timing	3°-10° ATDC
Secondary pickup timing	30° BTDC @ cranking speed
Maximum timing advance	30° BTDC @ 5500 rpm
Gearcase capacity	12.5 oz. (370 mL)

1. Electric start models are equipped with oil injection system. Oil injection is optional on manual start models.

TUNE-UP SPECIFICATIONS (50 AND 60 HP MODELS PRIOR TO SERIAL NO. D000750)

Cylinders	Inline 3
Bore	2.875 in.
Stroke	2.563 in.
Displacement	49.8 cu. in.
Fuel:oil ratio	Automatic oil injection
Idle speed (in forward gear)	600-700 rpm
Full throttle speed	5300-5800 rpm
Ignition type	Capacitor discharge (CDI)
Firing order	1-2-3
Spark plug	AC V40FFM or Champion L76V
Plug gap	Surface gap
Primary pickup timing	2° BTDC-2° ATDC
Maximum timing advance	33° BTDC @ 5500 rpm
Gearcase capacity	12.5 oz. (370 mL)

TUNE-UP SPECIFICATIONS (50 AND 60 HP SERIAL NO. D000750-ON)

Cylinders	Inline 3
Bore	
Serial No. D000750-D047798	2.9540 in.
Serial No. D047799-on	2.9553 in.
Stroke	2.520 in.
Displacement	51.8 cu. in.
Fuel:oil ratio	Automatic oil injection
Idle speed (in forward gear)	650-700 rpm
Full throttle speed	5000-5500 rpm
Ignition type	Capacitor discharge (CDI)
Firing order	1-3-2
Spark plug	NGK BU8H
Spark plug gap	Surface gap
Idle timing	2°-6° ATDC
Maximum timing advance	24° BTDC @ cranking speed 22° BTDC @ 5000 rpm
Gearcase capacity	11.5 oz. (340 mL)

TUNE-UP SPECIFICATIONS (75 AND 90 HP)

Cylinders	Inline 3
Bore	3.375 in.
Stroke	2.65 in.
Displacement	71.1 cu. in
Fuel:oil ratio	Automatic oil injection
Idle speed (in forward gear)	625-725 rpm
Full throttle speed	
75 hp	4750-5250 rpm
90 hp	5000-5500 rpm
Ignition type	Capacitor discharge (CDI)
Firing order	1-3-2
Spark plug	NGK BUHW-2, AC-V40FFK or Champion L78V
Spark plug gap	Surface gap
Idle timing	2°-4° BTDC
Maximum timing advance	28° BTDC @ cranking speed
	26° BTDC @ 5000 rpm
Gearcase capacity	22.5 oz. (665.4 mL)

TUNE-UP SPECIFICATIONS (100 AND 115 HP)

Cylinders	Inline 4
Bore	3.375 in.
Stroke	2.930 in.
Displacement	105 cu. in.
Fuel:oil ratio	Automatic oil injection
Idle speed (in forward gear)	625-725 rpm
Full throttle speed	4750-5250 rpm
Ignition type	Capacitor discharge (CDI)
Firing order	1-3-2-4
Spark plug	NGK BP8H-N
Spark plug gap	0.040 in.
Idle timing	2°-4° BTDC
Maximum timing advance	25° BTDC @ cranking speed
	23° BTDC @ 3000 rpm
Gearcase capacity	22.5 oz. (665.4 mL)

TUNE-UP SPECIFICATIONS (135 AND 150 HP)

Cylinders	V6
Bore	3.125 in.
Stroke	2.650 in.
Displacement	121.9 cu. in.
Fuel:oil ratio	Automatic oil injection
Idle speed (in forward gear)	600-700 rpm
Full throttle speed	5000-5600 rpm
Ignition type	Capacitor discharge (CDI)
Firing order	1-2-3-4-5-6
Spark plug	NGK BU8H
Spark plug gap	Surface gap
Idle/pickup timing	
Prior to serial No. D082000	2°-9° ATDC
Serial No. D082000-on	0°-9° ATDC
Maximum timing advance	19° BTDC @ cranking speed
	17° BTDC @ wide-open throttle
Gearcase capacity	22.5 oz. (665.4 mL)

TUNE-UP SPECIFICATIONS (1990-1991 150XR4 AND 175 HP; 1991 175XRi; 1990 200 HP AND 200 XRi

Cylinders	V6
Bore	3.375 in.
Stroke	2.650 in.
Displacement	142 cu. in.
Fuel:oil ratio	Automatic oil injection
Idle speed (in forward gear)	
150XR4	625-700 rpm
175, 200 hp	600-700 rpm
175XRi, 200XRi	600-675 rpm
Full throttle speed	
150XR4	5000-5600 rpm
175 hp	5300-5600 rpm
175XRi	5200-5700 rpm
200 hp	5300-5800 rpm
200XRi	5400-5900 rpm
Ignition type	Capacitor discharge (CDI)
Firing order	1-2-3-4-5-6
Spark plug	
200XRi	NGK BUZ8H
All others	NGK BU8H
Spark plug gap	Surface gap
Pickup timing	
150XR4	
Prior to serial No. C247591	4°-6° ATDC
After serial No. C247590	2°-9° ATDC
175 hp	2°-9° ATDC
175XRi	
Prior to serial No. C221500	10° ATDC
After serial No. C221499	4° ATDC
200 hp	2°-7° ATDC
200XRi	9° ATDC
Idle timing	
150XR4	
Prior to serial No. C247591	3°-11° ATDC
After serial No. C247590	2°-9° ATDC
175 hp	2°-9° ATDC
175XRi	
Prior to serial No. C221500	10° ATDC
After serial No. C221499	4° ATDC
200 hp	2°-7° ATDC
200XRi	9° ATDC
Maximum timing advance[1]	
150XR4	
Prior to serial No. C247591	22° BTDC @ cranking speed 26° BTDC @ wide-open throttle
Serial No. C247591-C254931	19° BTDC @ cranking speed 26° BTDC @ wide-open throttle
After serial No. C254931	19° BTDC @ cranking speed 20° BTDC @ wide-open throttle
175 hp	22° BTDC @ cranking speed 20° BTDC @ wide-open throttle

(continued)

TUNE-UP SPECIFICATIONS (1990-1991 150XR4 AND 175 HP; 1991 175XRi; 1990 200 HP AND 200 XRi (continued)

Maximum timing advance[1] (continued)	
175XRi	
Prior to serial No. D007414	22° BTDC @ cranking speed
After serial No. D007413	21° BTDC @ cranking speed
	20° BTDC @ 3000 rpm
	25° BTDC @ 5,100-5,600 rpm
200 hp	22° BTDC @ cranking speed
	26° BTDC @ wide-open throttle
200XRi	19° BTDC @ cranking speed-
	2,500 rpm
	25° BTDC @ 3500 rpm
Gearcase capacity	
150XR4	21 oz. (621 mL)
175-200 hp	24.25 oz. (717.1 mL)

1. Maximum ignition timing must be retarded 3° from listed specification on models (except 150XR4) with Idle Stabilizer Shift Kit (part No. 87-81428A1) installed as an accessory.

TUNE-UP SPECIFICATIONS (1992 AND 1993 150 XR6, 175 HP AND 175XRi; 1993 150XRi; 1991-1993 200 HP AND 200 XRi)

Cylinders	V6
Bore	3.500 in.
Stroke	2.650 in.
Displacement	153 cu. in.
Fuel:oil ratio	Automatic oil injection
Idle speed (in forward gear)	
150XR6	625-625 rpm
All others	600-700 rpm
Full throttle speed	
150XR6	5000-5600 rpm
200XRi	5000-5800 rpm
All others	5000-5600 rpm
Ignition type	Capacitor discharge (CDI)
Firing order	1-2-3-4-5-6
Spark plug	NGK BU8H
Spark plug gap	Surface gap
Idle timing	
All models prior to serial No. D082000	2°-9° ATDC
All models serial No. D082000-on	0°-9° ATDC
Pickup timing	
All models prior to serial No. D082000	2°-9° ATDC
All models serial No.	
D082000-D181999	0°-9° ATDC
150XRi, 175XRi, 200XRi serial No.	
D182000-on	4° ATDC
All others serial No. D182000-on	0°-9° ATDC
Maximum timing advance	
200 hp and 200XRi	
Serial No. C291520-D077246[1]	22° BTDC @ cranking speed
	20° BTDC @ wide-open throttle

(continued)

TUNE-UP SPECIFICATIONS (1992 AND 1993 150 XR6, 175 HP AND 175XRi; 1993 150XRi; 1991-1993 200 HP AND 200 XRi) (continued)

Maximum timing advance (continued)	
200 hp and 200XRi (continued)	
After serial No. D077247-D0819992	21° BTDC @ cranking speed
	25° BTDC @ wide-open throttle
200 hp serial No. D082000-on	21° BTDC @ cranking speed
	26° BTDC @ wide-open throttle
200XRi	
Serial No. D082000-on	20° BTDC @ cranking speed
	26° BTDC @ wide-open throttle
150XR6, 150XRi, 175 hp, 175XRi	
Serial No. D082000-on	19° BTDC @ cranking speed
	20° BTDC @ wide-open throttle
Gearcase capacity	
150XR6	21.0 oz. (621 mL)
All others	22.5 oz. (665.4 mL)

1. Equipped with idle stabilizer module.
2. Equipped with idle stabilizer/spark advance module.

TUNE-UP SPECIFICATIONS (250 AND 275 HP)

Cylinders	V6
Bore	3.74 in.
Stroke	3.14 in.
Displacement	207 cu. in.
Fuel:oil ratio	Automatic oil injection
Idle speed (in forward gear)	600-700 rpm
Full throttle speed	5000-5500 rpm
Ignition type	Capacitor discharge (CDI)
Firing order	1-2-3-4-5-6
Spark plug	NGK BU8H
Spark plug gap	Surface gap
Idle/pickup timing	
Prior to serial No. D082000	7° ATDC
Serial No. D082000-on	5° ATDC
Maximum timing advance	22° BTDC @ cranking speed
	20° BTDC @ wide-open throttle
Gearcase capacity	29 oz. (857.5 mL)

Chapter One

General Information

This detailed, comprehensive manual contains complete information on maintenance, tune-up, repair and overhaul. Hundreds of photos and drawings guide you through every step-by-step procedure.

Troubleshooting, tune-up, maintenance and repair are not difficult if you know what tools and equipment to use and what to do. Anyone not afraid to get their hands dirty, of average intelligence and with some mechanical ability, can perform most of the procedures in this book. See Chapter Two for more information on tools and techniques.

A shop manual is a reference. You want to be able to find information fast. Clymer books are designed with you in mind. All chapters are thumb tabbed and important items are indexed at the end of the book. All procedures, tables, photos, etc., in this manual assume that the reader may be working on the machine or using this manual for the first time.

Keep this book handy in your tool box. It will help you to better understand how your machine runs, lower repair and maintenance costs and generally increase your enjoyment of your marine equipment.

MANUAL ORGANIZATION

This chapter provides general information useful to marine owners and mechanics.

Chapter Two discusses the tools and techniques for preventive maintenance, troubleshooting and repair.

Chapter Three describes typical equipment problems and provides logical troubleshooting procedures.

Following chapters describe specific systems, providing disassembly, repair, assembly and adjustment procedures in simple step-by-step form. Specifications concerning a specific system are included at the end of the appropriate chapter.

NOTES, CAUTIONS AND WARNINGS

The terms NOTE, CAUTION and WARNING have specific meanings in this manual. A NOTE provides additional information to make a step or procedure easier or clearer. Disregarding a NOTE could cause inconvenience, but would not cause damage or personal injury.

A CAUTION emphasizes areas where equipment damage could result. Disregarding a CAUTION could cause permanent mechanical damage; however, personal injury is unlikely.

A WARNING emphasizes areas where personal injury or even death could result from negligence. Mechanical damage may also occur. WARNINGS *are to be taken seriously.* In some cases, serious injury or death has resulted from disregarding similar warnings.

TORQUE SPECIFICATIONS

Torque specifications throughout this manual are given in foot-pounds (ft.-lb.) and either Newton meters (N.m) or meter-kilograms (mkg). Newton meters are being adopted in place of meter-kilograms in accordance with the International Modernized Metric System. Existing torque wrenches calibrated in meter-kilograms can be used by performing a simple conversion: move the decimal point one place to the right. For example, 4.7 mkg = 47 N.m. This conversion is accurate enough for mechanics' use even though the exact mathematical conversion is 3.5 mkg = 34.3 N.m.

ENGINE OPERATION

All marine engines, whether 2- or 4-stroke, gasoline or diesel, operate on the Otto cycle of intake, compression, power and exhaust phases.

4-stroke Cycle

A 4-stroke engine requires two crankshaft revolutions (4 strokes of the piston) to complete the Otto cycle. **Figure 1** shows gasoline 4-stroke engine operation. **Figure 2** shows diesel 4-stroke engine operation.

2-stroke Cycle

A 2-stroke engine requires only 1 crankshaft revolution (2 strokes of the piston) to complete the Otto cycle. **Figure 3** shows gasoline 2-stroke engine operation. Although diesel 2-strokes exist, they are not commonly used in light marine applications.

FASTENERS

The material and design of the various fasteners used on marine equipment are not arrived at by chance or accident. Fastener design determines the type of tool required to work with the fastener. Fastener material is carefully selected to decrease the possibility of physical failure or corrosion. See *Galvanic Corrosion* in this chapter for more information on marine materials.

Threads

Nuts, bolts and screws are manufactured in a wide range of thread patterns. To join a nut and bolt, the diameter of the bolt and the diameter of the hole in the nut must be the same. It is just as important that the threads on both be properly matched.

The best way to determine if the threads on two fasteners are matched is to turn the nut on the bolt (or the bolt into the threaded hole in a piece of equipment) with fingers only. Be sure both pieces are clean. If much force is required, check the thread condition on each fastener. If the thread condition is good but the fasteners jam, the threads are not compatible.

Four important specifications describe every thread:

   a. Diameter.
   b. Threads per inch.
   c. Thread pattern.
   d. Thread direction.

Figure 4 shows the first two specifications. Thread pattern is more subtle. Italian and British

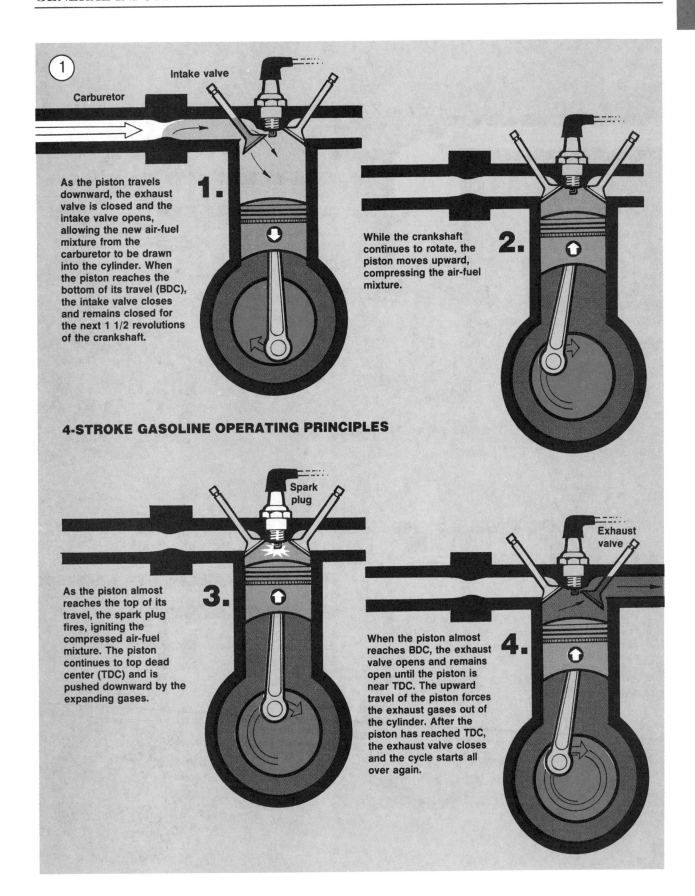

① **Carburetor** **Intake valve**

1. As the piston travels downward, the exhaust valve is closed and the intake valve opens, allowing the new air-fuel mixture from the carburetor to be drawn into the cylinder. When the piston reaches the bottom of its travel (BDC), the intake valve closes and remains closed for the next 1 1/2 revolutions of the crankshaft.

2. While the crankshaft continues to rotate, the piston moves upward, compressing the air-fuel mixture.

4-STROKE GASOLINE OPERATING PRINCIPLES

Spark plug

3. As the piston almost reaches the top of its travel, the spark plug fires, igniting the compressed air-fuel mixture. The piston continues to top dead center (TDC) and is pushed downward by the expanding gases.

Exhaust valve

4. When the piston almost reaches BDC, the exhaust valve opens and remains open until the piston is near TDC. The upward travel of the piston forces the exhaust gases out of the cylinder. After the piston has reached TDC, the exhaust valve closes and the cycle starts all over again.

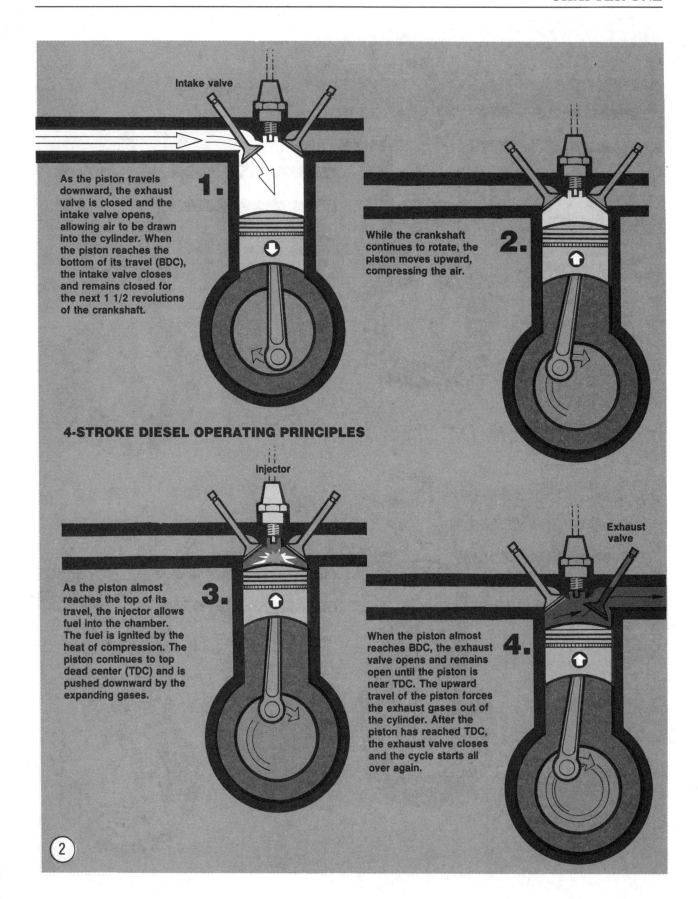

Intake valve

1. As the piston travels downward, the exhaust valve is closed and the intake valve opens, allowing air to be drawn into the cylinder. When the piston reaches the bottom of its travel (BDC), the intake valve closes and remains closed for the next 1 1/2 revolutions of the crankshaft.

2. While the crankshaft continues to rotate, the piston moves upward, compressing the air.

4-STROKE DIESEL OPERATING PRINCIPLES

Injector

3. As the piston almost reaches the top of its travel, the injector allows fuel into the chamber. The fuel is ignited by the heat of compression. The piston continues to top dead center (TDC) and is pushed downward by the expanding gases.

Exhaust valve

4. When the piston almost reaches BDC, the exhaust valve opens and remains open until the piston is near TDC. The upward travel of the piston forces the exhaust gases out of the cylinder. After the piston has reached TDC, the exhaust valve closes and the cycle starts all over again.

As the piston travels downward, it uncovers the exhaust port (A) allowing the exhaust gases to leave the cylinder. A fresh air-fuel charge, which has been compressed slightly in the crankcase, enters the cylinder through the transfer port (B). Since this charge enters under pressure, it also helps to push out the exhaust gases.

While the crankshaft continues to rotate, the piston moves upward, covering the transfer (B) and exhaust (A) ports. The piston compresses the new air-fuel mixture and creates a low-pressure area in the crankcase at the same time. As the piston continues to travel, it uncovers the intake port (C). A fresh air-fuel charge from the carburetor (D) is drawn into the crankcase through the intake port.

2-STROKE OPERATING PRINCIPLES

As the piston almost reaches the top of its travel, the spark plug fires, igniting the compressed air-fuel mixture. The piston continues to top dead center (TDC) and is pushed downward by the expanding gases.

As the piston travels down, the exhaust gases leave the cylinder and the complete cycle starts all over again.

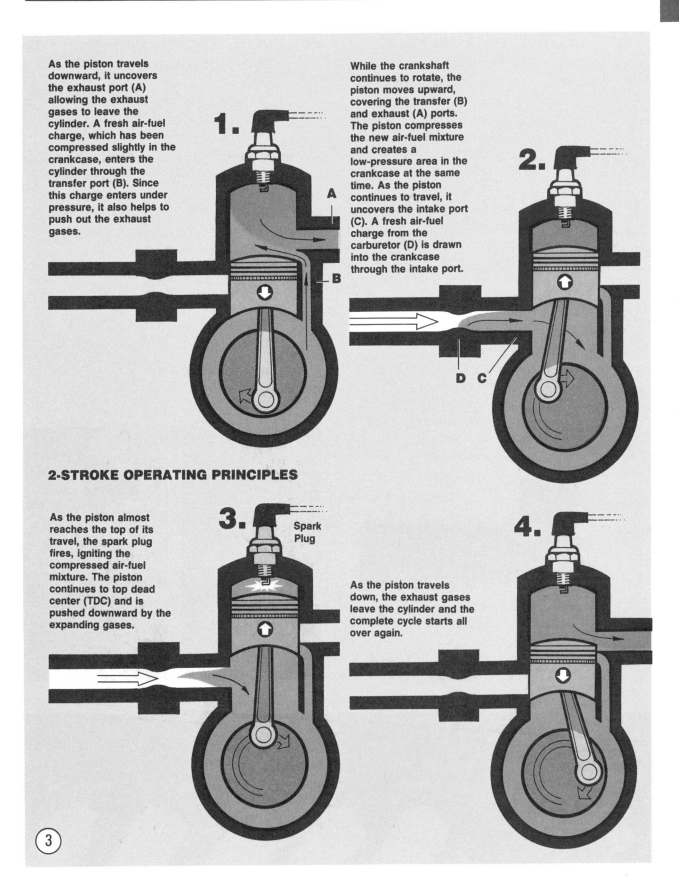

standards exist, but the most commonly used by marine equipment manufacturers are American standard and metric standard. The threads are cut differently as shown in **Figure 5**.

Most threads are cut so that the fastener must be turned clockwise to tighten it. These are called right-hand threads. Some fasteners have left-hand threads; they must be turned counterclockwise to be tightened. Left-hand threads are used in locations where normal rotation of the equipment would tend to loosen a right-hand threaded fastener.

Machine Screws

There are many different types of machine screws. **Figure 6** shows a number of screw heads requiring different types of turning tools (see Chapter Two for detailed information). Heads

are also designed to protrude above the metal (round) or to be slightly recessed in the metal (flat) (**Figure 7**).

Bolts

Commonly called bolts, the technical name for these fasteners is cap screw. They are normally described by diameter, threads per inch and length. For example, 1/4-20 × 1 indicates a bolt 1/4 in. in diameter with 20 threads per inch, 1 in. long. The measurement across two flats on the head of the bolt indicates the proper wrench size to be used.

Nuts

Nuts are manufactured in a variety of types and sizes. Most are hexagonal (6-sided) and fit

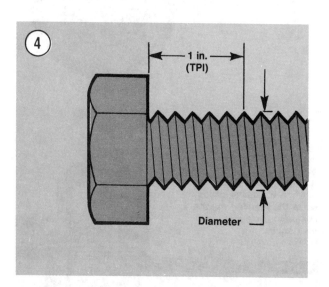

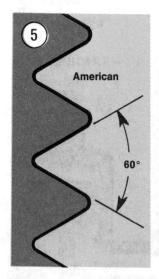

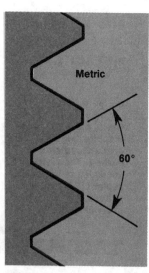

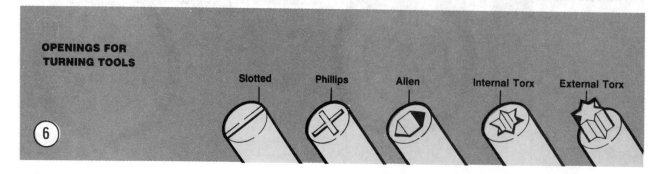

on bolts, screws and studs with the same diameter and threads per inch.

Figure 8 shows several types of nuts. The common nut is usually used with a lockwasher. Self-locking nuts have a nylon insert that prevents the nut from loosening; no lockwasher is required. Wing nuts are designed for fast removal by hand. Wing nuts are used for convenience in non-critical locations.

To indicate the size of a nut, manufacturers specify the diameter of the opening and the threads per inch. This is similar to bolt specification, but without the length dimension. The measurement across two flats on the nut indicates the proper wrench size to be used.

Washers

There are two basic types of washers: flat washers and lockwashers. Flat washers are simple discs with a hole to fit a screw or bolt. Lockwashers are designed to prevent a fastener from working loose due to vibration, expansion and contraction. **Figure 9** shows several types of lockwashers. Note that flat washers are often used between a lockwasher and a fastener to provide a smooth bearing surface. This allows the fastener to be turned easily with a tool.

Cotter Pins

Cotter pins (**Figure 10**) are used to secure special kinds of fasteners. The threaded stud

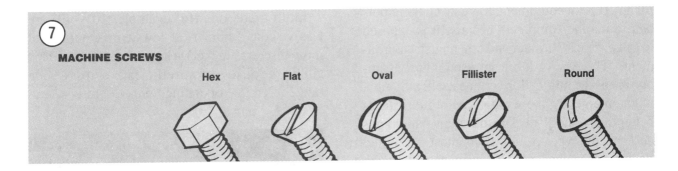

⑦

MACHINE SCREWS

| Hex | Flat | Oval | Fillister | Round |

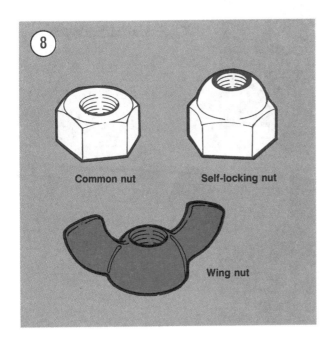

⑧

Common nut　　Self-locking nut

Wing nut

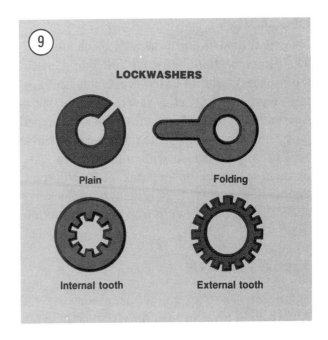

⑨

LOCKWASHERS

Plain　　Folding

Internal tooth　　External tooth

must have a hole in it; the nut or nut lock piece has projections that the cotter pin fits between. This type of nut is called a "Castellated nut." Cotter pins should not be reused after removal.

Snap Rings

Snap rings can be of an internal or external design. They are used to retain items on shafts (external type) or within tubes (internal type). Snap rings can be reused if they are not distorted during removal. In some applications, snap rings of varying thickness can be selected to control the end play of parts assemblies.

LUBRICANTS

Periodic lubrication ensures long service life for any type of equipment. It is especially important to marine equipment because it is exposed to salt or brackish water and other harsh environments. The *type* of lubricant used is just as important as the lubrication service itself; although, in an emergency, the wrong type of lubricant is better than none at all. The following paragraphs describe the types of lubricants most often used on marine equipment. Be sure to follow the equipment manufacturer's recommendations for lubricant types.

Generally, all liquid lubricants are called "oil." They may be mineral-based (including petroleum bases), natural-based (vegetable and animal bases), synthetic-based or emulsions (mixtures). "Grease" is an oil which is thickened with a metallic "soap." The resulting material is then usually enhanced with anticorrosion, antioxidant and extreme pressure (EP) additives. Grease is often classified by the type of thickener added; lithium and calcium soap are commonly used.

4-stroke Engine Oil

Oil for 4-stroke engines is graded by the American Petroleum Institute (API) and the So-

ciety of Automotive Engineers (SAE) in several categories. Oil containers display these ratings on the top or label (**Figure 11**).

API oil grade is indicated by letters, oils for gasoline engines are identified by an "S" and oils for diesel engines are identified by a "C." Most modern gasoline engines require SF or SG graded oil. Automotive and marine diesel engines use CC or CD graded oil.

Viscosity is an indication of the oil's thickness, or resistance to flow. The SAE uses numbers to indicate viscosity; thin oils have low numbers and thick oils have high numbers. A "W" after the number indicates that the viscosity testing was done at low temperature to simulate cold weather operation. Engine oils fall into the 5W-20W and 20-50 range.

Multi-grade oils (for example, 10W-40) are less viscous (thinner) at low temperatures and more viscous (thicker) at high temperatures. This allows the oil to perform efficiently across a wide range of engine operating temperatures.

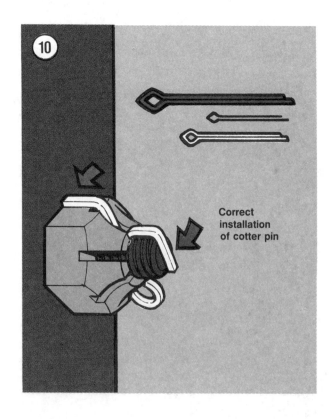

Correct installation of cotter pin

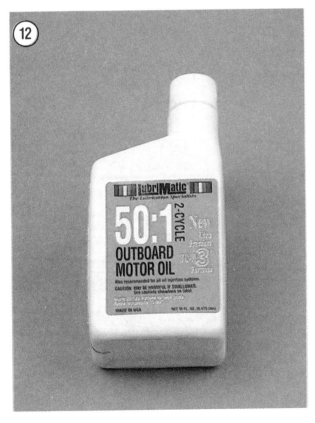

2-stroke Engine Oil

Lubrication for a 2-stroke engine is provided by oil mixed with the incoming fuel-air mixture. Some of the oil mist settles out in the crankcase, lubricating the crankshaft and lower end of the connecting rods. The rest of the oil enters the combustion chamber to lubricate the piston, rings and cylinder wall. This oil is then burned along with the fuel-air mixture during the combustion process.

Engine oil must have several special qualities to work well in a 2-stroke engine. It must mix easily and stay in suspension in gasoline. When burned, it can't leave behind excessive deposits. It must also be able to withstand the high temperatures associated with 2-stroke engines.

The National Marine Manufacturer's Association (NMMA) has set standards for oil used in 2-stroke, water-cooled engines. This is the NMMA TC-W (two-cycle, water-cooled) grade (**Figure 12**). The oil's performance in the following areas is evaluated:

a. Lubrication (prevention of wear and scuffing).
b. Spark plug fouling.
c. Preignition.
d. Piston ring sticking.
e. Piston varnish.
f. General engine condition (including deposits).
g. Exhaust port blockage.
h. Rust prevention.
i. Mixing ability with gasoline.

In addition to oil grade, manufacturers specify the ratio of gasoline to oil required during break-in and normal engine operation.

Gear Oil

Gear lubricants are assigned SAE viscosity numbers under the same system as 4-stroke engine oil. Gear lubricant falls into the SAE 72-250 range (**Figure 13**). Some gear lubricants are multi-grade; for example, SAE 85W-90.

Three types of marine gear lubricant are generally available: SAE 90 hypoid gear lubricant is designed for older manual-shift units; Type C gear lubricant contains additives designed for electric shift mechanisms; High viscosity gear lubricant is a heavier oil designed to withstand the shock loading of high-performance engines or units subjected to severe duty use. Always use a gear lubricant of the type specified by the unit's manufacturer.

Grease

Greases are graded by the National Lubricating Grease Institute (NLGI). Greases are graded by number according to the consistency of the grease; these ratings range from No. 000 to No. 6, with No. 6 being the most solid. A typical multipurpose grease is NLGI No. 2 (**Figure 14**). For specific applications, equipment manufacturers may require grease with an additive such as molybdenum disulfide (MOS^2).

GASKET SEALANT

Gasket sealant is used instead of pre-formed gaskets on some applications, or as a gasket dressing on others. Two types of gasket sealant are commonly used: room temperature vulcanizing (RTV) and anaerobic. Because these two materials have different sealing properties, they cannot be used interchangeably.

RTV Sealant

This is a silicone gel supplied in tubes (**Figure 15**). Moisture in the air causes RTV to cure. Always place the cap on the tube as soon as possible when using RTV. RTV has a shelf life of one year and will not cure properly when the shelf life has expired. Check the expiration date

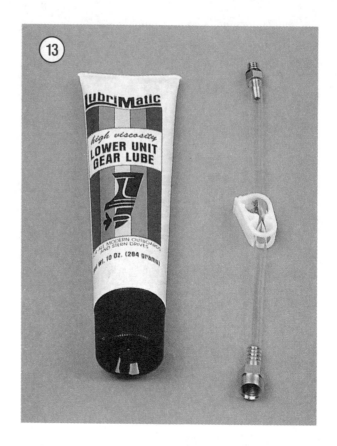

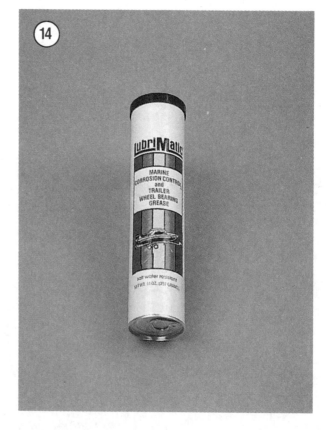

on RTV tubes before using and keep partially used tubes tightly sealed. RTV sealant can generally fill gaps up to 1/4 in. (6.3 mm) and works well on slightly flexible surfaces.

Applying RTV Sealant

Clean all gasket residue from mating surfaces. Surfaces should be clean and free of oil and dirt. Remove all RTV gasket material from blind attaching holes because it can create a "hydraulic" effect and affect bolt torque.

Apply RTV sealant in a continuous bead 2-3 mm (0.08-0.12 in.) thick. Circle all mounting holes unless otherwise specified. Torque mating parts within 10 minutes after application.

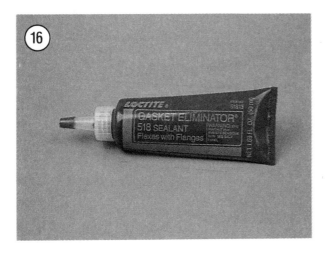

Anaerobic Sealant

This is a gel supplied in tubes (**Figure 16**). It cures only in the absence of air, as when squeezed tightly between two machined mating surfaces. For this reason, it will not spoil if the cap is left off the tube. It should not be used if one mating surface is flexible. Anaerobic sealant is able to fill gaps up to 0.030 in. (0.8 mm) and generally works best on rigid, machined flanges or surfaces.

Applying Anaerobic Sealant

Clean all gasket residue from mating surfaces. Surfaces must be clean and free of oil and dirt. Remove all gasket material from blind attaching holes, as it can cause a "hydraulic" effect and affect bolt torque.

Apply anaerobic sealant in a 1 mm or less (0.04 in.) bead to one sealing surface. Circle all mounting holes. Torque mating parts within 15 minutes after application.

GALVANIC CORROSION

A chemical reaction occurs whenever two different types of metal are joined by an electrical conductor and immersed in an electrolyte. Electrons transfer from one metal to the other through the electrolyte and return through the conductor.

The hardware on a boat is made of many different types of metal. The boat hull acts as a conductor between the metals. Even if the hull is wooden or fiberglass, the slightest film of water (electrolyte) within the hull provides conductivity. This combination creates a good environment for electron flow (**Figure 17**). Unfortunately, this electron flow results in galvanic corrosion of the metal involved, causing one of the metals to be corroded or eaten away by the process. The amount of electron flow (and, therefore, the amount of corrosion) depends on several factors:

a. The types of metal involved.

b. The efficiency of the conductor.

c. The strength of the electrolyte.

Metals

The chemical composition of the metals used in marine equipment has a significant effect on the amount and speed of galvanic corrosion. Certain metals are more resistant to corrosion than others. These electrically negative metals are commonly called "noble;" they act as the cathode in any reaction. Metals that are more subject to corrosion are electrically positive; they act as the anode in a reaction. The more noble metals include titanium, 18-8 stainless steel and nickel. Less noble metals include zinc, aluminum and magnesium. Galvanic corrosion

becomes more severe as the difference in electrical potential between the two metals increases.

In some cases, galvanic corrosion can occur within a single piece of metal. Common brass is a mixture of zinc and copper, and, when immersed in an electrolyte, the zinc portion of the mixture will corrode away as reaction occurs between the zinc and the copper particles.

Conductors

The hull of the boat often acts as the conductor between different types of metal. Marine equipment, such as an outboard motor or stern drive unit, can also act as the conductor. Large masses of metal, firmly connected together, are more efficient conductors than water. Rubber mountings and vinyl-based paint can act as insulators between pieces of metal.

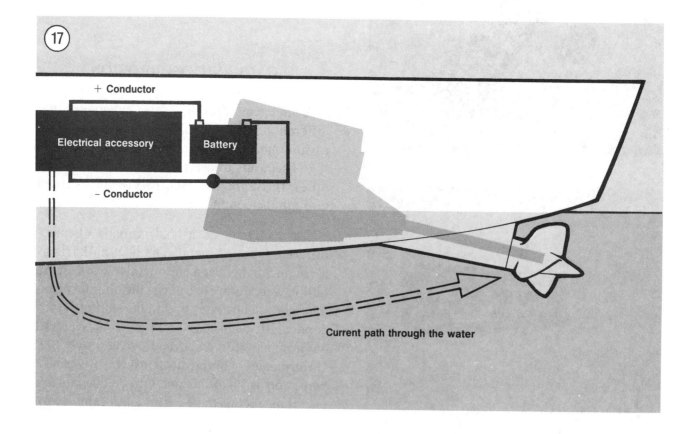

Electrolyte

The water in which a boat operates acts as the electrolyte for the galvanic corrosion process. The better a conductor the electrolyte is, the more severe and rapid the corrosion.

Cold, clean freshwater is the poorest electrolyte. As water temperature increases, its conductivity increases. Pollutants will increase conductivity; brackish or saltwater is also an efficient electrolyte. This is one of the reasons that most manufacturers recommend a freshwater flush for marine equipment after operation in saltwater, polluted or brackish water.

PROTECTION FROM GALVANIC CORROSION

Because of the environment in which marine equipment must operate, it is practically impossible to totally prevent galvanic corrosion. There are several ways by which the process can be slowed. After taking these precautions, the next step is to "fool" the process into occurring only where *you* want it to occur. This is the role of sacrificial anodes and impressed current systems.

Slowing Corrosion

Some simple precautions can help reduce the amount of corrosion taking place outside the hull. These are *not* a substitute for the corrosion protection methods discussed under *Sacrificial Anodes* and *Impressed Current Systems* in this chapter, but they can help these protection methods do their job.

Use fasteners of a metal more noble than the part they are fastening. If corrosion occurs, the larger equipment will suffer but the fastener will be protected. Because fasteners are usually very small in comparison to the equipment being fastened, the equipment can survive the loss of

material. If the fastener were to corrode instead of the equipment, major problems could arise.

Keep all painted surfaces in good condition. If paint is scraped off and bare metal exposed, corrosion will rapidly increase. Use a vinyl- or plastic-based paint, which acts as an electrical insulator.

Be careful when using metal-based antifouling paints. These should not be applied to metal parts of the boat, outboard motor or stern drive unit or they will actually react with the equipment, causing corrosion between the equipment and the layer of paint. Organic-based paints are available for use on metal surfaces.

Where a corrosion protection device is used, remember that it must be immersed in the electrolyte along with the rest of the boat to have any effect. If you raise the power unit out of the water when the boat is docked, any anodes on the power unit will be removed from the corrosion cycle and will not protect the rest of the equipment that is still immersed. Also, such corrosion protection devices must not be painted because this would insulate them from the corrosion process.

Any change in the boat's equipment, such as the installation of a new stainless steel propeller, will change the electrical potential and could cause increased corrosion. Keep in mind that when you add new equipment or change materials, you should review your corrosion protection system to be sure it is up to the job.

Sacrificial Anodes

Anodes are usually made of zinc, a far from noble metal. Sacrificial anodes are specially designed to do nothing but corrode. Properly fastening such pieces to the boat will cause them to act as the anode in *any* galvanic reaction that occurs; any other metal present will act as the cathode and will not be damaged.

Anodes must be used properly to be effective. Simply fastening pieces of zinc to your boat in random locations won't do the job.

You must determine how much anode surface area is required to adequately protect the equipment's surface area. A good starting point is provided by Military Specification MIL-A-818001, which states that one square inch of new anode will protect either:

a. 800 square inches of freshly painted steel.

b. 250 square inches of bare steel or bare aluminum alloy.

c. 100 square inches of copper or copper alloy.

This rule is for a boat at rest. When underway, more anode area is required to protect the same equipment surface area.

The anode must be fastened so that it has good electrical contact with the metal to be protected. If possible, the anode can be attached directly to the other metal. If that is not possible, the entire network of metal parts in the boat should be electrically bonded together so that all pieces are protected.

Good quality anodes have inserts of some other metal around the fastener holes. Otherwise, the anode could erode away around the fastener. The anode can then become loose or even fall off, removing all protection.

Another Military Specification (MIL-A-18001) defines the type of alloy preferred that will corrode at a uniform rate without forming a crust that could reduce its efficiency after a time.

Impressed Current Systems

An impressed current system can be installed on any boat that has a battery. The system consists of an anode, a control box and a sensor. The anode in this system is coated with a very noble metal, such as platinum, so that it is almost corrosion-free and will last indefinitely. The sensor, under the boat's waterline, monitors the potential for corrosion. When it senses that corrosion could be occurring, it transmits this information to the control box.

The control box connects the boat's battery to the anode. When the sensor signals the need, the control box applies positive battery voltage to the anode. Current from the battery flows from the anode to all other metal parts of the boat, no matter how noble or non-noble these parts may be. This battery current takes the place of any galvanic current flow.

Only a very small amount of battery current is needed to counteract galvanic corrosion. Manufacturers estimate that it would take two or three months of constant use to drain a typical marine battery, assuming the battery is never recharged.

An impressed current system is more expensive to install than simple anodes but, considering its low maintenance requirements and the excellent protection it provides, the long-term cost may actually be lower.

PROPELLERS

The propeller is the final link between the boat's drive system and the water. A perfectly

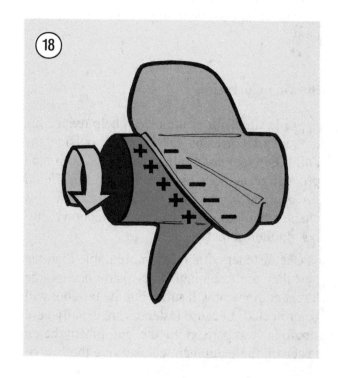

maintained engine and hull are useless if the propeller is the wrong type or has been allowed to deteriorate. Although propeller selection for a specific situation is beyond the scope of this book, the following information on propeller construction and design will allow you to discuss the subject intelligently with your marine dealer.

How a Propeller Works

As the curved blades of a propeller rotate through the water, a high-pressure area is created on one side of the blade and a low-pressure area exists on the other side of the blade (**Figure 18**). The propeller moves toward the low-pressure area, carrying the boat with it.

Propeller Parts

Although a propeller may be a one-piece unit, it is made up of several different parts (**Figure 19**). Variations in the design of these parts make different propellers suitable for different jobs.

The blade tip is the point on the blade farthest from the center of the propeller hub. The blade

tip separates the leading edge from the trailing edge.

The leading edge is the edge of the blade nearest to the boat. During normal rotation, this is the area of the blade that first cuts through the water.

The trailing edge is the edge of the blade farthest from the boat.

The blade face is the surface of the blade that faces away from the boat. During normal rotation, high pressure exists on this side of the blade.

The blade back is the surface of the blade that faces toward the boat. During normal rotation, low pressure exists on this side of the blade.

The cup is a small curve or lip on the trailing edge of the blade.

The hub is the central portion of the propeller. It connects the blades to the propeller shaft (part of the boat's drive system). On some drive systems, engine exhaust is routed through the hub; in this case, the hub is made up of an outer and an inner portion, connected by ribs.

The diffuser ring is used on through-hub exhaust models to prevent exhaust gases from entering the blade area.

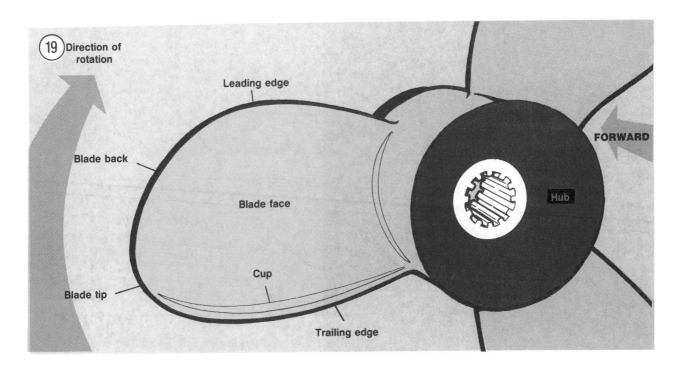

Direction of rotation

Leading edge

Blade back

Blade face

Cup

Blade tip

Trailing edge

FORWARD

Hub

Propeller Design

Changes in length, angle, thickness and material of propeller parts make different propellers suitable for different situations.

Diameter

Propeller diameter is the distance from the center of the hub to the blade tip, multiplied by

2. That is, it is the diameter of the circle formed by the blade tips during propeller rotation (**Figure 20**).

Pitch and rake

Propeller pitch and rake describe the placement of the blade in relation to the hub (**Figure 21**).

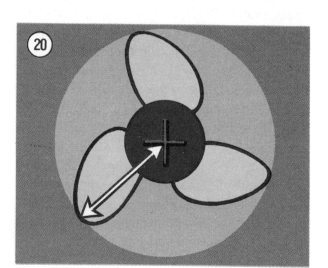

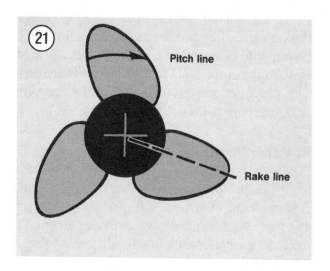

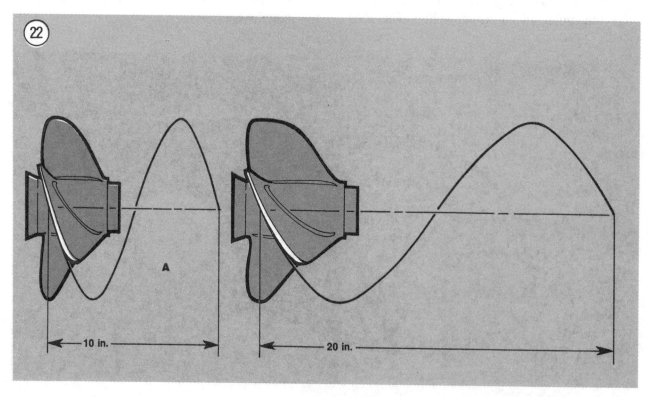

Pitch is expressed by the theoretical distance that the propeller would travel in one revolution. In A, **Figure 22**, the propeller would travel 10 inches in one revolution. In B, **Figure 22**, the propeller would travel 20 inches in one revolution. This distance is only theoretical; during actual operation, the propeller achieves about 80% of its rated travel.

Propeller blades can be constructed with constant pitch (**Figure 23**) or progressive pitch (**Figure 24**). Progressive pitch starts low at the leading edge and increases toward to trailing edge. The propeller pitch specification is the average of the pitch across the entire blade.

Blade rake is specified in degrees and is measured along a line from the center of the hub to the blade tip. A blade that is perpendicular to the hub (A, **Figure 25**) has 0° of rake. A blade that is angled from perpendicular (B, **Figure 25**) has a rake expressed by its difference from perpen-

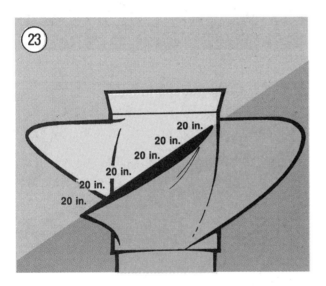

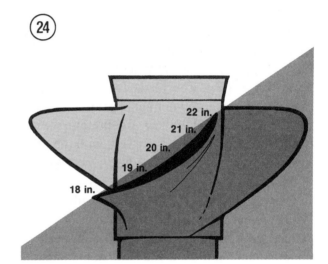

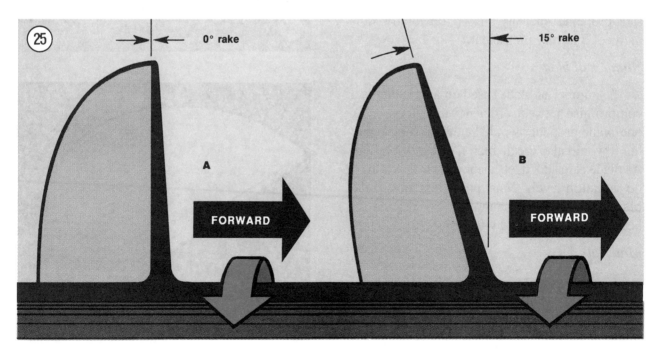

dicular. Most propellers have rakes ranging from 0-20°.

Blade thickness

Blade thickness is not uniform at all points along the blade. For efficiency, blades should be as thin as possible at all points while retaining enough strength to move the boat. Blades tend to be thicker where they meet the hub and thinner at the blade tip (**Figure 26**). This is to support the heavier loads at the hub section of the blade. This thickness is dependent on the strength of the material used.

When cut along a line from the leading edge to the trailing edge in the central portion of the blade (**Figure 27**), the propeller blade resembles an airplane wing. The blade face, where high pressure exists during normal rotation, is almost flat. The blade back, where low pressure exists during normal rotation, is curved, with the thinnest portions at the edges and the thickest portion at the center.

Propellers that run only partially submerged, as in racing applications, may have a wedge-shaped cross-section (**Figure 28**). The leading edge is very thin; the blade thickness increases toward the trailing edge, where it is the thickest. If a propeller such as this is run totally submerged, it is very inefficient.

Number of blades

The number of blades used on a propeller is a compromise between efficiency and vibration. A one-blade propeller would be the most efficient, but it would also create high levels of vibration. As blades are added, efficiency decreases, but so do vibration levels. Most propellers have three blades, representing the most practical trade-off between efficiency and vibration.

Material

Propeller materials are chosen for strength, corrosion resistance and economy. Stainless steel, aluminum and bronze are the most commonly used materials. Bronze is quite strong but

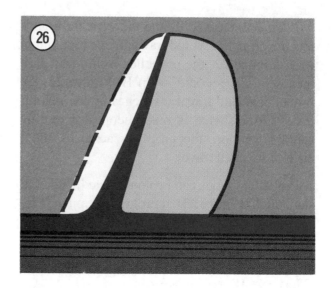

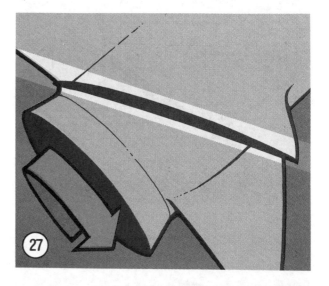

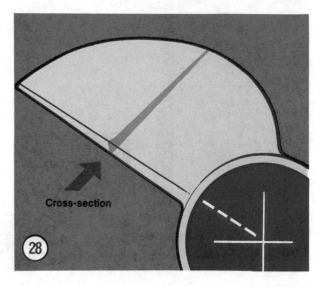

rather expensive. Stainless steel is more common than bronze because of its combination of strength and lower cost. Aluminum alloys are the least expensive but usually lack the strength of steel. Plastic propellers may be used in some low horsepower applications.

Direction of rotation

Propellers are made for both right-hand and left-hand rotation although right-hand is the most commonly used. When seen from behind the boat in forward motion, a right-hand propeller turns clockwise and a left-hand propeller turns counterclockwise. Off the boat, you can tell the difference by observing the angle of the blades (**Figure 29**). A right-hand propeller's blades slant from the upper left to the lower right; a left-hand propeller's blades are the opposite.

Cavitation and Ventilation

Cavitation and ventilation are *not* interchangeable terms; they refer to two distinct problems encountered during propeller operation.

To understand cavitation, you must first understand the relationship between pressure and the boiling point of water. At sea level, water will boil at 212° F. As pressure increases, such as within an engine's closed cooling system, the boiling point of water increases—it will boil at some temperature higher than 212° F. The opposite is also true. As pressure decreases, water will boil at a temperature lower than 212° F. If pressure drops low enough, water will boil at typical ambient temperatures of 50-60° F.

We have said that, during normal propeller operation, low-pressure exists on the blade back. Normally, the pressure does not drop low enough for boiling to occur. However, poor blade design

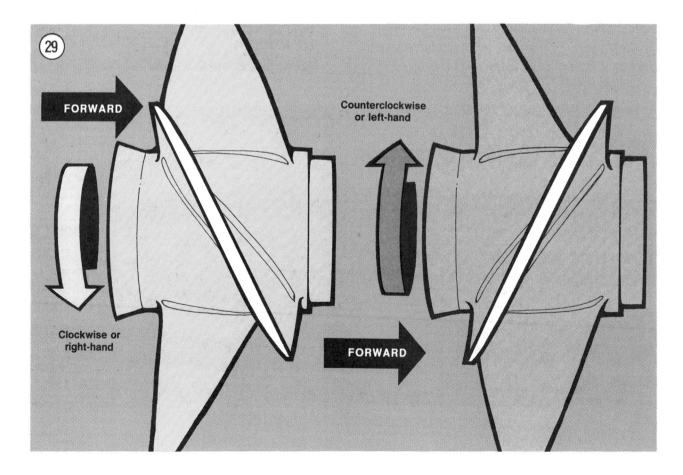

FORWARD

Counterclockwise or left-hand

Clockwise or right-hand

FORWARD

or selection, or blade damage can cause an unusual pressure drop on a small area of the blade (**Figure 30**). Boiling can occur in this small area. As the water boils, air bubbles form. As the boiling water passes to a higher pressure area of the blade, the boiling stops and the bubbles collapse. The collapsing bubbles release enough energy to erode the surface of the blade.

This entire process of pressure drop, boiling and bubble collapse is called "cavitation." The damage caused by the collapsing bubbles is called a "cavitation burn." It is important to remember that cavitation is caused by a decrease in pressure, *not* an increase in temperature.

Ventilation is not as complex a process as cavitation. Ventilation refers to air entering the blade area, either from above the surface of the water or from a through-hub exhaust system. As the blades meet the air, the propeller momentarily over-revs, losing most of its thrust. An added complication is that as the propeller over-revs, pressure on the blade back decreases and massive cavitation can occur.

Most pieces of marine equipment have a plate above the propeller area designed to keep surface air from entering the blade area (**Figure 31**). This plate is correctly called an "antiventilation plate," although you will often *see* it called an "anticavitation plate." Through hub exhaust systems also have specially designed hubs to keep exhaust gases from entering the blade area.

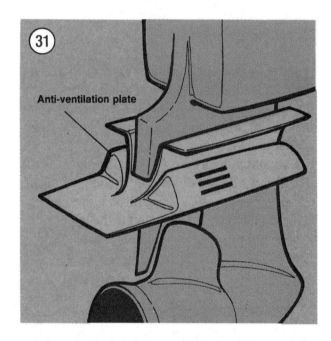

Anti-ventilation plate

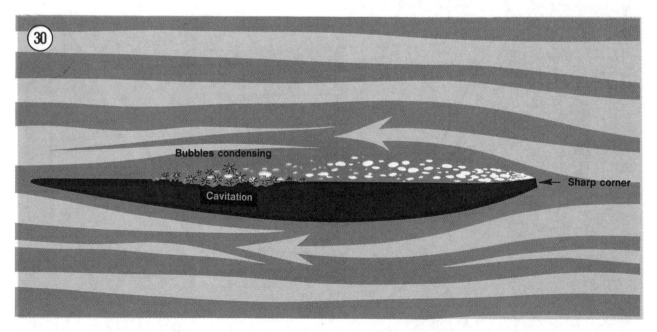

Bubbles condensing

Cavitation

Sharp corner

Chapter Two

Tools and Techniques

This chapter describes the common tools required for marine equipment repairs and troubleshooting. Techniques that will make your work easier and more effective are also described. Some of the procedures in this book require special skills or expertise; in some cases, you are better off entrusting the job to a dealer or qualified specialist.

SAFETY FIRST

Professional mechanics can work for years and never suffer a serious injury. If you follow a few rules of common sense and safety, you too can enjoy many safe hours servicing your marine equipment. If you ignore these rules, you can hurt yourself or damage the equipment.

1. Never use gasoline as a cleaning solvent.
2. Never smoke or use a torch near flammable liquids, such as cleaning solvent. If you are working in your home garage, remember that your home gas appliances have pilot lights.
3. Never smoke or use a torch in an area where batteries are being charged. Highly explosive hydrogen gas is formed during the charging process.

4. Use the proper size wrenches to avoid damage to fasteners and injury to yourself.
5. When loosening a tight or stuck fastener, think of what would happen if the wrench should slip. Protect yourself accordingly.
6. Keep your work area clean, uncluttered and well lighted.
7. Wear safety goggles during all operations involving drilling, grinding or the use of a cold chisel.
8. Never use worn tools.
9. Keep a Coast Guard approved fire extinguisher handy. Be sure it is rated for gasoline (Class B) and electrical (Class C) fires.

BASIC HAND TOOLS

A number of tools are required to maintain marine equipment. You may already have some of these tools for home or car repairs. There are also tools made especially for marine equipment repairs; these you will have to purchase. In any case, a wide variety of quality tools will make repairs easier and more effective.

Keep your tools clean and in a tool box. Keep them organized with the sockets and related drives together, the open end and box wrenches together, etc. After using a tool, wipe off dirt and grease with a clean cloth and place the tool in its correct place.

The following tools are required to perform virtually any repair job. Each tool is described and the recommended size given for starting a tool collection. Additional tools and some duplications may be added as you become more familiar with the equipment. You may need all standard U.S. size tools, all metric size tools or a mixture of both.

Screwdrivers

The screwdriver is a very basic tool, but if used improperly, it will do more damage than good. The slot on a screw has a definite dimension and shape. A screwdriver must be selected to conform with that shape. Use a small screwdriver for small screws and a large one for large screws or the screw head will be damaged.

Two types of screwdriver are commonly required: a common (flat-blade) screwdriver (**Figure 1**) and Phillips screwdrivers (**Figure 2**).

Screwdrivers are available in sets, which often include an assortment of common and Phillips blades. If you buy them individually, buy at least the following:

    a. Common screwdriver—5/16 × 6 in. blade.

    b. Common screwdriver—3/8 × 12 in. blade

    c. Phillips screwdriver—size 2 tip, 6 in. blade.

Use screwdrivers only for driving screws. Never use a screwdriver for prying or chiseling. Do not try to remove a Phillips or Allen head screw with a common screwdriver; you can damage the head so that the proper tool will be unable to remove it.

Keep screwdrivers in the proper condition and they will last longer and perform better. Always keep the tip of a common screwdriver in good condition. **Figure 3** shows how to grind the tip to the proper shape if it becomes damaged. Note the parallel sides of the tip.

Pliers

Pliers come in a wide range of types and sizes. Pliers are useful for cutting, bending and crimping. They should never be used to cut hardened objects or to turn bolts or nuts. **Figure 4** shows several types of pliers.

Each type of pliers has a specialized function. General purpose pliers are used mainly for holding things and for bending. Locking pliers are used as pliers or to hold objects very tightly, like a vise. Needlenose pliers are used to hold or bend small objects. Adjustable or slip-joint pliers can

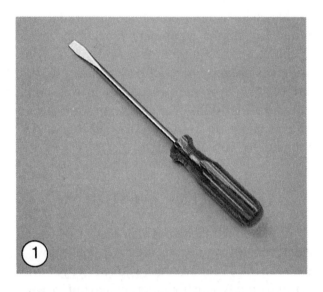

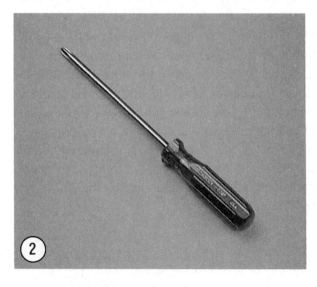

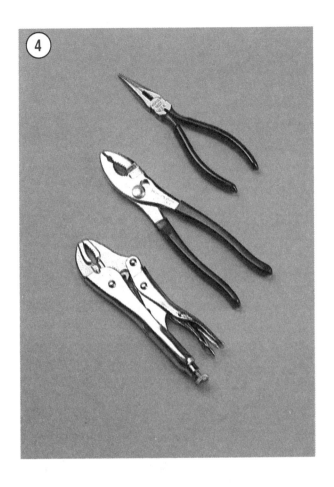

be adjusted to hold various sizes of objects; the jaws remain parallel to grip around objects such as pipe or tubing. There are many more types of pliers. The ones described here are the most commonly used.

Box and Open-end Wrenches

Box and open-end wrenches are available in sets or separately in a variety of sizes. See **Figure 5** and **Figure 6**. The number stamped near the end refers to the distance between two parallel flats on the hex head bolt or nut.

Box wrenches are usually superior to open-end wrenches. An open-end wrench grips the nut on only two flats. Unless it fits well, it may slip and round off the points on the nut. The box wrench grips all 6 flats. Both 6-point and 12-point openings on box wrenches are available. The 6-point gives superior holding power; the 12-point allows a shorter swing.

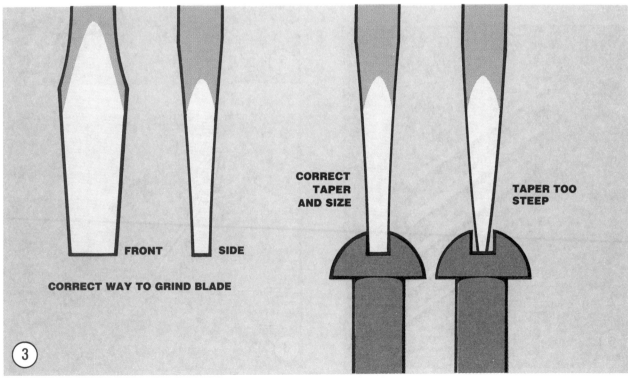

Combination wrenches, which are open on one side and boxed on the other, are also available. Both ends are the same size.

Adjustable Wrenches

An adjustable wrench can be adjusted to fit nearly any nut or bolt head. See **Figure 7**. However, it can loosen and slip, causing damage to the nut and maybe to your knuckles. Use an adjustable wrench only when other wrenches are not available.

Adjustable wrenches come in sizes ranging from 4-18 in. overall. A 6 or 8 in. wrench is recommended as an all-purpose wrench.

Socket Wrenches

This type is undoubtedly the fastest, safest and most convenient to use. See **Figure 8**. Sockets, which attach to a suitable handle, are available with 6-point or 12-point openings and use 1/4, 3/8 and 3/4 inch drives. The drive size indicates

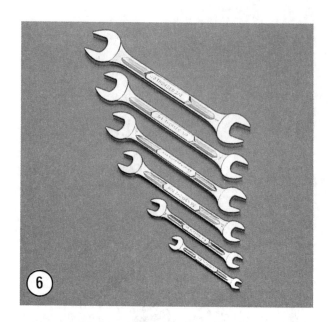

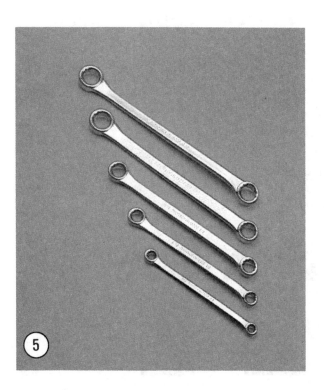

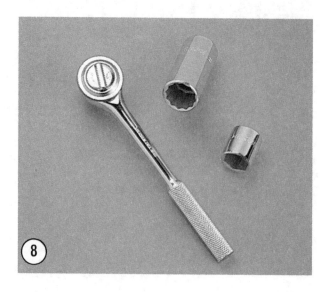

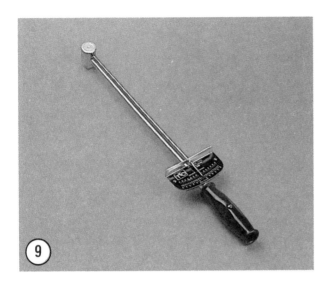

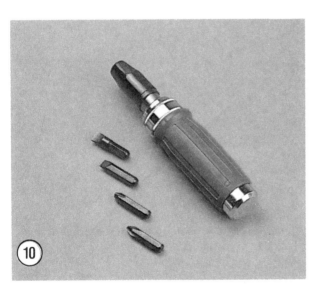

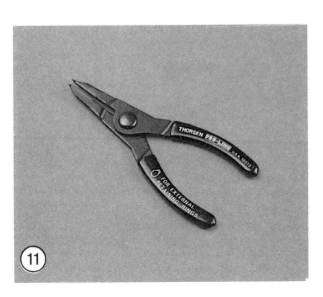

the size of the square hole that mates with the ratchet or flex handle.

Torque Wrench

A torque wrench (**Figure 9**) is used with a socket to measure how tight a nut or bolt is installed. They come in a wide price range and with either 3/8 or 1/2 in. square drive. The drive size indicates the size of the square drive that mates with the socket. Purchase one that measures up to 150 ft.-lb. (203 N•m).

Impact Driver

This tool (**Figure 10**) makes removal of tight fasteners easy and eliminates damage to bolts and screw slots. Impact drivers and interchangeable bits are available at most large hardware and auto parts stores.

Circlip Pliers

Circlip pliers (sometimes referred to as snap-ring pliers) are necessary to remove circlips. See **Figure 11**. Circlip pliers usually come with several different size tips; many designs can be switched from internal type to external type.

Hammers

The correct hammer is necessary for repairs. Use only a hammer with a face (or head) of rubber or plastic or the soft-faced type that is filled with buckshot (**Figure 12**). These are sometimes necessary in engine tear-downs. *Never* use a metal-faced hammer as severe damage will result in most cases. You can always produce the same amount of force with a soft-faced hammer.

Feeler Gauge

This tool has either flat or wire measuring gauges (**Figure 13**). Wire gauges are used to measure spark plug gap; flat gauges are used for all other measurements. A non-magnetic (brass) gauge may be specified when working around magnetized parts.

Other Special Tools

Some procedures require special tools; these are identified in the appropriate chapter. Unless otherwise specified, the part number used in this book to identify a special tool is the marine equipment manufacturer's part number.

Special tools can usually be purchased through your marine equipment dealer. Some can be made locally by a machinist, often at a much lower price. You may find certain special tools at tool rental dealers. Don't use makeshift tools if you can't locate the correct special tool; you will probably cause more damage than good.

TEST EQUIPMENT

Multimeter

This instrument (**Figure 14**) is invaluable for electrical system troubleshooting and service. It combines a voltmeter, an ohmmeter and an ammeter into one unit, so it is often called a VOM.

Two types of multimeter are available, analog and digital. Analog meters have a moving needle with marked bands indicating the volt, ohm and amperage scales. The digital meter (DVOM) is ideally suited for troubleshooting because it is easy to read, more accurate than analog, contains internal overload protection, is auto-ranging (analog meters must be recalibrated each time the scale is changed) and has automatic polarity compensation.

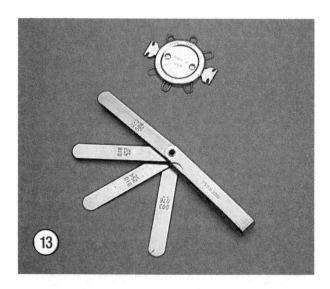

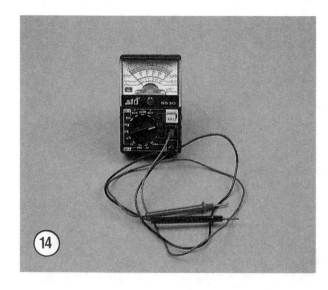

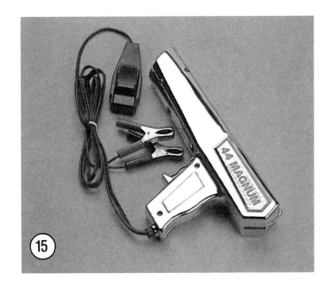

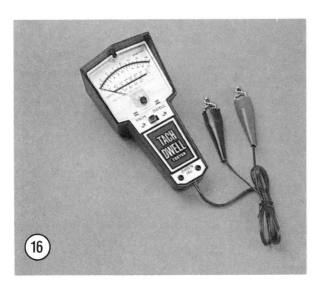

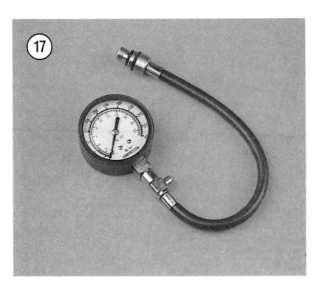

Strobe Timing Light

This instrument is necessary for dynamic tuning (setting ignition timing while the engine is running). By flashing a light at the precise instant the spark plug fires, the position of the timing mark can be seen. The flashing light makes a moving mark appear to stand still opposite a stationary mark.

Suitable lights range from inexpensive neon bulb types to powerful xenon strobe lights. See **Figure 15**. A light with an inductive pickup is best because it eliminates any possible damage to ignition wiring.

Tachometer/Dwell Meter

A portable tachometer is necessary for tuning. See **Figure 16**. Ignition timing and carburetor adjustments must be performed at the specified idle speed. The best instrument for this purpose is one with a low range of 0-1000 or 0-2000 rpm and a high range of 0-6000 rpm. Extended range (0-6000 or 0-8000 rpm) instruments lack accuracy at lower speeds. The instrument should be capable of detecting changes of 25 rpm on the low range.

A dwell meter is often combined with a tachometer. Dwell meters are used with breaker point ignition systems to measure the amount of time the points remain closed during engine operation.

Compression Gauge

This tool (**Figure 17**) measures the amount of pressure present in the engine's combustion chamber during the compression stroke. This indicates general engine condition. Compression readings can be interpreted along with vacuum gauge readings to pinpoint specific engine mechanical problems.

The easiest type to use has screw-in adapters that fit into the spark plug holes. Press-in rubber-tipped types are also available.

Vacuum Gauge

The vacuum gauge (**Figure 18**) measures the intake manifold vacuum created by the engine's intake stroke. Manifold and valve problems (on 4-stroke engines) can be identified by interpreting the readings. When combined with compression gauge readings, other engine problems can be diagnosed.

Some vacuum gauges can also be used as fuel pressure gauges to trace fuel system problems.

Hydrometer

Battery electrolyte specific gravity is measured with a hydrometer (**Figure 19**). The specific gravity of the electrolyte indicates the battery's state of charge. The best type has automatic temperature compensation; otherwise, you must calculate the compensation yourself.

Precision Measuring Tools

Various tools are needed to make precision measurements. A dial indicator (**Figure 20**), for example, is used to determine run-out of rotating parts and end play of parts assemblies. A dial indicator can also be used to precisely measure piston position in relation to top dead center; some engines require this measurement for ignition timing adjustment.

Vernier calipers (**Figure 21**) and micrometers (**Figure 22**) are other precision measuring tools used to determine the size of parts (such as piston diameter).

Precision measuring equipment must be stored, handled and used carefully or it will not remain accurate.

SERVICE HINTS

Most of the service procedures covered in this manual are straightforward and can be performed by anyone reasonably handy with tools.

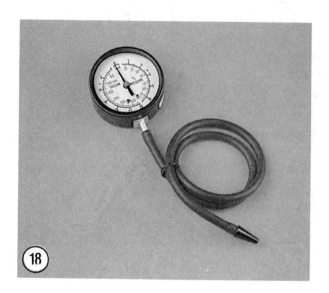

18

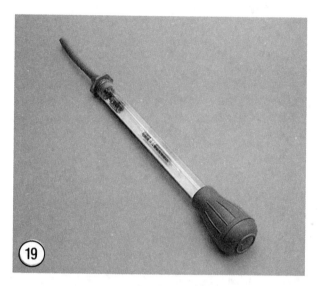

19

20

It is suggested, however, that you consider your own skills and toolbox carefully before attempting any operation involving major disassembly of the engine or gearcase.

Some operations, for example, require the use of a press. It would be wiser to have these performed by a shop equipped for such work, rather than trying to do the job yourself with makeshift equipment. Other procedures require precise measurements. Unless you have the skills and

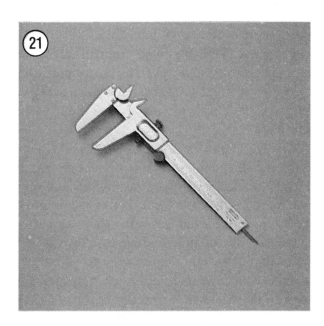

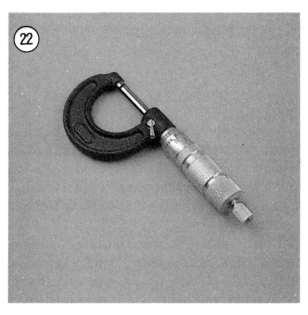

equipment required, it would be better to have a qualified repair shop make the measurements for you.

Preparation for Disassembly

Repairs go much faster and easier if the equipment is clean before you begin work. There are special cleaners, such as Gunk or Bel-Ray Degreaser, for washing the engine and related parts. Just spray or brush on the cleaning solution, let it stand, then rinse away with a garden hose. Clean all oily or greasy parts with cleaning solvent as you remove them.

WARNING
Never use gasoline as a cleaning agent. It presents an extreme fire hazard. Be sure to work in a well-ventilated area when using cleaning solvent. Keep a Coast Guard approved fire extinguisher, rated for gasoline fires, handy in any case.

Much of the labor charged for repairs made by dealers is for the removal and disassembly of other parts to reach the defective unit. It is frequently possible to perform the preliminary operations yourself and then take the defective unit in to the dealer for repair.

If you decide to tackle the job yourself, read the entire section in this manual that pertains to it, making sure you have identified the proper one. Study the illustrations and text until you have a good idea of what is involved in completing the job satisfactorily. If special tools or replacement parts are required, make arrangements to get them before you start. It is frustrating and time-consuming to get partly into a job and then be unable to complete it.

Disassembly Precautions

During disassembly of parts, keep a few general precautions in mind. Force is rarely needed to get things apart. If parts are a tight fit, such as a bearing in a case, there is usually a tool designed to separate them. Never use a screwdriver to pry apart parts with machined surfaces (such as cylinder heads and crankcases). You will mar the surfaces and end up with leaks.

Make diagrams (or take an instant picture) wherever similar-appearing parts are found. For example, head and crankcase bolts are often not the same length. You may think you can remember where everything came from, but mistakes are costly. There is also the possibility you may be sidetracked and not return to work for days or even weeks. In the interval, carefully laid out parts may have been disturbed.

Cover all openings after removing parts to keep small parts, dirt or other contamination from entering.

Tag all similar internal parts for location and direction. All internal components should be reinstalled in the same location and direction from which removed. Record the number and thickness of any shims as they are removed. Small parts, such as bolts, can be identified by placing them in plastic sandwich bags. Seal and label them with masking tape.

Wiring should be tagged with masking tape and marked as each wire is removed. Again, do not rely on memory alone.

Protect finished surfaces from physical damage or corrosion. Keep gasoline off painted surfaces.

Assembly Precautions

No parts, except those assembled with a press fit, require unusual force during assembly. If a part is hard to remove or install, find out why before proceeding.

When assembling two parts, start all fasteners, then tighten evenly in an alternating or crossing pattern if no specific tightening sequence is given.

When assembling parts, be sure all shims and washers are installed exactly as they came out.

Whenever a rotating part butts against a stationary part, look for a shim or washer. Use new gaskets if there is any doubt about the condition of the old ones. Unless otherwise specified, a thin coat of oil on gaskets may help them seal effectively.

Heavy grease can be used to hold small parts in place if they tend to fall out during assembly. However, keep grease and oil away from electrical components.

High spots may be sanded off a piston with sandpaper, but fine emery cloth and oil will do a much more professional job.

Carbon can be removed from the cylinder head, the piston crown and the exhaust port with a dull screwdriver. *Do not* scratch either surface. Wipe off the surface with a clean cloth when finished.

The carburetor is best cleaned by disassembling it and soaking the parts in a commercial carburetor cleaner. Never soak gaskets and rubber parts in these cleaners. Never use wire to clean out jets and air passages; they are easily damaged. Use compressed air to blow out the carburetor *after* the float has been removed.

Take your time and do the job right. Do not forget that the break-in procedure on a newly rebuilt engine is the same as that of a new one. Use the break-in oil recommendations and follow other instructions given in your owner's manual.

SPECIAL TIPS

Because of the extreme demands placed on marine equipment, several points should be kept in mind when performing service and repair. The following items are general suggestions that may improve the overall life of the machine and help avoid costly failures.

1. Unless otherwise specified, use a locking compound, such as Loctite Threadlocker, on all bolts and nuts, even if they are secured with lockwashers. Be sure to use the specified grade

of thread locking compound. A screw or bolt lost from an engine cover or bearing retainer could easily cause serious and expensive damage before its loss is noticed.

When applying thread locking compound, use a small amount. If too much is used, it can work its way down the threads and stick parts together that were not meant to be stuck together.

Keep a tube of thread locking compound in your tool box; when used properly, it is cheap insurance.

2. Use a hammer-driven impact tool to remove and install screws and bolts. These tools help prevent the rounding off of bolt heads and screw slots and ensure a tight installation.

3. When straightening the fold-over type lockwasher, use a wide-blade chisel, such as an old and dull wood chisel. Such a tool provides a better purchase on the folded tab, making straightening easier.

4. When installing the fold-over type lockwasher, always use a new washer if possible. If a new washer is not available, always fold over a part of the washer that has not been previously folded. Reusing the same fold may cause the washer to break, resulting in the loss of its locking ability and a loose piece of metal adrift in the engine.

When folding the washer, start the fold with a screwdriver and finish it with a pair of pliers. If a punch is used to make the fold, the fold may be too sharp, thereby increasing the chances of the washer breaking under stress.

These washers are relatively inexpensive and it is suggested that you keep several of each size in your tool box for repairs.

5. When replacing missing or broken fasteners (bolts, nuts and screws), always use authorized replacement parts. They are specially hardened for each application. The wrong 50-cent bolt could easily cause serious and expensive damage.

6. When installing gaskets, always use authorized replacement gaskets *without* sealer, unless designated. Many gaskets are designed to swell when they come in contact with oil. Gasket sealer will prevent the gaskets from swelling as intended and can result in oil leaks. Authorized replacement gaskets are cut from material of the precise thickness needed. Installation of a too thick or too thin gasket in a critical area could cause equipment damage.

MECHANIC'S TECHNIQUES

Removing Frozen Fasteners

When a fastener rusts and cannot be removed, several methods may be used to loosen it. First, apply penetrating oil, such as Liquid Wrench or WD-40 (available at any hardware or auto supply store). Apply it liberally and allow it penetrate for 10-15 minutes. Tap the fastener several times with a small hammer; do not hit it hard enough to cause damage. Reapply the penetrating oil if necessary.

For frozen screws, apply penetrating oil as described, then insert a screwdriver in the slot and tap the top of the screwdriver with a hammer. This loosens the rust so the screw can be removed in the normal way. If the screw head is too chewed up to use a screwdriver, grip the head with locking pliers and twist the screw out.

Avoid applying heat unless specifically instructed because it may melt, warp or remove the temper from parts.

Remedying Stripped Threads

Occasionally, threads are stripped through carelessness or impact damage. Often the threads can be cleaned up by running a tap (for internal threads on nuts) or die (for external threads on bolts) through threads. See **Figure 23**.

Removing Broken Screws or Bolts

When the head breaks off a screw or bolt, several methods are available for removing the remaining portion.

If a large portion of the remainder projects out, try gripping it with vise-grip pliers. If the projecting portion is too small, file it to fit a wrench or cut a slot in it to fit a screwdriver. See **Figure 24**.

If the head breaks off flush, use a screw extractor. To do this, centerpunch the remaining portion of the screw or bolt. Drill a small hole in the screw and tap the extractor into the hole. Back the screw out with a wrench on the extractor. See **Figure 25**.

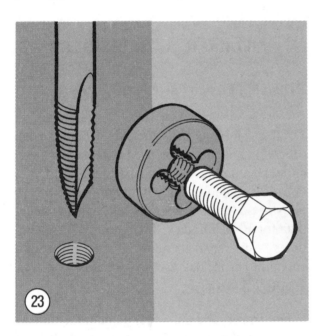

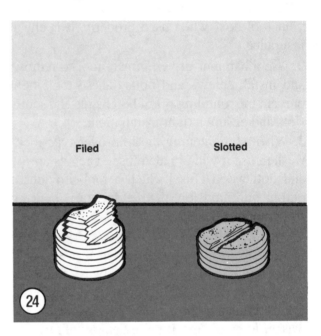

Filed   Slotted

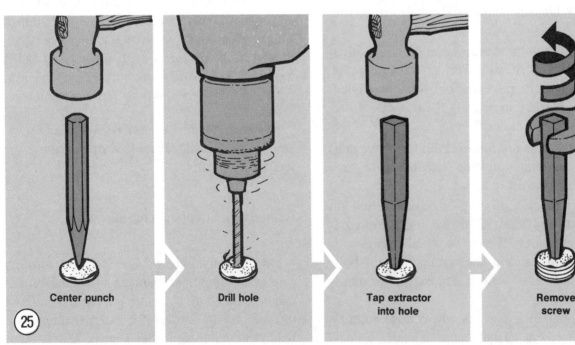

Center punch   Drill hole   Tap extractor into hole   Remove screw

Chapter Three

Troubleshooting

Troubleshooting is a relatively simple matter when done logically. The first step in any troubleshooting procedure is to define the symptoms as closely as possible and then localize the problem. Subsequent steps involve testing and analyzing those areas which could cause the symptoms. A haphazard approach may eventually solve the problem, but it can be very costly in terms of wasted time and unnecessary parts replacement.

Proper lubrication, maintenance and periodic tune-up as described in Chapter Four will reduce the necessity for troubleshooting. Even with the best of care, however, an outboard motor is prone to problems which will require troubleshooting. This chapter contains brief descriptions of each operating system and troubleshooting procedures to be used. **Table 1** provides the recommended battery cable gauge sizes. **Table 2** provides starter motor current draw specifications. **Tables 3-6** present typical problems with their probable causes and solutions. **Tables 1-6** are located at the end of this chapter.

OPERATING REQUIREMENTS

Every outboard motor requires 3 basic things to run properly: an uninterrupted supply of fuel and air in the correct proportions, proper ignition at the right time and adequate compression. If any of these are lacking, the motor will not run. The electrical system is generally the weakest link in the chain. More problems result from electrical malfunctions than from any other source. Keep this in mind before blaming the fuel system and making unnecessary carburetor repairs and adjustments.

If an outboard motor has been sitting for any length of time and refuses to start, check the condition of the battery first to make sure it is adequately charged, then inspect the fuel delivery system. This includes the fuel tank, fuel pump, fuel lines and carburetor(s). Rust may have formed in the tank, restricting fuel flow. Gasoline deposits may have gummed up carburetor jets and air passages. Gasoline tends to lose its potency after standing for long periods. Condensation may contaminate the fuel with water. Drain the old fuel and try starting with a fresh tankful.

STARTING SYSTEM

Description

High compression, multi-cylinder outboard motors use an electric starter motor (**Figure 1**) to crank the engine. The starter motor is mounted vertically on the engine. When battery voltage is supplied to the starter motor, its pinion gear is thrust upward to engage the teeth on the engine flywheel (**Figure 2**). When the engine starts, the pinion gear disengages from the flywheel.

The starting system requires a fully charged battery to provide the large amount of electrical current necessary to operate the starter motor. The battery may be charged externally or by an engine-driven alternator which maintains the battery charge during operation.

The starting system on outboard motors equipped with electric start consists of the battery, an ignition switch, starter solenoid (**Figure 3**), starter motor and related wiring. Turning the ignition switch to the START position allows current to flow through the solenoid coil. This causes the solenoid contacts to close, allowing current to flow from the battery through the solenoid to the starter motor. A neutral start switch in the starter circuit prevents current flow to the starter motor if the shift control is not in the NEUTRAL position.

> *CAUTION*
> *To prevent starter damage from overheating, do not operate the starter motor continuously for more than 30 seconds. Allow the motor to cool for at least 2 minutes between attempts to start the engine.*

Troubleshooting

If the following procedures do not locate the problem, refer to **Table 3** for more extensive testing. Before troubleshooting the starting circuit, be sure of the following:

   a. The battery is fully charged.

   b. The shift control lever is in the NEUTRAL position.

   c. All electrical connections are clean and tight.

   d. The wiring harness is in good condition, with no worn or frayed insulation.

   e. The fuse installed in the red lead between the ignition switch and starter solenoid, if so equipped, is not blown.

Starter Motor Turns Slowly

1. Make sure the battery is in acceptable condition and fully charged.

2. Inspect all electrical connections for looseness or corrosion. Clean and tighten as necessary.

3. Check for the proper size and length of battery cables. Refer to **Table 1** for recommended cable gauge sizes and lengths. Replace cables that are undersize or relocate the battery to shorten the

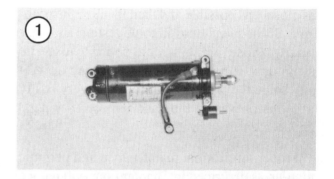

distance between the battery and starter sole-noid.

4. Check the starter motor current draw using a suitable ammeter or current indicator such as shown in **Figure 4**. Disconnect the spark plug leads and ground the leads to the engine. Crank the engine to check current draw. If excessive current draw is indicated (**Table 2**), repair or replace the starter motor.

Starter Motor Does Not Turn

Refer to **Figure 5** and perform the following test.

NOTE
Test points at starter solenoid will vary according to the solenoid used, as shown in ***Figure 5***.

Disconnect the yellow or black starter motor cable at the starter solenoid (test point 1, **Figure 5**) to prevent accidental cranking during the test procedure.

On some cranking circuits, there may be a 20-amp fuse installed in the red lead between the

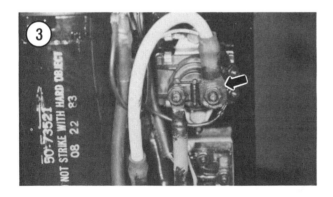

ignition switch and the starter solenoid (test points 5 and 6, **Figure 5**). Make sure the fuse is not blown on systems so equipped before proceeding with the test sequence.

Test No. 1

1. Disconnect the black ground wire at test point 2.
2. Connect a voltmeter between test point 2 and a good engine ground.
3. Turn the ignition switch to the START position while noting the voltmeter reading.
4A. If no voltage is noted, proceed to *Test No. 2*.
4B. If the voltmeter indicates battery voltage, check the black ground wire for an open circuit or poor connection. Reconnect the wire to the solenoid and proceed to *Test No. 6*.

Test No. 2

1. Connect the voltmeter between test point 3 and a good engine ground.
2. Turn the ignition switch to START and note the voltmeter.
3A. If no voltage is noted, proceed to *Test No. 3*.
3B. If battery voltage is noted, the starter sole-noid is defective and must be replaced.

Test No. 3

1. Connect the voltmeter between test point 4 and a good engine ground.
2. Turn the ignition switch to the START position while noting the voltmeter.
3A. If no voltage is noted, proceed to *Test No. 4*.
3B. If battery voltage is noted, check the neutral start switch for an open circuit. If the switch is acceptable, an open circuit is present in the yel-low or yellow/red wire between test points 3 and 4. Repair or replace the wire as necessary.

Test No. 4

1. Connect the voltmeter between test point 5 and a good engine ground.

2A. If no voltage is noted, proceed to *Test No. 5*.

2B. If battery voltage is present at test point 5, the ignition switch is defective and must be replaced.

Test No. 5

1. Connect the voltmeter between test point 6 and a good engine ground.

2A. If no voltage is noted, check the positive battery cable between the starter solenoid and battery for an open circuit, loose connection or excessive corrosion. Repair or replace battery cable as necessary.

2B. If battery voltage is present at test point 6, an open circuit (or blown fuse) is present in the wire between test points 5 and 6.

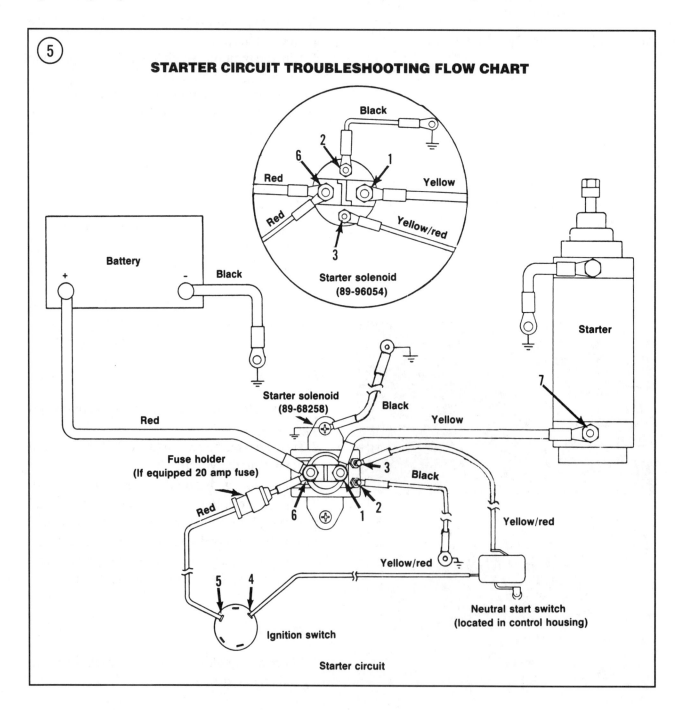

⑤

STARTER CIRCUIT TROUBLESHOOTING FLOW CHART

Test No. 6

1. Connect the voltmeter between test point 1 and a good engine ground.

2. Turn the ignition switch to the START position and note the voltmeter.

3A. If no voltage is noted, the starter solenoid is defective and must be replaced.

3B. If battery voltage is noted, proceed to *Test No. 7*.

Test No. 7

1. Reconnect the yellow or black starter cable to the starter solenoid.

2. Connect the voltmeter between test point 7 and a good engine ground.

3. Turn the ignition switch to the START position while noting the voltmeter.

4A. If no voltage is noted, check the cable between the starter solenoid and starter motor for an open circuit, loose connection or excessive corrosion. Repair or replace the cable as necessary.

4B. If the voltmeter indicates battery voltage and the starter does not operate, the starter motor is defective and must be repaired or replaced.

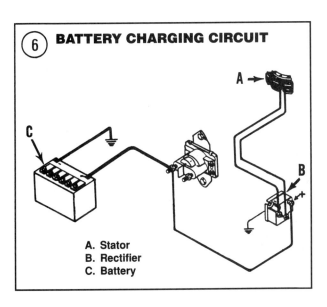

BATTERY CHARGING CIRCUIT

A. Stator
B. Rectifier
C. Battery

CHARGING SYSTEM

Description

Four basic charging systems are used on models covered in this manual:

a. 5 ampere (60 watt) unregulated charging system—Standard on 9.9-15 hp models equipped with electric start. Optional on 8 hp and 9.9-25 hp models equipped with manual start.

b. 9 ampere (127 watt) unregulated charging system—Standard on 40-60 hp models prior to 1993. On 1993 40-60 hp models, a 9 ampere (127 watt) system with a voltage regulator/rectifier is used.

c. 18 ampere (226 watt) charging system with voltage regulator/rectifier—Standard on all 75-115 hp models, 1990 and 1991 135, 150 and 175 hp models.

d. 40 ampere (564 watt) charging system with voltage regulator/rectifier—Optional on 1990 135, 150 and 175 hp models; standard on all other V6 models. Late V6 and some 75-115 hp models are equipped with dual voltage regulator/rectifiers.

A 4 amp AC lighting coil may be used on 4 and 5 hp models.

The charging system generally consists of permanent magnets located within the flywheel, a stator assembly, a rectifier (unregulated models), a voltage regulator or regulator/rectifier, the battery and related wiring. See **Figure 6** for a typical arrangement.

The 40 amp charging system with dual voltage regulator/rectifiers is basically 2 separate 20 amp charging systems. Half of the stator windings are connected to one regulator/rectifier assembly and the remaining stator windings are connected to the other regulator/rectifier. Should one regulator/rectifier fail, the charging system will still function, but at only one half of its rated output. Note that each regulator/rectifier assembly should be tested separately from the other.

3

A malfunction in the battery charging system generally causes the battery to remain undercharged. Since the stator assembly is protected by the flywheel, it is more likely that the battery, rectifier, voltage regulator (or rectifier/regulator) or connecting wiring will cause most charging system problems. The following conditions will cause rectifier or voltage regulator (or regulator/rectifier) damage:

a. Reversed battery cables.
b. Running the engine with battery cable(s) disconnected.
c. Broken wire or loose connection resulting in an open circuit.

CAUTION
If the outboard motor must be operated with the battery removed or disconnected, disconnect the stator wires from the rectifier or voltage regulator. Tape the ends of the wires to prevent accidental grounding.

System Inspection
(All Models)

Before performing the stator/rectifier troubleshooting procedure, check the following.
1. Make sure the battery is properly connected. If the battery polarity is reversed, the rectifier or voltage regulator will be damaged.
2. Check for loose or corroded connections. Clean and tighten as necessary.
3. Check the battery condition. Recharge or replace the battery as necessary.
4. Check the wiring harness between the stator and battery for cut, chafed or deteriorated insulation and corroded, loose or disconnected connections. Repair or replace the wiring harness as necessary.

Alternator Stator Resistance Test
(All Models)

The alternator stator assembly can be tested without removal from the power head on all models.

1. Disconnect the stator wires from the rectifier (**Figure 7**), terminal block or voltage regulator. The stator wires are yellow and gray on 8-15 hp models and yellow or yellow/red on all other models.
2. Calibrate ohmmeter on the R × 1 scale. Connect the ohmmeter between the disconnected stator wires and note resistance.

NOTE
Stator resistance should generally be less than 1 ohm, but may vary depending upon temperature. A very low resistance reading (resembling a short circuit) is acceptable.

3. Stator resistance should be 1.0-1.5 ohms or less.
4. Calibrate the ohmmeter on the R × 1000 scale. Connect the positive (red) ohmmeter lead to either stator wire. Connect the negative (black) ohmmeter lead to a good engine ground. No continuity should be present between either stator wire and ground.
5. Replace the stator if the resistance is not as specified. See Chapter Seven.

Rectifier Test
(All Models Except 40 Amp)

The rectifier can be tested without removal from the power head. Disconnect the battery cables from the battery before testing. Refer to **Figure 8** for terminal connections.

NOTE
Depending upon the internal polarity of the individual ohmmeter used during the following test, the results may be an exact opposite of what is described.

1. Disconnect all leads from the rectifier terminals.

2. Calibrate ohmmeter on the R × 1000 scale.

3. Connect the positive (red) ohmmeter lead to the rectifier ground and the negative (black) lead alternately to terminals A and C. The ohmmeter should indicate continuity.

4. Connect the negative ohmmeter test lead to the rectifier ground and the positive test lead alternately to terminals A and C. No continuity should be indicated.

5. Connect the negative ohmmeter lead to terminal B and the positive test lead alternately to terminals A and C. The ohmmeter should indicate continuity.

6. Connect the positive ohmmeter test lead to terminal B and the negative test lead alternately to terminals A and C. The ohmmeter should indicate no continuity.

7. Replace the rectifier if the ohmmeter readings are not as specified.

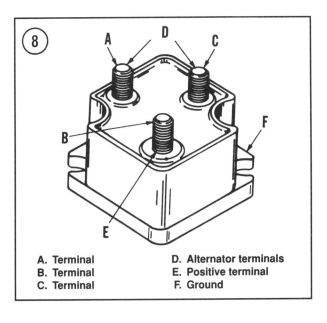

A. Terminal
B. Terminal
C. Terminal
D. Alternator terminals
E. Positive terminal
F. Ground

Alternator Output Test (9 Amp Charging System)

CAUTION
The outboard motor must be provided with an adequate supply of water while performing this procedure. Install a flushing device, place the engine in a test tank or perform the procedure with the boat in the water.

The rectifier must be functioning properly to obtain accurate output test results. Test the rectifier as described in this chapter.

1. If equipped with a voltage regulator, disconnect the regulator wires at the rectifier. Reinstall the rectifier terminal nut on the yellow stator wire.

2. Remove the red wire from the positive (+) rectifier terminal.

3. Connect an ammeter positive (+) test lead to the rectifier positive (+) terminal. Connect the ammeter negative (–) test lead to the disconnected red rectifier wire.

4. Start the engine and run at 3000 rpm while noting the ammeter reading.

5. Alternator output should be 7-9 amperes. If not, replace the stator assembly as described in Chapter Seven.

Voltage Regulator Test (9 Amp Charging System With Voltage Regulator/Rectifier and 16 Amp Charging System)

The voltage regulator can be tested without removal from the power head. A suitable ammeter and a 9-volt battery are necessary to perform the following test. Refer to **Figure 9** for this procedure.

CAUTION
The outboard motor must be provided with an adequate supply of water while performing this procedure. Install a flushing device, place the engine in a test tank or perform the procedure with the boat in the water.

1. Connect a voltmeter to the battery.

2. Start the engine and note the voltmeter.

3. If battery voltage exceeds 14.5 volts, replace the voltage regulator.

4. If the battery voltage is less than 14.5 volts, stop the engine, disconnect the battery cables from the battery and charge the battery.

5. Check battery voltage while cranking the engine. Replace the battery if it will not maintain 9.5 volts under cranking load.

6. If the cranking voltage is acceptable, disconnect the large red voltage regulator wire from the starter solenoid. See **Figure 9**.

7. Disconnect the small red voltage regulator wire (sense lead) from the starter solenoid. Connect the sense lead to the positive (+) terminal of a 9-volt battery (**Figure 9**). Connect the 9-volt battery negative (–) terminal to a good ground point on the outboard motor.

8. Connect the positive (red) ammeter lead to the large diameter red regulator wire and the negative (black) ammeter lead to the positive (+) terminal of the starter solenoid. See **Figure 9**.

CAUTION
Be certain all wires and ammeter leads are positioned away from the outboard flywheel while running the outboard.

9. Start the engine and note the ammeter.

10A. 9 amp charging system—The output current should be as follows:

  a. Idle speed—1 amp.

  b. 1000 rpm—4 amps.

  c. 2000 rpm—8 amps.

  d. 3000 rpm—9 amps.

10B. 18 amp charging system—The output current should be as follows:

  a. Idle speed—2 amps.

  b. 1000 rpm—10 amps.

  c. 2000 rpm—17 amps.

  d. 3000 rpm—18 amps.

11. If the output current is as specified, the charging system is performing properly. Make sure discharged battery is not due to excessive draw on the battery from too many accessories.

12. If the ammeter indicates less than specified at 3000 rpm, perform the alternator stator resistance test as described in this chapter. If the stator resistance is within the specified limit, replace the voltage regulator.

Alternator System Test (40 Amp Charging System)

The 40 amp charging system is optional on 1990 135, 150, 175 and 200 hp models and standard equipment on all other V6 models. The 40 amp system can be identified by a vented flywheel (for cooling purposes) and a water-cooled voltage regulator/rectifier assembly.

CAUTION
The outboard motor must be provided with an adequate supply of water while performing this procedure. Install a flushing device, place the engine in a test tank or perform the procedure with the boat in the water.

1. Make sure the battery is fully charged and in acceptable condition.

NOTE
Use an analog voltmeter to check battery voltage in the following steps. A digital voltmeter will not be accurate due to interference from the ignition system.

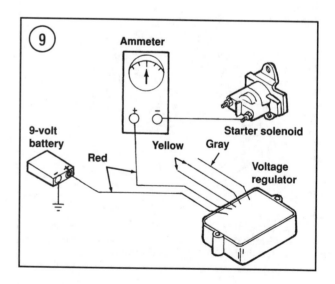

2. Connect an analog voltmeter to the battery. Note the battery voltage.

3. Start the motor and run at 1000 rpm while noting the voltmeter. Battery voltage should rise and then stabilize at approximately 14.5 volts. If so, the charging system is operating normally. If the voltage does not increase from the voltage noted in Step 2, proceed to *No Output*. If the voltage exceeds 16 volts, refer to *High Output*.

No output

NOTE
The tachometer receives its signal from the voltage regulator. It is possible for the tachometer to operate properly even with a defective voltage regulator.

1. Turn the ignition switch to the RUN position.
2. Disconnect the voltage regulator purple wire at the bullet connector.
3. Measure the voltage at the purple wire leading to the regulator. Battery voltage should be present at the wire. If not, the ignition switch or the wiring between the ignition switch and voltage regulator is defective.
4. Connect an AC voltmeter between the two yellow wire terminals at the voltage regulator. Start the engine and note the voltmeter.
5. If the voltage exceeds 16 volts AC, the regulator assembly is defective and should be replaced.

NOTE
The voltage regulator assembly has a thermal overload protection circuit designed to protect the voltage regulator from excessive heat. If the power head is not receiving adequate cooling water, the voltage regulator will not allow charging current to flow to the battery, preventing regulator overheating.

High output

1. Remove the flywheel as described in Chapter Eight. Inspect the stator assembly for burned windings or discoloration. Replace the stator assembly as necessary.

2. If the stator is in acceptable condition, reinstall the flywheel (Chapter Eight).

3. Connect an ammeter (40 amp minimum) in series with the red voltage regulator output wire between the terminal block above the voltage regulator and the starter solenoid.

4. Disconnect 1 yellow stator wire from the terminal block. Isolate the wire with electrical tape.

5. Start the engine and run at 1000-2000 rpm while noting the ammeter.

6. If no current output is noted, reconnect the yellow stator wire and disconnect the remaining yellow wire. Repeat Step 5.

7. If any current output is now noted, the stator assembly is shorted to ground and must be replaced as outlined in Chapter Seven.

8. If no current output is noted with either yellow wire disconnected, the voltage regulator is defective and must be replaced. See Chapter Seven.

Regulated voltage check

The battery must be in acceptable condition and fully charged for accurate regulated voltage test results.

CAUTION
The outboard motor must be provided with an adequate supply of water while performing this procedure. Install a flushing device, place the engine in a test tank or perform the procedure with the boat in the water.

1. Discharge the battery slightly by turning on all accessories and cranking the engine for 20 seconds with the lanyard switch turned off.

2. Connect an analog voltmeter to the battery. If a digital voltmeter must be used, keep the voltmeter as far from the power head as possible to prevent interference from the ignition system.

3. Start the engine and note the voltmeter. The voltage should rise slowly and stabilize at 14-14.5 volts. If not, test the stator and voltage regulator as previously described. If the regu-

3

lated voltage is as specified, the charging system is operating normally. Be sure that the discharged battery is not due to excessive current draw from operating too many accessories.

NOTE
*The voltage regulator/rectifier assemblies' 40 amp systems, including dual regulator systems, can be tested as described under **Voltage Regulator Test** in this chapter.*

IGNITION SYSTEM

The wiring harness used between the ignition switch and outboard motor is adequate to handle the electrical requirements of the outboard motor. It *will not* handle the electrical requirements of accessories. Whenever an accessory is added, run new wiring between the battery and the accessory, installing a separate fuse panel on the instrument panel.

If the ignition switch requires replacement, *never* install an automotive-type switch. A switch approved for marine use must always be used.

Description

A magneto breaker-point ignition system is used on 1990-1992 3 hp models. An alternator driven capacitor discharge ignition (CDI) system is used on all other models covered in this manual. General troubleshooting procedures are provided in **Table 4**.

Troubleshooting Precautions

Several troubleshooting precautions should be strictly observed to avoid damaging the ignition system.

1. Do not reverse the battery connections. Reverse battery polarity will damage the rectifier(s) and switchbox(es).
2. Do not "spark" the battery terminals with the battery cable connections to determine polarity.
3. Do not disconnect the battery cables with the engine running.

4. On models equipped with capacitor discharge ignition, do not crank or run the outboard if the switchbox(es) are not grounded to the power head.
5. Do not touch or disconnect any ignition components when the outboard is running, while the ignition switch is ON or while the battery cables are connected.
6. If the outboard must be started and run with the battery disconnected, disconnect the yellow or yellow/red stator wires from the rectifier, terminal block or voltage regulator. Tape each wire separately to prevent shorts.

Troubleshooting Preparation (All Models)

1. Test the ignition switch and mercury switch as described in this chapter to be certain they are not causing a problem.

NOTE
To test the wiring harness for poor solder connections in Step 2, bend the molded rubber connector while checking the continuity of the wire.

2. Check the wiring harness and all plug-in connections to make sure that all terminals are clean and tight, and the wiring insulation is in good condition.
3. Check all electrical components that are grounded to the engine for a clean tight ground connection.
4. Make sure all ground wires are properly connected, and the connections are clean and tight.
5. Check the remainder of the wiring harness for disconnected wires, short or open circuits. Repair wiring or replace the harness as necessary.
6. Make sure an adequate supply of fresh and properly mixed fuel is available to the power head.
7. Check the battery condition. Clean the terminal connections and recharge the battery if necessary. See Chapter Seven.

8. Check the spark plug lead routing. Make sure the leads are properly connected to their respective spark plugs.

9. Remove all spark plugs, keeping them in order. Check the condition of each plug. See Chapter Four.

10. Install spark gap tester Quicksilver part No. 91-63998A1 (or equivalent) to check for spark at each cylinder. If a spark tester is not available, reconnect the proper spark plug lead to its spark plug. Lay the plug against the cylinder head so its base makes a good connection and crank the engine. If weak or no spark is noted, check for loose wire connections at the ignition coil(s), battery and switchbox(es). Check the battery and starting system. The battery must be capable of maintaining at least 9.5 volts when cranking the engine with all spark plugs installed. If all are acceptable, an ignition system malfunction is likely.

BREAKER-POINT IGNITION TROUBLESHOOTING (1990-1992 3 HP MODELS)

Breaker point contacts are normally light gray in color. Dirty breaker point contacts should be cleaned with a suitable contact file. Do not use emery cloth to dress or clean breaker point contacts.

Badly burned or pitted breaker points should be replaced (Chapter Seven). Badly burned or pitted points usually indicate a problem elsewhere in the ignition system such as a defective condenser, improper point gap adjustment or oil or other contamination on the contact surfaces. Refer to Chapter Seven for breaker point replacement and adjustment procedures.

Stop Switch Test

If a no-spark condition is present, disconnect the stop switch and recheck the spark. If acceptable spark is now present at the spark plug, test the switch as follows:

1. Connect an ohmmeter between the disconnected stop switch wires. See **Figure 10**.
2. With the switch button not depressed, the meter should indicate no continuity.
3. Depress the switch button while noting the ohmmeter. With the button depressed, the meter should indicate continuity.
4. Replace the stop switch if test results are not as specified.

Primary Ignition Coil Test

The primary ignition coil is located under the flywheel.
1. Remove the flywheel as described in Chapter Eight.
2. Refer to **Figure 10** and disconnect the primary coil black/white wire.
3. Calibrate an ohmmeter on the R × 1 scale. Connect the ohmmeter positive (+) lead to the disconnected black/white wire and the negative (–) lead to the coil ground.
4. Primary coil resistance should be 1.5 ohms.
5. Replace the coil if resistance is not as specified. See Chapter Seven.

Secondary Ignition Coil Test

The secondary ignition coil is mounted on the side of the cylinder block and does not require removal for testing. Refer to **Figure 10** for this procedure.

NOTE
Resistance tests can only detect open or shorted windings in the secondary ignition coil. Replace the coil if resistance is not as specified in the following test. If the coil resistance is as specified, and the coil is still suspected as being defective, test the coil using a suitable magneto analyzer. Follow the instructions provided with the analyzer.

1. Disconnect the spark plug lead from the spark plug.
2. Disconnect the coil white/black primary wire from the connector leading to the primary coil.

3. Calibrate the ohmmeter on the R × 1 scale. Connect the ohmmeter positive lead to the disconnected black/white wire and the negative lead to the coil lamination (ground). The resistance should be 0.81-1.09 ohms.

4. Calibrate the ohmmeter on the R × 1000 scale. Connect the positive test lead to the spark plug terminal and the negative test lead to the coil lamination (ground). Resistance should be 4250-5750 ohms.

5. Replace the secondary ignition coil if resistance is not as specified.

CAPACITOR DISCHARGE IGNITION (CDI)

All models (except 1990-1992 3 hp) covered in this manual are equipped with an alternator-driven capacitor discharge ignition system. See Chapter Seven for a full description of the ignition systems. The switchbox(es) and ignition coil(s) cannot be tested using conventional test equipment. The manufacturer recommends using a Quicksilver Multi-Meter/DVA tester part No. 91-99750 (or equivalent) to test the ignition system, especially if the engine misfires, runs rough or if intermittent malfunctions are encountered.

NOTE
Multi-Meter Model 530 equipped with built-in DVA is available from Electronic Specialties Inc., 3148 South Chrysler, Tucson, Arizona 85713.

A conventional analog voltmeter can be used, providing it is capable of measuring 400 volts DC and is used with Quicksilver Direct Voltage Adapter (DVA) part No. 91-89045. Follow the instructions provided with the Multi-Meter/DVA tester or direct voltage adapter when testing the ignition system.

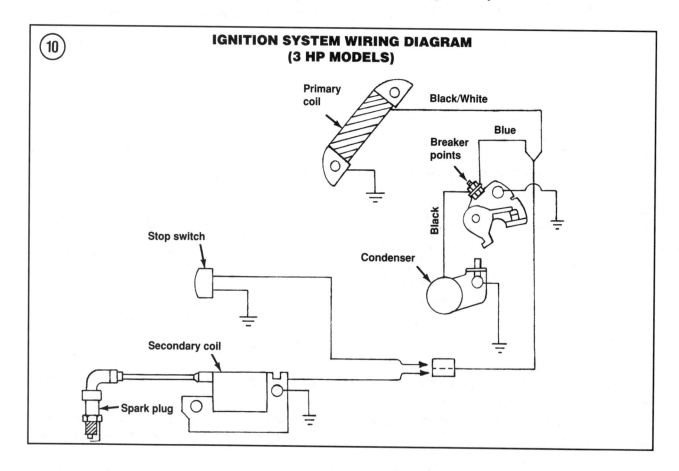

(10) IGNITION SYSTEM WIRING DIAGRAM (3 HP MODELS)

CAUTION
Unless specifically noted, all tests that involve cranking or running the engine must be performed with lead wires connected to their respective component(s). In addition, switchbox(es) must be securely grounded to the power head any time the engine is cranked or started or switchbox damage may result.

If the Quicksilver Multi-Meter/DVA tester or direct voltage adapter is not available, the ignition coil(s) on some models can be tested using a Model 9800 Merc-O-Tronic Magneto Analyzer. Follow the instructions and specifications provided with the magneto analyzer when testing ignition coils. The stator and trigger coil assemblies can be effectively tested using an ohmmeter. Refer to *Resistance Tests* in this chapter. If necessary, use a process of elimination and a suitable ohmmeter to troubleshoot the CDI system.

DIRECT VOLTAGE TESTS

A Quicksilver Multi-Meter/DVA tester part No. 91-99750 (or equivalent) or voltmeter capable of measuring 400 volts DC used with a Quicksilver Direct Voltage Adapter part No. 91-89045 is required to perform direct voltage tests.

NOTE
Unless otherwise noted, all direct voltage tests should be performed with the wires connected, but with the terminals exposed to accommodate test lead connection.

WARNING
High voltage is present during ignition system operation. Do not touch ignition components, wires or test leads while cranking or running the engine.

1-Cylinder Models

CAUTION
The outboard motor must be supplied with adequate cooling water if starting and running the engine. Place the out-board into a test tank or connect a flushing device to provide cooling water.

Ignition coil primary input

1. Check ignition coil primary input voltage by connecting the red test lead to a good engine ground. On 3.3 hp models, connect the black test lead to the orange wire at the bullet connector located between the ignition coil and CDI unit. On 4 and 5 hp models, connect the black test lead to the black/yellow ignition coil primary terminal. See **Figure 11**.

2. Position the DVA selector switch at DVA/400 VDC.

3. Crank or start the engine while noting the DVA meter. Ignition coil primary input voltage at 300-2000 rpm should be 100-320 volts on 3.3 hp models and 120-300 volts on 4 and 5 hp models.

4. If input voltage is below the specified voltage (Step 3), continue to *Switchbox Stop Circuit*. If input voltage is within specification (Step 3), continue at Step 5.

5. Disconnect the spark plug lead from the spark plug. Connect Quicksilver Spark Tester (part No. 91-63998A-1) or equivalent between the spark plug lead and engine ground. See **Figure 12**, typical.

6. Crank the engine while noting the spark tester. If weak or no spark is noted, the ignition coil is defective and must be replaced. See Chapter Seven.

7. If the spark is acceptable, inspect the condition of the spark plug and replace as necessary.

8. If the malfunction persists after replacing the spark plug, check the ignition timing as described in Chapter Five. If a sudden unexplained timing change is noted, check the trigger magnets in the hub of the flywheel for damage or a possible shift in magnet position. If the magnets are cracked or damaged or have shifted position, the flywheel must be replaced. See Chapter Eight. If the ignition timing is within specification, and the malfunction persists, the problem is not in the ignition system.

3

Switchbox stop circuit

1. On 3.3 hp models, connect the red test lead to a good engine ground and the black test lead to the brown or brown/white wire leading to the stop switch. On 4 and 5 hp models, connect the red test lead to the brown wire leading to the stop switch. Connect the black test lead to a good engine ground.

2. Set the meter selector switch to DVA/400 VDC.

3. Crank the engine while noting the test meter.

4. If the stop circuit voltage is within 120-320 volts (3.3 hp) or 175-300 volts (4 and 5 hp), continue at *Charge Coil Voltage* in this chapter.

5A. 3.3 hp—If the stop circuit voltage is above 320 volts, either the CDI unit or the charge/trigger coil assembly is defective. Test the charge/trigger coil as described under *Charge coil voltage* in this chapter. If the charge/trigger coil is in acceptable condition, replace the CDI unit as described in Chapter Seven.

5B. 4 and 5 hp—If the stop circuit voltage is above 300 volts, either the switchbox or the trigger coil is defective. Test the trigger coil as described in *RESISTANCE TESTS*. If the trigger coil is in acceptable condition, replace the switchbox as described in Chapter Seven.

> *WARNING*
> *To prevent the engine from starting in Step 6, disconnect the spark plug lead from the spark plug lead to the power head.*

6. If the stop circuit voltage is below 100 volts on 3.3 hp models or 175 volts on 4 and 5 hp models, disconnect the brown (4 and 5 hp) or brown/white (3.3 hp) stop switch wire from the CDI unit or switchbox at the bullet connector.

7. Repeat Step 3. If the stop circuit voltage is now within the specified range, the stop switch or stop switch wiring is defective. If the stop switch voltage is still below specifications, continue at *Charge coil voltage* in this chapter.

Charge coil voltage

The capacitor charge coil and trigger coil are a combined assembly on 3.3 hp models.

1A. 3.3 hp—Connect the red test lead to a good engine ground and the black test lead to the white charge/trigger coil wire at the bullet connector.

1B. 4 and 5 hp—Connect the red test lead to the black/red charge coil wire leading to the switchbox. Connect the black test lead to a good engine ground.

2. Set the meter selector switch to DVA/400 VDC.

3. Crank the engine and note the meter.

4A. 3.3 hp—Charge/trigger coil output should be 120-320 volts. If not, either the charge/trigger coil assembly or the CDI unit is defective. Test charge/trigger coil resistance as described under *Resistance Tests* in this chapter. If charge/trigger coil resistance is within specifications, replace the CDI unit.

4B. 4 and 5 hp—Charge coil output should be 150-325 volts. If the charge coil voltage is below 150 volts, either the charge coil or the switchbox is defective. Test charge coil resistance as described under *Resistance Tests* in this chapter. If charge coil resistance is within specification, replace the switchbox and retest.

2-Cylinder Models

> *CAUTION*
> *The outboard motor must be supplied with adequate cooling water if starting and running the engine. Place the outboard into a test tank or connect a flushing device to provide cooling water.*

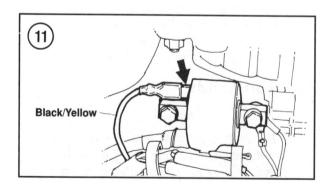

Ignition coil primary input

1A. Prior to serial No. D082000—Connect the red test lead to the No. 1 ignition coil negative terminal (black wire). Connect the black test lead to the coil positive terminal (green/yellow wire).

1B. Serial No. D082000-on—Connect the red test lead to the No. 1 ignition coil positive terminal (green/yellow wire) and the black test lead to the coil negative terminal (black wire).

2. Set the meter selector switch to DVA/400 VDC.

3. Crank or start the engine, note the meter reading, then discontinue cranking or stop the engine.

4A. Prior to serial No. D082000—Connect the red test lead to the No. 2 ignition coil negative terminal (black wire) and the red test lead to the positive coil terminal (green/wite wire). Repeat Step 3.

4B. Serial No. D082000-on—Connect the red test lead to the No. 2 ignition coil positive terminal (green/white wire) and the black test lead to the coil negative terminal (black wire). Repeat Step 3.

5. Ignition coil primary input voltage should be as follows:

    a. 8-25 hp prior to serial No. D0820000—100-250 volts at cranking and idle speed and 150-300 volts at 1000-4000 rpm.

    b. 8-15 hp serial No. D0820000-on—160-210 volts at cranking and idle speed and 200-230 volts at 1000-4000 rpm.

    c. 20 and 25 hp serial No. D0820000-on—160-285 volts at cranking and idle speed and 200-360 volts at 1000-4000 rpm.

6. If ignition coil input voltage is below specified voltage (Step 5) at either coil, continue at *Switchbox Stop Circuit*. If coil input voltage is within specified voltage, continue with Step 7.

7. Disconnect the number 1 spark plug lead from the ignition coil. Connect spark tester (Quicksilver part No. 91-63998A-1 or equivalent) between the ignition coil high tension terminal and a good engine ground.

8. Crank the engine while noting the spark tester. If weak, intermittent or no spark is noted, the ignition coil is defective and must be replaced (Chapter Seven).

9. Repeat Step 7 and Step 8 at the number 2 ignition coil.

10. If acceptable spark from both coils is noted in Step 8, replace the spark plugs. See Chapter Four.

11. If the malfunction persists after replacing the spark plugs, check the ignition timing as described in Chapter Five. If a sudden unexplained timing change is noted, check the trigger magnets in the flywheel hub for damage or a possible shift in magnet position. If the magnets are cracked or damaged or have shifted position in the flywheel hub, the flywheel must be replaced. See Chapter Eight. Check trigger advance linkage for worn, loose or damaged components and repair or replace as necessary. If the ignition timing is within specification, the problem is not in the ignition system.

Switchbox stop circuit

1. Connect the red test lead to a good engine ground. Connect the black test lead to the black/yellow switchbox wire between the switchbox and the stop switch (tiller handle and manual start models) or the wiring harness connector (remote control models).

2. Set the meter selector switch to DVA/400 VDC.

3. Crank or start the engine while noting the meter.

4. Switchbox stop circuit voltage should be 200-360 volts.

5. If the switchbox stop circuit voltage is within 200-360 volts, proceed to *Charge Coil Voltage* in this chapter.

6. If the stop switch voltage is higher than 360 volts, either the trigger coil or the switchbox is defective. Test trigger coil resistance as described under *Resistance Tests* in this chapter. Replace the trigger coil if resistance is not as specified. If the trigger coil resistance is within specification, replace the switchbox and retest the *Switchbox Stop Circuit*.

CAUTION
Only disconnect the ignition switch, stop switch and lanyard switch black/yellow wire in Step 7. The black/yellow wire leading to the stator assembly must remain connected to the switchbox during the following procedure.

7. If the switchbox stop circuit voltage (Step 3) is below 200 volts, disconnect the ignition switch, stop switch, lanyard switch and mercury switch (if so equipped) from the switchbox black/yellow wire or terminal.

WARNING
To prevent the engine from starting in Step 8, disconnect the spark plug leads from the spark plugs. Securely ground the spark plug leads to the engine.

8. With the ignition switch, stop switch, lanyard switch and mercury switch isolated from the switchbox, repeat Step 3. If the stop switch voltage is now within 200-360 volts, the ignition switch, stop switch, lanyard switch or mercury switch (and/or related wiring) is defective.

Charge coil voltage

1. To check the low-speed charge coil output to the switchbox, connect the red test lead to a good engine ground and the black test lead to black/yellow switchbox wire leading to the stator assembly.

2. Set the meter selector switch to DVA/400 VDC.

3. Crank or start the engine while noting the meter.

4. Low-speed charge coil output to the switchbox should be 200-360 volts.

5. To check the high-speed charge coil output to the switchbox, connect the red test lead to a good engine ground and the black test lead to the black/white switchbox wire leading to the stator assembly.

6. Make sure the meter selector switch is set at DVA/400 VDC.

7. Crank or start the engine while noting the meter.

8. High-speed charge coil output to the switchbox should be 10-100 volts at cranking and idle speed, and 100-300 volts at 1000-4000 rpm.

9. If either low-speed or high-speed charge coil output is below the specified voltage, either the stator assembly or the switchbox is defective. Check the stator resistance as described under *Resistance Tests* in this chapter. If the stator resistance is not as specified, replace the stator assembly (Chapter Seven). If the stator resistance is within specification, replace the switchbox and recheck charge coil output.

3- and 4-Cylinder Models

CAUTION
The outboard motor must be supplied with adequate cooling water if starting and running the engine. Place the outboard into a test tank or connect a flushing device to provide cooling water.

NOTE
Weak, intermittent or no spark at two cylinders usually indicates a defective trigger coil. Weak, intermittent or no spark at all cylinders usually indicates a defective stator assembly or switchbox. Weak, intermittent or no spark at any one cylinder usually indicates a defective spark plug, ignition coil or switchbox.

3

Ignition coil primary input

1. Connect the red test lead to the number 1 ignition coil positive primary terminal. Connect the black test lead to the number 1 coil negative primary terminal.

2. Set the meter selector switch to DVA/400 VDC.

3. Crank or start the engine, note the meter reading, then discontinue cranking or stop the engine.

4. Repeat Steps 1-3 on the remaining ignition coils.

5. Ignition coil primary input voltage at cranking and idle speed should be 160-250 volts on 40 hp models and 150-250 volts on 50-115 hp models. Ignition coil primary input voltage at 1000-4000 rpm should be 180-275 volts on 40 hp models and 180-280 on 50-115 hp models.

6. If primary input is below the specified voltage at any coil, proceed to *Switchbox Stop Circuit* in this chapter. If primary input is within the specified voltage, continue at Step 7.

7. If primary input voltage is within specification (Step 5), disconnect the spark plug lead from the number 1 ignition coil and spark plug.

8. Connect spark tester (Quicksilver part No. 91-63998A-1 or equivalent) to the coil high tension terminal and spark plug.

9. Crank or start the engine while noting the spark tester. If weak, intermittent or no spark output is noted, the ignition coil is defective and must be replaced (Chapter Seven).

10. Repeat Steps 7-9 on all remaining coils.

11. If acceptable spark is noted at all ignition coils, replace the spark plugs. See Chapter Four.

12. If the malfunction persists after replacing the spark plugs, check the ignition timing as described in Chapter Five. If a sudden unexplained timing change is noted, check the trigger magnets in the flywheel hub for damage or a possible shift in magnet position. If the magnets are cracked or damaged, or have shifted position in the flywheel hub, the flywheel must be replaced. See Chapter Eight. Check trigger advance link-

age for worn, loose or damaged components and repair or replace as necessary. If the ignition timing is within specification, the problem is not in the ignition system.

Switchbox stop circuit

1. Connect the red test lead to the black/yellow switchbox wire leading to the wiring harness connector or stop switch. Connect the black test lead to a good engine ground.

2. Set the meter selector switch to DVA/400 VDC.

3. Crank or start the engine, note the meter, then discontinue cranking or stop the engine.

4. Switchbox stop circuit voltage should be 200-360 volts.

5. If the stop circuit voltage is within 200-360 volts, proceed to *Charge Coil Voltage* in this chapter. If stop circuit voltage is above 360 volts, continue at Step 6. If stop switch voltage is below 200 volts, continue at Step 7.

6. If stop switch voltage is above 360 volts, either the trigger coil assembly or the switchbox is defective. Check trigger coil resistance as described under *RESISTANCE TESTS* in this chapter. Replace the trigger assembly if resistance is not as specified. If the trigger resistance is within specification, replace the switchbox, then recheck the switchbox stop circuit voltage.

WARNING
To prevent the engine from starting in Step 7, disconnect the spark plug leads from the spark plugs. Securely ground the spark plug leads to the engine.

7. If the switchbox stop circuit voltage is below 200 volts, disconnect the ignition switch, stop switch and mercury switch black/yellow wire(s) from the switchbox black/yellow terminal or wire. With the ignition switch, stop switch and mercury switch isolated from the switchbox, crank the engine and note the meter. If the stop circuit voltage is now within 200-360 volts, the ignition switch, stop switch or mercury switch

(and/or related wiring) is defective. Test the switches as described in this chapter.

Charge coil voltage

1. To check the low-speed charge coil output to the switchbox, connect the red test lead to the blue switchbox wire leading to the stator assembly. Connect the black test lead to a good engine ground.

2. Set the meter selector switch to DVA/400 VDC.

3. Crank or start the engine, note the meter, then discontinue cranking or stop the engine.

4. Low-speed charge coil output should be as follows:
   a. Three-cylinder models—200-300 volts at cranking and idle speeds, and 200-330 volts at 1000-4000 rpm.
   b. Four-cylinder models—210-310 volts at cranking and idle speeds, and 190-310 volts at 1000-4000 rpm.

5. To check high-speed charge coil output, move the red test lead to the red switchbox wire leading to the stator. Leave the black test lead connected to engine ground.

6. With the meter selector switch set at DVA/400 VDC, crank or start the engine, note meter, then discontinue cranking or stop the engine.

7. High-speed charge coil output should be as follows:
   a. 40 hp models—25-90 volts at cranking and idle speed and 140-310 volts at 1000-4000 rpm.
   b. 50-90 hp models—20-90 volts at cranking and idle speed and 130-300 volts at 1000-4000 rpm.
   c. 100 and 115 hp models—20-100 volts at cranking and idle speed and 140-310 volts at 1000-4000 rpm.

8. If either low- or high-speed charge coil output is below the specified voltage, either the stator assembly or the switchbox is defective. To determine which, check the stator resistance as described under *RESISTANCE TESTS* in this chapter. If the stator resistance is not within specifications, replace the stator assembly (Chapter Seven). If the stator resistance is as specified, replace the switchbox and repeat the charge coil output tests.

V6 Models

> *CAUTION*
> *The outboard motor must be supplied with adequate cooling water if starting and running the engine. Place the outboard into a test tank or connect a flushing device to provide cooling water.*

> *NOTE*
> *Weak, intermittent or no spark at two cylinders (one cylinder on each bank) usually indicates a defective trigger coil. Weak, intermittent or no spark at three cylinders (one complete bank) usually indicates a defective stator assembly or switchbox. Weak, intermittent or no spark at any one cylinder usually indicates a defective spark plug, ignition coil or switchbox.*

Ignition coil primary input

1. Connect the red test lead to the number 1 ignition coil positive primary terminal and the black test lead to the coil negative primary terminal. See **Figure 13**.

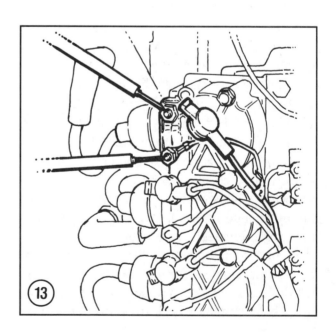

2. Set the meter selector switch to DVA/400 VDC.

3. Crank or start the engine, note the meter, then discontinue cranking or stop the engine.

4. Repeat Steps 1-3 on all remaining ignition coils.

NOTE
The 40 amp stator can be identified by the serrated, vented flywheel cover. The flywheel cover on models with 16 amp charging system is smooth and not vented.

5. Ignition coil primary input voltage should be as follows:

a. Cast iron flywheel 16 amp charging system—80-130 volts at cranking and idle speeds, 125-170 volts at 1000 rpm and 140-190 volts at 3000 rpm.

b. Flex plate flywheel 16 amp charging system—125-195 volts at cranking and idle speeds, 160-230 volts at 1000 rpm and 200-300 volts at 3000 rpm.

c. Forty amp charging system—90-145 volts at cranking and idle speeds, 125-175 volts at 1000 rpm and 175-240 volts at 3000 rpm.

6. If primary input voltage is as specified at all ignition coils, proceed to *Switchbox Stop Circuit* in this chapter. If primary input is below specified voltage, continue at Step 7.

7. Disconnect the spark plug lead from the number 1 ignition coil and spark plug. Connect spark tester (Quicksilver part No. 91-63998A-1 or equivalent) to the number 1 ignition coil high tension terminal and spark plug.

8. Crank or start the engine while noting the spark tester. If weak, intermittent or no spark is noted, the ignition coil is defective and must be replaced (Chapter Seven).

9. Repeat spark test (Step 7 and Step 8) on all remaining ignition coils.

10. If acceptable spark is noted at all ignition coils, replace the spark plugs. See Chapter Four.

11. If the malfunction persists after replacing the spark plugs, check the ignition timing as de-

scribed in Chapter Five. If a sudden unexplained timing change is noted, check the trigger magnets in the flywheel hub for damage or a possible shift in magnet position. If the magnets are cracked or damaged, or have shifted position in the flywheel hub, the flywheel must be replaced. See Chapter Eight. Check trigger advance linkage for worn, loose or damaged components and repair or replace as necessary. If the timing is erratic (shifts around) at cranking and idle speeds, proceed to *Switchbox Bias* in this chapter. If the timing is within specification, the problem is not in the ignition system.

Switchbox stop circuit

NOTE
The switchboxes on V6 models (except 250 and 275 hp) must be removed from the power head to gain access to the inner switchbox wire terminals.

1. Remove the 2 screws securing the switchboxes to the power head (**Figure 14**). Without disconnecting any switchbox wires, separate the inner and outer switchboxes, being careful not to lose the spacers located between switchboxes at each mounting screw.

CAUTION
The switchboxes must be grounded to the power head when cranking or starting the engine, or the switchboxes may be damaged. Be sure to connect a suitable jumper wire between BOTH switchboxes and a good engine ground before cranking the engine in the following tests.

2. Connect the red test lead to the outer (upper on 250 and 275 hp models) switchbox black/yellow wire terminal. See **Figure 15**. Connect the black test lead to a good engine ground.

3. Set the meter selector switch to DVA/400 VDC.

4. Crank or start the engine, note the meter, then discontinue cranking or stop the engine.

5. Move the red test lead to the inner (lower on 250 and 275 hp models) switchbox black/yellow

wire terminal. Be sure the black test lead is connected to a good engine ground. Repeat Step 4.

6. Switchbox stop circuit voltage should be as follows:

   a. Cast iron flywheel 16 amp charging system—175-275 volts at cranking and idle speeds and 225-375 volts at 1000-3000 rpm.

   b. Flex plate flywheel 16 amp charging system—200-300 volts at cranking and idle speeds and 290-400 volts at 1000-3000 rpm.

   c. Forty amp charging system—200-300 volts at cranking and idle speed and 225-400 volts at 1000-3000 rpm.

7. If stop circuit voltage is within the specified range at both switchboxes, proceed to *Charge Coil Voltage* in this chapter. If the stop circuit voltage is higher than the specified voltage at one or both switchboxes, continue at Step 8. If stop circuit voltage is below the specified voltage at one or both switchboxes, continue at Step 9.

8. If stop switch voltage is above the specified range at either or both switchboxes, the trigger coil assembly or one (or both) switchbox(es) is defective. To determine which, check trigger coil resistance as described under *RESISTANCE TESTS* in this chapter. Replace the trigger coil (Chapter Seven) if trigger resistance is not as specified. If trigger resistance is within specification, one or both switchbox(es) is defective. Replace the switchbox(es) that exhibited high stop circuit voltage (Chapter Seven) and repeat the stop circuit test.

WARNING
To prevent the engine from starting in Step 9, disconnect the spark plug leads from the spark plugs and securely ground the leads to the engine.

9. If switchbox stop circuit voltage is below the specified voltage at one or both switchboxes, isolate the ignition switch, stop switch and mer-

cury switch by disconnecting the black/yellow wires from each switchbox.

10. Recheck the stop circuit voltage at both switchboxes (Steps 2-5). If stop circuit voltage is still below specifications, proceed to *Charge Coil Voltage*. If stop circuit voltage is now within specifications, the ignition switch, stop switch or mercury switch (and/or related wiring) is defective. Test the switches as described in this chapter.

11. If the ignition system malfunction has been determined and repaired at this point, reattach the switchboxes to the power head (except 250 and 275 hp models). See Chapter Seven. If not, the switchboxes must remain detached to test charge coil output.

Charge coil output

CAUTION
The switchboxes must be grounded to the power head when cranking or starting

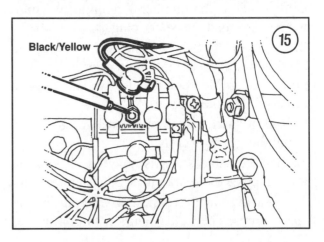

the engine, or the switchboxes may be damaged. Be sure to connect a suitable jumper wire between BOTH switchboxes and a good engine ground before cranking the engine in the following tests.

1. To test low-speed charge coil output to the outer (or upper on 250 and 275 hp models) switchbox, connect the red test lead to the blue terminal (**Figure 16**) of the outer (upper on 250 and 275 hp) switchbox. Connect the black test lead to a good engine ground.

2. Set the meter selector switch to DVA/400 VDC.

NOTE
A malfunctioning idle speed stabilizer or spark advance module may cause the following test results to be invalid. If so equipped, disconnect the idle speed stabilizer and/or spark advance module before performing charge coil output tests.

3. Crank or start the engine, note the meter, then discontinue cranking or stop the engine.

4. Low-speed charge coil output should be as follows:

  a. Cast iron flywheel 16 amp charging system—150-250 volts at cranking and idle speeds, 190-265 volts at 1000 rpm and 200-275 volts at 3000 rpm.

  b. Flex plate flywheel 16 amp charging system—250-480 volts at cranking and idle

speeds, 270-480 volts at 1000 rpm and 310-400 volts at 3000 rpm.

  c. Forty amp charging system—180-265 volts at cranking and idle speeds, 195-265 volts at 1000 rpm and 255-345 volts at 3000 rpm.

5. To test high-speed charge coil output to the outer (upper on 250 and 275 hp) switchbox, connect the red test lead to the outer (or upper) switchbox red wire terminal (**Figure 17**). Connect the black test lead to a good engine ground.

6. Set the meter selector switch to DVA/400 VDC.

7. Crank or start the engine, note the meter, then discontinue cranking or stop the engine.

8. High-speed charge coil output should be as follows:

  a. Cast iron flywheel 16 amp charging system—20-35 volts at cranking and idle speeds, 85-120 volts at 1000 rpm and 170-240 volts at 3000 rpm.

  b. Flex plate flywheel 16 amp charging system—25-50 volts at cranking and idle speeds, 65-105 volts at 1000 rpm and 250-375 volts at 3000 rpm.

  c. Forty amp charging system—25-50 volts at cranking and idle speeds, 120-160 volts at 1000 rpm and 230-320 volts at 3000 rpm.

9. Repeat Steps 1 through 8 on the inner (lower on 250 and 275 hp) switchbox.

10. If either low-speed or high-speed charge coil output is below the specified voltage at one or both switchboxes, check stator resistance as described under *RESISTANCE TESTS* in this chapter. Replace the stator assembly if resistance is not as specified (Chapter Seven). If stator resistance is within specifications, replace the switchbox that exhibited low charge coil output. If charge coil output is within specifications at both switchboxes, proceed to *Switchbox Bias* in this chapter.

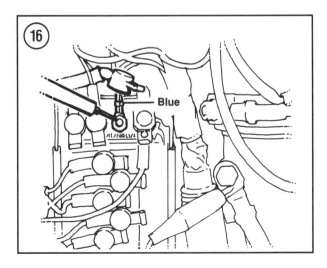

16

Blue

Switchbox bias

> *NOTE*
> *A malfunctioning idle speed stabilizer or spark advance module may cause the following test results to be invalid. If so equipped, disconnect the idle speed stabilizer and/or spark advance module before performing switchbox bias tests.*

Switchbox bias tests must be performed using a conventional voltmeter. If using a meter with a built-in DVA, set the meter selector switch to 20 VDC, instead of DVA/20 VDC.

1. Connect the red test lead to a good engine ground and the black test lead to the outer (upper on 250 and 275 hp) switchbox white/black wire terminal (**Figure 18**).
2. Crank or start the engine, note the meter, then discontinue cranking or stop the engine.
3. Switchbox bias on all models should be 1-6 volts at cranking and idle speeds, 3-15 volts at 1000 rpm and 10-30 volts at 3000 rpm.
4. If switchbox bias is below the specified voltage, one or both switchbox(es) is defective. Replace the outer (upper on 250 and 275 hp) switchbox (Chapter Seven) and retest bias voltage. If necessary, replace the inner (lower on 250 and 275 hp) switchbox and retest bias voltage.
5. If switchbox bias is within specifications, and the engine does not run or performs poorly, one or both switchbox(es), or the trigger assembly is defective. Check trigger resistance as described under *RESISTANCE TESTS* in this chapter. If trigger resistance is within specifications, replace switchbox(es) and repeat bias voltage test.

> *NOTE*
> *A frequent cause of switchbox bias failure is a poor ground to the adjacent switchbox. If repeated bias failure occurs in the same switchbox, the other switchbox ground should be closely inspected. If the ground is clean, tight and appears to be in acceptable condition, the manufacturer recommends replacing BOTH switchboxes.*

RESISTANCE TESTS

The switchbox(es) and ignition coils cannot be effectively tested using conventional test equipment. The stator and trigger coil, however, can be effectively tested using an ohmmeter. If necessary, use a process of elimination and a suitable ohmmeter to troubleshoot the CDI system. If the stator and trigger coil assemblies test good in the following procedures, the switchbox(es) and ignition coil(s) can be tested by a Mercury outboard dealer or other marine specialist.

The resistance values specified in the following test procedures are based on tests performed at room temperature. Actual resistance readings

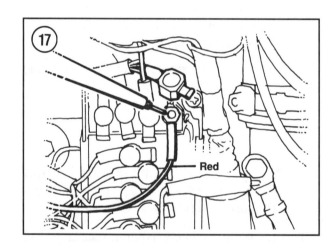

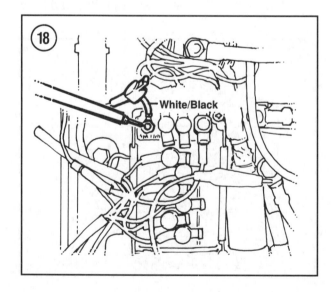

obtained during testing will generally be slightly higher if checked on hot components. In addition, resistance readings may vary depending on the manufacturer of the ohmmeter. Therefore, use discretion when failing any component that is only slightly out of specification.

Charge/Trigger Coil Test (3.3 hp)

1. Disconnect the charge/trigger coil white wire at its bullet connector between the coil and the CDI unit.
2. Attach the positive ohmmeter lead to the charge/trigger coil white wire and the black ohmmeter lead to a good engine grould
3. Charge/trigger coil resistance should be 300-400 ohms.
4. Replace the charge/trigger coil assembly (Chapter Seven) if resistance is not as specified.

CDI Unit Test (3.3 hp)

NOTE
Depending on the internal polarity of individual ohmmeters, the following test results may be the exact opposite of those specified.

1. Disconnect the white and orange CDI unit wires at their bullet connectors.

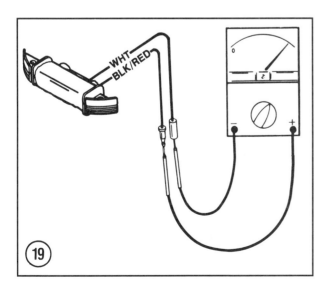

2. Calibrate the ohmmeter on the R × 1000 ohms scale.
3. Connect the positive ohmmeter lead to the white CDI unit wire and the negative ohmmeter lead to the orange CDI unit wire.
4. Continuity should be noted.
5. Next, switch the ohmmeter leads, positive lead to the orange wire and negative lead to the white wire.
6. No continuity should be noted.
7. Replace the CDI unit if the resistance is not as specified.

Charge Coil (Stator) Tests

NOTE
Wire color code abbreviations are embossed on the switchbox at each wire terminal. To remove the switchbox wires in the following procedures, unsnap the rubber cap and remove the nut holding each wire to be removed. Reinstall the nut on the terminal to prevent its loss.

4 and 5 hp

The charge coil can be tested on 4 and 5 hp models without removal from the power head.
1. Disconnect the black/red and white charge coil wires from the switchbox.
2. Connect an ohmmeter between the disconnected wires. See **Figure 19**.
3. Charge coil resistance should be 93-142 ohms. Replace the charge coil (Chapter Seven) if resistance is not as specified.

2-cylinder models (8, 9.9, 15, 20 and 25 hp)

The charge coil resistance can be checked without removal from the power head.

NOTE
Make sure the stator assembly is securely grounded to the power head.

1. Disconnect the black/yellow and black/white stator wires from the switchbox.

2. Connect the ohmmeter between the black/white stator wire and a good engine ground. Resistance should be 120-180 ohms.

3. Connect the ohmmeter between the black/yellow wire and a good engine ground. Resistance should be 3200-3800 ohms.

4. Connect the ohmmeter between the black/white and the black/yellow wires. Resistance should be 3100-3700 ohms.

5. Replace the stator assembly (Chapter Seven) if resistance is not as specified.

4-cylinder models (40, 100 and 115 hp)

The charge coils can be tested without removal from the power head. Make sure the stator black wire is securely grounded to the power head.

1. Disconnect the blue and blue/white stator wires (low-speed charge coil) from the switchbox.

2. Connect the ohmmeter between the blue and blue/white wires. Resistance should be 5700-8000 ohms on 40 hp models or 6800-7600 ohms on 100 and 115 hp models.

3. Disconnect the red and red/white stator wires (high-speed charge coil) from the switchbox.

4. Connect the ohmmeter between the red and red/white wires. Resistance should be 56-76 ohms on 40 hp models or 90-140 ohms on 100 and 115 hp models.

5. Connect the ohmmeter between a good engine ground and alternately to the red stator wire and the blue stator wire. No continuity should be noted between engine ground and the red and blue wires.

6. Replace the stator assembly (Chapter Seven) if the resistance is not as specified.

3-cylinder models (50, 60, 75 and 90 hp)

The charge coils can be tested without removal from the power head. Make sure the black stator wire is securely grounded to the power head.

1. Disconnect the blue and red stator wires from the switchbox.

2. Connect the ohmmeter between the blue and red stator wires (low- speed charge coil). Resistance should be as follows:
   a. 50 and 60 hp (prior to serial No. D000750)—5400-6200 ohms.
   b. 50 and 60 hp (serial No. D000750-on) and 75 and 90 hp—3600-4200 ohms.

3. Connect the ohmmeter between the red stator wire and the black stator ground wire or a good engine ground (high-speed charge coil). Resistance should be as follows:
   a. 50 and 60 hp (prior to serial No. D000750)—125-175 ohms.
   b. 50 and 60 hp (serial No. D000750-on) and 75 and 90 hp—90-140 ohms.

4. Replace the stator assembly if resistance is not as specified. See Chapter Seven.

V6 Models

The charge coils can be tested without removal from the power head. Make sure the stator black wire is securely grounded to the power head.

NOTE
The 40 amp stator can be identified by the serrated, vented flywheel cover. The flywheel cover used with the 16 amp stator is smooth and not vented.

1. Disconnect the blue, red, blue/white and red/white stator wires from the switchboxes.

2. Connect the ohmmeter between the blue and red stator wires. Resistance should be as follows:
   a. 135-200 hp 16 amp stator—4450-4650 ohms.
   b. 135-275 hp 40 amp stator—3500-4200 ohms.
   c. 250 and 275 hp 16 amp stator—3900-4400 ohms.

3. Connect the ohmmeter between the blue/white and red/white stator wires. Resistance should be as follows:

a. 135-200 hp 16 amp stator—4450-4650 ohms.

b. 135-275 hp 40 amp stator—3500-4200 ohms.

c. 250 and 275 hp 16 amp stator—3900-4400 ohms.

4. Connect the ohmmeter between the black stator ground wire and alternately to the red wire, then the red/white wire. Resistance should be 65-75 ohms on all models with a 16 amp stator, or 90-140 ohms on all models with a 40 amp stator.

5. Replace the stator assembly (Chapter Seven) if resistance is not as specified.

Trigger Coil Tests

> *NOTE*
> *Wire color code abbreviations are embossed on the switchbox at each wire terminal. To remove the switchbox wires in the following procedures, unsnap the rubber cap and remove the nut holding each wire to be removed. Reinstall the nut on the terminal to prevent its loss.*

3.3 hp

See *Charge/Trigger Coil Test* in this chapter.

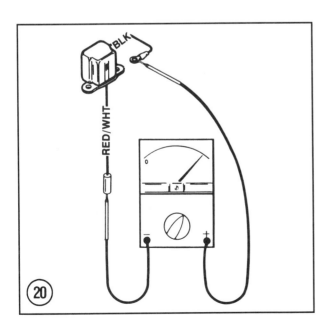

4 and 5 hp

The trigger coil can be tested without removal from the power head.

1. Disconnect the red/white trigger coil wire from the switchbox. Disconnect the black trigger coil ground wire installed under one of the trigger mounting screws.

2. Connect the ohmmeter between the red/white and black wires (**Figure 20**). Resistance should be 80-115 ohms.

3. Replace the trigger coil assembly (Chapter Seven) if resistance is not as specified.

2-cylinder models (8, 9.9, 15, 20 and 25 hp)

The trigger coil can be tested without removal from the power head.

1. Disconnect the brown/yellow and brown/white trigger wires from the switchbox.

2. Connect the ohmmeter between the brown/yellow and brown/white wires. Resistance should be 650-850 ohms.

3. Replace the trigger coil assembly if the resistance is not as specified.

3-cylinder models (50, 60, 75 and 90 hp)

The trigger coils can be tested without removal from the power head.

1. Disconnect the brown, white, white/black and violet trigger wires from the switchbox.

2. Connect one ohmmeter lead to the trigger white/black wire. Connect the other ohmmeter lead alternately to the brown, white and violet trigger wires, noting the meter reading at each connection. Resistance should be 1100-1400 ohms at each test connection.

3. Replace the trigger assembly if the resistance is not as specified.

4-cylinder models (40, 100 and 115 hp)

The trigger coils can be tested without removal from the power head.

1A. 100 and 115 hp—Disconnect the brown, white/black, white and violet trigger wires from the switchbox.

1B. 40 hp—Disconnect the brown, black, white and violet trigger wires from the switchbox.

2A. 100 and 115 hp—Connect the ohmmeter between the brown and white/black trigger wires.

2B. 40 hp—Connect the ohmmeter between the brown and black trigger wires.

3. Resistance should be 700-1000 ohms on all models.

4. All Models—Connect the ohmmeter between the white and violet trigger wires. Resistance should be 7000-1000 ohms.

5. Replace the trigger assembly (Chapter Seven) if resistance is not as specified.

V6 models

The trigger coils can be tested without removal from the power head.

1. Remove the 2 screws securing the inner and outer switchboxes (except 250 and 275 hp) to the power head. See **Figure 21**. Separate the switchboxes, being careful not to lose the spacers located between the switchboxes at each mounting screw.

2. Disconnect the brown, white and violet (with yellow sleeve) trigger wires from the outer or lower switchbox. Disconnect the brown, white and violet (without yellow sleeve) from the inner or upper switchbox.

3. Connect the ohmmeter between the brown (without yellow sleeve) and white (with yellow sleeve) trigger wires. Note meter reading.

4. Connect the ohmmeter between the white (without yellow sleeve) and violet (with yellow sleeve) trigger wires. Note the meter reading.

5. Connect the ohmmeter between the violet (without yellow sleeve) and brown (with yellow sleeve) trigger wires. Note the meter reading.

6. Trigger coil resistance should be 1100-1400 ohms at each test connection.

7. Replace the trigger assembly if resistance is not as specified. See Chapter Seven.

8. During reassembly, note that the trigger wires with the yellow sleeve must be connected to the lower switchbox on 250 and 275 hp models, or the outer switchbox on all other V6 models. Make sure the 2 spacers are properly located between the switchboxes (except 250 and 275 hp) and tighten the 2 switchbox mounting screws (**Figure 21**) securely.

Ignition Coil Tests

NOTE
Resistance tests can only detect open or shorted windings in an ignition coil. Re-

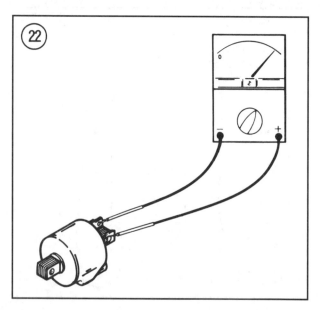

*place the ignition coil(s) if resistance is not as specified. If ignition resistance is within specifications, but still suspected as being defective, test the coil(s) as described under **Direct Voltage Tests** in this chapter, or test the coil using a suitable magneto analyzer, or have the coil tested by a Mercury dealership or other marine specialist.*

3.3 hp

1. Calibrate the ohmmeter on the R × 1 scale.

2. Disconnect the orange ignition coil wire at its bullet connector. Disconnect the spark plug lead from the ignition coil.

3. Connect the ohmmeter positive lead to the orange ignition coil wire and the negative lead to a good engine ground.

4. Coil primary winding resistance should be less than 1 ohm.

5. Calibrate the ohmmeter on the R × 1 000 scale.

6. Connect the ohmmeter positive lead to the coil high tension terminal and the negative lead to a good engine ground.

7. Coil secondary windings resistance should be 3000-4000 ohms.

8. Replace the ignition coil if resistance is not as specified.

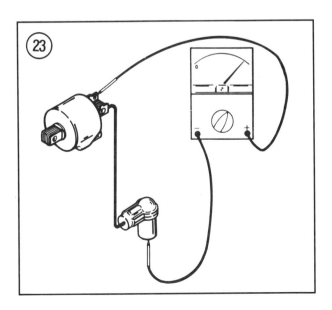

4 and 5 hp

1. Disconnect the black/yellow switchbox wire from the ignition coil.

2. Disconnect the spark plug high tension lead from the ignition coil.

3. Remove the 2 screws and washers securing the coil to the power head. Disconnect the black ground wire from behind the coil, then remove the coil from the power head.

4. Connect the ohmmeter between the negative and positive terminals as shown in **Figure 22** to check primary winding resistance. Primary resistance should be 0.02-0.38 ohm.

5. Connect the ohmmeter leads as shown in **Figure 23** to check secondary winding resistance. Secondary resistance should be 3000-4400 ohms.

6. Replace the ignition coil if resistance is not as specified.

8-275 hp

1. Disconnect the primary wires from the positive and negative ignition coil terminals.

2. Remove the spark plug lead from the high tension terminal.

3. To check primary winding resistance, connect the ohmmeter between the positive and negative coil primary terminals. Ignition coil primary resistance should be 0.02-0.04 ohm.

4A. Orange colored ignition coils:

   a. Connect the ohmmeter between the coil high tension terminal and either the positive or negative primary terminal. The meter should indicate no continuity.

   b. Connect the ohmmeter between the high tension terminal and a good engine ground (if mounted) or the coil ground wire at the rear of the coil (if removed). The meter should indicate 800-1100 ohms.

4B. Blue colored coils—Connect the ohmmeter between the coil high tension terminal and either the positive or negative primary terminal. The meter should indicate 800-1100 ohms.

5. Replace the coil(s) if resistance is not as specified (Chapter Seven).

Mercury (Tilt) Switch Test

See **Figure 24** for a typical mercury switch installation.

1. Remove the mercury switch mounting screw and black ground wire.

2. Connect an ohmmeter between the black ground wire and the black/yellow wire or terminal stud on the switch.

3. Hold the mercury switch as it would be positioned with the outboard motor in the DOWN position. The meter should indicate no continuity.

4. Tilt the mercury switch to the UP position. Tap the switch on its end with a finger. The meter should now indicate continuity.

5. Replace the mercury switch if it does not perform as specified in Step 3 and Step 4.

Push Button Stop Switch Test
(Models So Equipped)

Refer to the back of this manual for wiring diagrams on all models.

1. To test the push button stop switch, disconnect the stop switch black and black/yellow wires from the engine wiring.

2. Connect an ohmmeter between the disconnected stop switch wires.

3. With the stop switch not depressed, the meter should indicate no continuity.

4. Depress the stop switch and note the meter. It should now indicate continuity (1 ohm or less).

5. Replace the stop switch if it does not perform as specified.

Lanyard Switch Test
(Models So Equipped)

Refer to the wiring diagrams in the back of this manual.

1. Disconnect the lanyard switch black and black/yellow wires.

2. Connect an ohmmeter between the disconnected wires.

3. With the lanyard switch in the RUN position, the meter should indicate no continuity.

4. Place the switch in the OFF position. The meter should now indicate continuity (1 ohm or less).

5. Replace the lanyard switch if it does not perform as specified.

Ignition Switch Test
(Quicksilver "Commander" Remote Control)

The ignition switch is most easily tested at the remote control assembly wiring harness connector. Refer to the wiring diagrams (back of manual) for terminal location and identification. If the ignition switch is removed from the remote control, perform the test according to the wire color codes shown in **Figure 25**.

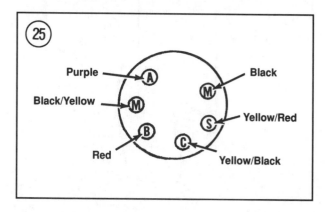

NOTE
The following procedure should be used to test the ignition switch and wiring on models equipped with a Quicksilver "Commander" remote control assembly. This test may not be valid on models equipped with an aftermarket remote control.

Refer to **Figure 25** for this procedure.

1. Disconnect the negative, then the positive battery cables from the battery.

2. Disconnect the remote control wiring harness and instrument panel connector.

3. Place the ignition switch in the OFF position.Connect an ohmmeter between the connector terminals M (black) and m (black/yellow). The meter should indicate continuity.

4. Place the switch in the RUN position. Connect the ohmmeter between terminals B (red) and A (purple). The meter should indicate continuity.

5. Hold the switch in the START position. Connect the ohmmeter between terminals B (red) and S (yellow/red), then between terminals A (purple) and S (yellow/red), then between terminals B (red) and A (purple). The meter should indicate continuity at each test connection.

6. Place the switch in the RUN or START position and depress the key to activate the choke circuit. Connect the ohmmeter between the following terminals: B (red) and C (yellow/red); B (red) and A (purple); C (yellow/black) and A (purple). The meter should indicate continuity at each test connection.

7. Check the ignition switch soldered connections if readings other than specified are obtained. If the connections and switch wiring are in acceptable condition, replace the ignition switch assembly.

SPEED LIMITER

Models 250 and 275 are equipped with a speed limiter module designed to prevent excessive engine rpm. Should engine speed exceed 6000-6200 rpm, the speed limiter module reduces ignition voltage to cylinders 2, 4 and 6 until engine speed drops below 6000 rpm. The speed limiter module is mounted to the starboard side of the power head below the switchboxes. Refer to the appropriate wiring diagrams in the back of this manual.

Use the following procedure to troubleshoot the speed limiter system.

1. If an intermittent ignition malfunction is noted at engine speeds of less than 6000 rpm, disconnect the orange speed limiter wire from the lower switchbox. If the engine now runs properly, the speed limiter is defective and should be replaced.

2. If sudden ignition failure to all 6 cylinders is noted at approximately 6000 rpm, the diode may be shorted to ground. See *Diode Test.*

3. If the engine continues to run on 3 cylinders after the ignition switch is turned off, the diode may be open or disconnected. See *Diode Test.*

4. If the engine continues to run on all 6 cylinders after the ignition switch is turned off, check the diode for correct installation (not backward). Refer to the appropriate wiring diagram in in the back of this manual.

NOTE
The speed limiter black wire must be securely connected to a good engine ground for proper speed limiter operation.

Diode Test

The diode is connected to the black/yellow terminal of the lower switchbox. Refer to the wiring diagrams in the back of this manual. Proceed as follows to test the diode.

1. Disconnect the diode from the lower switchbox and the bullet connector.

2. Connect an ohmmeter to the diode wires, note the reading, then reverse the ohmmeter leads.

3. The meter should indicate continuity in one direction and no continuity in the other. If the diode shows continuity in both directions or no continuity in both directions, replace the diode.

SPARK ADVANCE/IDLE STABILIZER MODULE TROUBLESHOOTING

Electronic Spark Advance Modules

V6 models may be equipped with an idle stabilizer or spark advance module. These solid-state modules are non-serviceable and should be replaced if they do not function as described.

Idle Stabilizer Test

When the engine speed drops below approximately 550 rpm, the idle stabilizer electronically advances ignition timing by up to 9°. The timing advance provided raises the engine speed to 550 rpm, at which time the module returns ignition timing to normal operation. The idle stabilizer is mounted to the power head and can be identified by its shape and wire color. See **Figure 26**. Proceed as follows to test the idle stabilizer:

1. With the engine in a test tank or mounted on a boat in the water, remove the engine cover and connect a timing light to the No. 1 (top starboard) spark plug lead. Connect an accurate tachometer to the engine.

2. Start the engine and run at idle speed above 600 rpm.

3. Slowly, pull forward on the spark advance lever to retard the timing. Using the timing light, observe the timing as the spark advance lever is moved.

NOTE
Due to variations in individual idle stabilizer modules, and in tachometers from different manufacturers, the engine speed at which timing advance/retard occurs may vary slightly.

4. If the ignition timing suddenly advances (as much as 9°) as the engine speed falls below 550 rpm (approximately), the idle stabilizer is operating properly. If timing advance is not noted, replace the idle stabilizer module.

Idle Stabilizer Shift System (150XR4 and 150XR6 Models)

The idle stabilizer shift system is designed to prevent stalling by advancing the ignition timing 3° when the outboard is shifted into forward gear.

NOTE
If the idle stabilizer shift system is installed on models other than 150XR4 and 150XR6 as an accessory, the ignition timing must be retarded 3°. Refer to Chapter Five for timing procedures.

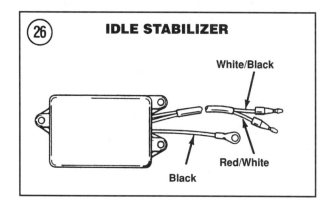

26 **IDLE STABILIZER**

White/Black

Red/White

Black

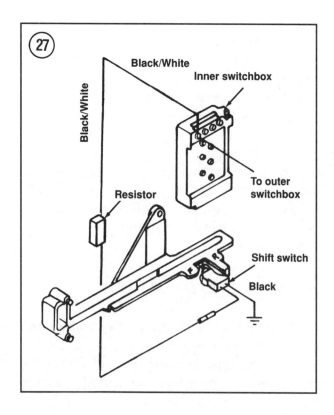

27

Black/White

Black/White

Inner switchbox

Resistor

To outer switchbox

Shift switch

Black

When the outboard motor is running at idle speed in neutral gear, the shift switch (**Figure 27**) is open. When shifted into gear, the shift switch closes and completes the switchbox bias circuit from each switchbox to ground, resulting in a 3° timing advance. If the 6800 ohm resistor (**Figure 27**) is open, or the shift switch remains open, the timing advance will not occur. In addition, full-throttle timing will be 3° retarded. Should the resistor or the black/white wire between the shift switch and the outer switchbox short to ground, the timing will be excessively advanced and could cause engine damage from detonation.

Idle Stabilizer Shift System Test

1. With the engine in a test tank or mounted on a boat in the water, remove the engine cover and connect a timing light to the No. 1 (top starboard) spark plug lead. Connect an accurate tachometer to the engine.
2. Start the engine and run at idle speed.
3. While observing the ignition timing, shift into forward gear. The idle stabilizer shift system is functioning properly if the timing advances 3° upon shifting into gear.

Low Speed/High Speed Spark Advance Module Test

The low speed/high speed spark advance module combines the functions of an idle stabilizer and a high speed spark advance module. See **Figure 28** to identify the module.

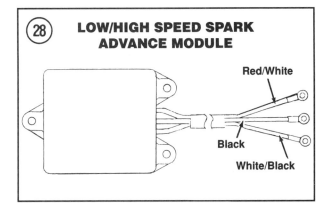

All functions of the idle stabilizer module are incorporated into the low speed/high speed spark advance module. In addition, the module electronically advances ignition timing by 6° if engine speed reaches 5000 rpm. The timing remains advanced until engine speed exceeds 5600 rpm. Should engine speed exceed 5600 rpm, the module electronically retards timing by 4°-6°. The timing remains retarded until engine speed falls below 5600 rpm.

NOTE
Due to variations in individual idle stabilizer modules, and in tachometers from different manufacturers, the engine speed at which timing advance/retard occurs may vary slightly.

1. With the outboard motor in a test tank or mounted on a boat in the water, remove the engine cover and connect a timing light to the No. 1 (top starboard) spark plug lead. Connect an accurate shop tachometer according to the manufacturer's instructions.
2. Test the low speed (idle stabilizer) capabilities as described under *Idle Stabilizer Test* in this chapter.
3. Increase engine speed while observing ignition timing. Timing should advance 6° at 5000 rpm, and retard 4°-6° at 5600 rpm.
4. If the low speed/high speed spark advance module does not operate as specified, it must be replaced.

FUEL SYSTEM

Many outboard owners automatically assume the carburetor is at fault when the engine does not run properly. While fuel system problems are not uncommon, carburetor adjustment is seldom the solution. In many cases, adjusting the carburetor only compounds the problem by making the engine run worse.

Fuel system troubleshooting should start at the fuel tank and work through the system, reserving the carburetor(s) as the final point. The majority of fuel system problems result from an empty fuel tank, sour fuel, plugged fuel filter or a malfunctioning fuel pump. **Table 5** provides a series of symptoms and causes that can be useful in localizing fuel system problems.

Troubleshooting

As a first step, check the fuel flow. Make sure fuel is present in the fuel tank, then disconnect and ground the spark plug lead(s) to prevent the engine from starting. Disconnect the fuel delivery hose at the carburetor and place it into a suitable container to collect discharged fuel. Check to be sure fuel flows freely from the hose when the primer bulb is squeezed. If no fuel flows from the hose, the fuel valve may be shut off, blocked by rust or foreign material, or the fuel line may be obstructed or kinked. If acceptable fuel flow is present, crank the engine to check fuel pump operation. The fuel pump should deliver a constant fuel flow from the hose. If the fuel flow varies from pulse to pulse, the fuel pump may be failing.

The carburetor choke can also present problems. A choke sticking open results in hard starting; a choke sticking closed results in an excessively rich fuel:air mixture.

During hot engine shut down, the fuel bowl temperature can rise above 200°F, causing the fuel inside the carburetor to boil. While all Mer-cury carburetors are vented to help prevent fuel boiling, some fuel may still percolate over the high-speed nozzle, causing flooding and an excessively rich fuel mixture.

A leaking carburetor inlet valve assembly or defective float allows an excessive amount of fuel into the fuel bowl. Pressure in the fuel line after the engine is shut down forces fuel past the leaking inlet valve, raising the fuel level inside the carburetor and allowing raw fuel to overflow into the intake manifold.

Excessive fuel consumption may not necessarily indicate an engine or fuel system problem. Marine growth on the boat hull, a bent or damaged propeller or a fuel leak will result in increased fuel consumption. Always check for obvious problems before servicing the carburetor(s).

ENGINE

Engine problems are generally symptoms of something wrong in another system, such as ignition, fuel or starting and/or charging. If properly maintained and serviced, the engine should experience no problems other than those caused by age and wear.

Overheating and Lack of Lubrication

Overheating and lack of lubrication cause the majority of engine mechanical problems. Out-

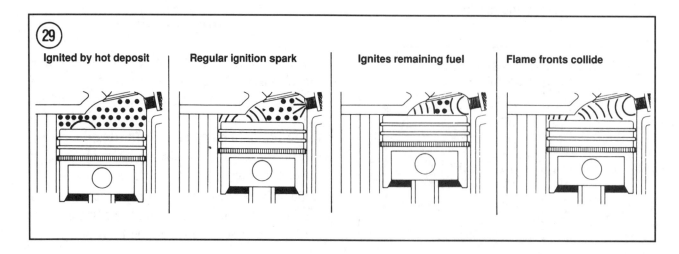

㉙

| Ignited by hot deposit | Regular ignition spark | Ignites remaining fuel | Flame fronts collide |

board motors are not designed to operate at a standstill for any length of time. Using a spark plug of the wrong heat range can burn a piston. Incorrect ignition timing or an excessively lean fuel mixture can cause the engine to overheat.

Preignition

Preignition is the premature burning of fuel and is caused by hot spots in the combustion chamber. See **Figure 29**. The fuel actually ignites before it is supposed to. Glowing deposits in the combustion chamber, inadequate cooling or overheated spark plugs can all cause preignition. Preignition is first noticed in the form of a power loss, but will eventually result in extensive damage to the internal engine components (especially pistons) because of excessive combustion chamber pressure and temperature.

Detonation

Commonly referred to as "spark knock" or "fuel knock," detonation is the violent explosion of fuel in the combustion chamber, as opposed to even burning of the fuel:air mixture that occurs during normal combustion. See **Figure 30**. When detonation occurs, combustion chamber pressure and temperature rise dramatically, creating severe shock waves in the engine. This can cause severe engine damage. The use of low octane gasoline is a common cause of detonation.

Even when high octane gasoline is used, detonation can still result from over-advanced ignition timing, lean fuel mixture, overheating, overpropping (excessive prop pitch), crossfiring spark plugs or excessive accumulation of combustion chamber deposits.

When the knock or detonation occurs at high speeds, it may not be noticed due to wind and other noises that are present during high-speed operation. Such inaudible detonation is often the cause when engine damage occurs for no apparent reason.

Poor Idle

Poor idling can be caused by incorrect carburetor adjustment, incorrect timing, ignition system malfunctions, intake or crankcase air leaks or fuel delivery problems. Make sure the fuel tank vent is not restricted.

Misfiring

Misfiring can be caused by a weak spark or dirty or worn out spark plugs. Check for fuel contamination. If misfiring only occurs under a heavy load, it is often caused by a defective spark plug or spark plug lead. Run the motor at night to check for spark leaks along the plug lead and under spark plug cap or use a spark leak tester (**Figure 31**).

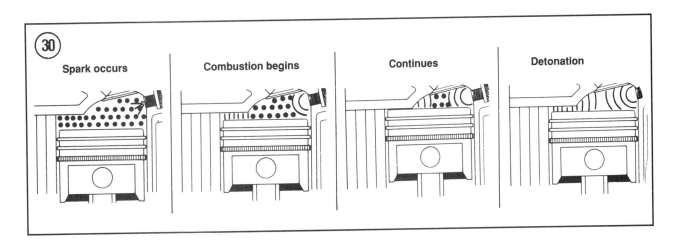

WARNING
Do not run the engine in a dark garage to check for spark leak. There is considerable danger of carbon monoxide poisoning.

Flat Spots

If the engine seems to hesitate or bog down when the throttle is opened and then recovers, check for a restricted main jet in the carburetor(s), water in the fuel or an excessively lean fuel mixture. Faulty accelerator pump operation on models so equipped can also result in hesitation during acceleration.

Water Leakage into Cylinder(s)

The fastest and easiest method to check for water leakage into a cylinder is to check the spark plugs. Water in the combustion chamber tends to clean the spark plug. If one spark plug in a multi-cylinder engine is clean and the others have normal deposits, a water leak is likely in the cylinder with the clean spark plug.

To determine if a water leak is present, install used spark plugs with normal deposits into each cylinder. Run the engine in a test tank or on the boat for 5-10 minutes. Stop the engine and remove the spark plugs. If one or more spark plugs are clean and all others show normal deposits, a water leak is present in that cylinder.

Water Damage in Power Head
Lower Cylinder

While water leakage into lower cylinders is generally caused by defective or failed gaskets, manifold plates or covers, water can also enter the lower end of a power head in several ways the casual observer would not consider:

a. When a steep unloading ramp or tilted trailer bed is used to launch the boat from a trailer, the boat enters the water quickly and at a steep angle. This can force water into the drive shaft housing and up through the exhaust chambers into the cylinders if the pistons are not covering the exhaust ports.

b. Sudden deceleration in the water can cause a wave to swamp the engine and enter the exhaust ports or into the lower carburetors. This is most prevalent with engines mounted on outboard transom brackets or twin engine installations. Since engine weight is considerably aft of the boat, the stern tends to sink lower into the water. Running the boat in REVERSE at high speed will cause a similar condition.

Water entering a cylinder can result in a bent connecting rod, a broken piston and/or piston pin, a cracked cylinder and/or cylinder head or any combination of these conditions. Even if no immediate physical damage is done to the power head, the entry of water will result in rusting and corrosion of the lower main bearing, crankshaft and/or connecting rod bearings.

The solution to this problem lies in changing the mounting of the engine on the transom or the use of an engine with an extra long shaft.

Power Loss

Several factors can cause a lack of power and speed. Check for air leaks in the fuel line or fuel pump, restricted fuel filter or choke/throttle valve(s) not operating properly. Retarded ignition timing is a frequent cause of low power.

A piston or cylinder that is galling, incorrect piston clearance or a worn/sticky piston ring may also be responsible for lower power. Check for loose bolts, defective gaskets or leaking machined mating surfaces on the cylinder head, cylinder or crankcase.

Piston Seizure

Piston seizure can be caused by incorrect piston-to-cylinder bore clearance, improper piston ring end gap, insufficient lubrication, improper spark plug heat range, preignition, detonation, incorrect ignition timing and overheating.

Excessive Vibration

Excessive vibration may be caused by loose motor mounts, worn bearings, a damaged propeller or a generally poor running engine.

Engine Noise

Experience is needed to diagnose engine noises accurately. Noises are difficult to differentiate and harder yet to describe. Deep knocking noises usually mean main bearing failure. A slapping noise generally comes from a loose piston. A light knocking noise during acceleration may be a worn connecting rod bearing. Pinging or spark knock should be corrected immediately or damage to the engine will result. A compression leak at the head-to-cylinder mating surface frequently sounds like a rapid on-and-off squeal.

3

Table 1 BATTERY CABLE LENGTHS AND MINIMUM SIZE REQUIREMENTS

Cable length	Cable gauge size (AWG)
To 3-1/2 ft.	4
3-1/2 to 6 ft.	2
6-7 to 1/2 ft.	1
7-1/2 to 9-1/2 ft.	0
9-1/2 to 12 ft.	00
12-15 ft.	000
15-19 ft.	0000

Table 2 STARTER MOTOR DRAW (AMPERES)

Starter motor part No.	No-load draw	Normal draw
A-50-44369	40	100
A-50-57465	55	190
A-50-64975	55	190
A-50-65436	40	145
A-50-66015	40	120
A-50-67341	40	120
A-50-72467	40	180
A-50-72521	40	100
A-50-73521	40	100
A-50-77141	40	175
A-50-79472	40	175
A-50-86976	20	190
A-50-90983	15	60

Table 3 STARTER TROUBLESHOOTING

Trouble	Cause	Remedy
Starter motor has low no-load speed and high current draw	Armature may be dragging on pole shoes from bent shaft, worn bearings or loose pole shoes.	Replace shaft or bearings and/or tighten pole shoes.
	Tight or dirty bearings.	Loosen or clean bearings.
High current draw with no armature rotation	A direct ground switch, at terminal or at brushes or field connections.	Replace defective parts.
	Frozen shaft bearings which prevent armature from rotating.	Loosen, clean or replace bearings.
Starter motor has grounded armature or field winding	Field and/or armature is burned or lead is thrown out of commutator due to excess leakage.	Raise grounded brushes from commutator and insulate them with cardboard. Use Magneto Analyzer (part No. C-91-25213) (Selector No. 3) and test points to check between insulated terminal or starter motor and starter motor frame (remove ground connection of shunt coils on motors with this feature). If analyzer shows resistance (meter needle moves to right), there is a ground. Raise other brushes from armature and check armature and fields separately to locate ground.
Starter motor has grounded armature or field winding abnormal.	Current passes through armature first, then to ground field windings.	Disconnect grounded leads, then locate any grounds in motor.
Starter motor fails to operate and draws no current and/or high resistance	Open circuit in fields or armature, at connections or brushes or between brushes and commutator.	Repair or adjust broken or weak brush springs, worn brushes, high insulation between commutator bars or a dirty, gummy or oily commutator.
High resistance in starter motor	Low no-load speed and a low-current draw and low developed torque.	Close "open" field winding on unit which has 2 or 3 circuits in starter motor (unit in which current divides as it enters, taking 2 or 3 parallel paths).
High free speed and high current draw	Shorted fields in starter motor.	Install new fields and check for improved performance. (Fields normally have very low resistance, thus it is difficult to detect shorted fields, since difference in current draw between normal starter mobor field windings would not be very great.
Excessive voltage drop.	Cables too small.	Install larger cables to accommodate high current draw.

(continued)

Table 3 STARTER TROUBLESHOOTING (continued)

Trouble	Cause	Remedy
High circuit resistance	Dirty connections.	Clean connections.
Starter does not operate	Run-down battery.	Check battery with hydrometer. If reading is below 1.230, recharge or replace battery.
	Poor contact at terminals.	Remove terminal clamps. Scrape terminals and clamps clean and tighten bolts securely.
	Wiring or key switch.	Coat with sealer to protect against further corrosion.
	Starter solenoid.	Check for resistance between: (a) positive (+) terminal of battery and large input terminal of starter solenoid, (b) large wire at top of starter motor and negative (–) terminal of battery, and (c) small terminal of starter solenoid and positive battery terminal. Key switch must be in START position. Repair all defective parts.
	Starter motor.	With a fully charged battery, connect a negative (–) jumper wire to upper terminal on side of starter motor and a positive jumper to large lower terminal of starter motor. If motor still does not operate, remove for overhaul or replacement.
Starter turns over too slowly	Low battery or poor contact at battery terminal.	See "Starter does not operate."
	Poor contact at starter solenoid or starter motor.	Check all terminals for looseness and tighten all nuts securely.
	Starter mechanism.	Disconnect positive (+) battery terminal. Rotate pinion gear in disengaged position. Pinion gear and motor should run freely by hand. If motor does not turn over easily, clean starter and replace all defective parts.
	Starter motor.	See "Starter does not operate."
Starter spins freely but does not engage engine	Low battery or poor contact at battery terminal; poor contact at starter solenoid or starter motor.	See "Starter does not operate."
	Dirty or corroded pinion drive.	Clean thoroughly and lubricate the spline underneath the pinion with multipurpose lubricant (part No. C-92-63250).
Starter does not engage freely	Pinion or flywheel gear.	Inspect mating gears for excessive wear. Replace all defective parts.

(continued)

Table 3 STARTER TROUBLESHOOTING (continued)

Trouble	Cause	Remedy
	Small anti-drift spring.	If drive pinion interferes with flywheel gear after engine has started, inspect anti-drift spring located under pinion gear. Replace all defective parts. NOTE: If drive pinion tends to stay engaged in flywheel gear when starter motor is in idle position, start motor at 1/4 throttle to allow starter pinion gear to release flywheel ring gear instantly.
Starter keeps on spinning after key is turned ON	Key not fully returned.	Check that key has returned to normal ON position from START position. Replace switch if key constantly stays in START position.
	Starter solenoid.	Inspect starter solenoid to see if contacts have become stuck in closed position. If starter does not stop running with small yellow lead disconnected from starter solenoid, replace starter solenoid.
	Wiring or key switch.	Inspect all wires for defects. Open remove control box and inspect wiring at switches. Repair or replace all defective parts.
Wires overheat	Battery terminals improperly connected.	Check that negative marking on harness matches that of battery. If battery is connected improperly, red wire to rectifier will overheat.
	Short circuit in wiring system.	Inspect all connections and wires for looseness or defects. Open remote control box and inspect wiring at switches.
	Short circuit in choke solenoid.	Repair or replace all defective parts. Check for high resistance. If blue choke wire heats rapidly when choke is used, choke solenoid may have internal short. Replace if defective.
	Short circuit in starter solenoid.	If yellow starter solenoid head overheats, there may be internal short (resistance) in starter solenoid. Replace if defective.
	Battery voltage low.	Battery voltage is checked with an ampere-volt tester only when battery is under a starting load. Battery must be recharged if it registers under 9.5 volts. If battery is below specified hydrometer reading of 1.230, it will not turn engine fast enough to start it.

Table 4 IGNITION TROUBLESHOOTING

Symptom	Probable cause
Engine won't start, but fuel and spark are okay	Defective spark plugs. Spark plug gap set too wide. Improper spark timing.
Engine misfires at idle	Incorrect spark plug gap. Defective or loose spark plugs. Spark plugs of incorrect heat range. Leaking or broken high tension wires. Weak armature magnets. Defective coil or condenser. Defective ignition switch. Spark timing out of adjustment.
Engine misfires at high speed	See "Engine misfires at idle." Coil breaks down. Coil shorts through insulation. Spark plug gap too wide. Wrong type spark plugs. Too much spark advance.
Engine backfires Through exhaust	Cracked spark plug insulator. Improper timing. Crossed spark plug wires.
Through carburetor	Improper ignition timing.
Engine preignition	Spark advanced too far. Incorrect type spark plug. Burned spark plug electrodes.
Engine noises (knocking at power head)	Spark advanced too far.
Ignition coil fails	Extremely high voltage. Moisture formation. Excessive heat from engine.
Spark plugs burn and foul	Incorrect type plug. Fuel mixture too rich. Inferior grade of gasoline. Overheated engine. Excessive carbon in combustion chambers.
Ignition causing high fuel consumption	Incorrect spark timing. Leaking high tension wires. Incorrect spark plug gap. Fouled spark plugs. Incorrect spark advance. Weak ignition coil. Preignition.

3

Table 5 FUEL SYSTEM TROUBLESHOOTING

Symptom	Probable cause
No fuel at carburetor	No gas in tank. Air vent in gas cap not open. Air vent in gas cap clogged. Fuel tank sitting on fuel line. Fuel line fittings not properly connected to engine or fuel tank. Air leak at fuel connection. Fuel pickup clogged. Defective fuel pump.
Flooding at carburetor	Choke out of adjustment. High float level. Float stuck. Excessive fuel pump pressure. Float saturated beyond buoyancy.
Rough operation	Dirt or water in fuel. Reed valve open or broken. Incorrect fuel level in carburetor bowl. Carburetor loose at mounting flange. Throttle shutter not closing completely. Throttle shutter valve installed incorrectly.
Engine misfires at high speed	Dirty carburetor. Lean carburetor adjustment. Restriction in fuel system. Low fuel pump pressure.
Engine backfires	Poor quality fuel. Air/fuel mixture too rich or too lean. Improperly adjusted carburetor.
Engine preignition	Excessive oil in fuel. Inferior grade of gasoline. Lean carburetor mixture.
Spark plugs burn and foul	Fuel mixture too rich. Inferior grade of gasoline.
High gas consumption: Flooding or leaking	Cracked carburetor casting. Leaks at line connections. Defective carburetor bowl gasket. High float level. Plugged vent hole in cover. Loose needle and seat. Defective needle valve seat gasket. Worn needle valve and seat. Foreign matter clogging needle valve. Worn float pin or bracket. Float binding in bowl. High fuel pump pressure.

(continued)

Table 5 FUEL SYSTEM TROUBLESHOOTING (continued)

Symptom	Probable cause
High gas consumption: (cont.) Overrich mixture	Choke lever stuck. High float level. High fuel pump pressure.
Abnormal speeds	Carburetor out of adjustment. Too much oil in fuel.

3

Table 6 OUTBOARD POWER TRIM/TILT TROUBLESHOOTING

Malfunction	Causes	Remedy
MECHANICAL **Outboard hydraulic system operate normally, but:**		
1. Will only trim part way up.	a. Internal resistance in cylinder. b. Tilt pin installed through safety strap.	a. Replace cylinder. b. Remove tilt pin and reinstall after tilting full up.
2. Will not pivot freely within clamp bracket flanges.	Clamp bracket flanges too close together.	Check for proper installation of spacer.
3. Will not trail out easily when going slowly over obstructions.	NOTE: Engine is held in position by reverse lock control at all times. Release by turning control knob fully in or trim unit out to clear obstructions.	
ELECTRICAL **Outboard hydraulic system operates normally, but:**		
1. Will only trim part way.	a. Low battery charge. b. Defective key, push button or rocker switch.	a. Charge battery. b. Test, replace defective parts.
2. Trims out beyond bracket flanges.	a. Limit switch not adjusted properly. b. Defective key, push button or rocker switch.	a. Refer to installation or service manual for adjustment procedure. b. Test, replace defective parts.
3. Pump motor runs only in "down" direction.	a. Improper wiring. b. Proper switch not operated. c. Limit switch open or disconnected. d. Solenoid inoperative. e. High resistance in wiring, grounds or solenoid. f. Defective pump motor. g. Defective key, push button or rocker switch.	a. Trace wire and correct connections. b. Use correct switch. c. Replace switch or reconnect leads. d. Test, replace defective parts. e. Test, replace defective parts. f. Test, replace defective parts. g. Test, replace defective parts.

(continued)

Table 6 OUTBOARD POWER TRIM/TILT TROUBLESHOOTING (continued)

Malfunction	Causes	Remedy
ELECTRICAL		
Outboard hydraulic system operates normally, but:		
4. Pump motor does not run.	a. Low battery charge. b. Improper wiring. c. High resistance in wiring, grounds or solenoid. d. Defective pump motor. e. Defective key, push button or rocker switch.	a. Charge battery. b. Trace wire and correct connections. c. Test, replace defective parts. d. Test, replace defective parts. e. Test, replace defective parts.
5. Unit tilts up while unattended	Moisture in key switch.	Test, replace defective parts.
HYDRAULIC		
Outboard hydraulic system operates normally, but:		
1. Will not hold trimmed position in FORWARD gear.	a. External leaks (fittings and parts leak). b. Internal cylinder leaks. c. Pump check valve leak (high pressure).* d. Dirt in system.*	a. Tighten fittings or replace if defective. b. Replace or repair cylinder. c. Replace pump base assembly. d. Flush system with clean oil, fill and bleed system.
2. Will not hold trimmed position in reverse gear.	a. External leaks (fittings and parts leak). b. Internal cylinder leaks. c. Control valve assembly inoperative. d. Reverse lock control turned full in.	a. Tighten fittings or replace if defective. b. Replace or repair cylinder. c. Replace assembly. d. Turn full out to engage reverse locks.
3. Will only trim part way up.	a. Oil level low. b. Too low or no pump pressure.	a. Add oil. b. Replace pump body assembly.
4. Will not tilt up manually.	a. Control valve assembly inoperative. b. Reverse control not turned fully in.	a. Replace assembly. b. Turn full in to disengage reverse locks.
5. Engine swings in and out when shifting from FORWARD to REVERSE to FORWARD.	Air in system.	Check for leaks and bleed system properly.
6. Will not release from power tilted "full up" position.	Too low or no "down" pump pressure.	Replace pump body assembly.
7. Trails out when backing off throttle from high speed.	a. Control valve assembly inoperative. b. Air in system.	a. Replace assembly. b. Check for leaks and bleed system properly.

(continued)

Table 6 OUTBOARD POWER TRIM/TILT TROUBLESHOOTING (continued)

Malfunction	Causes	Remedy
HYDRAULIC Outboard hydraulic system operates normally, but:		
	c. Reverse lock control knob turned full in.	c. Turn full out to activate reverse locks.
8. Oil foams out of pump vent.	a. Oil level low.	a. Add oil.
9. Will not remain tilted full up.	a. External leaks (fittings and parts leak).	a. Tighten fittings or replace if defective.
	b. Internal cylinder leaks.	b. Replace or repair cylinder.
	c. Pump check valve leak (high pressure).*	c. Replace or repair cylinder.
	d. Dirt in system.*	d. Flush system with clean oil, fill and bleed system.

*Pump check valve may contain entrapped foreign particles which can be cleared by operating system up and down several times when flushing system. If flushing system fails to correct the problem, the check valve is defective.

3

Chapter Four

Lubrication, Maintenance
And Tune-up

The modern outboard motor delivers more power and performance than ever before, with higher compression ratios, improved electrical systems and other design advances. Proper lubrication, maintenance and tune-up are increasingly important as ways to maintain a high level of performance, extend engine life and extract the maximum economy of operation.

You can do your own lubrication, maintenance and tune-up if you follow the correct procedures and use common sense. The following information is based on recommendations from Mercury Marine that will help you maintain your outboard motor operating at its peak performance level.

Tables 1-4 are at the end of this chapter.

LUBRICATION

Proper Fuel Selection

Two-stroke engines are lubricated by mixing oil with the fuel. The various components of the engine are thus lubricated as the fuel-oil mixture passes through the crankcase and cylinders. Since two-stroke fuel serves the dual function of producing combustion and distributing the lubrication, the use of marine white gasolines should be avoided due to their low octane rating and tendency to cause ring sticking and port plugging.

The recommended fuel for 3-25 hp models is any major brand of unleaded gasoline that will satisfactorily operate an automobile.

The recommended fuel for 40 hp through V6 models is any major brand of unleaded gasoline with a minimum pump octane rating of 87 (research octane number [RON] 90). Gasoline with injector cleaner added at the refinery is preferred to maintain internal engine cleanliness and prolong spark plug service life.

Sour Fuel

Fuel should not be stored for more than 60 days (under ideal conditions). As gasoline ages, it forms gum and varnish deposits that can restrict carburetor passages and other fuel system components. A fuel additive such as Quicksilver Gasoline Stabilizer part No. 92-817529A12 may be used to prevent gum and varnish formation during periods of non use, but it is preferred to drain the fuel system in such cases. Always use fresh gasoline when mixing fuel for your outboard motor.

Alcohol Extended Gasoline

Some gasoline sold for marine use contains alcohol, although this fact may not be advertised. Although the manufacturer *does not* recommend using alcohol extended gasoline, testing to date has found that it causes no major deterioration of fuel system components when consumed immediately after purchase.

Gasoline with alcohol slowly absorbs moisture from the atmosphere. When the moisture content of the fuel reaches approximately one half of one percent, it combines with the alcohol and separates (phase separation) from the gasoline. This separation does not normally occur in an automobile, as the fuel is generally consumed within a few days after purchase; however, because boats often remain idle for days or even weeks, the problem does occur in marine use.

Moisture and alcohol (especially methanol) become very corrosive when mixed and will cause corrosion of metal components and deterioration of rubber and plastic fuel system components. In addition, the alcohol and water mixture settles to the bottom of the fuel tank. If this mixture enters the engine, it will wash off the oil film and may result in corrosion and damage to the cylinders and other internal engine components. It will be necessary to drain the fuel tank, flush out the fuel system with clean gasoline, and if necessary, remove and clean the spark plugs before the motor can be started.

The following procedure is an accepted and widely used field procedure for detecting alcohol in gasoline. Note that the gasoline should be checked prior to mixing with oil. Use any small

transparent bottle or tube that can be capped and can be provided with graduations or a mark at approximately 1/3 full. A pencil mark on a piece of adhesive tape is sufficient.

1. Fill the container with water to the 1/3 full mark.
2. Add gasoline until the container is almost full. Leave a small air space at the top.
3. Shake the container vigorously, then allow it to sit for 3-5 minutes. If the volume of water appears to have increased, alcohol is present. If the dividing line between the water and gasoline becomes cloudy, reference from the center of the cloudy band.

This procedure can not differentiate between types of alcohol (ethanol or methanol), nor is it considered to be absolutely accurate from a scientific standpoint, but it is accurate enough to determine if sufficient alcohol is present to cause the user to take precautions.

Recommended Fuel Mixture

CAUTION
Some marinas are blending valve recession additives into their fuel to accommodate owners of older 4-stroke marine engines. Valve recession additives help to prevent premature valve seat wear on older 4-stroke engines. The valve recession additives may react with some outboard motor oils causing certain 2-stroke additives to precipitate. This precipitation resembles a gel-like substance that can plug fuel filters and smaller carburetor passages; therefore, the use of gasoline containing valve recession additives in outboard motors should be avoided.

The recommended oil for all Mercury outboard motors is Quicksilver Premium Blend 2-Cycle Outboard Oil. If Quicksilver Premium Blend is not available, use a good quality NMMA certified TCW-II engine oil. Follow the oil manufacturer's mixing instructions on the oil container, but *do not* exceed a 50:1 fuel-oil ratio (25:1 during engine break-in).

CAUTION
Do not, under any circumstances, use multigrade or other high detergent automotive oil or oil which contains metallic additives. This type of oil is harmful to 2-stroke engines. Oil designed for use in 4-stroke engines does not mix properly with gasoline, does not burn as 2-stroke oil does and leaves an ash residue, which may result in piston scoring, bearing failure or both.

3-25 hp (without AutoBlend system)

During engine break-in (first 30 gallons of fuel) and normal service, mix one 12-ounce container of Quicksilver Premium Blend 2-Cycle Outboard Oil with each 5 gallons of gasoline (or 8 ounces with each 3 gallons) to provide the required 50:1 fuel-oil mixture. On models with an engine mounted fuel tank, mix the fuel and oil in a separate container. On models equipped with a remote fuel tank, mix the fuel and oil directly into the remote fuel tank.

50 and 60 hp prior to serial No. D000750 (without AutoBlend system)

During the break-in period (first 30 gallons of fuel) of a new or rebuilt power head, mix two 12-ounce containers of Quicksilver Premium Blend 2-Cycle Outboard Oil with each 5 gallons of gasoline (or 16 ounces with each 3 gallons) to provide a 25:1 fuel-oil mixture. Mix the gasoline and oil directly into the remote fuel tank.

After the break-in period, mix one 12-ounce container of oil with each 5 gallons of gasoline into the remote fuel tank to provide a 50:1 fuel-oil mixture.

All models equipped with AutoBlend fuel and oil mixing system

AutoBlend fuel and oil mixing system is standard equipment on 50 and 60 hp models prior to serial No. D000750, and is an option of 5-25 hp models.

During the break-in period (first 30 gallons of fuel) of a new or rebuilt power head, mix one 12-ounce container of Quicksilver Premium Blend 2-Cycle Outboard Oil with each 5 gallons of gasoline (8 ounces with each 3 gallons) to provide a 50:1 fuel-oil mixture. Use this 50:1 fuel-oil mixture in the remote fuel tank in combination with the AutoBlend system to provide the additional lubrication required during engine break-in. After the break-in period, confirm that the oil mixing system is functioning properly, then switch to straight gasoline in the remote fuel tank.

All models equipped with oil injection (40 hp, 50 and 60 hp [serial No. D000750-on], 100 and 115 hp and V6)

During the break-in period (first 30 gallons of fuel) of a new or rebuilt power head, mix one 12-ounce container of Quicksilver Premium Blend 2-Cycle Outboard Oil with each 5 gallons of gasoline (or 8 ounces with each 3 gallons) to provide a 50:1 fuel-oil ratio. Use this 50:1 fuel-oil mixture in the remote fuel tank in combination with the normal oil injection system to provide the additional lubrication required during engine break-in. After the break-in period, confirm that the oil injection system is functioning properly, then switch to straight gasoline in the fuel tank.

Fuel Mixing Procedures

Mix the fuel and oil outside or in a well-ventilated inside location. Mix the fuel directly in the remote fuel tank.

> *WARNING*
> *Gasoline is an extreme fire hazard. Never use gasoline near heat, spark or flame. Do not smoke while mixing fuel.*

Measure the required amounts of gasoline and oil accurately. Pour a small amount of oil into the remote tank and add a small amount of gasoline. Mix it thoroughly by shaking or stirring vigorously; then add the balance of gasoline and oil and mix again.

Using less than the specified amount of oil can result in insufficient lubrication and serious engine damage. Using more oil than specified causes spark plug fouling, erratic carburetor operation, excessive smoking and rapid carbon accumulation. Cleanliness is of prime importance when mixing fuel. Even a very small particle of dirt can restrict carburetor passages. Always use fresh gasoline. Gum and varnish deposits tend to form in gasoline stored in a tank for any length

of time. Use of sour fuel can result in carburetor problems and spark plug fouling.

Consistent Fuel Mixtures

The carburetor idle mixture adjustment is sensitive to fuel mixture variations which result from the use of different oils and gasolines or due to inaccurate measuring and mixing. This may require readjustment of the idle mixture screw(s). To prevent the necessity of carburetor readjustment from one fuel batch to another, always be consistent when mixing fuel. Prepare each batch of fuel exactly the same as previous ones.

Pre-mixed fuel sold at some marinas is not recommended for use in Mercury outboard motors, since the quality and consistency of pre-mixed fuel can vary greatly. The possibility of engine damage resulting from use of an incorrect fuel mixture outweighs the convenience offered by pre-mixed fuel.

AutoBlend II Injection System

The AutoBlend II oil and gasoline mixing (injection) system is used on 50 and 60 hp models prior to serial No. D000750 and is optional on 5-25 hp models. The AutoBlend system is designed to deliver a constant 50:1 fuel-oil mixture to the power head at all speeds and load conditions. **Figure 1** shows the AutoBlend system.

A bracket-mounted tank with a 3.9 qt. (3.7 l) oil reservoir connects between the fuel tank and the engine fuel inlet. The diaphragm operated fuel and oil mixing chamber is actuated by vacuum pulsations provided by the power head-mounted fuel pump. The AutoBlend is equipped with a battery operated (9 volt) warning system that activates a warning horn (4, **Figure 2**) should the oil level drop to approximately 1/2 pint, or if the internal shuttle (mixing) valve sticks or is not operating properly. A battery test

4

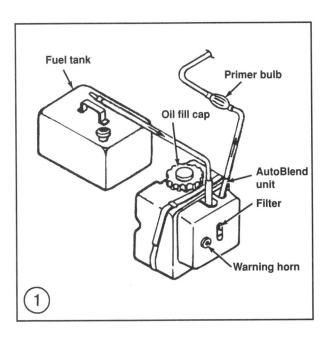

Fuel tank

Primer bulb

Oil fill cap

AutoBlend unit

Filter

Warning horn

①

button (9, **Figure 2**) is provided to determine if the 9-volt battery has sufficient voltage to activate the warning system. If the warning horn sounds when the test button (9) is depressed, the battery is in acceptable condition.

The drain plug (6, **Figure 2**) allows fuel to be drained before storage or service. Replace the drain plug O-ring if necessary.

The following inspection should be performed periodically to ensure the unit functions properly.

1. Check the oil level in the AutoBlend reservoir prior to using the outboard motor. Refill the reservoir with a recommended oil if necessary.

2. Make sure the fill cap is tightened securely after refilling the reservoir.

3. Remove the AutoBlend cover and check the translucent filter for sediment after each month of operation. Replace the filter (Chapter Eleven) once per season or as required whenever sediment is noted.

4. Check the low-oil warning system after refilling the reservoir as follows:

  a. Remove the AutoBlend unit from its mounting bracket. Invert the AutoBlend to activate the low-oil warning sensor.

  b. If the warning horn sounds, the low-oil warning system is functioning properly.

  c. If the horn does not sound, depress the battery test button (9, **Figure 2**). If the horn does not sound when the button is depressed, remove the 9-volt battery (Chapter Eleven) and check battery voltage. If battery voltage is less than 5.85 volts, replace the battery and retest.

  d. If the horn still does not sound, check the 2-pin connector (1, **Figure 2**) and receptacle for tightness, corrosion or other damage. Repair or replace the connector as necessary.

  e. If the 2-pin connector is in acceptable condition, connect a suitable jumper wire across the 2-pin connector (female side). If the horn sounds, the low-oil sensor is de-

fective. If the horn still does not sound, the electronic control module (8, **Figure 2**) is defective. Refer to Chapter Eleven.

5. Make sure the AutoBlend unit is mounted securely in its bracket.

6. Check the fuel hoses for cracks, deterioration, excessive stress or kinks. Make sure the fuel hose clamps are tightened securely.

7. Inspect the AutoBlend diaphragm at least once per season (Chapter Eleven).

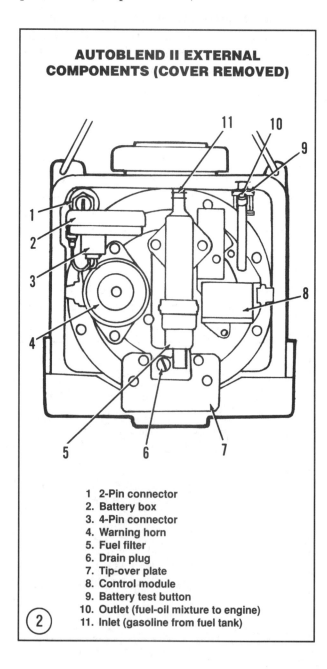

AUTOBLEND II EXTERNAL COMPONENTS (COVER REMOVED)

  1　**2-Pin connector**
  2　**Battery box**
  3　**4-Pin connector**
  4　**Warning horn**
  5　**Fuel filter**
  6　**Drain plug**
  7　**Tip-over plate**
  8　**Control module**
  9　**Battery test button**
  10　**Outlet (fuel-oil mixture to engine)**
  11　**Inlet (gasoline from fuel tank)**

②

Constant Ratio Oil Injection (40 hp and 50 and 60 hp [Serial No. D000750-on])

> *CAUTION*
> *If using an electric fuel pump, fuel pressure must not exceed 2 psi (13.8 kPa). If necessary, install a pressure regulator between the electric fuel pump and the power head. Adjust the pressure regulator to a maximum 2 psi (13.8 kPa) fuel pressure.*

The oil injection system used on 40 hp models and 50 and 60 hp (serial No. D000750-on) models provides a constant 50:1 fuel:oil ratio at all engine speeds and load conditions. The oil pump is driven by the engine crankshaft and injects oil into the fuel line ahead of the engine fuel pump. See **Figure 3**.

The engine mounted oil tank (**Figure 4**) capacity is 0.935 gal. (3.54 l) on 40 hp models and provides approximately 7 hours operation at wide-open throttle. The engine mounted oil tank capacity on 50 and 60 hp models is 3 qt. (2.8 l) providing approximately 10.5 hours of operation at wide-open throttle. The oil tank is equipped with an oil level sight gauge visible through an opening in the engine cowl.

An oil level sensor contained within the oil reservoir is designed to trigger the warning module to activate the warning horn should the oil level drop to 7.5 fl. oz. (222 mL) on 40 hp models or 14.5 fl. oz. (428.8 mL) on 50 and 60 hp models. The warning horn should sound briefly each time the ignition switch is turned ON to indicate the warning system is functioning. Refer to Chapter Eleven for injection system operation and service procedures.

The oil tank can be filled without removing the engine cowl. Remove the fill cap (**Figure 4**) and fill with Quicksilver Premium Blend 2-Cycle Outboard Oil or a suitable equivalent NMMA certified TCW-II engine oil. Reinstall the fill cap securely.

Variable Ratio Oil Injection (75, 90, 100 and 115 hp Models)

> *CAUTION*
> *If using an electric fuel pump, fuel pressure must not exceed 2 psi (13.8 kPa). If necessary, install a pressure regulator between the electric fuel pump and the power head. Adjust the pressure regulator to a maximum 2 psi (13.8 kPa) fuel pressure.*

Models 75, 90, 100 and 115 hp are equipped with the oil injection system shown in **Figure 5**. The engine-mounted oil reservoir capacity is 1 gallon and provides sufficient oil for 6 hours of operation at wide-open throttle. The reservoir is equipped with an oil level sight gauge (**Figure 6**), visible through an opening in the engine cowl. An oil level sensor contained within the oil reservoir activates the low-oil warning circuit when the oil level drops to 1 qt (0.95 l). When the low-oil warning horn sounds, enough oil for approximately 1 hour of wide-open throttle operation remains. To fill the oil reservoir, remove the engine cowl, remove the reservoir fill cap and fill with Quicksilver Premium Blend 2-Cycle Outboard Oil or a suitable NMMA certified TCW-II engine oil.

The oil pump is driven by the engine crankshaft and injects oil into the fuel stream at the fuel pump as shown in **Figure 5**. The oil pump delivers oil relative to carburetor throttle valve opening and engine speed. The fuel-oil ratio is approximately 80:1 at idle and approximately 50:1 at wide-open throttle. Refer to Chapter Eleven for injection system operation and service procedures.

Variable Ratio Oil Injection (V6 Models)

> *CAUTION*
> *If using an electric fuel pump, fuel pressure must not exceed 2 psi (13.8 kPa). If necessary, install a pressure regulator between the electric fuel pump and the*

power head. Adjust the pressure regulator to a maximum 2 psi (13.8 kPa) fuel pressure.

A 3 gallon (11.4 l) remote oil tank supplies oil to the reservoir mounted under the engine cowl (**Figure 7**). The reservoir oil capacity is 2.75 qts. (2.6 l) on 150 and 275 hp models and 0.94 qt. (0.9 l) on all other V6 models. The engine

mounted reservoir provides enough oil for approximately 30 minutes of wide-open throttle operation after the remote oil tank is empty.

The oil tank (1, **Figure 8**) is pressurized by crankcase pressure, causing oil from the tank to transfer to the engine mounted reservoir (3). Should the oil line between the tank (1) and reservoir (3) become restricted, the 2 psi (13.8

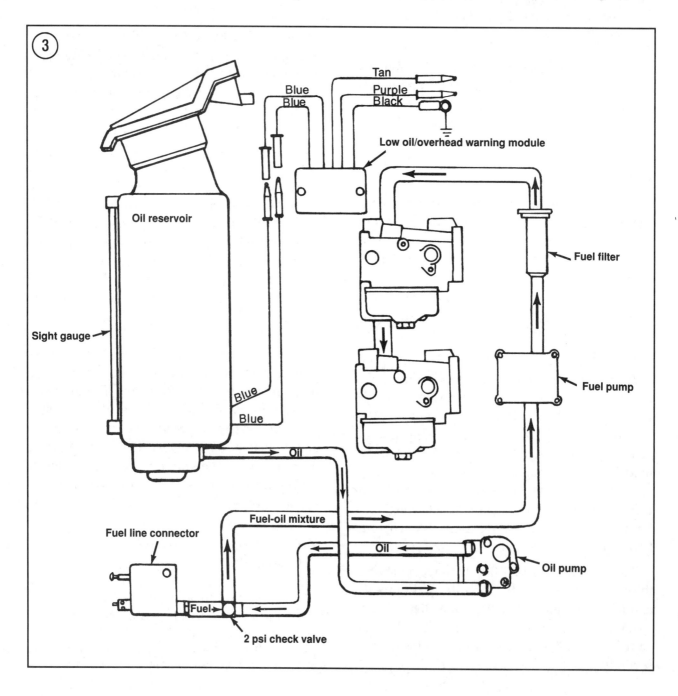

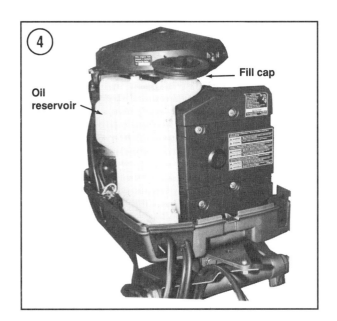

Fill cap

Oil reservoir

kPa) check valve (5) will unseat, allowing air to vent through hose (7) preventing the injection pump from creating a vacuum in the reservoir.

The injection pump (**Figure 9**) is mounted to the engine block and is driven by a gear on the crankshaft. The pump is synchronized with carburetor opening by mechanical linkage. The fuel-oil mixture is varied from approximately 100:1 (80:1 on 250 and 275 hp) at idle to approximately 50:1 at wide-open throttle. On carburetted models, the oil pump injects oil through a 2 psi (13.8 kPa) check valve (6, **Figure 8**) into the fuel stream, prior to the fuel pump. The check valve prevents the fuel pump from pumping gasoline into the oil delivery line. On EFI mod-

4

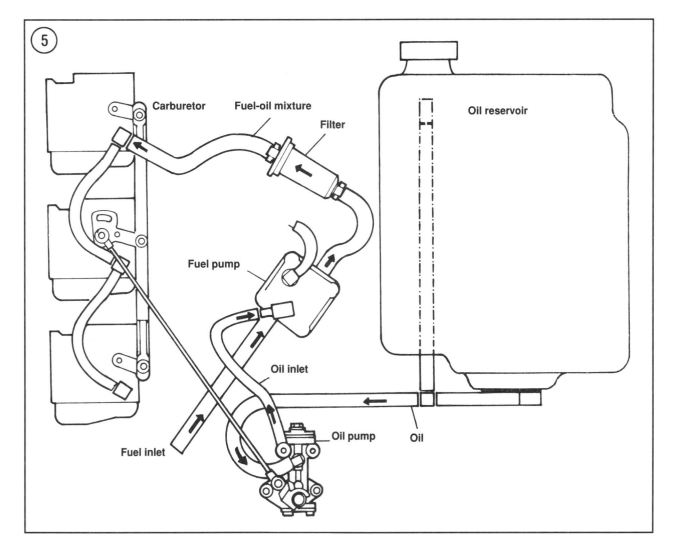

Carburetor   Fuel-oil mixture

Filter

Oil reservoir

Fuel pump

Oil inlet

Fuel inlet

Oil pump   Oil

els, the oil is injected into the fuel at the vapor separator assembly.

A low-oil sensor (**Figure 10**) attached to the reservoir fill cap activates the warning circuit if the oil level in the reservoir becomes low. In addition, a motion sensor (9, **Figure 8**) detects movement of a magnet inside the pump coupler and triggers the warning module (10, **Figure 8**) to sound the warning horn if pump shaft movement should stop due to binding or breakage.

The warning horn should sound briefly each time the ignition switch is turned ON to indicate that the warning system is functioning. If the horn does not sound, or if it remains on after the ignition is switched ON, do not start the engine. If the warning horn sounds intermittently when the engine is running, shut the engine off immediately. Refer to Chapter Eleven for oil injection system operation and service procedures.

Checking Lower Drive Unit Lubricant

The lower unit gear housing lubricant level should be checked after the initial 10 days of operation, then every 30 days thereafter. The recommended lubricant is Quicksilver Premium Blend Gear Lube.

CAUTION
Do not use regular automotive gear lubricant in the gear housing. The expansion and foam characteristics of automotive gear lube are not suitable for marine use.

1. Place the outboard motor in an upright (vertical) position. Locate and loosen (but do not remove) the gear housing drain/fill plug (**Figures 11-13**). Allow a small amount of lubricant to drain. If water is present inside the gear housing, it will drain before the lubricant. Retighten the drain/fill plug securely.

CAUTION
If water is present in the gear housing, it will be necessary to determine and re-

pair the cause of leakage before returning the unit to service.

2. Remove the gear housing vent plug(s). See **Figures 11-13**. Do not lose the gasket on each plug. The lubricant should be as follows:

   a. Level with the bottom of the rear vent plug hole on 50-115 hp models (**Figure 12**).

   b. Level with the lower vent plug hole on models 250 and 275 hp (**Figure 13**).

   c. Level with the vent plug hole on all other models (**Figure 11**).

CAUTION
The vent plug(s) is provided to vent displaced air while lubricant is added to the gear housing. Never attempt to fill or add lubricant to the gear housing without first removing the vent plug(s).

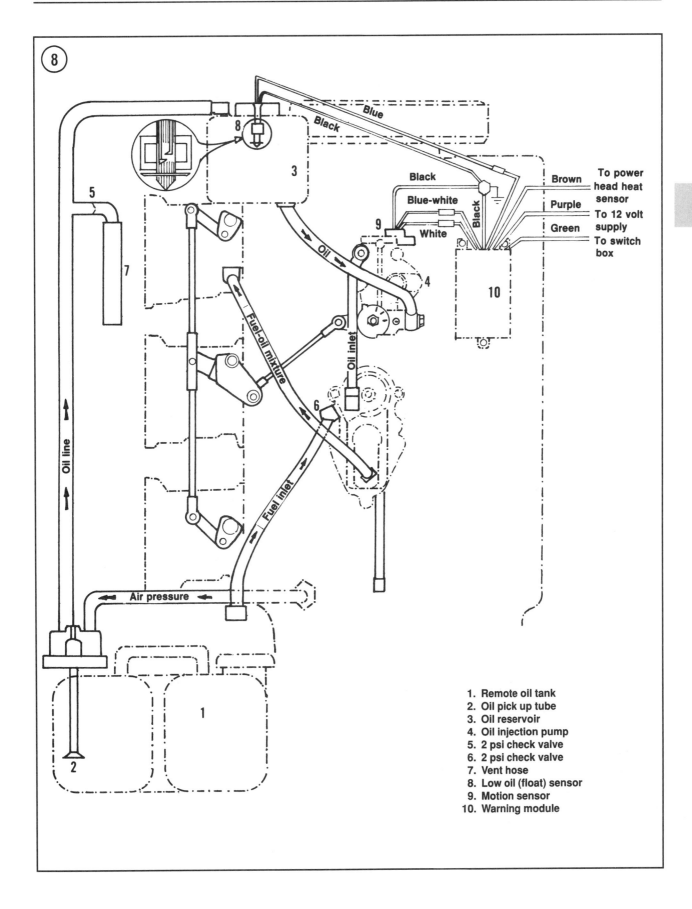

1. Remote oil tank
2. Oil pick up tube
3. Oil reservoir
4. Oil injection pump
5. 2 psi check valve
6. 2 psi check valve
7. Vent hose
8. Low oil (float) sensor
9. Motion sensor
10. Warning module

3. If the lubricant level is low, reinstall the vent plug(s) and remove the drain/fill plug. Insert the lubricant tube or pump into the drain/fill plug hole, then remove the vent plug(s).

4A. All models except 50-115 hp, 250 and 275 hp—Inject the recommended oil into the drain/fill plug hole until excess oil flows from the vent plug hole (**Figure 11**). Install and tighten the vent plug. Remove the lubricant tube and quickly install and tighten the drain/fill plug.

4B. 50-115 hp models—Inject the recommended oil into the drain/fill plug hole until oil flows from the front vent plug hole (**Figure 12**). Install and tighten the front vent plug. Continue adding oil until the oil flows from the rear vent plug hole. Without removing the lubricant tube from the drain/fill plug hole, install and tighten the rear vent plug. Remove the lubricant tube and quickly install and tighten the drain/fill plug.

NOTE
Due to the path the oil must travel to exit the vents on 250 and 275 models, oil will flow from the top vent plug hole first.

4C. 250 and 275 hp models—Inject the recommended oil into the drain/fill plug hole, until oil flows from the upper vent plug hole (**Figure 13**). Install and tighten the top vent plug. Continue to add lubricant until the oil flows from the lower vent plug hole. Allow any excess oil to drain from the lower vent plug hole. When the oil stops draining from the lower vent, install and tighten

the lower vent plug. Remove the lubricant tube and quickly install and tighten the drain/fill plug.

Lower Drive Unit Lubricant Change

The lower unit gear housing lubricant should be changed after the first 25 hours of operation and every 100 hours (or seasonally) thereafter. Refer to **Table 4** for gear housing lubricant capacities.

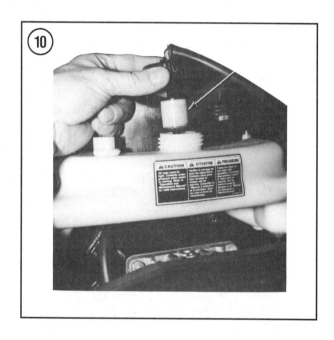

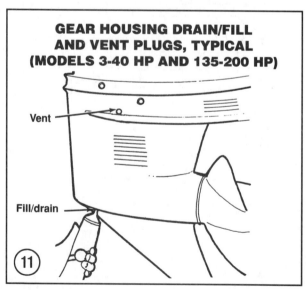

GEAR HOUSING DRAIN/FILL AND VENT PLUGS, TYPICAL (MODELS 3-40 HP AND 135-200 HP)

Vent

Fill/drain

Refer to **Figure 11** (all models except 50-115 hp, 250 and 275 hp), **Figure 12** (50-115 hp models) and **Figure 13** (250 and 275 hp models) for this procedure.

1. Remove the engine cover and disconnect the spark plug leads to prevent accidental starting.

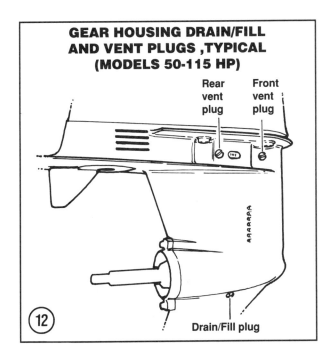

GEAR HOUSING DRAIN/FILL AND VENT PLUGS ,TYPICAL (MODELS 50-115 HP)

Rear vent plug — Front vent plug — Drain/Fill plug

⑫

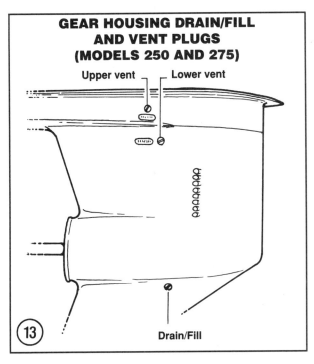

GEAR HOUSING DRAIN/FILL AND VENT PLUGS (MODELS 250 AND 275)

Upper vent — Lower vent — Drain/Fill

⑬

2. Place the outboard motor in an upright position. Place a suitable container under the gear housing.

3. Remove the drain/fill plug, then the vent plug(s). Allow the lubricant to drain into the container.

4. Inspect the lubricant for the presence of metallic particles. Note the color of the lubricant. A white or milky brown color indicates water in the lubricant. Check the drain container for water separation from the lubricant. If metallic particles or water contamination are noted in the lubricant, the gear housing must be repaired before returning the unit to service.

5. Refill the gear housing with the recommended lubricant as described under *Check Lower Drive Unit Lubricant* in this chapter. Refer to **Table 4** for gear housing lubricant capacities.

Propeller Shaft

To prevent corrosion and to ease the future removal of the propeller, the propeller shaft should be lubricated once each season during freshwater operation or every 60 days of saltwater operation. Remove the propeller (Chapter Nine) and thoroughly clean any corrosion or dried grease, then coat the propeller shaft splines with Quicksilver Special Lubricant 101, Quicksilver 2-4-C Marine Lubricant or a suitable anticorrosion grease.

Other Lubrication Points

Refer to **Figures 14-34** and **Table 1** and **Table 2** for other lubrication points, recommended lubrication intervals and recommended lubricants.

CAUTION
When lubricating the steering cable, make sure its core is fully retracted into the cable housing. Lubricating the cable while extended can cause a hydraulic lock to occur that could result in hard turning or loss of steering control.

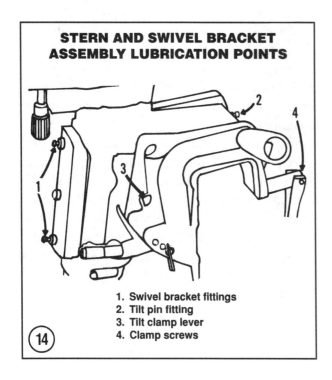

STERN AND SWIVEL BRACKET ASSEMBLY LUBRICATION POINTS

1. Swivel bracket fittings
2. Tilt pin fitting
3. Tilt clamp lever
4. Clamp screws

14

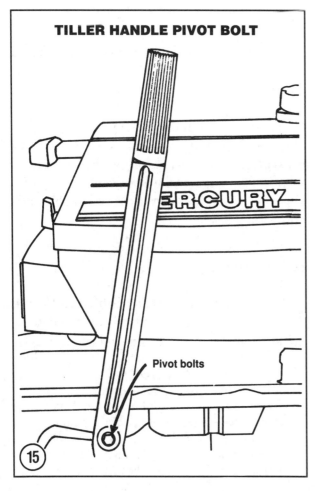

TILLER HANDLE PIVOT BOLT

Pivot bolts

15

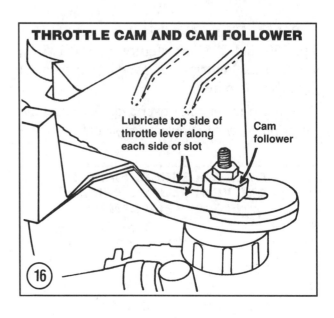

THROTTLE CAM AND CAM FOLLOWER

Lubricate top side of throttle lever along each side of slot

Cam follower

16

17

REVERSE LOCK LEVER ASSEMBLY LUBRICATION

Reverse lock lever shaft

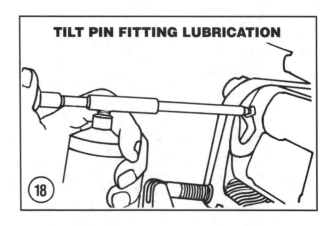

TILT PIN FITTING LUBRICATION

18

THROTTLE AND TIMING ADVANCE LINKAGE LUBRICATION POINTS

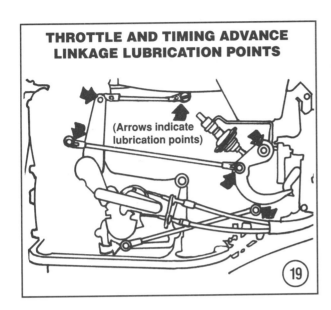

(Arrows indicate lubrication points)

⑲

CARBURETOR AND CHOKE MECHANISM LUBRICATION POINTS

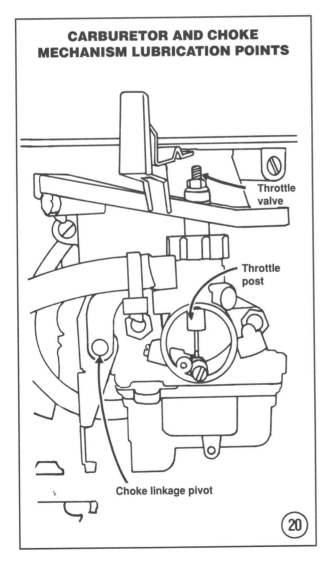

Throttle valve

Throttle post

Choke linkage pivot

⑳

THROTTLE AND SHIFT LINKAGE LUBRICATION POINTS

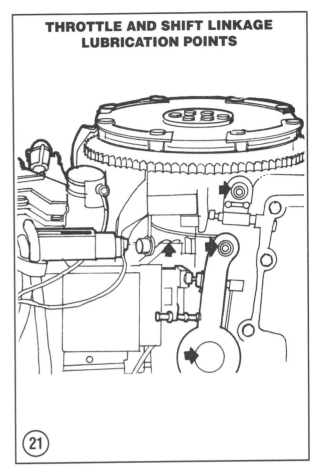

㉑

4

㉒ **STEERING CABLE/LINK ROD LUBRICATION**

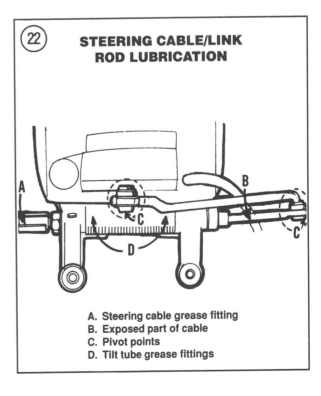

A
B
C
D

A. Steering cable grease fitting
B. Exposed part of cable
C. Pivot points
D. Tilt tube grease fittings

Saltwater Corrosion of Gear Housing Bearing Carrier/Nut

Saltwater corrosion that is allowed to accumulate between the propeller shaft bearing carrier and gear housing can eventually split the housing and destroy the lower unit assembly. If the out-

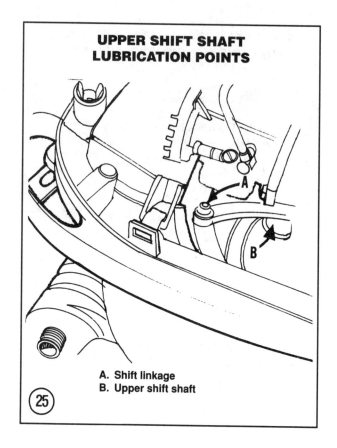

UPPER SHIFT SHAFT LUBRICATION POINTS

A. Shift linkage
B. Upper shift shaft

25

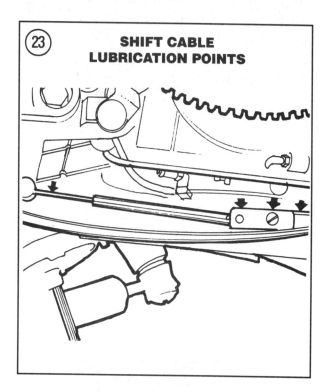

23 **SHIFT CABLE LUBRICATION POINTS**

26 **STARTER DRIVE GEAR ASSEMBLY LUBRICATION**

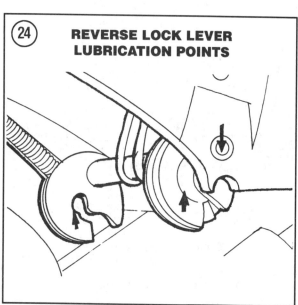

24 **REVERSE LOCK LEVER LUBRICATION POINTS**

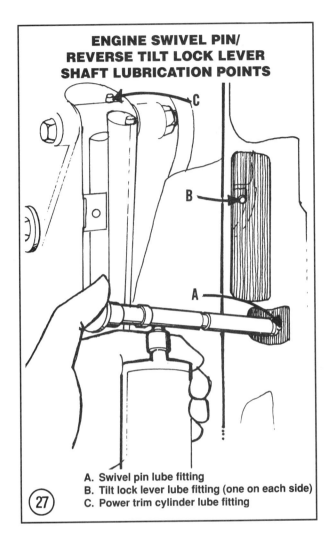

ENGINE SWIVEL PIN/ REVERSE TILT LOCK LEVER SHAFT LUBRICATION POINTS

A. Swivel pin lube fitting
B. Tilt lock lever lube fitting (one on each side)
C. Power trim cylinder lube fitting

㉗

board motor is operated in saltwater, remove the cover nut (or bearing carrier screws) and propeller shaft bearing carrier at least once per year. Refer to Chapter Nine for bearing carrier removal procedures for all models.

Thoroughly clean all corrosion and dried lubricant from each end of the carrier (**Figure 35**, typical).

4

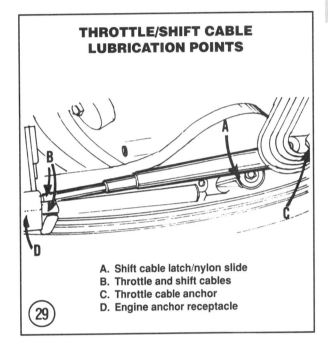

THROTTLE/SHIFT CABLE LUBRICATION POINTS

A. Shift cable latch/nylon slide
B. Throttle and shift cables
C. Throttle cable anchor
D. Engine anchor receptacle

㉙

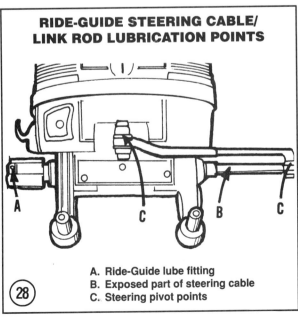

RIDE-GUIDE STEERING CABLE/ LINK ROD LUBRICATION POINTS

A. Ride-Guide lube fitting
B. Exposed part of steering cable
C. Steering pivot points

㉘

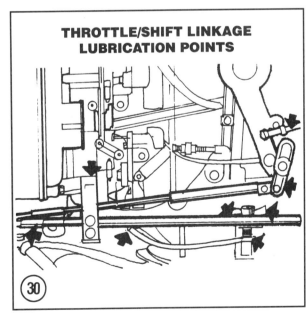

THROTTLE/SHIFT LINKAGE LUBRICATION POINTS

㉚

Clean the gear housing internal threads and cover nut external threads on models so equipped. Inspect the bearing carrier O-rings and propeller shaft seals and replace as necessary. Apply a liberal coating of Quicksilver Perfect Seal, Special Lubricant 101 or 2-4-C Marine Lubricant to each end of the carrier and to the gear housing and cover nut threads (if so equipped). If Quicksilver Perfect Seal is used, be careful not to allow any Perfect Seal into the propeller shaft bearings. Reinstall the bearing carrier as described in Chapter Nine.

STORAGE

The major consideration in preparing an outboard motor for storage is to protect it from rust, corrosion, dirt or other contamination. Mercury Marine recommends the following procedure.

1. Remove the engine cowling.

2. Remove the air box, if so equipped. **Figure 36** shows a typical installation.

3A. Except EFI Models:

  a. With the outboard in a test tank, in the water or connected to a suitable flushing device, start the engine and allow it to warm to normal operating temperature.

  b. Disconnect the fuel delivery hose or shut off the fuel valve (if so equipped) and run the engine at low speed while spraying approximately 2 oz. of Quicksilver Storage Seal into each carburetor throat. Allow the engine to stall indicating the carburetor(s) have run dry.

3B. EFI Models:

  a. Prepare a 50:1 fuel-oil mixture using a recommended oil and gasoline in the fuel tank. The engine should be run on the 50:1 fuel-oil mixture in combination with the normal oil injection system during the lay-up procedure.

  b. Place the outboard motor in a test tank, in the water or connect a suitable flushing device.

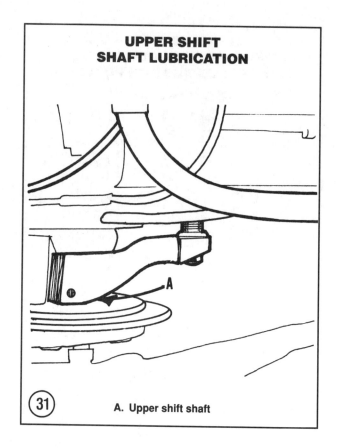

UPPER SHIFT SHAFT LUBRICATION

(31)

A. Upper shift shaft

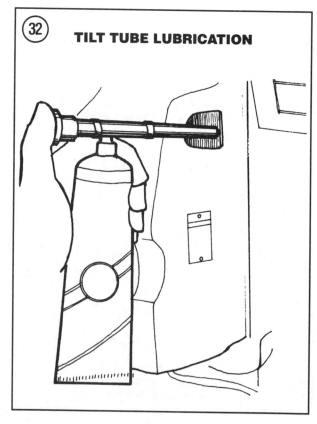

(32) **TILT TUBE LUBRICATION**

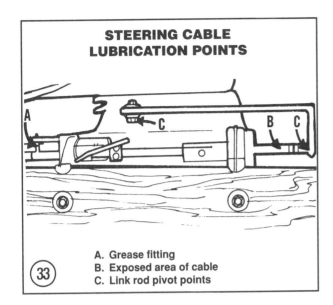

A. Grease fitting
B. Exposed area of cable
C. Link rod pivot points

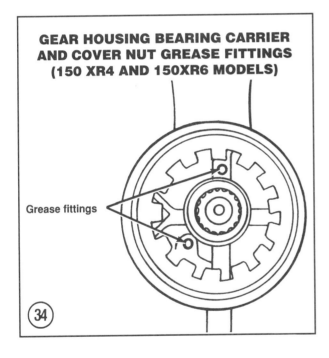

c. Start the engine and allow to run at idle speed for 10 minutes. After 10 minutes, disconnect the fuel delivery hose from the engine.

d. Allow the engine to stall after running out of fuel.

4. All Models—Remove the spark plugs as described in this chapter. Spray about one ounce of Quicksilver Storage Seal into each spark plug hole. Crank the engine by hand several revolutions to distribute the Storage Seal throughout the cylinders. Reinstall the spark plugs.

5. Service the remote fuel tank filter as follows:

a. Detach the fuel hose from the tank and remove the screws holding the cover in the tank. Remove the cover with the fuel outlet tube and filter assembly.

b. Clean the fine wire mesh filter by rinsing in clean solvent. Dry the filter with compressed air.

6A. On models equipped with an engine mounted fuel tank (3, 4 and 5 hp models), service the tank, filter and related components as follows:

a. Place the fuel valve in the OFF position.

b. Slide the rubber collar (**Figure 37**) away from the fuel valve. Lift the fuel valve rod off the valve.

c. Compress the hose clamp and disconnect the fuel hose from the fuel pump (**Figure 38**).

d. Remove the nuts and washers securing the fuel tank to its mounting brackets. Lift the tank off the power head along with the valve, hoses and inline filter.

e. Drain and properly dispose of any fuel present in the tank. If necessary, rinse out the tank using clean gasoline. Clean the fuel strainer (affixed to the tank fill cap) using clean solvent. Dry the strainer with compressed air.

f. Disconnect the fuel hoses from each side of the fuel filter (**Figure 38**) then remove and discard the filter. Install a new filter with the arrow facing toward the fuel pump. Replace the fuel hoses if softness, swelling or other deterioration is noted.

g. Loosen the clamp and remove the fuel valve from the tank. Inspect the filter screen inside the valve for sediment or other contamination, and if necessary clean the screen with clean solvent. If the screen is damaged or can not be thoroughly cleaned, replace the fuel valve.

h. Reassemble the fuel tank and related components in reverse order of disassembly.

6B. On models equipped with a sight bowl fuel filter (**Figure 39**), service the fuel filter as follows:

a. Pull downward on the filter assembly to disengage the ball mount (**Figure 40**) from the rubber handle rest.

b. Unscrew the sight bowl from the filter base.

c. Remove the filter element from the bowl. Clean the element in clean solvent and dry with compressed air.

d. Be sure the sight bowl seal is correctly positioned in the bowl. Reinstall the filter into the bowl and reinstall the bowl on the filter base. Tighten the bowl securely *by hand*.

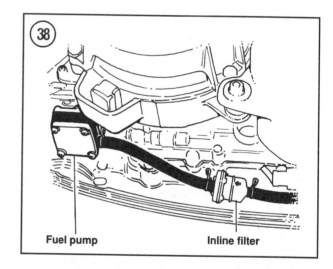

Fuel pump   **Inline filter**

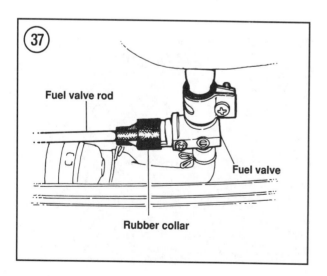

Fuel valve rod

Fuel valve

Rubber collar

e. Check the filter assembly for leakage by priming the fuel system with the primer bulb. Repair any leaks as necessary.

6C. On models equipped with an inline fuel filter (**Figure 41**, typical), service the filter as follows:

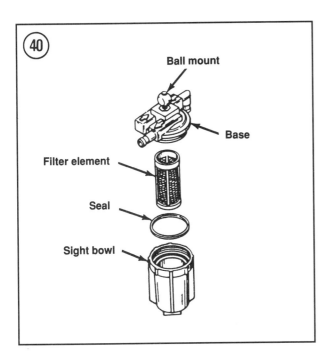

NOTE
Excessive filter contamination can be easily seen through the translucent filter housing.

a. Carefully cut the sta-strap clamps from each end of the filter.

b. Disconnect the fuel hoses from the filter. Discard the filter.

c. Connect the fuel hoses to a new filter. Fasten the hoses to the filter securely with new sta-straps.

6D. EFI Models—Service the water separating filter (**Figure 42**) on EFI models as follows:

a. Disconnect the tan water sensor wire from the bottom of the filter canister.

b. Remove the water separating fuel filter by unscrewing the filter from the filter base. Empty the contents of the filter into a suitable container. If the filter is not excessively contaminated, reinstall by reversing the removal procedure.

c. If excessive fuel contamination is noted, remove the water sensing probe from the bottom of the filter and discard the filter.

d. Install the water sensing probe into a new filter. Install the filter onto the filter base, tighten securely by hand, then reconnect the tan water sensor probe wire. Coat the wire

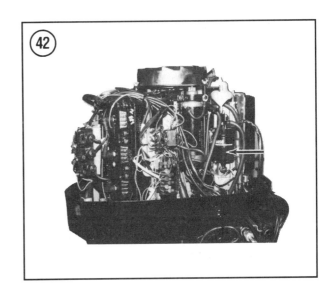

connection with Quicksilver Liquid Neoprene (part No. 92-25711).

7. Drain then refill the lower unit as described in this chapter. Check the condition of the vent and drain plug gaskets and replace as required.

8. Refer to **Figures 14-34** and **Tables 1-2** as appropriate and lubricate the outboard motor at all specified points.

9. Clean all exterior areas of the outboard motor, including all accessible power head parts. Spray the outboard motor including all electrical connections with Quicksilver Corrosion Guard. Install the engine cowling and spray a thin film of Quicksilver Corrosion Guard on all painted surfaces.

10. Remove the propeller as described in Chapter Nine. Lubricate the propeller shaft with Quicksilver Special Lubricant 101 or Quicksilver 2-4-C Marine Lubricant and reinstall the propeller.

CAUTION
Make certain all water drain holes in the gear housing are clear and open to allow water to drain. Water expands as it freezes and can crack the gear housing or water pump. If the boat is equipped with a speedometer, disconnect the pickup tube and allow it to drain completely, then reconnect the tube.

11. Drain the system completely to prevent damage from freezing.

12. Store the motor with the power head higher than the lower unit to prevent any water from entering the engine through the exhaust ports.

13. Prepare the battery for storage as follows:

 a. Disconnect the negative, then the positive battery cables.

 b. Remove all grease, sulfate or other contamination from the battery case.

 c. Check the electrolyte level in each battery cell and top up with distilled water if necessary. The electrolyte level in each cell should not be higher than 3/16 in. above the perforated baffles.

 d. Lubricate the terminals and terminal fasteners with a suitable grease or petroleum jelly.

CAUTION
A discharged battery can be damaged by freezing.

 e. With the battery in a fully-charged condition (specific gravity at 1.260-1.275), store the battery in a *cool, dry* location where the temperature will not drop below the freezing point.

 f. Recharge the battery every 45 days or whenever the specific gravity drops below 1.230. Before charging, cover the plates with distilled water, but not over 3/16 in. above the perforated baffles. The charge rate should not exceed 6 amps. Discontinue charging when the specific gravity reaches 1.260 at 80°F (27°C).

 g. Remove the grease on the battery terminals prior to returning the battery to service. Make sure the battery is installed in a fully-charged state.

ANTI-CORROSION MAINTENANCE

1. Flush the cooling system with freshwater as described in this chapter after each time the outboard is operated in saltwater. Wash the exterior with freshwater.

2. Dry the exterior of the outboard and apply primer over any paint nicks and scratches. Use only tin anti-fouling paint; do not use paints containing mercury or copper. Do not paint sacrificial anodes or the trim tab.

3. Spray the power head and all electrical connections with Quicksilver Corrosion Guard.

4. Check sacrificial anodes and trim tab. Replace if any are less than half their original size.

5. If the outboard motor is used consistently in saltwater, reduce lubrication intervals (**Tables 1-2**) by one half.

COMPLETE SUBMERSION

An outboard motor which has been lost overboard should be recovered as quickly as possible. Disassemble and clean it immediately—any delay will result in rust and corrosion of internal components. The following emergency steps should be accomplished immediately if the motor is submerged in freshwater.

If the outboard motor should fall overboard in saltwater, completely disassemble and clean the motor before any attempt to start the engine.

1. Wash the outside of the motor with clean water to remove weeds, mud and other debris.

2. Remove the engine cowling. Remove the spark plug(s) as described in this chapter.

3. Except EFI—Remove the carburetor float bowl(s). See Chapter Six.

> *CAUTION*
> *If there is a possibility that sand may have entered the power head, do not attempt to start the engine or severe internal damage could occur. If the outboard is lost overboard while running, internal engine damage is likely. Do not force the motor if it fails to turn over easily with the spark plug(s) removed. This is an indication of internal damage such as a bent connecting rod or broken piston.*

4. Drain as much water as possible from the power head by placing the motor in a horizontal position. Position the spark plugs facing downward and manually rotate the flywheel to expel water from the cylinder(s).

> *NOTE*
> *If an EFI equipped outboard motor is submerged in saltwater, the ECU assembly will most likely be damaged and will require replacement.*

5. EFI Models:
  a. Remove the electronic control unit (ECU) from the power head. Drain as much water as possible from the manifold absolute pressure (MAP) sensor. Do not attempt to remove the MAP sensor hose from the ECU.
  b. Place the ECU assembly in an oven and heat at 120°F (50°C) for approximately 2 hours to dry the ECU assembly. Remove the ECU from the oven and have it tested by a Mercury Marine dealer.

6. Pour alcohol into the spark plug holes and carburetor throats (except EFI) to displace water. Rotate the flywheel by hand to distribute the alcohol.

7. Pour approximately one teaspoon of engine oil into each cylinder through the spark plug hole(s). Rotate the flywheel by hand to distribute the oil.

8A. Except EFI—Position the outboard with the carburetor(s) facing upward. Pour engine oil into each carburetor throat while rotating the flywheel by hand to distribute the oil.

8B. EFI Models:
  a. Remove the fuel delivery hose at the electric fuel pump. Drain the contents of the vapor separator assembly. See Chapter Six.
  b. Position the outboard so the induction manifold is facing upward. Remove the induction manifold cover and pour one tablespoon of engine oil into each reed valve section. Rotate the flywheel by hand.
  c. Remove the final fuel filter and water separator filter as described in this chapter. Clean any contamination from the final filter. Empty the contents of the water separator filter into a suitable container.

9. Reinstall the spark plug(s) as described in this chapter.

10A. Except EFI—Reinstall the carburetor float bowls.

10B. EFI—Replace or reinstall the final fuel filter and water separator filter. Reinstall the induction manifold cover.

11. Attempt to start the engine using a 50:1 fuel-oil mixture in the fuel tank (including EFI and oil injection models). If the outboard motor

will start, allow it to run at least one hour to evaporate any remaining water inside the engine.

CAUTION
If it is not possible to disassemble and clean the motor immediately, resubmerge the outboard in water to prevent rust and corrosion until it can be properly serviced.

12. If the motor will not start in Step 11, attempt to diagnose the cause as fuel, electrical or mechanical and repair as necessary. If the engine cannot be started within 2 hours, disassemble, clean and oil all internal components as soon as possible.

FLUSHING THE COOLING SYSTEM

Periodic flushing with clean freshwater will prevent salt or silt deposits from accumulating in the cooling system passageways. The flushing procedure should be performed after each time the outboard is operated in saltwater or polluted or brackish water.

Keep the motor in an upright position during and after flushing. This prevents water from passing into the power head through the drive shaft housing and exhaust ports during the flushing procedure. It also eliminates the possibility of residual water being trapped in the drive shaft housing or other passages.

3-15 hp

Models 3-15 hp require a special flushing adapter. See your Mercury Marine dealer for application details.

1. Remove the propeller as described in Chapter Nine.

2. Compress the flush cup and slide the flush adapter over the antiventilation plate. Locate the cup over the water intake opening. See **Figure 43**.

3. Connect a garden hose between a water tap and the flushing device.

4. Open the water tap to provide full water pressure.

5. Shift the outboard into NEUTRAL, then start the engine.

6. Check the motor to make sure that water is being discharged from the "tell-tale" hole. If it is not, stop the motor immediately and determine the cause of the problem.

7. Flush the motor until the discharged water is clear. If the outboard is used in saltwater, flush for 3-5 minutes minimum.

8. Stop the engine, then shut off the water supply. Remove the flushing device from the outboard by compressing the cup and sliding it off the rear of the antiventilation plate.

9. Keep the outboard in an upright position to allow all water to drain from the drive shaft housing. If this is not done, water can enter the

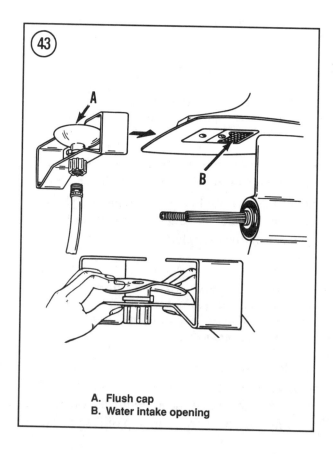

A. Flush cap
B. Water intake opening

power head through the drive shaft housing and exhaust ports.

20-275 hp

1. Attach the flushing device from the front of the lower unit according to the manufacturer's instructions. See **Figure 44**.

2. Connect a garden hose between a water tap and the flushing device.

3. Open the water tap partially. Adjust the water pressure until a significant amount of water escapes from around the flushing cups, but do not apply full pressure.

4. Shift the outboard into NEUTRAL gear, then start the motor. Maintain the engine speed below 2500 rpm.

5. Adjust the water flow so a slight loss of water around the rubber cups of the flushing device is noted.

6. Check the motor to be certain that water is being discharged from the "tell-tale" nozzle. If not, stop the motor immediately and determine the cause of the problem.

CAUTION
Flush the outboard for at least 5 minutes if used in saltwater.

7. Flush the outboard until the discharged water is clear.

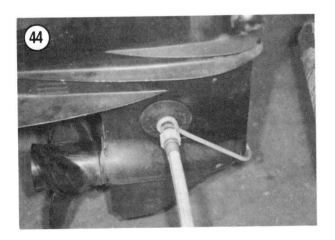

8. Stop the engine, then close the water tap. Remove the flushing device from the lower unit.

TUNE-UP

A tune-up consists of a series of inspections, adjustments and parts replacement to compensate for normal wear and deterioration of the outboard motor components. Regular tune-up is important to maintain the proper power, performance and economy. Mercury Marine recommends tune-up service be performed every 6 months or after 100 hours of operation. If the outboard is used on a limited basis, tune the engine at least once per year.

Since proper outboard motor operation depends upon a number of interrelated system functions, a tune-up consisting of only one or two corrections will seldom provide satisfactory results. For best results, a thorough and systematic procedure of analysis and correction is necessary.

Prior to performing a tune-up, flush the outboard cooling system as described in this chapter to check for proper water pump operation.

The tune-up sequence recommended by Mercury Marine includes the following:

a. Compression test.
b. Spark plug service.
c. Ignition system service (if required).
d. Lower unit and water pump check.
e. Fuel system service.
f. Battery, starter motor and solenoid check.
g. Alternator and rectifier check (if so equipped).
h. Wiring harness check.
i. Timing, synchronization and adjustment.
j. Performance test (on the boat).

Anytime the fuel or ignition system is adjusted or defective parts replaced, the engine timing, synchronization and adjustment *must* be checked and/or adjusted. These procedures are described in Chapter Five. Perform the timing, synchronization and adjustment procedure for your engine *before* running the performance test.

Compression Test

An accurate cylinder compression check provides an indication of the condition of the basic working parts of the engine. It is also an important first step in any tune-up; a motor with low or unequal compression between cylinders *cannot* be satisfactorily tuned. Any compression problem discovered during this test must be corrected before continuing with the tune-up procedure.

1. With the power head warm, remove the spark plug(s) as described in this chapter.

2. Securely ground the spark plug lead(s) to the engine to disable the ignition and prevent switch-box damage on models equipped with capacitor discharge ignition.

3. Following the compression gauge manufacturer's instructions, connect the gauge to the top spark plug hole (**Figure 45**, typical).

4. Place and hold the throttle in the wide-open position. Crank the engine through at least 4 compression strokes and record the gauge reading.

5. Repeat Step 3 and Step 4 for all remaining cylinders.

While minimum compression per cylinder should be no less than 100 psi (689 kPa), actual readings are not as important as the differences in readings when interpreting the results. A variation of more than 15 psi (103 kPa) between 2 cylinders indicates a problem with the lower reading cylinder, such as worn or sticking piston rings and/or scored pistons or cylinder walls. In such cases, pour a tablespoon of engine oil into the suspect cylinder and repeat Step 3 and Step 4. If the compression increases significantly (by 10 psi [69 kPa] in an old engine) the rings are worn and should be replaced.

Many outboard motors are plagued by hard starting and generally poor running for which

there seems to be no good cause. The carburetion and ignition systems are functioning properly. A compression test indicates the piston(s), rings and cylinder(s) are in acceptable condition. What a compression test does *not* show, however, is lack of primary compression. In a 2-stroke engine the crankcase must be able to seal alternately against pressure and vacuum. After the piston closes the intake ports, further downward movement of the piston causes the entrapped mixture to be pressurized so that it can rush quickly into the cylinder when the scavenging ports are opened. Upward piston movement creates a low pressure in the crankcase, enabling the fuel and air mixture from the carburetor to enter the crankcase.

When the crankshaft seals or case gaskets leak, the crankcase cannot hold pressure and

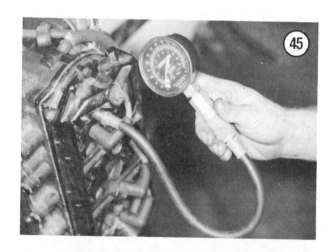

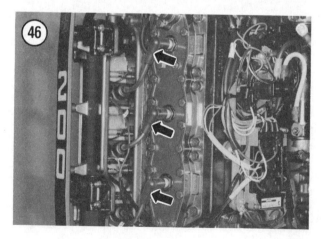

proper engine operation becomes impossible. Any other source of leakage, such as defective cylinder base gaskets or a porous or cracked crankcase casting will result in the same conditions.

If the power head shows signs of overheating (discolored or scorched paint), but the compression is normal, check the cylinders visually through the transfer ports for possible scoring. A cylinder can be slightly scored and still deliver a relatively good compression reading. Also, when overheating is evident, be sure to inspect the water pump and cooling system closely for a possible cause for overheating.

Spark Plug Replacement

Improper installation is a common cause of poor spark plug performance in outboard motors. The gasket on the plug must be fully compressed against a clean plug seat for heat transfer

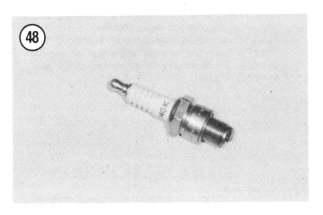

to take place effectively. This requires close attention to proper torquing during installation.

CAUTION
When the spark plugs are removed, dirt or other foreign material surrounding the spark plug hole(s) can fall into the cylinder(s). Foreign material inside the cylinders can cause engine damage when the engine is started.

1. Clean the area around the spark plugs using compressed air, if available. If not, use a can of compressed inert gas, available from photo stores.

2. Disconnect the spark plug leads (**Figure 46**, typical) by twisting the boot back and forth on the spark plug insulator while pulling outward. Pulling on the lead instead of the boot can cause internal damage to the lead.

3. Remove the spark plugs using an appropriate size spark plug socket. Arrange the spark plugs in order of the cylinder which they were removed.

4. Examine each spark plug. See **Figure 47** for surface gap plugs and **Figure 48** for conventional gap plugs. Compare spark plug condition to **Figure 49** (surface gap) or **Figure 50** (conventional gap). Spark plug condition is a good indicator of piston, rings and cylinder condition, and can provide a warning of developing trouble.

5. Check each plug for make and heat range. All should be of the same make and number or heat range.

6. Discard the spark plugs. Although they could be cleaned and reused if in good condition, new plugs are inexpensive and far more reliable.

7. Inspect the spark plug threads in the engine and clean them with a thread chaser (**Figure 51**) if necessary. Wipe the spark plug seats clean before installing new spark plugs.

8. Install new plugs with new gaskets and tighten to 20 ft.-lb. If a torque wrench is not available, seat the plugs finger tight, then tighten an additional 1/4 turn with a wrench.

4

9. Inspect each spark plug lead before reconnecting it to its spark plug. If the insulation is damaged or deteriorated, install a new plug lead. Push the boot onto the plug terminal making sure it is fully seated.

Spark Plug Gap Adjustment (Conventional Gap Only)

New spark plugs should be carefully gapped to ensure a reliable, consistent spark. Use a special spark plug gapping tool with round gauges. **Figure 52** shows a common type of gapping tool.

1. Install the gaskets on the spark plugs.

NOTE
*Some spark plug brands require that the terminal end be screwed on the plug before installation. See **Figure 53**.*

2. Insert the appropriate size round feeler gauge (**Table 3**) between the electrodes. If the gap is correct, there will be a slight drag as the wire is pulled through. To adjust the gap, bend the side electrode with the gapping tool (**Figure 54**), then remeasure the gap.

CAUTION
Never attempt to close the gap by tapping the spark plug on a solid surface. This can damage the spark plug. Always

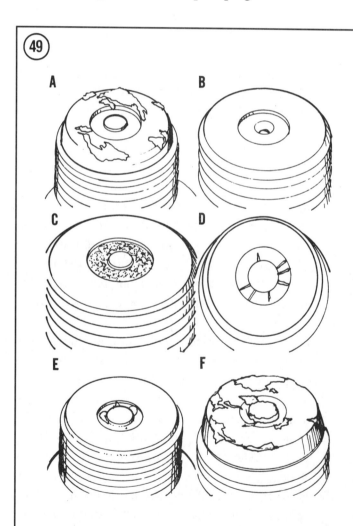

(49)

SPARK PLUG ANALYSIS (SURFACE GAP SPARK PLUGS)

A. Normal—Light tan or gray colored deposits indicate that the engine/ignition system condition is good. Elec trode wear indicates normal spark rotation.
B. Worn out—Excessive electrode wear can cause hard starting or a misfire during acceleration.
C. Cold fouled—Wet oil or fuel deposits are caused by "drowning" the plug with raw fuel mix during cranking, overrich carburetion or an improper fuel:oil ratio. Weak ignition will also contribute to this condition.
D. Carbon tracking—Electrically conductive deposits on the firing end provide a low-resistance path for the voltage. Carbon tracks form and can cause misfires.
E. Concentrated arc—Multi-colored appearance is normal. It is caused by electricity consistently following the same firing path. Arc path changes with deposit conductivity and gap erosion.
F. Aluminum throw-off—Caused by preignition. This is not a plug problem but the result of engine damage. Check engine to determine cause and extent of damage.

4

SPARK PLUG ANALYSIS
(CONVENTIONAL GAP SPARK PLUGS)

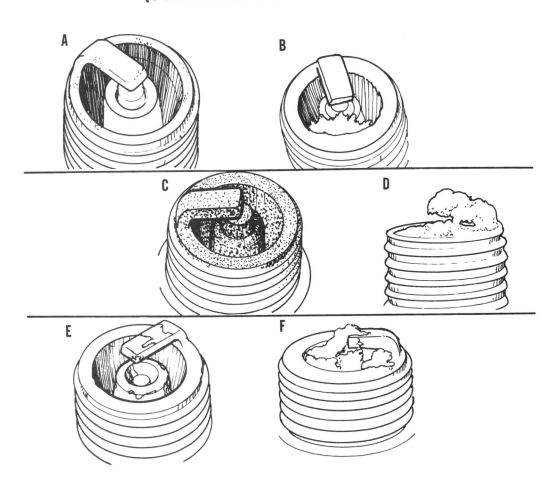

A. **Normal**—Light tan to gray color of insulator indicates correct heat range. Few deposits are present and the electrodes are not burned.

B. **Core bridging**—This defect is caused by excessive combustion chamber deposits striking and adhering to the firing end of the plug. In this case, they wedge or fuse between the electrode and core nose. They originate from the piston and cylinder head surfaces. Deposits are formed by one or more of the following:
   a. Excessive carbon in cylinder.
   b. Use of non-recommended oils.
   c. Immediate high-speed operation after prolonged trolling.
   d. Improper fuel:oil ratio.

C. **Wet fouling**—Damp or wet, black carbon coating over entire firing end of plug. Forms sludge in some engines. Caused by one or more of the following:
   a. Spark plug heat range too cold.
   b. Prolonged trolling.
   c. Low-speed carburetor adjustment too rich.

   d. Improper fuel:oil ratio.
   e. Induction manifold bleed-off passage obstructed.
   f. Worn or defective breaker points.

D. **Gap bridging**—Similar to core bridging, except the combustion particles are wedged or fused between the electrodes. Causes are the same.

E. **Overheating**—Badly worn electrodes and premature gap wear are indicative of this problem, along with a gray or white "blistered" appearance on the insulator. Caused by one or more of the following:
   a. Spark plug heat range too hot.
   b. Incorrect propeller usage, causing engine to lug.
   c. Worn or defective water pump.
   d. Restricted water intake or restriction somewhere in the cooling system.

F. **Ash deposits or lead fouling**—Ash deposits are light brown to white in color and result from use of fuel or oil additives. Lead fouling produces a yellowish brown discoloration and can be avoided by using unleaded fuels.

use the proper adjusting tool to open or close the gap.

Lower Unit and Water Pump Check

Overheating and extensive power head damage can result from a faulty water pump. Therefore, it is good practice to replace the water pump impeller, seals and gaskets at least once per year or whenever the lower unit is removed for service. See Chapter Nine.

Many outboard owners depend upon the visual indication provided by the "tell-tale" discharge to determine if the water pump is functioning. However, installation of a water pressure gauge kit (available from your Mercury Outboard dealer) is a more effective method to ensure that the pump is operating properly. The kit contains a fitting and hose that attaches to the engine block and a water pressure gauge for use in the boat.

After installing the pressure gauge kit, note the water pressure the first time the outboard is run. Water pressure under full throttle conditions should be at least 5 psi 34.5 kPa). If the pressure reading drops during subsequent use, service the water pump as soon as possible. See Chapter Nine.

Fuel System Service

The clearance between the carburetor body and the choke valve (on models so equipped) should not be greater than 0.015 in. (0.38 mm) when the choke is closed or hard cold starting will result. Refer to Chapter Six.

Fuel Lines and Hoses

1. Visually inspect all fuel lines and hoses for kinks, leaks, deterioration or other damage.
2. Disconnect fuel lines and blow out with compressed air to dislodge any contamination or foreign material.

NOTE
Brass line fuel fittings should only be sealed using Quicksilver Perfect Seal.

3. Coat fuel line fittings sparingly with Quicksilver Perfect Seal and reconnect the lines.

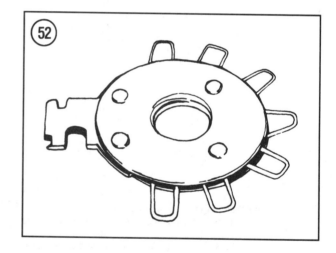

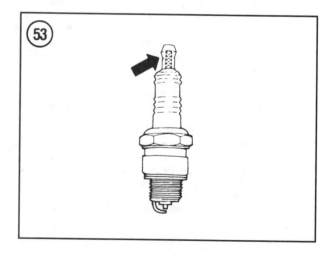

Engine Fuel Filter

The engine fuel filter should be inspected, cleaned or replaced during tune-up service. Four types of filters are used on models covered in this manual:

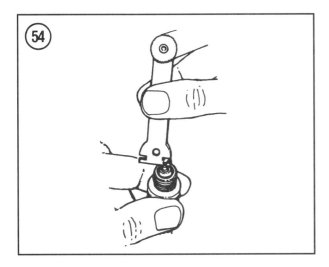

a. Inline filter (3-5 hp and 40-275 hp except EFI).
b. Sight bowl filter (8-25 hp).
c. Water separating filter (EFI models).
d. Final fuel filter (EFI models).

Inline filter

A translucent inline filter (**Figure 55**, typical) is installed between the fuel valve and the carburetor mounted fuel pump on 4 and 5 hp models or between the fuel pump and carburetors on 40-275 hp models. The translucent filter housing permits visual inspection to determine if water or contamination is present in the filter. To replace the inline filter:

1. On models equipped with an engine mounted fuel tank, set the fuel valve in the OFF position. Unclamp and disconnect the inlet and outlet holes from the filter. If sta-straps are used to clamp the fuel hoses, carefully cut and discard the sta-straps.
2. Remove and discard the fuel filter.
3. Install a new filter with the arrow on the filter housing facing toward the carburetor(s).
4. Install the hose clamps securely. If sta-straps are used to clamp the hoses, install new sta-straps and tighten securely.

Sight bowl filter

A sight bowl fuel filter (**Figure 56**) is used on 8-25 hp models. Service the sight bowl fuel filter as follows:

1. Pull downward on the filter assembly to disengage the ball mount (**Figure 57**) from the rubber handle rest.
2. Unscrew the sight bowl from the filter base.
3. Remove the filter element from the bowl. Clean the element in clean solvent and dry with compressed air. Replace the element if excessive contamination is present.
4. Be sure the sight bowl seal is correctly positioned in the bowl. Reinstall the filter in the bowl

and reinstall the bowl on the filter base. Tighten the bowl securely *by hand*.

5. Check the filter assembly for leakage by priming the fuel system with the primer bulb. Repair any leaks as necessary.

Water separating filter (EFI models)

A water separating fuel filter (**Figure 58**) is provided on electronic fuel injection (EFI) equipped models to prevent water or other contamination from damaging fuel injection components. The water separating filter assembly is equipped with a sensor that activates a warning light and horn should the water level in the filter become excessive. Service the water separating filter as follows:

1. Remove the tan water sensor probe wire from the bottom of the filter canister.

2. Unscrew the filter canister (**Figure 58**) from the filter base.

3. Empty the filter contents into a suitable container.

4. If excessive water or other contamination is noted, replace the filter.

   a. Remove the water sensor probe from the filter canister.

   b. Discard the canister, then reinstall the probe into a new filter canister.

5. Lubricate the filter canister seal with a light coat of engine oil and install onto the filter base. Tighten the filter securely *by hand*.

6. Reconnect the tan water sensor wire to the bottom of the filter canister. Coat the sensor wire connection with Quicksilver Liquid Neoprene (part No. 92-25711).

Final fuel filter (EFI models)

The final fuel filter (**Figure 59**) is installed in the fuel system between the electric fuel pump and the injector rail. The final filter prevents any fuel contamination from reaching the fuel injectors. Service the final fuel filter as follows:

WARNING
The fuel injection system is under pressure. Be certain to relieve the fuel pressure before any disassembly is performed.

1. Relieve the fuel system pressure by removing the cap from the fuel rail service port (**Figure 60**). Wrap a shop towel around the service port to catch the discharged fuel, then depress the valve inside the service port using a small screw-

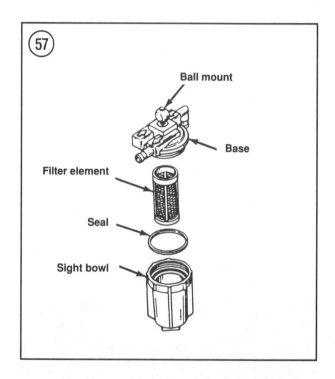

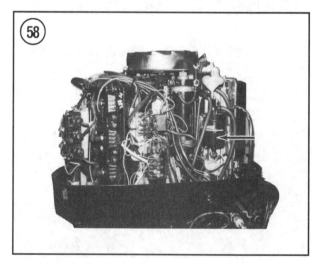

driver or similar tool. Allow the pressure to discharge into the shop towel.

2. Remove the final filter cover screw (G, **Figure 61**) and remove the cover.

3. Withdraw the filter element (C, **Figure 61**).

4. Clean the filter element in solvent and dry with compressed air. If excessive contamination is noted, replace the filter element.

5. Install new O-rings (B and D, **Figure 61**) into the filter element and cover. Install the element

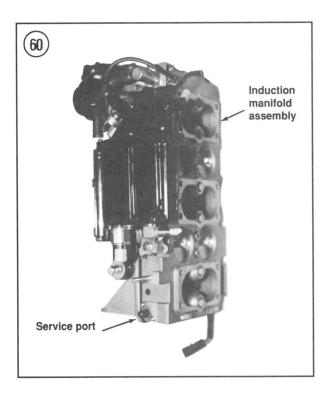

into the filter base, then install the filter cover. Tighten the cover screw securely.

Fuel Pump (Except EFI)

The fuel pump does not generally require service during a tune-up. However, if the engine has 100 or more hours of operation since the pump was last serviced, it is good practice to remove and disassemble the pump, inspect each component carefully for wear or damage and reassemble it with a new diaphragm. See Chapter Six.

> *NOTE*
> *Crankcase air leaks or any condition that causes low compression will have an adverse effect on fuel pump operation.*

A defective fuel pump diaphragm often produces symptoms that are diagnosed as an ignition system problem. A common malfunction results from a tiny pinhole in the diaphragm. This pinhole allows fuel to enter the crankcase and fuel foul the spark plug(s) at idle speed; however the problem usually disappears at speeds above idle.

Fuel pump flow can be tested by installing a clear fuel hose between the pump and carburetor(s). Place the outboard into a test tank or connect a flushing device and start the engine. If air bubbles are noted in the clear fuel hose, check the following:

    a. Fuel hose leaks.

    b. Fuel pump loose on the power head.

    c. Defective fuel pump gaskets or diaphragm.

    d. Loose fuel fitting or fuel hose connection.

Fuel pump pressure test

> *NOTE*
> *Fuel pump pressure cannot be tested on integral fuel pump/carburetor assemblies.*

1. Install pressure gauge part No. C-91-30692 (or equivalent) to the fuel hose between the pump and carburetor (upper carburetor on multi-carburetor models).

CAUTION
The outboard motor must be in a test tank or on a boat in the water to perform wide-open throttle fuel pump tests.

2. Place the outboard into a test tank or connect a flushing device.

3. Start the engine and allow to run at idle speed while noting fuel pump pressure. Fuel pump pressure should be:

   a. 40 hp—2.0-3.25 psi (14-22 kPa).

   b. 50 and 60 hp—3.0-5.0 psi (21-34 kPa).

   c. 75-200 hp—1.0-3.0 psi (7-21 kPa).

   d. 250 and 275 hp—5 psi (34 kPa).

4. Briefly, run the engine at wide-open throttle. Fuel pump pressure should be:

   a. 40 hp—5.5-6.5 psi (38-45 kPa).

   b. 50 and 60 hp prior to serial No. D000750—6.0-8.0 psi (41-55 kPa).

   c. 50 and 60 hp serial No. D000750-on—4.0-7.0 psi (28-48 kPa).

   d. 135-200 hp—3.0-10.0 psi (21-69 kPa).

   e. 250-275 hp—2.0-8.0 psi (14-55 kPa).

5. Repair or replace the fuel pump if pressure is not as specified.

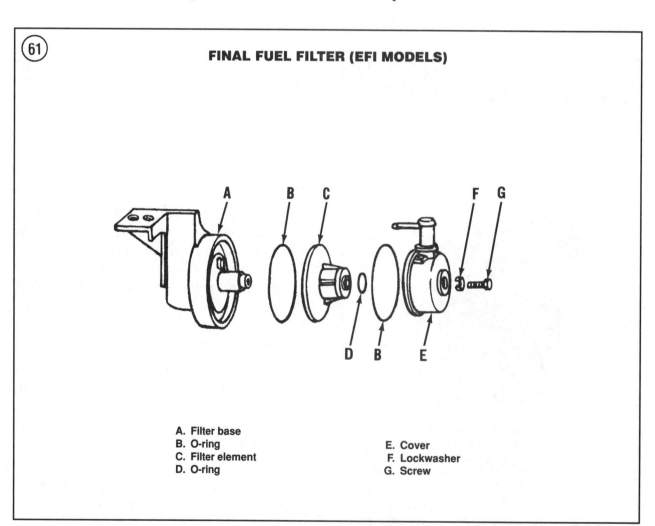

(61) FINAL FUEL FILTER (EFI MODELS)

A. Filter base
B. O-ring
C. Filter element
D. O-ring

E. Cover
F. Lockwasher
G. Screw

Ignition System Service

Replace the breaker points and condenser on 3 hp models as described in Chapter Seven. On all models, perform ignition timing, synchronizing and adjustment service as described in Chapter Five.

Battery and Starter Motor Check

1. Check the battery state of charge. See Chapter Seven.
2. Connect a voltmeter between the starter motor positive terminal and a good engine ground.
3. Turn the ignition switch to the START position while noting voltmeter.
4. If the voltage exceeds 9.5 volts and the starter motor does not operate properly, repair or replace the starter motor.
5. If the voltage is less than 9.5 volts, check the battery and all connections. Charge or replace the battery if necessary, and repeat the test procedure.

Starter Solenoid Check

Test the solenoid using a suitable ohmmeter.

TERMINALS ON SOLENOID

A. Connect small red test lead
B. "S" terminal
C. "T" terminal
D. Connect small black test lead

1. Disconnect all leads from the starter solenoid. See **Figure 62**.
2. Connect the meter test leads to the large solenoid terminals (A and D, **Figure 62**).
3. Connect a 12-volt battery between the small solenoid terminals (B and C, **Figure 62**). Note the ohmmeter reading.
4. The solenoid should make an audible click, and the ohmmeter should indicate continuity when the battery is connected. If the solenoid does not click, or if it does click but the ohmmeter shows no continuity, replace the solenoid.

Alternator and Rectifier Check

Test the stator and rectifier as described in Chapter Three.

Internal Wiring Harness Check

1. Check the wiring harness for frayed or chafed insulation.
2. Check for loose connections between the wires and terminal ends.
3. Check harness connector for bent electrical prongs.
4. Check harness connector and prongs for corrosion. Clean as required.
5. If harness is suspected of contributing to electrical malfunctions, check all wires for continuity and resistance between the harness connection and the terminal ends. Repair or replace the wiring harness as necessary.

Ignition Timing, Synchronization and Adjustment

See Chapter Five.

Performance Test (On the Boat)

Before performance testing the outboard motor, make sure that the boat bottom is cleaned of all marine growth and that no "hook" or "rocker" is present in the boat bottom. Any of these conditions will reduce the boat performance considerably.

The boat should be performance tested with an average load on board. The outboard motor should be tilted or trimmed at an angle that will produce optimum performance and balanced steering control. If equipped with an adjustable trim tab, it should be properly adjusted to allow the boat to steer in either direction with equal ease.

Check the engine rpm at full throttle. If engine speed is not within the specified range (Chapter Five), check the propeller pitch. Use a higher pitch propeller to reduce engine speed or a lower pitch to increase engine speed.

Adjust the idle speed and fuel mixture with the boat in the water, idling in forward gear to obtain optimum adjustment results.

Table 1 LUBRICATION[1] (3-25 HP MODELS)

Frequency[2]	Item	Quicksilver lubricant
Every 30 days (fresh or saltwater)	Gear housing lube level	Premium Blend Gear Lube
Every 60 days	Swivel pin/tilt pin fittings	2-4-C Marine Lubricant
	Clamp screws	2-4-C Marine Lubricant
	Reverse lock cam, lever and/or hook	2-4-C Marine Lubricant
	Steering cable, tube and pivot/ball joints	2-4-C Marine Lubricant
	Shift/throttle linkage pivot points	2-4-C Marine Lubricant
	Tiller handle knuckle and gears/U-joint	2-4-C Marine Lubricant
	Tilt stop lever	2-4-C Marine Lubricant
	Upper shift shaft	2-4-C Marine Lubricant
	Steering link rod pivot points	SAE 30 engine oil
	Ride-Guide Steering cable and cable end	2-4-C Marine Lubricant
Once per season or every 100 hours	Change gear housing lubricant	Premium Blend Gear Lube
	Starter motor pinion gear	SAE 10 engine oil
	Gear housing bearing carrier	Special Lubricant 101 or 2-4-C Marine Lubricant
	Propeller shaft	Special Lubricant 101 or 2-4-C Marine Lubricant
	Crankshaft-to-drive shaft splines	2-4-C Marine Lubricant

1. Complete list may not apply to all models. Perform only those items which apply to your specific model.
2. Double the lubrication intervals if outboard is operated consistently in saltwater or polluted or brackish water.

Table 2 LUBRICATION[1] (40-275 HP MODELS)

Frequency[2]	Item	Quicksilver lubricant
Every 30 days (fresh or saltwater)	Gear housing lube level	Premium Blend Gear Lube
Every 60 days	Throttle/shift linkage pivot points	2-4-C Marine Lubricant
	Upper shift shaft	2-4-C Marine Lubricant
	Tilt lock lever	2-4-C Marine Lubricant
	Swivel pin	2-4-C Marine Lubricant
	Ride Guide Steering cable	2-4-C Marine Lubricant
	Tilt tube	2-4-C Marine Lubricant
	Steering link rod pivot points	SAE 30 engine oil
	Trim rod ball ends	Special Lubricant 101
	Tilt lock lever shaft	SAE 30 engine oil
	Tilt lock lever locking brace	SAE 30 engine oil
Once per season or every 100 hours	Change gear housing lubricant	Premium Blend Gear Lube
	Starter motor pinion gear	SAE 10 engine oil
	Gear housing bearing carrier	Special Lubricant 101 or 2-4-C Marine Lubricant
	Crankshaft-to-drive shaft splines	2-4-C Marine Lubricant
	Propeller shaft	Special Lubricant 101 or 2-4-C Marine Lubricant
	Power trim/tilt fluid level	Power Trim & Steering Fluid
	Accelerator pump plunger and throttle cam	Special Lubricant 101

1. Complete list may not apply to all models. Perform only those items which apply to your specific model.
2. Double the lubrication intervals if outboard is operated consistently in saltwater or polluted or brackish water.

Table 3 RECOMMENDED SPARK PLUGS

Model	NGK	Champion	Gap
3 and 3.3 hp	BPR6HS-10	RL87YC	0.040 in. (1.0 mm)
4 and 5 hp	BP7HS-10	L82YC	0.040 in. (1.0 mm)
8 and 9.9 hp[1]	–	L82YC	0.040 in. (1.0 mm)
15 hp[1]	BP8HS-15	–	0.060 in. (1.5 mm)
20 and 25 hp	BU8H	L76V	Surface gap
40 hp	BUHW-2	–	Surface gap
50 and 60 hp	BU8H	L76V	Surface gap
75-115 hp	BUHW-2	L78V	Surface gap
135-275 hp	BU8H	L76V	Surface gap

1. Models equipped with standard ignition coils. Use NGK BUHW spark plugs on models equipped with high energy ignition coils.

Table 4 GEAR HOUSING LUBRICANT CAPACITIES

Model	Capacity
3 hp	3 oz. (88.7 mL)
3.3 hp	2.5 oz. (73.9 mL)
4-5 hp	6.6 oz. (195 mL)
8-15 hp	6.5 oz. (192 mL)
20-25 hp	7.6 oz. (225 mL)
40 hp	12.5 oz. (370 mL)
50-60 hp (prior to serial No. D000750)	12.5 oz. (370 mL)
50-60 hp (serial No. D000750-on)	11.5 oz. (340 mL)
75-115 hp	22.5 oz. (665 mL)
135-200 hp (except 150XR4 and 150XR6)	24.25 oz. (717 mL)
150XR4 and 150XR6	21 oz. (621 mL)
250-275 hp	29 oz. (857 mL)

Chapter Five

Timing, Synchronizing
And Adjusting

If an outboard motor is to deliver its maximum efficiency and peak performance, the carburetors or fuel injection system and the ignition timing must be properly adjusted. In addition, the ignition system must be properly synchronized with the throttle operation. The engine should be adjusted, timed and synchronized during a tune-up or whenever any fuel or ignition system components are replaced, serviced or adjusted.

Procedures for timing, synchronizing and adjusting Mercury outboard motors differ according to model and ignition system. This chapter is divided into self-contained sections dealing with particular models/ignition systems for fast and easy reference. Each section specifies the appropriate procedure and sequence to be followed and provides the necessary tune-up data. Read the general information at the beginning of the chapter, then select the section pertaining to your particular outboard motor.

NOTE
*Factory timing specifications provided by Mercury Marine are given in **Tables 1-13**. However, due to the low octane rating of available gasoline, Mercury Marine has occasionally found it necessary to modify their specifications during production of late-model outboards. If your engine has a decal attached to the power head or air box, always follow the specifications provided on the decal instead of the specifications in **Tables 1-13**.*

IGNITION TIMING AND SYNCHRONIZATION

Ignition timing advance and throttle opening must be synchronized to occur at the proper time for the engine to perform properly. Synchronizing is the process of timing the carburetor (or fuel injection) throttle operation to the ignition timing advance.

All models use some form of timing marks and can be timed using a suitable timing light. See **Figure 1**. This method is not always practical, however, as the outboard must be operated at full throttle in forward gear to adjust maximum timing advance. This requires the use of a test tank, as timing an engine while speeding across open water is neither easy nor safe.

Some models can be timed with a timing light while the engine is cranked. A test tank is not required in this procedure.

Required Equipment

> *CAUTION*
> *Never operate the outboard motor without water circulating through the lower unit to the power head. To do this will damage the water pump, and can cause power head damage.*

Some form of water supply is essential whenever the engine is operated during timing adjustment procedures. Using a test tank is the preferred and most convenient method, although the adjustments may be performed with the boat in the water or with a flushing device attached to the gear housing (**Figure 2**).

Static adjustment of the ignition timing requires the use of a suitable dial indicator to position the No. 1 piston at top dead center (TDC) accurately before making timing adjustments. TDC is determined by removing the No. 1 spark plug and installing the dial indicator in the spark plug hole. Refer to **Figure 3**.

Dynamic timing adjustment requires the use of a stroboscopic timing light connected to the No. 1 spark plug lead. As the engine is cranked or operated, the light flashes each time the spark plug fires. When the light is pointed at the moving flywheel, the mark on the flywheel appears to stand still. The appropriate timing marks will be aligned if the timing is correctly adjusted.

An accurate shop tachometer should be connected to the engine to determine engine speed during timing adjustments. Do not rely on the tachometer installed in a boat to provide accurate engine speed readings.

3 HP MODELS

Timing Adjustment

Refer to **Table 1** for tune-up data. Ignition timing and synchronization is not required on 3 hp models. The timing should be correct if the breaker points are in acceptable condition and the point gap is maintained at 0.012-0.016 in. (0.03-0.04 mm). Refer to Chapter Seven for breaker point replacement/adjustment procedures.

Idle Speed Adjustment

1. Start the engine and allow to warm to normal operating temperature.
2. Place the throttle lever in the slowest speed position.

3. Adjust the idle speed screw (**Figure 4**) to obtain 900-1000 rpm.

Throttle Jet Needle Adjustment

See Chapter Six.

4 AND 5 HP MODELS

Refer to **Table 2** for tune-up data. The ignition timing is advanced electronically on 4 and 5 hp models and is not adjustable. However, the timing should be checked periodically to ensure the ignition system is functioning properly.

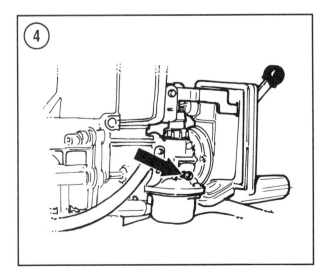

Checking Static Timing

1. Remove the spark plug and install dial indicator part No. 91-58222A1 (or equivalent) into the spark plug hole.
2. Rotate the flywheel in the normal direction of rotation to position the piston at TDC.
3. With the piston positioned at TDC, the TDC mark on the flywheel should be aligned with the cylinder block-to-crankcase cover split line.
4. If the split line and timing mark do not align:
   a. The dial indicator was incorrectly installed, set up or misread.
   b. The flywheel is incorrectly installed or the flywheel key is sheared.

Checking Dynamic Timing

1. Connect a suitable timing light to the spark plug lead.
2. Start the engine and allow to warm to normal operating temperature.
3. With the engine running at idle speed, shift into FORWARD gear.
4. Point the timing light at the flywheel. With the engine idling in forward gear, the TDC mark on the flywheel should be located 1/4 in. (6.4 mm) from the cylinder block-to-crankcase cover split line (5° BTDC).
5. Advance the throttle to wide-open throttle.
6. With the engine running at wide-open throttle in forward gear, the 30° BTDC mark on the flywheel should be aligned with the cylinder block-to-crankcase cover split line. If not, test the ignition system as described in Chapter Three.

Idle Speed and Mixture Adjustment

1. Connect an accurate shop tachometer to the engine according the manufacturer's instructions.
2. Start the engine and allow it to warm to normal operating temperature.

3. Place the throttle in the idle position, then shift into FORWARD gear.

4. Adjust the idle speed screw (A, **Figure 5**) to obtain 850 rpm (in forward gear).

5. Slowly turn the idle mixture screw (B, **Figure 5**) counterclockwise until the engine begins to run roughly due to an over-rich mixture.

6. Slowly turn the idle mixture screw clockwise until the engine speed increases and the engine runs smoothly. If the engine hesitates during acceleration, the mixture is too lean. Turn the mixture screw counterclockwise slightly to enrichen the mixture.

7. Recheck the idle speed and adjust as required.

High Speed Mixture Adjustment

The high speed mixture is adjusted by varying the size of the fixed main jet. Refer to Chapter Six.

8, 9.9 AND 15 HP MODELS

Refer to **Table 3** for tune-up data.

> *NOTE*
> *On tiller handle equipped models, loosen the throttle cable jam nuts and adjust the nuts to provide equal full-throttle travel in forward and reverse gears, and to remove any slack in the cables.*

Maximum Spark Advance Adjustment

1. Connect a timing light to the No. 1 (top) spark plug lead.

2. Start the engine and warm it to normal operating temperature.

3. Shift the outboard into FORWARD gear.

4. Point the timing light at the timing pointer above the carburetor. Advance the throttle to the wide-open throttle position and note the timing. The 3 dots (36° BTDC) on the flywheel should be aligned with the timing pointer. See **Figure 6**.

5. If adjustment is necessary, stop the engine and loosen the jam nut on the maximum advance screw (A, **Figure 7**). Restart the engine and adjust the screw (A) as necessary to align the 3 dots and timing pointer as described in Step 4. Stop the engine and retighten the jam nut securely.

Idle Timing Adjustment

1. Push the primer/fast idle knob (**Figure 8**) in fully, then turn the knob completely counterclockwise.

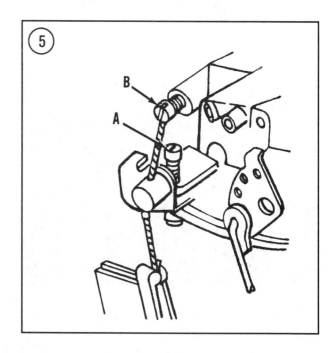

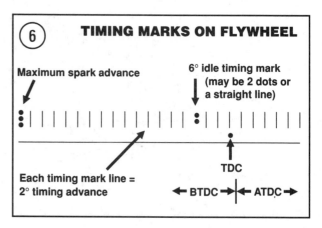

TIMING MARKS ON FLYWHEEL

Maximum spark advance

6° idle timing mark (may be 2 dots or a straight line)

Each timing mark line = 2° timing advance

TDC

← BTDC → ← ATDC →

2. Start the engine and run at idle speed, then shift into FORWARD gear. If necessary, adjust idle speed to obtain a smooth, stable idle.

3. Adjust the idle timing screw (B, **Figure 7**) to align the 2 dots (6° BTDC) on the flywheel with the timing pointer.

Idle Wire Adjustment

1. Push primer/fast idle knob (**Figure 8**) in fully then turn the knob completely counterclockwise.

2. Shift the outboard into NEUTRAL.

3. Adjust the screw (E, **Figure 7**) until all clearance is removed between the idle wire (E, **Figure 7**) and the trigger.

Idle Mixture Adjustment

1. Start the engine and run at fast idle until warmed to normal operating temperature. Throttle back to idle speed, shift into FORWARD gear and allow engine speed to stabilize.

2. Push primer/fast idle knob (**Figure 8**) in fully, then turn the knob completely counterclockwise.

3. Remove the access plug from the front top of the carburetor intake cover (if so equipped).

4. With the engine running at idle speed in forward gear, slowly turn the idle mixture screw (**Figure 9**) counterclockwise until the engine begins to run rough and misfire due to the over-rich idle mixture. Note the position of the mixture screw.

5. Slowly turn the idle mixture screw clockwise until the engine runs smoothly and idle speed increases. Continue turning the screw clockwise until the engine speed decreases and misfire occurs due to an excessively lean idle mixture. Note the position of the mixture screw.

6. Back out the idle mixture screw to a point halfway between the rich and lean settings.

CAUTION
To prevent engine damage, do not adjust the idle mixture leaner than necessary to provide a reasonably smooth idle. It is good practice to set the idle mixture slightly rich instead of too lean.

7. Reinstall the access plug into the carburetor intake cover (if so equipped).

Idle Speed Adjustment

NOTE
On models not equipped with an idle speed screw, the carburetor is calibrated

5

at the factory to idle at 600-700 rpm in forward gear.

On models so equipped, the idle speed screw is located on top of the throttle cam follower (D, **Figure 7**).

1. Push primer/fast idle knob (**Figure 8**) in fully, then turn the knob completely counterclockwise.
2. Connect an accurate shop tachometer to the engine per the manufacturer's instructions.
3. Start the engine, shift into FORWARD gear and allow to run at idle speed.
4. Adjust the idle speed screw to obtain 700-800 rpm.

High Speed Mixture Adjustment

The high speed fuel-air mixture is adjusted by varying the size of a fixed main jet. See Chapter Six.

20 AND 25 HP MODELS

Refer to **Table 4** for tune-up data.

1. Push the primer/fast idle knob fully inward, then turn the knob completely counterclockwise.
2. Adjust the idle speed fuel-air mixture as described under *Low Speed Mixture* in this chapter.

Full Throttle Timing Adjustment

1. Connect a timing light to the No. 1 (top) spark plug lead according to the manufacturer's instructions.
2. Connect an accurate shop tachometer to the engine according to the manufacturer's instructions.
3. Start the engine and shift into FORWARD gear.
4. Advance the throttle to the wide-open position and note the timing using the timing light. The 3 dot (25° BTDC) mark on the flywheel should be aligned with the timing pointer. See **Figure 10**.

CAUTION
Do not attempt to adjust link rod in Step 5 with the engine running. Serious personal injury could result if contact is made with the moving flywheel.

5. If adjustment is necessary, stop the engine and pry the end of the spark advance rod from the throttle lever (A, **Figure 11**) using a screwdriver or similar tool. Lengthen the link rod to advance timing or shorten the rod to retard timing.
6. Reconnect the spark advance link rod to the throttle lever. Start the engine and recheck the adjustment. Repeat Step 5 as necessary to align the timing marks as specified in Step 4.

Throttle Cam Adjustment

1. With the engine not running, loosen the jam nuts on the dashpot (D, **Figure 11**) and back dashpot away from the throttle cam.
2. Release the neutral rpm ratchet and back off the idle speed screw so the carburetor throttle valve is fully closed.
3. Move the throttle cam toward the throttle roller. The bottom mark on the throttle cam should just contact the roller as shown in **Figure 12**.
4. If adjustment is required, loosen the throttle cam bolt (B, **Figure 11**), reposition the cam on its elongated slot, then securely tighten the cam bolt. Recheck the adjustment as described in Step 3.

Pickup Timing Adjustment

NOTE
The throttle cam must be properly adjusted prior to checking pickup timing. See **Throttle Cam Adjustment** *in this chapter.*

1. Connect a timing light to the No. 1 (top) spark plug lead.
2. Start the engine and point the timing light at the flywheel.

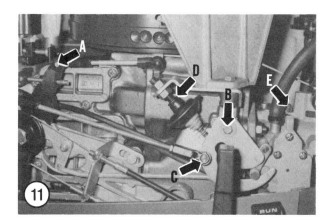

3. Move the throttle lever until the timing pointer is aligned with the 2° BTDC mark (**Figure 13**) on the flywheel. At this point, the bottom throttle cam mark should just contact the throttle roller as shown in **Figure 12**.

CAUTION
Do not disconnect the throttle link rod from the throttle cam in Step 4. Attempting to disconnect the rod at the throttle cam end can damage the cam.

5

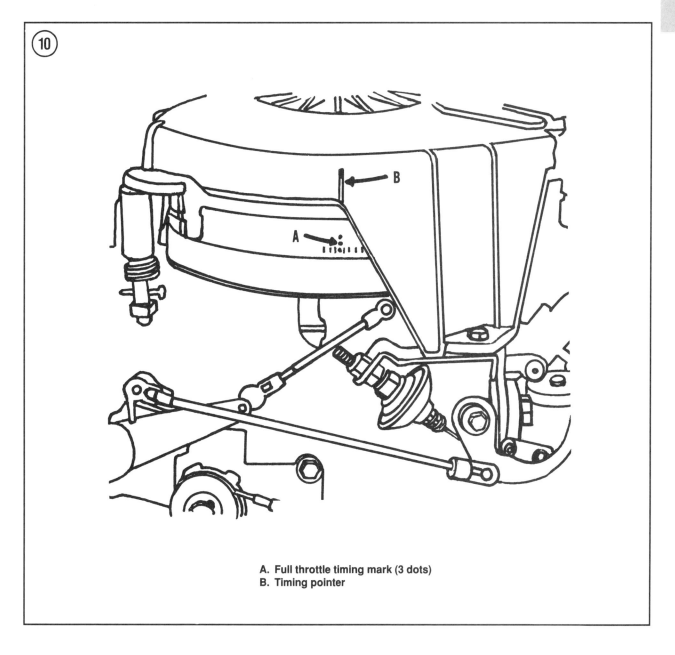

A. Full throttle timing mark (3 dots)
B. Timing pointer

4. If adjustment is required, stop the engine and disconnect the throttle link rod (C, **Figure 11**) from the throttle lever by prying with a screwdriver or similar tool.

5. Adjust the length of the link rod as necessary to position the throttle cam mark as described in Step 3.

6. Reconnect the link rod and repeat Step 2 and Step 3. Readjust the link rod as necessary.

Idle Speed Adjustment

1. Connect an accurate shop tachometer to the engine according to the manufacturer's instructions.

2. With engine running in forward gear, at normal operating temperature, adjust the idle speed screw to obtain 700-800 rpm.

3. If necessary, adjust idle mixture as described under *Idle Mixture Adjustment* in this chapter.

Dashpot Adjustment

1. Adjust the dashpot (D, **Figure 11**) so its plunger is fully depressed when the engine is running at the specified idle speed.

2. After adjustment, securely tighten the dashpot jam nuts.

Neutral Rpm Adjustment

1. Start the engine and allow to run at idle speed in NEUTRAL.

2. Set the primer/fast idle knob (A, **Figure 14**) to the center detent position.

3. Adjust ratchet (B, **Figure 14**) as necessary to obtain 1500-1700 rpm idle speed.

Starter Interlock Adjustment

1. Stop engine and shift outboard into NEUTRAL.

2. Pull the primer/fast idle knob to the fully out position.

3. Adjust starter interlock screw (E, **Figure 11**) so interlock lever clears the starter pulley ratchet. Check adjustment by making sure the rewind starter operates normally with the outboard in NEUTRAL gear.

Idle Mixture Adjustment

Do not adjust the idle speed fuel-air mixture leaner than necessary to provide a smooth idle. It is good practice to set the idle mixture slightly rich instead of too lean.

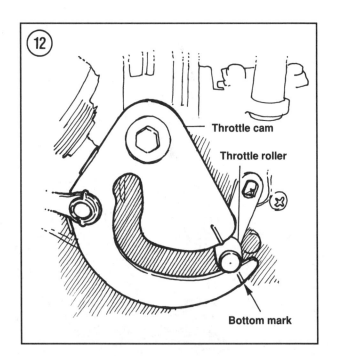

Throttle cam
Throttle roller
Bottom mark

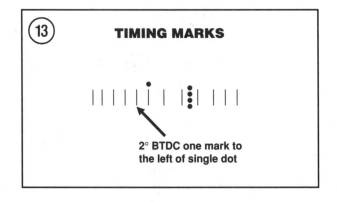

TIMING MARKS

2° BTDC one mark to the left of single dot

1. Start the engine and warm to normal operating temperature.

2. Allow engine speed to stabilize at idle for approximately 60 seconds, then shift into FORWARD gear.

3. Slowly turn the idle mixture screw (**Figure 15**) counterclockwise until the engine begins to run rough due to an over-rich mixture. Note the position of the mixture screw.

4. Slowly turn the idle mixture screw clockwise until the engine begins to run smoothly and rpm increases. Note the position of the mixture screw. Continue turning the screw clockwise until the engine begins to run rough and misfire occurs due to an excessively lean mixture.

5. Set the mixture screw at a halfway point between the rich and lean settings.

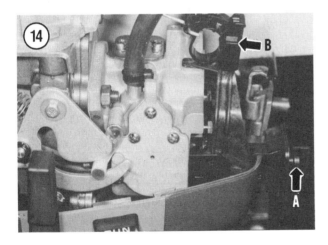

6. If necessary, readjust the idle speed as described in this chapter.

High Speed Mixture Adjustment

The high speed fuel-air mixture is adjusted by varying the size of a fixed main jet. See Chapter Six.

40 HP MODELS

Timing Adjustments

NOTE
The battery must be fully charged and the starting system functioning properly when checking static ignition timing on electric start models. Manual start models must be running to check ignition timing.

Refer to **Table 5** for tune-up data.

1. Remove the engine cowl.

2A. Electric start:

   a. Disconnect the spark plug leads and remove the spark plugs.

   b. Connect spark gap tester (part No. 91-63998A1 or equivalent) between the No. 1 (top) spark plug lead and a good engine ground.

   c. Connect a timing light to the No. 1 (top) spark plug lead.

2B. Manual start—Connect a timing light to the No. 1 (top) spark plug lead.

Throttle primary pickup adjustment

1. Crank the engine with the electric starter (or start the engine on manual start models) while pointing the timing light at the timing pointer window in the flywheel cover (**Figure 16**). Slowly advance the throttle/spark arm until the "0" (TDC) mark is aligned with the V-notch in the timing pointer window. Hold the throttle/spark arm in this position.

2. While holding the throttle/spark arm, turn the idle speed screw (**Figure 17**) until the screw just contacts its stop.

3. Repeat Step 1 to verify that the "0" timing mark is still aligned with the V-notch in the timing window while holding the throttle/spark arm against the idle speed screw stop. If adjustment is necessary, crank or start the engine and adjust the idle speed screw while noting the timing marks with the timing light.

NOTE
After primary, secondary and maximum advance ignition timing adjustments are completed, the idle speed screw will require readjustment to obtain the correct idle speed.

4. Stop the engine (manual start models). Loosen the 2 throttle plate actuator screws (**Figure 18**).

5. Hold the throttle/spark arm firmly against the idle speed screw stop. Rotate the actuator plate as required so the primary throttle cam just contacts the primary pickup arm on the carburetor cluster (**Figure 19**), then retighten the actuator plate screws.

Maximum timing adjustment

NOTE
The battery must be fully charged and the starting system functioning properly

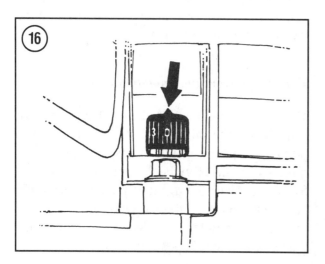

when checking static ignition timing on electric start models. Manual start models must be running to check ignition timing.

1A. Electric start:

  a. Advance the throttle/spark arm to position the maximum spark advance screw against its stop. See **Figure 20**.

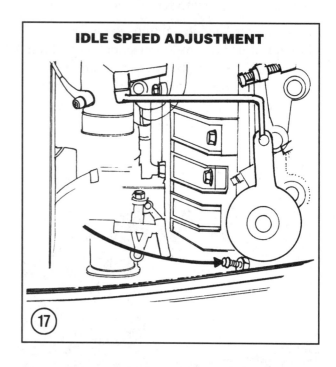

IDLE SPEED ADJUSTMENT

⑰

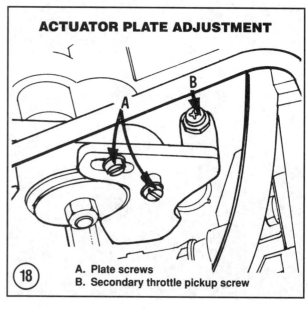

ACTUATOR PLATE ADJUSTMENT

⑱ A. Plate screws
B. Secondary throttle pickup screw

b. Crank the engine with the electric starter while noting the timing with the timing light.

c. Adjust the maximum spark advance screw (**Figure 20**) to align the 32° BTDC mark on the flywheel with the V-notch in the timing window.

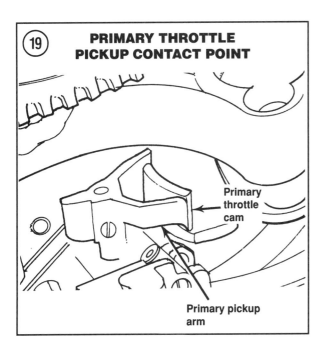

PRIMARY THROTTLE PICKUP CONTACT POINT

Primary throttle cam

Primary pickup arm

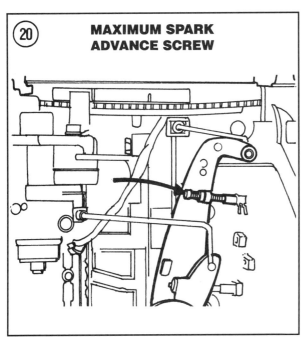

MAXIMUM SPARK ADVANCE SCREW

NOTE
Due to the electronic spark advance characteristics of this ignition system, the timing will retard slightly when running at wide-open throttle (5500 rpm). Therefore, the maximum timing should be adjusted to 32° BTDC at cranking speed to obtain the desired 30° BTDC when running at 5500 rpm. All timing adjustments made at cranking speed should be verified with the outboard running.

1B. Manual start:

a. Start the engine, warm to normal operating temperature and shift into FORWARD gear.

b. Advance the throttle/spark arm so the maximum spark advance screw (**Figure 20**) is against its stop and note the timing with the timing light.

c. Adjust the maximum spark advance screw (**Figure 20**) to align the 30° BTDC mark on the flywheel with the V-notch in the timing window.

2. Remove the timing light. On electric start models, remove the spark gap tester, reinstall the spark plugs and connect the plug leads.

Throttle secondary pickup adjustment

1. With the engine not running, advance the throttle until the maximum spark advance screw (**Figure 20**) is against its stop.

2. Adjust the secondary throttle pickup screw (**Figure 21**) so the screw just contacts the secondary lever of the carburetor cluster. See **Figure 22**.

Full throttle stop screw adjustment

1. With the engine not running, advance the throttle lever so the full throttle stop screw is against its stop. See **Figure 23**. Hold the throttle in this position.

5

2. Adjust the full throttle stop screw so the carburetor throttle valves are in the fully open position.

> *CAUTION*
> *The carburetor throttle valves must not serve as a throttle stop at wide-open throttle or damage to the carburetors will result. In the wide-open throttle position, 0.010-0.015 in. (0.25-0.38 mm) free play must be present between the secondary pickup screw and the carburetor cluster secondary lever (**Figure 24**). If insufficient free play is present, the full throttle stop screw **must** be readjusted to provide the specified clearance.*

Idle Mixture Adjustment

Do not adjust the idle speed fuel-air mixture leaner than necessary to provide a smooth idle. It is good practice to set the idle mixture slightly rich instead of too lean.

1. Start the engine and warm to normal operating temperature.

2. Allow engine speed to stabilize at idle for approximately 60 seconds, then shift into FORWARD gear.

3. Slowly turn the idle mixture screw counterclockwise until the engine begins to run rough due to an over-rich mixture. Note the position of the mixture screw.

4. Slowly turn the idle mixture screw clockwise until the engine begins to run smoothly and rpm increases. Note the position of the mixture screw. Continue turning the screw clockwise until the engine begins to run rough and misfire occurs due to an excessively lean mixture.

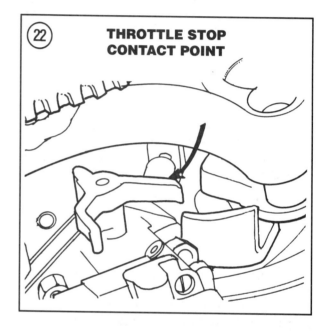

㉒ **THROTTLE STOP CONTACT POINT**

㉓ **FULL THROTTLE STOP SCREW**

SECONDARY PICKUP SCREW

㉑

5. Set the mixture screw at a halfway point between the rich and lean settings.

High Speed Mixture Adjustment

The high speed mixture is adjusted by varying the size of a fixed main jet. See Chapter Six.

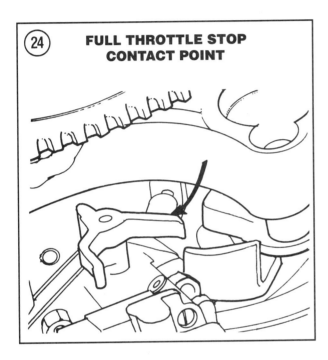

24 **FULL THROTTLE STOP CONTACT POINT**

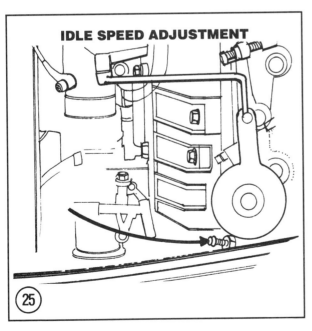

IDLE SPEED ADJUSTMENT

25

Idle Speed Adjustment

1. Start the engine and allow to run at fast idle for approximately 5 minutes.
2. Make sure the idle mixture is correctly adjusted as previously described.
3. Shift the outboard into FORWARD gear.
4. Remove the throttle cable barrel from the barrel retainer on the cable anchor bracket.
5. Adjust the idle speed screw (**Figure 25**) to obtain 600-700 rpm in forward gear.
6. Hold the throttle lever against the idle stop. Adjust the cable barrel to slip into the retainer with a very light preload of the throttle lever against the idle stop. Fasten the barrel in the retainer.

NOTE
Excessive preload in Step 6 will result in difficult shifting from FORWARD gear to NEUTRAL.

7. Check the throttle cable preload by inserting a thin piece of paper (such as a matchbook cover) between the idle stop and stop screw. If the preload is correct, a slight drag (without tearing) will be noted when removing the paper. Readjust the cable as required to obtain the desired preload.

50 AND 60 HP MODELS (PRIOR TO SERIAL NO. D000750)

Timing Pointer Adjustment

If the power head is equipped with an adjustable timing pointer, it should be adjusted before proceeding with ignition timing adjustments.
1. Remove the engine cowl.
2. Remove all spark plugs from the engine to prevent accidental starting.
3. Install a dial indicator in the No. 1 (top) spark plug hole (**Figure 26**).
4. Rotate the flywheel clockwise until the No. 1 piston is located at TDC, then zero the dial indicator.

5

5. Rotate the flywheel counterclockwise until the ".464" mark on the flywheel timing decal is about 1/4 turn past the timing pointer.

6. Rotate the flywheel clockwise until the dial indicator reads exactly 0.464 in.

7. The timing pointer groove should be aligned with the ".464" mark on the flywheel timing decal. If not, loosen the pointer adjusting screw (**Figure 27**), align the pointer with the specified timing mark, then retighten the screw.

8. Remove the dial indicator and reinstall the spark plugs.

Timing Adjustments

Refer to **Table 6** for tune-up data and timing specifications.

1. Place the outboard motor into a test tank or mount on a boat in the water. Connect the appropriate electrical harness and fuel line to the outboard motor.

2. Connect a timing light to the No. 1 spark plug lead.

3. Connect an accurate shop tachometer to the engine according to the manufacturer's instructions.

4. Lightly seat the carburetor idle mixture screws, then back the screws out 1-1/4 to 1-3/4 turns.

Maximum timing adjustment

1. Start the engine and shift into FORWARD gear. Advance the throttle to 5300-5800 rpm and note the ignition timing with the timing light.

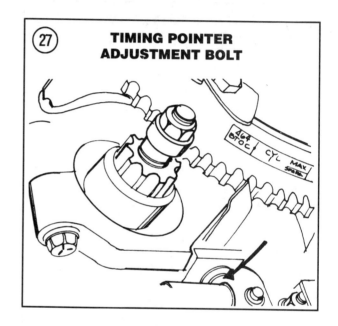

TIMING POINTER ADJUSTMENT BOLT

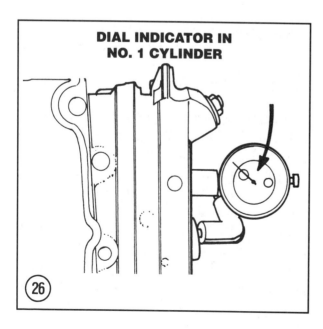

DIAL INDICATOR IN NO. 1 CYLINDER

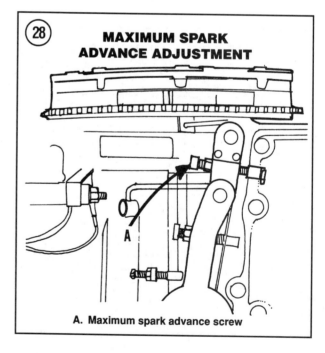

MAXIMUM SPARK ADVANCE ADJUSTMENT

A. Maximum spark advance screw

2. Adjust the maximum timing screw (**Figure 28**) to align the timing pointer with the 23° BTDC mark on the flywheel decal.

3. Throttle back to idle, stop the engine and remove the timing light.

4. With the engine not running, advance the throttle to the wide-open position. Adjust the full

throttle stop screw (**Figure 29**) to permit full throttle valve opening without allowing the throttle valve to act as a throttle stop. A 0.015-0.015 in. (0.25-0.38 mm) clearance must be present between the carburetor cluster pin and the throttle actuator cam at wide-open throttle. See **Figure 30**. Adjust the full throttle stop screw as necessary to provide the specified clearance.

Full throttle stop adjustment

1. With the engine not running, move the spark control lever to the maximum advance position.

2. Adjust the secondary pickup adjustment screw (**Figure 31**) so the carburetor cluster pin is located at the secondary pickup point on the throttle actuator cam as shown in **Figure 32**.

3. Return the throttle lever to the idle position.

Carburetor Adjustment

Idle mixture adjustment

Do not adjust the idle speed fuel-air mixture leaner than necessary to provide a smooth idle.

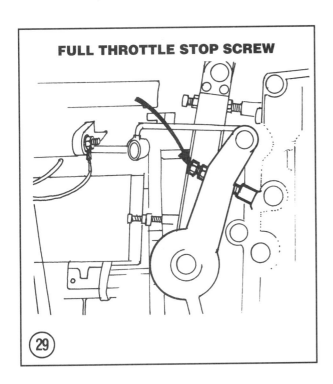

FULL THROTTLE STOP SCREW

(29)

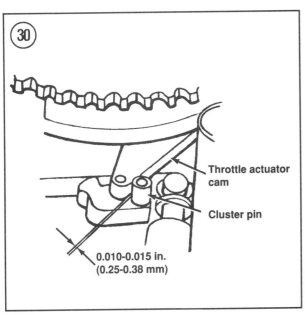

(30)

Throttle actuator cam

Cluster pin

0.010-0.015 in. (0.25-0.38 mm)

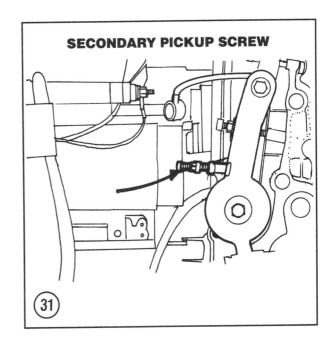

SECONDARY PICKUP SCREW

(31)

5

It is good practice to set the idle mixture slightly rich instead of too lean.

1. Start the engine, shift into forward gear and warm to normal operating temperature.

2. With engine running at idle speed in forward gear, slowly turn the idle mixture screw counterclockwise until the engine begins to run roughly due to an over-rich mixture. Note the position of the mixture screw.

3. Slowly turn the idle mixture screw clockwise until the engine begins to run smoothly and rpm increases. Note the position of the mixture screw. Continue turning the screw clockwise until the engine begins to run rough and misfire occurs due to an excessively lean mixture.

4. Set the mixture screw at a halfway point between the rich and lean settings. Richen the mixture slightly if the outboard hesitates during acceleration.

5. Adjust the idle speed as described in this chapter.

Idle speed adjustment

1. The outboard should be warmed to normal operating temperature and running at idle speed in forward gear to adjust idle speed. Make sure the idle mixture is properly adjusted as previously described.

2. Remove the throttle cable barrel from the barrel retainer on the cable anchor bracket.

3. Adjust the idle speed screw (**Figure 33**) to obtain 600-700 rpm in forward gear.

4. Hold throttle lever against the idle stop. Adjust the barrel to slip into the retainer with a very light preload of throttle lever against the idle stop.

> *NOTE*
> *Excessive preload in Step 5 will result in difficult shifting from FORWARD gear to NEUTRAL.*

5. Lock the barrel in position. Check the throttle cable preload by inserting a thin piece of paper (such as a matchbook cover) between the idle

stop and stop screw. If the preload is correct, a slight drag (without tearing) will be noted when removing the paper. Readjust the cable as required to obtain the desired preload.

50 AND 60 HP MODELS (SERIAL NO. D000750-ON)

Timing Pointer Adjustment

Refer to **Table 7** for tune-up data.

1. Remove the spark plugs to prevent accidental starting.

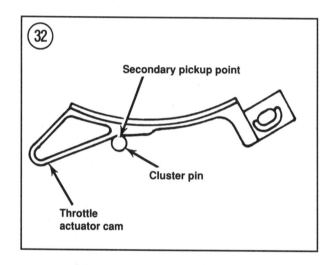

Secondary pickup point

Cluster pin

Throttle actuator cam

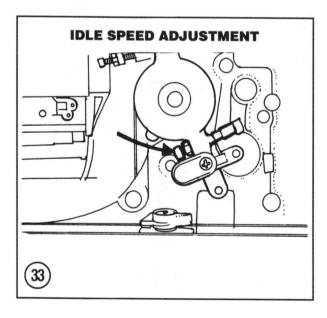

IDLE SPEED ADJUSTMENT

2. Install dial indicator part No. 91-58222A1 (or equivalent) into the No. 1 (top) spark plug hole (**Figure 34**).

3. Rotate the flywheel clockwise until the No. 1 (top) piston is at TDC. Zero the dial indicator.

4. Rotate the flywheel counterclockwise until the dial indicator reads 0.550 in. BTDC. Then, rotate the flywheel clockwise until the indicator reads exactly 0.459 in. BTDC.

5. At this point, the timing pointer (**Figure 35**) should be aligned with the ".459" timing mark on the flywheel. If not, loosen the 2 timing

pointer adjusting screws (A, **Figure 35**) and move pointer as necessary to align as specified. Retighten the screws (A) to 20 in.-lb. (2.2 N•m).

Carburetor Synchronization

1. Remove the 4 screws securing the carburetor sound box cover and remove the cover.

2. Loosen the cam follower adjusting screw (3, **Figure 36**).

3. Loosen the 4 carburetor synchronizing screws (4, **Figure 36**).

4. Make sure the throttle valves in all 3 carburetors are fully closed, then retighten the screws (4, **Figure 36**).

5

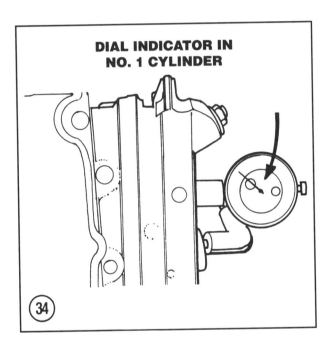

DIAL INDICATOR IN
NO. 1 CYLINDER

34

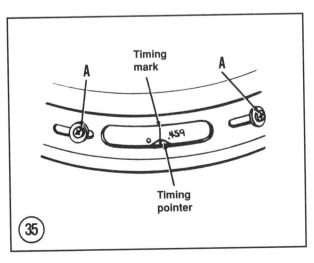

Timing mark

A   A

.459

Timing pointer

35

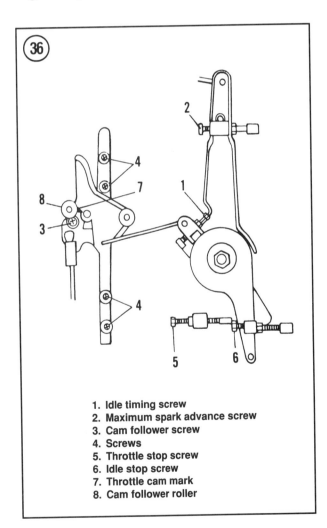

36

1. Idle timing screw
2. Maximum spark advance screw
3. Cam follower screw
4. Screws
5. Throttle stop screw
6. Idle stop screw
7. Throttle cam mark
8. Cam follower roller

5. Hold the idle stop screw (6, **Figure 36**) against its stop by pushing the throttle arm.

6. Position the cam follower roller (8, **Figure 36**) against the throttle cam. Adjust the idle stop screw (6) to align the throttle cam mark (7) with the center of the follower roller (8), then tighten the idle stop screw locknut.

7. While holding the throttle arm in the idle position, adjust the cam follower to set a 0.005-0.020 in. (0.13-0.51 mm) clearance between the cam follower roller and throttle cam. See **Figure 37**. Make sure the throttle cam mark is aligned with the center of the roller, then securely tighten the cam follower screw (A, **Figure 37**).

8. Hold the throttle arm so the full throttle stop screw (5, **Figure 36**) is against its stop. Adjust the full throttle screw so the carburetor throttle valves are fully open (wide-open throttle) while allowing for approximately 0.015 in. (0.38 mm) play in the throttle linkage. Be certain the throttle valves do not bottom out at wide-open throttle.

9. Reinstall the carburetor sound box cover.

Timing Adjustments

The ignition timing adjustments can be performed while cranking the engine with the electric starter. To prevent the engine from starting, remove the spark plugs and ground the spark plug leads to the engine. The battery must be fully charged and the electric starting system must be functioning properly when checking timing at cranking speed.

1. Attach spark gap tester part No. 91-63998A1 (or equivalent) between the No. 1 (top) spark plug lead and a good engine ground.

2. Connect a timing light to the No. 1 (top) spark plug lead.

3. Disconnect the fuel delivery hose from the engine and connect the remote control wiring harness to the engine harness.

4. Remove the throttle cable barrel from the barrel retainer.

Idle timing adjustment

1. Shift the outboard into NEUTRAL gear.

2. Hold the throttle arm in the idle position, crank the engine and note the timing. The timing pointer should be aligned with the 4° ATDC mark on the flywheel.

3. If adjustment is necessary, adjust the idle timing screw (1, **Figure 36**) to align the specified timing marks.

Maximum timing adjustment

1. Hold the throttle arm so the maximum advance screw (2, **Figure 36**) is against its stop.

2. Crank the engine while noting the timing with the timing light. Maximum timing should be 24° BTDC at cranking speed.

3. If adjustment is necessary, adjust maximum spark advance screw (2, **Figure 36**) to align the timing pointer with the specified timing mark on the flywheel.

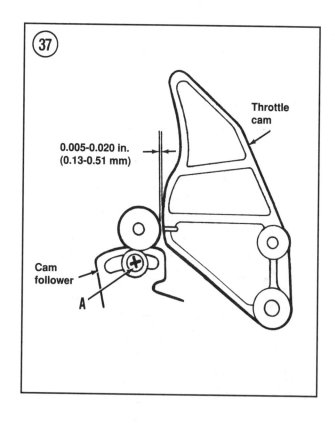

(37)

Throttle cam

0.005-0.020 in. (0.13-0.51 mm)

Cam follower

A

NOTE
Due to the electronic spark advance characteristics of this ignition system, the timing will retard slightly when running at wide-open throttle (5500 rpm). Therefore, the maximum timing should be adjusted to 24° BTDC at cranking speed to obtain the desired 22° BTDC when running at 5500 rpm. All timing adjustments made at cranking speed should be verified with the outboard running, and readjusted if necessary.

Idle Mixture Adjustment

1. Connect the fuel delivery hose to the engine.

2. Start the engine and allow to warm to normal operating temperature.

3. Shift the outboard into FORWARD gear.

4. Slowly turn idle mixture screw clockwise until the engine begins to misfire due to an excessively lean mixture.

5. Back the idle mixture screw out 1/4 turn and quickly accelerate the outboard. If the outboard hesitates and/or backfires during acceleration, the mixture is too lean. Back out the mixture screw slightly and check by quickly accelerating the engine.

6. Repeat the adjustment procedure on the remaining carburetors.

NOTE
Do not adjust the mixture any leaner than necessary to obtain a reasonably smooth idle. It is good practice to adjust the mixture slightly rich, rather than too lean.

High Speed Mixture Adjustment

The high speed mixture is adjusted by varying the size of a fixed main jet. See Chapter Six.

Idle Speed Adjustment

Be sure the idle mixture is properly adjusted prior to adjusting the idle speed.

1. Connect an accurate shop tachometer to the engine according to the manufacturer's instructions.

2. Start the engine and allow to warm for approximately 1 minute.

3. With the throttle cable barrel removed from its retainer, hold the throttle arm in the idle position.

4. Shift into FORWARD gear. Adjust idle timing screw (1, **Figure 36**) to obtain 650-750 rpm in forward gear.

Throttle Cable Installation

1. Connect the throttle cable to the throttle arm.

2. While holding the throttle arm against the idle stop, adjust the throttle cable barrel to slip into the barrel retainer on the cable anchor bracket with a slight preload of the throttle arm against the idle stop.

3. Lock the throttle cable barrel in place.

NOTE
Excessive preload in Step 4 will result in difficult shifting from FORWARD gear to NEUTRAL.

4. Check the throttle cable preload by inserting a thin piece of paper (such as a matchbook cover) between the idle stop and stop screw. If the preload is correct, a slight drag (without tearing) will be noted when removing the paper. Readjust the cable as required to obtain the desired preload.

75 AND 90 HP MODELS

Timing Pointer Adjustment

Refer to **Table 8** for tune-up data.

1. Remove the engine cowl and the aft cowl support bracket.

2. To prevent accidental starting, remove all spark plugs.

3. Install dial indicator part No. 91-58222A1 (or equivalent) into the No. 1 (top) spark plug hole.

4. Rotate the flywheel clockwise until the No. 1 piston is at TDC, then zero the dial indicator.

5. Rotate the flywheel counterclockwise until the dial indicator reads 0.550 in. BTDC. Then rotate the flywheel clockwise until the indicator reads exactly 0.491 in. BTDC.

6. Check the timing pointer position. The pointer groove should be aligned with the ".491" mark on the flywheel. If not, loosen the 2 timing pointer screws and reposition the pointer as required to align with the specified timing mark. Retighten the timing pointer screws to 20 in.-lb. (2.3 N•m).

7. Remove the dial indicator from the No. 1 spark plug hole. Reinstall the spark plugs.

Carburetor Synchronization

1. Remove the sound box cover.

2. Loosen the cam follower adjustment screw (3, **Figure 38**).

3. Loosen the 4 carburetor synchronizing screws (4, **Figure 38**).

4. Make sure all carburetor throttle valves are completely closed, then securely tighten the screws (4, **Figure 38**). Recheck the adjustment, making sure all carburetor throttle valves open and close at exactly the same time.

5. Hold the throttle arm so the idle stop screw (6, **Figure 38**) is against its stop.

6. While holding the cam follower roller (8, **Figure 38**) against the throttle cam, adjust the idle stop screw (6) to align the throttle cam mark (7) with the center of the cam follower roller (8).

7. While holding the throttle arm in the idle position, adjust the cam follower to provide a clearance of 0.025-0.050 in. (0.64-1.3 mm) between the cam follower roller and throttle cam as shown in **Figure 39**. Tighten the cam follower adjusting screw (3, **Figure 39**).

8. Hold the throttle arm so the full throttle stop screw (5, **Figure 38**) is against its stop. Adjust the full throttle stop screw so the carburetor throttle valves are fully open, while allowing for approximately 0.015 in. (0.38 mm) free play in the throttle linkage. Be sure the throttle valves do not bottom out at wide-open throttle; adjust the full throttle stop screw as necessary.

CAUTION
The carburetors can be damaged if the throttle valves act as throttle stops during full throttle operation.

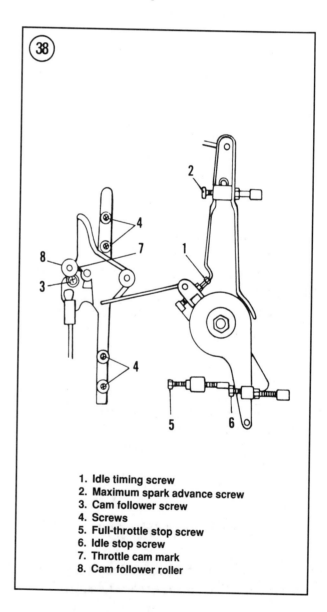

1. Idle timing screw
2. Maximum spark advance screw
3. Cam follower screw
4. Screws
5. Full-throttle stop screw
6. Idle stop screw
7. Throttle cam mark
8. Cam follower roller

Oil Pump Synchronization

1. Hold the throttle arm in the idle position.
2. The mark stamped in the oil pump control lever should be aligned with the stamped mark in the oil pump body. See B, **Figure 40**. A second mark (C, **Figure 40**) is stamped in the oil pump

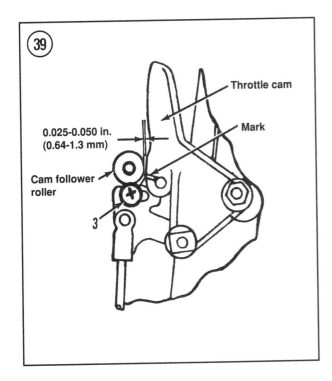

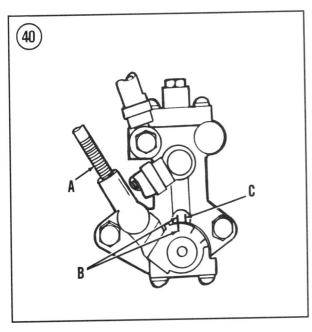

body on some models. *Do not* use this mark for oil pump synchronization.
3. If adjustment is necessary, disconnect the oil pump control rod (A, **Figure 40**) and adjust length of rod as necessary to align the marks.

Timing Adjustments

The ignition timing can be checked and adjusted while cranking the engine with the electric starter. The battery must be fully charged and the starting system functioning properly.
1. Remove the spark plugs. Attach spark gap tester part No. 91-63998A1 (or equivalent) between the No. 1 (top) spark plug lead and a good engine ground.
2. Disconnect the fuel delivery hose from the engine and connect the remote control wiring harness to the engine harness.
3. Remove the throttle cable barrel from the barrel retainer.
4. Connect a timing light to the No. 1 (top) spark plug lead.

Idle timing adjustment

1. Shift the outboard into NEUTRAL.
2. While holding the throttle arm in the idle position, crank the engine and note the timing with the timing light. Idle speed timing should be 2° BTDC.
3. If adjustment is necessary, adjust the idle timing screw (1, **Figure 38**) as required to align the timing pointer with the specified timing mark on the flywheel.

Maximum timing adjustment

1. Position the throttle arm so the maximum spark advance screw (2, **Figure 38**) is against its stop.
2. While cranking the engine, adjust the maximum advance screw (2, **Figure 38**) so the 28°

5

BTDC mark on the flywheel is aligned with the timing pointer.

NOTE
Due to the electronic spark advance characteristics of this ignition system, the timing will retard slightly when running at wide-open throttle (5000 rpm). Therefore, the maximum timing should be adjusted to 28° BTDC at cranking speed to obtain the desired 26° BTDC when running at 5000 rpm. All timing adjustments made at cranking speed should be verified with the outboard running, and readjusted if necessary.

Idle Mixture Adjustment

1. Start the engine and run at fast idle until warmed to normal operating temperature.

2. Allow the engine to run at idle speed for approximately 1 minute to stabilize the engine. Shift into FORWARD gear.

3. With engine running at idle speed in forward gear, slowly turn the low speed mixture screw clockwise until the engine begins to run roughly and misfire due to an excessively lean mixture.

4. Turn the mixture screw counterclockwise 1/4 turn, then quickly accelerate the engine. If the mixture is properly adjusted, the engine will accelerate cleanly without hesitation. If the engine hesitates and/or backfires during acceleration, the mixture is too lean.

CAUTION
Do not adjust the idle mixture any leaner than necessary to provide a reasonably smooth idle. It is good practice to adjust the mixture slightly rich rather than too lean.

5. Repeat the adjustment procedure on the remaining 2 carburetors.

High Speed Mixture Adjustment

The high speed mixture is adjusted by varying the size of a fixed main jet. See Chapter Six.

Idle Speed Adjustment

Make sure the idle mixture is properly adjusted before attempting to adjust idle speed.
1. Connect an accurate shop tachometer to the engine according to the manufacturer's instructions.
2. Start the engine and shift into FORWARD gear.
3. While holding the throttle arm in the idle position, adjust the idle timing screw (1, **Figure 38**) to obtain 625-725 rpm (in forward gear).

Throttle Cable Installation

1. Connect the throttle cable to the throttle arm.
2. While holding the throttle arm against the idle stop, adjust the throttle cable barrel to slip into the barrel retainer on the cable anchor bracket with a slight preload of the throttle arm against the idle stop.
3. Lock the throttle cable barrel in place.

NOTE
Excessive preload in Step 4 will result in difficult shifting from FORWARD gear to NEUTRAL.

4. Check the throttle cable preload by inserting a thin piece of paper (such as a matchbook cover) between the idle stop and stop screw. If the preload is correct, a slight drag (without tearing) will be noted when removing the paper. Readjust the cable as required to obtain the desired preload.

100 AND 115 HP MODELS

Refer to **Table 9** for tune-up data.

Timing Pointer Adjustment

1. Remove the spark plugs to prevent accidental starting. Ground the spark plug leads to the engine.

2. Remove the aft cowl support bracket.

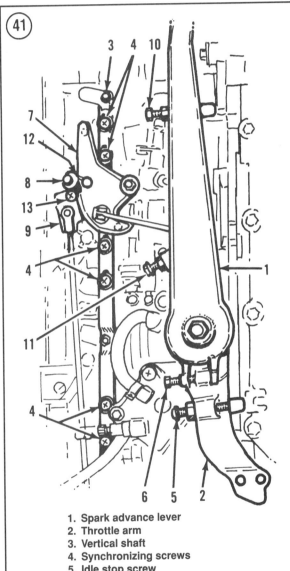

1. Spark advance lever
2. Throttle arm
3. Vertical shaft
4. Synchronizing screws
5. Idle stop screw
6. Idle timing screw
7. Throttle cam
8. Cam follower roller
9. Cam follower
10. Maximum spark advance screw
11. Full throttle stop screw
12. Throttle cam mark
13. Cam follower screw

3. Install dial indicator (part No. 91-58222A1, or equivalent) into the No. 1 (top) spark plug hole.

4. Rotate the flywheel clockwise until the No. 1 (top) is at TDC, then zero the dial indicator.

5. Rotate the flywheel counterclockwise until the indicator reads approximately 0.600 in. BTDC, then clockwise until the indicator reads exactly 0.554 in. BTDC.

6. At this point, the timing pointer should be aligned with the ".554" BTDC mark on the flywheel. If not, loosen the 2 timing pointer screws and reposition the pointer as necessary. Retighten the timing pointer screws securely.

Carburetor Synchronization

Refer to **Figure 41** for this procedure.

1. Remove the sound box cover.

2. Loosen the cam follower screw 1/4 to 1/2 turn.

3. Loosen 6 carburetor synchronizing screws.

4. Looking into the carburetor throats, make sure all throttle valves are fully closed, then retighten the synchronizing screws while applying light downward pressure on the vertical shaft.

5. Recheck adjustment by observing the carburetor throttle valves while opening and closing the throttle. Make sure all throttle valves open and close at the same time; repeat adjustment procedure as necessary.

6. Hold the throttle arm so the idle stop screw is against its stop.

7. Move the cam follower roller against the throttle cam and hold in that position. Adjust the idle stop screw to align the raised mark on the throttle cam with the center of the cam follower roller.

8. While holding the throttle cam in the idle position, adjust the cam follower to provide a 0.005-0.020 in. (0.13-0.51 mm) clearance between the throttle cam and cam follower roller as shown in **Figure 42**. Securely tighten the cam follower screw.

9. Hold the throttle arm in the wide-open throttle position. Adjust the full throttle stop screw to

position the carburetor throttle valves in the wide-open position while allowing for a small amount of free play in the throttle linkage.

CAUTION
The carburetors can be damaged if the throttle valves bottom out at wide-open throttle.

10. Hold the throttle arm in the wide-open throttle position. Loosen the 2 accelerator pump mounting screws and position the pump to provide 0.030 in. (0.76 mm) clearance between the throttle cam and the top of the pump casting as shown in **Figure 43**. Securely tighten the pump mounting screws.

NOTE
The throttle cam on some models (serial Nos. OB209468-OD028564) is made of a material that may stick to the accelerator pump plunger if sufficient lubricant is not present between the cam and pump plunger. This bonding can result in difficult throttle operation. If throttle cam-to-pump plunger bonding occurs, replace the throttle cam (marked 14518) with a new design cam marked 14518-C3).

Oil Pump Synchronization

1. Hold the throttle arm in the idle position.
2. The mark stamped in the oil pump control lever should be aligned with the stamped mark in the oil pump body. See B, **Figure 44**. A second mark (C, **Figure 44**) is stamped in the oil pump body on some models. *Do not* use this mark for oil pump synchronization.
3. If adjustment is necessary, disconnect the oil pump control rod (A, **Figure 44**) and adjust length of rod as necessary to align the marks.

Timing Adjustments

The ignition timing can be checked and adjusted while cranking the engine with the electric starter. The battery must be fully charged and the

starting system functioning properly. Refer to **Figure 41** for the following procedures.

1. Remove the spark plugs. Attach spark gap tester part No. 91-63998A1 (or equivalent) between the No. 1 (top) spark plug lead and a good engine ground.
2. Disconnect the fuel delivery hose from the engine and connect the remote control wiring harness to the engine harness.
3. Remove the throttle cable barrel from the barrel retainer.
4. Connect a timing light to the No. 1 (top) spark plug lead.

Idle timing adjustment

Refer to **Figure 41** for this procedure.

1. Shift the outboard into NEUTRAL.
2. While holding the throttle arm in the idle position, crank the engine and note the timing with the timing light. Idle speed timing should be 2°-4° BTDC.

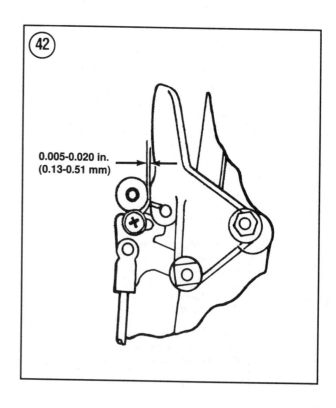

42

0.005-0.020 in.
(0.13-0.51 mm)

3. If adjustment is necessary, adjust the idle timing screw as required to align the timing pointer with the specified timing mark on the flywheel.

Maximum timing adjustment

Refer to **Figure 41** for this procedure.

1. Position the throttle arm so the maximum spark advance screw is against its stop.

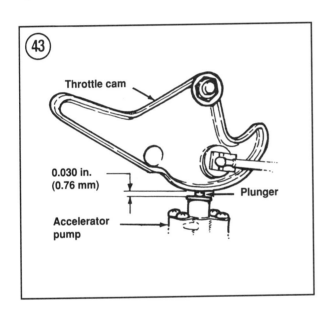

2. While cranking the engine, adjust the maximum advance screw to align the 25° BTDC mark on the flywheel with the timing pointer.

NOTE
Due to the electronic spark advance characteristics of this ignition system, the timing will retard slightly when running at wide-open throttle (5000 rpm). Therefore, the maximum timing should be adjusted to 25° BTDC at cranking speed to obtain the desired 23° BTDC when running at 5000 rpm. All timing adjustments made at cranking speed should be verified with the outboard running, and readjusted if necessary.

Idle Mixture Adjustment

NOTE
Only the top 2 carburetors are equipped with idle mixture adjustment screws on 100 and 115 hp models.

1. Start the engine and run at fast idle until warmed to normal operating temperature.
2. Allow the engine to run at idle speed for approximately 1 minute to stabilize the engine. Shift into FORWARD gear.
3. With engine running at idle speed in forward gear, slowly turn the low speed mixture screw clockwise until the engine begins to run roughly and misfire due to an excessively lean mixture.
4. Turn the mixture screw counterclockwise 1/4 turn, then quickly accelerate the engine. If the mixture is properly adjusted, the engine will accelerate cleanly without hesitation. If the engine hesitates and/or backfires during acceleration, the mixture is too lean. Adjust the mixture screws an additional 1/4 to 1/2 turn counterclockwise.

CAUTION
Do not adjust the idle mixture any leaner than necessary to provide a reasonably smooth idle. It is good practice to adjust the mixture slightly rich rather than too lean.

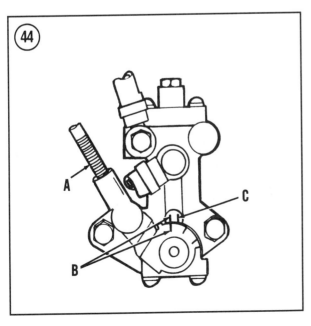

5. Repeat the adjustment procedure on the remaining carburetor.

High Speed Mixture Adjustment

The high speed mixture is adjusted by varying the size of a fixed main jet. See Chapter Six.

Idle Speed Adjustment

Make sure the idle mixture is properly adjusted before attempting to adjust idle speed. Refer to **Figure 41**.

1. Connect an accurate shop tachometer to the engine according to the manufacturer's instructions.
2. Start the engine and shift into FORWARD gear.
3. While holding the throttle arm in the idle position, adjust the idle timing screw to obtain 625-725 rpm (in forward gear).

Throttle Cable Installation

1. Connect the throttle cable to the throttle arm.
2. While holding the throttle arm against the idle stop, adjust the throttle cable barrel to slip into the barrel retainer on the cable anchor bracket with a slight preload of the throttle arm against the idle stop.
3. Lock the throttle cable barrel in place.

NOTE
Excessive preload in Step 4 will result in difficult shifting from FORWARD gear to NEUTRAL.

4. Check the throttle cable preload by inserting a thin piece of paper (such as a matchbook cover) between the idle stop and stop screw. If the preload is correct, a slight drag (without tearing) will be noted when removing the paper. Readjust the cable as required to obtain the desired preload.

135-200 HP (EXCEPT EFI) MODELS

Refer to **Tables 10-12** for tune-up data.

Timing Pointer Adjustment

1. Remove all spark plugs to prevent accidental starting during the following adjustment.
2. Install dial indicator (part No. 91-58222A1, or equivalent) into the No. 1 (top starboard) spark plug hole.
3. Rotate the flywheel clockwise until the No. 1 piston is positioned at TDC, then zero the indicator.

NOTE
On some models equipped with a cast iron flywheel, a "45" mark is stamped in

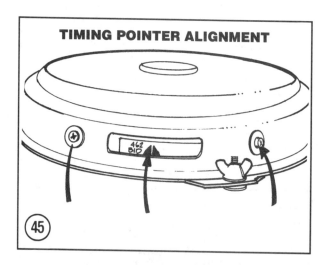

TIMING POINTER ALIGNMENT

45

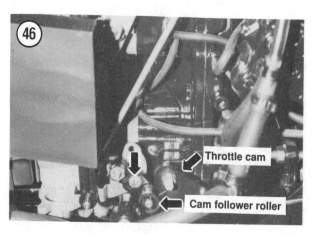

46

Throttle cam

Cam follower roller

the flywheel instead of the ".462" mark found on all flexplate type flywheels. The ".462" mark indicates 0.462 in. of piston travel and is equivalent to the "45" mark which indicates 45° of crankshaft rotation. Note that not all cast iron flywheels use the "45" mark; later production models use the ".462" marking.

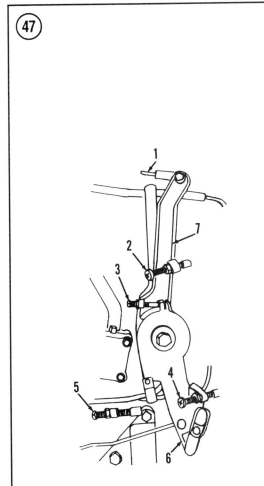

1. Trigger link rod
2. Maximum advance stop screw
3. Primary pickup screw
4. Idle stop screw
5. Full throttle stop screw
6. Throttle arm
7. Spark advance lever

4. Rotate the flywheel counterclockwise approximately 1/4 turn past the ".462" (or "45") BTDC reading on the indicator (**Figure 45**).

5. Rotate the flywheel clockwise until the dial indicator reads exactly 0.462 in. BTDC. The timing pointer should now be aligned with the ".462" (or "45") mark on the flywheel. If not, loosen the 2 timing pointer adjustment screws and reposition the timing pointer as required. Retighten the timing pointer screws securely.

Throttle Cam Adjustment

1. Loosen the cam follower adjusting screw (**Figure 46**) to allow the cam follower to move freely.

2. With the cam follower roller resting on the throttle cam, adjust the idle stop screw (4, **Figure 47**) so the raised mark on the throttle cam is aligned with the center of the cam follower roller. Do not tighten the cam follower screw at this point.

Carburetor Synchronization

Refer to **Figure 47** for this procedure.

1. Remove the air box cover.

2. Loosen the 2 carburetor synchronizing screws (**Figure 48**) allowing the carburetor throttle valves to close fully.

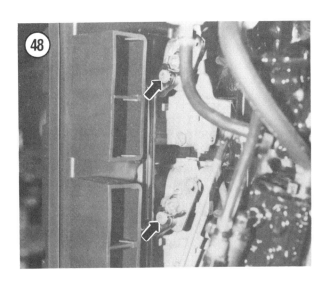

3. Position the throttle arm so the idle stop screw is against its stop. Move the throttle cam follower so the follower roller just contacts the throttle cam. While holding the roller in this position, securely tighten the cam follower screw (**Figure 46**) and the carburetor synchronizing screws (**Figure 48**).

4. Make sure that all carburetor throttle valves open and close simultaneously during throttle operation. Readjust the carburetor synchronization as necessary.

5. Hold the throttle arm in the wide-open throttle position.

6. Adjust the full throttle stop screw to position the carburetor throttle valves in the wide-open position while allowing for 0.010-0.015 in. (0.25-0.38 mm) free play between the throttle cam and cam follower roller.

> *CAUTION*
> *The carburetors can be damaged if the throttle valves bottom out at wide-open throttle.*

7. Reinstall the carburetor air box cover.

Oil Pump Synchronization

1. Place the throttle arm in the idle position.
2. With the throttle in the idle position, the marks (M, **Figure 49**) on the oil pump body and control lever should be aligned.
3. If adjustment is necessary, disconnect the pump control rod from the pump control lever and adjust the length of the rod as required to align the marks.

Timing Adjustments

The ignition timing can be checked and adjusted while cranking the engine with the electric starter. The battery must be fully charged and the starting system functioning properly. Refer to **Figure 47** for the following procedures.

1. Remove all spark plugs.

2. Attach spark gap tester (part No. 91-63998A1, or equivalent) to the No. 1 (top starboard) spark plug lead.

3. Disconnect the fuel delivery hose from the engine and connect the remote control wiring harness to the engine harness.

4. Remove the throttle cable barrel from the barrel retainer.

5. Check the trigger link rod length from the end of the rod to the locknut as shown in **Figure 50**. If length is not 11/16 in. (17.5 mm), disconnect link rod and adjust the length as necessary.

6. Disconnect the idle stabilizer module white/black wire bullet connector located on the starboard side of the engine. Isolate the disconnected wires with electrical tape.

7. Connect a timing light to the No. 1 spark plug lead.

Maximum timing adjustment

Refer to **Figure 47** for this procedure.

> *CAUTION*
> *On models (except 150XR4 and 150XR6) equipped with an Idle Stabilizer Shift Kit (part No. 87-814281A1)*

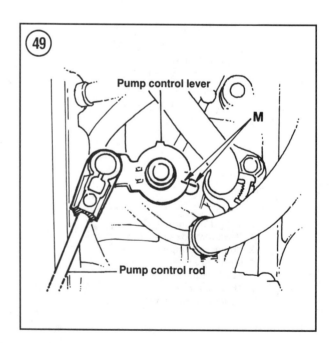

*installed as an accessory, the maximum ignition timing must be retarded 3° from the specifications listed in **Tables 10-12**. On 150XR4 and 150XR6 models, however, the Idle Stabilizer Shift Kit is installed at the factory as standard equipment and the timing specifications listed in **Tables 10-12** are correct.*

1. Shift the outboard into NEUTRAL and place the throttle arm in the wide-open throttle position. Hold the throttle arm so the maximum advance stop screw is against its stop.

2. Crank the engine and note the timing with the timing light.

3. Adjust the maximum advance stop screw to obtain the specified maximum advance timing (**Tables 10-12**).

NOTE
Due to the electronic spark advance/retard characteristics of the individual ignition systems, ignition timing adjusted at cranking speed will advance when running at full throttle on 150XR4 and XR6 models and retard at full throttle on all other models. Ignition timing adjusted at cranking speed should always be verified with the outboard running, and readjusted if necessary.

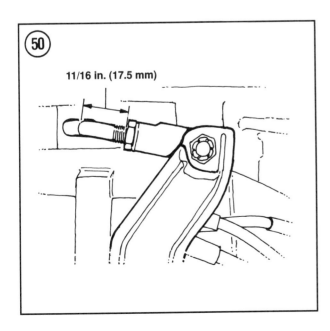

11/16 in. (17.5 mm)

Primary pickup timing adjustment

Refer to **Figure 47** for this procedure. The primary pickup screw is also used to adjust idle speed. See *Idle Speed Adjustment*.

1. Shift the outboard into NEUTRAL and hold the throttle arm so the idle stop screw is against its stop.

2. Crank the engine with the starter motor and note the ignition timing with the timing light.

3. Adjust the primary pickup screw to obtain the ignition timing as specified in **Tables 10-12**.

NOTE
Ignition timing adjusted at cranking speed should always be verified with the engine running, and readjusted if necessary.

4. Remove the timing light and spark gap tester.

5. Reinstall the spark plugs and tighten to 17 ft.-lb. (23.0 N·m).

6. Reconnect the idle stabilizer white/black wire at the bullet connector.

Idle Speed Adjustment

1. Connect an accurate shop tachometer to the engine according to the manufacturer's instructions.

2. Start the engine and warm to normal operating temperature.

3. With engine running at idle speed in FORWARD gear, adjust the primary pickup screw to obtain the idle speed specified in **Tables 10-12**.

CAUTION
Idle speed must never exceed 750 rpm in forward gear.

4. Connect the throttle cable to the throttle arm.

5. While holding the throttle arm against the idle stop, adjust the throttle cable barrel to slip into the barrel retainer on the cable anchor bracket with a slight preload of the throttle arm against the idle stop.

6. Lock the throttle cable barrel in place.

5

NOTE
Excessive preload in Step 7 will result in difficult shifting from FORWARD gear to NEUTRAL.

7. Check the throttle cable preload by inserting a thin piece of paper (such as a matchbook cover) between the idle stop and stop screw. If the preload is correct, a slight drag (without tearing) will be noted when removing the paper. Readjust the cable as required to obtain the desired preload.

8. If sufficient throttle cable barrel adjustment is not available, check for correct installation of the throttle arm-to-throttle cam link rod. The link rod must be threaded into its plastic retainers until bottomed out, then backed off just enough to install the link rod in the correct position. Note that all synchronizing and adjusting procedures must be repeated if the link rod is adjusted.

Idle Mixture Adjustment

Each carburetor is equipped with 2 idle mixture screws. See **Figure 51**. The idle mixture screws are set at the factory and plastic limiter caps are installed on each screw to limit adjustment range. See Chapter Six. When adjusting the idle mixture, be certain that all mixture screws are turned equal amounts in the same direction; clockwise rotation leans the fuel mixture and counterclockwise rotation richens the mixture. Do not remove the limiter caps to increase the adjustment range.

High Speed Mixture Adjustment

The high speed mixture is adjusted by varying the size of fixed main jets. See Chapter Six.

250 AND 275 HP MODELS

Timing Pointer Adjustment

Refer to **Table 13** for tune-up data.
1. Remove all spark plugs to prevent accidental starting during the following procedure.
2. Install dial indicator (part No. 91-58222A1, or equivalent) into the No. 1 (top starboard) spark plug hole.
3. Rotate the flywheel clockwise until the No. 1 piston is at TDC.
4. Rotate the flywheel counterclockwise approximately 1/4 turn past the ".557" indicator reading, then rotate the flywheel clockwise until the indicator reads exactly 0.557 in.
5. At this point, the timing pointer should be aligned with the ".557" mark on the flywheel. If

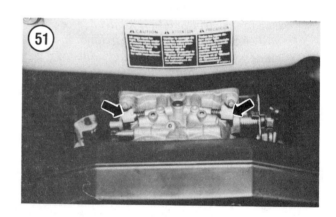

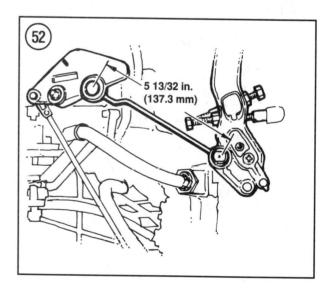

not, loosen the 2 timing pointer screws and re-position the pointer as necessary. Securely retighten the pointer screws.

6. Remove the dial indicator from the No. 1 spark plug hole.

Carburetor Synchronization

1. Disconnect the battery cables from the battery.

2. Measure the distance of the link rod between the throttle arm barrel and throttle cam at the points shown in **Figure 52**. The distance should be 5-13/32 in. (137.3 mm).

3. If adjustment is required, disconnect the link rod and adjust as required.

4. Remove 14 screws securing the sound box cover and remove cover.

5. Loosen the carburetor synchronizing screws (A, **Figure 53**). Allow the carburetor throttle valves to close freely.

6. Position the throttle arm so the idle stop screw (A, **Figure 54**) is against its stop and the cam follower roller (D, **Figure 53**) is lightly contacting the throttle cam (C, **Figure 53**).

5

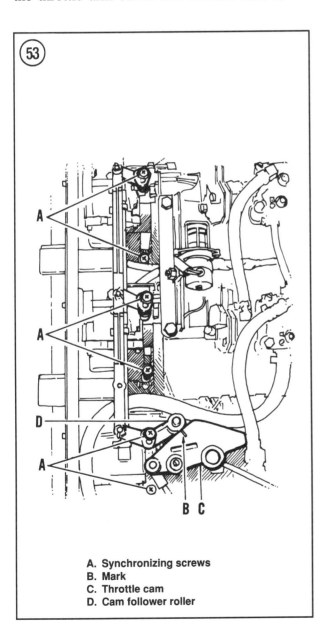

A. Synchronizing screws
B. Mark
C. Throttle cam
D. Cam follower roller

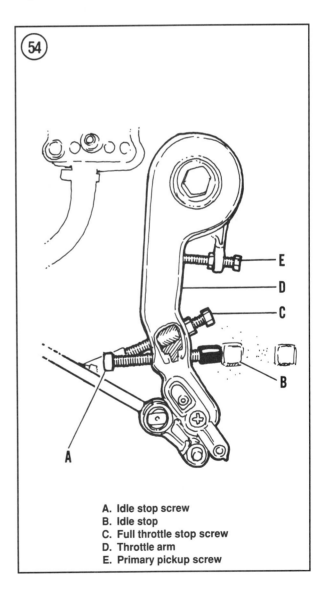

A. Idle stop screw
B. Idle stop
C. Full throttle stop screw
D. Throttle arm
E. Primary pickup screw

7. Adjust the idle stop screw (A, **Figure 54**) to align the throttle cam mark (B, **Figure 53**) with the center of the follower roller (D, **Figure 53**). Holding the follower roller in this position, tighten the carburetor synchronizing screws (A, **Figure 53**).

8. Make sure all carburetor throttle valves open and close simultaneously. Repeat Steps 5-7 as necessary. Reinstall the sound box cover.

Timing Adjustments

The ignition timing can be checked and adjusted while cranking the engine with the electric starter. The battery must be fully charged and the starting system functioning properly.

1. Check the trigger link rod length from the end of the rod to the locknut as shown in **Figure 55**. If length is not 11/16 in. (17.5 mm), disconnect link rod and adjust the length as necessary.

2. Remove all spark plugs from the engine.

3. Attach spark gap tester (part No. 91-63998A1, or equivalent) between the No. 1 (top starboard) spark plug lead and a good engine ground.

4. Disconnect the fuel delivery hose from the engine and connect the remote control wiring harness to the engine harness.

5. Remove the throttle cable barrel from the barrel retainer.

6. Connect a timing light to the No. 1 spark plug lead.

7. Shift into NEUTRAL and position the throttle arm so the idle stop screw is against its stop (**Figure 54**).

8. Crank the engine and adjust the primary pickup screw (**Figure 54**) to align the timing pointer with the specified mark (**Table 13**) on the flywheel.

9. Position the throttle arm so the maximum advance stop screw is against its stop (**Figure 56**).

10. Crank the engine and adjust the maximum advance stop screw (**Figure 56**) to align the

timing pointer with the 22° BTDC mark on the flywheel.

NOTE
Due to the electronic spark advance characteristics of this ignition system, the timing will retard slightly when running at wide-open throttle (5500 rpm). Therefore, the maximum timing should be adjusted to 22° BTDC at cranking speed to obtain the desired 20° BTDC when running at 5500 rpm. All timing adjustments made at cranking speed should be verified with the outboard running, and readjusted if necessary.

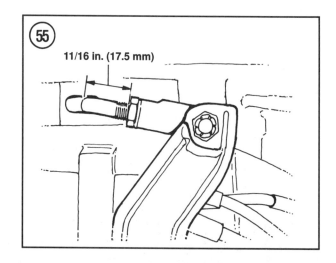

55 11/16 in. (17.5 mm)

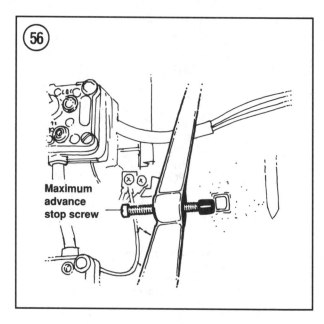

56 Maximum advance stop screw

11. Move the throttle arm so the full throttle stop screw (**Figure 54**) is against its stop.

12. Adjust the full throttle stop screw so the carburetor throttle valves are in the fully open position while allowing 0.010-0.015 in. (0.25-0.38 mm) clearance between the throttle cam and cam follower roller.

CAUTION
The carburetors can be damaged if the throttle valves bottom out during wide-open throttle operation.

Oil Pump Synchronization

Refer to **Figure 57** for this procedure.

1. Place the throttle arm in the idle position and note the alignment marks on the oil pump body and control lever.

2. With the throttle in the idle position, the alignment mark on the oil pump body should be aligned with the short mark on the pump control lever. If necessary, adjust the length of the pump control rod to align the marks as specified.

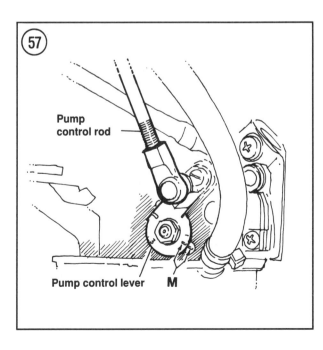

Idle Speed Adjustment

CAUTION
Idle speed must never exceed 750 rpm in gear.

1. With the outboard motor in the water, start the engine and allow it to warm to normal operating temperature.

2. Shift outboard into FORWARD gear.

3. With the engine idling in forward gear, adjust the primary pickup screw (**Figure 54**) to obtain 600-700 rpm.

4. Connect the throttle cable to the throttle arm.

5. While holding the throttle arm against the idle stop, adjust the throttle cable barrel to slip into the barrel retainer on the cable anchor bracket with a slight preload of the throttle arm against the idle stop.

6. Lock the throttle cable barrel in place.

NOTE
Excessive preload in Step 7 will result in difficult shifting from FORWARD gear to NEUTRAL.

7. Check the throttle cable preload by inserting a thin piece of paper (such as a matchbook cover) between the idle stop and stop screw. If the preload is correct, a slight drag (without tearing) will be noted when removing the paper. Readjust the cable as required to obtain the desired preload.

Mixture Adjustments

Idle and high speed fuel-air mixture is adjusted by varying the size of fixed jets. See Chapter Six.

150XRi, 175XRi AND 200XRi (EFI) MODELS

Refer to **Tables 11-12** for tune-up data.

5

Timing Pointer Adjustment

1. Remove all spark plugs to prevent accidental starting during the following adjustment.

2. Install dial indicator (part No. 91-58222A1, or equivalent) into the No. 1 (top starboard) spark plug hole.

3. Rotate the flywheel clockwise until the No. 1 piston is positioned at TDC, then zero the indicator.

> *NOTE*
> *On some models equipped with a cast iron flywheel, a "45" mark is stamped in the flywheel instead of the ".462" mark found on all flexplate type flywheels. The ".462" mark indicates 0.462 in. of piston travel and is equivalent to the "45" mark which indicates 45° of crankshaft rotation. Note that not all cast iron flywheels use the "45" mark; later production models use the ".462" marking.*

4. Rotate the flywheel counterclockwise approximately 1/4 turn past the ".462" (or "45") BTDC reading on the indicator.

5. Rotate the flywheel clockwise until the dial indicator reads exactly 0.462 in. BTDC. The timing pointer should now be aligned with the ".462" (or "45") mark on the flywheel. If not, loosen the 2 timing pointer adjustment screws and reposition the timing pointer as required. Retighten the timing pointer screws securely.

EFI Adjustments

The initial ignition timing is checked and adjusted while cranking the engine with the electric starter. The battery must be fully charged and the starting system functioning properly.

1. Check the trigger link rod length from the end of the rod to the locknut as shown in **Figure 58**. If length is not 11/16 in. (17.5 mm), disconnect link rod and adjust the length as necessary.

2. Remove all spark plugs except No. 1 (top starboard).

3. Disconnect the fuel delivery hose from the engine and connect remote control wiring harness to the engine harness.

4. Remove the throttle cable barrel from the barrel retainer.

5. Connect a timing light to the No. 1 (top starboard) spark plug lead.

Throttle cam adjustment

Refer to **Figure 59** for this procedure.

1. Loosen the cam follower screw and allow cam follower roller to slide freely against the throttle cam.

2. Adjust the idle stop screw so the throttle cam mark is aligned with the center of the cam follower roller.

3. With the mark on the throttle cam aligned as specified in Step 2, hold the throttle arm so the idle stop screw is against its stop, then tighten the cam follower screw.

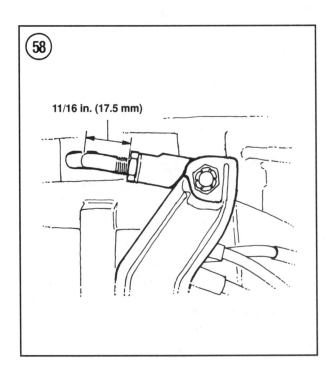

58

11/16 in. (17.5 mm)

Idle timing adjustment (cranking speed)

1. Disconnect the idle stabilizer module white/black wire at the bullet connector. Tape the ends of the disconnected wires to prevent grounding.

2. Disconnect the electronic control unit (ECU) wiring harness.

3. Hold the throttle arm so the idle stop screw is against its stop. Crank the engine and note the timing with the timing light.

4. Adjust the idle timing screw (6, **Figure 59**) to obtain the specified idle timing (**Table 11** and **Table 12**).

NOTE
Do not reconnect the idle stabilizer module or the ECU harness until after performing Maximum Timing Adjustment.

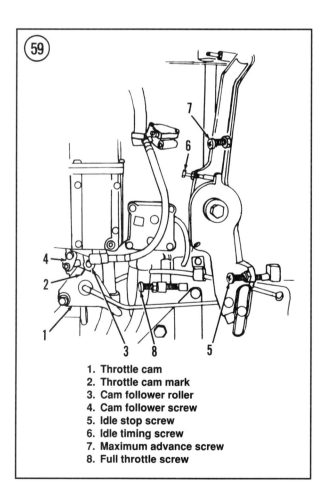

1. Throttle cam
2. Throttle cam mark
3. Cam follower roller
4. Cam follower screw
5. Idle stop screw
6. Idle timing screw
7. Maximum advance screw
8. Full throttle screw

Maximum timing adjustment (cranking speed)

1. Hold the throttle arm so the maximum advance screw (7, **Figure 59**) is against its stop.
2. Crank the engine while noting the timing with the timing light.
3. Adjust the maximum advance screw (7, **Figure 59**) to obtain the specified maximum timing (**Table 11** and **Table 12**).
4. Reconnect the idle stabilizer module white/black wire at the bullet connector. Reconnect the ECU harness and remove the timing light. Reinstall the spark plugs.

NOTE
Ignition timing adjusted at cranking speed should be verified with the engine running and readjusted if necessary.

Maximum throttle adjustment

1. Hold the throttle arm so the full throttle stop screw (8, **Figure 59**) is against its stop.
2. Adjust the full throttle stop screw so the induction chamber throttle valves are fully open while allowing for slight free play in the throttle linkage between the throttle shaft arm and the stop on the induction chamber.

CAUTION
To prevent the throttle linkage from binding at full throttle, be sure 0.010-0.015 in. (0.25-0.38 mm) clearance is present between the throttle cam and cam follower roller at wide-open throttle. Readjust the full throttle stop screw as necessary to provide some clearance.

Throttle position indicator (TPI) adjustment

CAUTION
The throttle position indicator (TPI) must only be adjusted using a digital meter. Using an analog (needle type) meter can damage the TPI.

5

1. Disconnect the TPI connector (**Figure 60**) from the EFI harness.

2. Connect TPI Test Lead Assembly (part No. 91-816085) between the TPI and EFI connectors.

3. Connect a digital voltmeter to the TPI Test Lead Assembly. Set the meter on 2 volts DC.

4. Disconnect the tan/blue cylinder head temperature sender leads (**Figure 61**).

5. Turn the ignition switch to the ON position.

6. Loosen the 2 TPI mounting screws (**Figure 60**).

7. Slowly rotate the TPI assembly to obtain a voltage reading of:

　a. ECU part No. 14632A13 and below—0.125-0.145 volt.

　b. ECU part No. 14632A15 and above—0.240-0.260 volt.

8. Tighten the TPI mounting screws, making sure the voltage reading does not change.

9. Slowly advance the throttle arm to wide-open throttle, then back to idle while observing the voltmeter. The voltage should increase and decrease smoothly.

10. Set the meter selector switch to the 20 volts DC position.

11. Advance the throttle to wide-open throttle. The voltage reading at wide-open throttle should not exceed 7.46 volts.

12. Remove the TPI Test Lead and reconnect the TPI to the ECU harness (**Figure 60**).

13. Reconnect the tan/blue cylinder head temperature sender wires (**Figure 61**).

14. Connect the remote control cable to the throttle arm.

NOTE
The TPI can be readjusted slightly if the outboard runs excessively rich or lean. Decreasing the TPI voltage leans the mixture while increasing the voltage richens the mixture.

Idle Speed Adjustment

1. Loosen the throttle cam follower screw (4, **Figure 59**).

2. Start the engine and warm it to normal operating temperature.

3. While holding the throttle arm in the idle position, adjust the idle speed screw (**Figure 62**) to the specified idle speed (**Table 11** and **Table 12**).

4. Retighten the cam follower screw.

Oil Pump Synchronization

Refer to **Figure 63** for this procedure.

1. Place the throttle arm in the idle position and note the alignment marks on the oil pump body and control lever.

2. With the throttle in the idle position, the alignment mark on the oil pump body should be

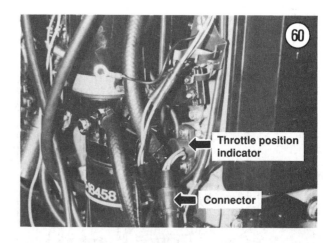

aligned with the short mark on the pump control lever. If necessary, adjust the length of the pump control rod to align the marks as specified.

Throttle Cable Installation

1. Connect the throttle cable to the throttle arm.
2. While holding the throttle arm against the idle stop, adjust the throttle cable barrel to slip into

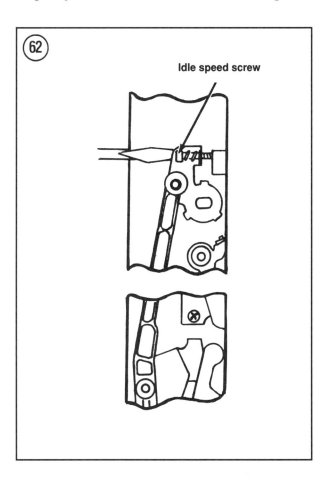

the barrel retainer on the cable anchor bracket with a slight preload of the throttle arm against the idle stop.
3. Lock the throttle cable barrel in place.

NOTE
Excessive preload in Step 4 will result in difficult shifting from FORWARD gear to NEUTRAL.

4. Check the throttle cable preload by inserting a thin piece of paper (such as a matchbook cover) between the idle stop and stop screw. If the preload is correct, a slight drag (without tearing) will be noted when removing the paper. Readjust the cable as required to obtain the desired preload.

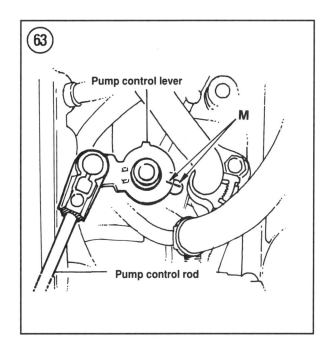

Tables 1-13 are on the following pages.

Table 1 TUNE-UP SPECIFICATIONS (3 and 3.3 HP)

Cylinders	1
Bore	1.85 in.
Stroke	1.69 in.
Displacement	4.6 cu. in.
Fuel:oil ratio	50:1
Idle speed (in gear)	900-1000 rpm
Full throttle speed	4500-5500
Compression pressure	90 psi min.
Firing order	Single cylinder
Ignition type	
3 hp	Magneto breaker point
3.3 hp	Capacitor discharge (CDI)
Spark Plug	NGK BPR6HS or
	Champion RL87YC
Spark plug gap	0.040 in.
Breaker point gap	0.012-0.016 in.
Ignition timing	Not adjustable
Gearcase capacity	3 oz. (88.7 mL)

Table 2 TUNE-UP SPECIFICATIONS (4 AND 5 HP)

Cylinders	1
Bore	2.165 in.
Stroke	1.693 in.
Displacement	6.2 cu. in.
Fuel:oil ratio	50:1
Idle speed (in gear)	800-900 rpm
Full throttle speed	4500-5500 rpm
Compression pressure	90 psi min.
Firing order	Single cylinder
Ignition type	Capacitor discharge (CDI)
Spark plug	NGK BP7HS-10 or
	Champion L82YC
Spark plug gap	0.040 in.
Idle timing	5° BTDC
Maximum timing advance	28°-32° BTDC
Gearcase capacity	6.6 oz. (195.2 mL)

Table 3 TUNE-UP SPECIFICATIONS (8, 9.9 AND 15 HP)

Cylinders	2
Bore	
8, 9.9 hp	2.125 in.
15 hp	2.375 in.
Stroke	1.77 in.
Displacement	
8, 9.9 hp	12.8 cu. in.
15 hp	16.0 cu. in.
Fuel:oil ratio	50:1
Idle speed (in forward gear)	
8 hp	600-700 rpm[1]
9.9, 15 hp	700-800[1]

(continued)

Table 3 TUNE-UP SPECIFICATIONS (8, 9.9 AND 15 HP) (continued)

Full throttle speed	
8 hp	4500-5500 rpm
9.9, 15 hp	5000-6000 rpm
Ignition type	Capacitor discharge (CDI)
Firing order	Alternate
Spark plug	
Standard ignition coils	
8 hp	Champion L82YC
9.9, 15 hp	NGK BP8HS-15
Spark plug gap	
8 hp	0.040 in.
9.9, 15 hp	0.060 in.
High energy ignition coils	NGK BUHW (surface gap)
Spark plug gap	Not adjustable
Idle timing	6° BTDC
Maximum timing advance	36° BTDC
Gearcase capacity	6.5 oz. (192.2 mL)

1. On models without an idle speed adjustment screw, the carburetors are factory calibrated to maintain idle speed of 600-700 rpm in forward gear.

Table 4 TUNE-UP SPECIFICATIONS (20 AND 25 HP)

Cylinders	2
Bore	2.56 in.
Stroke	2.38 in.
Displacement	24.4 cu. in.
Fuel:oil ratio[1]	50:1
Idle speed (in forward gear)	700-800 rpm
Full throttle speed	
20 hp	4500-5500
25 hp	5000-6000
Ignition type	Capacitor discharge (CDI)
Firing order	Alternate
Spark plug	NGK BUHW or
	Champion L76V
Spark plug gap	Not adjustable
Pickup timing	0°-2° BTDC
Full throttle timing	25° BTDC
Gearcase capacity	7.6 oz. (225 mL)

1. Some models may be equipped with an optional oil injection system.

Table 5 TUNE-UP SPECIFICATIONS (40 HP)

Cylinders	Inline 4
Bore	2.565 in.
Stroke	2.125 in.
Displacement	43.9 cu. in.
Fuel:oil ratio[1]	50:1
Idle speed (in forward gear)	600-700 rpm
Full throttle speed	5000-5500 rpm
Ignition type	Capacitor discharge (CDI)
Firing order	1-3-2-4
Spark plug	NGK BUHW-2
Spark plug gap	Surface gap

(continued)

5

Table 5 TUNE-UP SPECIFICATIONS (40 HP) (continued)

Primary pickup timing	2° ATDC-2° BTDC
Idle timing	3°-10° ATDC
Secondary pickup timing	30° BTDC @ cranking speed
Maximum timing advance	30° BTDC @ 5500 rpm
Gearcase capacity	12.5 oz. (370 mL)

1. Electric start models are equipped with oil injection system. Oil injection is optional on manual start models.

Table 6 TUNE-UP SPECIFICATIONS (50 AND 60 HP MODELS PRIOR TO SERIAL NO. D000750)

Cylinders	Inline 3
Bore	2.875 in.
Stroke	2.563 in.
Displacement	49.8 cu. in.
Fuel:oil ratio	Automatic oil injection
Idle speed (in forward gear)	600-700 rpm
Full throttle speed	5300-5800 rpm
Ignition type	Capacitor discharge (CDI)
Firing order	1-2-3
Spark plug	AC V40FFM or Champion L76V
Plug gap	Surface gap
Primary pickup timing	2° BTDC-2° ATDC
Maximum timing advance	33° BTDC @ 5500 rpm
Gearcase capacity	12.5 oz. (370 mL)

Table 7 TUNE-UP SPECIFICATONS (50 AND 60 HP SERIAL NO. D000750-ON)

Cylinders	Inline 3
Bore	
Serial No. D000750-D047798	2.9540 in.
Serial No. D047799-on	2.9553 in.
Stroke	2.520 in.
Displacement	51.8 cu. in.
Fuel:oil ratio	Automatic oil injection
Idle speed (in forward gear)	650-750 rpm
Full throttle speed	5000-5500 rpm
Ignition type	Capacitor discharge (CDI)
Firing order	1-3-2
Spark plug	NGK BU8H
Spark plug gap	Surface gap
Idle timing	2°-6° ATDC
Maximum timing advance	24° BTDC @ cranking speed
	22° BTDC @ 5000 rpm
Gearcase capacity	11.5 oz. (340 mL)

Table 8 TUNE-UP SPECIFICATIONS (75 AND 90 HP)

Cylinders	Inline 3
Bore	3.375 in.
Stroke	2.65 in.
Displacement	71.1 cu. in
Fuel:oil ratio	Automatic oil injection
Idle speed (in forward gear)	625-725 rpm

(continued)

Table 8 TUNE-UP SPECIFICATIONS (75 AND 90 HP) (continued)

Full throttle speed	
75 hp	4750-5250 rpm
90 hp	5000-5500 rpm
Ignition type	Capacitor discharge (CDI)
Firing order	1-3-2
Spark plug	NGK BUHW-2, AC-V40FFK or Champion L78V
Spark plug gap	Surface gap
Idle timing	0°-4° BTDC
Maximum timing advance	28° BTDC @ cranking speed
	26° BTDC @ 5000 rpm
Gearcase capacity	22.5 oz. (665.4 mL)

5

Table 9 TUNE-UP SPECIFICATIONS (100 AND 115 HP)

Cylinders	Inline 4
Bore	3.375 in.
Stroke	2.930 in.
Displacement	105 cu. in.
Fuel:oil ratio	Automatic oil injection
Idle speed (in forward gear)	625-725 rpm
Full throttle speed	4750-5250 rpm
Ignition type	Capacitor discharge (CDI)
Firing order	1-3-2-4
Spark plug	NGK BP8H-N
Spark plug gap	0.040 in.
Idle timing	2°-4° BTDC
Maximum timing advance	25° BTDC @ cranking speed
	23° BTDC @ 3000 rpm
Gearcase capacity	22.5 oz. (665.4 mL)

Table 10 TUNE-UP SPECIFICATIONS (135 AND 150 HP)

Cylinders	V6
Bore	3.125 in.
Stroke	2.650 in.
Displacement	121.9 cu. in.
Fuel:oil ratio	Automatic oil injection
Idle speed (in forward gear)	600-700 rpm
Full throttle speed	5000-5600 rpm
Ignition type	Capacitor discharge (CDI)
Firing order	1-2-3-4-5-6
Spark plug	NGK BU8H
Spark plug gap	Surface gap
Idle/pickup timing	
Prior to Serial No. D082000	2°-9° ATDC
Serial No. D082000-on	0°-9° ATDC
Maximum timing advance	
Prior to serial No. D082000	19° BTDC @ cranking speed
	17° BTDC @ wide-open throttle
Serial No. D082000-on	21° BTDC @ cranking speed
	19° BTDC @ wide-open throttle
Gearcase capacity	22.5 oz. (665.4 mL)

Table 11 TUNE-UP SPECIFICATIONS (1990-1991 150XR4 AND 175 HP; 1991 175XRi; 1990 200 HP AND 200 XRi)

Cylinders	V6
Bore	3.375 in.
Stroke	2.650 in.
Displacement	142 cu. in.
Fuel:oil ratio	Automatic oil injection
Idle speed (in forward gear)	
150XR4	625-700 rpm
175, 200 hp	600-700 rpm
175XRi, 200XRi	600-675 rpm
Full throttle speed	
150XR4	5000-5600 rpm
175 hp	5300-5600 rpm
175XRi	5200-5700 rpm
200 hp	5300-5800 rpm
200XRi	5400-5900 rpm
Ignition type	Capacitor discharge (CDI)
Firing order	1-2-3-4-5-6
Spark plug	
200XRi	NGK BUZ8H
All others	NGK BU8H
Spark plug gap	Surface gap
Pickup timing	
150XR4	
Prior to serial No. C247591	4°-6° ATDC
After serial No. C247590	2°-9° ATDC
175 hp	2°-9° ATDC
175XRi	
Prior to serial No. C221500	10° ATDC
After serial No. C221499	4° ATDC
200 hp	2°-7° ATDC
200XRi	9° ATDC
Idle timing	
150XR4	
Prior to serial No. C247591	3°-11° ATDC
After serial No. C247590	2°-9° ATDC
175 hp	2°-9° ATDC
175XRi	
Prior to serial No. C221500	10° ATDC
After serial No. C221499	4° ATDC
200 hp	2°-7° ATDC
200XRi	9° ATDC
Maximum timing advance[1]	
150XR4	
Prior to serial No. C247591	22° BTDC @ cranking speed
	26° BTDC @ wide-open throttle
Serial No. C247591-C254931	19° BTDC @ cranking speed
	26° BTDC @ wide-open throttle
After serial No. C254931	19° BTDC @ cranking speed
	20° BTDC @ wide-open throttle
175 hp	22° BTDC @ cranking speed
	20° BTDC @ wide-open throttle

(continued)

Table 11 TUNE-UP SPECIFICATIONS (1990-1991 150XR4 AND 175 HP; 1991 175XRi; 1990 200 HP AND 200 XRi (continued)

Maximum timing advance[1] (continued)	
175XRi	
Prior to serial No. D007414	22° BTDC @ cranking speed
After serial No. D007413	21° BTDC @ cranking speed
	20° BTDC @ 3000 rpm
	25° BTDC @ 5100-5600 rpm
200 hp	22° BTDC @ cranking speed
	26° BTDC @ wide-open throttle
200XRi	19° BTDC @ cranking speed-2500 rpm
	25° BTDC @ 3500 rpm
Gearcase capacity	
150XR4	21 oz. (621 mL)
175-200 hp	24-1/4 oz. (717.1 mL)

1. Maximum ignition timing must be retarded 3° from listed specifications on models (except 150XR4) with Idle Stabilizer Shift Kit (part No. 87-814281A1) installed as an accessory.

5

Table 12 TUNE-UP SPECIFICATIONS (1992 AND 1993 150XR6, 175 HP and 175 XRi; 1993 150XRi; 1991-1993 200 HP and 200XRi

Cylinders	V6
Bore	3.500 in.
Stroke	2.650 in.
Displacement	153 cu. in.
Fuel:oil ratio	Automatic oil injection
Idle speed (in forward gear)	
150XR6	625-725 rpm
All others	600-700 rpm
Full throttle speed	
150XR6	5000-5600 rpm
200XRi	5000-5800 rpm
All others	5000-5600 rpm
Ignition type	Capacitor discharge (CDI)
Firing order	1-2-3-4-5-6
Spark plug	NGK BU8H
Spark plug gap	Surface gap
Idle timing	
All models prior to serial No. D082000	2°-9° ATDC
All models serial No. D082000-on	0°-9° ATDC
Pickup timing	
All models prior to serial No. D082000	2°-9° ATDC
All models serial No. D082000-D181999	0°-9° ATDC
150XRi, 175 XRi, 200XRi serial No. D182000-on	4° ATDC
All others serial No. D182000-on	0°-9° ATDC
Maximum timing advance	
200 hp & 200XRi	
Serial No. C291520-D077246[1]	22° BTDC @ cranking speed
	20° BTDC @ wide-open throttle
Serial No. D077247-D081999[2]	21° BTDC @ cranking speed
	25° BTDC @ wide-open throttle

(continued)

Table 12 TUNE-UP SPECIFICATIONS (1992 AND 1993 150XR6, 175 HP and 175 XRi; 1993 150XRi; 1991-1993 200 HP and 200XRi (continued)

Maximum timing advance (continued)	
200 hp	
Serial No. D082000-on	21° BTDC @ cranking speed
	26° BTDC @ wide-open throttle
200XRi	
Serial No. D082000-on	20° BTDC @ cranking speed
	26° BTDC @ wide-open throttle
150XR6, 150XRi, 175 hp & 175XRi	
Serial No. D082000-on	19° BTDC @ cranking speed
	20° BTDC @ wide-open throttle
Gearcase capacity	
150XR6	21.0 oz. (621 mL)
All others	22.5 (665.4 mL)

1. Equipped with idle stabilizer module.
2. Equipped with idle stabilizer/spark advance module.

Table 13 TUNE-UP SPECIFICATIONS (250 AND 275 HP)

Cylinders	V6
Bore	3.74 in.
Stroke	3.14 in.
Displacement	207 cu. in.
Fuel:oil ratio	Automatic oil injection
Idle speed (in forward gear)	600-700 rpm
Full throttle speed	5000-5500 rpm
Ignition type	Capacitor discharge (CDI)
Firing order	1-2-3-4-5-6
Spark plug	NGK BU8H
Spark plug gap	Surface gap
Idle/pickup timing	
Prior to serial No. D082000	7° ATDC
Serial No. D082000-on	5° ATDC
Maximum timing advance	22° BTDC @ cranking speed
	20° BTDC @ wide-open throttle
Gearcase capacity	29 oz. (857.5 mL)

Chapter Six

Fuel System

This chapter contains removal, overhaul, installation and adjustment procedures for fuel pumps, carburetors, enrichener valves/choke solenoids, electronic fuel injection components, fuel tanks and connecting lines used with the Mercury outboard motors covered in this manual. Carburetor jet size recommendations are provided in **Tables 1-5** at the end of the chapter.

FUEL PUMP

The diaphragm-type fuel pump used on Mercury outboard motors is operated by crankcase pressure pulsations. Since this type of fuel pump cannot create sufficient pressure to draw fuel from the tank during starting, fuel is transferred to the carburetor for starting by hand operating the primer bulb installed in the fuel hose.

Pressure pulsations created by movement of the pistons reach the fuel pump through a passage between the crankcase and the fuel pump.

Upward piston movement creates a low pressure on the pump diaphragm. This low pressure opens the inlet check valve in the pump, drawing fuel from the line into the pump. At the same time, the low pressure draws the air-fuel mixture from the carburetor into the crankcase.

Downward piston movement creates a high pressure on the pump diaphragm. This pressure closes the inlet check valve and opens the outlet check valve, forcing the fuel into the carburetor and drawing the air-fuel mixture from the crankcase into the cylinder for combustion. **Figure 1** shows the operational sequence of a typical Mercury outboard fuel pump.

Mercury fuel pumps are extremely simple in design and reliable in operation. Diaphragm failures are the most common problem, although the use of dirty or improper fuel-oil mixtures in the fuel tank can cause check valve problems.

CAUTION
Fuel pump assemblies and internal fuel pump components vary between models. Be certain that the correct fuel pump or fuel pump components are used when replacing or overhauling the fuel pump. An incorrect fuel pump or internal components can cause poor performance or power head failure. Never interchange fuel pump components from another model.

Removal/Installation
All Models (Except Integral Fuel Pump Carburetor)

Figure 2 shows a typical fuel pump installation.

1. On 40 hp and 50-60 hp (serial No. D000750-on)—Remove the oil reservoir. See Chapter Eleven.

2. Remove and discard the sta-straps clamping the fuel hoses to the fuel pump.

3. Label the hoses at the pump for correct reinstallation. Disconnect all hoses from the pump assembly.

NOTE
The fuel pump is secured to the power head by 2 Phillips or slotted screws. The fuel pump components are held together by 2 hex-head screws. During fuel pump removal, do not remove the hex-head screws unless fuel pump disassembly is necessary.

4. Remove the two screws (A, **Figure 2**) securing the fuel pump assembly to the power head. Lift the pump off the power head.

NOTE
On 250-275 hp models, two fuel pumps connected in series are used. The bottom fuel pump delivers fuel to the top pump and the top pump delivers fuel to the carburetors.

5. If necessary, repeat Steps 2-4 to remove the remaining fuel pump on 250-275 hp models.

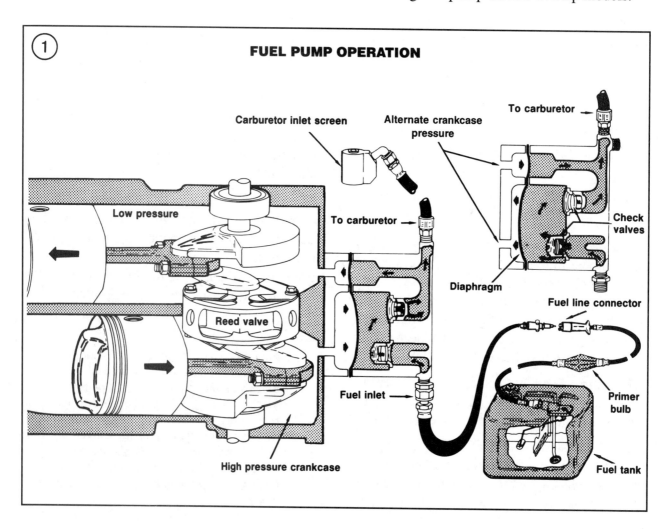

① **FUEL PUMP OPERATION**

Carburetor inlet screen

Alternate crankcase pressure

To carburetor

Low pressure

To carburetor

Check valves

Reed valve

Diaphragm

Fuel line connector

Fuel inlet

Primer bulb

High pressure crankcase

Fuel tank

6. Carefully clean the fuel pump-to-power head gasket from the power head or fuel pump.

7. Install a new gasket between the fuel pump and power head.

8. Install the pump on the power head and secure with the 2 screws. Tighten the pump mounting screws to 40 in.-lb. (4.5 N•m) on 50 and 60 hp models prior to serial No. D000750, or 50-60 in.-lb. (5.6-6.7 N•m) on all other models.

9. On 40 hp and 50-60 hp (serial No. D000750-on), reinstall the oil reservoir and bleed the injection system. See Chapter Eleven.

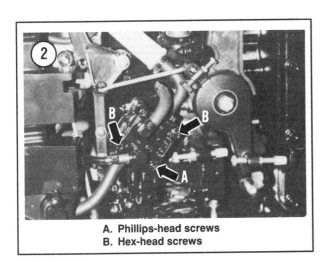

A. Phillips-head screws
B. Hex-head screws

Removal/Installation (Integral Fuel Pump Carburetor 4 and 5 hp)

NOTE
*All fuel pump gaskets should be replaced
if the pump is disassembled.*

The fuel pump can be removed for service without carburetor removal.

1. Disconnect the fuel delivery hose (A, **Figure 3**) from the pump inlet.

2. Remove the fuel pump mounting screws (B, **Figure 3**). Separate the pump cover, body and gasket from the carburetor.

3. Install a new gasket between the fuel pump and carburetor during installation.

4. Install the pump assembly on the carburetor making sure all components are properly aligned. Install the mounting screws (B, **Figure 3**) and tighten securely.

Removal/Installation (Integral Fuel Pump Carburetor 8-25 hp)

NOTE
*All fuel pump gaskets should be replaced
if the pump is disassembled.*

1. Remove the 5 screws securing the pump assembly to the carburetor. See **Figure 4**, typical.

2. Separate the pump assembly from the carburetor.

3. Replace the pump gasket(s) and diaphragm(s) during installation.

4. Install the pump assembly on the carburetor making sure all components are properly aligned.

5. Install the 5 pump mounting screws (**Figure 4**). Tighten the screws evenly and securely.

6

Disassembly/Reassembly
(All Models Except Integral Fuel Pump Carburetor)

NOTE
All fuel pump gaskets should be replaced any time the pump is disassembled.

1. Remove the hex-head screws holding the pump assembly together.

2. Referring to **Figure 5**, separate the pump cover, gaskets and diaphragms from the pump body and base. Discard the gaskets and diaphragms.

3. Using needlenose pliers, remove the check valve retainers (6, **Figure 5**) from the pump body. Remove the plastic discs and check valves from the retainers.

4. Remove the cap (12, **Figure 5**) and spring (13) from the pump cover.

5. Remove the cap (4, **Figure 5**) and spring (5) from the pump body.

6. To reassemble the pump, insert the check valve retainer into the plastic disc, then into the

check valve. See **Figure 6**. Repeat on the remaining check valve assembly.

7. Lubricate the check valve retainers with engine oil or soapy water. Insert the check valve and retainer assemblies into the pump body (**Figure 6**).

8. Bend the check valve retainer stem from side to side, until the stem breaks off flush with the retainer cap. See **Figure 7**. Repeat on the remaining check valve retainer.

9. Insert the broken retainer stem into the retainer as shown in **Figure 8**. Using a small hammer and punch, tap the stem into the retainer until flush with the retainer cap.

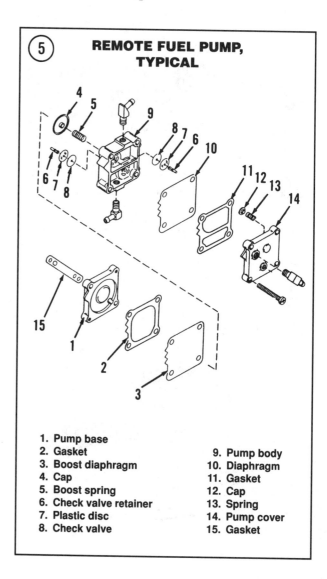

(5) REMOTE FUEL PUMP, TYPICAL

1. Pump base
2. Gasket
3. Boost diaphragm
4. Cap
5. Boost spring
6. Check valve retainer
7. Plastic disc
8. Check valve
9. Pump body
10. Diaphragm
11. Gasket
12. Cap
13. Spring
14. Pump cover
15. Gasket

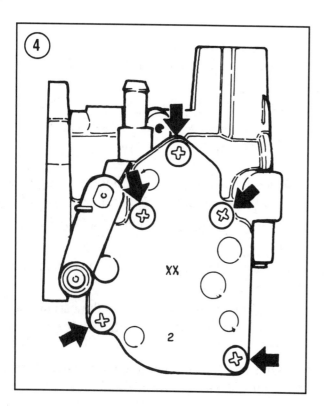

NOTE
Fuel pump components have one or more "V" tabs on one side for directional reference during assembly. Be certain the "V" tabs on all components are aligned. To ensure the correct alignment of pump components, use 1/4-in. bolts or dowels as guides. Insert the guides through the pump mounting screw holes.

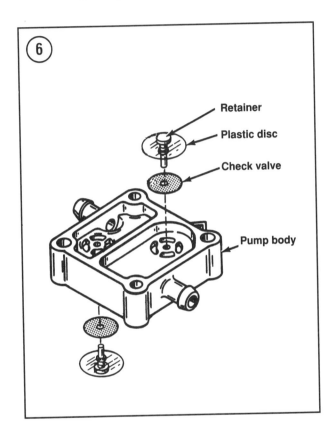

10. Referring to **Figure 5**, reassemble the pump by reversing the order of disassembly. Do not use gasket sealer on the pump gaskets or diaphragms. Be sure that all pump components are properly aligned.

CAUTION
*On 75-115 hp models, 2 oil holes are present in the boost diaphragm to permit oil from the oil pump to enter and mix with the gasoline flow. During pump assembly, be certain the "V" tab on the boost diaphragm (**Figure 9**) is properly aligned with the tab on the pump cover and body. Failure to do so will result in power head failure.*

11. Install the hex-head screws and tighten securely. If used, remove the 1/4 in. bolts or dowels.

Disassembly/Reassembly
(4 and 5 hp Integral Fuel Pump Carburetor)

Refer to **Figure 10** for this procedure.

1. Separate the pump cover, outer gasket and diaphragm from the pump body.

2. Remove the inner gasket and diaphragm from the pump body.

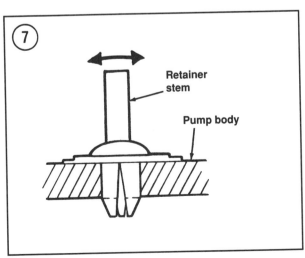

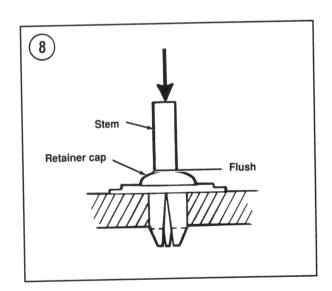

3. Inspect the check valves for cracks, chips or bends. If necessary, remove the nut and screw securing the check valves to the pump body and remove the check valves.

4. To reassemble the pump, install the check valves and secure with the nuts and screws. Make sure the valves are centered over the check valve seats.

5. Complete reassembly by reversing the order of disassembly. Make sure the gaskets and diaphragms are properly aligned. Do not use gasket sealer on the pump components. Tighten the pump mounting screws (B, **Figure 3**) securely.

Disassembly/Reassembly
(8-25 hp Integral Fuel Pump Carburetor)

Refer to **Figure 11** and **Figure 12** for this procedure.

1. After removing the fuel pump assembly from the carburetor, separate the pump cover, gasket(s) and diaphragm(s). Discard the gaskets.

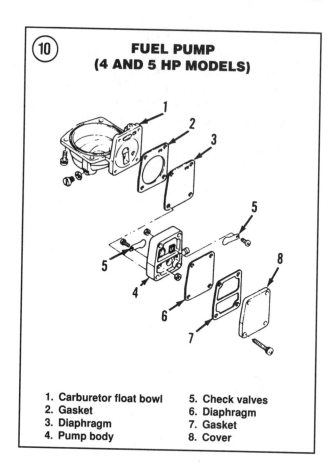

(10) **FUEL PUMP**
(4 AND 5 HP MODELS)

1. Carburetor float bowl	5. Check valves
2. Gasket	6. Diaphragm
3. Diaphragm	7. Gasket
4. Pump body	8. Cover

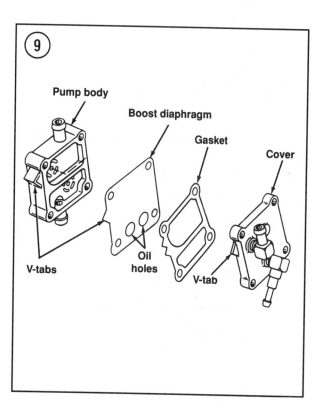

(9)

Pump body

Boost diaphragm

Gasket

Cover

V-tabs

Oil holes

V-tab

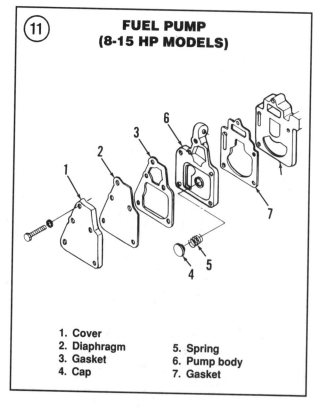

(11) **FUEL PUMP**
(8-15 HP MODELS)

1. Cover	
2. Diaphragm	5. Spring
3. Gasket	6. Pump body
4. Cap	7. Gasket

2. On 8-15 hp models, remove the cap (4, **Figure 11**) and spring (5) from the pump body (6).

3. Using new gasket(s), assemble the pump by reversing the disassembly procedure.

Cleaning/Inspection (All Models Except Integral Fuel Pump Carburetor)

1. Clean the pump components in a suitable solvent and dry with compressed air (except check valves).

2. Inspect check valves and plastic discs for cracks, holes or other damage. Replace as required.

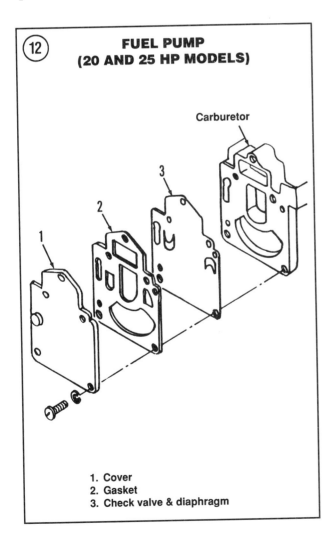

FUEL PUMP (20 AND 25 HP MODELS)

Carburetor

1. Cover
2. Gasket
3. Check valve & diaphragm

3. Inspect the fuel fittings on the pump cover or base for looseness, leakage or other damage. Tighten or replace the fittings as required.

Cleaning/Inspection (4 and 5 hp Integral Fuel Pump Carburetor)

1. Remove any diaphragm or gasket material from the mating surfaces.

2. Clean all components in a suitable solvent and dry with compressed air.

3. Inspect the pump body, cover and carburetor mounting flange for nicks, cracks or other damage.

4. Inspect the reed-type check valves for bends, cracks or other damage. Replace the check valves as required.

Cleaning/Inspection (8-25 hp Integral Fuel Pump Carburetor)

1. Clean all components in a suitable solvent and dry with compressed air.

2. Inspect the pump cover, body and carburetor mounting flange for cracks, nicks or other damage. Replace any component found to be defective or damaged.

3. Inspect the check valve diaphragm for holes, deterioration or other damage. Replace the diaphragm as necessary.

CARBURETORS

Carburetor Floats

A redesigned alcohol-resistant float of hollow plastic is installed in many late-model carburetors. The floats are also available as service replacements for earlier models. Read the instructions accompanying the plastic float carefully, as float settings may be changed on some models when the plastic float is installed.

6

Carburetor Adjustments

The engine must be provided with an adequate supply of cooling water when performing any procedures that involve starting and running the engine. Install a flushing device, place the engine in a test tank or mount the outboard on a boat and place in the water.

When performing carburetor adjustments (idle speed and fuel mixture), the outboard must be running in forward gear at normal operating temperature. The best results will be obtained if the motor is mounted on a boat, in the water, running in forward gear with boat movement unrestrained.

THROTTLE PLUNGER CARBURETOR (3 AND 3.3 HP MODELS)

Removal/Installation

1. Remove the knobs from the throttle and choke levers.
2. Remove the front intake cover from the carburetor.
3. Close the fuel shut-off valve.
4. Disconnect the fuel delivery hose from the carburetor.
5. Loosen the carburetor mounting clamp and remove the carburetor.
6. Make sure the carburetor gasket (26, **Figure 13**) is properly located inside the carburetor throat.
7. Install the carburetor and tighten the mounting clamp.
8. Reconnect the fuel delivery hose.
9. Complete installation by reinstalling the choke and throttle lever knobs, then reinstall the front intake cover.

Disassembly

Refer to **Figure 13** for this procedure.

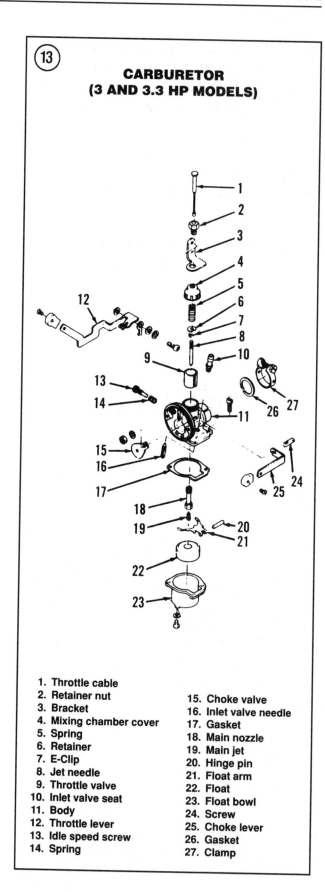

CARBURETOR (3 AND 3.3 HP MODELS)

1. Throttle cable
2. Retainer nut
3. Bracket
4. Mixing chamber cover
5. Spring
6. Retainer
7. E-Clip
8. Jet needle
9. Throttle valve
10. Inlet valve seat
11. Body
12. Throttle lever
13. Idle speed screw
14. Spring
15. Choke valve
16. Inlet valve needle
17. Gasket
18. Main nozzle
19. Main jet
20. Hinge pin
21. Float arm
22. Float
23. Float bowl
24. Screw
25. Choke lever
26. Gasket
27. Clamp

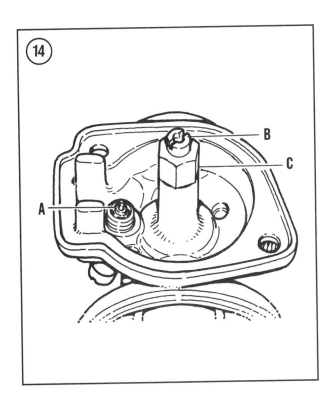

1. Remove the 2 float bowl attaching screws. Separate the float bowl from the carburetor. Remove and discard the float bowl gasket.

2. Invert the carburetor and lift off the float.

3. Remove the float hinge pin and the float arm.

4. Remove the inlet valve needle (A, **Figure 14**).

5. Remove the main jet (B, **Figure 14**) using a suitable wide-blade screwdriver.

6. Remove the main nozzle (C, **Figure 14**) with an appropriate size wrench.

7. Remove the throttle lever.

8. Loosen the retainer nut several turns, then unscrew the mixing chamber cover. Lift the throttle valve assembly (**Figure 15**) out of the carburetor body.

9. Compress the throttle valve spring and disconnect the throttle cable from the throttle valve. See **Figure 16**.

10. Remove the jet needle and jet retainer from the throttle valve. See **Figure 16**. Do not lose the jet needle E-ring.

11. Lightly seat the idle speed screw, counting the turns required for reference during reassembly. Remove the idle speed screw and spring to complete disassembly.

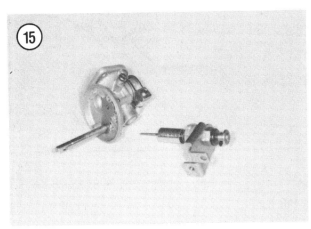

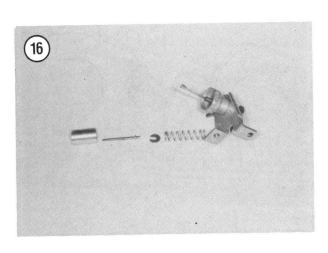

Cleaning and Inspection

1. Clean the carburetor body and metal parts in a carburetor cleaning solution to remove gum, dirt and varnish. Follow the instructions provided with the carburetor cleaner.

2. Rinse the carburetor components in clean solvent and dry with compressed air. Thoroughly blow out all orifices, nozzles and passages.

CAUTION
Do not use wire or drill bits to clean any carburetor passages. Doing so can alter calibration and ruin the carburetor.

3. Carefully inspect the carburetor body for cracks, stripped threads or other damage.

4. Inspect the float hinge and hinge pin for excessive wear and replace as required.

6

5. Inspect inlet valve needle and seat for excessive wear. Replace the valve needle and seat as an assembly if wear is noted.

6. Check the float for fuel absorption or deterioration and replace as necessary.

Reassembly

Refer to **Figure 13** for this procedure.

1. Slide the spring onto the idle speed screw. Install the screw into the carburetor body until lightly seated, then back out the number of turns noted during disassembly.

2. Insert the jet needle into the throttle valve. Place the needle retainer into the throttle valve over the needle E-ring. Align the retainer slot with the slot in the throttle valve. See **Figure 17**.

3. Reassemble the throttle valve components as follows:

   a. Place the throttle valve spring over the throttle cable.

   b. Compress the spring, then slide the throttle cable anchor through the slot and into position in the throttle valve. See **Figure 18**.

4. Align the slot in the throttle valve with the alignment pin in the carburetor body. Insert the throttle valve assembly into the body and tighten the mixing chamber cover. Tighten the cover retainer nut securely.

5. Reinstall the throttle lever.

6. Install the main nozzle (C, **Figure 14**) and main jet (B).

7. Install the inlet valve needle (A, **Figure 14**).

8. Install the float arm and hinge pin. Check float adjustment as described under *Float Adjustment* in this chapter.

9. Install the float.

10. Install the float bowl with a new gasket. Tighten the bowl screws securely.

Float Adjustment

1. With the float bowl removed, invert the carburetor and measure from the mating surface of the carburetor body (gasket installed) to the float arm as shown in **Figure 19**. The distance should be 0.090 in. (2.3 mm).

2. If adjustment is necessary, bend float arms evenly to obtain the specified measurement.

High-Speed Mixture Adjustment

High speed mixture is controlled by a fixed main jet and is not adjustable.

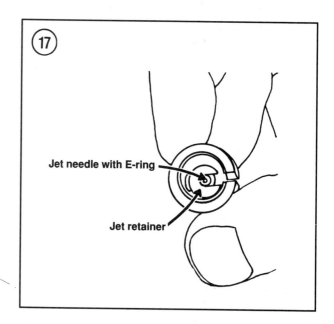

Jet needle with E-ring

Jet retainer

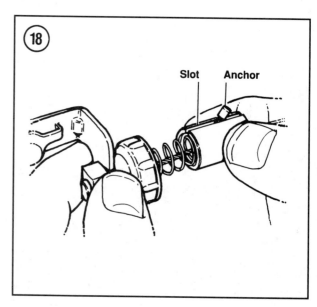

Slot   Anchor

Throttle Jet Needle Adjustment (Mid-range Mixture)

The position of the E-ring on the jet needle determines the proper mixture between 1/4 and 3/4 throttle opening. See **Figure 20**. The E-ring should normally be located in the second groove (from top). This setting should be acceptable for most operating conditions.

If an excessively rich or lean condition results from extreme changes in elevation, temperature or humidity, the E-ring location can be changed. The mixture becomes leaner as the E-ring is moved to the upper grooves. See **Figure 20**. Remember, it is always preferable to run a slightly rich mixture as opposed to one that is too lean.

1. Remove the carburetor as described in this chapter.
2. Remove and disassemble the throttle valve assembly as described in this chapter.
3. Relocate the E-ring as necessary, then reassemble and install the carburetor as described in this chapter.

Idle Speed Adjustment

1. Start the engine and allow to warm to normal operating temperature.
2. Place the throttle lever in the slowest position.
3. Adjust the idle speed screw to obtain 900-1000 rpm.

INTEGRAL FUEL PUMP CARBURETOR (4 AND 5 HP MODELS)

This carburetor uses an integral fuel pump assembly and a choke starting system.

Removal/Installation

1. Remove the engine cover.
2. Unclamp and disconnect the fuel hose at the carburetor fuel pump.
3. Loosen the screw (A, **Figure 21**) holding the throttle wire (B, **Figure 21**) to the carburetor throttle arm. Remove the wire from the throttle arm.
4. Disconnect the choke link rod (C, **Figure 21**) at the carburetor.
5. Remove 2 screws securing the baffle cover at the front of the carburetor. Remove the cover.
6. Remove 2 bolts (A, **Figure 22**) holding the baffle cover bracket (B, **Figure 22**) and the carburetor to the crankcase cover. Remove the bracket, carburetor and gasket. Discard the gasket.

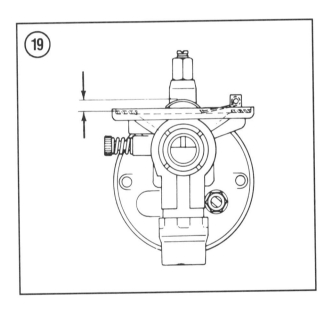

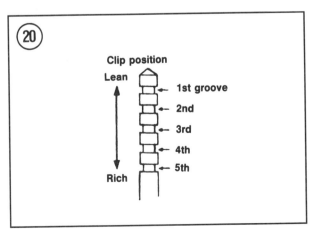

6

7. Using a new gasket, install the carburetor and baffle cover bracket to the crankcase cover. Tighten the bolts (A, **Figure 22**) evenly and securely.

8. Install the baffle cover.

9. Connect the choke link rod (C, **Figure 21**) to the carburetor.

10. Insert the throttle wire into the hole in the throttle arm retainer. Adjust the throttle wire as follows:

    a. Back the idle speed screw (D, **Figure 21**) off the throttle arm.

    b. Turn the idle speed screw inward until it just contacts the throttle arm, then turn inward an additional 2 complete turns. With the throttle arm in this position, pull any slack out of the throttle wire, then tighten the retainer screw (A, **Figure 21**).

Disassembly/Reassembly

Refer to **Figure 23** for this procedure.

1. Remove the lock clip (A, **Figure 24**).

2. Remove the idle mixture screw (B, **Figure 24**) and spring.

3. Remove the 2 screws holding the mixing chamber cover to the carburetor. Remove the cover.

4. Remove plug (A, **Figure 25**) and packing (B) from the mixing chamber casting.

5. Remove the 4 screws securing the fuel pump assembly to the carburetor float bowl. If fuel pump service is required:

    a. Separate the pump cover from the pump body. Discard the cover and body gaskets and the inner/outer diaphragms.

    b. Install new diaphragms on the pump body.

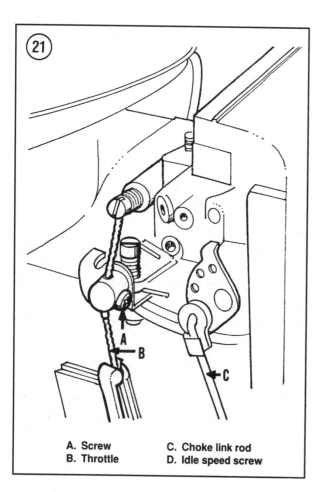

A. Screw   C. Choke link rod
B. Throttle   D. Idle speed screw

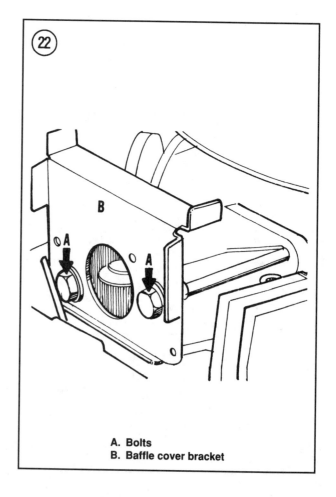

A. Bolts
B. Baffle cover bracket

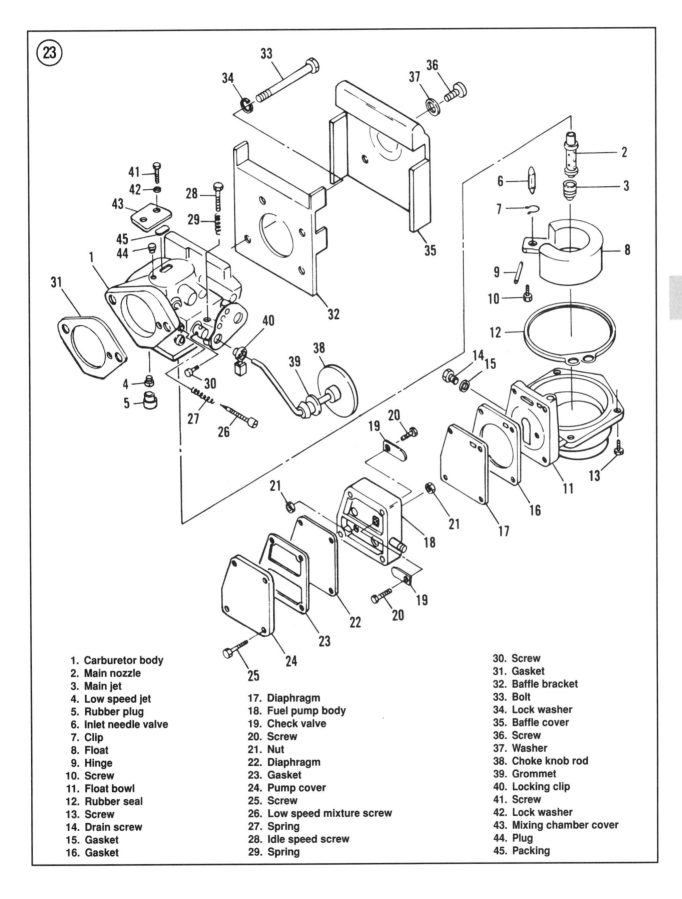

1. Carburetor body
2. Main nozzle
3. Main jet
4. Low speed jet
5. Rubber plug
6. Inlet needle valve
7. Clip
8. Float
9. Hinge
10. Screw
11. Float bowl
12. Rubber seal
13. Screw
14. Drain screw
15. Gasket
16. Gasket
17. Diaphragm
18. Fuel pump body
19. Check valve
20. Screw
21. Nut
22. Diaphragm
23. Gasket
24. Pump cover
25. Screw
26. Low speed mixture screw
27. Spring
28. Idle speed screw
29. Spring
30. Screw
31. Gasket
32. Baffle bracket
33. Bolt
34. Lock washer
35. Baffle cover
36. Screw
37. Washer
38. Choke knob rod
39. Grommet
40. Locking clip
41. Screw
42. Lock washer
43. Mixing chamber cover
44. Plug
45. Packing

c. Install the cover onto the pump body using a new gasket. Insert the pump mounting screws through the cover and body to maintain component alignment.

d. Install the pump assembly onto the carburetor float bowl using a new gasket.

6. Remove 4 screws (A, **Figure 26**) securing the float bowl (B, **Figure 26**) to the carburetor body. Remove the float bowl and discard the rubber bowl seal.

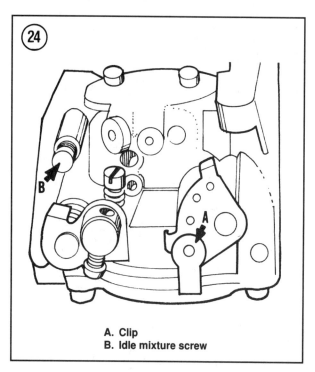

A. Clip
B. Idle mixture screw

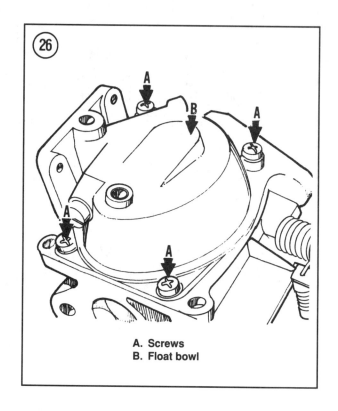

A. Screws
B. Float bowl

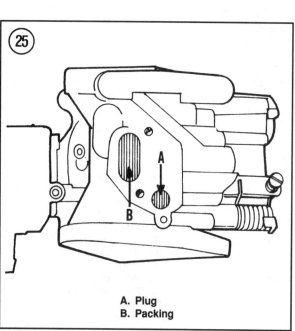

A. Plug
B. Packing

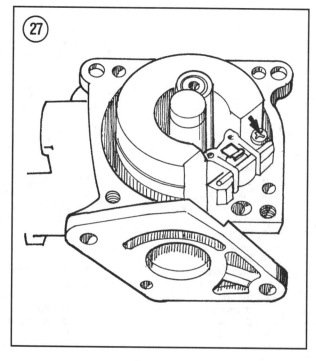

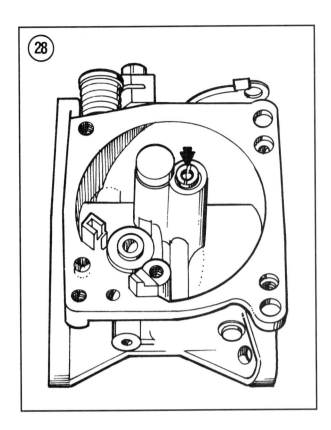

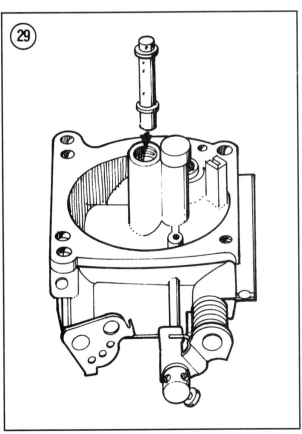

7. Remove the screw (**Figure 27**) holding the float assembly in the carburetor. Remove the float assembly.

8. Remove the float hinge pin and inlet needle valve from the float.

9. Remove the main jet (**Figure 28**). Remove the main nozzle located under the main jet (**Figure 29**).

10. Remove the plug (A, **Figure 30**) and low speed jet (B, **Figure 30**).

11. To reassemble the carburetor, first install the low speed jet (B, **Figure 30**) and plug (A).

12. Install the main nozzle (**Figure 29**) and the main jet (**Figure 28**).

13. Place the float hinge pin into the float arm. Install the inlet needle valve on the float.

14. Install the float, hinge pin and inlet valve assembly onto the carburetor body. Secure the hinge pin with the screw (**Figure 27**).

15. Adjust the float level as described in this chapter.

16. Place a new rubber float bowl seal into the bowl groove.

6

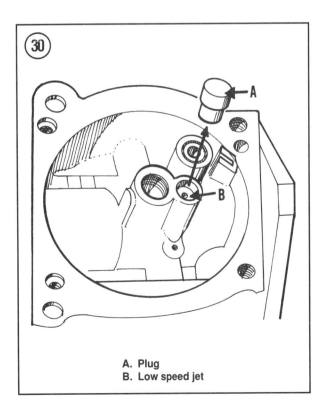

A. Plug
B. Low speed jet

17. Mount the float bowl on the carburetor body. Tighten the 4 screws evenly and securely.

18. Install the fuel pump assembly onto the float bowl. Tighten the 4 screws evenly and securely.

19. Install the low speed mixture screw (B, **Figure 24**). Turn in until lightly seated, then back out the number of turns noted during disassembly.

20. Complete the remaining reassembly by reversing the disassembly procedure.

Cleaning and Inspection

1. Clean the carburetor body and metal parts using a carburetor cleaning solution to remove gum, dirt and varnish. Follow the instructions provided with the cleaner.

2. Rinse the carburetor components in clean solvent and dry with compressed air. Be sure to blow out all orifices, nozzles and passages thoroughly.

> *CAUTION*
> *Do not use wire or drill bits to clean any carburetor passages. Doing so can alter calibration and ruin the carburetor.*

3. Check the carburetor body casting for stripped threads, cracks or other damage.

4. Check the float for fuel absorption, deterioration or other damage. Replace the float as necessary.

5. Check the inlet needle and seat for excessive wear. Replace the needle and seat as an assembly if necessary.

Float Adjustment

Check the float level from the float to the float bowl mating surface as shown in **Figure 31**. The top of the float should be 1/2 in. (12.7 mm) above the mating surface. If necessary, adjust by bending the float tang (**Figure 32**).

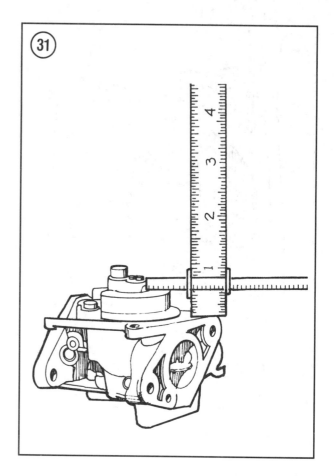

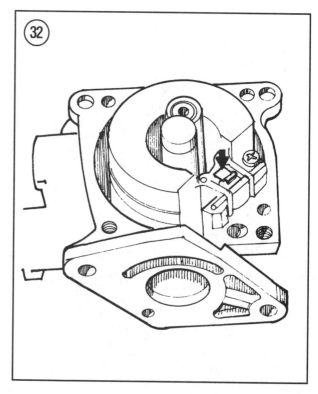

Idle Speed and Mixture Adjustment

1. Turn the idle mixture screw (B, **Figure 33**) inward until lightly seated, then back out 1-1/2 turns.

2. Start the engine and warm to normal operating temperature.

3. Throttle back to idle and shift into FORWARD gear.

4. Adjust the idle speed screw to obtain an idle speed of 850 rpm in forward gear.

5. Slowly turn the idle mixture screw (B, **Figure 33**) counterclockwise until the engine begins to run roughly and load up due to an overly rich mixture.

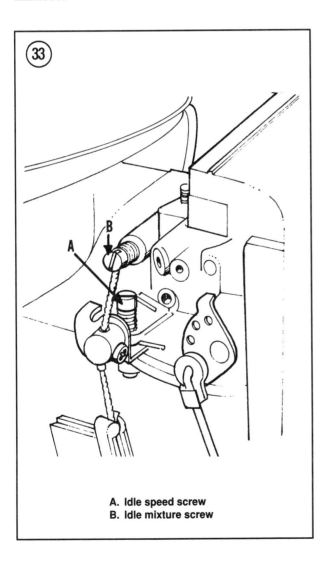

A. Idle speed screw
B. Idle mixture screw

6. Now slowly turn the idle mixture screw clockwise until the engine speed increases and runs smoothly.

7. Quickly accelerate the engine. If the engine hesitates and/or backfires, the idle mixture is too lean. Richen the mixture until the engine will accelerate cleanly without hesitation. It is good practice to adjust the mixture slightly rich instead of too lean.

8. Recheck the idle speed and readjust to 850 rpm in forward gear if necessary.

High Speed Mixture Adjustment

The high speed mixture is controlled by a fixed main jet. Normally, no adjustment is required. However, extreme changes in temperature, humidity or elevation may require a change in jet size. The standard main jet size for normal operation is 0.031 in. on 4 hp models and 0.032 in. on 5 hp models. Increasing main jet size richens the mixture while decreasing main jet size leans the mixture.

The standard main jet installed at the factory is acceptable for operation at sea level to 2500 ft. (762 m) above sea level. Refer to **Table 1** for recommended main jet sizes for different elevations.

INTEGRAL FUEL PUMP CARBURETOR WITH PRIMER SYSTEM (8-25 HP MODELS)

This carburetor uses an integral fuel pump and a diaphragm-operated primer system.

Removal/Installation (8-15 hp Models)

1. Remove the rewind starter housing assembly. Refer to Chapter Twelve.

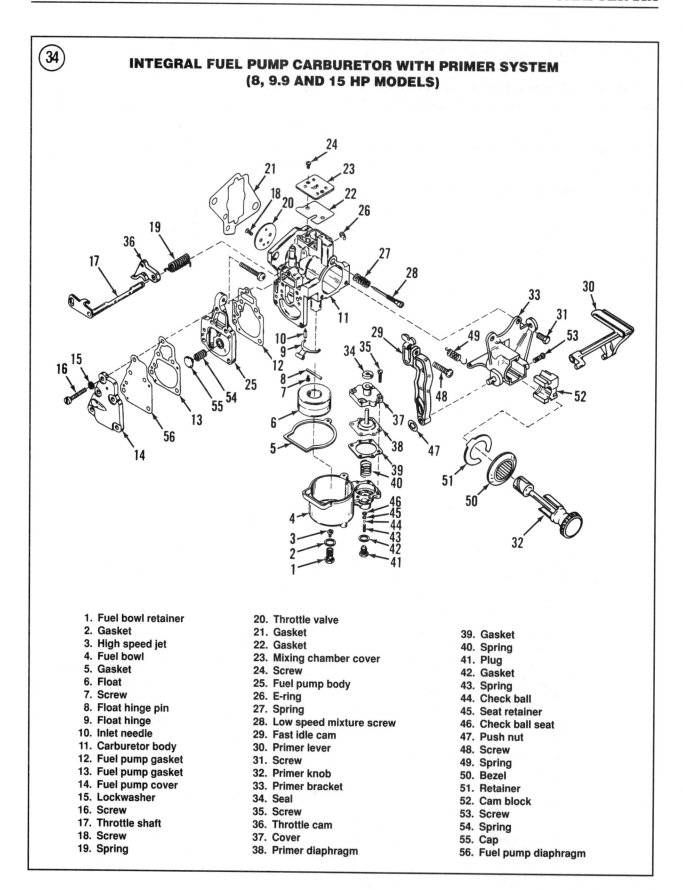

**INTEGRAL FUEL PUMP CARBURETOR WITH PRIMER SYSTEM
(8, 9.9 AND 15 HP MODELS)**

1. Fuel bowl retainer
2. Gasket
3. High speed jet
4. Fuel bowl
5. Gasket
6. Float
7. Screw
8. Float hinge pin
9. Float hinge
10. Inlet needle
11. Carburetor body
12. Fuel pump gasket
13. Fuel pump gasket
14. Fuel pump cover
15. Lockwasher
16. Screw
17. Throttle shaft
18. Screw
19. Spring
20. Throttle valve
21. Gasket
22. Gasket
23. Mixing chamber cover
24. Screw
25. Fuel pump body
26. E-ring
27. Spring
28. Low speed mixture screw
29. Fast idle cam
30. Primer lever
31. Screw
32. Primer knob
33. Primer bracket
34. Seal
35. Screw
36. Throttle cam
37. Cover
38. Primer diaphragm
39. Gasket
40. Spring
41. Plug
42. Gasket
43. Spring
44. Check ball
45. Seat retainer
46. Check ball seat
47. Push nut
48. Screw
49. Spring
50. Bezel
51. Retainer
52. Cam block
53. Screw
54. Spring
55. Cap
56. Fuel pump diaphragm

2. Loosen the cam block retaining screw and remove the large retaining clip holding the primer knob.

3. Depress the primer arm and pull the primer knob, bezel and slide block from the bottom cowl.

4. Disconnect the linkage from the fast idle lever.

5. Disconnect the fuel hose at the carburetor. Plug the hose to prevent leakage.

6. Remove the carburetor mounting nuts. Remove the carburetor and gasket. Discard the gasket.

7. Disconnect the bleed line from the fitting on the bottom of the carburetor, if so equipped.

8. To install the carburetor, install the primer components, and the air intake cover if so equipped, on the carburetor.

9. Reconnect the bleed hose to the carburetor.

10. Install the carburetor on the power head using a new gasket.

11. Attach the fuel hose to the carburetor.

12. Connect the fast idle lever linkage.

13. While pushing down on the primer arm, install the primer knob, bezel and cam block into the primer assembly. Securely tighten the cam block retaining screw.

14. Align the notch in the rear of the bezel with the tab on the lower cowl. Secure the bezel with the retaining clip.

15. Install the rewind starter housing assembly as described in Chapter Twelve.

Removal/Installation (20 and 25 hp)

1. Remove the bottom engine cowl as follows:
   a. Loosen the electrical harness clamp. Slide the clamp off the hook.
   b. If equipped with remote control cables, pull the front part of the rubber seal from the starboard bottom cowl to permit cowl removal without disconnecting the cables.
   c. Remove the 2 bolts holding the rear cowl latch. Remove the latch.
   d. Disconnect the "tell tale" hose at the bottom cowling fitting.
   e. Remove the hex nut holding the fuel hose connector to the bottom cowl.
   f. Remove the 2 bolts holding the front cowl latch and remove the latch.
   g. Separate the bottom cowl halves and remove from the engine. The fuel hose connector will drop out the port side when the cowl is removed.

2. Disconnect the fuel hose at the carburetor. Plug the hose to prevent leakage.

3. Remove the carburetor mounting nuts. Remove the carburetor and discard the gasket. Disconnect the idle wire from the ratchet adjustment lever.

4. Installation is the reverse of removal.

Disassembly/Reassembly

Refer to **Figure 34** (8, 9.9 and 15 hp) or **Figure 35** (20 and 25 hp) for this procedure.

1. Remove the primer knob and shaft components from the carburetor.

2. On 8-15 hp models so equipped, remove 2 screws and the air intake cover from the carburetor.

3. Remove the slow speed mixture screw and spring (**Figure 36**).

4. Invert the carburetor, remove the fuel bowl retainer (**Figure 37**) and lift off the fuel bowl (**Figure 38**). Note that the high speed jet is screwed into the fuel bowl retainer (**Figure 37**).

5. Lift the float off the carburetor body (**Figure 38**).

6. Remove the primer cover screws. Remove the cover, diaphragm, gasket and spring (**Figure 39**). Discard the gasket.

7. Remove the plug from the bottom of the primer housing. Remove the gasket, spring and check ball (**Figure 40**).

8. Remove the screw (A, **Figure 41**) holding the float hinge pin. Remove the pin and float hinge,

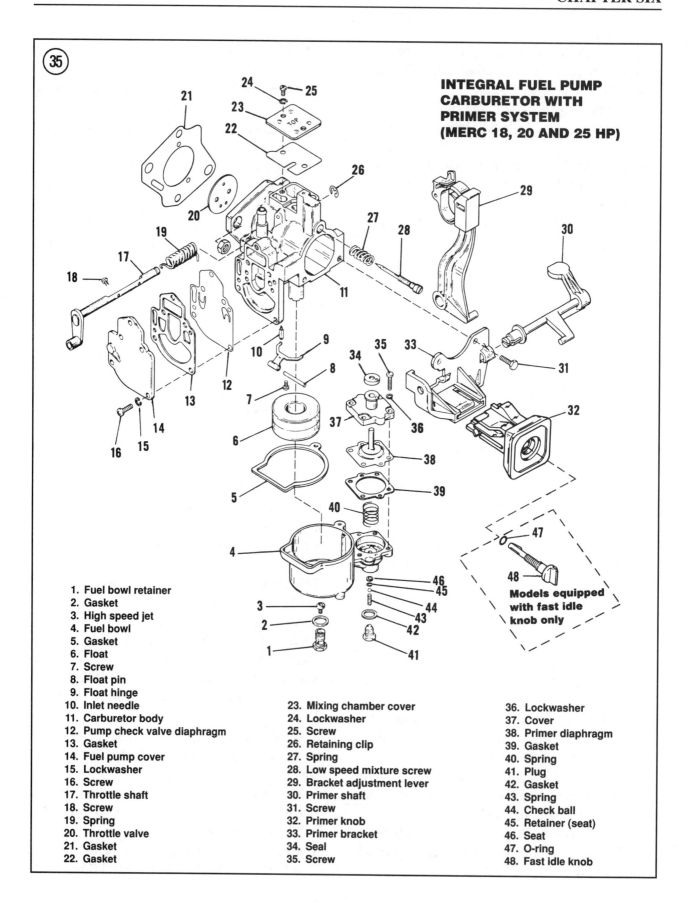

INTEGRAL FUEL PUMP CARBURETOR WITH PRIMER SYSTEM (MERC 18, 20 AND 25 HP)

Models equipped with fast idle knob only

1. Fuel bowl retainer
2. Gasket
3. High speed jet
4. Fuel bowl
5. Gasket
6. Float
7. Screw
8. Float pin
9. Float hinge
10. Inlet needle
11. Carburetor body
12. Pump check valve diaphragm
13. Gasket
14. Fuel pump cover
15. Lockwasher
16. Screw
17. Throttle shaft
18. Screw
19. Spring
20. Throttle valve
21. Gasket
22. Gasket
23. Mixing chamber cover
24. Lockwasher
25. Screw
26. Retaining clip
27. Spring
28. Low speed mixture screw
29. Bracket adjustment lever
30. Primer shaft
31. Screw
32. Primer knob
33. Primer bracket
34. Seal
35. Screw
36. Lockwasher
37. Cover
38. Primer diaphragm
39. Gasket
40. Spring
41. Plug
42. Gasket
43. Spring
44. Check ball
45. Retainer (seat)
46. Seat
47. O-ring
48. Fast idle knob

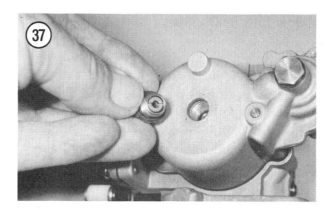

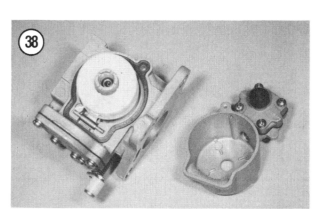

then the inlet needle. Remove the fuel bowl gasket (B, **Figure 41**).

> *NOTE*
> *The inlet needle valve seat is not serviceable. If the seat is worn or damaged, the carburetor body must be replaced.*

9. Remove the mixing chamber cover and gasket (**Figure 42**). Discard the gasket.

10. Remove the 5 screws holding the fuel pump to the carburetor. Remove the pump assembly. See **Figure 43**.

11. Reassembly is the reverse of disassembly. Replace all gaskets during reassembly. Adjust the float level as described in this chapter.

Cleaning and Inspection

1. Clean the carburetor body and metal parts using a carburetor cleaning solution to remove

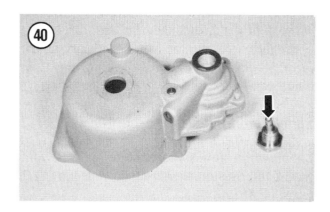

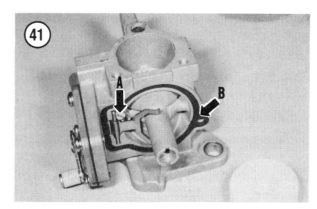

gum, dirt and varnish. Follow the instructions provided with the cleaner.

2. Rinse the carburetor components in clean solvent and dry with compressed air. Be sure to blow out all orifices, nozzles and passages thoroughly.

> *CAUTION*
> *Do not use wire or drill bits to clean any carburetor passages. Doing so can alter calibration and ruin the carburetor.*

3. Check the carburetor body casting for stripped threads, cracks or other damage.

4. Check the float for fuel absorption, deterioration or other damage. Replace the float as necessary.

5. Check the inlet needle and seat for excessive wear. Replace the needle if necessary. If the seat is worn or damaged, replace the carburetor body assembly.

Float Adjustment

Check the float level as shown in **Figure 44**. The top of the float should be 1 in. (25.4 mm) above the carburetor casting. If necessary, adjust the float level by carefully bending the float hinge. See A, **Figure 44**.

Slow Speed Mixture Adjustment

1. Screw the slow speed mixture screw inward until lightly seated, then back out 1-1/4 to 1-1/2 turns.

2. Start the engine and run at fast idle (in neutral) until warmed up to normal operating temperature. Throttle back to idle for approximately 1 minute to stabilize engine speed.

3. Push the primer/fast idle knob in completely and turn knob fully clockwise.

4. Shift into FORWARD gear.

5. Turn the slow speed mixture screw counterclockwise until the engine begins to run roughly due to an over-rich mixture. Note the position of the screw.

6. Turn the slow speed mixture screw clockwise until the engine begins to idle smoothly and engine speed increases. Continue turning clockwise until the engine begins to misfire due to an excessively lean mixture. Again, note the position of the screw.

7. Set the mixture screw at a half-way point between too rich and too lean. Do not adjust mixture any leaner than necessary to obtain a reasonably smooth idle condition. It is good practice to adjust the mixture slightly rich instead of too lean.

Idle Speed Adjustment (Models Equipped With Idle Speed Screw)

1. Push the primer/fast idle knob in completely and turn knob fully clockwise.

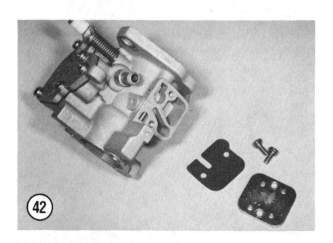

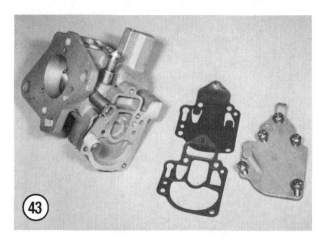

2. With the engine running at idle speed in forward gear, adjust the idle speed screw to obtain 600-700 rpm on 8 hp models or 700-800 rpm on 9.9-25 hp models.

High Speed Mixture Adjustment

The high speed mixture is controlled by a fixed main jet. Normally, no adjustment is required. However, extreme changes in temperature, humidity or elevation may require a change in jet size. The standard main jet for normal operation is as follows:

   a. 8 hp—0.046 in.
   b. 9.9 hp—0.056 in.
   c. 15 hp—0.066 in.
   d. 20 hp—0.046 in.
   e. 25 hp—0.080 in.

Increasing main jet size richens the mixture while decreasing main jet size leans the mixture.

The standard main jet installed at the factory should be acceptable for operation at sea level to 2500 ft. (762 m) above sea level. Refer to **Table 1** for recommended main jet sizes for different elevations.

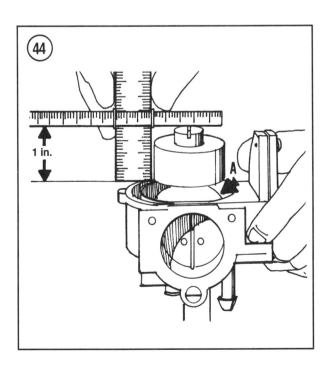

WMA CARBURETOR (40 HP MODELS)

The 40 hp models use a dual carburetor arrangement with each carburetor providing fuel for 2 cylinders. An electrically operated cold-start enrichment system is used in place of a conventional choke. A vent jet (back draft) circuit is used for improved mid-range fuel economy, and the high speed fuel mixture is metered by fixed main jets.

Removal/Installation

If necessary, remove the fuel pump as described in this chapter, for better access to the carburetors.

1. Remove the oil reservoir. See Chapter Eleven.
2. Remove and discard the sta-strap clamping the fuel delivery hose to the top carburetor. Disconnect the fuel hose.
3. Disconnect the primer hose from the top carburetor.
4. Remove the 4 nuts (2 at each carburetor) securing the carburetors to the power head, then remove both carburetors as an assembly. Remove and discard the carburetor gaskets.
5. Install the carburetors by reversing the removal procedure. Use new gaskets and tighten the mounting nuts to 110 in.-lb. (12.4 N•m). Securely clamp the fuel delivery and primer hoses using new sta-straps.
6. Install the oil reservoir and bleed the injection system as described in Chapter Eleven.

Disassembly

Refer to **Figure 45** for this procedure. The following describes disassembly procedures for the top carburetor. The bottom carburetor is identical except the float bowl retainer.

1. Disconnect the fuel and primer hoses and the throttle linkage between the upper and lower carburetors. See **Figure 46**.

6

2. Remove the 4 screws securing the cover plate to the carburetor. Remove the cover plate and gasket.

3. Remove the primer fitting/float bowl retainer, float bowl and float bowl gasket from the carburetor.

4. Remove the float pin and float. Remove the inlet needle and baffle. See **Figure 47**.

5. Remove the main jet (**Figure 47**).

> *NOTE*
> *On WMA9 carburetors, the main jet is screwed into the bottom of the body casting.*

6. Remove the main nozzle (**Figure 48**) using a wide-blade screwdriver. Remove the venturi from the carburetor throat.

7. Remove the vent jet and the idle mixture screw and spring (**Figure 49**).

> *NOTE*
> *Further disassembly is not necessary for normal cleaning and inspection. Proceed to Step 8 only if the throttle shaft or throttle valve requires replacement.*

8. Remove the throttle return spring (10, **Figure 45**) from the throttle shaft.

9. Remove the 2 screws securing the throttle valve to the throttle shaft. Remove the throttle valve, then pull the shaft out the top of the carburetor.

Cleaning and Inspection

1. Clean the carburetor body and metal parts using a carburetor cleaning solution to remove gum, dirt and varnish. Follow the instructions provided with the cleaner.

2. Rinse the carburetor components in clean solvent and dry with compressed air. Be sure to blow out all orifices, nozzles and passages thoroughly.

> *CAUTION*
> *Do not use wire or drill bits to clean any carburetor passages. Doing so can alter calibration and ruin the carburetor.*

3. Check the carburetor body casting for stripped threads, cracks or other damage.

4. Check the float for fuel absorption, deterioration or other damage. Replace the float as necessary.

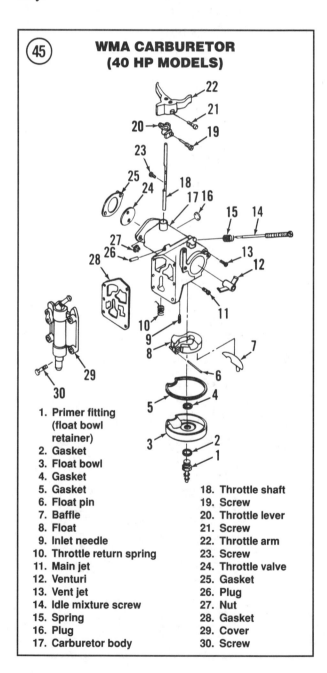

WMA CARBURETOR (40 HP MODELS)

1. Primer fitting (float bowl retainer)
2. Gasket
3. Float bowl
4. Gasket
5. Gasket
6. Float pin
7. Baffle
8. Float
9. Inlet needle
10. Throttle return spring
11. Main jet
12. Venturi
13. Vent jet
14. Idle mixture screw
15. Spring
16. Plug
17. Carburetor body
18. Throttle shaft
19. Screw
20. Throttle lever
21. Screw
22. Throttle arm
23. Screw
24. Throttle valve
25. Gasket
26. Plug
27. Nut
28. Gasket
29. Cover
30. Screw

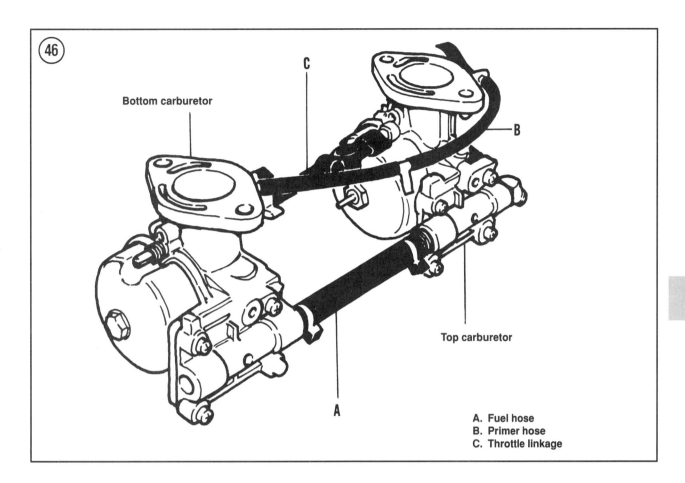

Bottom carburetor

Top carburetor

A. Fuel hose
B. Primer hose
C. Throttle linkage

6

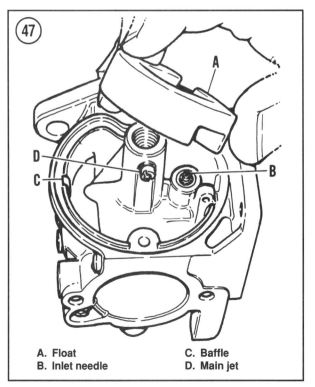

A. Float
B. Inlet needle
C. Baffle
D. Main jet

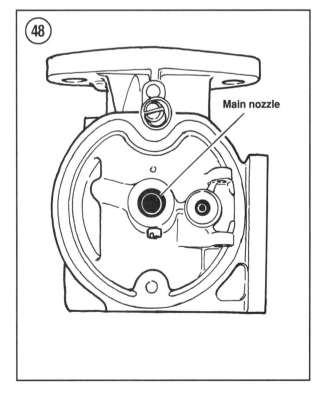

Main nozzle

5. Check the inlet needle and seat for excessive wear. Replace the needle and seat as an assembly if necessary.

Reassembly

Refer to **Figure 45** for this procedure.

1. If removed, insert the throttle shaft into the carburetor body.

2. Apply a suitable thread locking compound to the threads of the throttle valve screws, then install the screws and tighten securely.

3. Install the throttle return spring to the throttle shaft.

4. Install the idle mixture screw and spring (**Figure 49**). Turn the screw inward until lightly seated, then back out 1-1/4 turns.

5. Install the vent jet (**Figure 49**). Tighten the vent jet to 14 in.-lb. (1.6 N.m).

6. Install the main nozzle (**Figure 48**) into the carburetor body. Tighten the nozzle securely.

7. Install the main jet (**Figure 47**) and tighten to 6 in.-lb. (0.7 N.m).

8. Install the float baffle (**Figure 47**) into the carburetor body.

9. Attach the inlet needle to the float using the retaining wire. Lower the inlet needle into its seat, locate the float in the proper position and install the float pin. Securely seat the splined area of the pin into the mounting hole.

10. Check the float adjustment as described in this chapter.

11. Install the float bowl using a new gasket. Tighten the primer fitting (or bowl retainer on the bottom carburetor) to 33 in.-lb. (3.7 N.m).

12. Install the cover plate using a new gasket. Tighten the 4 cover screws to 18 in.-lb. (2.0 N.m).

13. Connect the throttle linkage (**Figure 46**).

14. Connect the fuel and primer hoses to the carburetors. Securely clamp the hoses using new sta-straps.

15. Install the carburetors as described in this chapter.

Float Level and Drop Adjustment

1. With the float bowl removed and the carburetor inverted, measure the float level as shown in **Figure 50**. The measurement from the bowl mating surface to the bottom of the float should be 1/4 in. (6.4 mm) on Model WMA-7B carburetors or 11/16 in. (17.5 mm) on Model WMA-9 carburetors. Bend the adjustment tab as required to set the float.

NOTE
*Bending the metal adjustment tab (A, **Figure 50**) toward the inlet needle (with the float installed) decreases float level.*

2. Position the carburetor upright and measure the float drop as shown in **Figure 51**. The distance from the bottom of the float to the top of the main jet should be 1/32 to 1/16 in. (0.79-1.6 mm). Float drop is not adjustable. If the drop measurement is not as specified, the float must be replaced.

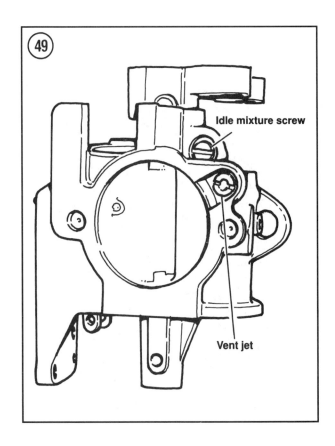
(49) Idle mixture screw / Vent jet

Idle Speed Adjustment

Adjust idle speed as described under *40 HP MODELS* in Chapter Five.

Idle Mixture Adjustment

1. Make sure the idle mixture screw is turned 1-1/4 turns out from a lightly seated position.
2. Place the outboard into a test tank or on the boat in the water.
3. Start the engine and allow it to warm to normal operating temperature. With the engine running at idle speed, shift into FORWARD gear.
4. Slowly turn the idle mixture screw counterclockwise until the engine runs roughly due to an over-rich mixture. Next, turn the mixture

screw clockwise until the engine speed begins to increase.
5. Continue turning the screw clockwise until the engine begins to misfire due to an excessively lean mixture. Note the position of the screw.
6. Turn the idle mixture screw to a position 1-1/4 to 1-3/4 turns out from the lean position noted in Step 5. Do not adjust the idle mixture any leaner than necessary to provide a reasonably smooth idle. It is always good practice to adjust the mixture slightly rich rather than too lean.

Vent Jet Adjustment

The vent jet (**Figure 49**) is used to provide improved mid-range fuel economy by reducing the atmospheric pressure inside the float bowl. A smaller vent jet will lean mid-range fuel-air mixture. To richen mid-range mixture, increase (or remove jet) vent jet size.

The standard vent jet size for normal operation at sea level to 2500 ft. (762 m), is 0.098 in. Refer

6

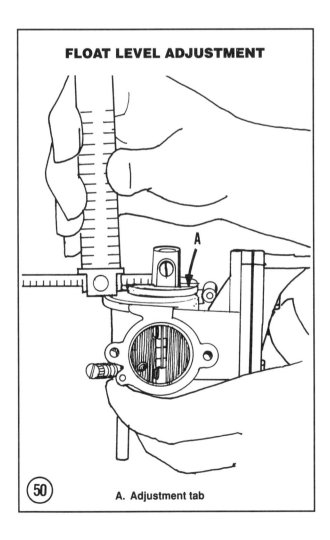

FLOAT LEVEL ADJUSTMENT

A. Adjustment tab

⑤⓪

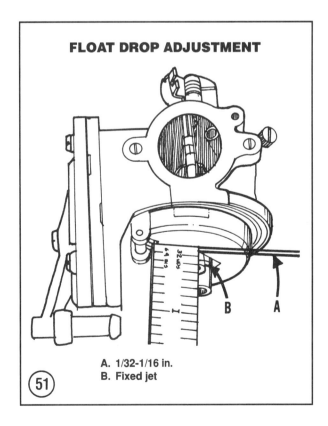

FLOAT DROP ADJUSTMENT

A. 1/32-1/16 in.
B. Fixed jet

⑤①

to **Table 2** for recommended jet sizes at different elevations.

High Speed Mixture Adjustment

The high speed mixture is controlled by the fixed main jet. Normally, no adjustment is required. However, extreme changes in temperature, humidity or elevation may require a change in jet size.

The standard main jet size for normal operation is 0.057 in. and should be acceptable for operation at sea level to 2500 ft. (762 m) above sea level. Increasing main jet size richens the mixture while decreasing main jet size leans the mixture. Refer to **Table 2** for recommended main jet sizes for different elevations.

MERCARB CENTER BOWL CARBURETOR (50 AND 60 HP MODELS PRIOR TO SERIAL NO. D000750)

Removal/Installation

1. Remove 8 screws securing the air box cover to the air box. Remove the air box cover.

2. Remove the nut and disconnect the ground wire from the mounting stud adjacent to the starter motor.

3. Remove the starter solenoid mounting fasteners, but do not disconnect solenoid wires.

4. If so equipped, remove the power trim solenoid fasteners, but do not disconnect the solenoid wires.

5. Remove the nut and disconnect the ground wire from the mounting stud at top of the air box on the port side.

6. Disconnect the yellow/black wire from the choke solenoid.

7. Remove the bolt and washer from the fuel connector.

8. Remove the air box from the outboard. Allow the choke solenoid linkage to remain connected to the carburetors.

9. Remove the 4 Phillips screws securing the carburetor plate to the carburetors. See **Figure 52**. Remove the plate.

10. If removing both carburetors, disconnect the linkage at A, **Figure 53**. To remove only one carburetor, disconnect linkage at B (top carburetor) or at C (bottom carburetor).

11. Disconnect the fuel hose at the fuel pump if removing both carburetors. If removing only the top carburetor, disconnect the fuel hose at D, **Figure 53**. If removing only the bottom carburetor, disconnect the fuel hose at E, **Figure 53**.

12. Remove 2 bolts holding each carburetor to the power head (F, **Figure 53**). Remove the carburetors and gaskets from the power head.

13. If both carburetors are removed, disconnect the choke linkage (A, **Figure 54**) and remove the

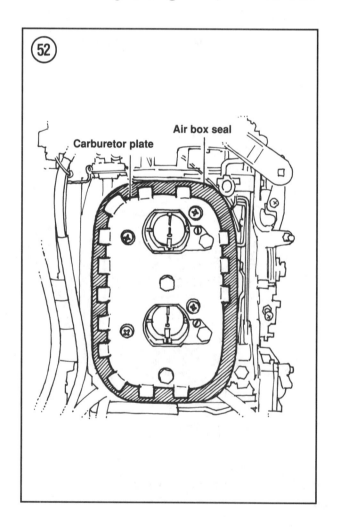

(52)

Carburetor plate   Air box seal

fuel hoses from the carburetor inlet fittings (B, **Figure 54**).

14. Install new carburetor flange gaskets during reinstallation. Do not use gasket sealant on the gaskets.

15. Install the carburetor(s) and mounting bolts (F, **Figure 53**). Tighten the bolts to 110 in.-lb. (12.4 N.m).

16. Connect the fuel hoses and securely clamp using new sta-straps.

17. Install new gaskets (without sealant) between the carburetors and carburetor plate, then install the carburetor plate and secure with the Phillips screws (**Figure 52**).

18. While guiding the choke solenoid plunger into the solenoid, install the air box onto the carburetor plate and mounting studs.

19. Connect the yellow/black wires to the choke solenoid. Secure with a lockwasher and nut.

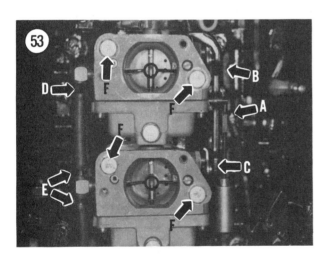

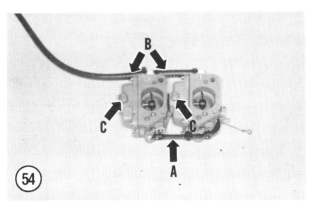

20. Attach the ground wires to the mounting studs, then install the washers and nuts. Tighten the nuts securely.

21. Attach the fuel connector to the air box.

22. Mount the starter solenoid and power trim solenoids (if so equipped) to the air box. Make sure the solenoid ground wires are properly connected.

23. Install the air box cover using 8 screws to complete installation.

Disassembly

Refer to **Figure 55** for this procedure.

1. Remove the main jet plug and gasket (C, **Figure 54**) from the fuel bowl.

2. Remove the screws and lockwashers holding the fuel bowl to the carburetor body. Separate the fuel bowl from the carburetor (**Figure 56**).

3. Remove and discard the fuel bowl gasket.

4. Push the float hinge pins toward the outer side of the carburetor with a small punch. Remove the hinge pins and float assembly. Remove the float lever hinge pin by pushing the pin toward the rear of the carburetor using a small punch. Remove the pin and lever (**Figure 57**).

5. Remove the inlet needle from seat (A, **Figure 58**). Remove the inlet seat using an appropriate size wrench. Remove and discard the metal gasket under the seat.

NOTE
The fuel inlet fitting is a press fit on late models and can not be removed from the carburetor body in Step 6.

6. Remove the fuel inlet fitting (B, **Figure 58**). Check the inlet screen in the carburetor body. If the screen is loose, torn or damaged, remove the screen.

7. Remove the screw and lockwasher holding the enrichment valve assembly to the carburetor body. Remove the valve assembly (**Figure 59**).

8. Remove the idle mixture screw and spring (**Figure 60**).

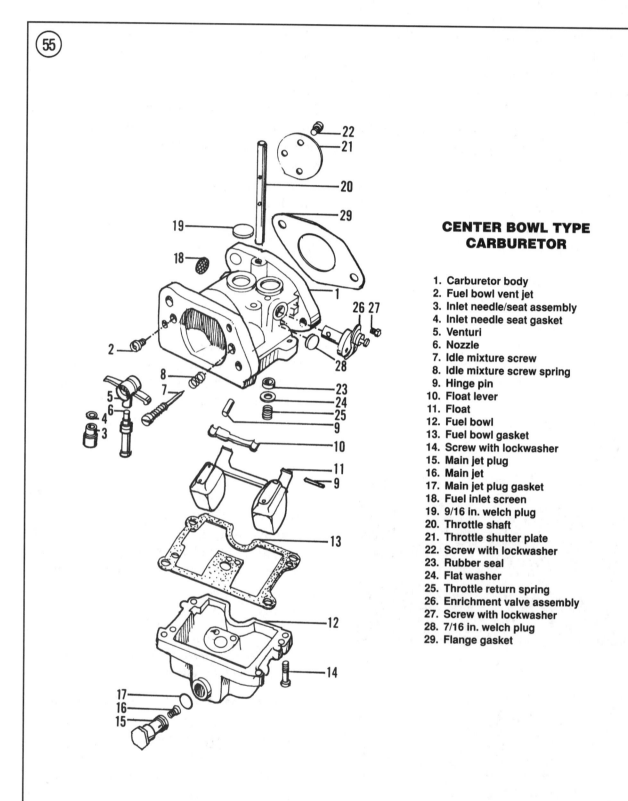

**CENTER BOWL TYPE
CARBURETOR**

1. Carburetor body
2. Fuel bowl vent jet
3. Inlet needle/seat assembly
4. Inlet needle seat gasket
5. Venturi
6. Nozzle
7. Idle mixture screw
8. Idle mixture screw spring
9. Hinge pin
10. Float lever
11. Float
12. Fuel bowl
13. Fuel bowl gasket
14. Screw with lockwasher
15. Main jet plug
16. Main jet
17. Main jet plug gasket
18. Fuel inlet screen
19. 9/16 in. welch plug
20. Throttle shaft
21. Throttle shutter plate
22. Screw with lockwasher
23. Rubber seal
24. Flat washer
25. Throttle return spring
26. Enrichment valve assembly
27. Screw with lockwasher
28. 7/16 in. welch plug
29. Flange gasket

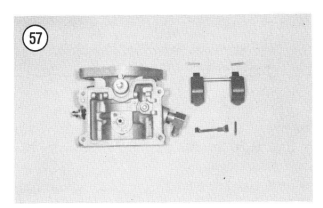

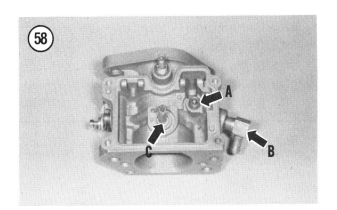

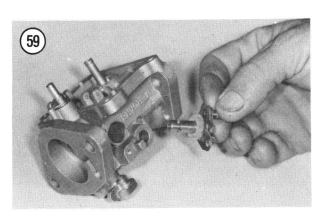

9. Remove the fuel bowl vent jet (arrow, **Figure 60**) from the carburetor with a jet wrench or a suitable screwdriver.

CAUTION
The carburetor nozzle is a press fit on later models and cannot be removed in Step 10. If the nozzle on such models is damaged, the carburetor body must be replaced.

10. Remove the nozzle (C, **Figure 58**) from the carburetor body using a wide-blade screwdriver.

11. After removing the nozzle, remove the plastic venturi. **Figure 61** shows the nozzle and venturi removed.

12. Remove the throttle return spring, flat washer and rubber seal from the bottom of the throttle shaft.

CAUTION
When removing the welch plugs in Step 13, do not allow the drill to pass into the

6

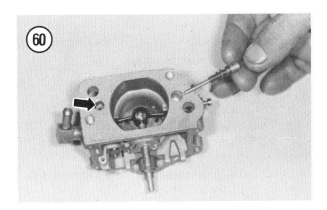

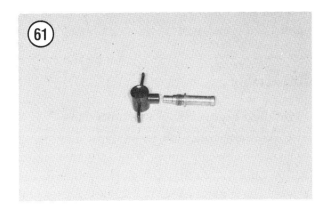

carburetor casting or the discharge ports may be damaged.

13. Remove the 3 welch plugs covering the bypass holes in the carburetor body. Carefully drill a 1/8 in. hole into each plug and pry the plug from the body with a pointed punch or similar tool. This completes the necessary disassembly for cleaning and inspection.

14. Inspect the throttle valve and shaft for excessive wear or damage. If the throttle valve or shaft requires replacement, remove the 2 screws holding the valve to the shaft. Remove the valve from the carburetor throat, then pull the shaft out of the carburetor.

Cleaning and Inspection

1. Clean the carburetor body, fuel bowl and metal parts in a carburetor cleaning solution to remove gum, dirt and varnish. Follow the instructions provided with the cleaner.

2. Rinse the carburetor components thoroughly with hot water, then clean solvent and dry with compressed air. Be sure to blow through all orifices, nozzles and passages.

CAUTION
Do not use wire or drill bits to clean carburetor passages. Doing so can alter calibration and ruin the carburetor.

3. Check the float for fuel absorption or deterioration. Replace the float as necessary.

4. Check the inlet needle and seat for excessive wear or other damage. If necessary, replace the inlet needle and seat as an assembly.

Reassembly

Refer to **Figure 55** for this procedure.

1. Install new welch plugs (convex side facing out) into the casting bores. With a suitable punch and hammer, carefully flatten the plugs in the bores to provide a tight seal. Coat the plug and

bore with fingernail polish to provide additional sealing ability.

2. If removed, insert the throttle shaft with the lever attached into the carburetor body.

3. Position the throttle valve into the shaft with the stamped numbers on the valve facing outward (toward rear of carburetor). Install new throttle valve screws and lockwashers. Tighten the screws securely.

4. Install the rubber seal onto the throttle shaft with the lip facing toward the carburetor.

NOTE
During throttle return spring installation, be sure the strongest spring (0.034 in. wire diameter) is installed to the top carburetor.

5. Install the flat washer and throttle return spring. Hold the throttle valve closed and connect the spring.

6. Install the idle mixture screw and spring. Turn the screw in until lightly seated, then back out 1 full turn.

7. Install the fuel bowl vent jet into the carburetor body and tighten securely.

8. Install the enrichment valve assembly and tighten the screw securely.

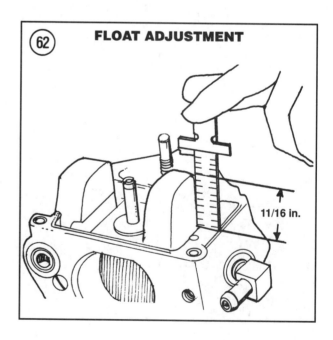

(62) **FLOAT ADJUSTMENT**

11/16 in.

9. Install the venturi in the carburetor bore slots. Install the nozzle through the top of the carburetor and into the venturi. Tighten the nozzle securely using a wide-blade screwdriver.

NOTE
The ridged side of the rubber insert must face away from the inlet needle when installed in the needle seat assembly in Step 10.

10. Install the rubber insert into the inlet needle seat. Make sure the smooth side of the insert is facing the inlet needle point.

11. Install the float lever into the carburetor body and secure with the hinge pin. Push the hinge pin into the carburetor body holes (toward the front of carburetor) until the knurled end of the pin is flush with the body.

12. Install the float assembly into the carburetor body and insert the hinge pins toward the center of the carburetor. Push the hinge pins in until the knurled ends of the pins are flush with outer edge of the carburetor body holes.

13. Check float adjustment as described in this chapter.

14. Using a new gasket, install the fuel bowl onto the carburetor body. Tighten the screws securely.

15. Screw the main jet into the main jet plug. Using a new gasket, install the main jet plug into the fuel bowl.

16. If necessary, install a new filter screen into the carburetor body inlet.

17. Install the fuel inlet fitting (if removed) into the carburetor body and tighten securely.

Float Adjustment

1. With the fuel bowl removed, invert the carburetor. Measure the distance from the fuel bowl mating surface to the bottom of the float as shown in **Figure 62**. The distance should be 11/16 in. (17.5 mm).

2. If adjustment is necessary, carefully bend the float lever within the area shown in **Figure 63** as required to obtain the specified distance (**Figure 62**).

Fuel Bowl Vent Adjustment

The carburetor is equipped with a fixed vent jet. The jet size for normal operation at sea level to 2500 ft. (762 m) above sea level is 0.096 in. Refer to **Table 2** for recommended jet sizes for different elevations.

High Speed Mixture Adjustment

The high speed mixture is controlled by the fixed main jet. Normally, no adjustment is required. However, extreme changes in temperature, humidity or elevation may require a change in jet size.

The standard main jet size is 0.058 in. on 50 hp models and 0.0785 in. for the top carburetor and 0.072 in. for the bottom carburetor on 60 hp models.

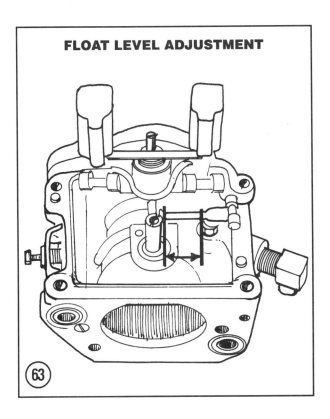

FLOAT LEVEL ADJUSTMENT

63

The standard main jet should be acceptable for operation at sea level to 2500 ft. (762 m) above sea level. Increasing main jet size richens the mixture while decreasing main jet size leans the mixture. Refer to **Table 2** for recommended main jet sizes for different elevations.

Idle Adjustments

NOTE
For best results, perform the final carburetor adjustments with the outboard mounted on a boat in the water, the correct propeller installed, running at idle speed in forward gear with boat movement unrestrained.

Do not adjust idle mixture any leaner than necessary to provide a reasonably smooth idle. It is always good practice to adjust the mixture slightly rich rather than too lean.

1. Make sure the idle mixture screws are 1 turn out from a lightly seated position.

2. With the outboard in a test tank or installed on a boat in the water, start the engine and warm it to normal operating temperature.

3. Shift into FORWARD gear. With the engine running at idle speed (550-600 rpm in forward gear), slowly turn the idle mixture screw counterclockwise until the engine begins to run roughly due to an over-rich mixture.

4. Turn the idle mixture screw clockwise until the engine speed increases and idles smoothly. The engine should accelerate cleanly without hesitation. If hesitation and/or backfiring are noted during acceleration, the mixture is too lean.

5. Adjust the idle speed as described in Chapter Five.

6. Accelerate the engine to approximately 4000-5000 rpm to clear any excess fuel from the crankcase, then recheck the idle speed.

WME CARBURETOR (50 AND 60 HP SERIAL NO. D000750-ON, 75, 90, 100 AND 115 HP MODELS)

WME type carburetors are used on 50 and 60 hp models after serial No. D000749, 75 and 90 hp 3-cylinder models and 100 and 115 hp 4-cylinder models. One carburetor per cylinder is used. A float bowl vent (back draft) jet is used to improve mid-range fuel economy. High speed fuel mixture is metered by a fixed main jet. All models are equipped with an electrically operated cold-start enrichment system to aid cold starting. See *Enrichment Valve And Choke Solenoid Systems* in this chapter.

NOTE
WME carburetors can be identified by the number stamped in the face of the air box mounting flange (early models) or in the top of the carburetor mounting flange (later models). Each identification number includes a suffix number 1 to 3 (3-cylinder models) or 1 to 4 (4-cylinder models). This suffix number indicates carburetor position on the power

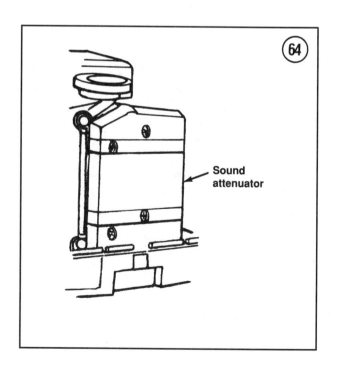

Sound attenuator

head with the top carburetor being No. 1. Each carburetor must be installed in the correct location according to its suffix number.

On 100 and 115 hp models, cylinders 3 and 4 are inoperative at engine speeds below approximately 1600-2000 rpm due to reduced fuel flow from their respective carburetors. On the carburetors used on cylinders 3 and 4, the off idle discharge ports are relocated farther from the power head so the fuel-air mixture at idle speeds is too lean for combustion to occur, yet adequate for proper engine lubrication. As the engine speed reaches approximately 1600-2000 rpm (depending on engine load), air flow through the carburetors increases and the fuel-air mixture to cylinders 3 and 4 becomes sufficient to support combustion, resulting in all 4 cylinders being operational. An accelerator pump system injects fuel into cylinders 3 and 4 during acceleration to

prevent hesitation during the transition from 2 cylinder to 4 cylinder operation.

This system is known as Mercury 2+2 concept and is used to reduce smoke and hydrocarbon emissions at idle speeds while improving fuel economy during trolling.

Removal/Installation (50 and 60 hp)

1. Disconnect the battery and spark plug leads.
2. Remove 4 screws and lift off the sound attenuator assembly (**Figure 64**).
3. Remove the 6 carburetor mounting screws (A, **Figure 65**), then remove the attenuator mounting plates (B) and carburetors as an assembly.
4. Disconnect the throttle linkage and primer hoses from the carburetors.
5. Install the carburetors by reversing the removal procedure. Use new carburetor gaskets (without sealant). Tighten the 6 carburetor mounting screws (**Figure 65**) to 100 in.-lb. (11.3 N.m).
6. Complete timing, synchronizing and adjustment procedures as described in Chapter Five.

Removal/Installation (75 and 90 hp)

1. Disconnect the battery and spark plug leads.
2. Disconnect the wiring harness retainer clamp and fuel connector from the front cowl bracket. Remove 2 cowl bracket bolts, then remove the front cowl bracket.
3. Remove 8 screws retaining the air box cover, then remove the cover.
4. Remove the oil reservoir lower support bolt and the 2 reservoir upper neck brace bolts.
5. Remove 6 air box/carburetor mounting nuts and remove the air box.
6. Disconnect the oil lines from the oil reservoir. Plug the lines and remove the reservoir.
7. Disconnect the throttle linkage from the center carburetor ball socket.

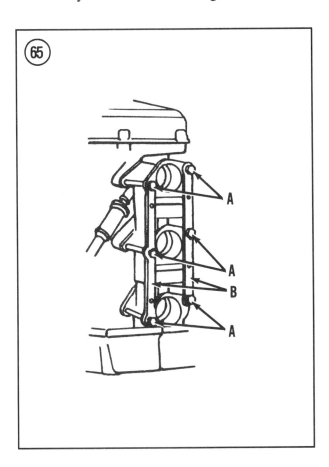

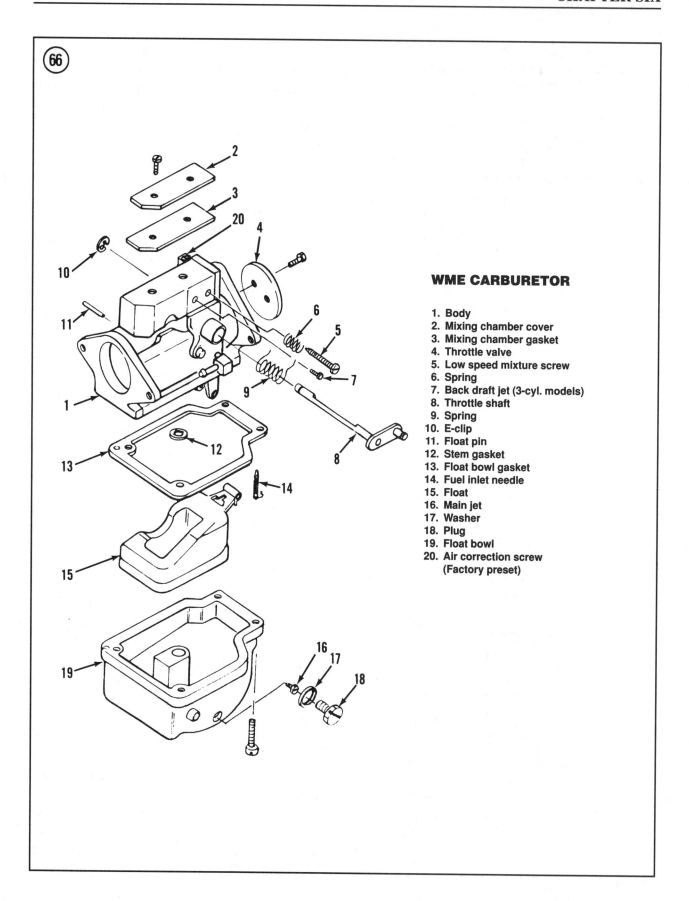

WME CARBURETOR

1. Body
2. Mixing chamber cover
3. Mixing chamber gasket
4. Throttle valve
5. Low speed mixture screw
6. Spring
7. Back draft jet (3-cyl. models)
8. Throttle shaft
9. Spring
10. E-clip
11. Float pin
12. Stem gasket
13. Float bowl gasket
14. Fuel inlet needle
15. Float
16. Main jet
17. Washer
18. Plug
19. Float bowl
20. Air correction screw
    (Factory preset)

8. Disconnect the fuel delivery and primer hoses from the top carburetor.

9. Withdraw the carburetors and throttle linkage as a unit.

10. Separate the carburetors from the throttle linkage.

11. Installation is the reverse of removal while noting the following:

   a. Use new carburetor mounting gaskets and new air box gaskets. Do not use sealant on the gaskets.

   b. Tighten the 6 air box/carburetor mounting nuts to 100 in.-lb. (11.3 N•m).

12. Complete timing, synchronizing and adjustment procedures as described in Chapter Five.

Removal/Installation (100 and 115 hp)

1. Disconnect the battery and spark plug leads.

2. Disconnect the fuel delivery hose from the engine bayonet fitting.

3. Remove the 2 oil reservoir upper neck brace bolts.

4. Remove the 2 bottom cowl support bracket bolts.

5. Remove the vapor return hose from the "T" fitting located between the fuel deliver bayonet fitting and the fuel pump.

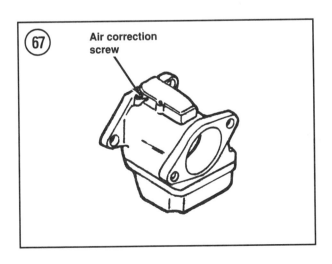

6. Remove the bayonet fitting retaining bolt at the bottom cowl support bracket, then withdraw the support bracket.

7. Remove 10 air box cover screws and remove the cover.

8. Remove the oil reservoir front support bracket bolt.

9. Remove the 8 air box/carburetor mounting nuts and remove the air box.

10. Disconnect the fuel hoses from the carburetor fittings.

11. Withdraw the carburetor assemblies and throttle linkage as a unit.

12. Separate the carburetors from the throttle linkage.

13. Installation is the reverse of removal while noting the following:

   a. Use new carburetor mounting gaskets and new air box gasket. Do not use sealer on the gaskets.

   b. Tighten the 8 air box/carburetor mounting nuts to 100 in.-lb. (11.3 N•m).

14. Complete timing, synchronizing and adjusting as described in Chapter Five.

Disassembly

Refer to **Figure 66** for this procedure.

NOTE
*Do not remove or attempt to adjust the air correction screw (**Figure 67**). This screw is preset by the manufacturer and should not require additional adjustment. Conventional carburetor cleaning solutions will not affect the sealant securing the screw adjustment.*

1. Remove 4 screws and remove the float bowl and gasket.

2. Remove the float pin, float and inlet needle. The inlet needle should be attached to the float with a wire clip.

3. Remove the stem gasket.

4. Remove 2 screws securing the mixing chamber cover (**Figure 68**) to the carburetor body. Remove the cover and gasket.

NOTE
On 100 and 115 hp models, only the top carburetors (Nos. 1 and 2) are equipped with low speed mixture screws. The bottom 2 carburetors have plugs installed in place of mixture screws.

5. Remove the low speed mixture screw and spring (**Figure 68**).
6. 3-Cylinder models—Remove the vent (back draft) jet. See **Figure 68**.
7. Remove the main jet plug and gasket from the float bowl, then remove the main jet. See **Figure 69**.

NOTE
Further disassembly is not necessary for normal cleaning and inspection.

8. Inspect the throttle shaft and valve for excessive wear or damage. If throttle shaft or valve removal is necessary, remove the shaft E-clip (10, **Figure 66**). Next, remove the 2 screws securing the valve to the shaft. Remove the throttle valve, then pull the shaft from the carburetor body.

Cleaning and Inspection

1. Clean the carburetor body, float bowl and metal parts in a carburetor cleaning solution to remove gum, dirt and varnish. Follow the instructions provided with the cleaner.
2. Rinse the carburetor components thoroughly with hot water and blow dry with compressed air. Be sure to blow through all orifices, nozzles and passages.

CAUTION
Do not use wire or drill bits to clean carburetor passages. Doing so can alter calibration and ruin the carburetor.

3. Check the plastic float for fuel absorption or deterioration. If available, weigh the float using a gram scale. If the float weighs more than 7-8 grams, it has absorbed fuel and must be replaced.

4. Inspect the carburetor body and float bowl for cracks, damaged threads, restricted passages or other damage. Replace as necessary.

5. Check the inlet needle for excessive wear or damage and replace as necessary.

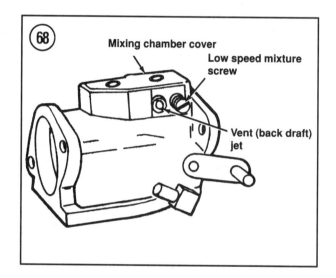

68 Mixing chamber cover
Low speed mixture screw
Vent (back draft) jet

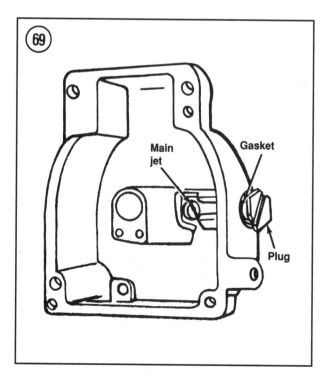

69 Main jet
Gasket
Plug

Reassembly

Refer to **Figure 66** for this procedure.

1. If removed, insert the throttle shaft into the carburetor body. Install the throttle shaft E-clip.

   a. Spray the threads of the throttle valve screws with Loctite Primer N.

   b. Allow the primer to air dry, then apply a suitable thread locking compound to the screw threads.

   c. Install the throttle valve (numbers facing outward) and secure with the 2 screws. Make sure the throttle shaft return spring is properly engaged with the throttle lever and the boss on the carburetor body.

2. Install the main jet and fuel bowl plug, using a new gasket (**Figure 69**).

3. 3-Cylinder models—Install the vent (back draft) jet (**Figure 68**).

4. Install the low speed mixture screw and spring. Turn the screw in until lightly seated, then back out:

   a. 1-1/4 turns—50 and 60 hp.

   b. 1-1/2 turns—75, 90 and 115 hp.

   c. 1-3/4 turns—100 hp.

5. Install the mixing chamber cover using a new gasket. Tighten the cover screws securely.

6. Install a new stem gasket.

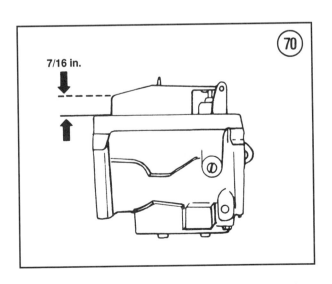

7. Attach the inlet needle wire clip over the metal float tab. Install the float, making sure the inlet needle properly enters the inlet valve seat.

8. Install the float pin.

9. Perform the float adjustment as outlined in this chapter.

10. Install the float bowl using a new gasket. Tighten the bowl screws evenly and securely.

Float Adjustment

1. With the float bowl removed and the carburetor inverted, measure the float height as shown in **Figure 70**.

2. The measurement should be 7/16 in. (11.1 mm).

3. If adjustment is necessary, carefully bend the metal float tab as required.

Idle Speed Adjustment

Adjust the idle speed as described under the appropriate model in Chapter Five.

Low Speed Mixture Adjustment

NOTE
For best results, perform the final carburetor adjustments with the outboard mounted on a boat in the water, the correct propeller installed, running at idle speed in forward gear with boat movement unrestrained.

Do not adjust the low speed mixture any leaner than necessary to provide a reasonably smooth idle. It is always good practice to adjust the mixture slightly rich rather than too lean.

1. With the outboard mounted in a test tank or on a boat in the water, start the engine and run at fast idle until warmed to normal operating temperature.

2. Throttle back to idle for approximately 1 minute to allow the engine to stabilize, then shift into FORWARD gear.

NOTE
The bottom 2 carburetors on 4-cylinder models are not equipped with low speed mixture screws.

3. Turn each low speed mixture screw clockwise until the engine begins to run poorly and misfire due to an excessively lean mixture.
4. Back out the mixture screws 1/4 turn.

NOTE
On 100 and 115 hp models, be sure the accelerator pump is properly adjusted as described in Chapter Five.

5. Quickly accelerate the engine. If the engine hesitates and/or backfires, the mixture is too lean. Back out the mixture screws slightly. Adjust the mixture on each carburetor equally. The engine will accelerate cleanly without hesitation if the mixture is correct.
6. Recheck the idle speed as described in Chapter Five.

Vent (back draft) Jet Adjustment

The carburetor is equipped with a fixed vent (back draft) jet. The vent jet is used to improve mid-range fuel economy. The standard jet size for normal operation should be:
   a. 50 hp—0.092 in.
   b. 60 hp—0.090 in.
   c. 75-90 hp—0.094 in.
   d. 100-115 hp—not installed.
The standard jet size should be acceptable for operation at sea level to 2500 ft. (762 m) above sea level. Refer to **Table 3** for recommended jet sizes for different elevations.

High Speed Mixture Adjustment

The high speed mixture is controlled by the fixed main jet. Normally, no adjustment is required. However, extreme changes in temperature, humidity or elevation may require a change in jet size.

The standard main jet size for normal operation at sea level to 2500 ft. (762 m) above sea level is:
   a. 50 hp—0.052 in.
   b. 60 hp—0.070 in.
   c. 75 hp—0.068 in.
   d. 90 hp—0.072 in.
   e. 100 hp—0.054 in.
   f. 115 hp—0.076 in.
Increasing main jet size richens the mixture while decreasing main jet size leans the mixture. Refer to **Table 3** for recommended main jet sizes for different elevations.

WMH CARBURETOR (135-200 HP MODELS)

WMH carburetors are a 2-barrel center-bowl type used on V6 models (except 250 and 275 hp). The starboard side of the carburetor meters fuel

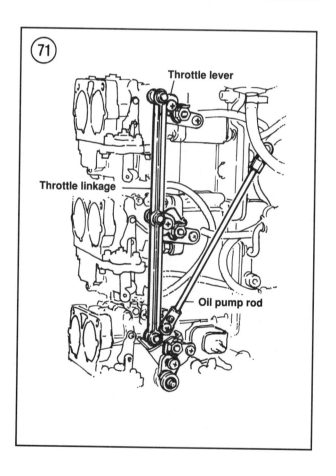

71

Throttle lever

Throttle linkage

Oil pump rod

to the port cylinders and the port side of the carburetor meters fuel to the starboard cylinders. One vent (back draft) jet and one idle air jet are used and affect both cylinder banks.

WMH carburetors can be identified by the letters (WMH) stamped in the top of the starboard side of the carburetor near the air box mounting flange and the numbers stamped in the port side near the air box mounting flange. Each identification number includes a suffix number (1 to 3). This suffix number indicates carburetor position on the power head with the top carburetor being No. 1. Each carburetor must be installed in the correct location according to its suffix number.

A thermal air valve located in the starboard cylinder head (under the No. 3 spark plug), restricts air in the idle circuit during cold engine operation (below 100°F). The air restriction results in a richer fuel mixture and eliminates the need to activate the enrichment circuit frequently during cold operation. When the engine temperature exceeds 100°F, the valve opens allowing normal fuel metering.

On 1990 and 1991 models, a linkage actuated accelerator pump injects fuel into the carburetor throats to prevent hesitation or backfiring during acceleration. The fuel is pumped from the float bowl, past a check valve assembly into 2 discharge tubes located in each carburetor throat. The check valve assembly prevents pump discharge during smooth acceleration.

Removal/Installation

1. Mark each carburetor for reinstallation in the same location as removed.
2. Remove the air box cover. Remove the 6 screws securing the air box to the carburetors. Remove the air box.
3. Carefully pry the throttle linkage away from the throttle lever at each carburetor (**Figure 71**).
4. Disconnect the oil pump control rod (**Figure 71**) from the bottom carburetor throttle lever.
5. Disconnect the fuel delivery hose, enrichener valve hose and thermal air valve hoses from the carburetors. See **Figure 72**.
6. Remove 2 nuts and 2 Allen screws from each carburetor to be removed. Remove and discard the carburetor gaskets.
7. To reinstall the carburetor(s), place new carburetor gaskets onto the mounting studs and install the carburetor(s) at their original locations.
8. Install the nuts and Allen screws and tighten evenly and securely.
9. Connect the fuel delivery hoses, enrichener hoses and thermal air valve hoses to their fittings (**Figure 72**). Securely clamp the hoses with new sta-straps.
10. Install the throttle linkage and connect the oil pump control rod (**Figure 71**).
11. Perform timing, synchronizing and adjusting procedures as described in Chapter Five.

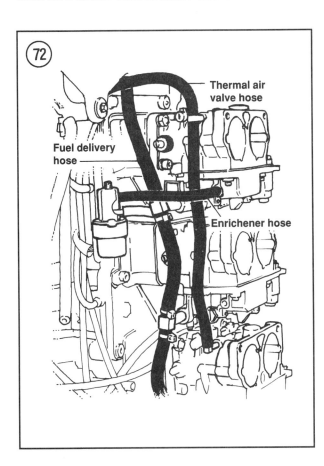

72

Thermal air valve hose

Fuel delivery hose

Enrichener hose

6

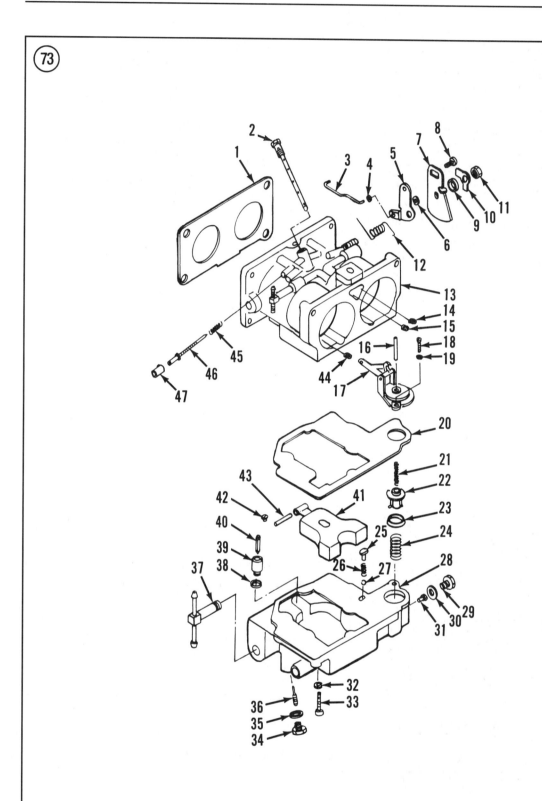

**WMH CARBURETOR
(135-200 HP MODELS)**

1. Gasket
2. Emulsion tube
3. Link rod
4. Bushing
5. Accelerator pump lever
6. E-ring
7. Throttle lever
8. Screw
9. Spacer
10. Tab washer
11. Nut
12. Spring
13. Carburetor body
14. Vent (back draft) jet
15. Idle air jet
16. Plunger
17. Accelerator pump cover
18. Screw
19. Lockwasher
20. Gasket
21. Pump override spring (1991 & 1992 models)
22. Accelerator pump cup (1991 & 1992 models)
23. Pump cup seal (1991 & 1992 models)
24. Pump return spring (1991 & 1992 models)
25. Retainer (1991 & 1992 models)
26. Spring (1991 & 1992 models)
27. Check ball (1991 & 1992 models)
28. Float bowl
29. Plug
30. Gasket
31. Main jet
32. Lockwasher
33. Screw
34. Plug
35. Gasket
36. Off idle tube
37. Fuel inlet fitting
38. Gasket
39. Inlet valve seat
40. Inlet valve needle
41. Float
42. Screw
43. Float pin
44. Off idle (progression) air jet
45. Spring
46. Idle mixture screw
47. Limiter cap

Disassembly

Refer to **Figure 73** for this procedure. If disassembling 2 or more carburetors, be sure to keep individual components with their respective carburetors. Do not interchange parts between carburetor assemblies.

1. Remove the off idle tube plug and gasket. Remove the off idle tube.

2. Remove the main jet plugs and gaskets, then remove the main jets.

3. Remove the off idle air jets (**Figure 74**).

NOTE
The back draft jet is absent on some models.

4. Remove the idle air bleed and back draft jets (**Figure 74**).

5. 1990 and 1991 models:

  a. Remove the E-ring (**Figure 75**) and disconnect the accelerator pump link rod from the pump lever.

  b. Remove the 2 screws (**Figure 75**) securing the accelerator pump cover to the float bowl. Lift the pump assembly from the float bowl.

6. Remove the emulsion tube from the carburetor body.

6

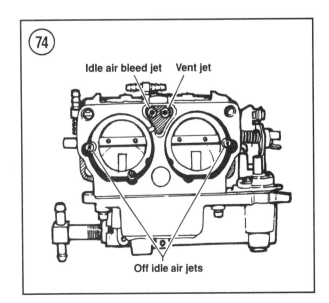

Idle air bleed jet   Vent jet

Off idle air jets

7. Remove 5 screws securing the float bowl to the carburetor body. Separate the float bowl from the body. Remove and discard the bowl gasket.

8. Remove the float pin retaining screw. Lift the float and pin out of the float bowl.

9. Remove the inlet needle. Remove the inlet valve seat using a wide-blade screwdriver. Remove and discard the seat gasket.

10. Using needlenose pliers, extract the check ball retainer (25, **Figure 73**) from the float bowl. Invert the bowl and remove the spring and check ball.

NOTE
Further disassembly is not required for normal cleaning and inspection. If the throttle shaft is excessively worn or damaged, continue at Step 11. Should it become necessary to rmove the air

calibration screws for carburetor cleaning, continue at Step 12.

11. If throttle shaft removal is required, refer to **Figure 76** and proceed as follows:

  a. Bend the tab washer away from the nut.

  b. Remove the nut, tab washer, spacer and throttle lever.

  c. Remove the throttle lever screw and throttle lever.

  d. Remove the throttle valve screws (2 each valve), remove the valves from the carburetor throats and pull the throttle shaft from the carburetor body.

CAUTION
*The air calibration screws located behind the 2 welch plugs (**Figure 77**) are preset at the factory for optimum performance and efficiency. The screws do*

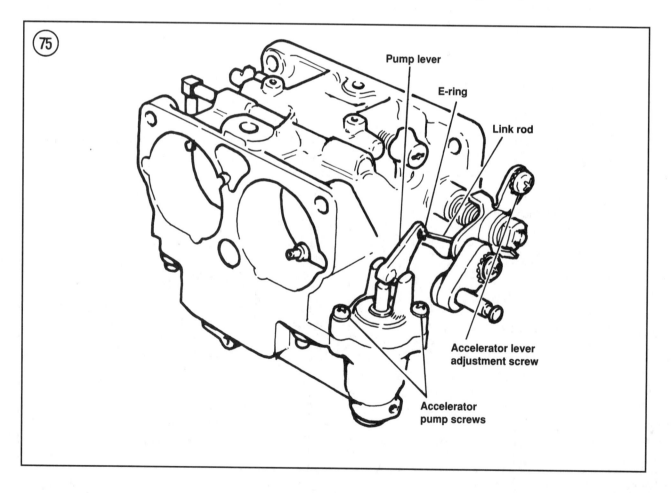

(75)

Pump lever

E-ring

Link rod

Accelerator lever adjustment screw

Accelerator pump screws

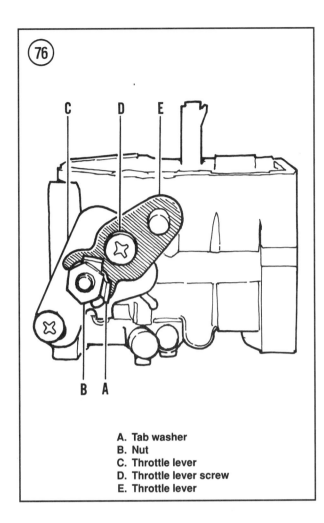

A. Tab washer
B. Nut
C. Throttle lever
D. Throttle lever screw
E. Throttle lever

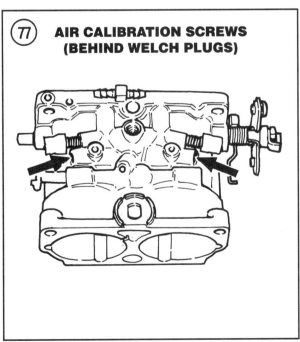

**AIR CALIBRATION SCREWS
(BEHIND WELCH PLUGS)**

not normally require removal or adjustment and should not be tampered with. However, if the screws must be removed for cleaning the carburetor, turn the screws inward and record the number of turns required to lightly seat the screws prior to removal. Apply a suitable thread locking compound to the threads of the screws during installation.

12. If necessary, carefully drill a small hole into the welch plugs (**Figure 77**), then pry the welch plugs out using a small punch or similar tool.

13. Turn the air calibration screws inward, while counting the number of turns required to seat the screws lightly. Record the number of turns, then remove the screws.

14. If necessary, pry the plastic limiter caps off the idle mixture screws, then remove the screws and springs.

Cleaning and Inspection

1. Clean the carburetor body, float bowl and metal parts in a carburetor cleaning solution to remove gum, dirt and varnish. Follow the instructions provided with the cleaner. Do not place floats or any other rubber or plastic component in carburetor cleaner.

2. Rinse the carburetor components thoroughly with hot water, then clean solvent. Blow dry with compressed air. Be sure to blow through all orifices, nozzles and passages.

CAUTION
Do not use wire or drill bits to clean carburetor passages. Doing so can alter calibration and ruin the carburetor.

3. Check the plastic float for fuel absorption or deterioration. Replace the float as necessary.

4. Inspect the carburetor body and float bowl for cracks, damaged threads, restricted passages or other damage. Repair or replace as necessary.

5. Check the inlet needle and seat for excessive wear or damage. Replace the inlet needle and seat as an assembly only.

6

6. Inspect the accelerator pump cup seal. Replace the cup seal if excessively worn, cut, deteriorated or damaged.

Reassembly

1. If removed, insert the throttle shaft into the carburetor body.

2. Install the throttle valves onto the shaft. Make sure the throttle valve screws are clean, then apply a suitable thread locking compound to the screw threads. Install the screws and tighten securely.

3. Refer to **Figure 76**. Install the throttle spring, throttle lever, spacer, tab washer and nut. Bend the tab washer over to secure the nut.

4. Install the check ball and spring into the float bowl. Install the retainer to secure the spring and ball in place.

5. Using a new gasket, install the inlet valve seat into the float bowl.

6. Place the inlet valve needle into the valve seat.

7. Insert the float pin into the float. Install the float and pin assembly into the float bowl and secure with the pin retaining screw.

8. Adjust the float level as described in this chapter.

9. Install the emulsion tube into the carburetor body.

10. If removed, reinstall the air calibration screws as follows:

  a. Apply a suitable thread locking compound to the threads of the screws.

  b. Install the screws and turn inward until lightly seated. Back out the screws the number of turns recorded during disassembly.

  c. Place new welch plugs into the screw bores (convex side facing outward). Using a hammer and punch, carefully flatten the plugs to provide a tight seal. If necessary, seal the plug and area around the plug with fingernail polish.

11. Invert the carburetor body and place a new float bowl gasket onto the body. Install the float bowl and the 5 bowl screws. Tighten the screws evenly and securely.

12. 1990 and 1991 models:

  a. Assemble and install the accelerator pump in the order shown in **Figure 78**. Secure the cover with the 2 screws.

  b. Install the accelerator pump link rod to the pump lever. Secure the rod with the E-ring.

  c. Loosen the accelerator lever adjustment screw (**Figure 75**). Adjust the lever so the pump lever just contacts the pump plunger, then retighten the screw.

13. Install the idle air and back draft jets (if so equipped). See **Figure 74**.

14. Install the off idle air jets (**Figure 74**).

15. Install the main jets. Install the main jet plugs with new gaskets.

16. Install the off idle tube. Install the tube plug with a new gasket.

17. Install the idle mixture screws. Turn the screws inward until lightly seated, then back out 1-3/4 turns on carburetors with identification WMH4-__A and WMH6__A, and 1-1/2 turns on all other models. With the mixture screws in this position, install the limiter caps with the tabs facing straight upward.

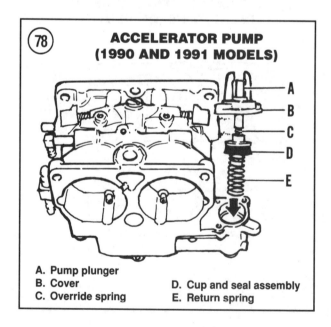

(78) **ACCELERATOR PUMP (1990 AND 1991 MODELS)**

A. Pump plunger
B. Cover
C. Override spring
D. Cup and seal assembly
E. Return spring

Float Adjustment

1. With the float bowl removed and the inlet needle, seat and float installed in the bowl, invert the float bowl.

2. Place a machinist's scale or a straightedge across the float bowl as shown in **Figure 79**. The float should be flush with the float bowl mating surface.

3. If adjustment is necessary, carefully bend the metal float tab as necessary.

Idle Speed Adjustment

Refer to the appropriate section in Chapter Five.

Idle Mixture Adjustment

Fuel mixture at idle speed is controlled by 2 mixture screws. The mixture screws are fitted with plastic limiter caps to limit the adjustment range. Do not remove the limiter caps to increase adjustment range. When adjusting idle mixture, both screws on each carburetor must be turned equally in the same direction. Turning the screws to the full clockwise limit from the straight up position will lean the idle mixture the equivalent

of 4 jet sizes. Turning the screws to the full counterclockwise limit from the straight up position will richen the idle mixture the equivalent of 4 jet sizes.

Each carburetor is equipped with 1 idle air bleed jet located adjacent to the back draft jet (if so equipped). See **Figure 74**. Installing a smaller air bleed jet richens the idle mixture; installing a larger jet leans the mixture.

Off Idle Mixture Adjustment

Off idle (above idle to just below full throttle) fuel mixture is controlled by off idle air jets located in each carburetor throat. See **Figure 74**. Installing a smaller off idle air jet leans the off idle fuel mixture. Refer to **Table 4** for standard jet sizes and recommended jet sizes for different elevations. The standard jet size is for normal operation at sea level to 5000 ft. (1524 m) above sea level.

Back Draft (Vent) Jet Adjustment

The back draft jet (if so equipped) is located adjacent to the off idle air jet. See **Figure 74**. The back draft circuit is designed to reduce atmospheric pressure on the fuel in the float bowl which improves mid-range fuel economy. Installing a smaller back draft jet will lean the mid-range fuel mixture. Refer to **Table 4** for standard jet sizes and recommended jet sizes for different elevations. The standard jet size should be acceptable for normal operation at sea level to 5000 ft. (1524 m) above sea level.

High Speed Mixture Adjustment

The high speed fuel mixture is controlled by fixed main jets located inside the float bowl. During full-throttle operation, fuel is drawn from the float bowl through the main discharge tubes.

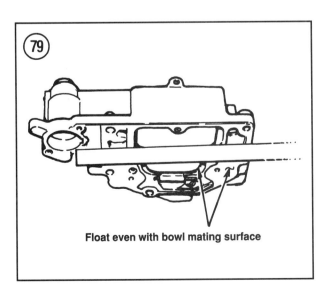

Float even with bowl mating surface

Normally, no adjustment is required. However, extreme changes in temperature, humidity or elevation may require a change in jet size. Refer to **Table 4** for standard jet sizes and recommended jet sizes for different elevations. The standard main jet size should be acceptable for normal operation at sea level to 5000 ft. (1524 m) above sea level. Installing smaller main jets will lean the high speed fuel mixture.

MERCARB CENTER BOWL CARBURETOR (250 AND 275 HP MODELS)

Six MerCarb center bowl carburetors are used on 250 and 275 hp models. A cross-over type intake manifold is used—the port side carburetors supply fuel to the starboard cylinders and the starboard carburetors supply fuel to the port cylinders. An electrically operated enrichment system provides additional fuel during cold starts. Idle, mid-range and high speed mixtures are controlled by fixed jets.

The carburetors are identified by the letters and numbers stamped in the top of the carburetor mounting flange. Each number includes a suffix number from 1 to 6. The suffix number indicates the installed position of the carburetor on the power head (not the cylinder number), with the No. 1 carburetor at the top. Each carburetor must be installed in the correct location according to its suffix number.

Removal/Installation

1. Remove the remote fuel tank connector from the lower cowl.
2. Remove the air box cover.
3. Remove the 12 nuts securing the attenuator cover and remove the cover.
4. Disconnect carburetor fuel delivery hose from the upper fuel pump.
5A. Individual carburetors—Disconnect the fuel hose(s) and throttle linkage from the carbure-

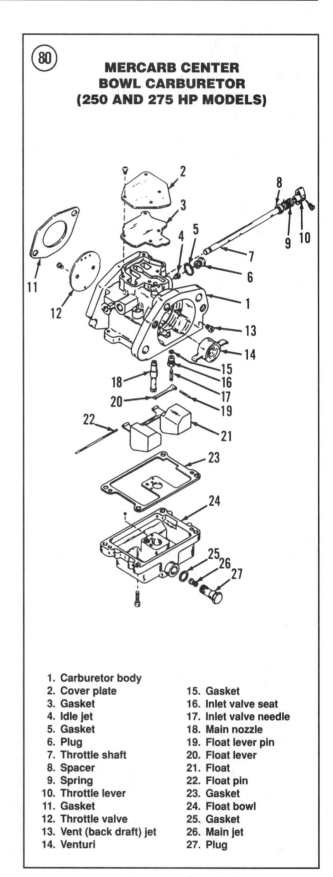

MERCARB CENTER BOWL CARBURETOR (250 AND 275 HP MODELS)

1. Carburetor body
2. Cover plate
3. Gasket
4. Idle jet
5. Gasket
6. Plug
7. Throttle shaft
8. Spacer
9. Spring
10. Throttle lever
11. Gasket
12. Throttle valve
13. Vent (back draft) jet
14. Venturi
15. Gasket
16. Inlet valve seat
17. Inlet valve needle
18. Main nozzle
19. Float lever pin
20. Float lever
21. Float
22. Float pin
23. Gasket
24. Float bowl
25. Gasket
26. Main jet
27. Plug

tor(s) being removed. Remove the carburetor(s) from the power head.

5B. All carburetors—Remove the 6 carburetors along with the throttle linkage and fuel hoses as an assembly. Remove the throttle linkage and fuel hoses to separate carburetors.

6. Clean any old gasket material from the carburetors and intake manifold.

7. To reinstall, connect the fuel hoses and throttle linkage to the carburetors.

8. Place new carburetor flange gaskets onto the carburetor mounting studs. Install the carburetor(s) at their original locations.

9. Install the fuel delivery hose onto the fuel pump. Securely clamp the hose with a new sta-strap.

10. Connect the enrichener hose to the float bowl fitting on the top port side carburetor. Clamp the hose with a new sta-strap.

11. Reinstall the attenuator cover. Install the 12 flat washers and nuts. Tighten the nuts to 60 in.-lb. (6.8 N.m).

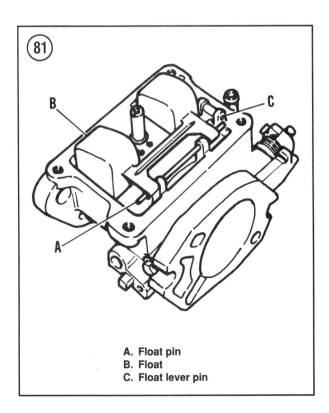

A. Float pin
B. Float
C. Float lever pin

12. Install the air box cover and gasket. Apply a suitable thread locking compound to the threads of the cover screws. Tighten the cover screws to 60 in.-lb. (6.8 N.m).

13. Apply thread locking compound to the remote fuel tank connector mounting screw. Install the connector and tighten the screw to 60 in.-lb. (6.8 N.m).

14. Perform timing, synchronization and adjusting procedures as described in Chapter Five.

Disassembly

Refer to **Figure 80** for this procedure. Be sure to note the size and location of each jet during disassembly. If disassembling 2 or more carburetors, keep all individual components with their respective carburetor. Do not interchange carburetor components.

1. Remove the main jet plug and gasket from the float bowl. Unscrew the main jet and remove from the plug.

2. Remove the idle jet plug and gasket from the carburetor body. Remove the idle jet.

3. Remove the float bowl and gasket.

4. Remove the float pin (A, **Figure 81**), then lift off the float (B).

5. Remove the float lever pin (C, **Figure 81**) and float lever.

6. Remove the inlet valve needle. Remove the inlet valve seat using an appropriate size wrench. Remove and discard the seat gasket.

7. Remove the main nozzle (**Figure 82**) from the carburetor body. Once the nozzle is removed, remove the venturi from the carburetor throat.

> *NOTE*
> *Further disassembly is not necessary for normal carburetor cleaning and inspection. If the throttle shaft requires removal, proceed at Step 8.*

8. Remove the 2 screws securing the throttle valve to the throttle shaft. Remove the valve.

9. Remove the throttle lever retaining screw (**Figure 83**), then slide the throttle lever off the shaft. Remove the return spring and spacer.

10. Pull the throttle shaft from the carburetor body to complete disassembly.

Cleaning and Inspection

1. Clean the carburetor body, float bowl and metal parts in a carburetor cleaning solution to remove gum, dirt and varnish. Follow the instructions provided with the cleaner. Do not place floats or any other rubber or plastic component in carburetor cleaner.

2. Rinse the carburetor components thoroughly with hot water, then clean solvent. Blow dry with compressed air. Be sure to blow through all orifices, nozzles and passages.

> *CAUTION*
> *Do not use wire or drill bits to clean carburetor passages. Doing so can alter calibration and ruin the carburetor.*

3. Check the plastic float for fuel absorption or deterioration. Replace the float as necessary.

4. Inspect the carburetor body and float bowl for cracks, damaged threads, restricted passages or other damage. Repair or replace as necessary.

5. Check the inlet needle and seat for excessive wear or damage. Replace the inlet needle and seat as an assembly only.

6. Inspect the accelerator pump cup seal. Replace the cup seal if excessively worn, cut, deteriorated or damaged.

Reassembly

1. If removed, insert the throttle shaft into the carburetor body. Place the plastic spacer over the throttle shaft, then install the return spring, throttle lever and lever retaining screw. Tighten the screw securely.

2. Apply a suitable thread locking compound to the throttle valve screws. Place the throttle valve

onto the flat area of the throttle shaft, insert the screws (with lockwashers) and tighten securely.

3. Place the venturi into the carburetor throat, then install the main nozzle. See **Figure 82**.

4. Using a new gasket, install the inlet valve seat into the carburetor body. Tighten the seat securely. Place the inlet needle into the seat.

5. Install the float lever and secure with the lever pin. Push the pin into position until the knurled end is flush with the mount (**Figure 81**).

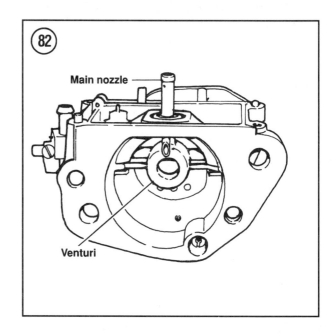

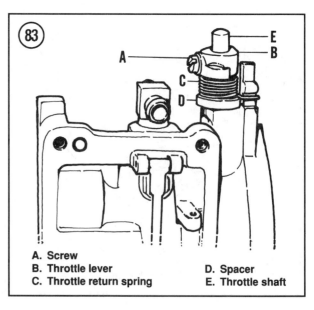

A. Screw
B. Throttle lever
C. Throttle return spring
D. Spacer
E. Throttle shaft

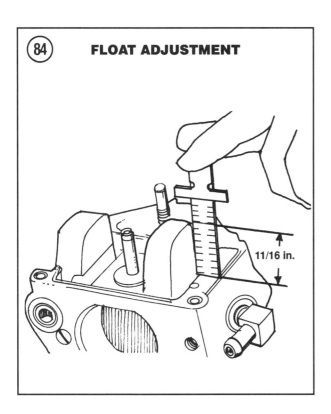

FLOAT ADJUSTMENT

11/16 in.

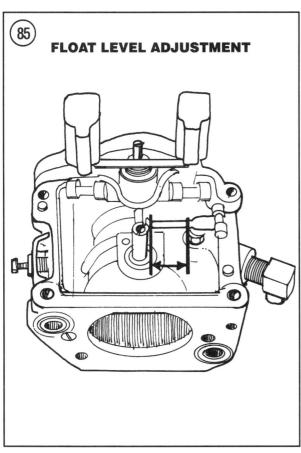

FLOAT LEVEL ADJUSTMENT

6. Install the float and secure with the float pin (**Figure 81**).

7. Adjust the float level as described in this chapter.

8. Place a new float bowl gasket onto the carburetor body. Install the float bowl. Tighten the bowl screws evenly and securely.

9. Install the main jet into the main jet plug. Install the plug and jet assembly (with new gasket) into the float bowl.

10. Install the back draft jet into the carburetor body.

11. Install the idle jet into the carburetor body. Place a new gasket onto the idle jet plug and install the plug.

6

Float Adjustment

1. With the float bowl removed, invert the carburetor and measure the float level as shown in **Figure 84**.

2. The measurement should be 11/16 in. (17.5 mm).

3. If adjustment is necessary, carefully bend the float lever in the area shown in **Figure 85**.

4. Recheck the float level. Repeat Step 3 as necessary.

Idle Mixture Adjustment

Fuel mixture at idle speed is controlled by a fixed idle jet (4, **Figure 80**). Installing a smaller jet will lean idle mixture; installing a larger jet richens the idle mixture. The standard idle jet should be acceptable for normal operation at sea level to 2500 ft. (762 m) above sea level. Refer to **Table 5** for standard jet sizes and recommended jet sizes for different elevations.

Vent Jet Adjustment

The vent (13, **Figure 80**) jet is designed to lower atmospheric pressure on the fuel in the float bowl, resulting in improved mid-range fuel economy. If a smaller vent jet is installed the mid-range fuel mixture becomes leaner; if a larger vent jet is installed, the mid-range fuel mixture becomes richer. The standard vent jet should be acceptable for normal operation at sea level to 2500 ft. (762 m) above sea level. Refer to **Table 5** for standard jets and recommended jet sizes for operation at different elevations.

High Speed Mixture Adjustment

The high speed fuel mixture is controlled by a fixed main jet (26, **Figure 80**). Normally, no adjustment is required. However, extreme changes in temperature, humidity or elevation may require a change in jet size. Refer to **Table 5** for standard jet sizes and recommended jet sizes for different elevations. The standard main jet size should be acceptable for normal opera-

tion at sea level to 2500 ft. (762 m) above sea level. Installing smaller main jets will lean the high speed fuel mixture.

To remove the main jet, remove the main jet plug (27, **Figure 80**), then unscrew the main jet from the plug. Reverse removal to install the main jet.

THERMAL AIR VALVE (135-200 HP MODELS)

The thermal air valve is installed in the starboard cylinder (below the No. 3 spark plug). During cold engine operation (below 100°F), the

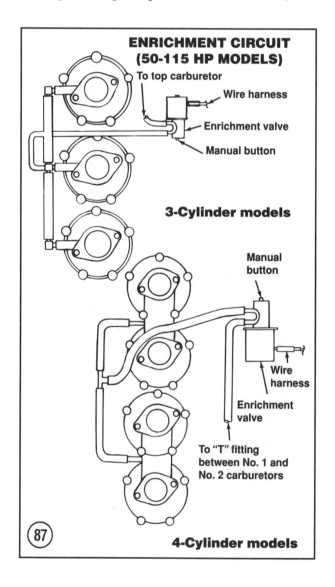

thermal air valve closes, causing an air restriction to the carburetors. This restriction results in a richer mixture, eliminating the need to activate the enrichment circuit periodically to keep the engine running. When the engine warms up, the thermal air valve opens, permitting normal fuel metering.

ENRICHMENT VALVE AND CHOKE SOLENOID SYSTEMS

The electrically operated enrichment valve provides additional fuel for easier cold starts. Fuel is gravity fed from the top carburetor to the enrichment valve. When the key or choke button is depressed and held, the valve opens and allows fuel from the fuel bowl of the top carburetor to flow to the remaining carburetor(s), intake manifold or balance tube (on some models). The valve can be operated manually by depressing and

holding the button located on the valve. Typical enrichment system hose routing is shown in **Figures 86-89**.

Enrichment Valve Test

1. Depress the key or choke button and listen for the valve to click. If the valve clicks, squeeze the primer bulb until it is firm, then remove the hose at the bottom of the valve. Hold a suitable container under the valve fitting. Depress and hold the key or choke button and check for fuel flow from the fitting:

    a. If fuel flows, the valve is acceptable.

    b. If fuel does not flow, disconnect the top carburetor hose at the valve.

    c. If fuel flows from this hose, replace the valve; if not, check all hoses and fittings for restrictions.

6

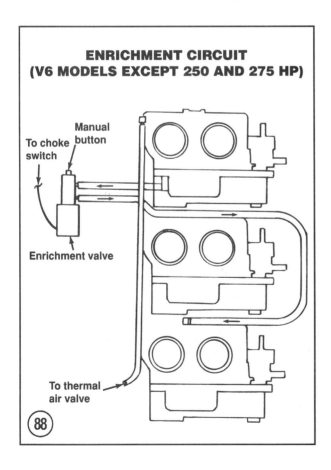

ENRICHMENT CIRCUIT (V6 MODELS EXCEPT 250 AND 275 HP)

To choke switch
Manual button
Enrichment valve
To thermal air valve

88

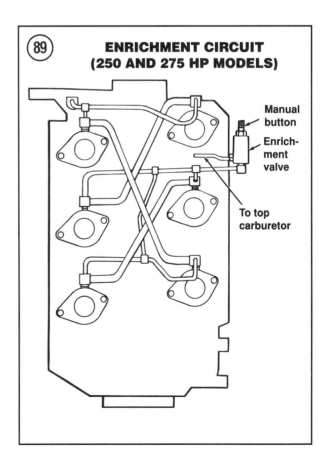

89

ENRICHMENT CIRCUIT (250 AND 275 HP MODELS)

Manual button
Enrichment valve
To top carburetor

2. If the valve does not click in Step 1, connect a voltmeter between the valve yellow/black wire at the terminal block and a good engine ground. Depress the key or choke button and note the voltmeter:

    a. If no voltage is noted, check for an open circuit in the yellow/black wire.

    b. If voltage is present, clean and tighten the engine harness yellow/black and enrichment valve black wire connections at the terminal block. Make sure that the remaining enrichment valve black wire is properly grounded at the terminal block.

    c. After repairing the connections as necessary, depress the key or choke button again. Replace the valve if it still does not click.

Enrichment Valve Replacement

1. Disconnect the enrichment valve wires at the terminal block or bullet connectors.

2. Disconnect the fuel hoses at the valve.

3. Remove the fasteners holding the valve to the mounting bracket (**Figure 90**, typical). Remove the valve and bracket assembly.

4. Separate the valve from the bracket. Apply Loctite 222 or 242 to the threads of the screws and install new valve to the bracket.

5. Note the location and direction of the fuel fittings, then remove the fittings from the old valve. Apply Quicksilver Gasket Sealer to the threads of the fittings, then install the fittings to the new valve. Tighten the fittings in the same position as the old valve.

6. Connect the fuel hoses to the new valve. Apply Loctite 222 or 242 to the threads of the valve bracket mounting fasteners. Install the valve and bracket assembly, tightening the fasteners securely.

7. Reconnect the valve wires at the bullet connectors or to the terminal block.

Choke Solenoid Replacement

1. If necessary, remove the top and rear cowl frame supports.

2. Disconnect the manual choke linkage at the choke rod.

3. Disconnect the choke wire at the solenoid terminal or bullet connector.

4. Disconnect the solenoid plunger linkage from the choke rod.

5. Remove the screws and wire harness clamp holding the solenoid to the front support frame.

6. Installation is the reverse of removal. Apply Quicksilver Multipurpose Lubricant to the plunger hole and choke linkage grommets.

ANTI-SIPHON DEVICES

In accordance with industry safety standards, late model boats equipped with a built-in fuel tank must have some form of anti-siphon device installed between the fuel tank outlet and the outboard fuel inlet. This device is designed to shut off the fuel supply to the engine should the boat capsize or be involved in an accident. Quite often, the malfunction of such devices leads to the replacement of a fuel pump in the belief that it is defective.

Anti-siphon devices can malfunction in one of the following ways:

a. Anti-siphon valve—orifice in the valve is too small or plugs easily; valve sticks in the closed or partially closed position; valve fluctuates between open and closed position; thread sealer, metal filings or dirt/debris plugs the orifice or lodges in the relief spring.

b. Solenoid-operated fuel shut-off valve—solenoid fails with the valve in the closed position; solenoid malfunctions, leaving the valve in the partially closed position.

c. Manually-operated fuel shut-off valve—valve is left in the completely closed position; valve is not fully opened.

The easiest method to determine if an anti-siphon valve is defective is to bypass it by operating the engine with a remote fuel supply. If a fuel system problem is suspected, check the fuel filter first. See Chapter Four. If the filter is not plugged or restricted, bypass the anti-siphon device. If the engine runs properly with the anti-siphon device bypassed, contact the boat manufacturer for replacement of the anti-siphon device.

FUEL FILTER

Refer to Chapter Four for fuel filter service procedures.

FUEL TANK

Figure 91 shows the components of the integral fuel tank assembly used on 3-5 hp models, including the inline fuel filter and in-tank strainer. **Figure 92** shows the metal remote fuel tank components and **Figure 93** shows the newer plastic remote fuel tank components.

When some oils are mixed with gasoline and stored in a warm place, a bacterial substance may form. This substance is clear in color and covers the fuel pickup, restricting fuel flow through the fuel system. Bacterial formation can be removed by using Quicksilver Engine Cleaner. To remove any dirt or water that may have entered the tank

during refilling, clean the inside of the tank once each season by flushing with clean gasoline or kerosene.

To check the fuel filter for possible restrictions, remove the cover and withdraw the outlet tube from the tank. The filter on the end of the outlet tube can be cleaned by rinsing in clean solvent or kerosene.

FUEL HOSE AND PRIMER BULB

Figure 94 shows the fuel hose and primer bulb components. The hose and bulb should be checked periodically for cracks, breaks, restrictions, chafing or other damage. Make sure all fuel hose connections are tight and securely clamped.

ELECTRONIC FUEL INJECTION (EFI)

The 1990 200XRi, 1991-1993 175XRi and 200XRi and 1993 150XRi are equipped with a sequential, multi-point electronic fuel injection system. This section includes basic EFI operation, a description of the EFI components and service procedures for parts of the EFI system that should be attempted by the home mechanic.

Typical of complex electronic systems, most parts can not be repaired, only replaced. The majority of the components should be serviced by a Mercury dealer, either due to any applicable warranty or because they require expensive, complicated electronic troubleshooting equipment and a thorough knowledge of the EFI system. Some of these components are very expensive and can be damaged by improper testing or service procedures. Many components or assemblies can be removed and taken to a dealer for bench testing.

Servicing the EFI system requires special precautions to prevent damage to the expensive electronic control unit (ECU). Common electrical system service procedures acceptable on

6

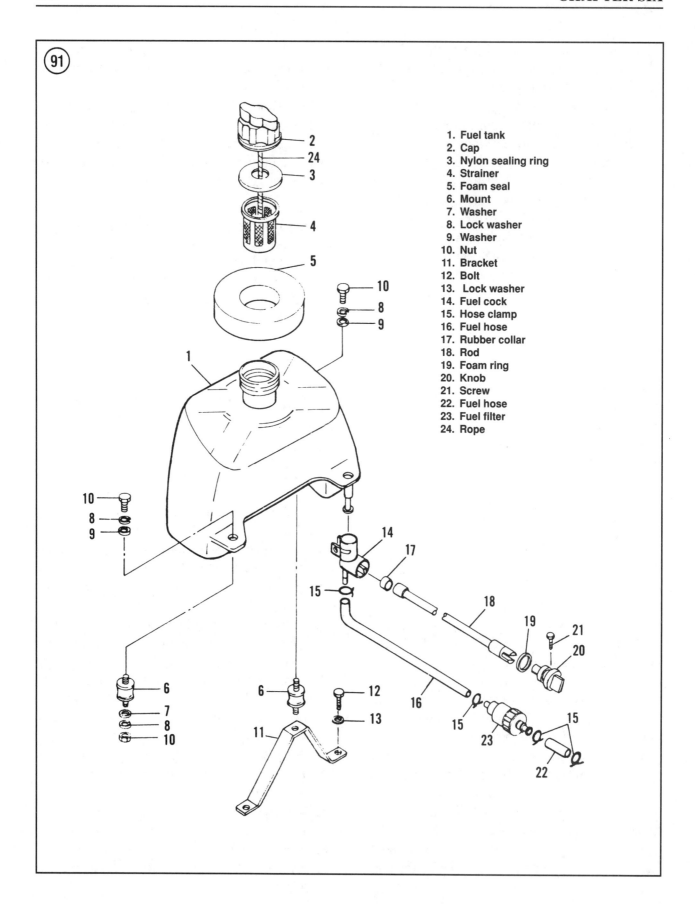

1. Fuel tank
2. Cap
3. Nylon sealing ring
4. Strainer
5. Foam seal
6. Mount
7. Washer
8. Lock washer
9. Washer
10. Nut
11. Bracket
12. Bolt
13. Lock washer
14. Fuel cock
15. Hose clamp
16. Fuel hose
17. Rubber collar
18. Rod
19. Foam ring
20. Knob
21. Screw
22. Fuel hose
23. Fuel filter
24. Rope

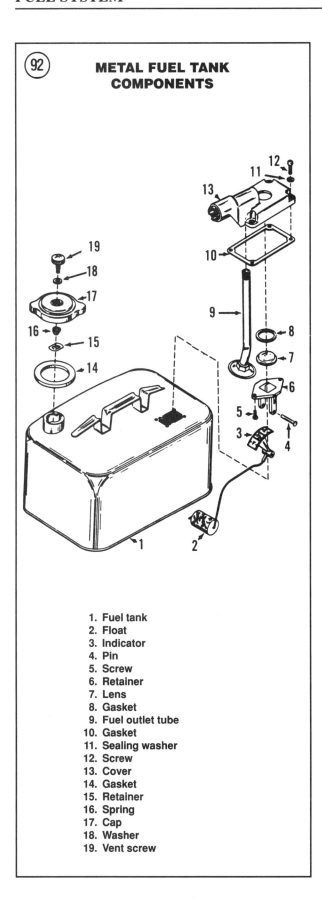

METAL FUEL TANK COMPONENTS

1. Fuel tank
2. Float
3. Indicator
4. Pin
5. Screw
6. Retainer
7. Lens
8. Gasket
9. Fuel outlet tube
10. Gasket
11. Sealing washer
12. Screw
13. Cover
14. Gasket
15. Retainer
16. Spring
17. Cap
18. Washer
19. Vent screw

other fuel systems may cause damage to several parts of the EFI system.

1. Unless otherwise specified in a procedure, do not start the outboard while any electrical connectors are disconnected. Do not disconnect the battery cables or any electrical connector while the ignition switch in ON. The electronic control unit will be damaged and require replacement.

2. Turn the ignition switch to the OFF position and disconnect the battery before disconnecting any electrical connector.

6

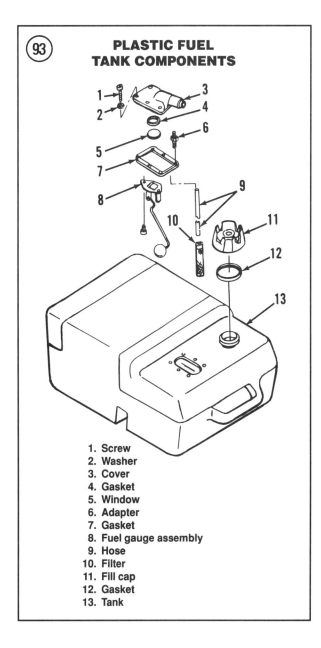

PLASTIC FUEL TANK COMPONENTS

1. Screw
2. Washer
3. Cover
4. Gasket
5. Window
6. Adapter
7. Gasket
8. Fuel gauge assembly
9. Hose
10. Filter
11. Fill cap
12. Gasket
13. Tank

3. Do not disconnect the battery while the engine is running.

4. Do not apply anything other than a 12 volt battery to the electrical system. The battery must be removed before attaching a battery charger.

Testing the EFI electronic circuits and components require the use of an expensive Quicksilver Fuel Injection Tester, part No. 91-11001A2. Improper testing procedures can destroy sensitive (and expensive) electronic components. If an EFI system malfunction occurs, it is highly recommended to take the outboard to a Mercury outboard motor dealer to be tested by a trained technician.

The following can be checked or inspected prior to troubleshooting the EFI system:

a. Make sure the ignition system is functioning properly. See Chapter Three.

b. Make sure the battery is in acceptable condition and fully charged. Make sure the battery terminal connections are clean and tight. Low battery voltage can result in erratic EFI system operation.

c. Make sure the ignition timing, synchronization and adjustments are correctly set. EFI models are very sensitive to set-up adjustments.

d. Make sure all wiring is in good condition. All wiring connections, especially grounds, must be clean and tight.

e. Route all EFI sensor wires away from any source of high voltage such as spark plug leads. High voltage can create radio frequency interference (RFI) that may alter sensor inputs to the ECU, or outputs from the ECU.

f. Attempt to operate the outboard using a remote fuel tank containing fresh unleaded gasoline. This will eliminate plugged or restricted fuel hoses, a malfunctioning anti-siphon valve or poor quality gasoline.

EFI Operation

During operation, the fuel injection system monitors engine condition by input signals from

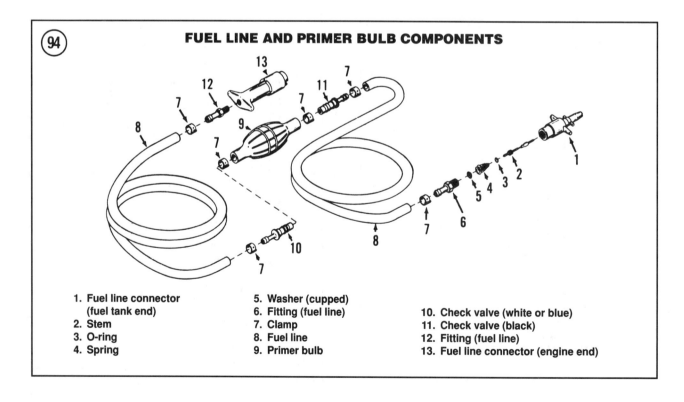

FUEL LINE AND PRIMER BULB COMPONENTS

1. Fuel line connector (fuel tank end)
2. Stem
3. O-ring
4. Spring
5. Washer (cupped)
6. Fitting (fuel line)
7. Clamp
8. Fuel line
9. Primer bulb
10. Check valve (white or blue)
11. Check valve (black)
12. Fitting (fuel line)
13. Fuel line connector (engine end)

various sensors within the system. The electronic control unit (ECU) processes this data to determine the optimum amount of fuel needed for the engine's current condition.

The fuel is delivered under pressure, at a constant rate to the fuel rail and injectors. The injectors are opened and closed electrically by the ECU. The time interval the injectors are open is called the pulse width; the mixture becomes richer as the pulse width widens, or leaner as the pulse width narrows.

EFI Component Description

A brief description of the fuel injection system will help to familiarize you with the system and describe the function of each component. A basic understanding of how the EFI components function and their relation to each other is helpful for pinpointing a source of EFI related problems.

Diaphragm fuel pump

A conventional diaphragm-type fuel pump is mounted on the crankcase. The pump draws fuel from the fuel tank and delivers it to the water separating filter, then to the vapor separator. Fuel

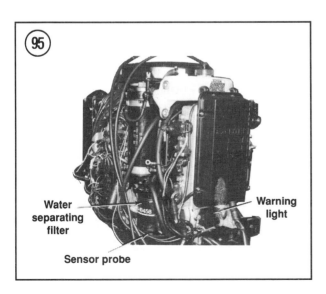

95

Water
separating
filter

Sensor probe

Warning
light

pressure should be 6-8 psi (41-55 kPa) at 5000 rpm.

Water separating filter

The water separating filter (**Figure 95**) is provided to prevent water contamination from damaging the fuel injection components. The water separating filter assembly is equipped with a sensor that activates a warning light (**Figure 95**) and horn should the water level in the filter canister reach the level of the sensor probe.

Any moisture that may be present in the fuel is separated from the fuel and accumulates in the bottom of the filter. Voltage is always present at the water sensor probe. If the accumulated water reaches the top of the probe, it completes the circuit to ground and activates the warning system.

To determine if the water sensing system is functioning properly, place the ignition switch in the ON position, disconnect the tan wire from the sensor probe (**Figure 95**) and connect it to a good engine ground for 10 seconds. The warning light should glow and the horn should sound if the system is functioning properly. Refer to Chapter Four for water separating filter service procedures.

Vapor separator

The vapor separator (**Figure 96**) is mounted on the induction manifold and serves as a reservoir where fuel from the diaphragm fuel pump and oil from the oil pump are blended and circulated. Unused fuel from the fuel rail bleed system is also returned to the vapor separator for recirculation. The fuel level in the vapor separator is regulated by a float and needle and seat valve assembly. If the float should become stuck in the up position, fuel flow into the vapor separator will be restricted. If the float should become stuck in the down position, fuel will overflow the

6

vapor separator resulting in an excessively rich mixture.

Bleed system

At idle speeds, unburned fuel from the crankcase is delivered to the vapor separator for recirculation. At off idle speeds (above 2000 rpm) the bleed system flow is shut off by the throttle linkage actuated bleed shut off valve. An inline bleed system filter (**Figure 96**) prevents contamination from entering the vapor separator assembly. A plugged bleed system filter will cause an excessively rich mixture at idle and hesitation during acceleration.

Electric fuel pump

The electric fuel pump (**Figure 96**) delivers fuel under pressure to the fuel rail. Any unused fuel is recirculated back to the vapor separator. When the ignition switch is in the ON position (engine not running), the ECU activates the pump for approximately 30 seconds to pressurize the fuel system.

Contained inside the ECU is a fuel pump driver circuit that controls the pump. With the ignition in the ON position, battery voltage is present at the pump positive (red) terminal. The ECU grounds the red/purple wire completing the circuit causing the pump to operate. The pump has 2 speeds which are controlled by the ECU assembly. The pump generally runs at the low speed during slow speed operation (under 2000 rpm).

Fuel pressure regulator

The electric fuel pump is capable of developing approximately 90 psi (621 kPa) fuel pressure inside the fuel rail. The fuel pressure regulator (**Figure 96**) is mounted on top of the vapor separator and regulates the pressure to the fuel injectors to a continuous 36-39 psi (248-269 kPa).

Final fuel filter

The final fuel filter is mounted above the electric fuel pump and prevents contamination from entering the fuel rail. Refer to Chapter Four for final fuel filter service.

Fuel injectors

The fuel injectors are connected to the fuel rail and are located inside the induction manifold assembly. See **Figure 97** for a view of the injectors with the induction manifold removed. Each injector consists of an electric solenoid that actuates a pintle valve assembly. The time duration the pintle valve is lifted off its seat, allowing fuel to flow, is called injector pulse width. The ECU determines injector pulse width according to input signals from the various sensors and widens (richens) or narrows (leans) the pulse width to accommodate all operating conditions. The ECU determines when to fire the injectors by referencing the primary ignition circuits.

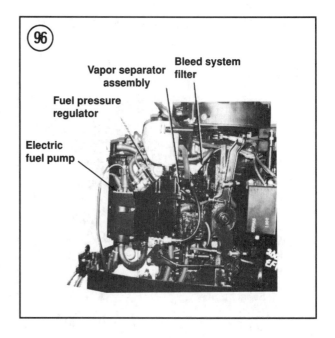

96

Vapor separator assembly

Bleed system filter

Fuel pressure regulator

Electric fuel pump

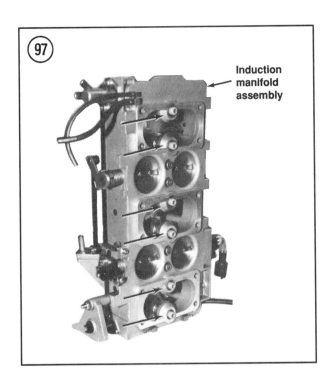

Induction manifold assembly

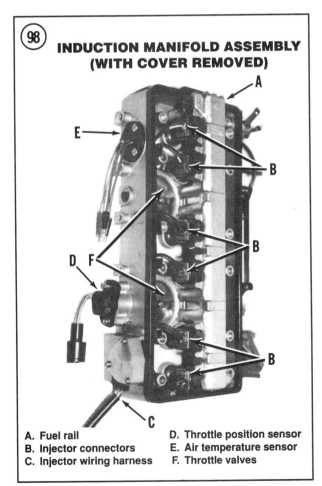

INDUCTION MANIFOLD ASSEMBLY (WITH COVER REMOVED)

A. Fuel rail
B. Injector connectors
C. Injector wiring harness
D. Throttle position sensor
E. Air temperature sensor
F. Throttle valves

The injectors are connected to the ECU by a 4-wire harness. During operation, the red wire provides battery voltage to the injectors. The ECU actuates the injectors by grounding either the white (cylinders 1 and 2), blue (cylinders 3 and 4) or yellow (cylinders 5 and 6) wires.

Induction manifold

The induction manifold assembly (**Figure 98**) contains 4 throttle valves mounted on 2 throttle shafts. The manifold assembly contains the fuel rail, fuel injectors, throttle position sensor and air temperature sensor. A fuel rail service port is located on the lower port side of the manifold and is used to measure fuel pressure inside the rail.

Electronic control unit

The electronic control unit (ECU) monitors engine temperature, throttle opening, detonation control, induction air temperature and barometric pressure data input from the various sensors. The ECU processes this information and determines the pulse width necessary for optimum performance during all engine operating conditions such as cranking, cold starting, climatic and altitude variation, acceleration and deceleration. The ECU is mounted to the induction manifold assembly as shown in **Figure 99**. The ECU can only be tested using the Quicksilver EFI Tester part No. 91-11001A1.

Air temperature sensor

The air temperature sensor (**Figure 98**) provides air temperature information to the ECU. As air temperature increases, the sensor resistance decreases, causing the ECU to lean the fuel mixture. If the sensor is disconnected (open circuit), the fuel mixture will richen by 10 percent.

6

If the sensor is grounded (short circuit), the fuel mixture will lean by 10 percent.

Manifold absolute pressure (MAP) sensor

The MAP sensor detects changes in manifold pressure and is connected to the intake manifold by a vacuum hose. The sensor is mounted inside the ECU and is non-serviceable. The ECU uses manifold pressure information from the MAP sensor to compensate for engine load condition and changes in barometric pressure and elevation.

Creating a vacuum on the MAP sensor hose will cause the ECU to lean the fuel mixture, varying engine operation or speed. If no change in engine speed or operation occurs when applying a vacuum on the hose, the sensor is not functioning properly and the ECU assembly must be replaced.

Engine head temperature sensor

The engine head temperature sensor provides the ECU with engine temperature information. The ECU uses this information to calculate the correct fuel enrichment during cold starts and during warm up. The ECU stops the enrichment process when the engine temperature reaches 90°F (32°C).

The sensor is located directly below the No. 2 (top port) spark plug. An open circuit in the temperature sensor will result in up to a 40 percent increase in fuel flow. If no change occurs with the sensor disconnected, the sensor is not functioning properly. The sensor must make a clean, tight contact with the cylinder head or an over-rich fuel mixture can occur.

Throttle position indicator

The throttle position indicator (TPI) is a variable resistor that provides throttle position infor-

mation to the ECU. The TPI (**Figure 100**) is mounted to the side of the induction manifold and is engaged with the lower throttle valve shaft. The sensor inputs throttle position information to the ECU as a voltage signal. Disconnecting (open circuit) the TPI will result in a 40 percent increase in fuel flow at idle, but does not affect wide-open throttle. The fuel mixture becomes richer as the TPI resistance increases. Refer to Chapter Five for TPI adjustment procedures.

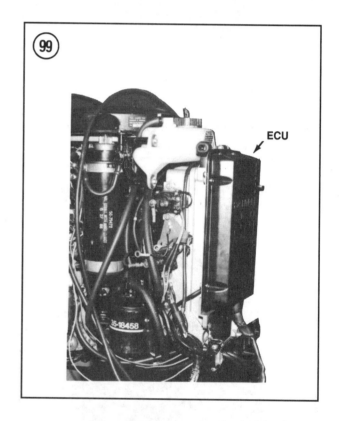

Detonation sensor

The detonation (knock) control system includes the detonation sensor mounted on the port cylinder head and the detonation control module mounted on the power head. The detonation sensor consists of a piezoelectric sensor that senses engine noise or vibrations and transmits a voltage signal to the control module. When the engine is started, the control module takes a 1 millisecond look at the sensor output, and retains this signal as a reference value. During operation, the ignition timing is electronically advanced by 6° at approximately 2500-3500 rpm, depending on engine load. If detonation occurs, the sensor output exceeds a predetermined level above the reference value and the timing is retarded (up to 8°) and the fuel mixture is richened (up to 15 percent) until the knock condition is eliminated.

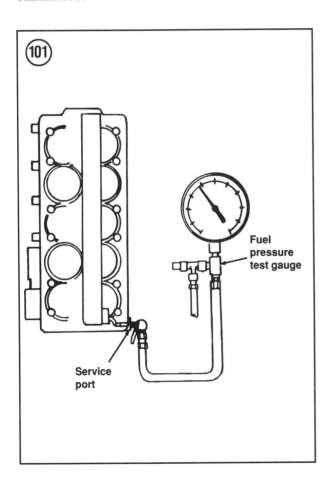

FUEL MANAGEMENT TESTS

Fuel Rail Pressure Test

The following test can be performed to determine if fuel under sufficient pressure is available to the injectors. The test can help isolate a malfunction as either a fuel delivery problem or an electrical system failure.

It is normal for fuel pressure to vary between approximately 34-39 psi (214-269 kPa) when checking fuel pressure while the engine is running.

1. Remove the plastic cap from the fuel rail service port located on the lower port side of the induction manifold.

2. Connect fuel pressure gauge assembly (part No. 91-16850, or equivalent) to the service port as shown in **Figure 101**. Note that **Figure 101** shows the induction manifold with the cover removed. It is not necessary to remove the cover to perform this test.

3. Place the ignition switch in the ON position (engine not running) and allow the electric fuel pump to operate for approximately 10 seconds. Note the pressure gauge reading.

NOTE
When the ignition switch is turned to ON (engine not running), the electric fuel pump will operate for approximately 30 seconds. If the ignition switch is turned OFF for 30 seconds, then back ON, the pump will run for another 30 seconds.

4. Fuel pump operation can be considered acceptable if the fuel pressure is within 36-39 psi (248-269 kPa). Fuel pressure well below 36 psi (248 kPa) is the result of a failed electric fuel pump, insufficient fuel delivered to the pump or other related problem. Refer to *Vapor Separator Fuel Delivery Test*. If fuel pressure exceeds 39 psi (269 kPa), the pressure regulator may be plugged or defective. Refer to *Fuel Pressure Regulator Test*. If the fuel pump will not run, refer to *Fuel Pump Voltage Test*.

6

Vapor Separator Fuel Delivery Test

The vapor separator fuel delivery test will determine if the components in the low pressure fuel delivery system are functioning properly and make sure sufficient fuel flow is available to the electric fuel pump.

1. Remove the sta-strap and disconnect the fuel delivery hose from the electric pump inlet port. See **Figure 102**. Direct the hose into a clean container and note the fuel flow from the hose.

2. If fuel flows from the hose, fuel is available to the electric fuel pump. The problem may be a plugged or restricted final fuel filter. See *Final Fuel Filter Check*. If little or no fuel flow is noted, proceed at Step 3.

3. Using a jumper wire, connect the mercury switch black/yellow wire terminal to a good engine ground to prevent the engine from starting.

4. Turn the ignition switch to the START position. Crank the engine for 10-20 seconds while noting fuel flow from the disconnected hose.

5. If a steady stream of fuel is discharged from the hose, check the final filter for plugging or restrictions (Chapter Four). If little or no fuel flows from the hose, proceed at *Vapor Separator Float Test*.

6. Reconnect the fuel delivery hose to the electric pump inlet fitting. Securely clamp the hose with a new sta-strap. If testing is completed, remove the jumper wire from the mercury switch.

Vapor Separator Float Test

The vapor separator float test will determine if the float is stuck in the UP position. If the float is stuck in the UP position, little or no fuel will flow through the vapor separator. If the float is stuck in the DOWN position, fuel will overflow the vapor separator and an excessively rich condition will result.

1. Remove the sta-strap and disconnect the fuel delivery hose from the vapor separator inlet. See

Figure 103. Direct the disconnected hose into a clean container.

2. Using a jumper wire, connect the mercury switch black/yellow wire terminal to a good engine ground to prevent the engine from starting.

3. Crank the engine for 15-20 seconds while observing the disconnected hose.

4. If fuel flows from the hose in Step 3, the vapor separator float is stuck in the up position, preventing fuel from entering the separator. Remove and disassemble the vapor separator as described in this chapter.

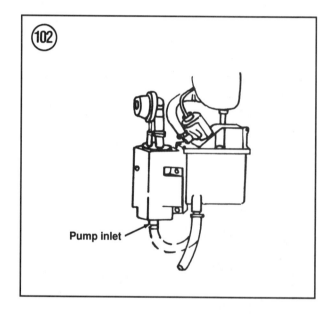

Pump inlet

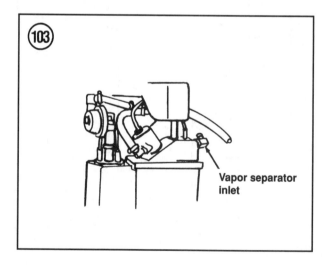

Vapor separator inlet

5. If little or no fuel flows from the hose in Step 3, proceed to *Water Separating Filter Flow Test* in this chapter.

Water Separating Filter Flow Test

This test will determine if the water separating filter is plugged.

1. Remove the sta-strap and disconnect the fuel delivery hose at the water separating filter inlet fitting. Direct the hose into a clean container.

2. Using a jumper wire, connect the mercury switch black/yellow wire terminal to a good engine ground to prevent the engine from starting.

3. Crank the engine for 10-20 seconds while observing the disconnected hose.

4. If fuel flows freely from the hose in Step 3, the water separating filter is plugged and must be replaced. See Chapter Four.

5. If little or no fuel flows from the hose in Step 3, disconnect the fuel delivery hose from the diaphragm pump inlet.

6. Squeeze the primer bulb several times and check for fuel flow at the disconnected hose.

7. If fuel flows freely in Step 6, remove, disassemble and inspect the diaphragm fuel pump as described in this chapter.

8. If little or no fuel flows from the hose in Step 6, check for plugging, loose connections and

Fuel hose

leaks in the fuel supply hose. Check the anti-siphon valve on the fuel tank for proper operation.

Final Fuel Filter Check

Refer to Chapter Four for final fuel filter service procedures.

Pressure Regulator Test

The pressure regulator test will determine if low fuel pressure (below 36 psi) is caused by a weak, restricted or open pressure regulator assembly.

1. Remove the plastic cap from the fuel rail service port located on the lower port side of the induction manifold.

2. Connect fuel pressure gauge assembly (part No. 91-16850, or equivalent) to the service port as shown in **Figure 101**. Note that **Figure 101** shows the induction manifold with the cover removed. It is not necessary to remove the cover to perform this test.

3. Remove the 2 pressure regulator mounting screws (**Figure 104**). Remove the pressure regulator from the vapor separator assembly, but do not disconnect any hoses.

4. Direct the discharge end of the pressure regulator into a clean container.

5. Turn the ignition switch to ON and check for fuel flow at the pressure regulator while noting the pressure gauge.

6. If a consistent fuel flow is noted in Step 5, but the fuel pressure is not within 36-39 psi (248-269 kPa), replace the pressure regulator.

7. If little or no fuel flows from the regulator in Step 5, and the fuel pressure is below 36 psi (248 kPa), refer to *Electric Fuel Pump Test* in this chapter.

6

Electric Fuel Pump Pressure Test

The electric fuel pump test will determine if the pump is capable of developing sufficient pressure for normal operation.

1. Remove the plastic cap from the fuel rail service port located on the lower port side of the induction manifold.

2. Connect fuel pressure gauge assembly (part No. 91-16850, or equivalent) to the service port as shown in **Figure 101**. Note that **Figure 101** shows the induction manifold with the cover removed. It is not necessary to remove the cover to perform this test.

3. Place the ignition switch in the ON position. Note the fuel pressure gauge reading within 30 seconds.

CAUTION
Do not close the fuel hose completely in Step 4 or fuel pump or hose damage may occur.

4. Partially restrict the fuel hose (**Figure 104**) to the pressure regulator by squeezing the hose with pliers. Note the gauge reading.

5. If the fuel pressure increases as the fuel hose is restricted, the electric fuel pump can be considered acceptable. If no pressure increase is noted in Step 4, the fuel pump may be defective. Perform the *Fuel Pump Voltage Test*.

Fuel Pump Voltage Test

This test will determine if the proper voltage is available to the fuel pump.

CAUTION
Use only a digital-type voltmeter during the following tests. Use of an analog (needle-type) voltmeter can damage sensitive ECU circuits.

1. With the ignition switch in the OFF position connect a voltmeter red test lead to the positive terminal (red) of the fuel pump. Connect the voltmeter black lead to a good engine ground.

2. The meter should indicate 12-13.5 volts. If not, check the battery state of charge and terminal connections. Charge or replace the battery as required. Clean and tighten the terminal connections as required.

3. With the ignition switch in the OFF position, move the red voltmeter lead to the negative fuel pump terminal. The meter should indicate the same reading as in Step 2. If not, the ECU may be defective. Remove the ECU and have it bench tested by a Mercury Dealer.

4. With the black meter lead connected to a good engine ground and the red lead connected to the negative fuel pump terminal, perform the following tests:

   a. Place the ignition switch in the ON position (engine not running). The meter should indicate 2 volts or less, then increase to 12-13.5 volts after 30 seconds. If not, either the fuel pump or the ECU is defective.

   b. Crank the engine while noting the meter. The meter should indicate 2 volts or less. If not, either the fuel pump or the ECU is defective.

CAUTION
Make sure sufficient cooling water is available during the remaining tests. Connect a flushing device, place the outboard into a test tank or perform the test in the water.

   c. Start the engine and run below 2000 rpm while noting the voltage reading. The meter should indicate 2 volts or less, then increase to 5 volts after 30 seconds. If not, either the fuel pump or the ECU is defective.

   d. Run the engine above 2000 rpm while noting the voltage reading. the meter should indicate 2 volts or less. If not, either the fuel pump or the ECU is defective.

5. Replace the fuel pump if the voltages are as specified, but the pump does not run, or if the pump pressure is low. See *Electric Fuel Pump Pressure Test* in this chapter.

Injector Harness Test

This test will determine if an open circuit is present in the injector wiring harness.

CAUTION
Use only a digital ohmmeter in the following test. Use of an analog (needle-type) ohmmeter can damage sensitive circuits.

1. Disconnect the injector harness 4-pin connector.
2. Set the digital ohmmeter on the 200 ohm scale.
3. Connect the red ohmmeter lead to the No. 2 terminal (red wire) in the injector harness. Connect the black ohmmeter lead to:
   a. The No. 4 terminal (white wire) for cylinders 1 and 2 injectors.
   b. The No. 3 terminal (blue wire) for cylinders 3 and 4 injectors.
   c. The No. 1 terminal (yellow wire) for cylinders 5 and 6 injectors.
4. The reading at each connection should be 0.9-1.3 ohms. If the resistance is 2.0-2.4 ohms at any one connection, one injector circuit has an open circuit.

Air Temperature Sensor Test

1. Disconnect and remove the air temperature sensor from the induction manifold.

CAUTION
Use only a digital ohmmeter in the following test. Use of an analog (needle-type) ohmmeter can damage sensitive circuits.

2. Set the digital ohmmeter on the 20K ohm scale.
3. Connect the ohmmeter between the sensor wires. Sensor resistance should be approximately 8500 ohms at 68°F (20°C).
4. Place the sensor into a container of ice water and note resistance.

5. The resistance should change inversely with the temperature (resistance increases as temperature decreases). If not, the sensor is defective and should be replaced.

Engine Cylinder Head Temperature Sensor Test

1. Disconnect and remove the cylinder head temperature sensor.

CAUTION
Use only a digital ohmmeter in the following test. Use of an analog (needle-type) ohmmeter can damage sensitive circuits.

2. Set the digital ohmmeter to the 2K ohm scale. Connect the ohmmeter between the sensor wires. The resistance should be approximately 1200-1300 ohms at 68°F (20°C).
3. Place the sensor into a container of ice water and note the resistance.
4. The resistance should change inversely with the temperature (resistance increases as temperature decreases). If not, the sensor is defective and should be replaced.

Cylinder Head Temperature Sensor Removal/Installation

1. Make sure the ignition switch is OFF. Disconnect the battery cables from the battery.
2. Remove the screw and retainer securing the sensor to the port cylinder head (under the No. 2 spark plug).
3. Disconnect the 2 sensor wires at the bullet connectors.
4. Install by reversing the order of removal. Make sure the sensor makes clean, secure contact with the cylinder head or the sensor may not function properly. Tighten the retaining screw securely.

6

Electronic Control Unit (ECU) Removal/Installation

1. Make sure the ignition switch is OFF. Disconnect the battery cables at the battery.

2. Disconnect the ECU wiring harness connector (**Figure 105**).

3. Remove the screws (B, **Figure 105**) and remove the water sensing module.

4. Remove the nuts (A, **Figure 105**) and screw (C).

5. Lift the ECU upward off the studs. Disconnect the MAP sensor hose and the manifold fitting and remove the ECU.

6. To reinstall, connect the MAP sensor hose to the manifold fitting and mount the ECU on the power head.

7. Install the water sensing module. Make sure the 2 ground wires are installed under the outer module screw.

8. Install the nuts (A, **Figure 105**) and screw (C). Tighten securely.

9. Reconnect the ECU wiring harness connector.

Water Separating Filter Assembly Removal/Installation

1. Remove the inlet and outlet hoses from the water separator filter assembly. See **Figure 106**.

2. Remove the tan wire from the water sensor probe at the bottom of the filter canister (**Figure 106**).

3. Remove the 2 screws securing the filter base to the induction manifold and remove the filter assembly.

4. If necessary, service the filter assembly as described in Chapter Four.

5. Reverse the order of removal to reinstall the filter assembly.

Throttle Position Indicator (TPI) Removal/Installation

1. Make sure the ignition switch is OFF and disconnect the battery cables at the battery.

2. Place match marks on the TPI base and induction manifold for reference during reinstallation. See **Figure 107**. The TPI should be reinstalled as closely as possible to its original position.

3. Disconnect the TPI 3-pin connector.

4. Remove the 2 mounting screws and remove the TPI and guide sleeve (**Figure 108**).

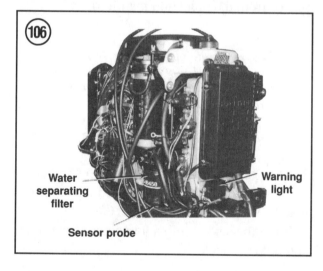

5. To reinstall the TPI, place the guide sleeve onto the TPI shaft.

6. Install the TPI on the induction manifold, making sure the TPI shaft properly engages the throttle shaft.

7. Align the match marks made during removal and lightly tighten the mounting screws.

8. Perform TPI adjustment procedures as described in Chapter Five.

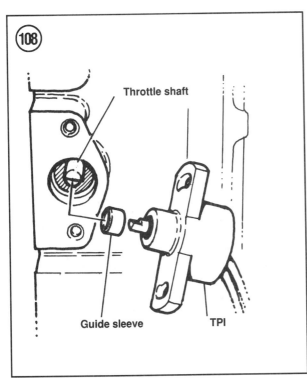

Throttle shaft

Guide sleeve   TPI

Air Temperature Sensor Removal/Installation

1. Make sure the ignition switch is OFF. Disconnect the battery cables at the battery.

2. Remove the water separating filter assembly as outlined in this chapter.

3. Disconnect the 2 sensor wires at the bullet connectors.

NOTE
Figure 109 shows the induction manifold removed from the power head. It is not necessary to remove the manifold to remove/install the air temperature sensor.

4. Remove the 3 screws securing the sensor (**Figure 109**) to the induction manifold. Remove and discard the O-ring from the inner surface of the sensor.

5. Reverse the removal procedure to reinstall the sensor. Install a new O-ring onto the inner sensor surface. Tighten the sensor mounting screws securely.

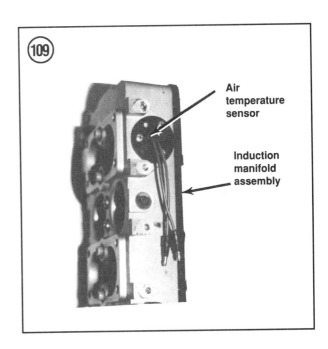

Air temperature sensor

Induction manifold assembly

Final Filter
Removal/Installation

Refer to Chapter Four for final filter removal, service and installation procedures.

Electric Fuel Pump
Removal/Installation

1. Make sure the ignition switch is OFF. Disconnect the battery cables at the battery.

2. Remove the 4 screws (A, **Figure 110**) securing the fuel pump cover and remove the cover.

CAUTION
Make sure the battery is disconnected when prying back the wire boot covers in Step 3. Battery voltage is present at both fuel pump terminals with the ignition switch OFF and the battery connected. Fuel pump and/or ECU damage can result if the pump terminals are shorted.

3. Pry the fuel pump wire boot covers away from the wire terminals. Disconnect the positive and negative pump wires.

4. Remove the final filter screw (C, **Figure 110**) and separate the filter cover from the filter base.

5. Disconnect the fuel pump inlet hose from the bottom of the pump.

6. Remove the fuel pump mounting screws (D, **Figure 110**). Remove the pump assembly, final filter base and rubber blanket around the pump.

7. If pump replacement is necessary, remove the clamp and disconnect the pump discharge hose from the pump and separate the pump from the final filter base. Connect a new pump to the discharge hose and secure with a new clamp.

8. To reinstall the pump, mount the pump and rubber blanket into position.

9. Connect the fuel pump inlet hose. Clamp securely with a new sta-strap.

10. Connect the pump positive and negative wires and slide the wire boot covers down into position.

11. Install the pump mounting screws.

12. Reinstall the final filter cover.

13. Install the pump cover. Tighten the 4 cover screws securely.

Vapor Separator
Removal/Installation

1. Remove the oil reservoir. See Chapter Eleven.

2. Remove the electric fuel pump as described in this chapter.

NOTE
Figure 111 *shows the vapor separator and induction manifold removed from the power head for illustrative purposes.*

3. Disconnect the fuel rail recirculation hose from the manifold fitting (A, **Figure 111**).

4. Disconnect vacuum hose (B, **Figure 111**) from the fuel pressure regulator.

5. Disconnect the bleed hose (C, **Figure 111**) from the vapor separator.

6. Disconnect the vacuum hose (D, **Figure 111**) from the vapor separator.

7. Disconnect the oil inlet hose at the bottom of the vapor separator assembly.

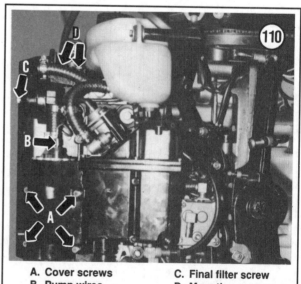

| A. Cover screws | C. Final filter screw |
| B. Pump wires | D. Mounting screws |

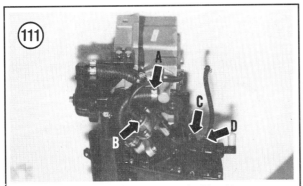

A. Fuel recirculation hose
B. Fuel pressure regulator vacuum hose
C. Bleed hose
D. Vapor separator vacuum hose

VAPOR SEPARATOR ASSEMBLY

1. Retainer plate
2. Screw
3. Lockwasher
4. Fuel pressure regulator assembly
5. O-ring
6. Cover assembly
7. Screw
8. Lockwasher
9. Flat washer
10. Inlet valve seat
11. Inlet valve needle
12. Wire clip
13. Float
14. Float pin
15. Seal
16. Bowl & bracket assembly
17. Check valve
18. Check valve
19. Bracket
20. Screws
21. Lockwasher

8. Remove the 3 screws securing the vapor separator to the induction manifold and remove the vapor separator assembly.

9. To reinstall the vapor separator, mount the vapor separator on the induction manifold and secure with the 3 screws. Tighten the screws securely.

10. Connect the oil delivery hose to the fitting on the bottom of the separator. Secure the hose with a hose clamp.

11. Connect the bleed and vacuum hoses (**Figure 111**).

12. Connect the fuel pressure regulator vacuum hose (**Figure 111**).

13. Connect the fuel recirculation hose (**Figure 111**). Secure the hose with a hose clamp.

14. Install the electric fuel pump as described in this chapter.

Vapor Separator
Disassembly/Reassembly

Refer to **Figure 112** for this procedure.

1. Remove the 2 pressure regulator mounting screws. Remove the regulator retainer plate, then the regulator. Remove the regulator O-ring seal.

2. Remove the vapor separator cover screws and lift off the cover assembly.

3. Remove the float pin using needlenose pliers. Remove the float and inlet needle.

4. Remove the cover seal from the bowl and bracket assembly.

5. To reassemble, attach the inlet needle to the float with the wire clip.

6. Install the float, making sure the inlet needle enters the seat, then install the float pin.

7. Install a new cover seal into the bowl and bracket assembly.

8. Install the cover assembly onto the bowl, install the cover screws and tighten securely.

9. Install the pressure regulator using a new O-ring. Place the retainer plate over the regulator and secure with the 2 screws.

6

Induction Manifold
Removal/Installation

1. Make sure the ignition switch is off. Disconnect the battery cables at the battery.

2. Remove the ECU assembly as described in this chapter.

3. Remove the water separating filter assembly as described in this chapter.

4. Disconnect the throttle position indicator at the 3-pin connector.

5. Disconnect the air temperature sensor at the bullet connectors.

6. Disconnect the fuel injector harness at the 4-pin connector.

7. Remove the oil reservoir as described in Chapter Eleven.

8. Remove the vapor separator assembly as described in this chapter.

9. Disconnect the throttle link rod from the throttle cam.

10. Disconnect the oil injection control rod from the injection pump control arm.

11. Note the location of the ground wires (**Figure 113**) for reference during installation.

12. Remove the 12 manifold cover screws and remove the manifold cover (**Figure 113**).

13. Disconnect the bleed hose from the bleed shut off valve. Pull the manifold away from the power head enough to disconnect the bleed hoses from the fittings at the bottom of the manifold assembly.

14. Remove the induction manifold assembly from the power head.

15. To reinstall the induction manifold, first place a new gasket onto the manifold-to-engine mating surface.

16. Hold the manifold in position while connecting the bleed hoses to the bleed shut off valve and the bleed fittings at the bottom of the manifold. Install the manifold onto the power head and secure with the 12 screws.

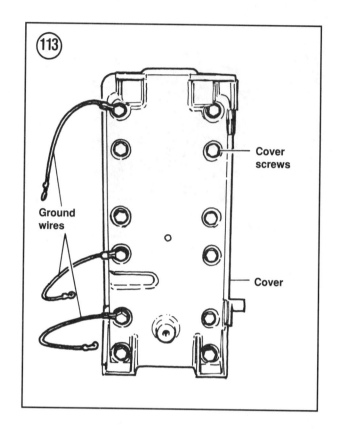

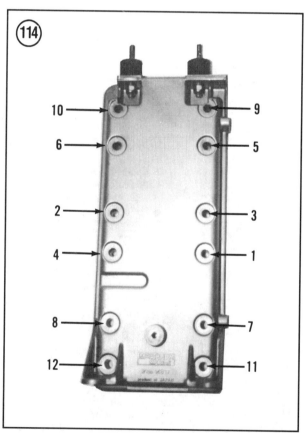

17. Tighten the manifold screws to 80-100 in.-lbs. (9-11 N•m) in the sequence shown in **Figure 114**.

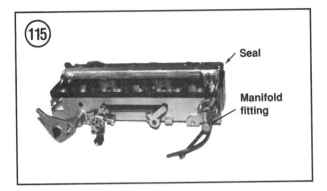

Seal

Manifold fitting

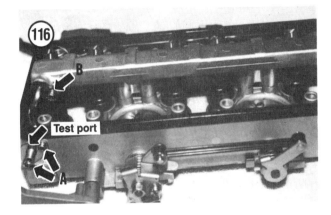

Test port

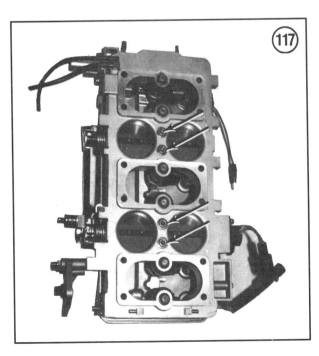

18. Make sure the oil injection pump control arm is rotated clockwise from center, then connect the oil pump control rod to the pump arm.

19. Connect the throttle link rod to the throttle cam.

20. Install the vapor separator as described in this chapter.

21. Install the electric fuel pump as described in this chapter.

22. Install the oil reservoir as described in Chapter Eleven.

23. Reconnect the throttle position indicator, air temperature sensor and fuel injector wiring harness.

24. Install the water separating filter and ECU assembly as described in this chapter.

25. Perform timing, synchronizing and adjusting procedures as described in Chapter Five.

26. Carefully inspect all fuel connections for leakage and repair as necessary.

Induction Manifold Disassembly/Reassembly (Replace Fuel Injectors)

1. Place the induction manifold assembly on a clean work surface.

2. Remove the induction manifold cover seal (**Figure 115**).

3. Remove the manifold fitting (**Figure 115**) mounting screws. Remove the fitting. Remove and discard the fitting O-rings seals.

4. Remove the 2 screws (A, **Figure 116**) securing the test port outer plate to the manifold.

5. Remove the screw (B, **Figure 116**) securing the test port inner plate to the fuel rail.

6. Remove the test port assembly from the manifold. Remove and discard the test port O-rings.

7. Remove the 4 fuel rail mounting screws (**Figure 117**) and remove the fuel rail from the manifold.

8. Lift the wire clip that secures the injector connectors to the injectors, from its groove. Disconnect the injector connectors.

6

9. Remove the injectors by lifting straight up from the manifold.

10. To reassemble, install the injector seals, O-ring and insert injector filter into the injector. See **Figure 118**.

11. Install the injectors into the manifold. Attach the injector connectors to the injectors and install the wire clips (A, **Figure 119**) to secure the connectors.

12. Install new O-rings on the fuel rail plugs, tube support and tubes. See **Figure 120**.

13. Install the fuel rail to the manifold. Install the 4 fuel rail screws (**Figure 117**) and tighten to 35 in.-lb. (3.9 N•m).

14. Install new O-rings on the service port tube, install the tube and tighten the screws securely.

15. Install new O-rings on the manifold fitting. Install the fitting to the manifold (**Figure 115**). Tighten the screws securely.

16. Install the induction manifold assembly as described in this chapter.

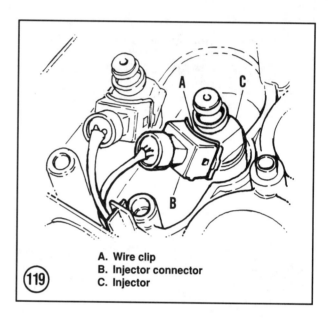

A. Wire clip
B. Injector connector
C. Injector

(119)

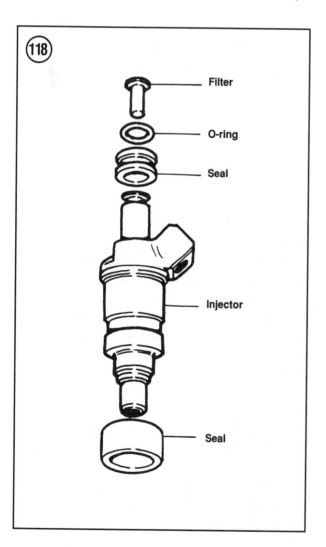

(118)

Filter

O-ring

Seal

Injector

Seal

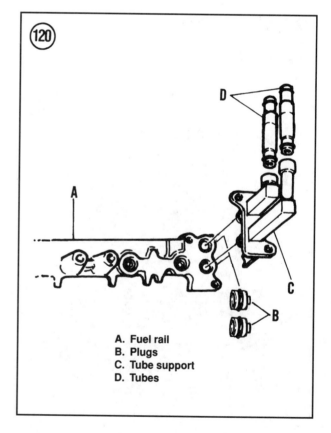

(120)

A. Fuel rail
B. Plugs
C. Tube support
D. Tubes

Table 1 CARBURETOR JET SIZES (4-25 HP MODELS)

Model	Jet type	Sea level to 2500 ft.	2500-5000 ft.	5000-7500 ft.	7500 ft. and up
4 hp	Main	0.031 in.	0.029 in.	0.027 in.	0.025 in.
5 hp	Main	0.032 in.	0.030 in.	0.028 in.	0.026 in.
8 hp	Main	0.046 in.	0.044 in.	0.042 in.	0.040 in.
9.9 hp	Main	0.056 in.	0.054 in.	0.052 in.	0.050 in.
15 hp	Main	0.066 in.	0.064 in.	0.062 in.	0.060 in.
20 hp	Main	0.046 in.	0.044 in.	0.042 in.	0.040 in.
25 hp	Main	0.080 in.	0.078 in.	0.076 in.	0.074 in.

Table 2 CARBURETOR JET SIZES (40 HP AND 50-60 HP [PRIOR TO SERIAL NO. D000750] MODELS)

Model	Jet type	Sea level to 2500 ft.	2500-5000 ft.	5000-7500 ft.	7500 ft. and up
40 hp					
WMA-7B	Main	0.057 in.	0.055 in.	0.053 in.	0.051 in.
	Vent	0.098 in.	0.096 in.	0.094 in.	0.092 in.
WMA-9	Main	0.050 in.	0.048 in.	0.046 in.	0.044 in.
	Vent	0.098 in.	0.096 in.	0.094 in.	0.092 in.
50 hp	Main	0.058 in.	0.054 in.	0.052 in.	0.050 in.
	Vent	0.096 in.	0.094 in.	0.092 in.	0.090 in.
60 hp					
Top	Main	0.0785 in.	0.076 in.	0.074 in.	0.072 in.
Bottom	Main	0.072 in.	0.070 in.	0.068 in.	0.066 in.
	Vent	0.096 in.	0.094 in.	0.092 in.	0.090 in.

Table 3 CARBURETOR JET SIZES (50-60 HP [D000750-ON], 75, 90, 100 AND 115 HP MODELS)

Model	Jet type	Sea level to 2500 ft.	2500-5000 ft.	5000-7500 ft.	7500 ft. and up
50 hp					
WME-23	Main	0.052 in.	0.050 in.	0.048 in.	0.046 in.
	Vent	0.092 in.	0.090 in.	0.088 in.	0.086 in.
WME-26	Main	0.048 in.	0.046 in.	0.044 in.	0.042 in.
	Vent	0.090 in.	0.088 in.	0.086 in.	0.084 in.
60 hp					
WME-22,					
WME-23	Main	0.070 in.	0.068 in.	0.066 in.	0.064 in.
	Vent	0.090 in.	0.088 in.	0.086 in.	0.084 in.
WME-28	Main	0.062 in.	0.060 in.	0.058 in.	0.056 in.
	Vent	0.090 in.	0.088 in.	0.086 in.	0.084 in.
75 hp[1]					
WME-8,					
WME-17	Main	0.068 in.	0.066 in.	0.064 in.	0.062 in.
	Vent	0.094 in.	0.092 in.	0.090 in.	0.088 in.
90 hp[1]					
WME-10	Main	0.072 in.	0.070 in.	0.068 in.	0.066 in.
	Vent	0.094 in.	0.092 in.	0.090 in.	0.088 in.
WME-19	Main	0.066 in.	0.064 in.	0.062 in.	0.060 in.
	Vent	0.094 in.	0.092 in.	0.090 in.	0.088 in.

(continued)

6

**Table 3 CARBURETOR JET SIZES (50-60 HP [D000750-ON],
75, 90, 100 AND 115 HP MODELS) (continued)**

Model	Jet type	Sea level to 2500 ft.	2500- 5000 ft.	5000- 7500 ft.	7500 ft. and up
100 hp WME-11, WME-20	Main	0.054 in.	0.052 in.	0.050 in.	0.048 in.
	Vent	None	None	None	None
115 hp WME-14, WME-21	Main	0.076 in.	0.074 in.	0.072 in.	0.070 in.
	Vent	None	None	None	None

1. On 75 and 90 hp models, the following high-altitude modifications should be performed in addition to jet changes: Idle timing should be advanced 2-3° at 5000 ft. and above, the engine should be propped to run near the top of the recommended full-throttle speed range and the idle fuel mixture should be adjusted slightly leaner.

Table 4 CARBURETOR JET SIZES (135-200 HP MODELS)

Model Carb. No.	Jet type	Sea level to 5000 ft.	5000- 7500 ft.	7500- 10,000 ft.	10,000 ft. and up
135 hp WMH-5	Main	0.050 in.	0.050 in.	0.046 in.	0.046 in.
	Off idle air	0.036 in.	0.040 in.	0.040 in.	0.040 in.
	Idle air	0.048 in.	0.048 in.	0.048 in.	0.048 in.
	Vent	0.070 in.	0.070 in.	0.070 in.	0.070 in.
WMH-8	Main	0.050 in.	0.050 in.	0.046 in.	0.046 in.
	Off idle air	0.040 in.	0.044 in.	0.044 in.	0.044 in.
	Idle air	0.048 in.	0.048 in.	0.048 in.	0.048 in.
	Vent	None	None	None	None
WMH-8 A	Main	0.050 in.	0.050 in.	0.046 in.	0.046 in.
	Off idle air	0.040 in.	0.044 in.	0.044 in.	0.044 in.
	Idle air	0.048 in.	0.048 in.	0.048 in.	0.048 in.
	Vent	None	None	None	None
WMH-12	Main	0.064 in.	0.064 in.	0.060 in.	0.058 in.
	Off idle air	0.070 in.	0.076 in.	0.076 in.	0.076 in.
	Idle air	0.052 in.	0.052 in.	0.052 in.	0.052 in.
	Vent	0.060 in.	0.060 in.	0.060 in.	0.060 in.
WMH-12 B	Main	0.060 in.	0.060 in.	0.056 in.	0.054 in.
	Off idle air	0.050 in.	0.056 in.	0.056 in.	0.056 in.
	Idle air	0.050 in.	0.050 in.	0.050 in.	0.050 in.
	Vent	0.090 in.	0.090 in.	0.090 in.	0.090 in.
WMH-24	Main	0.060 in.	0.060 in.	0.056 in.	0.054 in.
	Off idle air	0.050 in.	0.056 in.	0.056 in.	0.056 in.
	Idle air	0.056 in.	0.056 in.	0.056 in.	0.056 in.
	Vent	0.090 in.	0.090 in.	0.090 in.	0.090 in.
WMH-28 B	Main	0.062 in.	0.062 in.	0.058 in.	0.056 in.
	Off idle air	0.050 in.	0.056 in.	0.056 in.	0.056 in.
	Idle air	0.056 in.	0.056 in.	0.056 in.	0.056 in.
	Vent	None	None	None	None

(continued)

Table 4 CARBURETOR JET SIZES (135-200 HP MODELS) (continued)

Model Carb. No.	Jet type	Sea level to 5000 ft.	5000-7500 ft.	7500-10,000 ft.	10,000 ft. and up
150 hp					
WMH-1[1]	Main	0.062 in.	0.062 in.	0.058 in.	0.058 in.
	Off idle air	0.044 in.	0.050 in.	0.050 in.	0.050 in.
	Idle air[2]	0.048 in.	0.048 in.	0.048 in.	0.048 in.
	Vent	0.084 in.	0.084 in.	0.084 in.	0.084 in.
WMH-7	Main	0.062 in.	0.062 in.	0.058 in.	0.058 in.
	Off idle air	0.034 in.	0.040 in.	0.040 in.	0.040 in.
	Idle air	0.040 in.	0.040 in.	0.040 in.	0.040 in.
	Vent	None	None	None	None
WMH-13	Main	0.064 in.	0.064 in.	0.060 in.	0.058 in.
	Off idle air	0.070 in.	0.076 in.	0.076 in.	0.076 in.
	Idle air	0.050 in.	0.050 in.	0.050 in.	0.050 in.
	Vent	0.096 in.	0.096 in.	0.096 in.	0.096 in.
WMH-13 B	Main	0.064 in.	0.064 in.	0.060 in.	0.058 in.
	Off idle air	0.048 in.	0.054 in.	0.054 in.	0.054 in.
	Idle air	0.050 in.	0.050 in.	0.050 in.	0.050 in.
	Vent	0.096 in.	0.096 in.	0.096 in.	0.096 in.
WMH-23	Main	0.060 in.	0.060 in.	0.056 in.	0.054 in.
	Off idle air	0.050 in.	0.056 in.	0.056 in.	0.056 in.
	Idle air	0.054 in.	0.054 in.	0.054 in.	0.054 in.
	Vent	0.094 in.	0.094 in.	0.094 in.	0.094 in.
150XR4					
WMH-4	Main	0.062 in.	0.062 in.	0.058 in.	0.058 in.
	Off idle air	0.030 in.	0.034 in.	0.034 in.	0.034 in.
	Idle air	0.044 in.	0.044 in.	0.044 in.	0.044 in.
	Vent	None	None	None	None
WMH-4 A	Main	0.062 in.	0.062 in.	0.058 in.	0058 in.
	Off idle air	0.030 in.	0.034 in.	0.034 in.	0.034 in.
	Idle air	0.040 in.	0.040 in.	0.040 in.	0.040 in.
	Vent	None	None	None	None
WMH-6 A	Main	0.062 in.	0.062 in.	0.058 in.	0.058 in.
	Off idle air	0.030 in.	0.034 in.	0.034 in.	0.034 in.
	Idle air	0.040 in.	0.040 in.	0.040 in.	0.040 in.
	Vent	None	None	None	None
WMH-10	Main	0.062 in.	0.062 in.	0.058 in.	0.058 in.
	Off idle air	0.040 in.	0.044 in.	0.044 in.	0.044 in.
	Idle air	0.040 in.	0.040 in.	0.040 in.	0.040 in.
	Vent	None	None	None	None
150XR6					
WMH-14	Main	0.054 in.	0.054 in.	0.050 in.	0.048 in.
	Off idle air	0.050 in.	0.050 in.	0.052 in.	0.052 in.
	Idle air	0.052 in.	0.052 in.	0.052 in.	0.052 in.
	Vent	0.086 in.	0.086 in.	0.086 in.	0.086 in.
WMH-25	Main	0.060 in.	0.060 in.	0.056 in.	0.054 in.
	Off idle air	0.050 in.	0.050 in.	0.052 in.	0.052 in.
	Idle air	0.050 in.	0.050 in.	0.050 in.	0.050 in.
	Vent	0.086 in.	0.086 in.	0.086 in.	0.086 in.
175 hp					
WMH-2	Main	0.064 in.	0.064 in.	0.060 in.	0.060 in.
	Off idle air	0.044 in.	0.050 in.	0.050 in.	0.050 in.
	Idle air	0.052 in.	0.052 in.	0.052 in.	0.052 in.
	Vent	0.080 in.	0.080 in.	0.080 in.	0.080 in.

(continued)

6

Table 4 CARBURETOR JET SIZES (135-200 HP MODELS) (continued)

Model Carb. No.	Jet type	Sea level to 5000 ft.	5000-7500 ft.	7500-10,000 ft.	10,000 ft. and up
175 hp (continued)					
WMH-2 A	Main	0.064 in.	0.064 in.	0.060 in.	0.060 in.
	Off idle air	0.044 in.	0.050 in.	0.050 in.	0.050 in.
	Idle air	0.044 in.	0.044 in.	0.044 in.	0.044 in.
	Vent	0.080 in.	0.080 in.	0.080 in.	0.080 in.
WMH-11	Main	0.064 in.	0.064 in.	0.060 in.	0.060 in.
	Off idle air	0.070 in.	0.076 in.	0.076 in.	0.076 in.
	Idle air	0.048 in.	0.048 in.	0.048 in.	0.048 in.
	Vent	0.080 in.	0.080 in.	0.080 in.	0.080 in.
WMH-11 A	Main	0.064 in.	0.064 in.	0.060 in.	0.060 in.
	Off idle air	0.070 in.	0.076 in.	0.076 in.	0.076 in.
	Idle air	0.048 in.	0.048 in.	0.048 in.	0.048 in.
	Vent	0.080 in.	0.080 in.	0.080 in.	0.080 in.
WMH-15	Main	0.064 in.	0.064 in.	0.060 in.	0.058 in.
	Off idle air	0.070 in.	0.076 in.	0.076 in.	0.076 in.
	Idle air	0.054 in.	0.054 in.	0.054 in.	0.054 in.
	Vent	0.080 in.	0.080 in.	0.080 in.	0.080 in.
WMH-22	Main	0.064 in.	0.064 in.	0.060 in.	0.058 in.
	Off idle air	0.040 in.	0.046 in.	0.046 in.	0.046 in.
	Idle air	0.052 in.	0.052 in.	0.052 in.	0.052 in.
	Vent	0.098 in.	0.098 in.	0.098 in.	0.098 in.
WMH-22 A	Main	0.064 in.	0.064 in.	0.060 in.	0.058 in.
	Off idle air	0.040 in.	0.046 in.	0.046 in.	0.046 in.
	Idle air	0.050 in.	0.050 in.	0.050 in.	0.051 in.
	Vent	0.098 in.	0.098 in.	0.098 in.	0.098 in.
200 hp					
WMH-3 B	Main	0.066 in.	0.066 in.	0.060 in.	0.060 in.
	Off idle air	0.034 in.	0.036 in.	0.038 in.	0.038 in.
	Idle air	0.040 in.	0.040 in.	0.040 in.	0.040 in.
	Vent	0.082 in.	0.082 in.	0.082 in.	0.082 in.
WMH-3 C	Main	0.066 in.	0.066 in.	0.060 in.	0.060 in.
	Off idle air	0.034 in.	0.036 in.	0.038 in.	0.038 in.
	Idle air	0.040 in.	0.040 in.	0.040 in.	0.040 in.
	Vent	0.082 in.	0.082 in.	0.082 in.	0.082 in.
WMH-16	Main	0.066 in.	0.066 in.	0.060 in.	0.060 in.
	Off idle air	0.050 in.	0.046 in.	0.046 in.	0.046 in.
	Idle air	0.058 in.	0.058 in.	0.058 in.	0.058 in.
	Vent	0.090 in.	0.090 in.	0.090 in.	0.090 in.
WMH-21	Main	0.064 in.	0.064 in.	0.058 in.	0.058 in.
	Off idle air	0.050 in.	0.056 in.	0.056 in.	0.056 in.
	Idle air	0.046 in.	0.046 in.	0.046 in.	0.046 in.
	Vent	0.096 in.	0.096 in.	0.096 in.	0.096 in.

1. On some WMH-1 carburetors, 0.040 in. idle air jets are installed during manufacture.

2. In addition to changing jet sizes, the idle mixture screw should be turned in (clockwise) 30° if operated at 5000-10,000 ft. or 60° at 10,000 ft. and above. It may be necessary to reduce the lower unit gear ratio for satisfactory high-altitude operation.

Table 5 CARBURETOR JET SIZES (250 AND 275 HP MODELS)

Model Carb. No.	Jet type	Sea level to 2500 ft.	2500-5000 ft.	5000-7500 ft.	7500 ft. and up
250 hp					
WO-8-1					
WO-8-2					
WO-8-3					
WO-8-4					
WO-8-6	Main	0.078 in.	0.076 in.	0.074 in.	0.072 in.
	Idle	0.060 in.	0.058 in.	0.056 in.	0.054 in.
	Vent	0.080 in.	0.078 in.	0.076 in.	0.074 in.
WO-8-5	Main	0.084 in.	0.082 in.	0.080 in.	0.078 in.
	Idle	0.060 in.	0.058 in.	0.056 in.	0.054 in.
	Vent	0.080 in.	0.078 in.	0.076 in.	0.074 in.
275 hp					
WO-9-1					
WO-9-2					
WO-9-4					
WO-9-6	Main	0.082 in.	0.080 in.	0.078 in.	0.076 in.
	Idle	0.060 in.	0.058 in.	0.056 in.	0.054 in.
	Vent	None	None	None	None
WO-9-3	Main	0.084 in.	0.082 in.	0.080 in.	0.078 in.
	Idle	0.060 in.	0.058 in.	0.056 in.	0.054 in.
	Vent	None	None	None	None
WO-9-5	Main	0.088 in.	0.086 in.	0.084 in.	0.082 in.
	Idle	0.060 in.	0.058 in.	0.056 in.	0.054 in.
	Vent	None	None	None	None

6

Chapter Seven

Ignition and Electrical Systems

This chapter provides service procedures for the battery, starter motor and ignition systems used on outboard motors covered in this manual. Wiring diagrams are included at the end of the book. **Tables 1-4** are at the end of this chapter.

BATTERY

Batteries used in marine applications endure far more rigorous treatment than those used in automotive electrical systems. Marine batteries have a thicker exterior case to cushion the plates during tight turns and rough water operation. Thicker plates are also used, with each one individually fastened within the case to prevent premature failure. Spill-proof caps on the battery cells prevent electrolyte from spilling into the bilge.

Automotive batteries are not designed to be discharged and recharged repeatedly. For this reason, they should be used in a boat *only* during an emergency situation when a suitable marine battery is not available.

CAUTION
Sealed or maintenance-free batteries are ***not*** *recommended for use with the unregulated charging systems used on some Mercury outboard motors. Excessive charging during continued high-speed operation will cause the electrolyte to boil, resulting in its loss. Since water cannot be added to such batteries, the battery will be ruined.*

Separate batteries may be used to provide power for any accessories such as lighting, fish finders and depth finders. To determine the required capacity of such batteries, calculate the

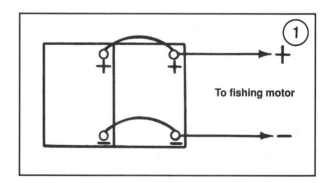

To fishing motor

accessory current (amperage) draw rate of the accessory and refer to **Table 1**.

Two batteries may be connected in parallel to double the ampere-hour capacity while maintaining the required 12 volts. See **Figure 1**. For

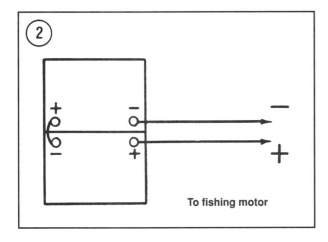

To fishing motor

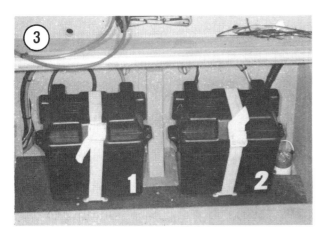

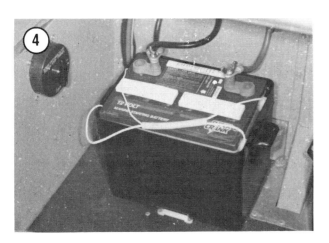

accessories which require 24 volts, batteries may be connected in series (**Figure 2**), but only accessories specifically requiring 24 volts should be connected to the system. If charging becomes necessary, batteries connected in a parallel or series circuit should be disconnected and charged individually.

Battery Installation in Aluminum Boats

If the battery is not properly secured and grounded when installed in an aluminum boat, it may contact the hull and short to ground. This will burn out remote control cables, tiller handle cables or wiring harnesses.

The following preventive steps should be observed when installing a battery in any boat, and especially a metal boat.

1. Choose a location as far as practical from the fuel tank while providing access for maintenance.

2. Install the battery in a plastic battery box with cover and tie-down strap.

3. If a covered battery box is not used, cover the positive battery terminal with a nonconductive shield or boot.

4. Make sure the battery is secured inside the battery box and the box is fastened in position with a suitable tie-down strap or fixture.

Care and Inspection

1. Remove the battery tray or container cover. See **Figure 3** for a typical installation.

2. Disconnect the negative battery cable, then the positive battery cable. See **Figure 4**.

NOTE
*Some batteries have a built-in carry strap (**Figure 5**) for use in Step 3.*

3. Attach a battery carry strap to the terminal posts. Remove the battery from the battery tray or container.

7

4. Check the entire battery case for cracks, holes or other damage.

5. Inspect the battery tray or container for corrosion and clean if necessary with a solution of baking soda and water.

NOTE
Do not allow the baking soda cleaning solution to enter the battery cells in Step 6 or the electrolyte will be severely weakened.

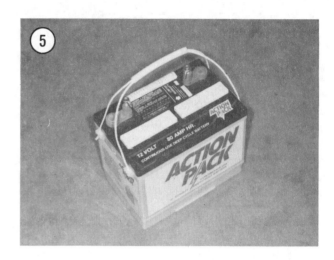

6. Clean the top of the battery with a stiff bristle brush using the baking soda and water solution (**Figure 6**). Rinse the battery case with clear water and wipe dry with a clean cloth or paper towel.

7. Position the battery in the battery tray or container.

8. Clean the battery cable clamps with a stiff wire brush.

9. Reconnect the positive battery cable first, then the negative cable.

CAUTION
Be sure the battery cables are connected to their proper terminals. Reversing the battery polarity will result in rectifier and ignition system damage.

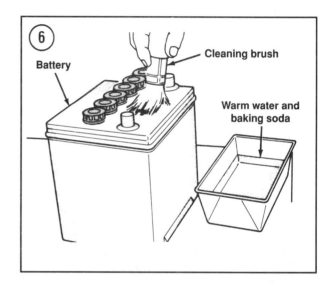

10. Securely tighten the battery connections. Coat the connections with petroleum jelly or a light grease to minimize corrosion.

NOTE
Do not overfill the battery cells in Step 11. The electrolyte expands due to heat from the charging system and will overflow if the level is more than 3/16 in. above the battery plates.

11. Remove the filler caps and check the electrolyte level. Add distilled water, if necessary, to bring the level up to 3/16 in. above the plates in the battery case. See **Figure 7**.

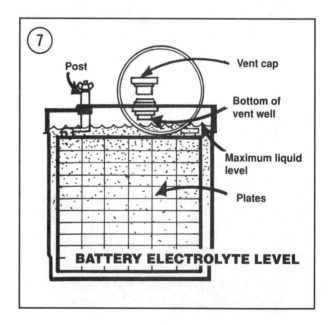

Testing

Hydrometer testing is the best method to check the battery state of charge (specific gravity). Use a hydrometer with numbered graduations from 1.100-1.300 points rather than one with color-coded bands. To use the hydrometer, squeeze the rubber bulb, insert the tip into a cell, then release the bulb to fill the hydrometer. See **Figure 8**.

NOTE
Do not test specific gravity immediately after adding water to the battery cells, as the water will dilute the electrolyte and lower the specific gravity. To obtain ac-

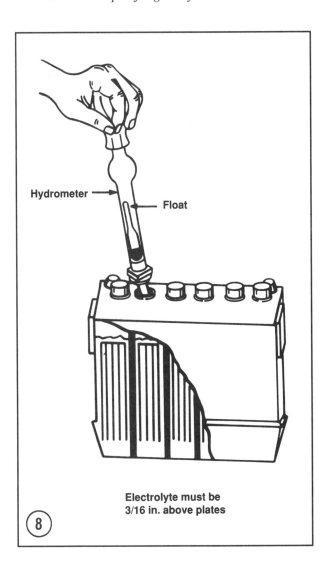

Hydrometer — Float

Electrolyte must be
3/16 in. above plates

⑧

accurate hydrometer readings, the battery must be charged after adding water.

Draw sufficient electrolyte to raise the float inside the hydrometer. When using a temperature-compensated hydrometer, discharge the electrolyte back into the battery cell and repeat the process several times to adjust the temperature of the hydrometer to that of the electrolyte.

Hold the hydrometer upright and note the number on the float that is even with the surface of the electrolyte (**Figure 9**). This number is the specific gravity for the cell. Discharge the electrolyte into the cell from which it came.

The specific gravity of a cell is the indicator of the cell's state of charge. A fully charged cell will read 1.260 or more at 80°F (26.7°C). A cell that is 75 percent charged will read from 1.220-1.230 while a cell with a 50 percent charge will read from 1.170-1.180. Any cell reading 1.120 or less should be considered discharged. All cells should be within 30 points specific gravity of each other. If over 30 points variation is noted, the battery condition is questionable. Charge the battery and recheck the specific gravity. If 30 points or more variation remains between cells after charging, the battery has failed and should be replaced.

NOTE
If a temperature-compensated hydrometer is not used, add 4 points specific gravity to the actual reading for every 10° above 80°F (26.7°C). Subtract 4 points specific gravity for every 10° below 80°F (26.7°C).

Battery Storage

Wet cell batteries slowly discharge when stored. They discharge faster when warm than when cold. Before storing a battery, clean the case with a solution of baking soda and water. Rinse with clear water and wipe dry. The battery should be fully charged (no change in specific gravity when 3 readings are taken 1 hour apart)

7

and then stored in a cool, dry location. Check electrolyte level and state of charge frequently during storage. If specific gravity falls to 40 points or more below full charge (1.260), recharge the battery.

Charging

A good state of charge should be maintained in batteries used for starting. Check the battery with a voltmeter as shown in **Figure 10**. Any battery that cannot deliver at least 9.6 volts under starting load should be charged. Replace the battery if it still cannot deliver at least 9.6 volts under cranking load after recharging.

The battery does not have to be removed from the boat for charging, but it is a recommended safety procedure, since a charging battery releases highly explosive hydrogen gas. In many boats, the area around the battery is not well ventilated and the gas may remain in the area for hours after the charging process has been completed. Sparks or flames occurring near the battery can cause it to explode, spraying battery acid over a wide area. For this reason, it is important to observe the following precautions:

a. Never smoke around batteries that are charging, or that have been recently charged.

b. Do not disconnect a live circuit at the battery creating a spark that can ignite any hydrogen gas that may be present.

Disconnect the negative battery cable first, then the positive cable. Make sure the electrolyte is at the proper level.

Connect the charger to the battery, negative charger lead to the negative battery terminal and positive charger lead to the positive battery terminal. If the charger output is variable, select a 4 ampere setting. Set the voltage switch to 12 volts and switch the charger on.

WARNING
Be extremely careful not to create any sparks around the battery when connecting the battery charger.

If the battery is severely discharged, allow it to charge for at least 8 hours. **Table 2** provides

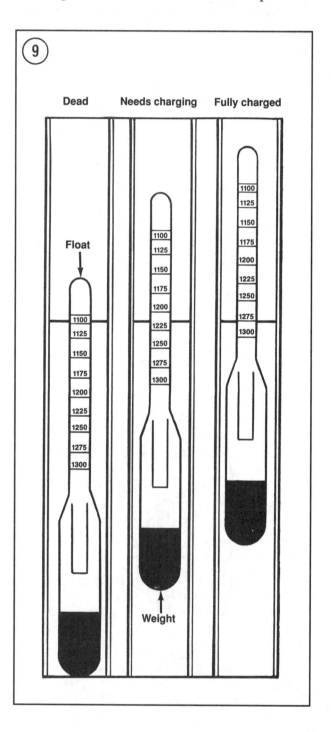

approximate charge rates for batteries used primarily for engine starting. Check the charging process with a hydrometer. The battery should be considered fully charged when the specific gravity of all cells does not increase when checked 3 times at 1 hour intervals, and all cells are gassing freely.

Jump Starting

If the battery becomes severely discharged, it is possible to "jump start" the engine from another battery. If the proper procedure is not followed, however, jump starting can be dangerous. Check the electrolyte level of the discharged battery before attempting the jump start. If the electrolyte is not visible or if it appears to be frozen, do not jump start the discharged battery.

WARNING
*Use extreme caution when connecting a booster battery to one that is discharged to avoid personal injury or damage to the system. **Be certain** the jumper cables are connected in the correct polarity.*

1. Connect the jumper cables in the order and sequence shown in **Figure 11**.

WARNING
An electrical arc may occur when the final connection is made. This could cause an explosion if it occurs near the battery. For this reason, the final connection should be made to a good engine ground, away from the battery and not to the battery itself.

2. Check that all jumper cables are out of the way of moving engine parts.

3. Start the engine. Once it starts, run it at a moderate speed.

CAUTION
Running the engine at high speed with a discharged battery can damage the charging system.

4. Remove the jumper cables in the exact reverse of the order shown in **Figure 11**. Remove the cable at point 4, then 3, 2 and 1.

7

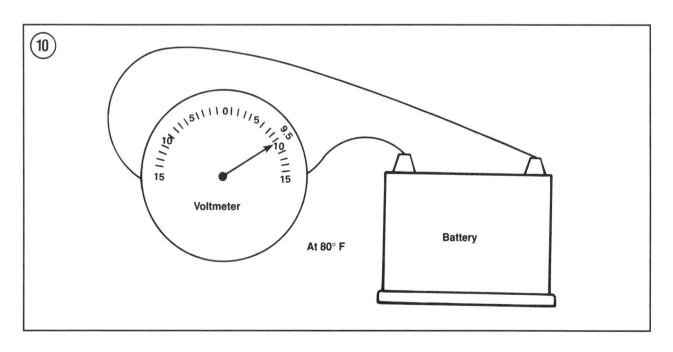

BATTERY CHARGING SYSTEM

The battery charging system used on Mercury outboard motors generally consists of a stator, rectifier and battery. See **Figure 12**. On 75-275 hp and some 40 hp models, a voltage regulator/rectifier assembly is used.

Alternating current (AC) created by the alternator stator is converted to direct current (DC) by the rectifier and used to charge the battery.

A malfunction in the battery charging system usually results in an undercharged battery. Perform the following visual inspection to determine the cause of the problem. If the visual inspection proves satisfactory, test the charging system as described in See Chapter Three.

1. Make sure that the battery cables are connected properly. The red cable (positive) must be connected to the positive battery terminal. If the polarity is reversed, check for a damaged rectifier.

2. Inspect the battery terminals for loose or corroded connections. Tighten or clean as necessary.

3. Inspect the physical condition of the battery. Look for bulges or cracks in the case, leaking electrolyte and corrosion build up.

4. Carefully check the wiring between the stator and battery for chafing, deterioration or other damage.

5. Check the circuit wiring for corroded, loose or disconnected connections. Clean, tighten or reconnect as necessary.

6. Determine if the accessory load on the battery is greater than the charging system and battery capacity.

STARTING SYSTEM

Marine starter motors are very similar in design and operation to those found on automotive engines. The starter motors used on outboards covered in this manual have an inertia-type drive in which external spiral splines on the armature

shaft mate with internal splines on the drive assembly.

The starter motor is capable of producing a very high torque, but only for a brief time, due to rapid heat buildup. To prevent overheating, never operate the starter motor continuously for more than 30 seconds. Allow the motor to cool for at least 2 minutes before further operation.

If the starter motor does not crank the engine, check the battery and all connecting wiring for loose or corroded connections, shorted or open

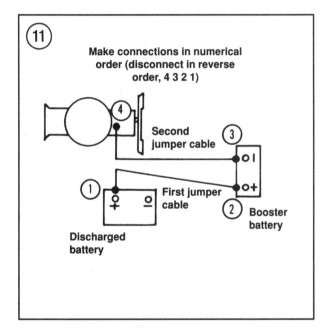

⑪ Make connections in numerical order (disconnect in reverse order, 4 3 2 1)

Second jumper cable

First jumper cable

Discharged battery

Booster battery

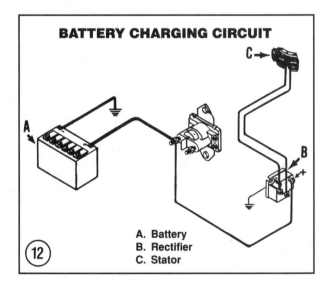

BATTERY CHARGING CIRCUIT

A. Battery
B. Rectifier
C. Stator

⑫

circuits, or other defects. If this inspection does not determine the problem, test the starting system as described in Chapter Three.

Starter Motor Removal/Installation (8-25 hp)

1. Disconnect the battery cables from the battery.

2. Remove the 2 starter motor mounting bolts.

3. Disconnect the yellow wire at the starter motor positive terminal and remove the starter motor.

4. Installation is the reverse of removal. Tighten the mounting bolts to specification (**Table 4**).

Starter Motor Removal/Installation (50 and 60 hp Prior to Serial No. D000750)

1. Disconnect the battery cables from the battery.

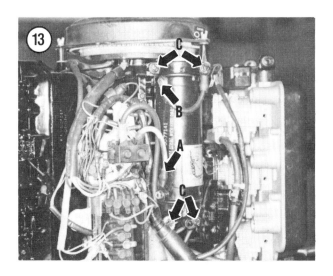

2. Disconnect the spark plug leads from the spark plugs.

3. Remove the nut from the lower air box mounting stud. Remove one end of the ground wire from the mounting stud.

4. Remove the nut from the upper air box mounting stud. Disconnect one end of the ground wire from the mounting stud.

5. Remove the mounting bolt and fuel connector from the air box.

6. Pull the air box away from the power head sufficiently to access the starter motor.

7. Disconnect the yellow cable (A, **Figure 13**, typical) at the starter motor positive terminal.

8. Disconnect the black ground cable at the starter (B, **Figure 13**, typical).

9. Note the location of the timing pointer behind the inside upper starter mounting bolt for reference during installation. Remove the 4 bolts (C, **Figure 13**, typical) holding the upper and lower starter mounting clamps. Remove the starter motor assembly.

10. Remove the starter mounting clamps along with the rubber mounting collars and spacer (if so equipped) from the starter motor. See **Figure 14**.

11. To reinstall, place the rubber collar and mounting clamp on the lower end of the motor.

12. Install the spacer (if so equipped), rubber collar and mounting clamp on the upper end of the starter.

13. Install the starter motor on the power head. Tighten the 4 mounting bolts to specification (**Table 4**). Make sure the timing pointer is properly positioned under the upper bolt as noted during removal.

14. Attach the black ground cable to the starter motor.

15. Connect the yellow cable to the starter motor positive terminal.

16. Mount the air box assembly onto the upper and lower mounting studs. Connect the ground wires to the studs and install the nuts.

7

17. Attach the fuel connector to the air box with the bolt and washer. Tighten the bolt securely.

**Starter Motor Removal/Installation
(50 and 60 hp [Serial No. D000750-on])**

1. Disconnect the battery cables from the battery.
2. Remove the black ground cable (A, **Figure 15**) from the starter motor.
3. Remove the black positive cable (C, **Figure 15**) from the starter terminal.
4. Remove the starter mounting bolts (B, **Figure 15**) and mounting clamp. Remove the starter motor from the power head.
5. Remove the rubber collars from each end of the motor. Remove the 2 rubber bumpers from the upper end of the motor.
6. Reverse the removal procedure to reinstall the starter motor. Tighten the mounting bolts securely.

**Starter Motor Removal/Installation
(40 hp and 75-275 hp)**

1. Disconnect the battery cables from the battery.

2. 275 hp—Remove the oil reservoir as described in Chapter Eleven. Note that 2 starter motor mounting bolts are removed during oil reservoir removal.

3. Disconnect the black ground cable (B, **Figure 13**, typical) from the starter motor.

4. Disconnect the yellow or black positive cable (A, **Figure 13**, typical) from the starter terminal.

5A. 275 hp—Remove the 2 remaining starter motor mounting bolts.

5B. All others—Remove the 4 starter motor mounting bolts.

6. Remove the starter motor along with the upper and lower mounting clamps.

7. Remove the rubber collars from each end of the starter motor.

⑮

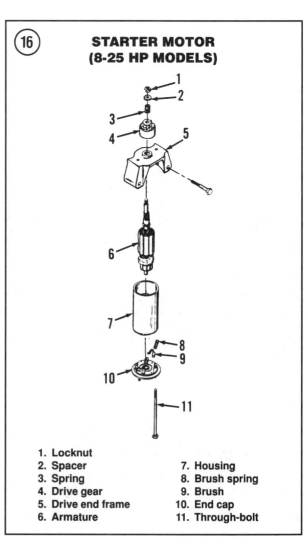

⑯ **STARTER MOTOR
(8-25 HP MODELS)**

1. Locknut
2. Spacer
3. Spring
4. Drive gear
5. Drive end frame
6. Armature
7. Housing
8. Brush spring
9. Brush
10. End cap
11. Through-bolt

8. Installation is the reverse of removal. Tighten the starter motor mounting bolts to specification (**Table 4**).

9. 275 hp—Reinstall the oil reservoir. Bleed the oil injection system. See Chapter Eleven.

Starter Motor Disassembly/Reassembly (Prestolite Starter Motor)

1. Remove the starter motor as described in this chapter.

2. Place match marks on the drive end frame, housing and end cap for alignment reference during reassembly. Remove the 2 through-bolts from the starter.

3. Lightly tap on the drive end of the armature shaft with a rubber mallet until the lower end cap separates from the starter housing. Remove the end cap, taking care not to lose the brush springs.

4. Lightly tap on the drive end frame to loosen the frame from the housing. Slide the starter housing off the armature assembly.

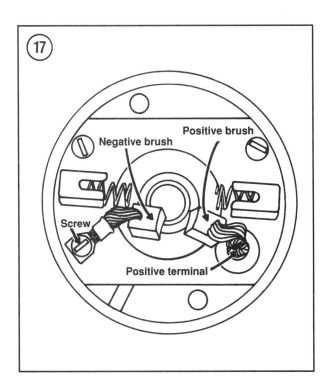

NOTE
It is not necessary to remove the starter drive assembly in Step 5 unless the drive requires replacement.

5. If starter drive replacement is necessary, secure the armature using strap wrench (part No. 91-24937A1, or equivalent). Loosen and remove the starter drive locknut, then remove the drive components from the armature shaft. See **Figure 16**.

6. To remove the brushes, remove the screw holding the negative brush lead to the end cap (**Figure 17**). Remove the negative brush.

7. Remove the hex nut and washers from the positive terminal. Remove the positive terminal and positive brush from the end cap. See **Figure 17**.

8. Install a new positive brush and positive terminal assembly into the end cap.

9. Install a new negative brush. Tighten the screw securely.

CAUTION
Do not overlubricate the starter bushings in Step 10. The starter will not operate properly and can be ruined if oil contaminates the commutator and brushes.

10. Lubricate the bushings in the drive end frame and end cap with a drop of SAE 10 oil. *Do not overlubricate.*

11. Insert the armature into the drive end frame. Install the starter drive gear, spring, spacer and a *new* locknut. See **Figure 16**. Secure the armature using strap wrench (part No. 91-24937A1, or equivalent) and tighten the locknut securely.

12. Place the starter housing over the armature. Align the match marks and mate the housing up against the end frame.

13. Fit the brush springs and brushes into the brush holders. Press the brushes into the holders and use a strip of flexible metal as shown in **Figure 18** as a tool to hold the brushes in place.

7

14. Push the drive end of the armature shaft into the housing so the commutator end extends out the housing.

15. Install the end cap onto the armature shaft. Remove the brush holding tool, then push the end cap up against the frame assembly.

16. Align the match marks on the end cap and housing. Install the through-bolts and tighten to specification (**Table 4**).

Cleaning and Inspection

1. Inspect the starter brushes in the end cap. See **Figure 17**.

2. Replace both brushes if either is pitted, chipped, oil soaked or worn to 3/16 in. (4.8 mm) or less.

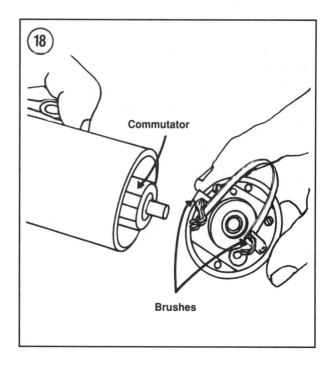

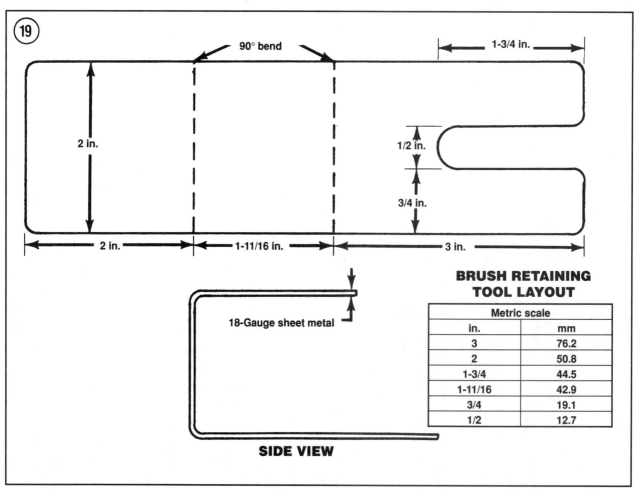

BRUSH RETAINING TOOL LAYOUT

Metric scale	
in.	mm
3	76.2
2	50.8
1-3/4	44.5
1-11/16	42.9
3/4	19.1
1/2	12.7

18-Gauge sheet metal

SIDE VIEW

3. Clean the starter drive components using clean solvent. Inspect the drive assembly for excessive wear or other damage.

4. Clean the commutator using 00 sandpaper. Clean any copper particles or other comtamination from between the commutator segments.

5. If the commutator is pitted, rough or worn unevenly, have the commutator resurfaced on a lathe. Have the armature checked for shorted windings using an armature growler. Most automotive electrical shops can perform commutator resurfacing and armature testing service.

Starter Motor Disassembly/Reassembly (Bosch Starter Motor)

A brush retaining tool should be fabricated from 18-gauge sheet metal to the dimensions

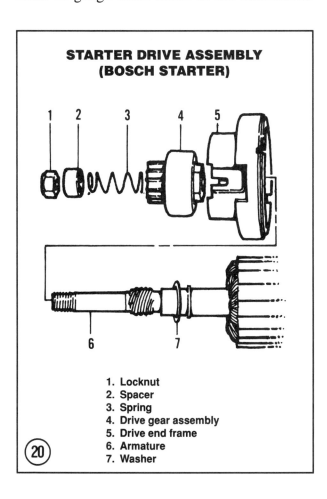

STARTER DRIVE ASSEMBLY (BOSCH STARTER)

1. Locknut
2. Spacer
3. Spring
4. Drive gear assembly
5. Drive end frame
6. Armature
7. Washer

⑳

shown in **Figure 19**. This tool is necessary to position the brushes properly and prevent damaging them when reassembling the starter end cap to the housing.

1. Remove the starter motor as described in this chapter.

2. If necessary, place match marks on the drive end frame, starter housing and end cap for alignment reference during reassembly.

3. Remove the 2 through-bolts, then remove the starter end cap.

4. Lift the armature and drive gear assembly from the starter housing.

NOTE
Do not remove the drive assembly in Step 5 and Step 6 unless the drive assembly or end frame requires replacement.

5. Place an appropriate size wrench on the hex area located on the back side of the drive gear. See **Figure 20**.

6. Remove the drive assembly locknut and slide the drive components and end frame off the armature shaft.

7. Remove the screws securing the brush holder and negative brushes to the end cap. Lift the brush holder from the end cap. See **Figure 21**.

8. Remove the negative brushes from the brush holder.

9. Remove the hex nut and washers from the positive terminal. Remove the positive terminal and positive brushes from the end cap as an assembly.

10. To reassemble, install new positive brushes and terminal assembly into the end cap. The longest brush lead should be located as shown in **Figure 22**.

11. Install the negative brushes into the brush holder. Install the brush holder into the end cap. Tighten the fasteners securely.

12. Fit the springs and brushes into the brush holder. Hold the brushes in place with the brush retaining tool (**Figure 23**).

7

13. Lubricate the armature shaft splines and drive end frame bushing with SAE 10 oil.

14. Install the drive components (**Figure 20**) onto the armature shaft. Tighten locknut securely while holding the drive gear with an appropriate size wrench.

15. Place the armature and end frame assembly into the starter housing. Be sure the commutator end of the armature is located at the end of the housing with the magnets recessed 1 in. (25.4 mm). Align the match marks on the housing and end frame.

16. With the brushes held in position with the brush retaining tool (**Figure 23**), install the end

cap onto the armature and up against the starter housing. Remove the brush retaining tool, align the match marks on the end cap and housing, then install the through-bolts. Tighten the through-bolts to specification (**Table 4**).

Cleaning and Inspection

1. Thoroughly clean all starter motor components with clean solvent. Dry with compressed air.

2. Check the starter drive gear for chipped teeth, cracks or excessive wear. Replace the drive assembly as necessary.

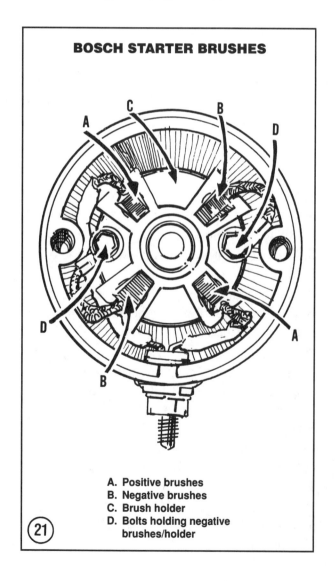

BOSCH STARTER BRUSHES

A. Positive brushes
B. Negative brushes
C. Brush holder
D. Bolts holding negative brushes/holder

㉑

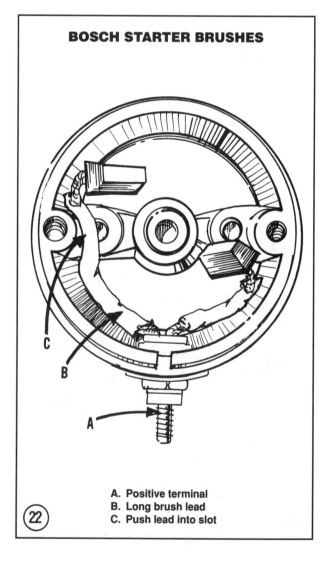

BOSCH STARTER BRUSHES

A. Positive terminal
B. Long brush lead
C. Push lead into slot

㉒

3. Inspect the brushes and replace all brushes if any are chipped, pitted, oil soaked or worn to 1/4 in. (6.4 mm) or less.

4. Inspect the armature shaft bushing in the end cap for excessive wear or other damage. Replace the bushing as necessary.

5. Inspect the commutator for excessive or uneven wear. If necessary, have the commutator resurfaced on a lathe. Most automotive electrical shops can perform this service.

6. If necessary, have the armature checked for shorted windings on an armature growler. Most automotive electrical shops can perform this service.

7. Using an ohmmeter, check for continuity between each commutator segment and the armature shaft and core. The armature must be replaced if any continuity is noted.

8. Undercut the insulation between the commutator segments using a broken hacksaw blade or similar tool. The undercut should be the full width of the insulation and 1/32 in. (0.8 mm) deep. Use caution not to damage the commutator

segments during the undercutting process. Thoroughly clean any copper particles from between the commutator segments after undercutting.

9. Clean and smooth the commutator after undercutting using 00 sandpaper. Make sure all burrs are removed from the commutator.

MAGNETO BREAKER POINT IGNITION

The 3 hp models are equipped with a conventional magneto breaker point ignition system. Major components include the flywheel, breaker points, condenser, primary coil, secondary coil, stator plate and spark plug. See **Figure 24**.

Operation

As the flywheel rotates, permanent magnets located around its inner diameter create a magnetic field in the primary coil (under the flywheel) while the breaker points are closed. When the breaker points open, the magnetic field in the primary coil is discharged into the primary windings of the secondary coil. At the same time the condenser discharges its stored voltage into the primary windings. The magnetic field in the primary windings then collapses, inducing voltage into the secondary windings. The secondary windings create a very high voltage which is directed to the spark plug. The stop switch grounds the primary coil output to stop the engine.

Flywheel Removal/Installation (3 hp)

1. Disconnect the spark plug lead from the spark plug to prevent accidental starting.

2. Remove the rewind starter assembly. See Chapter Twelve.

3. Remove the 3 screws securing the rope cup to the flywheel. Remove the rope cup.

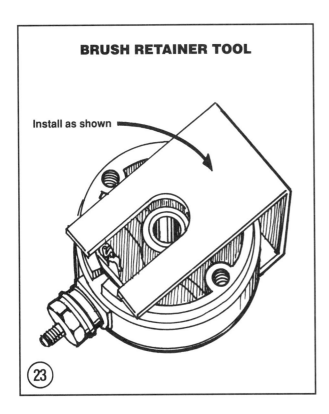

BRUSH RETAINER TOOL

Install as shown

(23)

7

4. Hold the flywheel using flywheel holder part No. 91-83163M (or equivalent) and loosen the flywheel nut. See **Figure 25**, typical.

5. Install flywheel puller part No. 91-83164M (or equivalent) on the flywheel as shown in **Figure 26**, typical. Tighten the puller center screw until the flywheel breaks free of the crankshaft taper.

6. Remove the flywheel puller. Remove the flywheel and Woodruff key in the crankshaft. See **Figure 27**.

7. To install, place the Woodruff key into the key slot in the crankshaft.

8. Lower the flywheel onto the crankshaft, making sure the key slot in the flywheel aligns with the Woodruff key.

9. Install the flywheel washer and nut. Hold the flywheel using flywheel holder part No. 91-83163M (**Figure 25**) and tighten the flywheel nut to specification (**Table 4**).

10. Reverse Steps 1-3 to complete flywheel installation.

Primary Coil Removal/Installation (3 hp)

Refer to **Figure 24** for this procedure.

1. Remove the flywheel as described in this chapter.

2. Disconnect the black/white primary coil wire at the stop switch and secondary coil connector.

3. Remove the stator plate mounting screws (A, **Figure 28**).

4. Lift the stator plate assembly off the power head.

5. Remove the 2 screws securing the primary coil to the stator plate. Invert the stator plate and remove the screw clamping the primary coil wire to the bottom of the stator plate.

6. To reinstall, mount the primary coil on the stator plate. Make sure the ground wire is positioned under the coil mounting screw (**Figure 28**) and tighten the mounting screws securely.

7. Clamp the primary coil wire to the bottom of the stator plate, then install the stator plate on the power head.

8. Apply Loctite 242 to the threads of the stator plate mounting screws. Install the screws and tighten securely. Reconnect the primary coil black/white wire.

9. Reinstall the flywheel as described in this chapter.

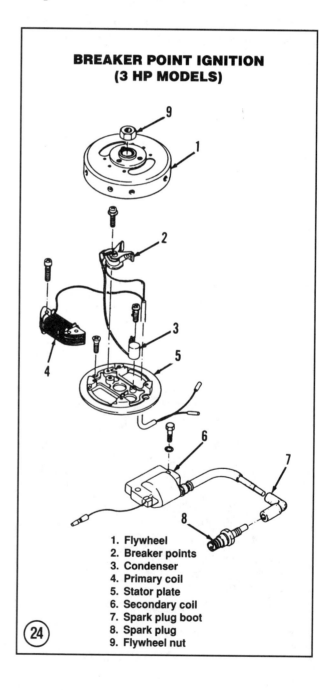

BREAKER POINT IGNITION (3 HP MODELS)

1. Flywheel
2. Breaker points
3. Condenser
4. Primary coil
5. Stator plate
6. Secondary coil
7. Spark plug boot
8. Spark plug
9. Flywheel nut

24

Secondary Coil Removal/Installation
(3 hp)

1. Disconnect the spark plug lead from the spark plug.

2. Disconnect the coil primary wire (black/white).

3. Remove the 2 screws securing the coil to the power head. Remove the secondary coil assembly.

4. To reinstall, reverse the removal procedure. Tighten the coil mounting screws securely.

Breaker Points and Condenser Removal/Installation
(3 hp)

1. Remove the flywheel as described in this chapter.

2. Remove the breaker point mounting screw (A, **Figure 29**).

3. Remove the E-ring retainer (B, **Figure 29**).

4. Disconnect the breaker point and condenser wires (C, **Figure 29**) from the points. Remove the breaker points.

5. Remove the screw (D, **Figure 29**) and lift the condenser from the stator plate.

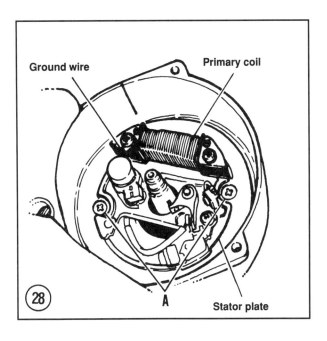

6. Place a drop or two of light oil on the felt wick attached to the condenser. Install the condenser on the stator plate, install the screw and tighten securely.

7. Install the breaker points, install the E-ring retainer and mounting screw. Connect the breaker points and condenser wires.

8. Install the flywheel as described in this chapter.

9. Rotate the flywheel so the high point on the breaker point cam is against the breaker point rubbing block (points open fully).

10. Using a feeler gauge, measure the breaker point gap by inserting the feeler gauge through the slot in the flywheel. The gap should be 0.012-0.016 in. (0.3-0.4 mm).

11. If necessary, loosen the breaker point screw (A, **Figure 29**) and move the point base as required to obtain the specified gap. Retighten the breaker point screw securely and recheck the gap.

CAPACITOR DISCHARGE IGNITION (CDI) (1993 3.3 HP MODELS)

The 3.3 hp models (1993) are equipped with a capacitor discharge ignition (CDI) system. The major components include the flywheel, capacitor charge/trigger coil assembly, CDI unit, ignition coil, spark plug, stop switch and related circuitry. See **Figure 30**.

Operation

A series of permanent magnets is contained along the outer rim of the flywheel. As the flywheel rotates, alternating current (AC) is induced into the charge coil windings of the unit where the AC current is converted (rectified) into direct current (DC) and stored in a capacitor contained inside the DCI unit. As the flywheel continues to rotate, a small voltage is induced into the trigger coil windings of the charge/trigger coil assembly. This voltage pulse causes an electronic switch (SCR) inside the CDI unit to

close, allowing the stored voltage in the capacitor to discharge into the ignition coil. The ignition coil amplifies this voltage and discharges it into the spark plug lead. This sequence of events is repeated with each revolution of the flywheel. Ignition timing advance is accomplished electronically and is not adjustable.

Flywheel Removal/Installation (3.3 hp)

1. Disconnect the spark plug lead from the spark plug to prevent accidental starting.

2. Remove the rewind starter assembly. See Chapter Twelve.

3. Remove the screws securing the rope cup to the flywheel. Remove the rope cup.

4. Hold the flywheel using flywheel holder part No. 91-83163M (or equivalent) and loosen the flywheel nut. See **Figure 25**, typical.

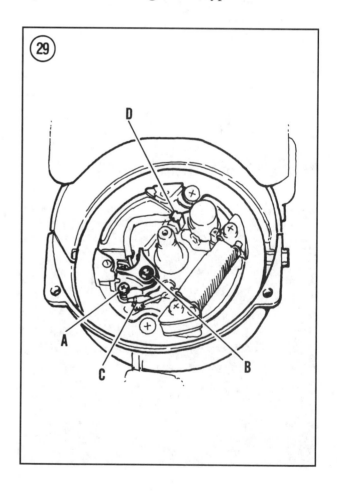

(29)

5. Install flywheel puller part No. 91-83164M (or equivalent) on the flywheel as shown in **Figure 26**, typical. Tighten the puller center screw until the flywheel breaks free of the crankshaft taper.

6. Remove the flywheel puller. Lift the flywheel off the crankshaft and remove the Woodruff key from the crankshaft. See **Figure 27**, typical.

7. To install, make certain the flywheel and crankshaft tapers are clean and dry. Place the Woodruff key into the key slot in the flywheel.

8. Lower the flywheel onto the crankshaft, making sure the key slot in the flywheel aligns with the Woodruff key.

9. Install the flywheel washer and nut. Hold the flywheel using the flywheel holder (part No.

91-83163M) and tighten the flywheel nut to specification.

10. Reverse Steps 1-3 to complete flywheel installation.

Capacitor Charge Coil/Trigger Coil Assembly Removal/Installation (3.3 hp)

Refer to **Figure 30** for this procedure.

1. Remove the flywheel as described in this chapter.

2. Disconnect the charge/trigger coil white wire at its bullet connector. Remove any screws,

7

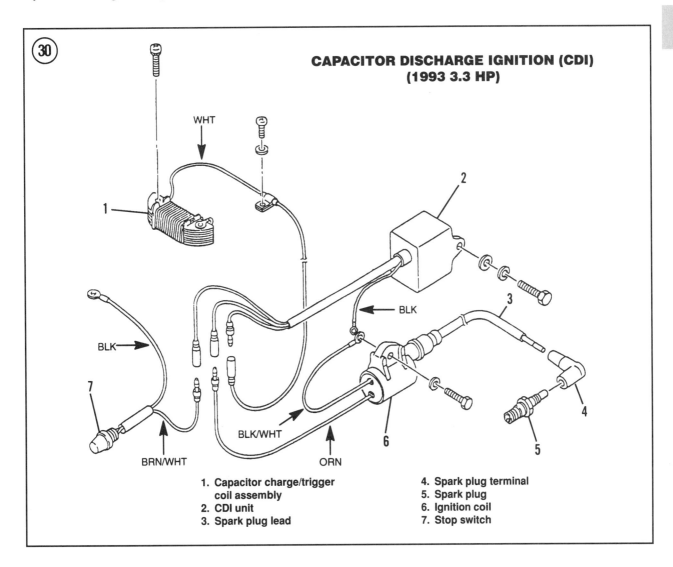

CAPACITOR DISCHARGE IGNITION (CDI)
(1993 3.3 HP)

1. Capacitor charge/trigger coil assembly
2. CDI unit
3. Spark plug lead
4. Spark plug terminal
5. Spark plug
6. Ignition coil
7. Stop switch

clamps or sta-straps securing the white wire to the power head.

3. Remove the 2 screws securing the charge/trigger coil to the stator plate. Remove the coil assembly.

4. To reinstall, mount the coil on the stator plate. Make sure the coil ground wire is properly positioned under the coil mounting screw. Install the coil mounting screws and tighten securely.

5. Complete installation by reversing the removal procedure.

Ignition Coil Removal/Installation (3.3 hp)

1. Disconnect the spark plug lead from the spark plug.

2. Disconnect the orange coil primary wire at its bullet connector.

3. Remove the ignition coil mounting fastener and lift the coil off the power head.

4. To install, reverse the removal procedure. Make sure the coil and CDI unit ground wires (black) are properly positioned under the coil mounting screw.

CDI Unit Removal/Installation

1. Remove the ignition coil mounting fastener to remove the CDI unit ground wire.

2. Disconnect the brown/white, orange and white CDI unit wires at their bullet connectors.

3. Remove the CDI unit mounting fastener and lift the unit off the power head.

4. Installation is the reverse of removal. Make sure the CDI unit black ground wire is securely fastened under the ignition coil mounting screw.

CAPACITOR DISCHARGE IGNITION (CDI) (4-275 HP MODELS)

All models covered in this manual (except 3 hp) are equipped with an alternator-driven ca-

pacitor discharge ignition system (CDI). Major components include the flywheel, stator assembly (charge coil[s]), trigger assembly, switchbox(es), ignition coil(s) spark plugs and connecting wiring. Refer to Chapter Three for testing and troubleshooting procedures and the back of this manual for wiring diagrams.

A series of permanent magnets is contained along the outer rim of the flywheel. As the flywheel rotates, alternating current (AC) is induced into the stator charge coil windings. The AC current flows to the switchbox where it is converted (rectified) into direct current (DC) and stored in the capacitor contained within the switchbox.

Permanent magnets mounted to the flywheel hub rotate inside the trigger assembly and induce a low voltage signal into the trigger coil(s). This voltage pulse causes an electronic switch (SCR) in the switchbox to close, allowing the stored voltage in the capacitor to discharge into the ignition coil at the correct time and in the correct firing order. The ignition coil greatly amplifies the voltage and discharges it into the high tension lead to the spark plug. This sequence of events is duplicated for each cylinder of the engine, and is repeated upon each revolution of the flywheel.

Ignition timing on all models except 4 and 5 hp is advanced and retarded by rotating the po-

sition of the trigger assembly in relation to the magnets on the flywheel inner hub. On 4 and 5 hp models, ignition timing is advanced electronically.

Component Wiring

Modern outboard motor electrical systems are quite complex, especially on the higher output engines. **Figure 31** shows a typical Mercury V6 switchbox assembly, starter motor, rectifier and associated wiring. For this reason, electrical wiring is color-coded, and the terminals on the components to which each wire connects are embossed with the correct wire color. When used in conjunction with the correct electrical diagram, incorrect wire connections should be held to a minimum.

In addition, wire routing is very important to prevent possible electrical interference and/or damage to the wiring harnesses from moving engine parts or vibration. Mercury outboards are shipped from the factory with all wiring harnesses and leads properly positioned and secured with "J" clamps and plastic sta-straps.

Should component replacement become necessary, it is highly recommended that you take the time to either carefully draw a sketch of the area to be serviced, noting the positioning of all

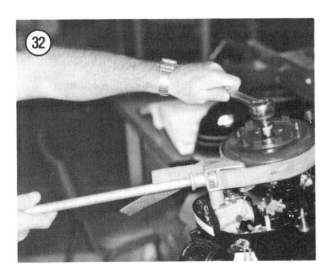

wire harnesses involved, or use an instant camera to take several photographs at close range of the harness routing and location. Either method can be invaluable when it comes time to reroute the harnesses for reassembly. Be sure to reinstall "J" clamps and new sta-straps where necessary to maintain the correct wire routing.

Flywheel Removal/Installation (4 and 5 hp)

1. Disconnect the spark plug lead from the spark plug to prevent accidental starting.
2. Remove the rewind starter assembly. See Chapter Twelve.
3A. Early style—Hold the flywheel by wrapping strap wrench part No. 91-24937A1 (or equivalent) around the flywheel as shown in **Figure 32**. Loosen and remove the flywheel nut.
3B. Late style—Hold the flywheel by wrapping strap wrench part No. 91-24937A1 around the starter rope cup. Loosen and remove the flywheel nut. Remove 3 screws securing the rope cup to the flywheel. Remove the cup (**Figure 33**).
4. Install flywheel puller part No. 91-83164M (or equivalent) onto the flywheel. Tighten the puller screw until the flywheel is dislodged from the crankshaft taper.
5. Lift the flywheel off the crankshaft. Remove the flywheel key from the crankshaft key slot.
6. To reinstall the flywheel, insert the flywheel key into the crankshaft key slot.
7. Place the flywheel onto the crankshaft, making sure the key slot in the flywheel is aligned with the flywheel key.
8A. Early style—Install the flywheel nut onto the crankshaft. Hold the flywheel using the strap wrench (**Figure 32**) and tighten the flywheel nut to specification (**Table 4**).
8B. Late style:
   a. Install the rope cup (**Figure 33**) on the flywheel. Tighten the rope cup fasteners to 70 in.-lb. (8 N·m).

b. Install the flywheel onto the crankshaft. Make sure the flywheel key slot is aligned with the flywheel key.

c. Install the flywheel nut. Hold the flywheel by wrapping the strap wrench around the rope cup and tighten the flywheel nut to specification (**Table 4**).

9. Reinstall the rewind starter assembly as described in Chapter Twelve.

Flywheel Removal/Installation (8-25 hp)

1. On electric start models, disconnect the negative battery cable from the battery.

2. Disconnect the spark plug leads from the spark plugs to prevent accidental starting.

3. Hold the flywheel using strap wrench part No. 91-24937A1 (manual start models) or flywheel holder part No. 91-52344 (electric start models). Loosen and remove the flywheel nut (8-15 hp models) or bolt (20-25 hp models).

> *NOTE*
> *If the flywheel is retained by a bolt, thread the bolt into the crankshaft 3/4-way for use with the flywheel puller.*

> *CAUTION*
> *Do not thread puller bolts more than 1/2 in. into the flywheel in Step 4 or damage may result to the stator or trigger assemblies located under the flywheel.*

4. Install flywheel puller part No. 91-13661A1 (or equivalent) on the flywheel. Tighten the puller screw until the flywheel is dislodged from the crankshaft taper. Remove the puller assembly from the flywheel. Remove the flywheel bolt on models so equipped.

5. Lift the flywheel off the crankshaft. Remove the flywheel key from the crankshaft slot.

6. To reinstall the flywheel, insert the flywheel key into the crankshaft key slot.

7. Place the flywheel onto the crankshaft. Make sure the flywheel key slot is properly aligned with the flywheel key.

8. Install the flywheel nut or bolt. Hold the flywheel using the strap wrench or flywheel holder. Tighten the nut or bolt to specification (**Table 4**).

Flywheel Removal/Installation (40-275 hp)

1A. Electric start models—Disconnect the negative battery cable from the battery. Remove the

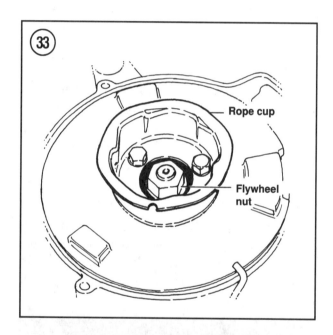

3 fasteners securing the flywheel cover and remove the cover.

1B. Manual start models—Remove the rewind starter as described in Chapter Twelve.

2. Disconnect the spark plug leads from the spark plugs.

3. On 50 and 60 hp models prior to serial No. D000750 equipped with electric start, remove the ignition timing pointer.

4A. Manual start models—Hold the flywheel using strap wrench part No. 91-24937A1 (or

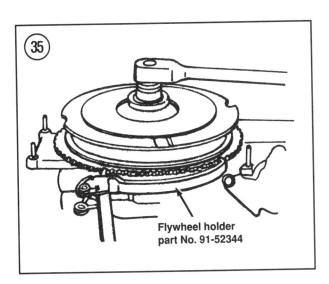

Flywheel holder part No. 91-52344

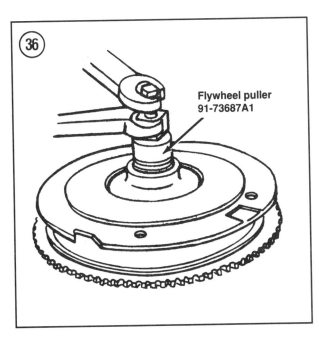

Flywheel puller 91-73687A1

equivalent). Remove the flywheel nut and washer. See **Figure 34**.

4B. Electric start models—Hold the flywheel using flywheel holder 91-52344. Remove the flywheel nut and washer. See **Figure 35**.

CAUTION
Flywheel removal without the use of a protector cap on the end of the crankshaft can cause crankshaft damage.

5. Install crankshaft protector cap (part No. 91-24161, or equivalent) on the end of the crankshaft.

CAUTION
Do not apply heat or strike the puller screw with a hammer while removing the flywheel in Step 6. Heat or hammering can damage the ignition components under the flywheel.

6. Install flywheel puller 91-73687A1 (**Figure 36**) into the flywheel. Hold the puller with one wrench and tighten the puller screw until the flywheel is dislodged from the crankshaft taper.

NOTE
The flywheel on 135-200 hp models serial No. D167373-on, has 3 holes (8 mm) to acommodate a universal type flywheel puller.

7. Lift the flywheel off the crankshaft. Remove the flywheel key from the crankshaft slot.

8. To reinstall the flywheel, insert the flywheel key into the crankshaft slot.

9. Place the flywheel onto the crankshaft aligning the flywheel key slot with the flywheel key.

10. Install the flywheel nut and washer. Hold the flywheel with the strap wrench (manual start) or the flywheel holder (electric start) and tighten the flywheel nut to specification (**Table 4**).

11. Install the ignition timing pointer on early 50 and 60 hp models.

12. Install the rewind starter on manual start models. Install the flywheel cover on electric start models.

Charge Coil Removal/Installation (4 and 5 hp)

Models 4 and 5 hp may be equipped with an optional AC lighting coil. The capacitor charge coil and the lighting coil are both replaced using the same procedure. Refer to **Figure 37** for this procedure.

1. Remove the flywheel as described in this chapter.

2. Disconnect the wires of the coil to be replaced from the CDI unit.

3. Remove the screw and clamp holding the wires in place.

4. Remove the 2 screws holding the coil to the power head. Remove the coil.

5. Installation is the reverse of removal. Be sure the coil wires are properly routed and clamped. Apply Loctite 222 or equivalent to the threads of the coil fasteners and tighten to 14 in.-lb. (1.6 N.m).

Stator and Alternator Removal/Installation (8-25 hp)

Models 8-25 hp may be equipped with an optional AC lighting coil attached to the stator assembly. The stator assembly includes a low-speed and a high-speed charge coil which are not serviceable separately.

1. Remove the flywheel as described in this chapter.

2. Remove the 5 screws (A, **Figure 38**) securing the stator and alternator assembly to the power head. If not equipped with an alternator, the stator is mounted with 4 screws.

3. Disconnect the stator wires from the switchbox.

4. Remove the stator wire clamp (B, **Figure 38**).

5. Remove the stator and alternator assembly from the power head.

6. To reinstall, mount the stator or stator and alternator assembly on the power head.

7. Install the fasteners and tighten to specification (**Table 4**).

8. Route the stator wires behind the switchbox, then reconnect the wires to the correct switchbox terminals.

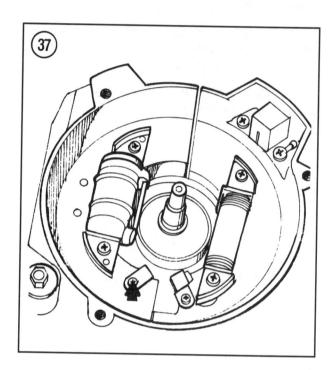

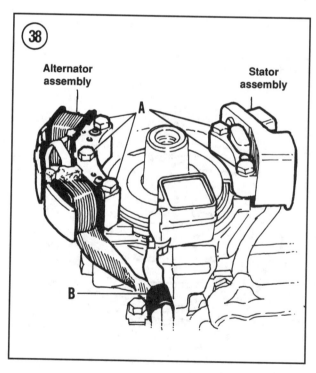

Alternator assembly

Stator assembly

9. The remaining installation is the reverse of removal.

Stator Assembly Removal/Installation (40-275 hp)

The stator assembly is mounted below the flywheel and contains 2 capacitor charge coils on 3- and 4-cylinder models and 4 capacitor charge coils on V6 models. In addition, the stator assembly contains the battery charging coils (alternator).

Refer to the appropriate wiring diagram at the end of the manual.

1. Remove the flywheel as described in this chapter.

2. Note the stator wire routing in relation to the end cap. Make a drawing or take an instant picture of the wiring for reference during reinstallation.

3. Remove the 4 stator assembly mounting screws. Remove the electrical component box cover, if so equipped.

4A. 135-200 hp V6 models—Remove the outer switchbox mounting screws. Separate the outer and inner switchboxes. Do not lose the spacers located between the switchboxes. Disconnect the stator wires from the switchboxes and rectifier. Disconnect stator ground wires.

4B. 75-115 hp models—Remove the starter motor as described in this chapter. Disconnect the

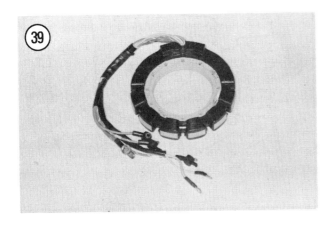

stator wires at the switchbox and rectificer and remove the stator assembly.

4C. All others—Disconnect the stator wires from the switchbox(es) and rectifier or terminal block. Disconnect stator ground wires.

5. Remove the stator assembly from the engine. See **Figure 39**.

6. Position new stator on the power head upper end cap.

7. Clean the stator mounting screws with Loctite Primer T and allow to air dry. Apply Loctite 222 to the threads of the screws.

8. Install the stator screws and tighten to specification (**Table 4**).

9. Route the stator wires as noted during removal.

10. Connect the stator wires to their respective terminals. Refer to the wiring diagrams at the end of the manual. On 250-275 hp models, make sure the stator wires with the yellow identification sleeve are connected to the lower switchbox. On 135-200 hp models, make sure the stator wires with the yellow identification sleeve (if so equipped) are connected to the outer switchbox.

11. V6 (135-200 hp) models—Install the outer switchbox over the inner switchbox. Make sure the spacers are properly located and securely tighten the switchbox mounting screws. Make sure the switchbox(es) are properly grounded on all models.

12. 75-115 hp models—Install the starter motor as described in this chapter.

13. Install the electrical component box cover if so equipped. Reinstall the flywheel as described in this chapter.

Trigger Coil Removal/Installation (4 and 5 hp)

A single trigger coil is mounted on the power head adjacent to the outer rim of the flywheel.

1. Disconnect the red/white trigger coil wire at the CDI unit.

7

2. Remove the 2 screws holding the trigger coil in the housing.

3. Pull the trigger coil from the housing.

4. Insert the new trigger coil wires through the rubber grommet and connect the red/white wire to the CDI unit.

5. Seat the trigger coil in the housing, connect the black ground wire under one coil mounting screw, then tighten the screw securely.

Trigger Coil Removal/Installation (8-25 hp)

A single trigger coil is mounted under the flywheel. Note trigger wiring harness routing for reference during reinstallation.

1. Remove the flywheel as described in this chapter.

2. Remove the stator mounting screws, but do not disconnect the stator wires.

3. Remove any wire harness clamps securing the trigger wires. Disconnect the trigger wires from the switchbox.

4. Lift the stator assembly upward so the trigger can be removed without interfering.

5. Pry the spark advance rod end from the trigger using a screwdriver or similar tool. See **Figure 40**.

6. Lift the trigger assembly off the power head and disconnect the link rod (**Figure 40**). Remove the trigger assembly.

7. To install the trigger, install the link rod into the trigger (**Figure 40**) and place the trigger assembly on the power head.

8. Install the spark advance rod (**Figure 40**).

9. Route the trigger wire harness as noted during removal. Install any harness clamps removed during removal. Connect the trigger wires to their respective switchbox terminals. Refer to the appropriate wiring diagram in Chapter Fourteen, if necessary.

10. Reinstall the stator mounting screws as described in this chapter.

11. Reinstall the flywheel as described in this chapter.

Trigger Plate Removal/Installation (40 hp and 50-60 hp Prior to Serial No. D000750)

The trigger plate assembly is mounted below the flywheel and contains 2 trigger coils. Each trigger coil controls 2 cylinders. Note the trigger wire harness routing for reference during reinstallation. Refer to the appropriate wiring diagram at the end of the manual.

1. Remove the flywheel as described in this chapter.

2. Remove the 4 stator assembly mounting screws, but do not disconnect the stator wires. Lift the stator off the upper end cap and lay aside.

3. Remove the locknut securing the link rod to the spark advance arm. **Figure 41**, typical shows the link rod with the flywheel installed. Pull the link rod from the spark advance arm.

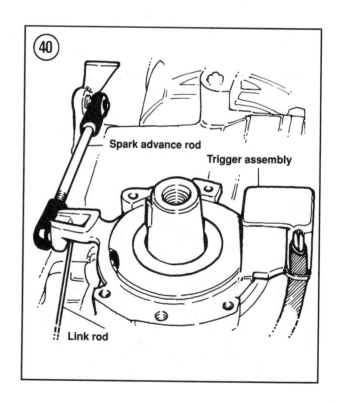

Spark advance rod
Trigger assembly
Link rod

4. 40 hp models—Remove the 6 electrical box cover screws and remove the cover.

5. Disconnect the trigger wires from the switchbox. Remove any wiring harness clamps or sta-straps securing the trigger wire harness. Remove the trigger plate assembly.

6. Remove the link rod from the trigger plate, if necessary, to install on a new trigger plate.

7. If removed, install the link rod on the trigger plate assembly.

8. Place the trigger plate assembly into the upper end cap.

9. Install the link rod into the spark advance lever (**Figure 41**, typical).

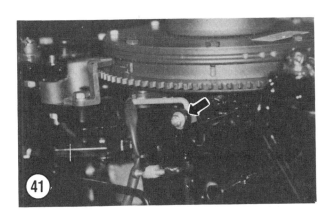

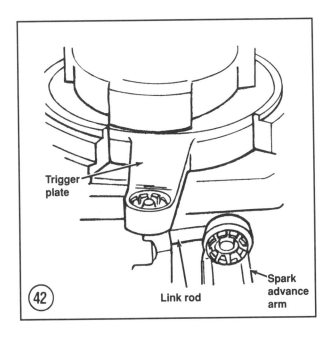

10. Route the trigger wire harness as noted during removal. Secure the harness using the necessary clamps and sta-straps.

11. Reconnect the trigger wires to their respective switchbox terminals. Refer to the appropriate wiring diagram at the end of the manual.

12. 40 hp models—Install the electrical box cover. Tighten the 6 cover screws securely.

13. Install the stator as described in this chapter.

14. Install the flywheel as described in this chapter.

Trigger Plate Removal/Installation (50 hp [Serial No. D000750-on]; 75, 90, 100 and 115 hp)

7

The trigger plate assembly is mounted under the flywheel and contains 3 trigger coils on 3-cylinder models and 2 trigger coils on 4-cylinder models. On 3-cylinder models, each trigger coil controls 1 cylinder. On 4-cylinder models, each trigger coil controls 2 cylinders. Note the trigger plate wire harness routing for reference during reinstallation. Refer to the appropriate wiring diagram in at the end of the manual.

1. Remove the flywheel as described in this chapter.

2. Remove the 4 stator mounting screws. Lift the stator off the upper end cap and lay aside.

3. Disconnect the trigger link rod from the spark advance arm (**Figure 42**).

4A. 50 and 60 hp:

  a. Disconnect the 4 trigger wires from the switchbox at their bullet connectors.

  b. Remove any clamps or sta-straps securing the wiring harness and remove the trigger plate assembly.

4B. 75-115 hp models:

  a. Remove the starter motor as described in this chapter.

  b. Disconnect the 4 trigger wires at the switchbox.

c. Remove any clamps or sta-straps securing the trigger wiring harness and remove the trigger plate assembly.

5. If necessary, remove the link rod (**Figure 42**) for installation on a new trigger plate.

6. To install, place the trigger plate into the upper end cap.

7. Route the trigger wires as noted during removal. Install the necessary clamps and sta-straps to secure the harness.

8. Connect the trigger wires to their respective switchbox terminals.

9. 75-115 hp models—Install the starter motor.

10. Install the stator and flywheel as described in this chapter.

Trigger Plate Removal/Installation (V6 Models)

The trigger plate assembly is mounted below the flywheel and contains 3 trigger coils. Each trigger coil controls 2 cylinders. Note the trigger wire harness routing for reference during installation. Refer to the appropriate wiring diagram at the end of the manual.

1. Remove the flywheel as described in this chapter.

2. Remove the 4 stator mounting screws. Lift the stator off the upper end cap and lay aside.

3. Remove the locknut securing the link rod to the spark advance lever, then pull the link rod from the arm.

4. 135-200 hp models—Remove the 2 switchbox mounting screws. Separate the outer and inner switchboxes. Do not lose the metal spacers located between the switchboxes.

5. Disconnect the trigger wires from the switchboxes. Remove any clamps and sta-straps securing the wiring harness. Remove the trigger plate assembly from the upper end cap.

6. If necessary, remove the link rod swivel for installation on a new trigger plate. Loosen the locknut and unscrew the swivel from the link rod. See **Figure 43**.

7. If removed, screw the locknut and swivel onto the link rod. Position the swivel to provide 11/16 in. (17.5 mm) between the locknut and the center of the trigger pivot as shown in **Figure 43**. Tighten the locknut securely.

8. Install the trigger plate into the upper end cap. Connect the link rod swivel to the spark advance lever. Install the locknut and tighten securely.

9. Route the trigger wiring harness as noted during removal. Connect the trigger wires to their respective switchbox terminals. The trigger wires with the yellow identifications sleeves must be connected to the outer switchbox on 135-200 hp models or the lower switchbox on 250 and 275 hp models.

10. Install the necessary clamps and sta-straps to secure the trigger wiring harness.

> *CAUTION*
> *The switchboxes must be grounded to the power head or switchbox damage will result when the engine is cranked or started. Make sure the switchboxes are grounded through the mounting screws and spacers, and ground wires if so equipped.*

11. 135-200 hp models—Install the inner and outer switchboxes to the power head. See *Switchbox Removal/Installation* in this chapter.

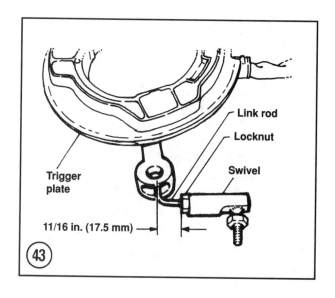

Link rod

Locknut

Swivel

Trigger plate

11/16 in. (17.5 mm)

(43)

Be certain the switchboxes are properly grounded to the engine.

12. Install the stator and flywheel as described in this chapter.

Ignition Coil Removal/Installation (4 and 5 hp)

1. Disconnect the black/yellow CDI unit lead at the ignition coil.

2. Disconnect the high tension lead from the spark plug.

3. Remove the 2 bolts and washers holding the coil to the power head. Disconnect the black ground wires from the behind the coil, then remove the coil from the power head.

4. Installation is the reverse of removal. Be sure the ground wires are properly installed.

Ignition Coil Removal/Installation (8-25 hp)

The ignition coils have short wires extending from the back side of the coils. These wires must be positioned across the rubber portion on the back of the coil to ensure proper grounding to the engine when installed.

1. Disconnect the spark plug wire(s) from the coil(s) to be removed (A, **Figure 44**, typical).

2. Disconnect the switchbox wire(s) at the positive coil terminal(s). Disconnect the black ground wire(s) at the negative coil terminal(s). See B, **Figure 44**, typical.

3. Remove the coil cover bolts with washers (C, **Figure 44**, typical). Remove the coil cover with the coils from the engine.

4. Remove the defective coil(s) from the coil cover.

5. Installation is the reverse of removal. Coat the coil terminal connections with Quicksilver Liquid Neoprene (part No. 92-25711).

Ignition Coil Removal/Installation (40-275 hp)

Orange colored coils have a short wire which extends from the back side of each coil. The wires must be positioned across the rubber portion on the back of the coil to ensure proper grounding to the engine when installed.

1. Remove the electrical box access cover on models so equipped.

2. 250 and 275 hp—Remove the rear cowl support bracket from the engine.

3. Disconnect the spark plug wire from the coil(s) to be replaced.

4. Disconnect the switchbox wire(s) at the positive coil terminal(s). Disconnect the black ground wire(s) at the coil negative terminal(s).

5. Remove the coil cover screws and washers (**Figure 45**, typical). Remove the coil cover with the coils (and coil plate, if so equipped) from the engine.

6. Remove the defective coil(s) from the coil cover.

7. Installation is the reverse of removal. On orange colored coils, make sure the short wire extending from the rear of each coil is positioned over the rubber portion of the coil. Coat the coil positive and negative terminal connections with Quicksilver Liquid Neoprene (part No. 92-25711).

7

Switchbox Removal/Installation

Although the wiring is color coded and the switchbox terminals are embossed with the proper coding, it is good practice to take special note of the wire routing and terminal connections before disconnecting any wires. The dual switchbox installation (**Figure 46**) can be visually confusing and might result in improper wire connections. The wiring diagrams at the end of the manual will assist in reconnecting the wires properly, but not in routing them correctly. The correct wire routing is very important to prevent insulation and wire damage from vibration or interference with moving engine parts.

4 and 5 hp

The switchbox leads are permanently attached to the rear of the switchbox (CDI unit) and must be removed at their bullet connectors encased in plastic sleeves.

1. Disconnect the 4 CDI unit wires at the bullet connectors.
2. Disconnect the black/yellow CDI wire at the ignition coil.
3. Remove the black CDI unit ground under 1 ignition coil mounting bolt.
4. Slide the CDI unit out of its rubber mounting bracket.
5. Installation is the reverse of removal.

8-15 hp

The switchbox wires are permanently attached to the switchbox and must be disconnected at the bullet connectors. Refer to the appropriate wiring diagram at the end of the manual.

1. Disconnect the 4 switchbox wires at their bullet connectors.
2. Disconnect the switchbox ground wire.
3. Remove the switchbox mounting screws and remove the switchbox.

4. Installation is the reverse of removal.

20 and 25 hp

Refer to **Figure 47** for this procedure.

1. Unsnap the neoprene cap on each switchbox terminal. Pull the caps back and remove the nuts holding the wires to the terminals. Remove the wires from the switchbox.
2. Remove the switchbox mounting screws and remove the switchbox.
3. Installation is the reverse of removal. Make sure the switchbox is properly grounded to the engine. Coat switchbox terminal connections

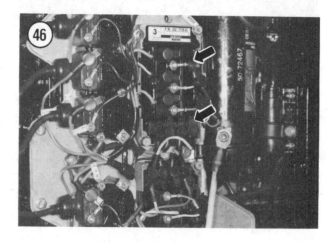

with Quicksilver Liquid Neoprene (part No. 92-25711).

40-115 hp

Refer to the appropriate wiring diagram at the end of the manual. Take special note of any ground wires located under the switchbox

mounting screws or attached to the power head. The switchbox will be damaged if not properly grounded.

1. Make sure the ignition switch is OFF and disconnect the battery cables from the battery.

2. 40 hp models—Remove the electrical box access cover.

3A. 50 and 60 hp serial No. D000750-on—Disconnect the switchbox wires at their bullet connectors.

3B. All others—Unsnap the neoprene cap on each switchbox wire terminal. Pull back the caps and remove the nuts holding the wires to the terminals. Disconnect the wires from the switchbox.

4. Remove the switchbox mounting screws and remove the switchbox.

5. Apply Loctite 242 to the threads of the switchbox mounting screws.

6. Install the switchbox on the power head using the mounting screws. Be sure to install the switchbox ground wires under the appropriate mounting screw. Tighten the mounting screws to specification (**Table 4**).

7A. 50 and 60 hp serial No. D000750-on—Reconnect the switchbox wires at their respective bullet connectors.

7B. All others—Reconnect the switchbox wires at their respective terminals. Tighten the terminals nuts to 30 in.-lb. (3.4 N•m).

8. 40 hp—Reinstall the electrical access cover. Tighten the 6 screws securely.

135-200 V6

Refer to the appropriate wiring diagram at the end of the manual. The switchboxes are grounded to the power head through the mounting screws and metal spacers, and ground wires, if so equipped.

1. Make sure the ignition switch is OFF and disconnect the battery cables from the battery.

2. Remove the 3 screws securing the ignition plate cover (**Figure 48**) and remove the cover.

3. Remove the 2 switchbox mounting screws (**Figure 49**). Separate the inner and outer switchboxes and remove the metal spacers between the switchboxes.

4. Unsnap the neoprene cap on each wire terminal. Pull the caps back and remove the terminal nuts. Disconnect the wires from the terminals and remove the switchboxes.

5. Reconnect the wires to the correct switchbox terminals. The wires with the yellow identification sleeves must be connected to the outer switchbox. Connect a ground wire (if so equipped) to each switchbox using a screw.

6. Apply Loctite 242 to the threads of the switchbox mounting screws. Install the switchboxes to the power head using the mounting screws and spacers. See **Figure 50**. Be certain the switchboxes are properly grounded to the power head or the switchboxes will be damaged when the engine is cranked or started.

7. Tighten the switchbox mounting screws to specification (**Table 4**).

8. Complete the remainder of the installation by reversing the removal procedure.

250 and 275 hp V6

Refer to the appropriate wiring diagram at the end of the manual. The switchboxes are

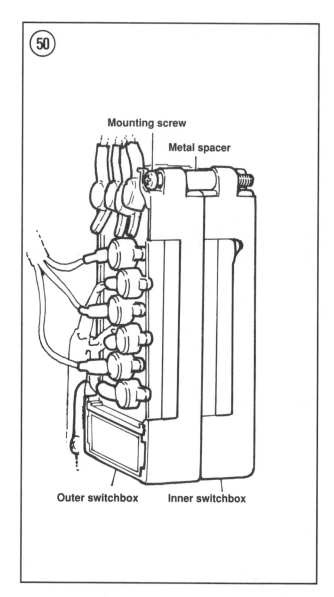

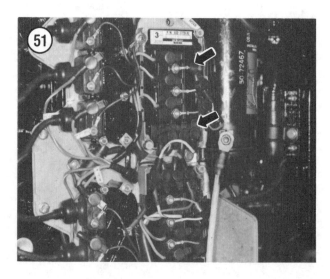

grounded to the power head through the mounting screws and ground wires. The switchboxes must be properly grounded to the power head or they will be damaged when the engine is cranked or started.

1. Make sure the ignition switch is OFF. Disconnect the battery cables from the battery.

2. Unsnap the neoprene cap on each switchbox terminal. See **Figure 51**, typical. Pull back the caps and remove the terminal nuts and disconnect the wires from the switchbox(es).

3. Remove 2 mounting screws from each switchbox and remove the switchbox(es).

4. Install the switchbox(es) to the power head. Install 2 mounting screws into each switchbox.

5. Reconnect the wires to their respective switchbox terminals. Attach ground wires to each switchbox using screws. The wires with the yellow identification sleeves must be connected to the lower switchbox.

6. Complete the remaining installation by reversing the removal procedure.

Table 1 BATTERY CAPACITY (HOURS)

Accessory draw	80 Amp-hour battery provides continuous power for:	Approximate recharge time
5 amps	13.5 hours	16 hours
15 amps	3.5 hours	13 hours
25 amps	1.8 hours	12 hours
Accessory draw	105 Amp-hour battery provides continuous pwer for:	Approximate recharge time
5 amps	15.8 hours	16 hours
15 amos	4.2 hours	13 hours
25 amps	2.4 hours	12 hours

Table 2 BATTERY CHARGE PERCENTAGE

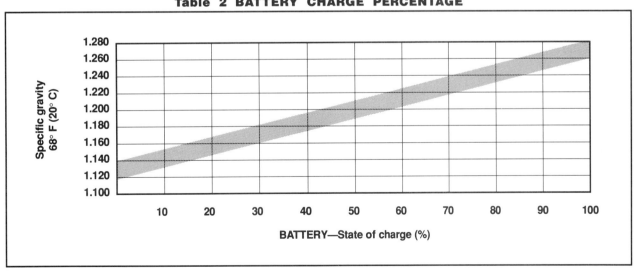

Table 3 BATTERY CABLE LENGTHS AND MINIMUM SIZE REQUIREMENTS

Cable length	Cable gauge size (AWG)
To 3-1/2 ft.	4
3-1/2 to 6 ft.	2
6-7 to 1/2 ft.	1
7-1/2 to 9-1/2 ft.	0
9-1/2 to 12 ft.	00
12-15 ft.	000
15-19 ft.	0000

Table 4 TIGHTENING TORQUES

Fastener	in.-lb.	ft.-lb	N·m
Charge/lighting coil			
4 and 5 hp	30		3.4
Ignition coil terminal			
nuts	30		3.4
Switchbox terminal nuts	30		3.4
Flywheel nut or bolt			
3 hp		30	41
4 and 5 hp		40	54.2
8-25 hp		50	67.8
50-60 (prior to serial			
No. D000750)		85	115.2
50-60 (serial No.			
D000750-on		120	162.7
75-115 hp, V6 (except			
250 and 275 hp		120	162.7
250-275 hp		100	135.6
Starter motor-to-crankcase			
8-25 hp	200		22.6
All others	180		20.3
Starter through–bolts	70		7.9
Stator screws			
8-25 hp	30		3.4
40 hp	35		3.9
50-60 hp (prior to			
serial No. D000750)	30		3.4
50-60 (serial No.			
D000750-on), 75-115			
& 135-200 hp	60		6.8
250-275 hp	150		16.9

Chapter Eight

Power Head

Basic repair of Mercury outboard power heads is similar from model to model, with minor differences. Some procedures require the use of special tools, which can be purchased from a Mercury outboard dealer. Certain tools may be fabricated by a local machinist, often at substantial savings. Power head stands are available from specialty shops and marine product distributors. Make sure the engine stand is of sufficient capacity to support the size of the engine.

Work on the power head requires considerable mechanical ability. Carefully consider your capabilities before attempting any operation involving major disassembly of the engine.

Much of the labor charge for dealer repairs involves the removal and disassembly of other parts to reach the defective component. Even if you decide not to tackle the entire power head overhaul after studying the text and illustrations in this chapter, it can be financially beneficial to perform the preliminary operations yourself and then take the power head to your dealer. Since many marine dealers have lengthy waiting lists for service (especially during the spring and summer seasons), this practice can reduce the time your unit is in the shop. If you have done much of the preliminary work, your repairs can be scheduled and performed much quicker.

Repairs proceed much faster and easier if your motor is clean before starting work. There are special cleaners for washing the motor and related parts. Just spray or brush on the cleaning solution, allow it to stand, then rinse thoroughly with clean water. Clean all oily or greasy parts with fresh solvent as you remove them.

> *WARNING*
> *Never use gasoline as a cleaning agent. Gasoline presents an extreme fire hazard. Be sure to work in a well-ventilated area when using cleaning solvents. Keep a fire extinguisher rated for gasoline and oil fires nearby in case of an emergency.*

Once you have decided to do the job yourself, read this chapter thoroughly until you have a good idea of what is involved in completing the repair satisfactorily. Make arrangements to buy or rent any special tools necessary and obtain replacement parts before starting. It is frustrating and time-consuming to start an overhaul and then be unable to finish because the necessary tools or parts are not at hand.

Before beginning the job, re-read Chapter Two of this manual. You will do a better job with this information fresh in your mind.

Since this chapter covers a large range of models over a lengthy time period, the procedures are somewhat generalized to accommodate all models. Where individual differences occur, they are specifically pointed out. The power heads shown in the accompanying pictures are current designs. While it is possible that the components shown in the pictures may not be identical with those being serviced, they are representative and the step-by-step procedures may be used with all models covered in this manual. **Tables 1-6** are at the end of the chapter.

ENGINE SERIAL NUMBER

Mercury outboard motors are often identified by the engine serial number instead of model year. The serial number is stamped on a plate riveted to the transom clamp. The serial number is also stamped on a welch plug installed on the power head (**Figure 1**, typical). Exact location of the transom clamp plate and welch plug varies according to the model.

The serial number identifies the outboard motor and indicates if there are unique parts or if internal changes have been made during the model run. The serial number should always be used when ordering replacement parts for the outboard.

GASKETS AND SEALANTS

The following sealants are recommended by the manufacturer for use during power head service:
   a. Loctite Master Gasket Sealant Kit (part No. 92-12564-1).
   b. Permatex #2 Form-A-Gasket (part No. 92-72592-1).
   c. Quicksilver Perfect Seal (part No. 92-34277-1).
   d. RTV (room temperature vulcanizing) sealant.

Loctite Master Gasket Sealant is used to seal the crankcase cover-to-cylinder block mating surfaces on models without a gasket. Apply the sealant in a continuous 1/16 in. (1.6 mm) bead. The sealant bead should be applied to the inside of all crankcase cover screw holes.

Permatex #2 is used to seal the crankcase cover-to-cylinder block mating surfaces on models with a gasket. Apply the sealant in a thin, even coat covering the entire mating surface.

When sealing the crankcase cover/cylinder block, both mating surfaces must be free of all sealant residue, dirt, oil or other contamination. Locquic Primer T (part No. 92-59327-1), lacquer thinner, acetone or similar solvents work well when used in conjunction with a broad, flat scraper or a somewhat dull putty knife. Solvents with an oil, wax or petroleum base should not be used. Clean the aluminum surfaces carefully to avoid nicking them with the scraper or putty knife.

In addition to the previously mentioned sealants, a suitable thread locking compound should be applied to any fastener used on moving or rotating engine components. Some common thread locking compounds recommended by the manufacturer are Loctite 222, 242 and 271. Loctite Retaining Compound 635 is used to retain roller bearings on some models. Apply Loctite 222 or 242 to the outer diameter of all metal

cased seals to secure the seal in place and to provide a good seal.

FASTENERS AND TORQUE

Always replace a worn or damaged fastener with one of the same size, type and torque requirement. Power head tightening torques are listed in **Tables 1-3**.

The cylinder head fasteners should be retorqued after 1/2 to 1 hour of operation. Back off the fasteners in the reverse order of the tightening sequence (described in this chapter), then retighten to the specified torque.

Other power head fasteners should be tightened in 2 steps. Tighten to 50 percent of the specified torque in the first step, then to 100 percent in the second step.

When spark plugs are installed after an overhaul, tighten the plugs to the specified torque. Warm the engine to normal operating temperature, allow it to cool, then retighten the plugs to the recommended torque.

POWER HEAD

The removal and installation procedures in this chapter represent the most efficient sequence for removing the power head while preparing for complete disassembly. If complete disassembly is not necessary, stop disassembly at the appropriate point, then begin reassembly where disassembly stopped. The power head should be removed as an assembly if major repairs are to be performed. Power head removal is not required for certain service procedures such as cylinder wall inspection, cylinder head and exhaust cover removal, ignition component replacement, fuel system component replacement and reed block removal.

Removal/Installation (3 and 3.3 hp)

1. Remove the engine cover.
2. Disconnect the spark plug lead and remove the spark plug.
3. Remove the rewind starter as described in Chapter Twelve.
4. Remove the flywheel, magneto stator plate and ignition coil as described in Chapter Seven.
5. Drain all the fuel from the fuel tank.
6. Remove the fuel tank, fuel shut-off valve and carburetor as described in Chapter Six.
7. Remove the 6 bolts holding the power head to the drive shaft housing.
8. Lift the power head off the drive shaft housing and place on a clean bench or mount into a suitable holding fixture.
9. Thoroughly clean any gasket material from the drive shaft housing and power head mating surfaces.
10. Install a new gasket on the drive shaft housing.
11. Lubricate the drive shaft splines with Quicksilver 2-4-C Marine Lubricant.
12. Install the power head onto the drive shaft housing. Rotate the propeller shaft as necessary to align the crankshaft and drive shaft splines.
13. Apply Permatex #2 to the threads of the power head mounting bolts. Install the bolts and tighten to specification (**Table 1**).
14. Install the ignition coil, magneto stator plate and flywheel as described in Chapter Seven.
15. Complete the remaining installation by reversing the removal procedure.

Removal/Installation (4 and 5 hp)

1. Remove the engine cover.
2. Disconnect the spark plug lead and remove the spark plug.
3. 4 hp—Close the fuel shutoff valve. Siphon all fuel from the engine-mounted fuel tank.

8

4. Remove the rewind starter from the power head (Chapter Twelve).

5. Remove the flywheel, CDI unit and ignition coil as described in Chapter Seven.

6. Remove the fuel tank mounting nuts. Remove the fuel tank.

7. Remove the carburetor as described in Chapter Seven.

8. Remove the 6 bolts holding the power head to the drive shaft housing.

9. Rock the power head to break the gasket seal between the drive shaft housing and power head. Remove the power head from the drive shaft housing and place on a clean bench or mount into a suitable holding fixture.

10. Thoroughly clean all gasket material from the power head and drive shaft housing mating surfaces.

11. Lubricate the drive shaft splines with Quicksilver 2-4-C Marine Lubricant.

12. Place a new gasket onto the drive shaft housing.

13. Install the power head onto the drive shaft housing. Install the 6 power head mounting bolts and tighten to specification (**Table 1**).

14. Complete the remaining installation by reversing Steps 1-7.

15. Perform timing, synchronizing and adjustment procedures. See Chapter Five.

Removal/Installation (8, 9.9 and 15 hp)

1. Remove the engine cover.

2. Disconnect the spark plug leads and remove the spark plugs.

3. Remove the rewind starter as described in Chapter Twelve.

4. Remove the flywheel and stator assembly as described in Chapter Seven.

5. Remove the ignition coil and switchbox. See Chapter Seven.

6. Remove the carburetor. See Chapter Six.

7. Remove the throttle and shift linkage.

8. Remove the 4 bolts and 2 nuts holding the power head to the drive shaft housing.

9. Rock the power head to break the gasket seal between the drive shaft housing and power head. Remove the power head and place on a clean bench or mount into a suitable holding fixture.

10. Thoroughly clean all gasket material from the drive shaft housing and power head mating surfaces.

11. Lubricate the drive shaft splines with Quicksilver 2-4-C Marine Lubricant.

12. Place a new gasket onto the drive shaft housing. Install the power head on the drive shaft housing. If necessary, rotate the crankshaft to align the crankshaft and drive shaft splines.

13. Apply Loctite 242 or 271 to the threads of the power head mounting bolts and studs. Tighten the mounting fasteners to specification (**Table 1**).

14. Perform timing, synchronizing and adjustment procedures as described in Chapter Five.

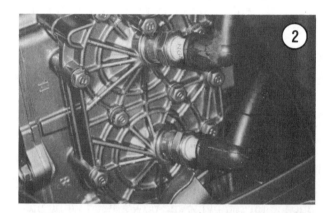

**Removal/Installation
(20 and 25 hp)**

1. Remove the top and bottom cowls.

2. Disconnect the battery cables from the battery on models so equipped.

3. Disconnect the spark plug leads (**Figure 2**). Remove the spark plugs.

4. Detach the sight bowl fuel filter from the rewind starter housing. See Chapter Six.

5. Remove the rewind starter assembly from the power head as described in Chapter Twelve.

6. Remove the flywheel, stator assembly, trigger plate, switchbox and ignition coils. See Chapter Seven.

7. Place the shift linkage into the neutral position.

8. Loosen the jam nuts holding the control cables to the anchor bracket (**Figure 3**). Remove the cables from the bracket.

9. Disconnect the lower cable (**Figure 3**) from the throttle/shift gear. Rotate the tiller handle twist grip fully clockwise, then disconnect the upper cable (**Figure 3**) from the throttle/shift gear.

10. Disconnect the fuel hoses (**Figure 4**). Remove the carburetor as described in Chapter Six.

11. Remove the screw holding the shift shaft coupler to the shift shaft, then slide the coupler off the shaft. See **Figure 5**.

12. Remove the 6 bolts holding the power head to the drive shaft housing.

13. Carefully pry the power head loose from the drive shaft housing. Place the power head on a clean bench or mount into a suitable holding fixture.

14. Thoroughly clean all gasket material from the drive shaft housing and power head mating surfaces.

15. Place a new gasket on the drive shaft housing and install the power head. If necessary, shift the gear housing into gear and rotate the propeller shaft to align the drive shaft and crankshaft splines.

16. Apply Loctite 271 to the threads of the power head mounting bolts. Install the bolts and tighten to specification (**Table 1**).

17. Reverse Steps 1-11 to complete the remaining installation.

18. Perform timing, synchronizing and adjustment procedures as described in Chapter Five.

**Removal/Installation
(40 hp)**

1. Remove the engine cover.

2. Disconnect the spark plug leads and remove the spark plugs.

3. Disconnect the alternator leads (manual start) or battery cables (electric start) from the battery.

4. Disconnect the control cable retainer. Remove the throttle cable from the throttle/spark lever. Remove the shift cable from the shift lever.

8

5. Remove the fuel connector from the lower cowl.

6. Remove the ground wire(s) and the "tell-tale" hose from the rear starboard of the lower cowl.

7A. Manual start:

   a. Disconnect the black/yellow stop switch wires at their bullet connectors.

   b. Remove the "tell-tale" hose from the lower cowl.

   c. Disconnect the fuel hoses from the enrichment valve.

   d. Remove the neutral interlock cable from the rewind starter. Remove the rewind starter assembly as described in Chapter Twelve.

7B. Electric start:

   a. Disconnect the remote control harness connector from the engine harness. See A, **Figure 6**. Disconnect the blue/white and green/white power trim/tilt wires (if so equipped) from the remote control (B, **Figure 6**).

   b. Remove the starter motor as described in Chapter Seven.

   c. Disconnect the engine mounted power trim switch blue/white and green/white wires at their bullet connectors.

   d. Disconnect the 2 blue oil level wires at their bullet connectors on the starboard side of the outboard.

   e. Disconnect the oil delivery hose from the oil pump. Plug the hose to prevent leakage.

   f. Remove the 3 screws holding the flywheel cover to the engine. Remove the cover and oil reservoir assembly.

8. Remove 4 screws holding the trim cover to the lower cowl. Remove the cover.

NOTE
Insufficient clearance will prevent the removal of the 2 front (1 each side) power head mounting nuts in Step 9. Loosen the 2 front nuts, remove all others, then lift the power head with the hoist to gain access to the front nuts.

9. Remove 8 nuts securing the power head to the drive shaft housing.

10. Remove the plastic cap from the center of the flywheel. Install lifting eye part No. 91-75132 (or equivalent) into the flywheel as far as possible. Attach a hoist to the lifting eye and lift the power head off the drive shaft housing. Place the power head on a clean bench or a suitable holding fixture.

11. Thoroughly clean all gasket material from the power head and drive shaft housing mating surfaces. The mating surfaces must be clean and smooth.

CAUTION
Do not apply grease to the top of the drive shaft in Step 12. If grease is present on the top of the drive shaft, a hydraulic lock may occur preventing complete engagement of the drive shaft and crankshaft splines.

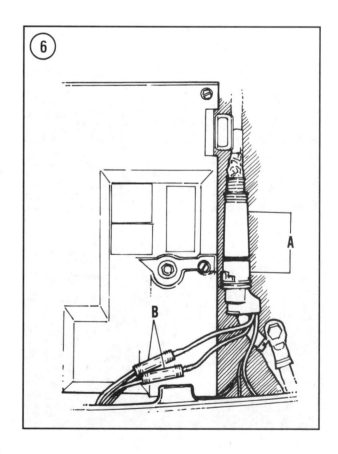

12. Lubricate the drive shaft splines with Quicksilver 2-4-C Marine Lubricant.

13. Shift the gearcase into NEUTRAL. The propeller should turn freely in both directions.

14. Install a new gasket on the drive shaft housing.

15. Thread the lifting eye part No. 91-75132 (or equivalent) into the flywheel 5 turns minimum. Attach a hoist to the lifting eye.

> *NOTE*
> *Start the 2 front power head mounting nuts (1 each side) on their studs before the power head is fully lowered onto the drive shaft housing.*

16. Install the power head on the drive shaft housing. Rotate the engine flywheel to align the crankshaft and drive shaft splines. Install the power head mounting nuts. Tighten the nuts evenly in 3 progressive steps, to the specified torque (**Table 2**).

17. Reverse Steps 1-8 to complete the remaining installation.

18. Perform timing, synchronizing and adjustment procedures as described in Chapter Five.

Removal/Installation
(50 and 60 hp Prior to Serial No. D000750)

1. Remove the front cover, clam-shell cowl and top cowl support bracket.

2. Disconnect the battery cables from the battery.

3. Disconnect the spark plug leads and remove the spark plugs.

4. Disconnect the fuel hose from the fuel pump.

5. Disconnect the remote control harness at the engine (**Figure 7**, typical).

6. Remove any clamps and sta-straps holding hoses and wiring harnesses to the power head.

7. Remove the fasteners and ground strap holding the rear cowl support bracket to the power head. Remove the bracket.

8. Shift the outboard into NEUTRAL.

> *NOTE*
> *Insufficient clearance will prevent the removal of the 2 front (1 each side) power head mounting nuts in Step 9. Loosen the 2 front nuts, remove all others, then lift the power head with the hoist (Step 12) to gain access to the front nuts.*

9. Loosen and remove the 4 bolts and 8 nuts securing the power head to the drive shaft housing.

10. Remove the shift cable latch assembly locknut. Remove the latch, flat washer and nylon wear plate from the control cable anchor bracket.

11. Remove the plastic cap from the center of the flywheel. Install lifting eye part No. 91-75132 (or equivalent) into the flywheel as far as possible.

12. Attach a hoist to the lifting eye and raise the power head enough to remove the front 2 power head mounting nuts.

13. Pull the shift linkage slightly from its neutral position while lifting the power head from the drive shaft housing. This prevents the link from pulling out of the drive shaft housing. Lift the power head off the drive shaft housing and place on a clean bench or mount into a suitable holding fixture.

14. Make sure the drive shaft housing and power head mating surfaces are clean.

8

CAUTION
Do not apply grease to the top of the drive shaft in Step 15. If grease is present on the top of the drive shaft, a hydraulic lock may occur preventing complete engagement of the drive shaft and crankshaft splines.

15. Coat the drive shaft splines with Quicksilver 2-4-C Marine Lubricant.

16. Install the power head onto the drive shaft housing. Place the gear housing into gear and rotate the propeller shaft to align the drive shaft and crankshaft splines.

NOTE
Start the 2 front power head mounting nuts (1 each side) on their studs before the power head is fully lowered onto the drive shaft housing.

17. Install the power head fasteners and tighten to specification (**Table 2**).

18. Reverse Steps 1-10 to complete the remaining installation.

19. Perform timing, synchronizing and adjusting as described in Chapter 5.

Removal/Installation (50 and 60 hp Serial No. D000750-on)

1. Disconnect the battery cables from the battery. Remove the engine cowl. Disconnect the spark plug leads from the spark plugs.

2. Disconnect the fuel hose from the fuel hose connector.

3. Disconnect the remote control power trim/tilt wiring harness from the engine power trim/tilt connector. See **Figure 8**.

4. Disconnect the engine mounted trim switch (**Figure 8**) and relay wires at their bullet connectors (blue/white, green/white and red/black).

5. Remove the remote control throttle and shift cables from the power head.

6. Remove the bolt securing the fuel connector to the lower cowl, then lift the fuel connector

rubber grommet out of the lower cowl. See **Figure 9**.

7. Remove the electrical box cover.

8. Disconnect the positive battery cable from the starter motor relay. Disconnect the negative battery cable (ground) from the starter motor mounting clamp and remove the clamp. See **Figure 10**.

9. Remove the oil reservoir as described in Chapter Eleven.

10. Remove the screw securing the low-oil warning module ground wire to the power head (next to the bottom spark plug).

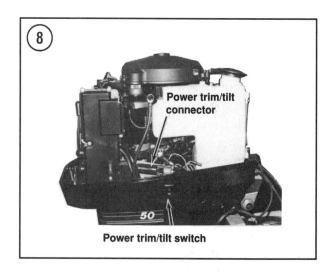

Power trim/tilt switch

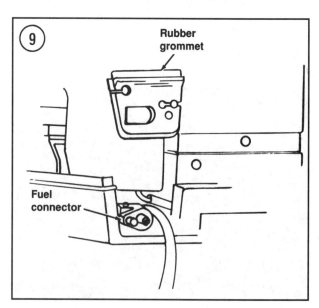

11. Remove the 4 screws securing the trim cover to the lower engine cowl. Remove the trim cover to gain access to the power head mounting bolts.

12. Thread lifting eye part No. 91-90455 (or equivalent) into the flywheel as far as possible.

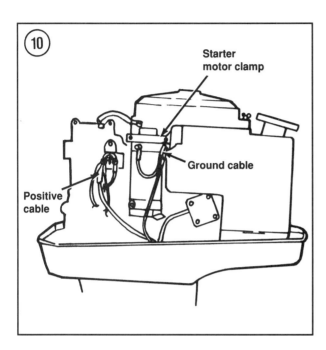

13. Remove the 6 power head mounting screws (**Figure 11**). Attach a hoist to the lifting eye and lift the power head off the drive shaft housing allowing the shift linkage to slide off the shift rail. Place the power head on a clean bench or mount into a suitable holding fixture.

CAUTION
Do not apply grease to the top of the drive shaft in Step 14. If grease is present on the top of the drive shaft, a hydraulic lock may occur preventing complete engagement of the drive shaft and crankshaft splines.

14. Apply Quicksilver 2-4-C Marine Lubricant to the drive shaft splines.

15. Install the power head onto the drive shaft housing. Rotate the propeller shaft (gear housing in gear) to align the drive shaft and crankshaft splines. Slide the shift linkage onto the shift rail while lowering the power head.

16. Install the 6 power head mounting bolts and tighten to specification (**Table 2**). Install the trim cover and screws.

17. Connect the low-oil module ground wire to the power head.

18. Install the oil reservoir (Chapter Eleven). Connect the reservoir oil level sensor wires.

19. Attach the positive battery cable to the starter relay. Install the starter motor clamp and connect the battery ground cable to the clamp using a starter mounting bolt. Install the electrical box cover.

20. Attach the remote control shift and throttle cables to the engine.

21. Complete the remaining installation by reversing the removal procedure. Be sure to route all wires and harnesses as noted during removal. Install the necessary wire harness clamps and sta-straps.

22. Bleed oil injection system as described in Chapter Eleven.

23. Perform timing, synchronizing and adjustment procedures as described in Chapter Five.

8

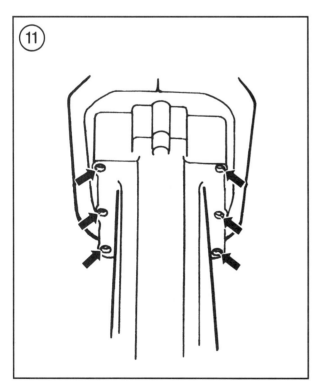

**Removal/Installation
(75 and 90 hp)**

1. Remove the engine cover.
2. Disconnect the battery cables from the battery. Disconnect the spark plug leads from the spark plugs.
3. Remove the front cowl support bracket.
4. Remove the 8 screws retaining the air box cover, then remove the cover.
5. Remove the oil reservoir lower support screw and the 2 oil reservoir neck brace screws.
6. Remove the 6 nuts retaining the air box. Remove the air box.
7. Disconnect the oil hoses from the oil reservoir. Plug the hoses to prevent leakage. Remove the oil reservoir.
8. Disconnect the throttle linkage from the center carburetor ball socket.
9. Disconnect the fuel supply hose and fuel primer hose from the top carburetor.
10. Withdraw the carburetor assemblies and actuating linkage as a complete unit.
11. Remove the flywheel cover.

NOTE
It is recommended that you make a series of drawings or take instant pictures prior to begining Step 12 to provide reference during reassembly and installation.

12. Disconnect all electrical and ignition wiring as necessary and remove with component mounting plates.
13. Loosen and remove the fasteners holding the power head to the drive shaft housing.
14. Remove the shift arm linkage.
15. Thread lifting eye part No. 91-90455 (or equivalent) into the flywheel as far as possible. Attach a hoist to the lifting eye.
16. Remove any component not previously noted that will interfere with power head removal.
17. Lift the power head from the drive shaft housing and place on a clean bench or mount into a suitable holding fixture.

18. Thoroughly clean all gasket material from the power head and drive shaft housing mating surfaces.
19. Install a new gasket onto the locating dowels on the drive shaft housing.
20. Apply Quicksilver 2-4-C Marine Lubricant to the drive shaft splines.
21. Make sure lifting eye (part No. 91-90455) is screwed into the flywheel at least 5 turns. Attach the hoist to the lifting eye and install the power head on the drive shaft housing. Rotate the engine flywheel as necessary to align the crankshaft and drive shaft splines.
22. Clean the power head mounting screws with Locquic Primer T and allow to air dry. Apply Loctite 271 to the threads of the mounting screws. Install the power head mounting screws and tighten in 3 steps to the specified tightness (**Table 2**).
23. Complete installation by reversing Steps 1-14. Bleed the oil injection system as described in Chapter Eleven. Perform timing, synchronizing and adjusting procedures as described in Chapter Five.

**Removal/Installation
(100 and 115 hp)**

1. Remove the engine cowl.
2. Disconnect the battery cables and spark plug leads. Remove the spark plugs.
3. Disconnect the "tell-tale" water hose from the aft cowl support bracket.
4. Remove the 4 bolts retaining the aft cowl support bracket, then remove the bracket.
5. Remove the 4 screws retaining the ignition plate cover, then remove the cover.
6. Disconnect the negative battery cable from the starter motor mounting bolt and positive battery cable from the starter solenoid.
7. Disconnect the power trim/tilt wires from their respective relays on the ignition plate. Remove the trim/tilt fuse located at the top of the starter motor.

8. Remove the 2 screws and clamp retaining the supply wiring harness assembly to the bottom cowl support bracket at the front of the engine.

9. Disconnect the supply wiring harness from the engine wiring harness at the ignition plate connector, then disconnect any wire connection not previously noted that will interfere with wiring harness removal. Remove the harness assembly.

10. Disconnect the fuel supply hose from the engine fuel connector.

11. Disconnect the throttle and shift cables from the engine mounting bracket.

12. Remove the shift arm linkage.

13. Install lifting eye part No. 91-90455 (or equivalent) into the flywheel. The eye must be threaded into the flywheel 5 turns minimum. Attach a hoist to the lifting eye.

14. Loosen and remove the 8 nuts and washers (4 each side) holding the power head to the drive shaft housing.

15. Lift the power head off the drive shaft housing. Place the power head on a clean bench or mount into a suitable holding fixture.

16. Make sure the power head and drive shaft housing mating surfaces are clean and smooth.

17. Screw lifting eye into the flywheel 5 turns minimum. Attach the hoist to the lifting eye.

18. Place a new power head gasket onto the locating dowels in the drive shaft housing.

19. Apply a small amount of Quicksilver 2-4-C Marine Lubricant to the drive shaft splines.

20. Install the power head onto the drive shaft housing. Rotate the flywheel as necessary to align the crankshaft and drive shaft splines.

21. Install the 8 power head mounting nuts and washers. Tighten the nuts to specification (**Table 2**).

22. Complete reinstallation by reversing Steps 1-12. Coat the electrical connections at the power trim/tilt relays with Liquid Neoprene (part No. 92-25711). Bleed the oil injection system as described in Chapter Eleven. Perform timing, synchronizing and adjustment procedures as described in Chapter Five.

Removal/Installation (135-200 hp V6)

1. Disconnect the battery cables from the battery.

2. Remove the engine cowling. Disconnect the spark plug leads and remove the spark plugs.

3. Disconnect the remote fuel tank hose from the outboard motor.

4. Disconnect the remote oil tank hose connector from the engine mounted oil reservoir.

5. Remove the remote control harness retainer. Disconnect the remote control harness from the power head harness connector.

6. Remove the ignition plate connector.

7. Disconnect the red, blue/white and green/white power trim/tilt wires at their bullet connectors. Disconnect the tan overheat warning wire at its bullet connector.

8. Remove the ignition coil/solenoid cover.

9. Disconnect the blue, green and black power trim/tilt wires from the trim relays.

10. Shift the outboard into NEUTRAL.

11. Remove the locknut holding the shift cable latch assembly. Remove the latch, washer, nylon wear plate and the spring from the control cable anchor bracket.

12. Disconnect the fuel delivery hose from the fuel pump.

13. Disconnect the "tell-tale" water hose from the exhaust plate elbow fitting. Unbolt and remove the rear cowl support bracket from the power head (**Figure 12**).

14. Remove the 4 screws holding the lower engine cowl halves together, then remove the lower cowl.

15. Remove the 10 nuts and lockwashers (5 each side) holding the power head to the drive shaft housing. See **Figure 13**.

16. Remove the plastic cap from the center of the flywheel. Thread lifting eye part No. 91-90455 (or equivalent) into the flywheel 5 turns minimum. Attach a hoist to the lifting eye.

17. Lift the power head off the drive shaft housing. Place the power head on a clean bench or mount into a suitable holding fixture.

18. To install the power head, make sure the lifting eye is threaded into the flywheel at least 5 turns. Attach the hoist to the lifting eye.

19. Thoroughly clean the power head and drive shaft housing mating surfaces.

20. Place a new power head gasket onto the power head studs and into position on the power head.

CAUTION
Do not apply grease to the top of the drive shaft in Step 21. If grease is present on the top of the drive shaft, a hydraulic lock may occur preventing complete engagement of the drive shaft and crankshaft splines.

21. Apply a small amount of Quicksilver 2-4-C Marine Lubricant to the drive shaft splines.

22. Using the hoist, lower the power head onto the drive shaft housing. Rotate the flywheel to align the crankshaft and drive shaft splines.

23. Install the power head mounting nuts and flat washers. Tighten the nuts in 3 steps to the specified torque (**Table 3**). Remove the hoist, remove the lifting eye and reinstall the plastic cap in the center of the flywheel.

24. With the spring and guide block installed on the shift link rod, insert the shift link rod into the control cable anchor bracket. Guide block must be installed with the anchor pin facing forward.

25. Secure the shift link rod with wear plate, latch, flat washer and locknut. Thread the locknut onto the shift link rod until 2 or 3 threads are exposed beyond the top of the nut. Adjust the shift linkage as described in Chapter Nine.

26. Complete the installation by reversing Steps 1-14. Bleed the oil injection system as described in Chapter Eleven. Perform timing, synchronizing and adjustment procedures as described in Chapter Five.

Removal/Installation
(250 and 275 hp V6)

1. Disconnect the battery cables from the battery.

2. Disconnect the remote fuel tank fuel hose from the engine.

3. Remove the engine cowl.

4. Disconnect the throttle and shift cables from the engine.

5. Disconnect the spark plug leads and remove the spark plugs.

6. Disconnect the remote control wiring harness from the engine harness (**Figure 14**).

7. Disconnect the "tell-tale" water hose from the aft cowl support bracket. Remove the 4 screws securing the aft cowl support bracket and remove the bracket.

8. Disconnect the remote oil tank hoses from the engine. Plug the hoses to prevent leakage or contamination.

9. Using an appropriate size punch and hammer, drive out the roll pin (**Figure 15**) securing the shift arm to the vertical shift shaft. Remove the shift arm from the vertical shaft.

10. Remove 6 nuts and lockwashers (3 each side) and 1 bolt from the base of the power head.

11. Remove the flywheel cover from the engine.

12. Thread lifting eye part No. 91-090455 (or equivalent) into the flywheel 5 turns minimum. Attach a hoist to the lifting eye.

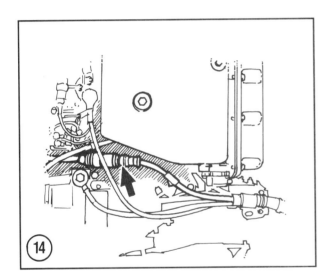

13. Using the hoist, lift the power head off the drive shaft housing and place on a clean bench or mount into a suitable holding fixture.

14. If removed, install the splined nylon tube (**Figure 16**) onto the drive shaft, then install the rubber seal onto the drive shaft with the splined side facing the nylon tube.

CAUTION
Do not apply grease to the top of the drive shaft in Step 15. If grease is present on the top of the drive shaft, a hydraulic lock may occur preventing complete engagement of the drive shaft and crankshaft splines. Any grease on top of the drive shaft must be removed prior to installing the power head.

15. Apply a light coat of Quicksilver 2-4-C Marine Lubricant to the drive shaft splines. Wipe off any grease present on top of the drive shaft.

8

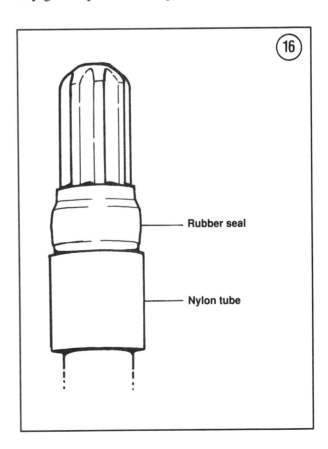

Rubber seal

Nylon tube

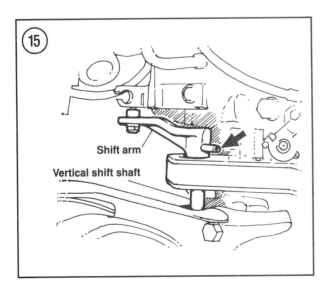

Shift arm

Vertical shift shaft

16. Make sure the lifting eye (part No. 91-90455) is threaded into the flywheel at least 5 turns. Attach the hoist to the lifting eye.

17. Thoroughly clean the power head and drive shaft housing mating surfaces. Install a new power head gasket.

18. Using the hoist, lower the power head onto the drive shaft housing. Rotate the flywheel as necessary to align the crankshaft and drive shaft splines.

19. Remove the hoist, then unscrew the lifting eye from the flywheel.

20. Install the flywheel cover and secure with 4 wingnuts.

CAUTION
Water leakage between the power head and drive shaft housing may occur if the power head mounting fasteners are not tightened in the correct sequence (Step 21).

21. Install the power head mounting nuts and bolt (with lockwashers). Tighten the fasteners to specification (**Table 3**) in the sequence shown in **Figure 17**.

22. Shift the gear housing into NEUTRAL. Install the shift arm (**Figure 15**) onto the vertical shift shaft so the roll pin hole is parallel to the front of the engine. Secure the shift arm with a new roll pin (**Figure 15**).

23. Complete installation by reversing Steps 1-8. Bleed the oil injection system as described in Chapter Eleven. Perform timing, synchronizing and adjustment procedures as described in Chapter Five.

Disassembly
(3 and 3.3 hp)

Refer to **Figure 18** for this procedure.

1. Remove the lower end cap.
2. Remove the cylinder head.
3. Remove the 6 crankcase cover screws and remove the crankcase cover from the cylinder

block, while allowing the crankshaft assembly to remain in the cylinder block.

4. Remove the 2 screws securing the reed stops and reed petals to the crankcase cover.
5. Remove the crankshaft, connecting rod and piston assembly from the cylinder block.
6. Slide the seals and retainer rings from each end of the crankshaft.

Disassembly
(4 and 5 hp)

Refer to **Figure 19** for this procedure.

1. Remove the 2 screws holding the seal housing to the power head. Gently tap the oil seal housing tube with a soft-face mallet to break the seal and remove the assembly from the power head. Discard the gasket.

2. Remove the 5 cylinder head bolts. Remove the cylinder head and discard the gasket.

3. Remove the 6 bolts holding the crankcase cover to the cylinder block.

4. Insert a screwdriver blade under the tab locations on each side of the crankcase cover. Carefully pry at the tab pry points to break the crankcase seal, then remove the crankcase cover from the cylinder block.

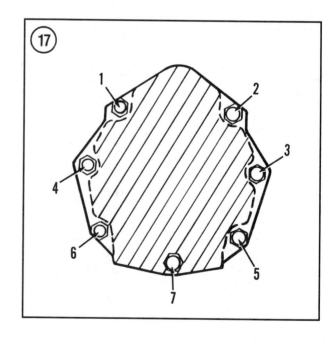

5. If reed valve service is necessary, remove the 2 screws holding the reed valve assembly to the crankcase cover. Remove the reed stop and reed petals.

6. Remove the oil seals and locating washers from each end of the crankshaft.

7. Lift the crankshaft assembly straight up and remove it from the cylinder block.

Disassembly
(8, 9.9 and 15 hp)

Refer to **Figure 20** for this procedure.

1. Remove the 3 screws holding the reed block assembly to the power head. If necessary, rap the assembly with a soft-face mallet to break the

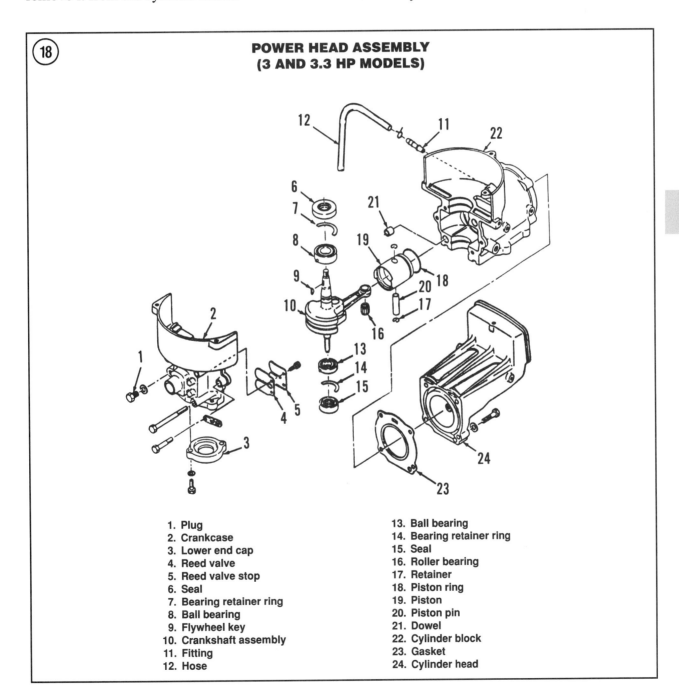

POWER HEAD ASSEMBLY
(3 AND 3.3 HP MODELS)

1. Plug
2. Crankcase
3. Lower end cap
4. Reed valve
5. Reed valve stop
6. Seal
7. Bearing retainer ring
8. Ball bearing
9. Flywheel key
10. Crankshaft assembly
11. Fitting
12. Hose
13. Ball bearing
14. Bearing retainer ring
15. Seal
16. Roller bearing
17. Retainer
18. Piston ring
19. Piston
20. Piston pin
21. Dowel
22. Cylinder block
23. Gasket
24. Cylinder head

8

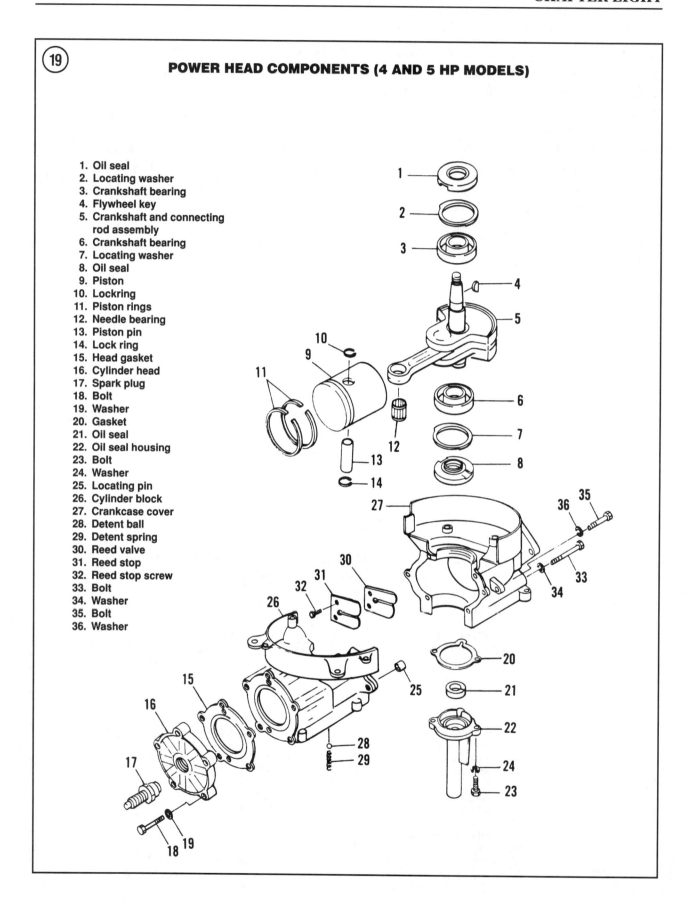

⑲ **POWER HEAD COMPONENTS (4 AND 5 HP MODELS)**

1. Oil seal
2. Locating washer
3. Crankshaft bearing
4. Flywheel key
5. Crankshaft and connecting rod assembly
6. Crankshaft bearing
7. Locating washer
8. Oil seal
9. Piston
10. Lockring
11. Piston rings
12. Needle bearing
13. Piston pin
14. Lock ring
15. Head gasket
16. Cylinder head
17. Spark plug
18. Bolt
19. Washer
20. Gasket
21. Oil seal
22. Oil seal housing
23. Bolt
24. Washer
25. Locating pin
26. Cylinder block
27. Crankcase cover
28. Detent ball
29. Detent spring
30. Reed valve
31. Reed stop
32. Reed stop screw
33. Bolt
34. Washer
35. Bolt
36. Washer

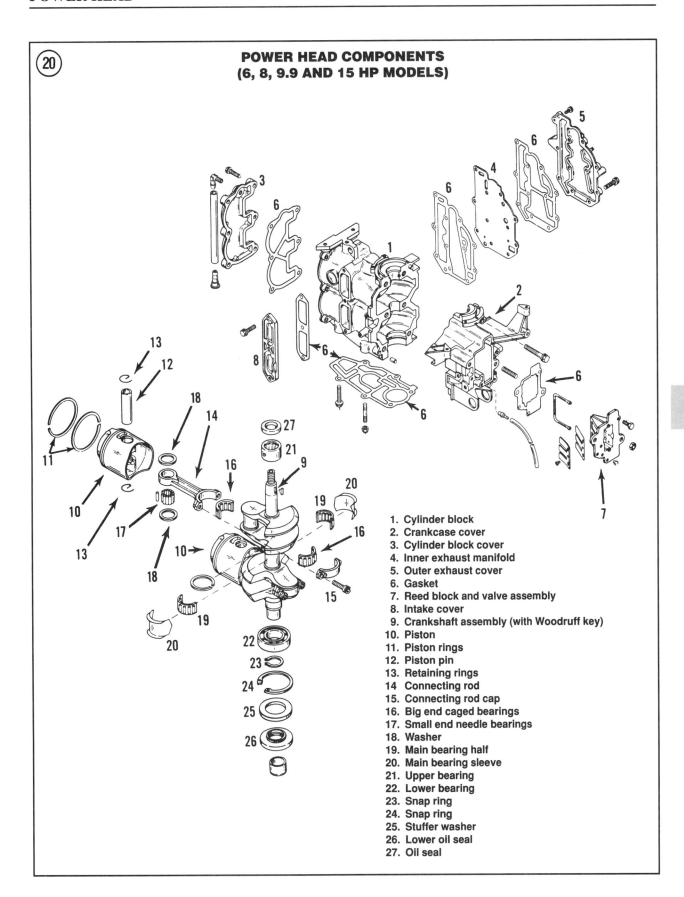

**POWER HEAD COMPONENTS
(6, 8, 9.9 AND 15 HP MODELS)**

1. Cylinder block
2. Crankcase cover
3. Cylinder block cover
4. Inner exhaust manifold
5. Outer exhaust cover
6. Gasket
7. Reed block and valve assembly
8. Intake cover
9. Crankshaft assembly (with Woodruff key)
10. Piston
11. Piston rings
12. Piston pin
13. Retaining rings
14. Connecting rod
15. Connecting rod cap
16. Big end caged bearings
17. Small end needle bearings
18. Washer
19. Main bearing half
20. Main bearing sleeve
21. Upper bearing
22. Lower bearing
23. Snap ring
24. Snap ring
25. Stuffer washer
26. Lower oil seal
27. Oil seal

8

gasket seal. Remove the reed block assembly, then remove and discard the gasket.

2. Remove the 6 screws holding the cylinder block cover to the power head. Remove the cover and discard the gasket.

3. Remove the 11 screws holding the exhaust cover to the cylinder block. If necessary, tap the

assembly gently with a soft-face mallet to break the gasket seal. Separate the exhaust cover and manifold assembly. Discard the gaskets.

4. Remove the intake cover. Remove and discard the gasket.

5. Remove the 6 screws holding the crankcase cover to the cylinder block. Carefully tap the

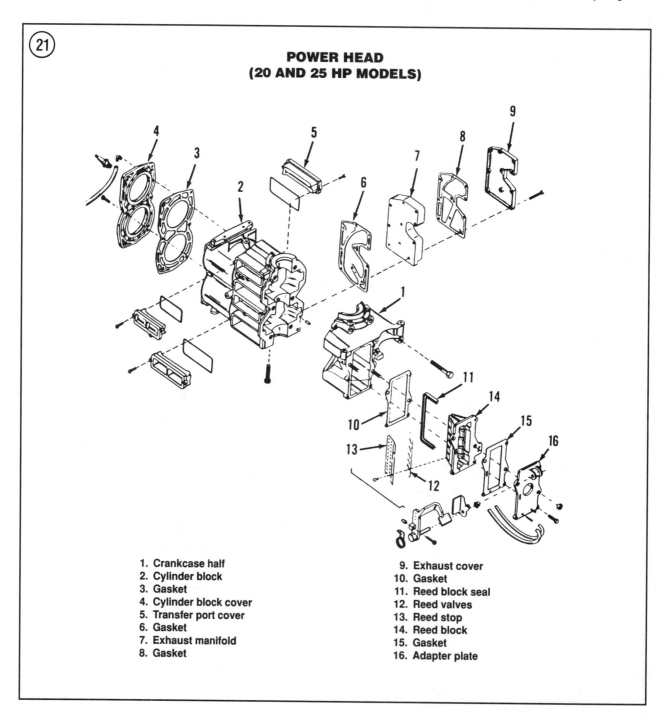

㉑ **POWER HEAD**
(20 AND 25 HP MODELS)

1. Crankcase half
2. Cylinder block
3. Gasket
4. Cylinder block cover
5. Transfer port cover
6. Gasket
7. Exhaust manifold
8. Gasket
9. Exhaust cover
10. Gasket
11. Reed block seal
12. Reed valves
13. Reed stop
14. Reed block
15. Gasket
16. Adapter plate

crankcase cover with a soft-face mallet to break the gasket seal. Remove the crankcase cover from the cylinder block.

6. Lift the crankshaft assembly straight up and remove it from the cylinder block. Place the

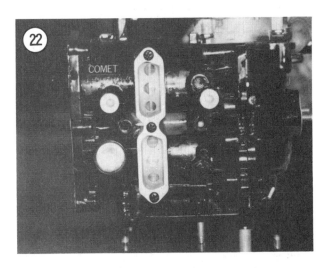

crankshaft upright into a power head stand mounted in a vise.

NOTE
*The reed valve assembly can be inspected without disassembly. See **Cleaning and Inspection (Reed Blocks)**. If inspection indicates component replacement is necessary, continue at Step 7.*

7. Remove the 3 screws securing each set of reed stop and valves to the reed block. Remove the reed stops and valves.

8. Remove the reed block rubber seal.

Disassembly
(20 and 25 hp)

Refer to **Figure 21** for this procedure.

1. Remove the carburetor adaptor plate, reed block assembly and gasket. Discard the gasket.

2. Remove the transfer port covers. See **Figure 22**, typical (covers removed).

3. Remove the cylinder block cover (**Figure 23**, typical).

4. Remove the exhaust cover and manifold (**Figure 24**, typical). Separate the exhaust cover from the manifold. Remove and discard the gaskets.

5. Remove 6 crankcase cover attaching screws. Carefully tap on the side of the crankcase cover with a soft-face mallet to break the seal between the cover and cylinder block. Remove the crankcase cover (**Figure 25**).

6. Lift the crankshaft straight up and remove it from the cylinder block. See **Figure 26**. Place the crankshaft assembly upright into a power head stand mounted in a vise.

NOTE
*The reed valve assembly can be inspected without disassembly. See **Cleaning and Inspection**. If inspection indicates component replacement is necessary, continue at Step 7.*

8

7. Remove the screws securing the reed stops and reed valves to the reed block. Remove the reed stops and valves. See **Figure 27**.

Disassembly
(40 hp)

1. Remove the rewind starter as described in Chapter Twelve.

2. Remove the flywheel, stator assembly, trigger plate assembly, switchbox and ignition coils as described in Chapter Seven.

3. Remove the starter motor as described in Chapter Seven.

4. Remove the carburetors, fuel pump and fuel enrichment valve as described in Chapter Six.

5. Remove the 2 Allen screws securing the oil injection pump to the crankcase cover. Remove the pump and driven gear. See Chapter Eleven. If the driven gear remains inside the crankcase cover, it can be removed after separating the crankcase cover and cylinder block.

6. Remove the 3 screws securing the throttle actuator assembly to the crankcase cover. See **Figure 28**. Remove the throttle actuator assembly.

7. Remove the bolt (**Figure 29**) securing the throttle/spark arm assembly to the exhaust manifold cover. Remove the throttle/spark arm assembly.

8. Remove the 4 screws securing the upper end cap to the cylinder block and crankcase cover.

9. Remove the 3 screws securing the lower end cap to the cylinder block and crankcase cover.

10. Bend back the locking tabs on the reed cage bolts and the center main bolt. See **Figure 30**. Remove the reed cage bolts and the center main bearing bolt.

11. Remove 17 screws securing the crankcase cover to the cylinder block.

CAUTION
The crankcase cover and cylinder block are a matched, align-bored unit. Do not

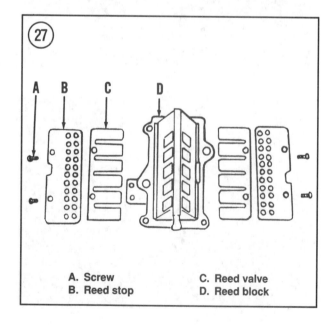

A. Screw
B. Reed stop
C. Reed valve
D. Reed block

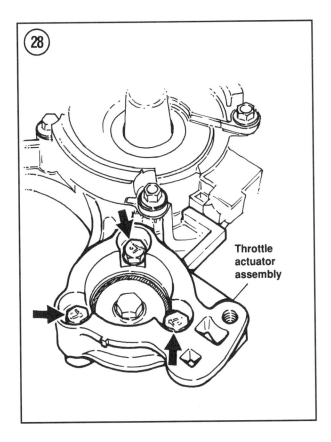

28

Throttle actuator assembly

scratch, nick or damage the machined, mating surfaces.

12. Using screwdrivers or similar tools, carefully pry at the pry points provided (**Figure 31**) to separate the crankcase cover from the cylinder block. *Do not* damage the crankcase cover and cylinder block mating surfaces. Remove the crankcase cover.

13. Using a soft-face mallet, carefully tap the upper and lower end caps free of the cylinder block. Slide the end caps off the crankshaft (**Figure 32**, typical).

14. On models so equipped, slide the oil pump drive gear (**Figure 33**) off the crankshaft.

15. Pad the crankcase mating surfaces near the ends of the crankshaft with clean shop cloths. Loosen the main bearing supports/reed blocks from the cylinder block locating pins with a pair of pry bars or screwdrivers. See **Figure 34**. Lift the crankshaft assembly straight up and remove

8

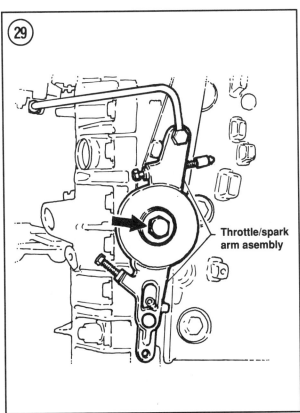

29

Throttle/spark arm asembly

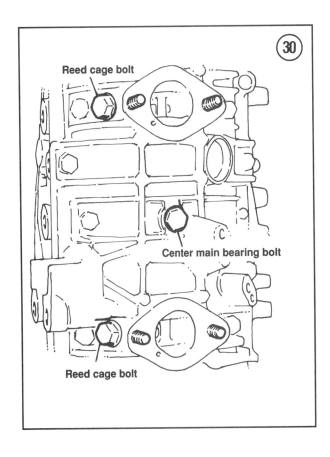

30

Reed cage bolt

Center main bearing bolt

Reed cage bolt

it from the cylinder block. Install the crankshaft upright on a power head stand mounted in a vise.

16. Remove the transfer port cover from the cylinder block. See **Figure 35**. Remove the discard the gasket.

17. Remove the balance tube and fittings from the cylinder block. See **Figure 35**. On some models, the primer fitting is attached to the balance tube.

18. Remove the bleed hose and bleed check valve from the cylinder block (**Figure 35**).

19. Remove the 10 screws securing the cylinder block cover to the cylinder block. Remove the cover and discard the gasket. Remove the temperature switch (next to the No. 1 spark plug hole) from the cylinder block.

20. Remove the 15 screws securing the exhaust cover to the cylinder block. Remove the cover

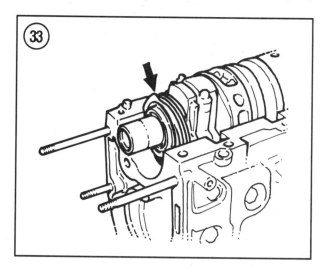

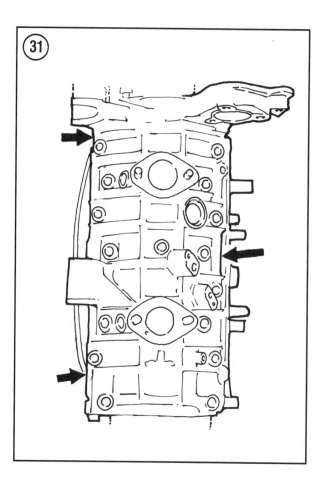

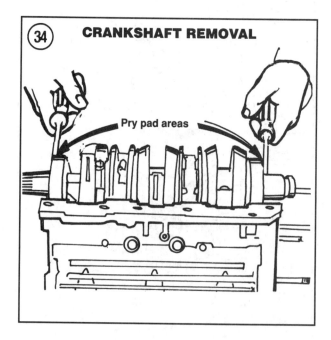

CRANKSHAFT REMOVAL

Pry pad areas

㉟ **CRANKCASE AND CYLINDER BLOCK ASSEMBLY (40 HP MODELS)**

8

1. Seal	13. Elbow fitting	24. Screw
2. Screw	14. Balance tube	25. Crankcase cover
3. Upper end cap	15. Primer fitting	26. Dowel pin
4. O-ring	16. Gasket	27. Reed cage bolt
5. Shim	17. Transfer port cover	28. Tab washer
6. Ball bearing	18. Screw	29. Stud
7. Cylinder block	19. Ball bearing	30. Center main bearing bolt
8. Gasket	20. Seals	31. Gasket
9. Cylinder block cover	21. O-ring	32. Exhaust baffle plate
10. Bleed hose connector	22. Shim	33. Gasket
11. Bleed hose	23. Lower end cap	34. Exhaust cover
12. Check valve		

and baffle plate from the cylinder block. Remove and discard the gaskets.

21. Using a suitable punch and hammer, drive the oil seals from the upper and lower end caps. Remove the end cap O-rings and shims.

NOTE
Do not remove the ball bearings from the end caps unless replacement is necessary. See **Cleaning and Inspection (End Caps).**

Disassembly
(50 and 60 hp Prior to Serial No. D000750)

1. Remove the flywheel. See Chapter Seven.

2. Remove the manual choke cable screw and push the cable down through the air box opening.

3. Disconnect the throttle lever linkage. Reinstall the bushing, flat washer and locknut on the end of the linkage.

4. Remove the stator and trigger assemblies. See Chapter Seven.

5. Disconnect all switchbox wires. See **Figure 36**.

6. Remove the starter motor. See Chapter Seven.

7. Unclamp the high tension leads and pull out from behind the fuel line.

8. Remove the fuel pump, filter and carburetors as an assembly. See Chapter Six.

9. Remove the air box, switchbox and ignition coils as an assembly.

10. Unbolt and remove the throttle actuator and linkage as an assembly.

11. Remove the crankcase cover screws. Remove the screws from the upper and lower end caps (**Figure 37**, typical).

CAUTION
The crankcase cover and cylinder block are a matched align-bored unit. Do not scratch, nick or damage the crankcase cover and cylinder block mating surfaces.

12. Split the crankcase cover gasket seal carefully with a putty knife. Remove the crankcase cover.

13. Using a soft-face mallet, tap the end caps off the crankcase (**Figure 38**). Do not damage the shims located under the end caps.

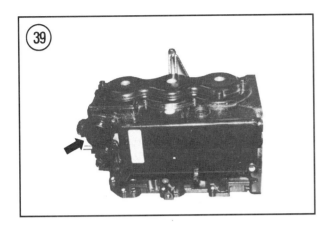

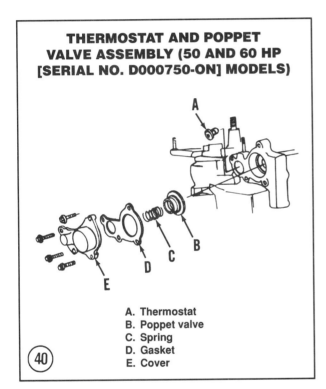

**THERMOSTAT AND POPPET
VALVE ASSEMBLY (50 AND 60 HP
[SERIAL NO. D000750-ON] MODELS)**

A. Thermostat
B. Poppet valve
C. Spring
D. Gasket
E. Cover

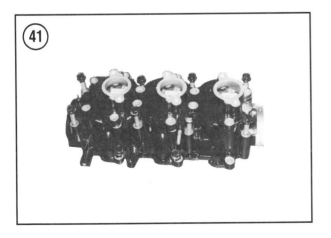

14. Pad the crankcase mating surfaces near the ends of the crankshaft with clean shop cloths. Loosen the main bearing supports/reed blocks from the cylinder block locating pins with a pair of pry bars or screwdrivers. See **Figure 34**. Lift the crankshaft straight up and remove it from the cylinder block. Install the crankshaft assembly upright into a power head stand.

15. Remove the exhaust cover from the cylinder block. Remove and discard the gasket.

16. Carefully pry the exhaust baffle from the cylinder block with a putty knife. Remove and discard the gasket.

17. Remove the transfer port cover. Remove and discard the gasket.

18. Remove the cylinder block cover. Remove and discard the gasket.

**Disassembly
(50 and 60 hp Serial No. D000750-on)**

1. Remove the flywheel. See Chapter Seven.

2. Remove the stator and trigger assemblies, switchbox and ignition coils. See Chapter Seven.

3. Remove the starter motor and starter relay. See Chapter Seven.

4. Remove the carburetors and linkage. Remove the fuel pump and enrichment valve. See Chapter Six.

5. Remove the oil injection pump. See Chapter Eleven.

6. Remove the remote control cable anchor bracket and shift cable latch assembly.

7. Remove the 4 thermostat cover screws (**Figure 39**). Remove the cover and withdraw the thermostat, poppet valve spring and poppet valve. See **Figure 40**. Remove and discard the cover gasket.

8. Remove the intake manifold mounting screws. Remove the intake manifold (**Figure 41**) and reed block assembly (**Figure 42**). If necessary, separate the reed block assembly from the intake

8

manifold. Remove and discard the manifold and reed block gaskets.

9. Lift the 2 check valves from the crankcase cover. See **Figure 43**.

10. Remove the screws securing the lower end cap. Remove the end cap.

11. Remove the crankcase cover screws (**Figure 43**). Remove the crankcase cover from the cylinder block.

12. Lift the crankshaft assembly straight up and remove it from the cylinder block. Place the crankshaft assembly into a power head stand (part No. 91-25821A1) mounted in a vise.

Disassembly
(75 and 90 hp)

1. Remove the flywheel. See Chapter Seven.

2. Remove the fuel pump with the inlet and outlet hoses. See Chapter Six.

3. Remove the oil injection pump with the inlet and outlet hoses. See Chapter Eleven. Remove the pump driven gear and housing.

4. Remove the intake manifold mounting screws. Remove the 3 intake manifolds as a unit with the balance tube connected.

5. Carefully pry the reed block assemblies from the crankcase cover. Pry only at the pry points provided. See **Figure 44**. Remove and discard the reed block gaskets.

6. Remove the 4 screws securing the rear cowl mounting bracket to the power head. Remove the bracket.

7. Remove the stator and trigger plate assemblies. See Chapter Seven.

8. Remove the starter motor, starter solenoid, electrical components mounting plate, spark plug leads and temperature sensor. See Chapter Seven.

9. Remove the thermostat housing. Remove the thermostat and pressure relief valve assembly. See **Figure 45**.

10. Remove the cylinder block cover screws. Remove the cover (**Figure 46**) from the cylinder

block by prying at the pry points located at the bottom of the cover on each side. Remove and discard the cover gasket.

11. Remove the exhaust cover screws. Remove the exhaust cover and divider plate. See **Figure 46**. Pry only at the pry point located at the bottom aft end of the exhaust cover. Remove and discard the gaskets.

12. Remove the crankcase cover screws and the lower end cap screw that threads into the crankcase cover.

13. Remove the crankcase cover by prying at the pry points located at the bottom of the cover on each side.

14. Remove the remaining 2 lower end cap screws and remove the end cap. Remove and discard the end cap O-ring. Remove the seal

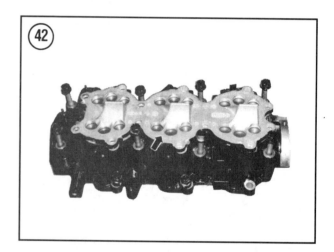

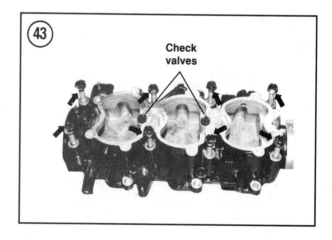

Check valves

from the end cap by carefully tapping out with a hammer and punch.

15. Lift the crankshaft assembly straight up and remove it from the cylinder block. Install the crankshaft assembly upright into a crankshaft holding fixture mounted in a vise.

Disassembly
(100 and 115 hp)

1. Remove the screw and retainer holding the overheat sensor in the cylinder block (**Figure 47**). Insert a small screwdriver between the sensor and cylinder block to break the grommet-to-cylinder block seal, then pull the sensor from the cylinder block.

2. Remove the starter motor. See Chapter Seven.

3. Disconnect the 2 light blue low-oil warning module wires at their bullet connectors. Remove the 2 low-oil warning module mounting screws.

4. Remove the 2 screws from the oil reservoir upper support bracket.

5. Remove the 2 screws from the bottom cowl support bracket.

6. Remove the accelerator pump return hose from the "T" fitting in the fuel hose.

7. Remove the fuel delivery hose from the fuel pump.

8. Remove the bottom cowl support bracket.

9. Remove the 10 screws securing the air box cover to the air box. Remove the cover.

10. Remove the front (bottom) oil reservoir support bracket.

11. Remove the 8 air box nuts and washers, then remove the air box.

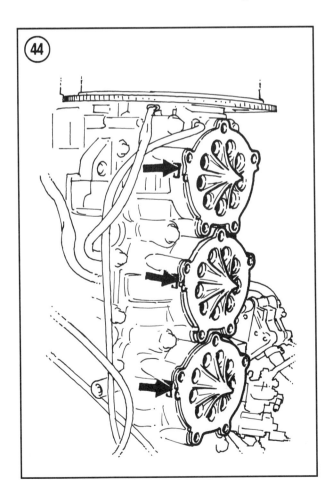

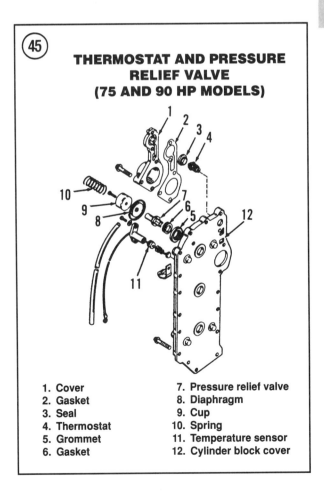

THERMOSTAT AND PRESSURE RELIEF VALVE (75 AND 90 HP MODELS)

1. Cover	7. Pressure relief valve
2. Gasket	8. Diaphragm
3. Seal	9. Cup
4. Thermostat	10. Spring
5. Grommet	11. Temperature sensor
6. Gasket	12. Cylinder block cover

8

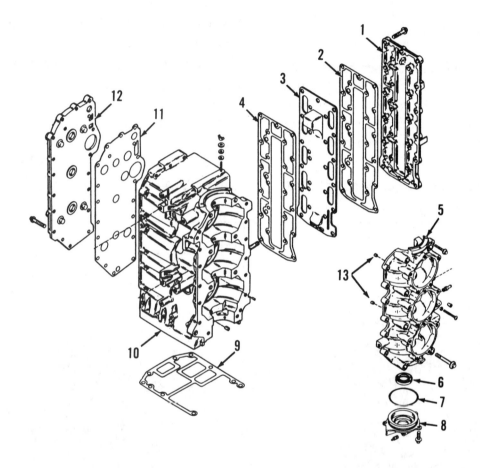

**CRANKCASE ASSEMBLY
(75 AND 90 HP MODELS)**

1. Exhaust cover
2. Gasket
3. Divider plate
4. Gasket
5. Crankcase cover
6. Seal
7. O-ring
8. Lower end cap
9. Gasket
10. Cylinder block
11. Gasket
12. Cylinder block cover
13. Check valves

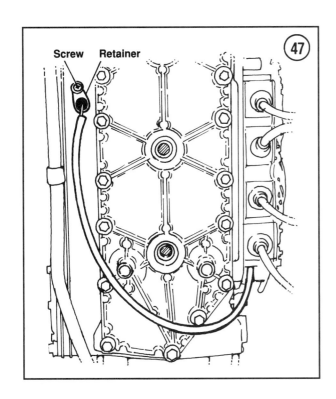

Screw Retainer

(47)

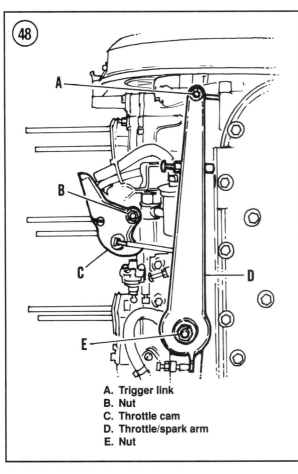

(48)

A
B
C
D
E

A. Trigger link
B. Nut
C. Throttle cam
D. Throttle/spark arm
E. Nut

12. Remove the fuel hose from the top carburetor. Disconnect the fuel inlet hose from the enrichener valve. Disconnect the fuel inlet hose from the accelerator pump.

13. Disconnect the oil pump control rod. Remove the 4 carburetors as an assembly.

14. Disconnect the clear oil delivery hose from the oil injection pump. Plug the hose to prevent leakage.

15. Remove the oil reservoir rear support screw. Remove the oil reservoir.

16. Disconnect the trigger link (A, **Figure 48**) from the spark advance arm.

17. Remove the throttle cam nut and washer (B, **Figure 48**). Remove the throttle/spark arm nut (E, **Figure 48**), then remove the throttle/spark arm and throttle cam as an assembly.

18. Disconnect the 2 fuel enrichment hoses from the intake manifolds. Remove the enrichment valve mounting screw. With the hose and wires still connected, move the enrichment valve around and below the ignition plate.

19. Remove the 2 accelerator pump mounting screws. With the fuel hose attached to the pump, move the pump over to the ignition plate side of the power head.

20. Remove the flywheel. See Chapter Seven.

21. Remove the intake manifold fasteners. Remove the intake manifolds and reed blocks as an assembly. Pry points are provided on the starboard side of each manifold to ease removal.

22. Remove the 4 stator mounting screws. Lift off the stator and lay aside. See Chapter Seven.

23. Remove the trigger plate assembly and lay aside. See Chapter Seven.

24. Remove the 4 screws securing the ignition plate assembly. Remove the ignition plate, stator, trigger, low-oil warning module, fuel enrichment valve and temperature sensor as an assembly.

25. Disconnect the accelerator pump hoses from No. 3 and No. 4 cylinder check valve fittings, then remove the check valves. Clean and test each check valve as follows:

8

a. Clean the valves by spraying WD-40 (or equivalent) into the barbed end of the valves, then blow dry with compressed air directed into the barbed end of the valves.

b. Using a hand-held pressure tester, apply air pressure to the barbed end of the check valves. The check valves should open at 11-14 psi (76-96 kPa) and should maintain at least 5 psi (34.5 kPa) for 30 seconds.

c. The check valve(s) should be replaced if they fail the pressure test or if excessive contamination is noted.

26. Disconnect the fuel pump pulse hose from the fitting on the power head.

27. Disconnect the clear oil injection pump hose from the fuel pump.

28. Remove the fuel pump assembly. See Chapter Six.

29. Bend back the locking tab washers on the throttle/shift bracket fasteners. Remove the 2 screws securing the throttle/shift bracket and remove the bracket. Discard the locking tab washers.

30. Remove the oil injection pump and drive assembly. See Chapter Eleven.

31. Disconnect the bleed hose from the fittings on the upper and lower end caps.

32. Remove the 3 lower end cap fasteners.

33. Remove the 16 small crankcase cover screws, then the 10 large crankcase cover screws.

34. Remove the crankcase cover by prying at the pry points. Do not nick, scratch or damage the crankcase cover and cylinder block mating surfaces.

35. Remove the thermostat cover. Remove the thermostat, pressure relief valve and related components. See **Figure 49**. Remove and discard the cover gasket.

36. Remove 18 screws securing the cylinder block cover. See **Figure 50**. Remove the cover by prying at the pry points located at the top and bottom of the cover.

37. Remove the 35 screws securing the exhaust cover (**Figure 50**). Remove the cover, baffle plate and gaskets. Pry points are provided at the top and bottom of the forward side of the cover to ease removal. Remove and discard the gaskets.

38. Lift the crankshaft straight up and remove it from the cylinder block. Place the crankshaft assembly upright on a power head stand mounted in a vise.

**Disassembly
(135-200 hp)**

1. Remove the flywheel. See Chapter Seven.

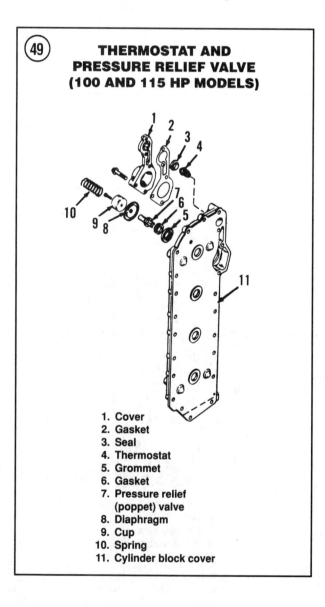

(49)   **THERMOSTAT AND PRESSURE RELIEF VALVE (100 AND 115 HP MODELS)**

1. Cover
2. Gasket
3. Seal
4. Thermostat
5. Grommet
6. Gasket
7. Pressure relief (poppet) valve
8. Diaphragm
9. Cup
10. Spring
11. Cylinder block cover

NOTE
All electrical and ignition components should remain attached to the electrical mounting plate. Remove the plate and electrical components as an assembly.

2. Disconnect all electrical and ignition wire connections on the power head. Make diagrams or take instant pictures of terminal connections and harness routing for reference during reassembly.

3. Remove the starter motor, starter solenoid, switchboxes, ignition coils, voltage regulator/rectifier(s), stator assembly and trigger assembly. See Chapter Seven.

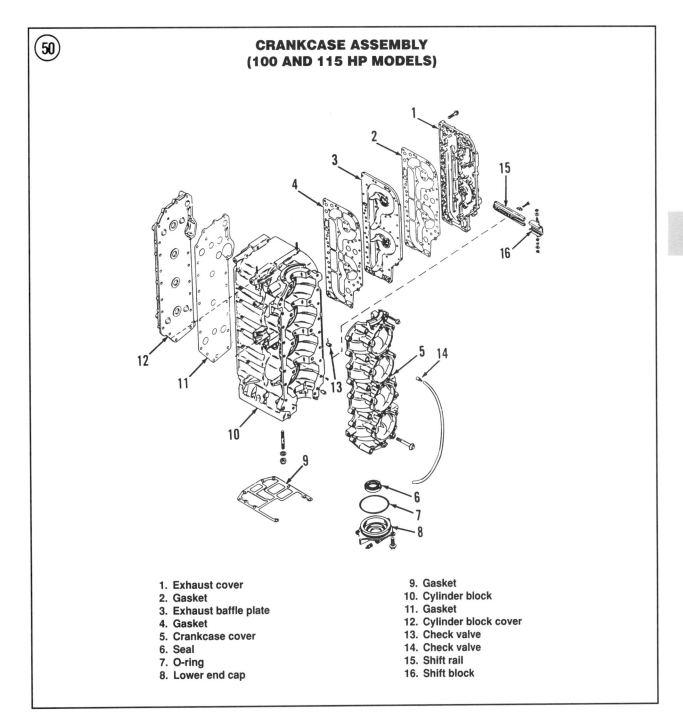

**CRANKCASE ASSEMBLY
(100 AND 115 HP MODELS)**

1. Exhaust cover
2. Gasket
3. Exhaust baffle plate
4. Gasket
5. Crankcase cover
6. Seal
7. O-ring
8. Lower end cap
9. Gasket
10. Cylinder block
11. Gasket
12. Cylinder block cover
13. Check valve
14. Check valve
15. Shift rail
16. Shift block

4. Remove the idle stabilizer or low speed/high speed spark advance module, if so equipped, from the top of the air silencer. Remove the air silencer.

5. Remove the carburetors, linkage and fuel pump. See Chapter Six.

6. Remove the shift cable latch assembly. Remove the control cable anchor bracket.

7. Remove the oil injection warning module, engine mounted oil reservoir and injection pump. See Chapter Eleven.

8. EFI models—Remove the fuel injection induction manifold assembly. See Chapter Six.

9. Remove the thermostat covers and thermostats. Remove and discard the cover gaskets.

10. Remove the cylinder heads. See **Figure 51**.

11. Remove the exhaust manifold cover, divider plate, divider plate seal and gaskets. Discard the gasket and seal.

12. Remove the reed block housing and gasket from the engine. Place the housing on a flat surface to prevent damage to the reed valve assemblies. See **Figure 52**.

13. Remove the end cap screws. See **Figure 53** (upper end cap) and **Figure 54** (lower end cap).

14. Remove the screws securing the crankcase cover to the cylinder block. Locate the pry points at each end of the cover and carefully pry the cover from the cylinder block. See **Figure 55**. Do not nick, scratch or damage the crankcase cover and cylinder block mating surfaces.

15. Rotate the crankshaft to position one connecting rod cap at the bottom of its stroke. Using

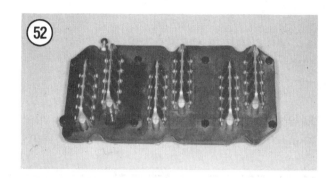

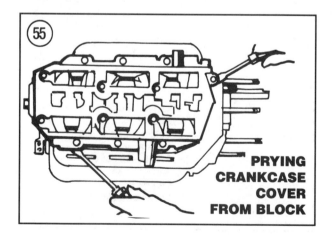

PRYING CRANKCASE COVER FROM BLOCK

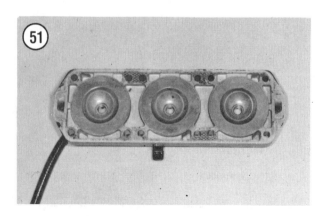

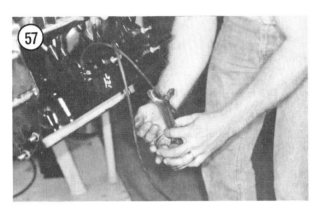

an awl or electric pencil, mark each connecting rod with its respective cylinder number.

16. Loosen the connecting rod cap bolts (**Figure 56**) using a 12-point socket. Remove the rod cap, bearings and bearing cage from the connecting rod.

17. Place one hand under the cylinder block to catch the piston and push it out with the other hand. See **Figure 57**.

CAUTION
Each connecting rod and cap is a matched assembly and must not be mismatched.

18. Reassemble the rod cap to its connecting rod.

19. Repeat Steps 15-17 to remove the remaining piston and connecting rod assemblies.

20. Remove the upper and lower end caps from the crankshaft. See **Figure 58**.

21. Carefully lift the crankshaft straight up and out of the cylinder block. See **Figure 59**. Place the crankshaft upright on a power head stand mounted in a vise.

Disassembly (250 and 275 hp)

1. Disconnect the black overheat warning wire and the tan/black oil warning module wires from the terminal block adjacent to the starter relay.

2. Remove the oil delivery hose from the oil pump. Plug the hose to prevent leakage.

3. Remove the oil reservoir from the engine.

4. Remove the carburetors as described in Chapter Six.

5. Remove the flywheel. See Chapter Seven.

6. Remove the oil pump control rod from the throttle cam. Remove the nut securing the throttle cam to the power head.

7. Remove the nut (A, **Figure 60**) and disconnect the spark advance link rod from the spark advance lever. Remove the bolt (C, **Figure 60**) from the throttle/spark advance arm and remove the arm and throttle cam as an assembly. Rein-

8

stall the bolt (C) into the throttle/spark advance arm, then install a nut on the back side of the bolt to hold the throttle/spark advance arm together.

8. Disconnect the 2 fuel pump pulse hoses from the crankcase cover fittings.

9. Remove the fuel pumps. See Chapter Six.

10. Disconnect the fuel enrichment valve wires (D, **Figure 60**) from the terminal block.

11. Disconnect the enrichment valve discharge hose from the "T" fitting.

> *NOTE*
> *The 2 screws holding the enrichment valve bracket to the power head are locked with thread locking compound at the factory. If necessary, apply heat to the screws using a heat gun or torch lamp to loosen the compound in Step 12.*

12. Remove the 2 enrichment valve bracket fasteners. Remove the valve and bracket as an assembly.

> *NOTE*
> *The screws securing the shift cable support bracket are locked with thread locking compound at the factory. If necessary, loosen the compound by applying heat with a heat gun or torch lamp.*

13. Remove the 2 screws securing the shift cable support bracket and remove the bracket.

14. Remove 4 screws from each carburetor adapter plate. Remove the adapter plates.

15. Remove the voltage regulator from the exhaust cover.

16. Remove the 17 screws securing the exhaust cover. Remove the exhaust cover with the 3 ignition coils as an assembly. If necessary, break the cover gasket seal by tapping the cover with a soft-face mallet.

17. Remove the stator assembly. See Chapter Seven.

18. Remove the starter motor. See Chapter Seven.

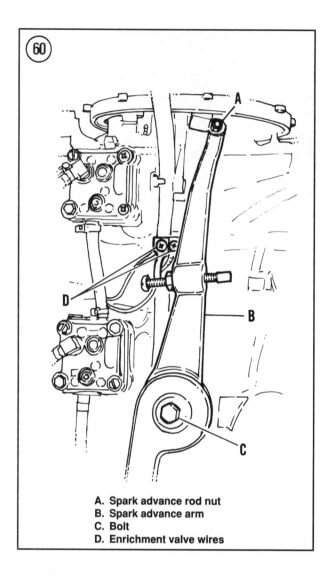

A. Spark advance rod nut
B. Spark advance arm
C. Bolt
D. Enrichment valve wires

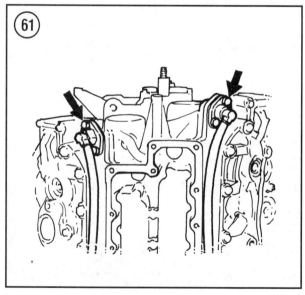

19. Remove the 3 screws securing the ignition plate to the power head. Remove the ignition plate with the stator, trigger, speed limiter, relays and switchboxes as an assembly.

20. Remove the thermostat covers and thermostats. See **Figure 61**.

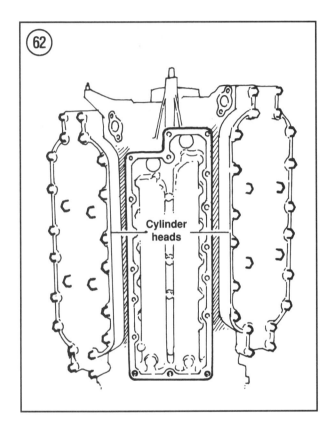

21. Remove 24 screws from each cylinder head (**Figure 62**). Remove the cylinder heads.

22. Remove 2 nuts from the aft bottom side of the power head (**Figure 63**).

23. Lay the power head on its side and remove the exhaust extension plate nuts (**Figure 64**). Remove the exhaust extension plate.

24. Remove the oil injection pump. See Chapter Eleven.

25. Remove 13 screws and 1 nut from the crankcase cover.

26. Remove the 4 screws from the lower end cap.

27. Using a soft-face mallet, tap the crankcase cover to break the gasket seal. Remove the crankcase cover and the lower end cap.

28. Rotate the crankshaft to position one connecting rod at the bottom of its stroke. Check the rod and cap for cylinder identification numbers. If none are present, scribe the respective cylinder number on the connecting rod and cap using an awl or electric pencil. Loosen the connecting rod cap bolts (**Figure 65**) evenly and equally to prevent the rod cap from cocking during removal. Remove the rod cap, bearings and bearing cages. Note that 16 bearing rollers are present in each rod bearing.

8

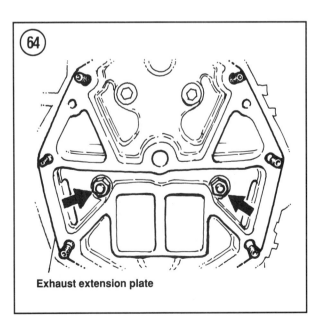

Exhaust extension plate

NOTE
The connecting rods and caps are the fractured design. The rod caps must be kept with their respective connecting rods.

29. Place one hand under the cylinder block to catch the piston and push it out with the other hand **Figure 66**). Reassemble the rod cap to its connecting rod.

30. Repeat Steps 28 and 29 to remove the remaining piston and connecting rod assemblies.

31. Lift the crankshaft straight up and remove it from the cylinder block. Install the crankshaft upright on a power head stand mounted in a vise.

**Crankshaft Disassembly
(3 and 3.3 hp)**

Refer to **Figure 67** for this procedure.

WARNING
Suitable eye protection must be worn while prying piston pin retainers from the piston.

1. Remove and discard the piston pin retainers from each end of the piston pin bore.

2. Push the piston pin out of the piston.

3. Remove the piston and the caged roller bearing from the connecting rod.

4. Remove the piston ring from the piston using Piston Ring Expander part No. 91-24697 (or equivalent).

5. Upper and lower crankshaft bearings are pressed in place and should not be removed unless replacement is necessary. See crankshaft

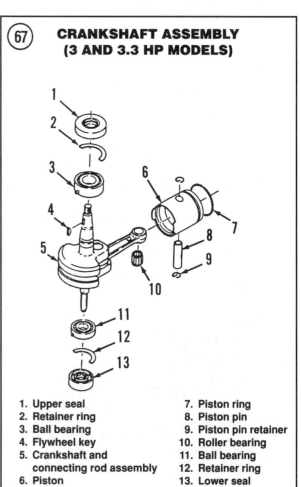

**CRANKSHAFT ASSEMBLY
(3 AND 3.3 HP MODELS)**

1. Upper seal
2. Retainer ring
3. Ball bearing
4. Flywheel key
5. Crankshaft and connecting rod assembly
6. Piston
7. Piston ring
8. Piston pin
9. Piston pin retainer
10. Roller bearing
11. Ball bearing
12. Retainer ring
13. Lower seal

Cleaning and Inspection in this chapter. If necessary to replace one or both bearings:

   a. Install protector cap on the crankshaft end and remove the upper bearing with a universal bearing press plate and an arbor press.

   b. Remove the lower bearing with a universal bearing press plate, a suitable mandrel and an arbor press.

6. The connecting rod is not removable from the crankshaft. If the connecting rod is excessively worn or damaged, the crankshaft assembly must be replaced.

Crankshaft Disassembly
(4 and 5 hp)

Refer to **Figure 68** for this procedure.

WARNING
Suitable eye protection must be worn while prying the piston pin lockrings from the piston.

1. Remove and discard the piston pin lockring from each end of the piston pin bore.

2. Push the piston pin from the bore.

3. Remove the piston and caged needle roller bearing from the connecting rod.

4. Remove the piston rings from the piston with ring expander part No. 91-24697 (or equivalent).

5. Upper and lower crankshaft bearings are pressed in place and should not be removed unless replacement is necessary. See crankshaft *Cleaning and Inspection* in this chapter. If necessary to replace one or both bearings:

   a. Install a suitable protector cap on the upper crankshaft end and remove the upper bearing with a universal bearing press plate and an arbor press.

   b. Remove the lower bearing with a universal bearing press plate, a suitable mandrel and an arbor press.

6. The connecting rod is not removable from the crankshaft. If the connecting rod is excessively

worn or damaged, the crankshaft assembly must be replaced.

Crankshaft Disassembly
(8, 9.9 and 15 hp)

Refer to **Figure 69** for this procedure.

1A. Except 15 hp—Remove the center main bearing outer race halves and bearing halves.

1B. 15 hp—Remove the main bearing retaining ring (B, **Figure 70**) from the groove of the outer race. Remove the outer race halves and bearing.

2. Slide the upper crankshaft seal and bearing off the crankshaft.

3. Remove the lower crankshaft seal, stuffer washer and large retaining snap ring.

4. Remove the coupling seal with a pair of pliers. Discard the seal.

5. Remove the snap ring from the lower bearing.

6. Remove the sealing ring from the crankshaft center journal.

7. Mark the corresponding cylinder number on the pistons and connecting rods with an indelible marker.

NOTE
Always store piston pins, piston pin bearings, locating washers, connecting rod bearings, rod caps and rod cap screws together with their respective piston and connecting rod so they can be reinstalled in their original locations.

8. Remove and discard the piston pin lockrings from each end of the piston pin bores.

9. Place the piston pin tool (part No. 91-13663) into the top of the piston pin bore. Support the bottom of the piston with one hand and drive the pin tool and pin from the piston. See **Figure 71**.

NOTE
Cleanliness is absolutely essential in Step 10. Do not get dirt or lint on the needle bearings.

10. Remove the piston from the connecting rod. Remove the locating washers and 24 needle

8

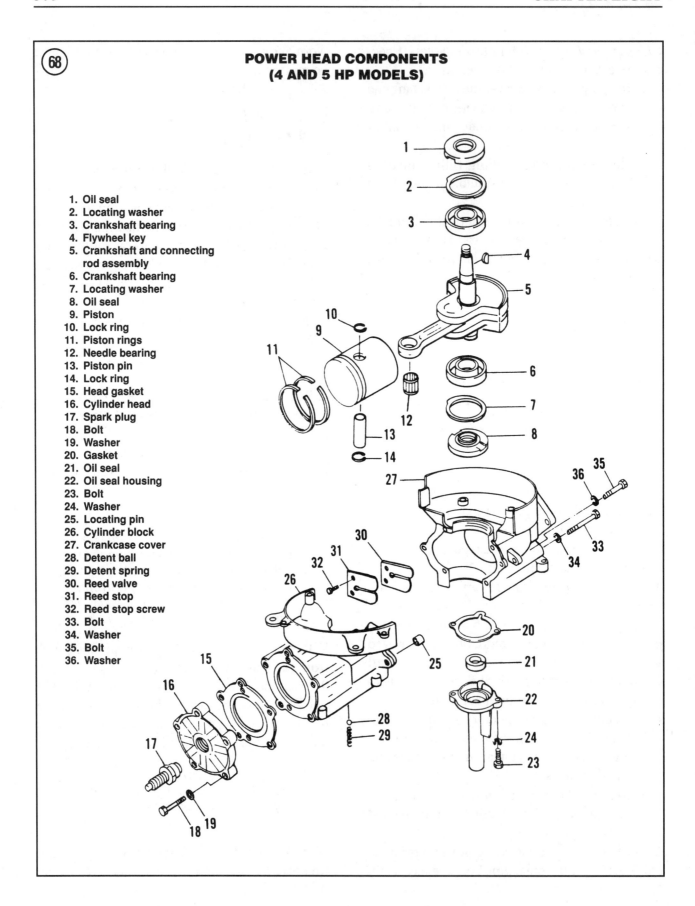

**POWER HEAD COMPONENTS
(4 AND 5 HP MODELS)**

1. Oil seal
2. Locating washer
3. Crankshaft bearing
4. Flywheel key
5. Crankshaft and connecting rod assembly
6. Crankshaft bearing
7. Locating washer
8. Oil seal
9. Piston
10. Lock ring
11. Piston rings
12. Needle bearing
13. Piston pin
14. Lock ring
15. Head gasket
16. Cylinder head
17. Spark plug
18. Bolt
19. Washer
20. Gasket
21. Oil seal
22. Oil seal housing
23. Bolt
24. Washer
25. Locating pin
26. Cylinder block
27. Crankcase cover
28. Detent ball
29. Detent spring
30. Reed valve
31. Reed stop
32. Reed stop screw
33. Bolt
34. Washer
35. Bolt
36. Washer

bearing rollers (**Figure 72**). Store bearings in clean numbered containers corresponding to the piston/connecting rod number.

11. Repeat Steps 9 and 10 to remove the remaining piston.

12. Remove the connecting rod cap screws. Tap the rod cap screws with a mallet to separate the cap from the rod. Remove the cap, then remove the caged roller bearings from the crankshaft. Store the bearing cages in clean numbered containers corresponding to the rod number. Repeat this step to remove the remaining connecting rod and bearing.

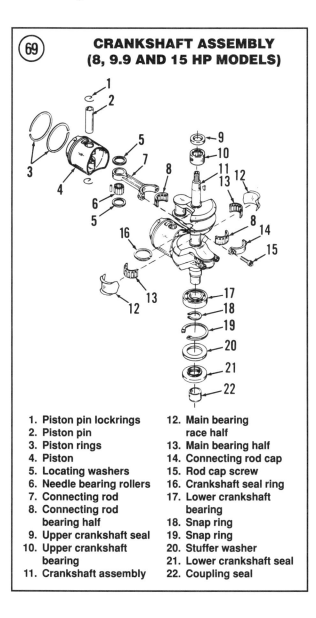

CRANKSHAFT ASSEMBLY (8, 9.9 AND 15 HP MODELS)

1. Piston pin lockrings
2. Piston pin
3. Piston rings
4. Piston
5. Locating washers
6. Needle bearing rollers
7. Connecting rod
8. Connecting rod bearing half
9. Upper crankshaft seal
10. Upper crankshaft bearing
11. Crankshaft assembly
12. Main bearing race half
13. Main bearing half
14. Connecting rod cap
15. Rod cap screw
16. Crankshaft seal ring
17. Lower crankshaft bearing
18. Snap ring
19. Snap ring
20. Stuffer washer
21. Lower crankshaft seal
22. Coupling seal

13. Do not remove the lower crankshaft bearing unless replacement is necessary. If replacement is necessary, remove the bearing with a universal bearing puller plate and arbor press.

Crankshaft Disassembly (20 and 25 hp)

Refer to **Figure 73** for this procedure.

1. Slide the upper oil seal and bearing off the crankshaft. Slide the lower oil seal and bearing off the crankshaft. Discard the oil seals.

2. Remove the piston rings with ring expander part No. 91-24697 (or equivalent). Discard the piston rings.

3. Mark the corresponding cylinder number on the pistons and connecting rods with an indelible marker. If reused, the pistons and connecting rods must always be reinstalled in the same location and in the same direction as removed.

NOTE
Always store piston pins, piston pin bearings, locating washers, connecting

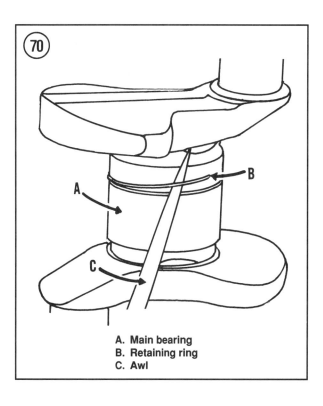

A. Main bearing
B. Retaining ring
C. Awl

rod bearings, rod caps and rod cap screws together with their respective piston and connecting rod so they can be reinstalled in their original locations.

4. Remove the piston pin lockrings from each piston pin bore. Discard the piston pin lockrings.

5. Place piston pin tool part No. 91-76160A2 into the top of the piston pin. Support the bottom of the piston with one hand and drive the pin tool and pin from the piston. See **Figure 71**.

6. Remove the piston, locating washers and 27 needle bearing rollers from the connecting rod. See **Figure 72**. Store the bearings in clean numbered containers corresponding to the piston/connecting rod number.

7. Remove the connecting rod cap screws. Separate the rod cap from the connecting rod and remove the caged bearing halves. Store the bearings in clean numbered containers corresponding to the connecting rod number. Reinstall the rod cap to the connecting rod.

8. Remove the main bearing race retaining ring (B, **Figure 70**) from the bearing race grooves. Remove the outer races and needle bearings (**Figure 74**). Store the bearings and outer races in a clean container.

Crankshaft Disassembly (40 hp and 50-60 hp Prior to Serial No. D000750)

Refer to **Figure 75** for this procedure.

> *WARNING*
> *Suitable eye protection must be worn while removing piston rings and piston pin lockrings.*

1. Remove the piston rings with ring expander part No. 91-24697 (or equivalent). See **Figure 76**. Discard the piston rings.

2A. 40 hp—Remove the piston pin lockrings using needlenose pliers. Discard the lockrings.

2B. 50 and 60 hp—Remove the piston pin lockrings using lockring removal tool part No. 91-52952A1 (**Figure 77**). Discard the lockrings.

3. Using an indelible marker, mark the pistons and connecting rods with the corresponding cylinder number. See **Figure 78**. If reused, the pistons and connecting rods must always be

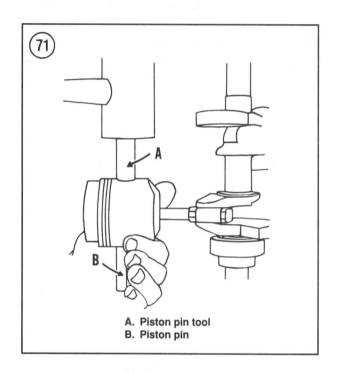

A. Piston pin tool
B. Piston pin

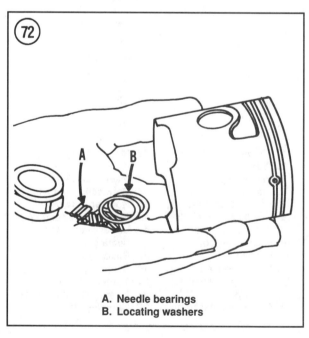

A. Needle bearings
B. Locating washers

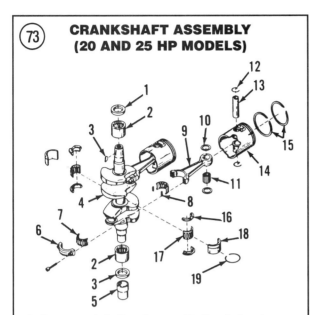

CRANKSHAFT ASSEMBLY (20 AND 25 HP MODELS)

1. Upper crankshaft seal
2. Upper crankshaft bearing
3. Flywheel key
4. Crankshaft
5. Crankshaft carrier
6. Connecting rod cap
7. Connecting rod bearing half
8. Bearing rollers
9. Connecting rod
10. Locating washer
11. Needle bearing
12. Piston pin lockring
13. Piston pin
14. Piston
15. Piston rings
16. Thrust washer half
17. Main bearing half
18. Main bearing outer race half
19. Bearing race retaining ring

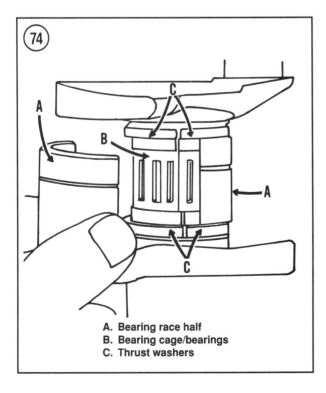

A. Bearing race half
B. Bearing cage/bearings
C. Thrust washers

reinstalled in the same location and in the same direction as removed.

4A. 40 hp—Place piston pin tool part No. 91-76160A2 into the top of the No. 1 cylinder piston pin. Support the bottom of the piston with one hand and drive the pin tool and the pin from the piston. See **Figure 71**.

WARNING
The lamp used in Step 4B produces an intense light. Wear the glasses included with the lamp and do not look directly at the lamp. Wear suitable hand protection to handle the piston or wrap it in several folds of shop towels.

4B. 50 and 60 hp—Using torch lamp (part No. 91-63209, or equivalent), heat the piston crown to approximately 190°F (88°C). See **Figure 79**. This should take 60-90 seconds. Turn the lamp off and place it out of the way. Immediately support the piston and drive the pin from the piston using a mallet and pin tool part No. 91-76159A1.

5. Remove the piston, piston pin bearing rollers and 2 locating washers from the connecting rod. See **Figure 72**. Store the bearing rollers and locating washers in clean numbered containers corresponding to the piston/connecting rod number.

NOTE
The manufacturer recommends replacing the connecting rod bearing rollers upon reassembly. However, if the bearings are reused, be certain they are installed in their original locations. Do not intermix needle bearing rollers with those from another connecting rod. Never intermix new bearing rollers with used rollers on the same connecting rod.

6. Repeat Step 4A or 4B, and Step 5 to remove the remaining pistons.

7. Loosen the connecting rod screws evenly in small increments, then remove and discard the screws.

8

CRANKSHAFT ASSEMBLY
(40 HP MODELS)

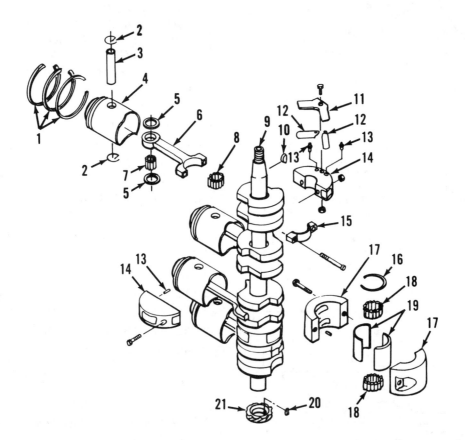

1. Piston rings
2. Piston pin lockring
3. Piston pin
4. Piston
5. Washer
6. Connecting rod
7. Needle bearing
8. Needle bearing
9. Crankshaft assembly
10. Key
11. Reed stop

12. Reed valves
13. Dowel pins
14. Reed block
15. Connecting rod cap
16. Retainer ring
17. Center main bearing support
18. Needle bearing
19. Center main bearing outer race
20. Key
21. Oil pump drive gear

8. Separate the connecting rod cap from the connecting rod and remove the bearings and cages (50 and 60 hp) or the loose bearing rollers (40 hp). Store the bearings in clean numbered containers corresponding to the cylinder number. Reinstall the rod cap onto the rod to prevent mixup. Repeat Steps 7 and 8 to remove the remaining connecting rods and bearings.

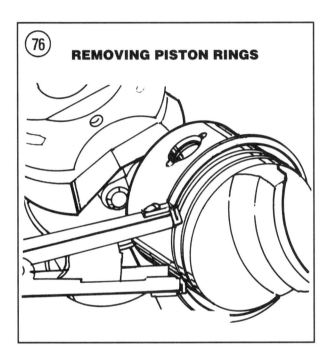

REMOVING PISTON RINGS

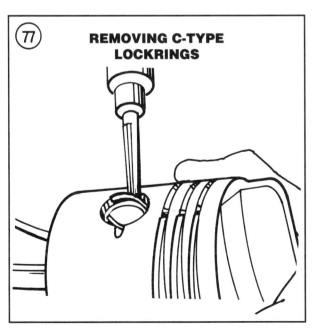

REMOVING C-TYPE LOCKRINGS

9. Mark the reed blocks for direction and location. Remove the 2 bolts and nuts holding the reed block together. See **Figure 80**, typical. Separate the reed block halves (**Figure 81**) and remove from the crankshaft. Reassemble each reed block as it is removed to ensure correct match during reassembly.

10. Repeat Step 9 to remove the remaining reed block assembly.

11. Remove the 2 bolts holding the center main bearing support halves together. See **Figure 82**.

12. Separate and remove the main bearing support (**Figure 83**).

13. Remove the main bearing outer race retaining ring using an awl or similar tool. See **Figure 84**. Remove the bearing outer race halves and the loose bearing rollers. Store the bearing rollers

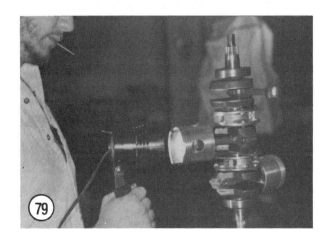

and outer races in a clean container for reinstallation on the same crankshaft journal.

**Crankshaft Disassembly
(50 and 60 hp [Serial No. D000750-on];
75, 90, 100 and 115 hp)**

Refer to **Figure 85** for this procedure. **Figure 85** shows the crankshaft and related components used on 4-cylinder models. Three-cylinder models are essentially the same. In addition, a seal carrier and seal are used in place of wear sleeve (19) and O-ring (20) on some models.

NOTE
The crankshaft main bearing rollers are loose when the outer races are removed in Step 1. Do not lose any bearing rollers or a new set will have to be installed.

1. Remove the retainer ring from the top main bearing outer race using an awl or similar tool.

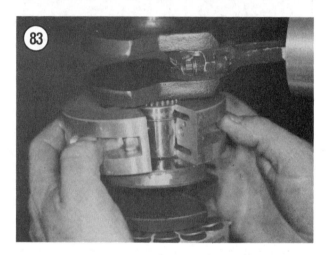

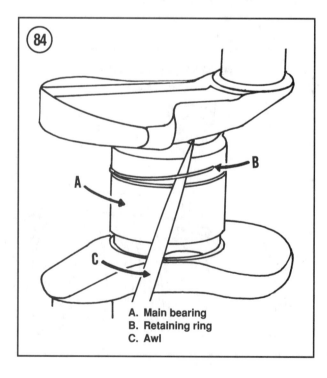

A. Main bearing
B. Retaining ring
C. Awl

8

85 **CRANKSHAFT ASSEMBLY (50 AND 60 [SERIAL NO. D000750-ON], 75, 90, 100 AND 115 HP MODELS)**

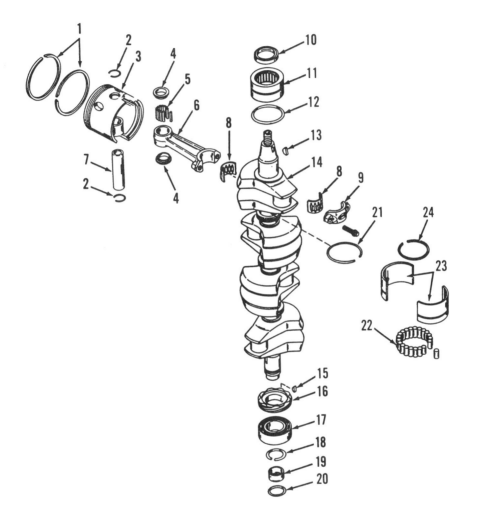

1. Piston rings	13. Key
2. Piston pin lockrings	14. Crankshaft
3. Piston	15. Key
4. Locating washers	16. Oil pump drive gear
5. Piston pin needle bearing	17. Lower main bearing
6. Connecting rod	18. Snap ring
7. Piston pin	19. Wear sleeve (except 50 and 60 hp)
8. Crankpin bearing	20. O-ring (except 50 and 60 hp)
9. Connecting rod cap	21. Seal ring
10. Upper crankshaft seal	22. Main bearing rollers
11. Upper main bearing	23. Main bearing outer race
12. O-ring	24. Retaining ring

See **Figure 86**. Remove the bearing outer race halves and the bearing rollers. Store the outer race and bearing rollers in clean numbered containers corresponding to their location on the crankshaft.

2. Repeat Step 1 to remove the remaining main bearing assemblies.

3. Using an indelible marker, number the pistons to match their respective connecting rods and cylinders. See **Figure 78**.

3. Using an awl, scribe an identification mark on each connecting rod and rod cap indicating location and direction. If reused, all components must be reinstalled in their original locations, facing the same direction.

4. Using a 3/8 in. 12-point socket, loosen the connecting rod cap screws evenly in small increments.

5. Remove each connecting rod and piston assembly, rod cap, bearings and bearing cages from the crankpin journals, one assembly at a time. Reinstall the rod caps onto their respective connecting rods in the same direction as removed. Temporarily install the rod cap screws to secure the rod caps. Store the bearings and cages in clean numbered containers corresponding to their respective cylinder and connecting rod.

NOTE
The connecting rod cap screws should not be used during final assembly. Always install new rod cap screws.

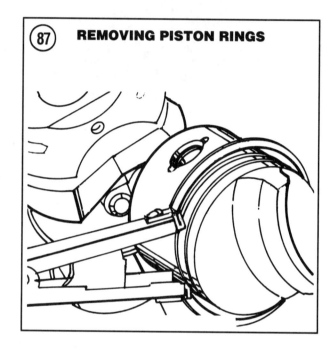

87. REMOVING PISTON RINGS

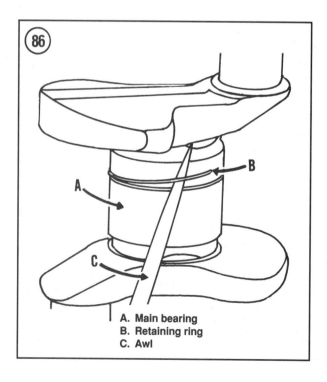

86.

A. Main bearing
B. Retaining ring
C. Awl

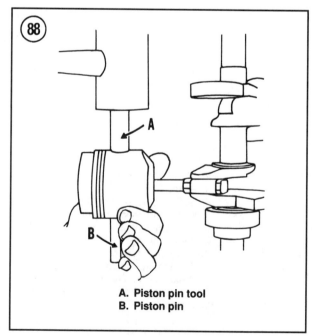

88.

A. Piston pin tool
B. Piston pin

6. Remove the main bearing seal rings from the crankshaft.

WARNING
Suitable eye protection must be worn while removing piston rings (Step 7) and piston pin lockrings (Step 8).

7. Remove the piston rings using ring expander part No. 91-24697 (or equivalent). See **Figure 87**, typical.

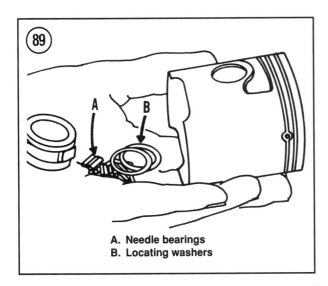

A. Needle bearings
B. Locating washers

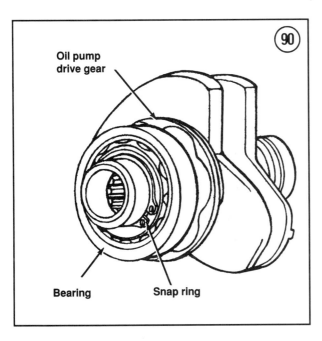

Oil pump drive gear

Bearing   Snap ring

8. Remove the piston pin lockrings from both sides of the pin bore on the top piston. Use an awl or similar tool to pry out the lockrings. Discard the lockrings.

9. Insert piston pin tool part No. 91-74607A2 into the piston pin. Support the piston with one hand and drive the piston pin and the pin tool from the piston. See **Figure 88**, typical.

10. Remove the piston, 2 locating washers and 29 loose needle bearing rollers. See **Figure 89**. Store the bearings and washers in clean numbered containers corresponding to the piston/cylinder number.

11. Repeat Steps 8-10 to remove the remaining pistons.

12. The lower main bearing is a press fit on the crankshaft and should not be removed unless the bearing or the oil pump drive gear requires replacement.

13A. 50 and 60 hp:
   a. To remove the lower main bearing, remove the snap ring securing the main bearing to the crankshaft. See **Figure 90**.
   b. Insert the power head/crankshaft stand into the bottom of the crankshaft, then remove the bearing using an arbor press and a universal press plate. See **Figure 91**. The oil pump drive gear can now be slipped off the crankshaft. Be sure to retrieve the drive gear key.

NOTE
*The snap ring (18, **Figure 85**) is not used on 75 and 90 hp models with serial No. C259434-on and 100 and 115 hp models with serial No. C259722-on.*

13B. 75, 90, 100 and 115 hp:
   a. To remove the lower main bearing, remove the snap ring (if so equipped) securing the bearing to the crankshaft.
   b. Insert the power head/crankshaft stand into the bottom of the crankshaft and press the bearing off the crankshaft using an arbor press and a universal press plate. See **Fig-**

8

ure 91. The oil pump drive gear can now be slipped off the crankshaft. Be sure to retrieve the drive gear key.

c. If the crankshaft is equipped with a lower seal and seal carrier (**Figure 92**), remove and discard the seal. If seal carrier requires replacement, pry the carrier from the crankshaft using an awl or screwdriver.

d. If the crankshaft is equipped with a wear sleeve (some 75 and 90 and all 100 and 115 hp models), remove the O-ring (20, **Figure 85**) using a small screwdriver or similar tool. If grooves, pitting or corrosion is noted on the wear sleeve, remove it from the crankshaft with pliers. It may be necessary to heat the sleeve lightly to ease removal.

**Crankshaft Disassembly
(V6 Models)**

1. Number the pistons with an indelible marker to indicate the cylinder from which they were removed.

2. Scribe identification marks on the connecting rods indicating direction and the cylinder from which they were removed.

> *WARNING*
> *Suitable eye protection should be worn during piston ring and piston pin lock-ring removal.*

3. Remove the piston rings using ring expander part No. 91-24697 (or equivalent).

4. Remove the piston pin lockrings from each pin bore using lockring tool part No. 91-52952A1. See **Figure 93**. Discard the lockrings.

> *NOTE*
> *It may be helpful to heat the piston crown lightly with a torch lamp to ease piston pin removal in Step 5.*

5. Insert piston pin tool part No. 91-76159A1 (135-200 hp models) or 91-92973A1 (250 and 275 hp models) into the piston pin. Support the

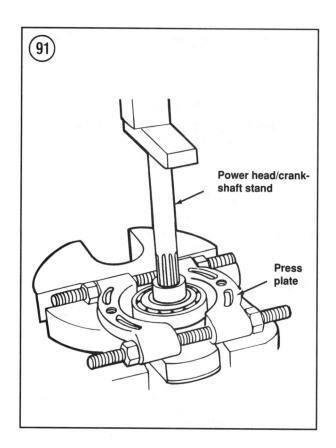

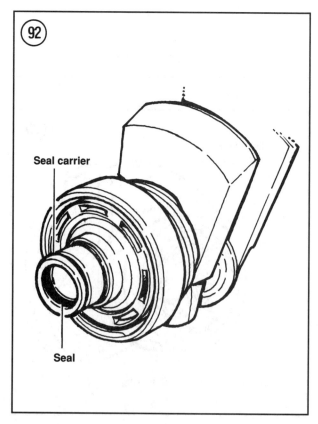

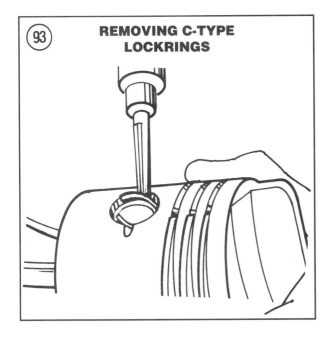

REMOVING C-TYPE LOCKRINGS

piston with one hand and drive the piston pin and pin tool from the piston.

6. Remove the piston, locating washers and piston pin needle bearing rollers. See **Figure 89**. Store the locating washers and bearing rollers in clean numbered containers corresponding to the piston/connecting rod number for reference during reassembly.

7. Repeat Steps 4-6 to separate each remaining piston from its connecting rod.

NOTE
The bearing rollers are loose when the outer races are removed in Step 8. Do not lose any rollers or a new set will have to be installed.

8. Remove the main bearing outer race retaining ring (A, **Figure 94**) from the upper bearing race. Remove the outer bearing race halves and roller bearings and bearing roller cages if so equipped, from the crankshaft journal. Store the bearings and race in a clean numbered container corresponding to the location of the journal from which they were removed. Repeat this step to remove the remaining bearing assembly.

9. Check the crankshaft sealing rings (B, **Figure 94**) for breakage or other damage. Do not remove the seal rings from the crankshaft unless replacement is necessary. Piston ring expander part No. 91-24697 (or equivalent) can be used to remove the seal rings from the crankshaft.

NOTE
On 135-200 hp models (serial No. D050182-on), the crankshaft seal ring above the lower main roller bearing is no longer used.

10A. 135-200 hp—Inspect the oil pump drive gear. On 135-200 hp models, do not remove the gear from the crankshaft unless it is damaged and replacement is required. If removal is necessary, remove the drive gear retaining screw (**Figure 95**), spread the gear at the split and remove it from the crankshaft. Discard the retaining screw.

8

10B. 250 and 275 hp—Slip the oil pump drive gear off the lower end of the crankshaft. Inspect the gear for chips, cracks or excessive looseness and replace as required.

NOTE
Do not remove the crankshaft bottom ball bearing unless replacement is necessary.

11. To remove the lower ball bearing, remove the snap ring (if so equipped) securing the bearing to the crankshaft.

12. Place the power head/crankshaft stand into the crankshaft and press the bearing from the shaft using an arbor press and a universal press plate. See **Figure 91**.

NOTE
On some 150-200 hp models, a shim is located above the crankshaft lower bearing. The shim is 0.030 in. (0.76 mm) thick, with a 3.5 in. (89 mm) outside diameter and 3.25 in. (83 mm) inside diameter. On models so equipped, be certain the shim is reinstalled if the lower ball bearing is removed. However, if the cylinder block is replaced, but the original crankshaft is reused, the shim can be discarded.

Cleaning and Inspection Cylinder Block/Crankcase Cover (All Models)

Mercury outboard cylinder blocks and crankcase covers are matched, align-bored assemblies. For this reason, do not attempt to assemble an engine with parts salvaged from other blocks. If the following inspection procedure indicates that the block or cover requires replacement, replace the entire cylinder block/crankcase as an assembly.

1. Clean the cylinder block, heads, exhaust cover and crankcase cover thoroughly with solvent and brush.

2. Carefully remove all gasket and sealant material from mating surfaces.

3. Check exhaust ports and remove any carbon deposits or varnish with a carbon removing solution or a fine wire brush and electric drill. Do not scratch, nick or gouge the exhaust ports or combustion chamber.

4. Check cylinder block, heads and covers for cracks, fractures, warpage, stripped threads or other damage.

5. Inspect gasket mating surfaces for nicks, grooves, cracks or distortion. Any of these defects will cause leakage.

6. Check all water and oil passages in the block and cover for obstructions. Make sure all plugs are installed tightly.

NOTE
Restrictors or check valves should be removed from the transfer bleed holes if it is necessary to submerge the

Check valves

cover/block in a strong cleaning solution. Be sure to install new restrictors after cleaning. Remove the bleed system to prevent damage to the hoses and check valves.

7A. 50 and 60 hp (prior to serial No. D000750)—Inspect the transfer port bleed holes to make sure the restrictors (**Figure 96**) are in place and in acceptable condition. Note that the bottom cylinder does not use a restrictor. Missing restrictors will cause cylinder flooding and poor idle.

7B. 50 and 60 (serial No. D000750-on), 75, 90, 100 and 115 hp:

a. If not previously removed, remove the 2 check valve and holder assemblies on 50, 60, 75 and 90 hp models, or 3 check valve

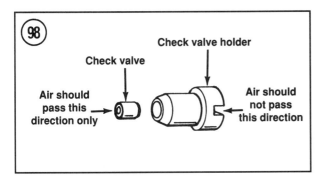

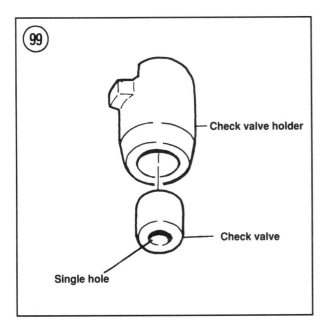

and holder assemblies on 100 and 115 hp models. See **Figure 97**, typical.

b. Look into the check valve assembly. If light is visible, the nylon check ball is missing (melted) and the check valve must be replaced. If light is not visible, insert a fine wire into the valve to check for slight movement of the check ball. Replace the check valve if movement is not possible. Replace the check valve holder if the valve holder is burned or damaged.

c. To replace the check valve, remove the valve from the rubber holder. On 50 and 60 hp models, insert the check valve into the holder so air will pass through the valve only in the direction shown in **Figure 98**. On 75-115 hp models, insert the check valve into the holder so the side with the single hole is facing the crankshaft (**Figure 99**).

NOTE
Chrome plated cylinder bores cannot be rebored or honed. No oversize pistons are available for chrome bore models. However, scored or damaged chrome cylinder bores can be replated to standard dimensions (V6 only). For details, contact U.S. Chrome Corporation of Wisconsin, P.O. Box 1536, 650 Oak Park Avenue, Fond du Lac, Wisconsin, 54935.

8A. Chrome cylinder bore (20, 25, 250 and 275 hp):

a. Inspect the cylinder bores for flaking, grooving, scoring, aluminum transfer (from the piston) or other damage.

NOTE
*Chrome plated cylinder bores have a porous appearance. See **Figure 100**. Do not mistake this for cylinder damage.*

b. Replace the cylinder block and crankcase cover if damage that penetrates through the chrome plating is present, or have the cylinder bores replated.

8

8B. Cast iron cylinder bore (all others):

  a. Inspect the cylinder bores for scoring, scuffing or other damage, and for aluminum transfer from the pistons.

NOTE
It is recommended that cylinder bore honing be performed by a dealer or a qualified machine shop.

  b. If the cylinders are in acceptable condition, lightly hone the cylinders to remove any glaze and to ensure the new piston rings will properly seat to the cylinders. Light scoring or scuffing can generally be cleaned up by honing the cylinders. Use a rigid-type hone. Do not use spring-type or bead hones. Follow the hone manufacturer's instructions when using the hone. After honing, the cylinder block must be thoroughly cleaned using hot water, detergent and a stiff bristle brush. Make certain all abrasive material from the honing process is removed. After washing, coat the cylinder walls with 2-stroke engine oil to prevent rusting.

WARNING
Use suitable hand and eye protection when using muriatic acid products. Avoid breathing the vapors. Use only in a well-ventilated area. Do not allow the muriatic acid to come into contact with aluminum areas of the cylinder block.

9. All models—If the cylinder bore(s) have aluminum transfer from the piston(s), clean loose deposits from the bore with a stiff bristle brush. Apply a small quantity of diluted muriatic acid (toilet bowl cleaner) to the aluminum deposits. A bubbling action indicates the aluminum is being dissolved. Wait 1-2 minutes, then thoroughly wash the cylinder with hot water and detergent. Repeat this procedure until the aluminum deposits are removed. Lightly oil the cylinder wall to prevent rust. Cast iron cylinders can now be honed to remove cylinder wall glazing.

10A. 8, 9.9 and 15 hp:

  a. Measure the cylinder bores using an inside micrometer (**Figure 101**, typical). Take 2 measurements near the top of the piston ring travel, 90° apart. Repeat measurements at the center, then the bottom of the bore (6 measurements total).

  b. Standard cylinder bore diameter is 2.375 in. (60.3 mm) on 8 and 9.9 hp models and 2.125 in. (53.98 mm) on 15 hp models. Oversize pistons and rings are not available.

  c. If the cylinder bores are worn, tapered or out-of-round more than 0.004 in. (0.10 mm), replace the cylinder block and crankcase cover.

10B. 20 and 25 hp:

  a. Measure the cylinder bore diameters using an inside micrometer. Take 2 measurements one-half way between the top of the cylinder and exhaust ports, 45° apart.

  b. Replace the cylinder block and crankcase cover if the cylinder(s) are tapered or out-of-round more than 0.003 in. (0.08 mm).

10C. 250 and 275 hp:

  a. Measure the cylinder bores with an inside micrometer (**Figure 101**, typical). Take 4 measurements at a point 1/2 in. (12.7 mm) from the top of each cylinder bore, 45° apart.

  b. If the bores are tapered or out-of-round more than 0.006 in. (0.15 mm), replace the

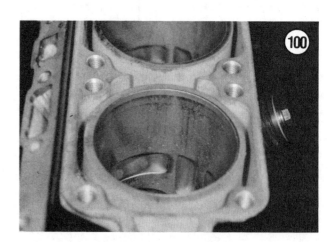

cylinder block and crankcase cover, or have the bores replated to the original diameter.

10D. All others (cast iron bore):

a. Measure the cylinder bore diameters with an inside micrometer (**Figure 101**, typical). Take 2 measurements at the top of the ring travel, 90° apart. Repeat measurements at the center, then the bottom of the ring travel (6 measurements total).

NOTE
Pistons and rings are available in 0.020 in. oversize on 3-5 hp models, 0.015 and 0.030 in. oversizes on 40 hp, 50 and 60 (prior to serial No. D000750) hp, 75-115 hp models and 0.015 in. oversize on 50 and 60 (serial No. D000750-on) hp, 150XR4, 150XR6 175 and 200 hp models.

b. Maximum allowable cylinder bore wear, taper and out-of-round is: 0.002 in. (0.05 mm) on 3 and 3.3 hp models; 0.003 in. (0.08 mm) on 4 and 5 hp, 50 and 60 (serial No. D000750-on) hp and 75-115 hp models; 0.004 in. (0.10 mm) on 40 hp and 50 and 60 (prior to serial No. D000750) hp; 0.006 in. (0.15 mm) on 135-200 hp models.

c. If cylinder bore wear, taper or out-of-round is more than specified from the standard cylinder block finish hone diameter (**Table 4**), the cylinder block should be bored to the next oversize dimension.

NOTE
*On V6 models, the crankshaft seal rings cause grooves to wear in the cylinder block and crankcase cover. The grooves should not be a problem unless the crankshaft is replaced. If the seal rings on a new crankshaft do not align with the seal grooves in the original cylinder block/crankcase cover assembly, the crankshaft may bind. Refer to **V6 Power Head Assembly** in this chapter.*

Cleaning and Inspection
Pistons (3-25 hp)

1. Inspect pistons for scoring, cracking, cracked or worn piston pin bosses or metal damage. Replace the piston and pin as necessary.

NOTE
The piston and piston pin are not available separately.

2. Check piston ring grooves for distortion, loose ring locating pins and excessive wear.

CAUTION
Do not use an automotive ring groove cleaning tool in Step 3 as it can damage the ring grooves and loosen the ring locating pins.

3. Clean the piston crown, ring grooves and skirt. Use the recessed end of a broken ring to remove any carbon deposits from the ring grooves.

4. Immerse the pistons in a carbon removal solution to remove any carbon deposits. If the solution does not remove all deposits, carefully use a bristle brush to finish cleaning. Avoid burring or rounding the machined edges. Polish piston skirts with crocus cloth on 3-15 hp models, or 320 carborundum on 20 and 25 hp models.

5A. 3 and 3.3 hp—Using a micrometer, measure the piston skirt at a 90° angle to the piston pin bore. Then measure the cylinder bore diameter using an inside micrometer. Subtract the piston diameter from the maximum cylinder bore diameter to obtain piston clearance. If the piston clearance is not within 0.002-0.005 in. (0.05-0.13 mm), replace the piston, and/or bore the cylinder to the next oversize.

5B. 4 and 5 hp—Using a micrometer, measure the piston skirt diameter 5/8 in. (16 mm) up from the bottom of the skirt, at a 90° angle to the piston pin bore. Measure the cylinder diameter using an inside micrometer. Subtract piston diameter from the maximum cylinder bore diameter to determine piston clearance. Refer to **Table 4** for piston and cylinder bore specifications. If piston clearance is not as specified, replace the piston, and/or bore the cylinder to the next oversize dimension.

5C. 8-25 hp—These models are equipped with barrel-shaped pistons. Oversize pistons and rings are not available. Using a micrometer, measure the piston skirt diameter 0.010 in. (2.5 mm) up from the bottom of the skirt, at a 90° angle to the piston pin bore. On 8-15 hp models, subtract piston diameter from the cylinder bore diameter to determine piston clearance. If piston clearance is not as specified (**Table 5**), replace the piston and/or cylinder block. On 20 and 25 hp models, replace the pistons if diameter is not as specified (**Table 4**).

> *NOTE*
> *Pistons and piston pins are available only as a unit assembly.*

Cleaning and Inspection
Pistons (40 hp and 50-60 hp
Prior to Serial No. D000750)

1. Inspect pistons for scoring, cracking, cracked or worn piston pin bosses or metal damage. Replace the piston and pin as necessary.

> *NOTE*
> *The piston and piston pin are not available separately.*

2. Check piston ring grooves for distortion, loose ring locating pins and excessive wear.

> *CAUTION*
> *Do not use an automotive ring groove cleaning tool in Step 3 as it can damage the ring grooves and loosen the ring locating pins. Replacement pistons on 50 and 60 hp models are equipped with 2 half keystone (tapered on top) rings in place of the 3 rectangular rings previously used. Be sure the correct type ring is used to clean the ring grooves in Step 3.*

3. Clean the piston crown, ring grooves and skirt. Use the recessed end of a broken ring to remove any carbon deposits from the ring grooves.

4. Immerse the pistons in a carbon removal solution to remove any carbon deposits. If the solution does not remove all deposits, carefully use a bristle brush to finish cleaning. Avoid burring or rounding the machined edges. Polish piston skirts with crocus cloth.

> *NOTE*
> *The pistons have a tapered, cam profile shape and are not a true diameter.*

5. After the pistons are thoroughly cleaned, check each piston for the correct dimensions using a micrometer.

6A. 40 hp—Measure the bottom of the piston skirt at a 90° angle to the piston pin bore. Replace the piston(s) if not within specification in **Table 4**.

6B. 50 and 60 hp—Measure the bottom of the piston skirt at a 90° angle to the piston pin bore. The skirt diameter should be:

  a. Standard piston—2.872 in. (72.95 mm).

  b. 0.015 in. oversize piston—2.887 in. (73.34 mm).

  c. 0.030 in. oversize piston—2.902 in. (73.71 mm).

Next, measure the piston crown diameter (above the piston rings) inline with the piston pin and at 90° to the pin. The piston crown diameter should be:

  a. Standard piston—2.863 in. (72.72 mm).

b. 0.015 in. oversize piston—2.878 in. (73.10 mm).

c. 0.030 in. oversize piston—2.893 in. (73.48 mm).

Replace the piston(s) if not as specified.

NOTE
Replacement pistons for 50 and 60 hp models (prior to Serial No. D000750) are equipped with 2 half keystone (tapered on the top) piston rings in place of the 3 rectangular rings used previously. It is acceptable to mix the new piston design and the previously used pistons in the same power head.

Cleaning and Inspection
Pistons (50 and 60 hp [Serial No. D000750-on]; 75, 90, 100 and 115 hp)

1. Inspect pistons for scoring, cracking, cracked or worn piston pin bosses or metal damage. Replace the piston and pin as necessary.

NOTE
The piston and piston pin are not available separately.

2. Check piston ring grooves for distortion, loose ring locating pins and excessive wear. Piston ring locating pins must be tight.

CAUTION
The pistons are equipped with half keystone (tapered on the top) rings. Do not use an automotive ring groove cleaning tool in Step 3 as it can damage the ring grooves and loosen the ring locating pins. Use caution not to scratch or nick the side surfaces of the ring grooves. Scratching the groove sides will damage the piston.

3. Clean the piston crown, ring grooves and skirt. Use the recessed end of a broken keystone ring to remove any carbon deposits from the ring grooves. Grind off enough of the ring taper to allow the inside edge of the broken ring to reach the inside diameter of the ring groove.

4. Immerse the pistons in a carbon removal solution to remove any remaining carbon deposits. If the solution does not remove all deposits, carefully use a bristle brush to finish cleaning. Avoid burring or rounding the machined edges. Polish piston skirts with crocus cloth.

5. After the pistons are thoroughly cleaned, measure the piston diameters using a micrometer.

6. Measure the piston skirt 1/2 in. (12.7 mm) up from the bottom of the skirt at a 90° angle to the piston pin bore. Compare to the specifications in **Table 4** and replace the piston(s) if worn below the specified diameter.

Cleaning and Inspection
Pistons (V6 Models)

1. Inspect pistons for scoring, cracking, cracked or worn piston pin bosses or metal damage. Replace the piston and pin as necessary.

NOTE
The piston and piston pin are not available separately.

2. Check piston ring grooves for distortion, loose ring locating pins and excessive wear. Piston ring locating pins must be tight.

NOTE
On 135 and 150 hp models, the top ring is a keystone type (tapered both sides) and the bottom ring is a conventional rectangular type. Two keystone rings are used on 150XR4 and 150XR6, 175 hp and 175XRi models. Two half-keystone (tapered top side) rings are used on 200 hp and 200XRi and 2 rectangular rings are used on 250 and 275 hp models.

3. Clean the piston crown, skirt and ring grooves.

CAUTION
Do not use an automotive ring groove cleaning tool to clean the ring grooves as it can damage the grooves and loosen the ring locating pins. Use the end of a

8

broken piston ring and carefully scrape any carbon deposits from the ring groove. Make sure the ring used matches the ring groove. Use caution not to scratch or nick the side surfaces of the ring grooves or the piston will be damaged.

4. Use the recessed end of a broken ring to remove any carbon deposits from the ring grooves. On keystone rings, grind off enough of the ring taper to allow the inside edge of the broken ring to reach the inside diameter of the ring groove.

5. Immerse the pistons in a carbon removal solution to remove any remaining carbon deposits. If the solution does not remove all deposits, carefully use a bristle brush to finish cleaning. Avoid burring or rounding the machined edges. Polish piston skirts with crocus cloth.

6. After the pistons are thoroughly cleaned, measure the piston diameters using a micrometer.

7A. 121.9 cid engine—Measure the piston diameter at the points shown in **Figure 102**. Dimension "A" should be:

a. Standard piston—3.113-3.117 in. (79.07-79.17 mm).

b. 0.015 in. oversize piston—3.128-3.132 in. (79.45-79.55 mm).

c. 0.030 in. oversize piston—3.143-3.147 in. (79.83-79.93 mm).

Dimension "B" should be within 0.008 in. (0.20 mm) of dimension "A." If not, replace the piston and pin assembly.

7B. 142.2 and 153 cid engine—Measure the piston diameter at the points shown in **Figure 103**. Dimension "A" should be:

a. 142.2 cid engine

Standard piston—3.3705-3.3715 in. (85.61-85.64 mm).

0.015 in. oversize piston—3.3855-3.3865 in. (85.99-86.02 mm).

b. 153 cid engine

Standard piston—3.4934-3.4944 in. (88.73-88.76 mm).

0.015 in. oversize piston—3.5084-3.5094 in. (89.11-89.14 mm).

Dimension "B" should be within 0.008 in. (0.20 mm) of dimension "A." If not replace the piston and pin assembly.

7C. 250 and 275 hp (207 cid engine)—Measure the piston diameter at the points shown in **Figure 104**. Dimension "A" should be 3.731-3.733 in. (94.77-85.68 mm). Dimension "B" should be

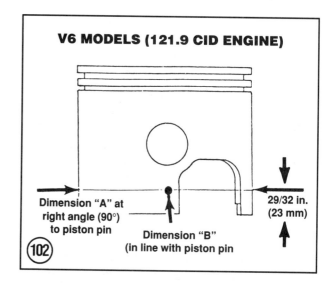

V6 MODELS (121.9 CID ENGINE)

Dimension "A" at right angle (90°) to piston pin

Dimension "B" (in line with piston pin

29/32 in. (23 mm)

(102)

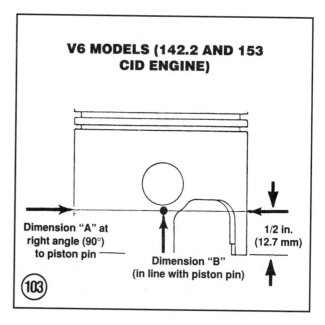

V6 MODELS (142.2 AND 153 CID ENGINE)

Dimension "A" at right angle (90°) to piston pin

Dimension "B" (in line with piston pin)

1/2 in. (12.7 mm)

(103)

within 0.003 in. (0.08 mm) of dimension "A." If not, replace the piston and pin assembly.

Cleaning and Inspection
Connecting Rods (All Models)

1. Check the connecting rods for straightness. Place each rod/cap assembly on a smooth, flat surface plate and press downward on rod. The rod should not wobble under pressure. Try inserting a 0.002 in. feeler gauge between the machined surfaces of the rod and the flat surface plate. If the feeler gauge can be inserted between any machined surface of the rod and the surface plate, the rod is bent and must be replaced.

2. Check the connecting rod bearings for rust or bearing failure.

3. Check the connecting rod big and small end bearing surfaces for rust, water marks, spalling, chatter marks, heat discoloration and excessive or uneven wear.

4. Slight defects noted in Step 3 may be cleaned up as follows:

   a. Reassemble the connecting rod cap to the rod with match marks aligned. Tighten the cap screws evenly and securely.

CAUTION
Use only crocus cloth and 320 carborundum as specified in the following steps. Do not substitute any other abrasive cloth to clean the connecting rod bearing surfaces.

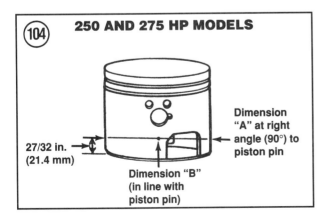

(104) **250 AND 275 HP MODELS**

27/32 in. (21.4 mm)

Dimension "A" at right angle (90°) to piston pin

Dimension "B" (in line with piston pin)

   b. On 8-25 hp models, clean the big end and small end bearing surfaces with crocus cloth.

   c. On 40-275 hp models, clean the big end bearing surface using crocus cloth and the small end bearing surface using 320 grit carborundum cloth.

   d. Wash the connecting rod thoroughly in clean solvent to remove any abrasive grit, then recheck the bearing surfaces.

   e. Replace any rod and cap assembly that does not clean up properly.

   f. Lightly oil the connecting rod bearing surfaces with 2-stroke engine oil to prevent rust.

Cleaning and Inspection
Crankshaft (3-5 hp)

1. Check the splines on the drive shaft end of the crankshaft for damage or wear. Check the connecting rod for straightness. Replace the crankshaft assembly as necessary.

2. Check crankshaft oil seal surfaces for grooving, pitting or scratches.

3. Check crankshaft bearing surfaces for grooves, pitting, scratches and evidence of overheating. Minor marks may be cleaned up with crocus cloth.

4. Clean the connecting rod small end bearing surfaces using crocus cloth.

5. Grasp the inner race of the crankshaft ball bearing and attempt to work it back and forth. Replace the bearing if excessive play is noted.

6. Lubricate ball bearings with a light oil and rotate the outer race. Replace the bearing if it sounds or feels rough, or if it does not rotate smoothly.

7. Support the crankshaft assembly as shown in **Figure 105**. Mount a dial indicator at the check points shown, then rotate the crankshaft assembly and check runout. Replace the crankshaft if runout exceeds 0.001 in. (0.025 mm) on 3 hp

8

models or 0.002 in. (0.05 mm) on 4 and 5 hp models.

8A. 3 and 3.3 hp—Determine connecting rod, crankpin and crankpin bearing wear by checking the connecting rod small end play (A, **Figure 106**). Replace the crankshaft assembly if play (A) is not within 0.022-0.056 in. (0.6-1.5 mm).

8B. 4 and 5 hp—Check the connecting rod side clearance by inserting a feeler gauge between the rod big end and crankshaft. Replace the crankshaft assembly if the side clearance is not within 0.005-0.015 in. (0.13-0.38 mm).

Cleaning and Inspection
Crankshaft (8-275 hp)

1. Check the crankshaft splines (drive shaft end) for damage or excessive wear. Replace the crankshaft as necessary.

2. Check the crankshaft oil seal surfaces for grooving, pitting or scratches.

3. Check the crankshaft bearing surfaces for rust, water marks, chatter marks and excessive or uneven wear. Minor rust and water or chatter marks may be cleaned up with 320 grit carborundum cloth (20-40 hp and 50 and 60 [prior to serial No D000750] hp) or crocus cloth (all other models).

4. Thoroughly clean the crankshaft in clean solvent and recheck the crankshaft surfaces. Replace the crankshaft if it cannot be properly cleaned. If the crankshaft is in acceptable condition, lightly oil the crankshaft (except bearings) to prevent rust.

5. Grasp the outer race of the crankshaft ball bearing(s) and attempt to work the race in and out. Replace the bearing if excessive play is noted.

6. Lightly oil ball bearing(s) and rotate the bearing. Replace the bearing if it feels or sounds rough or does not rotate smoothly.

> *CAUTION*
> *Do not replace individual bearing rollers in Step 7. If any rollers require re-*

placement or are lost, replace the entire bearing assembly.

7. Clean the center main bearing rollers with clean solvent. Check bearings for rust, galling or discoloration. Replace bearings if any defects are noted. The manufacturer recommends replacing all needle bearings during reassembly.

Cleaning and Inspection
Reed Valve Assembly (3-5 hp)

1. Clean the reed valve assemblies thoroughly with clean solvent.

2. Inspect the reeds for cracks, chips or evidence of fatigue. The reeds should be flush (or nearly

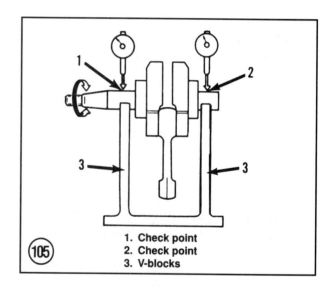

1. Check point
2. Check point
3. V-blocks

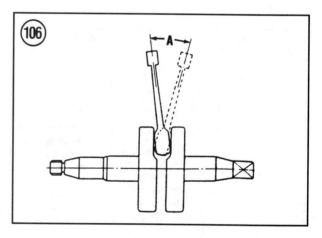

flush) to the seat along their entire length without being preloaded against the seat. Replace the reeds as necessary. See **Power Head Assembly** in this chapter.

3. Check for indentation (wear) on the face of the seat area in the crankcase cover. If the reeds have worn indentations in the seat, the cylinder block and crankcase cover must be replaced.

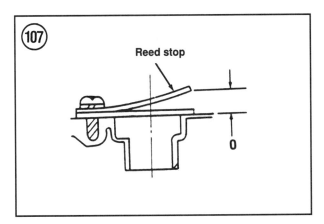

NOTE
Do not remove the reeds and reed stop unless replacement is necessary. Never turn reeds over for reuse. On 4/Sailpower models, one reed stop is flat causing one reed valve to be inoperative.

4. Check the reed stop as shown in **Figure 107**. On 3 and 3.3 hp models, replace the reed stop if the opening (O) is not within 0.236-0.244 in. (6.0-6.2 mm). On 4 and 5 hp models, carefully bend the reed stop to obtain 0.24-0.248 in. (6.1-6.3 mm) opening (O).

Cleaning and Inspection
Reed Valve Assembly (8-25 hp)

NOTE
Do not remove the reeds and reed stops from the reed block assembly unless replacement is necessary. Never remove the reeds and turn over for reuse. The reeds should always be replaced in entire sets.

1. Thoroughly clean the reed block assembly in clean solvent.

2. Check for excessive wear (indentations), cracks or grooves in the seat area of the reed block. Replace the reed block as necessary.

3. Check the valves for chipped or broken reeds. Replace reeds as necessary.

NOTE
Always replace reeds in entire sets. Never turn reeds over for reuse.

4. Check the gap between the reeds and seat area of the reed block. See **Figure 108** (8-15 hp models) or **Figure 109** (20 and 25 hp models). Replace the reeds if they are preloaded (stick tightly to the reed block) or stand open more than 0.007 in. (0.18 mm).

5. 8-15 hp—Check the reed stop opening by measuring from the inside of the reed stop to the top of the a closed reed. Carefully bend the reed

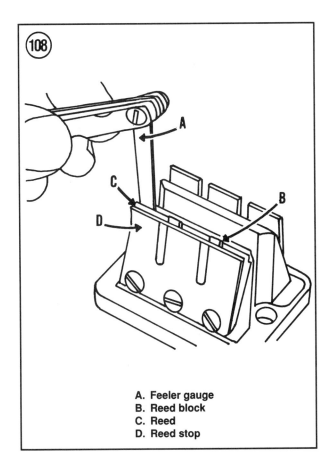

A. Feeler gauge
B. Reed block
C. Reed
D. Reed stop

stop to obtain 7/32 in. (5.6 mm) on 8 and 9.9 hp models or 19/64 in. (7.6 mm) on 15 hp models.

6. To remove the reeds, remove the screws attaching the reeds and stops to the block. To reinstall, apply Loctite 242 to the threads of the screws and tighten to 20 in.-lb. (2.3 N•m) on 8-15 hp models and 25 in.-lb. (2.8 N•m) on 20 and 25 hp models.

Cleaning and Inspection
Reed Valve Assembly (40 hp and 50-60 hp Prior to Serial No. D000750)

NOTE
Do not remove the reeds from the reed block unless replacement is necessary. Always replace reeds in complete sets. Never turn a reed over for reuse.

1. Clean reed block assemblies thoroughly in clean solvent.

2. Check the condition of the nylon locating pins (**Figure 110**) in the reed block halves. Locating pins that have been subjected to overheating (melted) will adversely affect the starting, idle and overall engine operation. If the pins are not perfect, replace the reed block.

3. Assemble the reed block halves and secure with the appropriate fasteners.

4. Check each reed block face for indentations indicating excessive wear. If the reeds have indented the reed block seat, replace the entire reed valve assembly.

5. Check the reed block labyrinth seal area (inside diameter) for excessive wear. Replace the reed block as necessary.

6. Check for chipped or broken reeds.

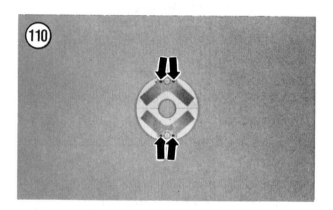

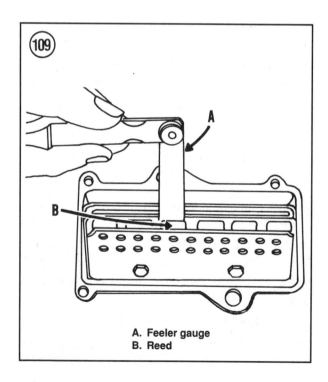

A. Feeler gauge
B. Reed

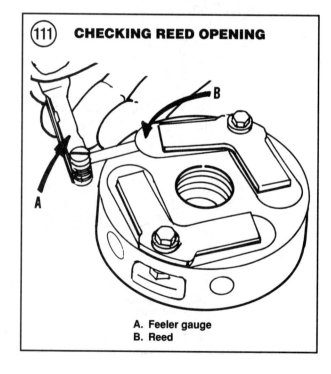

CHECKING REED OPENING

A. Feeler gauge
B. Reed

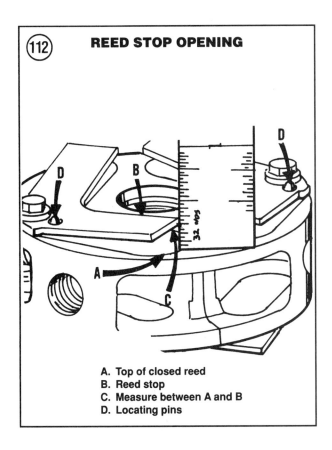

112 REED STOP OPENING

A. Top of closed reed
B. Reed stop
C. Measure between A and B
D. Locating pins

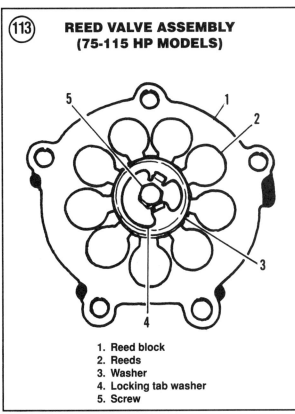

**113 REED VALVE ASSEMBLY
(75-115 HP MODELS)**

1. Reed block
2. Reeds
3. Washer
4. Locking tab washer
5. Screw

7. Check the gap between the reeds and reed block seat using a feeler gauge. See **Figure 111**. Replace the reeds if they stick tightly to the reed block (preloaded) or the gap exceeds 0.007 in. (0.18 mm).

8. Check each reed stop opening by measuring from the top of a closed reed to the inside of the reed stop. See **Figure 112**. Reed stop opening should be 5/32 in. (3.97 mm) on 40 hp models and 3/16 in. (4.8 mm) on 50 and 60 hp models. Carefully bend the reed stop to obtain the specified opening.

9. To replace the reeds, remove the reed retaining screw from each reed block half, then remove the reed stops and reeds. Reassemble the reed valve assembly by reversing this procedure. Apply Loctite 242 to the retaining screws and tighten to 30 in.-lb. (3.4 N·m).

Cleaning and Inspection
Reed Valve Assemblies (50-60 hp [Serial No. D000750-on]; 75, 90, 100 and 115 hp)

8

NOTE
Do not remove the reeds from the reed block unless replacement is necessary. Always replace reeds in complete sets. Never turn a reed over for reuse or attempt to straighten a damaged reed.

Separate reed block assemblies for each cylinder are used on 75-115 hp models (**Figure 113**). On 50 and 60 hp models, the reed valves are affixed to one common reed block (**Figure 114**).

1. Thoroughly clean the reed valve assemblies using clean solvent.

2. Check for chipped or broken reeds. The reeds should be flat and smooth along their entire seating surface. Replace the reeds as necessary.

3. Check the gap between the reeds and the reed block seating surface using a feeler gauge. See **Figure 115**. Replace the reeds if the gap exceeds 0.020 in. (0.51 mm).

4. To replace the reeds, bend back the locking tab washer and remove the screw securing the reeds and retaining washer.

CAUTION
Do not reuse the locking tab washer upon reassembly. Always install a new washer.

5. Reassembly is the reverse of disassembly. Make sure the reeds and the washer correctly engage the alignment pins. Install a new locking tab washer and tighten the retaining screw to 60 in.-lb. (6.8 N·m). If necessary, continue to tighten the screw to align a flat on the screw head with the locking tab on the washer, but do not exceed 100 in.-lb. (11.3 N·m). Secure the screw by bending the locking tab firmly against the screw head.

Cleaning and Inspection
Reed Valve Assemblies (V6 Models)

NOTE
Do not remove the reeds from the reed block unless replacement is necessary. Always replace reeds in complete sets. Never turn a reed over for reuse or attempt to straighten a damaged reed.

1. Clean the gasket surfaces of the reed blocks and reed block housing thoroughly.

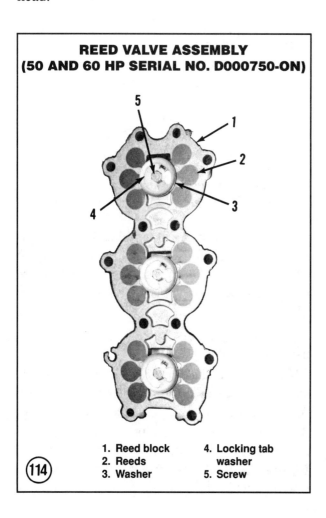

REED VALVE ASSEMBLY (50 AND 60 HP SERIAL NO. D000750-ON)

1. Reed block	4. Locking tab
2. Reeds	washer
3. Washer	5. Screw

(114)

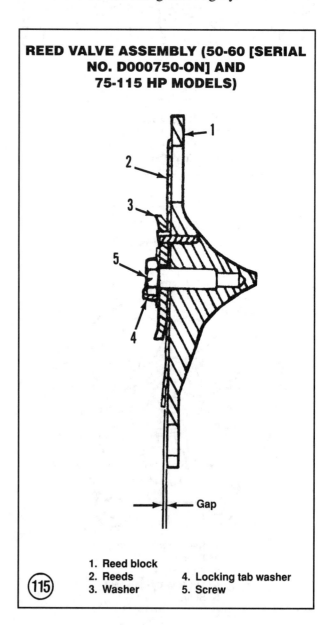

REED VALVE ASSEMBLY (50-60 [SERIAL NO. D000750-ON] AND 75-115 HP MODELS)

Gap

1. Reed block	
2. Reeds	4. Locking tab washer
3. Washer	5. Screw

(115)

2. Check the reed blocks and housing for distortion, cracks, deep grooves or any other damage that may cause leakage. Replace as necessary.

3. Check each reed block face for indentations indicating excessive wear. If the reeds have indented the surface of the block seating area, replace the entire reed valve assembly.

4. Check for chipped or broken reeds. See **Figure 116**, typical (5-petal reed shown).

5. Check the gap between the reeds and the reed block seating surface using a flat feeler gauge. See **Figure 117**, typical. If the gap exceeds 0.020 in. (0.51 mm), replace the reed set.

6. If the reed block is fitted with reed stops (250 and 275 hp models), measure the reed stop opening as shown in **Figure 118**. Reed stop opening should be 0.130 in. (3.3 mm). Carefully bend the reed stops to adjust the opening to the specified dimension.

Cleaning and Inspection
Lower Oil Seal Housing (4 and 5 hp)

1. Place the lower oil seal housing in a vise. Pad the housing with shop cloths to prevent damage.

2. Using puller part No. 91-83165M (or equivalent), remove the upper seal, spacer and lower seal. See **Figure 119**. Early models are equipped with 1 seal in place of the 2 seals and spacer.

8

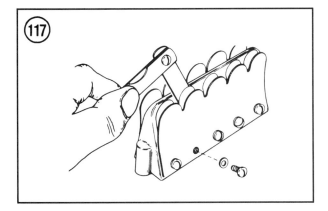

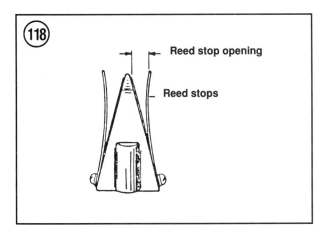

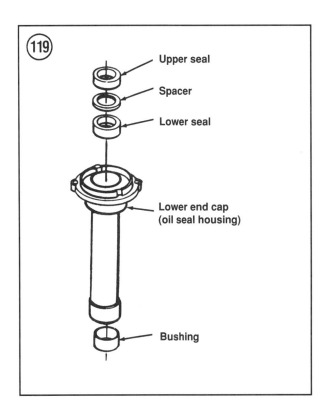

Upper seal

Spacer

Lower seal

Lower end cap
(oil seal housing)

Bushing

3. If necessary, drive the bushing (**Figure 119**) out the bottom of the housing using a suitable punch and hammer.

4. Clean the oil seal housing in clean solvent and inspect for wear or damage.

5A. Early models—With the oil seal housing supported in a vise, install the oil seal into the housing. Note that the seal lip must face down. Lubricate the seal lip with Quicksilver 2-4-C Marine Lubricant.

5B. Late models—Install the bushing (**Figure 119**) into the seal housing using a suitable driver. Install the lower seal, spacer and upper seal using a suitable driver. Both seals should have the lips facing down. Lubricate the seal lips with Quicksilver 2-4-C Marine Lubricant.

Cleaning and Inspection
End Caps (40 hp)

Do not remove the ball bearings from the end caps unless inspection determines that the bearings require replacement. If upper or lower bearing failure has occurred, closely inspect the respective end cap for excessive wear or damage. A loose bearing-to-end cap fit will result in premature bearing and/or crankshaft failure.

1. Support the upper end cap and drive out the seal using a suitable punch and hammer. Repeat the procedure on the lower end cap. Discard the seals. Remove and discard the O-rings from end caps.

2. Clean the end caps in clean solvent and dry with compressed air.

3. Move the bearing inner race in and out to check for excessive end play. Lubricate the bearing with light oil and rotate the inner race. If the bearing sounds noisy or feels rough, remove the bearing with a suitable puller and arbor press. Heat may be applied using a torch lamp or heat gun to ease bearing removal. Do not use open flame to heat bearing cap(s).

4A. Upper end cap—To install the upper bearing, invert the end cap and support it on an arbor

press. Using a suitable press block, press the bearing into the end cap until flush with the bottom surface of the end cap. Press from the numbered side of the bearing, on the outer race only. Place the end cap upright on the press. Apply Loctite 271 on the upper seal outer race and install the seal into the end cap. Note that the seal lip must face the bearing. Lubricate the bearing with 2-stroke engine oil. Lubricate the seal lip with Quicksilver 2-4-C Marine Lubricant. Install a new O-ring on the end cap.

4B. Lower end cap—Apply Loctite 271 to the outside diameter of both lower seals. Press the bottom seal (lip facing down) into the end cap until fully seated. Press the top bearing into the end cap until the top of the seal is just below the end cap bleed hole. Wipe off any excess Loctite and lubricate the seals with Quicksilver 2-4-C Marine Lubricant. If removed, press the lower bearing into the end cap until flush with the upper surface of the end cap. Press from the numbered side of the bearing, on the outer race only. Install a new O-ring on the end cap.

Cleaning and Inspection
End Caps (50 and 60 hp
Prior to Serial No. D000750)

1. Remove and discard the O-rings from the upper and lower end caps.

2. Using a suitable punch and hammer, drive the seals from the upper and lower end caps. Discard the seals.

3. Clean the end caps in clean solvent. Closely inspect the end caps for wear or damage.

4A. Upper end cap—Apply Loctite 271 to the outside diameter of the upper end cap seal. Press the seal (lip facing toward cylinder block) into the end cap until seated. Wipe off any excess Loctite. Install a new O-ring onto the end cap. Lubricate the O-ring and the seal with Quicksilver 2-4-C Marine Lubricant.

4B. Lower end cap—Press the outer seal (lip facing away from cylinder block) into the lower end cap until seated. Press the inner seal (lip facing away from cylinder block) into the end cap until the seal surface is flush with the bottom of the bearing bore. Remove any excess Loctite. Install a new O-ring onto the end cap. Lubricate the seals and the O-ring with Quicksilver 2-4-C Marine Lubricant.

Cleaning and Inspection
Lower End Cap (50 and 60 hp Serial No. D000750-on)

1. If not previously removed, remove and discard the end cap O-ring. Invert the end cap and drive the 2 seals from the end cap using a suitable punch and hammer. Discard the seals.

2. Thoroughly clean the end cap using clean solvent. Make sure the end cap mating surface is clean and all gasket sealant is removed.

3. Closely inspect the end cap for wear or damage.

4. Press the new seals into the end cap using a suitable mandrel and arbor press. Press the small seal (lip facing away from the power head) into the end cap until fully seated. Press the large seal (lip facing power head) into the end cap until fully seated.

5. Install a new O-ring onto the end cap.

6. Lubricate the seal lips and the O-ring with 2-stroke engine oil.

Cleaning and Inspection
Lower End Cap (75-155 hp)

1. Remove and discard the end cap O-ring. Invert the end cap and drive out the seal using a suitable punch and hammer. Discard the seal.

2. Thoroughly clean the end cap in clean solvent, especially the mating surface and O-ring groove. Make sure all gasket sealant is removed.

3. Apply Loctite 271 to the outer diameter of a new seal. Using a suitable mandrel and arbor press, install the seal (lip facing power head) into the end cap until fully seated. Wipe off any excess Loctite.

4. Install a new O-ring into the end cap groove. Lubricate the O-ring and seal lip with 2-stroke engine oil.

Cleaning and Inspection
End Caps (135-200 hp)

1. Remove and discard the O-rings from the upper and lower end caps. See **Figure 120** (lower) and **Figure 121** (upper).

2. Using a suitable punch and hammer, remove the 2 seals from the lower end cap and 1 seal from the upper end cap. Discard the seals.

3. Clean the end caps in clean solvent.

4. Closely inspect the roller bearing in the upper end cap. If the bearing is rusted, galled, worn, discolored or if loose rollers are noted inside the end cap, replace the bearing and upper end cap as an assembly. Inspect the lower end cap for wear or other damage.

5A. Upper end cap—Apply Loctite 271 to the outer diameter of a new upper seal. Using a suitable mandrel and an arbor press, install the seal (lip facing power head) into the upper end cap until bottomed on the end cap lip. See **Figure 122**. Wipe away any excess Loctite.

5B. Lower end cap—Apply Loctite 271 to the outer diameter of new lower seals. Using a suitable mandrel and arbor press, press the outer seal (lip facing down) into the end cap until fully seated. Remove any excess Loctite, then press the inner seal into the end cap until fully seated on the outer seal. See **Figure 123**. Remove any excess Loctite.

6. Install new O-rings into the end cap grooves. Lubricate the O-rings and seal lips with Quicksilver Needle Bearing Assembly Grease (part No. 92-42649A-1).

Cleaning and Inspection
End Cap and Upper Bearing Carrier
(250 and 275 hp)

1. Invert the lower end cap and tap the seal out using a suitable punch and hammer. Discard the seal. Remove and discard the O-ring.

2. Clean the end cap in clean solvent. Inspect the end cap for wear or damage.

3. Apply Loctite 271 to the outer diameter of a new lower seal. Using a suitable mandrel and arbor press, install the seal (lip facing down) into the end cap until fully seated. See **Figure 124**. Install a new O-ring into the end cap groove. Lubricate the O-ring and seal lip with Quicksilver Needle Bearing Assembly Grease (part No. 92-42649A-1).

4. Invert the upper bearing carrier and tap out the seal using a suitable punch and hammer. Discard the seal. Remove and discard the carrier O-ring.

5. Thoroughly clean the bearing and carrier assembly in clean solvent, then dry with compressed air.

6. Closely inspect the roller bearing in the carrier for excessive or uneven wear, chipped, broken or

loose rollers, rust, spalling, discoloration or other damage. If necessary, press the roller bearing from the carrier using a suitable mandrel and arbor press. Press a new bearing into the carrier until flush with the bottom of the carrier outer surface. Press the bearing from the lettered side only. Lubricate the bearing with Quicksilver

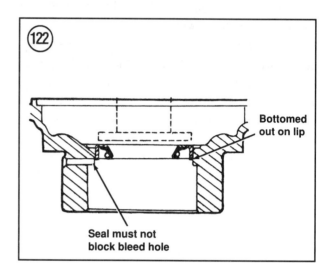

122

Bottomed out on lip

Seal must not block bleed hole

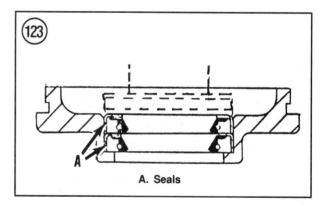

123

A

A. Seals

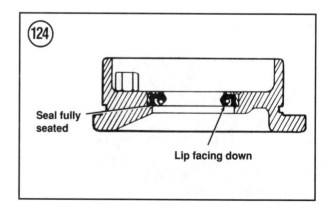

124

Seal fully seated

Lip facing down

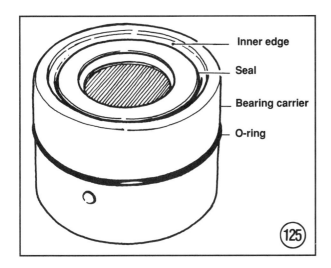

Inner edge

Seal

Bearing carrier

O-ring

(125)

(126)

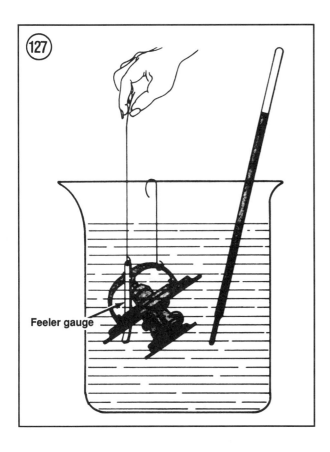

(127)

Feeler gauge

Needle Bearing Assembly Grease (part No. 92-42649A-1).

7. Apply Loctite 271 to the outer diameter of a new upper seal. Using a suitable mandrel and arbor press, install the seal (lip facing down) into the carrier until flush with the inner edge as shown in **Figure 125**. On 275 hp models after the following serial numbers, press the seal into the carrier until flush with the top surface of the carrier.

   a. 20 in. shaft—D086818-on.

   b. 25 in. shaft—D086876-on.

   c. 30 in. shaft—D090719-on.

8. Install a new O-ring into the carrier groove. Lubricate the O-ring and seal with Quicksilver Needle Bearing Assembly Grease (part No. 92-42649A-1).

Cleaning and Inspection
Thermostat (Models So Equipped)

1. Clean all gasket material from the thermostat and cylinder head covers.

2. Check thermostat covers for cracks or corrosion damage and replace as necessary.

3. Wash thermostat (**Figure 126**) with clean water.

4. Suspend the thermostat and a thermometer in a container of water that can be heated. See **Figure 127**.

NOTE
Support the thermostat with wire so it does not touch the sides or bottom of the container.

5. Heat the water and note the temperature at which the thermostat starts to open. The thermostat should begin to open at approximately:

   a. 8, 9.9, 15, 50 and 60 (serial No. D041952-on), 250 and 275 hp models—120°F (49°C).

   b. 50 and 60 (serial No. D000750-D041951) and 75-200 hp models—140°-145°F (60°-63°C).

8

NOTE
Models 75-115 hp are normally equipped with a 143°F (62°C) thermostat. If operated at idle speed for long periods in temperatures 80°F (27°C) and above, the manufacturer recommends installing a 120°F (49°C) thermostat (part No. 14586).

6. Replace the thermostat(s) if it fails to open at the specified temperature or if it does not open completely.

Crankshaft Assembly
(3 and 3.3 hp)

NOTE
Use Quicksilver Premium Blend or Premium Plus Blend 2-Cycle Outboard Oil whenever the procedure specifies lubrication with a light oil. A torque wrench is essential for proper fastener tightening. Do not use any grease inside the power head that is not gasoline soluble.

1. Using an arbor press and suitable mandrel, press the crankshaft ball bearings onto the crankshaft. Note that the side of the bearings with the alignment pins must face the bottom of the crankshaft. Press on the bearing inner race only.
2. Lubricate the piston pin needle bearing with Quicksilver Needle Bearing Assembly Grease (part No. 92-42649A-1), then install the bearing into the connecting rod.

NOTE
The piston must be installed on the connecting rod so the arrow on the piston crown is facing the exhaust port (down).

3. Install the piston on the connecting rod (arrow on crown facing down) and push the piston pin through the piston and connecting rod.
4. Using needlenose pliers, secure the piston pin with new "G" type lockrings. Make sure the lockrings are properly located in their grooves.
5. Before installing the piston ring on the piston, place the new piston ring inside the cylinder.

Push the ring into the cylinder with the piston to position the ring squarely inside the cylinder. Measure the gap between the ring ends using a feeler gauge as shown in **Figure 128**. The ring end gap should be 0.006-0.012 in. (0.18-0.33 mm). If the gap is excessive, replace the ring or check the cylinder bore diameter. If the gap is insufficient, carefully file the ring ends until the specified gap is obtained.

6. Using ring expander part No. 91-24697 (or equivalent), install the piston ring on the piston. Install the ring with the grooved ends facing up (toward piston crown). See **Figure 129**. Make sure the ring end gap properly engages the piston ring locating pin inside the ring groove.

7. Using a feeler gauge, measure the clearance between the piston ring and the side of the ring groove. The ring side clearance should be 0.0003-0.0010 in. (0.01-0.05 mm). If the clearance is excessive, replace the piston.

8. Lubricate the crankshaft seal lips with Quicksilver Needle Bearing Assembly Grease (part No. 92-42649A-1). Install the upper and lower seals onto the crankshaft so their lips are facing the center of the crankshaft.

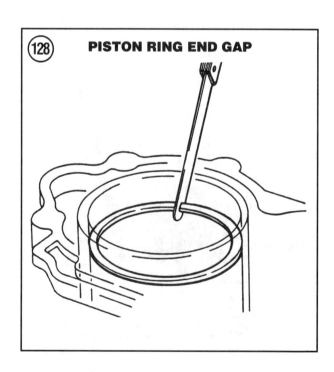

(128) **PISTON RING END GAP**

Crankshaft Assembly
(4 and 5 hp)

Refer to **Figure 19** for this procedure.

NOTE
Use Quicksilver Premium Blend or Premium Plus Blend 2-Cycle Outboard Oil whenever the procedure specifies lubrication with a light oil. A torque wrench is essential for proper fastener tightening. Do not use any grease inside the power head that is not gasoline soluble.

1. If the crankshaft upper or lower bearings are removed, install new bearings (numbered side facing away from the counterweight) with a suitable mandrel and an arbor press. Press against the bearing inner race until the bearing is seated against the shoulder on the crankshaft counterweight.

2. Before installing the piston rings on the piston, check piston ring end gap as follows:

   a. Place one piston ring into the cylinder. Using the piston skirt, push the ring approximately 1/2 in. (12.7 mm) into the cylinder bore.

   b. Measure the piston ring end gap using a feeler gauge as shown in **Figure 128**. Repeat the procedure on the remaining ring.

   c. Piston ring end gap should be 0.008-0.016 in. (0.2-0.4 mm). If gap is excessive, check

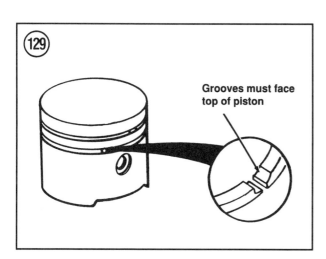

(129)

Grooves must face top of piston

the gap on another new ring until a ring within specification is found. If the gap is insufficient, carefully file the ring ends until the specified gap is obtained.

NOTE
*The piston rings must be installed on the piston so the grooved side of the end gap is facing the piston crown. See **Figure 129**.*

3. Fit the bottom piston ring into the ring expander part No. 91-24697 (or equivalent) and spread the ring just enough to slip over the piston from the top. Install the ring in the bottom groove. Repeat this step to install the top ring. Using a feeler gauge, measure the clearance between the piston rings and ring groove sides. Ring side clearance should be 0.0012-0.0028 in. (0.03-0.07 mm) on the top ring and 0.0008-0.0024 in. (0.02-0.06 mm) on the bottom ring. If ring gap is excessive, replace the piston.

4. Check rings for free rotation, lubricate with light oil and center the ring groove locating pins in the ring end gaps.

5. Lightly oil the piston pin caged bearing, then insert the bearing into the connecting rod small end.

6. Lightly oil the piston pin. Position the piston onto the connecting rod (up mark on piston crown facing flywheel end of crankshaft) and slide the pin through the piston and bearing. Center the pin in the piston.

7. Using needlenose pliers, install a new lockring into each piston pin bore. Make sure the lockrings are properly engaged in their grooves.

Crankshaft Assembly
(8, 9.9 and 15 hp)

NOTE
Use Quicksilver Premium Blend or Premium Plus Blend 2-Cycle Outboard Oil whenever the procedure specifies lubrication with a light oil. A torque wrench is essential for proper fastener tighten-

8

ing. Do not use any grease inside the power head that is not gasoline soluble.

Refer to **Figure 20** for this procedure.

1. If the crankshaft lower bearing is removed, install a new bearing (open side of ball retainer facing crankshaft) using the power head stand (part No. 91-13662A-1) and bearing sleeve as a mandrel and an arbor press. Be sure to press only on the bearing inner race. Seat the bearing inner race against the crankshaft shoulder and install a new snap ring to secure the ball bearing.

2. Lightly lubricate the lip of a new coupling seal with Quicksilver 2-4-C Marine Lubricant. Position the seal in the end of the crankshaft and press into place using the power head stand (part No. 91-13662A-1) as a pressing tool.

3. Install a new crankshaft sealing ring on the crankshaft center journal.

4. Secure the power head stand in a vise, then install the crankshaft onto the power head stand.

CAUTION
If crankshaft bearings are reused, be certain to install in original locations.

5. Lubricate both halves of one crankpin bearing with Quicksilver Needle Bearing Assembly Grease. Place the bearing halves onto the crankpin.

CAUTION
To prevent premature power head failure, the manufacturer recommends replacing connecting rod screws.

6. Clean the new connecting rod screws using clean solvent. Dry with compressed air. Do not oil the screw threads.

7. Remove the rod caps from the connecting rods. Discard the original screws.

8. Position the connecting rod with its lobe side facing the flywheel end of the crankshaft. Fit the rod onto the crankpin and install the rod cap, making sure the fracture lines on the rod cap and rod align properly. When properly aligned, the rod and cap fracture line will be nearly invisible.

9. Apply Loctite 271 to the threads of the rod cap screws. Install the screws and tighten evenly to 100 in.-lb. (11.3 N·m).

10. Repeat Steps 5-9 to install the remaining connecting rod.

11. Install the piston rings onto each piston using ring expander 91-24697 (or equivalent). Install the bottom ring first, then the top ring, expanding each one just enough to slip over the piston.

12. Lightly lubricate the sleeve portion of piston pin tool (part No. 91-13663A-1) with Quicksilver Needle Bearing Assembly Grease (part No. 92-42649A-1). Place the lower locating washer on the tip of your finger and hold it under the connecting rod piston pin bore, inserting the sleeve from the top of the bore.

13. Install the 24 needle bearing rollers between the insert and the piston pin bore, then fit the upper locating washer on top. Holding the assembly with one hand, slide the piston over the connecting rod and center the piston pin bore over the sleeve.

14. Insert the piston pin tool up through the piston pin bore to remove the sleeve.

15. Lubricate the piston pin with Quicksilver Needle Bearing Assembly Grease (part No. 92-

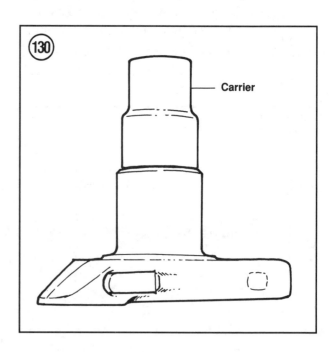

Carrier

42649A-1), then insert it through the piston pin bore until it contacts the tool. Support the bottom of the piston and the piston pin tool with one hand and drive the piston pin in flush with the piston surface using a soft-face mallet.

16. Remove the piston pin tool from the bottom of the piston, then insert it into the top of the piston pin bore and gently tap it until the pin is centered in the pin bore.

17. Using needlenose pliers, install a new lock-ring into each piston pin bore. Make sure the lockrings properly engage their grooves.

18. Repeat Steps 11-17 to install the remaining piston.

19. Install the retaining ring with its taper away from the lower crankshaft bearing. Install the stuffer washer and lower crankshaft oil seal.

20. Install the upper crankshaft roller bearing and a new oil seal.

21. Apply a thick coat of Needle Bearing Assembly Grease to the crankshaft center bearing journal, then install the caged center bearing halves.

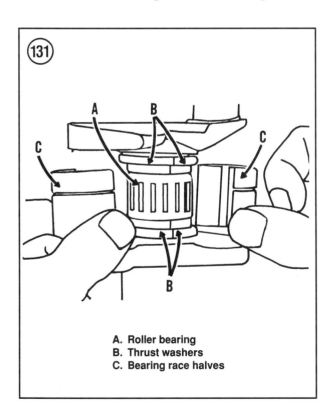

131

A. Roller bearing
B. Thrust washers
C. Bearing race halves

Crankshaft Assembly
(20 and 25 hp)

Refer to **Figure 73** for this procedure.

> *NOTE*
> *Use Quicksilver Premium Blend or Premium Plus Blend 2-Cycle Outboard Oil whenever the procedure specifies lubrication with a light oil. A torque wrench is essential for proper fastener tightening. Do not use any grease inside the power head that is not gasoline soluble.*

1. If removed, install the crankshaft carrier as follows:

    a. Apply Loctite 271 to the carrier surface on the crankshaft.

    b. Place the carrier onto the crankshaft. Make sure the carrier is started squarely.

    c. Place a 7/8 in. deep-well socket (or equivalent) over the carrier and drive onto the crankshaft by tapping the socket with a hammer. See **Figure 130**. Use caution not to damage the carrier. Wipe off any excess Loctite.

2. Secure the power head stand in a vise. Install the crankshaft on the power head stand.

3. Coat the crankshaft roller bearing and thrust washers with light oil.

4. Install the roller bearing with the thrust washers on the crankshaft, then install the bearing race halves. See **Figure 131**. Install the retaining ring into the bearing race groove. Make sure the retaining ring end gap is not aligned with the bearing race split line.

5. Push the thrust washers and bearing toward one end of the crankshaft. Check the clearance between the crankshaft and thrust washers with a feeler gauge. If the clearance exceeds 0.030 in. (0.76 mm), install new thrust washers.

6. Clean the new connecting rod cap screws with clean solvent. Dry with compressed air. Do not oil the screw threads.

7. Apply a thick coat of Quicksilver Needle Bearing Assembly Grease (part No. 92-42649A-

8

1) to either crankpin journal and its respective connecting rod big end and cap.

8. Install the 12 crankpin bearing rollers and the 2 bearing cage halves on the crankpin.

9. Install the connecting rod and cap. Make sure each connecting rod and cap is installed in its original location and direction. The notch in the rod and cap should face upward (or in the same direction as removed).

10. Install the connecting rod cap screws and tighten to specification (**Table 1**).

11. Repeat Steps 7-10 to install the remaining connecting rod and bearing assembly.

12. Place a piece of clean paper on the workbench. Align the needle bearing rollers from one piston/pin assembly (27 required) in a row.

13. Install the appropriate sleeve onto the piston pin tool (part No. 91-76160A2). Apply a thick coat of Quicksilver Needle Bearing Assembly Grease to the sleeve.

14. Roll the sleeve end of the piston pin tool over the aligned bearing rollers. This should pick up the rollers evenly around the sleeve. If it does not, see Step 16.

15. Position the lower locating washer under the piston pin bore. Slide the sleeve with attached bearings up through the washer and into the piston pin bore.

16. If the sleeve did not pick up all the bearing rollers in Step 14, insert the remaining rollers now. Position the upper locating washer over the piston pin tool sleeve and slide the tool out of the sleeve. The sleeve and washers will hold the bearing rollers in the piston pin bore.

17. Install the appropriate piston onto the connecting rod. Be sure the "UP" mark on the piston crown is facing the flywheel end of the crankshaft. Align the piston pin bore with the sleeve, then slide the pin tool through the upper pin bore and into the sleeve.

18. Lubricate the appropriate piston pin with light oil. Insert the piston pin into the lower piston pin bore. Hold the piston pin tool with one hand and drive the pin into the bore with a

soft-face mallet until the tool and sleeve are pushed out of the piston.

19. Center the pin in the piston. Using needlenose pliers, secure the piston pin with new piston pin lockrings. Be certain the lockrings are seated in their grooves.

20. Repeat Steps 12-19 to install the remaining piston to its connecting rod.

21. Install the piston rings on each piston using ring expander part No. 91-24697 (or equivalent). Install the bottom ring first, then the top ring. Expand the rings just enough to slip over the piston. Make sure the rings rotate freely in their grooves. If not, remove the rings and determine the cause. Lubricate the rings with light oil.

22. Lubricate the crankshaft upper and lower main bearings with Quicksilver Needle Bearing Assembly Grease. Slide the bearings onto each end of the crankshaft.

23. Lubricate the lips of new crankshaft upper and lower seals with Quicksilver Needle Bearing Assembly Grease. Install the seals onto each end of the crankshaft.

Crankshaft Assembly
(40 hp and 50-60 hp
Prior to Serial No. D000750)

Refer to **Figure 75** for this procedure.

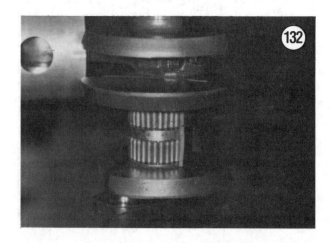

1. 50-60 hp—If removed, install the upper and lower ball bearings onto the crankshaft using an arbor press.

2. Apply a thick coat of Quicksilver Needle Bearing Assembly Grease to the crankshaft center main bearing journal. Install the center main bearing rollers on the crankshaft journal. See **Figure 132**.

3. Install the center main bearing outer race halves. The bearing race retaining ring groove should be toward the top of the crankshaft. Install the bearing race retaining ring. Make sure the

retaining ring end gap is not aligned with the bearing race split line.

4. 40 hp—Install the main bearing support onto the main bearing. The locating pin inside the support must engage the alignment hole in the bearing. See **Figure 133**. Install the bearing support screws and tighten to 80 in.-lb. (9.0 N•m).

5. Lubricate the reed block inner diameter with light oil. Install the reed block halves to the crankshaft. **Figure 134**, typical shows one half installed. Align the locating pins with the holes in the reed blocks. Apply Loctite 271 to the threads of the reed block fasteners, then install the fasteners and tighten to 55 in.-lb. (6.2 N•m).

CAUTION
Always use new connecting rod screws during reassembly.

6. Clean new connecting rod screws with solvent. Dry with compressed air. Do not oil the screw threads.

7. Apply a thick coat of Quicksilver Needle Bearing Assembly Grease (part No. 92-42649A-1) to one crankpin journal and to its respective connecting rod and cap.

8A. 40 hp—Place 25 loose crankpin bearing rollers around the appropriate crankpin journal.

8B. 50-60 hp—Place the crankpin bearing cage halves into the connecting rod and rod cap. Install the crankpin bearing rollers into the cage halves.

9. Install the connecting rod and cap to its crankpin journal. Apply Loctite 271 to the threads of the rod cap screws and install the screws.

10. Tighten the rod cap screws finger tight and check the rod and cap alignment. If properly aligned, the rod and cap fracture line will be nearly invisible. If necessary, loosen the screws and realign the rod and cap.

11. After the correct connecting rod-to-cap alignment is obtained, tighten the rod cap screws evenly in 3 progressive steps to 200 in.-lb. (22.6 N•m) on 40 hp models, or 180 in.-lb. (20.3 N•m) on 50 and 60 hp models. After tightening the

8

screws, recheck the rod-to-cap alignment. If necessary, loosen the screws and realign the rod and cap. If perfect alignment can not be obtained, the rod and cap must be replaced.

12. Repeat Steps 6-11 to install the remaining connecting rods to the crankshaft.

13. Place a piece of clean paper on the workbench. Align the needle bearing rollers from one piston/pin assembly in a row.

14. Install the sleeve on the piston pin tool part No. 91-76160A-2 (40 hp) or part No. 91-76159A-1) and coat it liberally with Quicksilver Needle Bearing Assembly Grease.

15. Roll the sleeve end of the piston pin tool over the aligned bearings. This should pick up the bearings evenly around the sleeve. If it does not, see Step 17.

16. Position the lower locating washer under the connecting rod piston pin bore. Slide the sleeve with attached bearings up through the washer and into the rod bore.

17. If the sleeve did not pick up all the bearing rollers in Step 15, insert the remaining rollers now. Position the upper locating washer over the piston pin tool sleeve and slide the tool out of the sleeve. The sleeve and washers will hold the bearing rollers in the rod bore.

18. Install the piston on the connecting rod as follows:

   a. 40 hp—The long sloping side of the piston crown must face exhaust ports.

   b. 50-60 hp—The concave side the deflector on the piston crown must face the intake ports.

19. Align the piston pin bore with the sleeve, then slide the pin tool through the upper pin bore and into the sleeve.

20. Lubricate the piston pin with light oil.

WARNING
The lamp used in Step 21 produces an intense light. Wear the glasses provided with the lamp and do not look directly at the lamp. Wear suitable hand protection while handling the hot piston.

21. 50-60 hp—Heat the piston crown to approximately 190°F (88°C) using a torch lamp (part No. 91-63209).

22. Insert the piston pin into the lower piston boss. Insert the piston pin tool through the upper piston boss and into the sleeve. Hold the piston pin tool with one hand and drive the pin into the bore with a mallet until the tool and sleeve are pushed out of the piston.

23A. 40 hp—Center the piston pin in the piston. Using needlenose pliers, install new piston pin lockrings into each side of the piston. Be certain the lockrings are seated in their grooves.

23B. 50-60 hp—Fit a new "C" type lockring inside the installer end of the lockring tool (part No. 91-52952A-1) with needlenose pliers as shown in **Figure 135**. Assemble the tool and insert it into the piston pin bore. Support the piston with one hand and press the installer handle downward quickly. See **Figure 136**. The

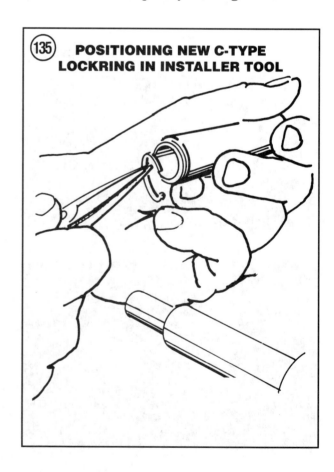

(135) **POSITIONING NEW C-TYPE LOCKRING IN INSTALLER TOOL**

tool will automatically install the lockring into the groove in the piston pin bore. Repeat this step to install the other lockring, supporting the piston with one hand and pushing the installer upward quickly.

24. Repeat Steps 20-23 to install the remaining pistons to their connecting rods.

25. Install the piston rings on each piston using ring expander part No. 91-24697 (or equivalent). Install the bottom ring first. Expand the rings just enough to slip over the piston. Lubricate the rings with light oil and align the ring end gaps with the locating pins in the ring grooves.

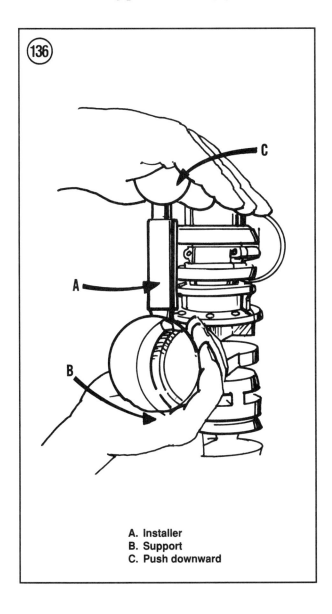

A. Installer
B. Support
C. Push downward

Crankshaft Assembly (50-60 hp [Serial No. D000750-on]; 75, 90, 100 and 115 hp)

Refer to **Figure 85** for this procedure. **Figure 85** shows the crankshaft and related components used on 4-cylinder models, however, 3-cylinder models are essentially the same.

NOTE
Use Quicksilver Premium Blend or Premium Plus Blend 2-Cycle Outboard Oil whenever the procedure specifies lubrication with a light oil. A torque wrench is essential for proper fastener tightening. Do not use any grease inside the power head that is not gasoline soluble.

1. If removed, install the oil injection pump drive gear onto the crankshaft, making sure the gear key slot is aligned with the key in the crankshaft.

2. Press the lower main ball bearing onto the crankshaft until seated against the oil pump drive gear. Press on the bearing inner race (numbered side) only.

3. On all 50-60 hp models, 75-90 hp models (prior to serial No. C259434), and 100 and 115 hp models (prior to serial No. C259722), install the lower main bearing snap ring (**Figure 137**). Make sure the snap ring is properly seated in its groove.

NOTE
Models 75 and 90 hp (serial No. C259434-on) and 100 and 115 hp models (serial No. C259722-on) do not use a snap ring below the lower main ball bearing.

4A. 75-90 hp equipped with lower crankshaft seal carrier (**Figure 138**):

a. If removed, install the seal carrier by tapping it into the crankshaft using a suitable piece of wood and a hammer. Be sure the carrier enters the crankshaft squarely.

b. Install a new seal into the seal carrier. Lubricate the seal with Quicksilver 2-4-C Marine Lubricant.

8

4B. 75-90 hp equipped with a lower crankshaft wear sleeve and all 100-115 hp:

  a. If removed, apply Loctite 271 to the inner diameter of the crankshaft wear sleeve (19, **Figure 85**).

CAUTION
The wear sleeve is easily distorted during installation. Be sure it is aligned squarely then tap it onto the crankshaft gently.

  b. Place the wear sleeve on the crankshaft squarely. Using a suitable piece of wood and hammer, tap the wear sleeve onto the crankshaft until seated. Remove any excess Loctite.

  c. Install a new O-ring (20, **Figure 85**) into the bottom of the wear sleeve. Lubricate the O-ring with Quicksilver 2-4-C Marine lubricant.

5. Each center main journal contains 2 seal rings. Install the seal rings and position the ring end gaps 180° apart.

6. Apply a thick coat of Quicksilver Needle Bearing Assembly Grease (part No. 92-42649A-1) to one crankshaft center main journal, then place the main bearing rollers around the journal. Each journal contains 28 bearing rollers on 50-60 hp models and 32 bearing rollers on 75-115 hp models. Install the bearing outer race halves around the bearing rollers. The holes in the bearing race must face the bottom of the crankshaft. Secure each race with a retaining ring. Make sure the retaining ring end gap is not aligned with the race split line.

7. Repeat Step 6 to install the remaining center main bearings.

8. Lubricate the top main bearing with light oil. Place a new O-ring around the bearing. With the hole in the bearing outer race facing the bottom of the crankshaft, slide the bearing onto the top of the crankshaft.

9. Place the bearing rollers for one piston/pin assembly on a clean piece of paper (29 rollers per piston). Liberally coat the bearing rollers with Quicksilver Needle Bearing Assembly Grease (part No. 92-42649A-1).

10. Install the sleeve portion of piston pin tool part No. 91-74607A-1 (75-115 hp) or 91-74607A-2 (50-60 hp) into the connecting rod piston pin bore. Center the sleeve in the bore.

11. Install the piston pin bearing rollers around the sleeve.

12. Position the locating washers on the connecting rod, then install the piston over the connecting rod. Make sure the match marks on the connecting rod and piston (made during disassembly) are aligned.

13. Insert the smaller diameter end of the piston pin tool through the piston pin bore in the piston and push out the sleeve portion of the tool.

14. Lubricate the piston pin with light oil. Place the pin on the small diameter end of the piston pin tool, then use a soft-face mallet to drive the piston pin into the piston while driving out the pin tool from the opposite side.

15. Fit a new "C" type lockring inside the installer end of the lockring tool (part No. 91-77109A-1) with needle nose pliers as shown in **Figure 135**.

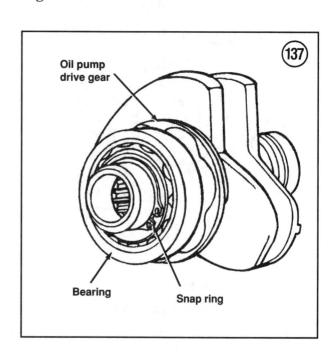

137

Oil pump drive gear

Bearing

Snap ring

NOTE
*On 50-60 hp models, the shaft of the lockring tool (part No. 91-77109A-1) must be modified to the dimension shown in **Figure 139**.*

16. Assemble the lockring tool and insert it into the piston pin bore (**Figure 136**). Hold the piston/rod assembly with one hand and press the installer handle downward. The tool will automatically install the lockring into the piston. Repeat the procedure to install the other lockring. Make certain the lockrings are securely seated in their grooves.

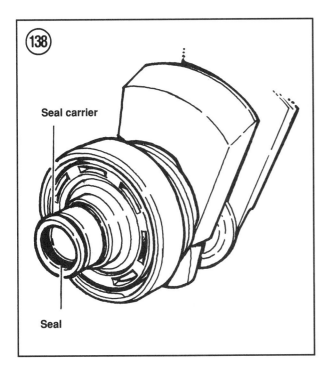

Seal carrier

Seal

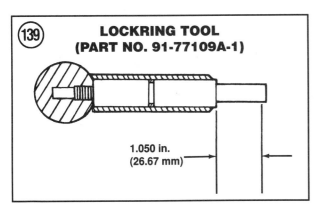

**LOCKRING TOOL
(PART NO. 91-77109A-1)**

1.050 in.
(26.67 mm)

17. Repeat Steps 9-16 to install each remaining piston to its respective connecting rod.

NOTE
The "T" mark on the piston rings must face piston crown when installed.

18. Install new piston rings onto the pistons using ring expander part No. 91-24697 (or equivalent). Install the bottom ring first. Expand the rings just enough to slip over the piston.

19. Make sure the piston rings rotate freely in the grooves. Align each ring end gap with the locating pin in the ring grooves.

20. Match each piston with the cylinder from which it was removed.

NOTE
The pistons can be installed into the cylinder block without the use of a piston ring compressor.

21. Install the pistons into their respective cylinder bores from the crankcase cover side of the block. Make sure the "UP" mark on the piston crown is facing the flywheel end of the cylinder block.

22. Insert a thin screwdriver through the exhaust port of each cylinder and depress each piston ring. If the ring does not spring back when the screwdriver is removed, it was probably broken during piston installation. Remove the piston and check ring condition. Replace any broken or damaged rings.

23. Apply a thick coat of Quicksilver Needle Bearing Assembly Grease to the bearing surface of each connecting rod. Install each connecting rod bearing cage and rollers.

24. Make sure all locating pins in the cylinder block are properly installed. If not, install new pins in the block.

25. Position all connecting rods toward one side of the cylinder block.

26. Carefully lower the crankshaft into place in the cylinder block. Gently push the crankshaft into place, rotating the main bearing races as

8

required to engage the bearing holes with the locating pins in the block.

27. Apply a thick coat of Quicksilver Needle Bearing Assembly Grease (part No. 92-42649A-1) to the crankpin journals.

28. Pull each connecting rod assembly into position on its respective crankpin journal, then install the remaining rod bearing cages and rollers on the correct crankpin.

29. Install each connecting rod cap on its respective connecting rod. Make sure the match marks on the rod and cap (made during disassembly) are aligned.

NOTE
The connecting rod and rod cap are both threaded on 75-115 hp models prior to serial No. D037620. The rod and cap must be properly aligned and held together tightly when installing the rod cap screws on these models. Be certain the rod and cap are still aligned and together tight after installing the screws.

30. Install the rod cap screws and tighten finger tight, then check rod-to-cap alignment. If alignment is acceptable, tighten the screws evenly to 15 in.-lb. (1.7 N·m) and recheck rod-to-cap alignment. If alignment is acceptable, proceed as follows:

 a. 50-60 hp with 1/4 in. screws—Tighten 1/4 in. screws to 180 in.-lb. (20 N·m). Recheck rod-to-cap alignment. If necessary, loosen the screws and realign the cap and rod.

 b. 50-60 hp with 5/16 in. screws—Tighten 5/16 in. screws to 27 ft.-lb. (37 N·m). Recheck rod-to-cap alignment. If necessary, loosen the screws and realign the rod and cap.

 c. 75-115 hp—Tighten the screws to 30 in.-lb. (40.7 N·m) and recheck rod-to-cap alignment. If alignment is acceptable, tighten the screws an additional 90° (after 30 ft.-lb. is obtained). Recheck rod-to-cap alignment. If necessary, loosen the screws and realign the rod and cap.

31. If perfect connecting rod-to-cap alignment can not be obtained, replace the rod assembly.

Crankshaft Assembly (V6 Models)

NOTE
Use Quicksilver Premium Blend or Premium Plus Blend 2-Cycle Outboard Oil whenever the procedure specifies lubrication with a light oil. A torque wrench is essential for proper fastener tightening. Do not use any grease inside the power head that is not gasoline soluble.

1. If removed, press the crankshaft lower ball bearing onto the crankshaft. Press only against the bearing inner race (from the numbered side). Be sure the bearing is fully seated, then install the bearing retaining ring using suitable snap ring pliers.

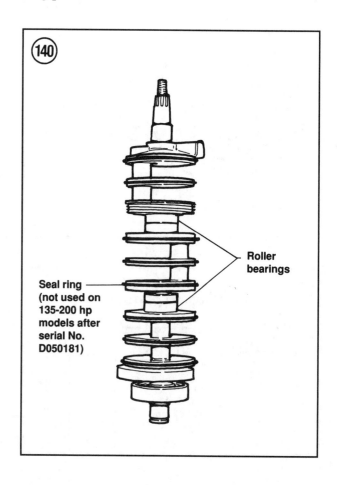

(140)

Roller bearings

Seal ring (not used on 135-200 hp models after serial No. D050181)

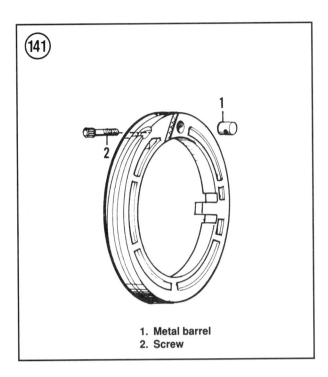

1. Metal barrel
2. Screw

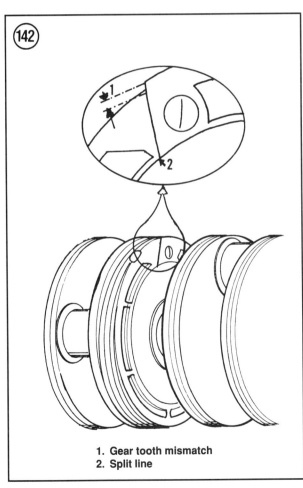

1. Gear tooth mismatch
2. Split line

NOTE
*On 135-200 hp models (serial No. D050182-on), the crankshaft seal ring previously located above the lower crankshaft roller bearing is no longer used. See **Figure 140**.*

2. If one or more crankshaft seal rings were removed, expand the new ring(s) just enough to fit around the crankpin journal. Then install the ring(s) into the crankshaft groove(s) using piston ring expander part No. 91-24697 (or equivalent).

3A. 135-200 hp—If the oil injection pump drive gear is removed from the crankshaft:

  a. Heat the new gear in hot water for about 4 minutes, then dry the gear.

  b. With the lip on the gear facing the top of the crankshaft, spread the gear at the split and install onto the crankshaft.

  c. Install the metal barrel into the gear center hole, aligning the barrel hole with the gear hole. See **Figure 141**.

  d. Apply Loctite 271 to the threads of the retaining screw. Install the screw and tighten to 8 in.-lb. (0.9 N•m). Gear split line must be drawn together tightly.

  e. Measure the gear tooth mismatch as shown in **Figure 142**. The mismatch must not exceed 0.030 in. (0.76 mm) or the gear will fail. If the mismatch is excessive, the gear lip is not fully seated in the crankshaft groove.

3B. 250-275 hp—Install the oil pump drive gear onto the crankshaft with the chamfer on the gear facing the lower crankshaft ball bearing.

4. Lubricate the center main roller bearings with light oil. Install the roller bearing and cage halves to their appropriate crankshaft main journal. Install the bearing outer races as follows:

  a. 135-200 hp—Install the bearing outer race halves with the larger of the 3 holes facing the drive shaft end of the crankshaft.

  b. 250-275 hp—Install the bearing outer race halves with the retaining ring grooves facing the drive shaft end of the crankshaft.

8

5. Install the center main bearing retaining rings. Be sure the retaining rings are fully seated in their grooves and that the ring end gap is not aligned with the bearing race split line.

6. 250-275 hp—Lubricate the crankshaft upper main bearing and seal with Quicksilver Needle Bearing Assembly Grease (part No. 92-42649A-1). Install a new O-ring around the main bearing carrier, then slide the bearing carrier assembly onto the top of the crankshaft.

NOTE
*This completes crankshaft assembly. The following steps will prepare the piston/connecting rod assemblies for installation during **Power Head Assembly.***

7. Place the piston/pin needle bearing rollers for one piston assembly on a clean piece of paper. Lubricate the bearing rollers liberally with Quicksilver Needle Bearing Assembly Grease (part No. 92-42649A-1). On 135-200 hp models, each connecting rod contains 29 piston pin bearing rollers. On 250 and 275 hp models, each connecting rod contains 34 piston pin bearing rollers.

8. Place the sleeve from the piston pin tool part No. 91-74607A-1 (135-200 hp) or 91-92973A-1 (250-275 hp) into the piston pin bore. Insert the piston pin bearing rollers around the sleeve.

9. Place the locating washers on the connecting rod (1 each side).

10. Carefully position the piston over the end of the connecting rod. Make sure the match marks (made during disassembly) on the piston and connecting rod are aligned. Make sure the locating washers remain in place.

11. Insert the piston pin tool part No. 91-74607A-1 (135-200 hp) or 91-92973A-1 (250-275 hp) into the piston pin bore and push out the sleeve.

12. Lubricate the piston pin with light oil. Place the pin on the piston pin tool. Using a soft-face mallet, drive the piston pin into the piston until the piston pin tool is pushed out of the piston. Center the pin inside the piston.

13. Fit a "C" type lockring inside the installer end of the lockring tool part No. 91-77109A-1 (135-200 hp) or part No. 91-93004A-1 (250-275 hp). Use needlenose pliers as shown in **Figure 135**.

14. Assemble the lockring tool and insert it into the piston pin bore (**Figure 136**, typical). Hold the piston assembly with one hand and press the installer handle quickly. The installer will automatically install the lockring into the groove in the piston. Install the other lockring in the other side of the piston. Be certain the lockrings are fully seated in their grooves.

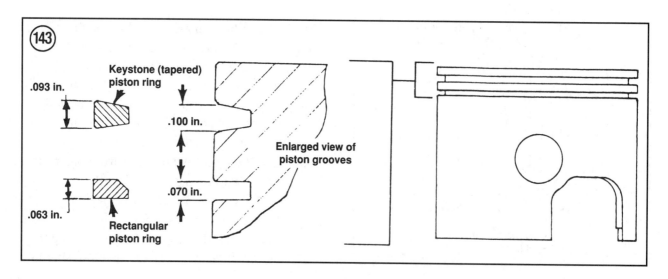

15. Repeat Steps 7-14 to install the remaining pistons to their respective connecting rods.

NOTE
On 121.9 and 207 cu. in. engines, the top piston ring is a keystone (tapered) design and the bottom ring is rectangular shape (Figure 143). On 142.2 cu. in. engines, both piston rings are keystone design (Figure 144). On 153 cu. in. engines, both piston rings are half keystone (tapered on top side) design.

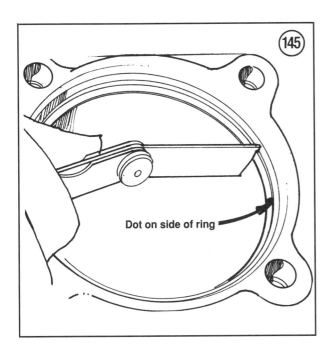

Dot on side of ring

16. Before installing the new piston rings on the pistons, insert each ring (one at a time) into its respective cylinder. Push the ring into the bore approximately 1/2 in. (12.7 mm) using the piston crown to ensure the ring is square with the bore. Measure the ring end gap using a feeler gauge as shown in **Figure 145**. Piston ring end gap should be 0.018-0.025 in. (0.46-0.63 mm) on 135-200 hp models and 0.012-0.024 in. (0.30-0.61 mm) on 250 and 275 hp models.

   a. If gap is excessive, try other new rings until one within specification is found.

   b. If gap is insufficient, carefully file the ring ends until the specified gap is obtained. Remove all rough edges or burrs after the filing process.

17. Install the rings that were checked in the No. 1 cylinder onto the No. 1 piston. Using ring expander part No. 91-24697 (or equivalent), install the bottom ring first, then the top. On 135-200 hp models, the side of the piston rings with the dot (**Figure 146**) must face toward the piston crown. On 250 and 275 hp models, install the rings with the sloped side of the ring ends facing toward the piston crown.

18. Repeat Step 17 to install each set of rings onto the piston corresponding to the cylinder in which they were checked.

8

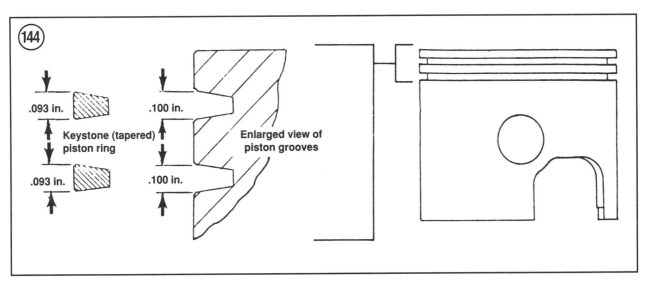

19. Make sure the rings rotate freely in their grooves. Align the end gap of each ring with the locating pin in the ring groove.

Power Head Assembly
(3 and 3.3 hp)

Refer to **Figure 18** for this procedure.

NOTE
Use Quicksilver Premium Blend or Premium Plus Blend 2-Cycle Outboard Oil whenever the procedure specifies lubrication with a light oil. A torque wrench is essential for proper fastener tightening. Do not use any grease inside the power head that is not gasoline soluble. Replace all gaskets and seals during reassembly.

1. Install the crankshaft bearing retainers into the cylinder block.
2. Lubricate the piston ring, piston and cylinder bore with light oil.
3. Make sure the piston ring end gap is properly aligned with the ring locating pin in the ring groove.
4. While maintaining the crankshaft in a horizontal position, push the piston into the cylinder bore. Carefully push the crankshaft assembly into position in the cylinder block. Rotate the crankshaft bearings so the locating pins are properly positioned in the notches in the block.
5. Insert a thin screwdriver blade into the exhaust port and depress the piston ring. If the ring fails to spring back when released, it probably was broken during installation. If necessary, remove the crankshaft and piston assembly and replace the ring if damaged or broken.
6. If removed, apply Loctite 242 to the threads of the reed valve screws. Install the reed valve, reed stop and attaching screws into the crankcase cover. Tighten the screws securely.
7. Using clean solvent, clean all oil from the cylinder block and crankcase cover mating surfaces.

8. Apply a continuous bead of Loctite Master Gasket Sealant (part No. 92-12564-1) to the mating surface of the cylinder block. Run the sealant bead along the inside of all bolt holes. Make sure the bead is continuous.
9. Install the crankcase cover into position on the cylinder block. Install the 6 crankcase cover screws and tighten to 50 in.-lb. (6 N.m).
10. Install the cylinder head with a new gasket. Tighten the cylinder head screws to 85 in.-lb. (10 N.m).
11. Install the lower end cap. Tighten the 2 screws to 50 in.-lb. (6 N.m).
12. Rotate the crankshaft several revolutions to check for binding or unusual noise. If binding or noise is noted, the power head must be disassembled and repaired before proceeding.

Power Head Assembly
(4 and 5 hp)

NOTE
Use Quicksilver Premium Blend or Premium Plus Blend 2-Cycle Outboard Oil whenever the procedure specifies lubrication with a light oil. A torque wrench is essential for proper fastener tightening. Do not use any grease inside the power head that is not gasoline soluble. Replace all gaskets and seals during reassembly.

1. If removed, install the locating pins in the cylinder block and crankcase cover.

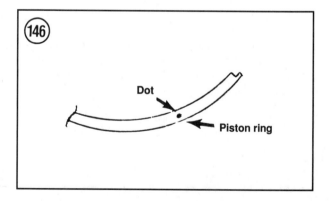

2. Lubricate the cylinder bore, piston and rings with light oil. Make sure the piston ring end gaps are aligned with the locating pins in the ring grooves. With the crankshaft positioned horizontally over the cylinder block, guide the piston into the cylinder bore. If necessary, squeeze the piston rings together to ease installation.

3. Align the crankshaft bearing locating pins in the cylinder block notches. With the larger diameter facing down, push the crankshaft locating washers into their grooves in the cylinder block.

4. Lubricate the new crankshaft seals with Quicksilver 2-4-C Marine Lubricant. Install the seals on each end of the crankshaft. The seal lip on both seals should face the center of the crankshaft.

5. Reach through the exhaust port with a small screwdriver and lightly depress each piston ring. The ring should spring back when released. If not, the ring was probably broken during installation. Remove the crankshaft and piston and replace the rings if broken or damaged.

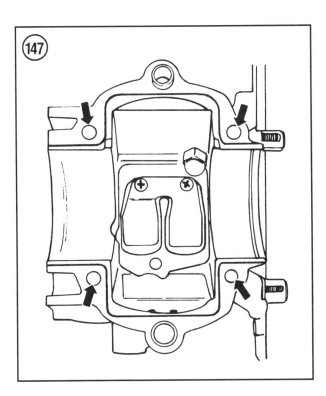

6. Rotate the crankshaft several revolutions and check for binding or unusual noise. If binding or noise is noted, the power head must be disassembled and repaired before proceeding with assembly.

7. If removed, apply Loctite 242 to the threads of the reed valve attaching screws. Install the reeds, reed stops and attaching screws. Tighten the screws to 9 in.-lb. (1.0 N•m).

8. Apply a continuous bead of Loctite Master Gasket Sealant (part No. 92-12564-1) to the mating surface of the crankcase cover. Make sure the sealant bead is run along the inside of the mounting screw holes (arrows, **Figure 147**).

9. Install the crankcase cover to the cylinder block. Install and tighten the 6 mounting screws in a crossing pattern to 91 in.-lb. (10.3 N•m).

10. Install the cylinder using a new gasket. Tighten the 5 cylinder head screws in a crossing pattern to 215 in.-lb. (24.3 N•m).

11. Lubricate the oil seal housing seal lips with Quicksilver 2-4-C Marine Lubricant. Install the seal housing, using a new gasket. Tighten the housing screws to 70 in.-lb. (8.0 N•m).

8

Power Head Assembly (8, 9.9 and 15 hp)

NOTE
Use Quicksilver Premium Blend or Premium Plus Blend 2-Cycle Outboard Oil whenever the procedure specifies lubrication with a light oil. A torque wrench is essential for proper fastener tightening. Do not use any grease inside the power head that is not gasoline soluble. Replace all gaskets and seals during reassembly.

Refer to **Figure 20** for this procedure.

1. Lubricate the cylinder bores, pistons and rings with light oil. Make sure the piston ring end gaps are properly aligned with the locating pins in the ring grooves.

2. With the crankshaft positioned horizontally over the cylinder block, guide the pistons into

the cylinders. Do not fully seat the crankshaft in the cylinder block at this time.

3A. 8 and 9.9 hp—Install one half of the center main bearing outer sleeve into the center block.

3B. 15 hp—Align the hole in the center main bearing outer race with the locating pin in the cylinder block.

4. Position the upper crankshaft bearing alignment pin into the notch in the cylinder block.

5. Seat the crankshaft assembly in the cylinder block. Push the crankshaft retaining ring (between lower bearing and seal) into its groove in the cylinder block. Carefully push inward on the crankshaft seals to ensure they are properly seated.

6. Insert a small screwdriver through the exhaust ports and lightly depress each piston ring. The ring should spring back when the pressure is released. If not, the ring was probably broken during installation. Remove the crankshaft and pistons and replace broken or damaged rings.

7. 8 and 9.9 hp—Install the other half of the center main bearing sleeve so it will align with the bearing sleeve in the block when the crankcase cover is installed.

8. Apply a continuous bead of Loctite Master Gasket Sealant (part No. 92-12564-1) on the mating surface of the crankcase cover. Run the bead along the inside of all mounting screw holes. See **Figure 148**.

9. Install the crankcase cover on the cylinder block. Tighten the 6 cover mounting screws to 200 in.-lb. (22.6 N•m) following the sequence shown in **Figure 149**.

10. Rotate the crankshaft several revolutions to check for binding or unusual noise. If binding or noise is noted, the power head must be disassembled and repaired before proceeding with reassembly.

11. Install a new rubber seal onto the reed block assembly. Pull the seal ends down into the holes at each end. Apply Quicksilver RTV sealant to the ends of the seal. Lubricate the remaining area

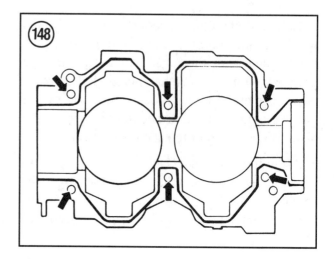

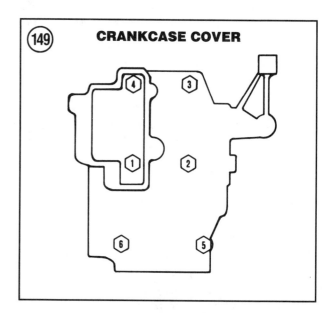

CRANKCASE COVER

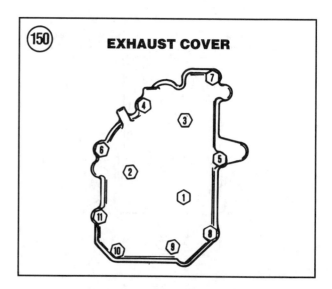

EXHAUST COVER

of the seal with Quicksilver Needle Bearing Assembly Grease.

12. Install the reed block assembly using a new gasket. Tighten the 3 mounting screws to 60 in.-lb. (6.8 N·m).

13. Install the intake cover with a new gasket. Tighten the mounting screws to 60 in.-lb. (6.8 N·m).

14. Sandwich the exhaust manifold between new gaskets. Fit the exhaust cover on top of the manifold and install the assembly on the power

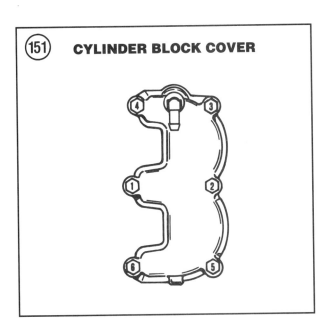

(151) **CYLINDER BLOCK COVER**

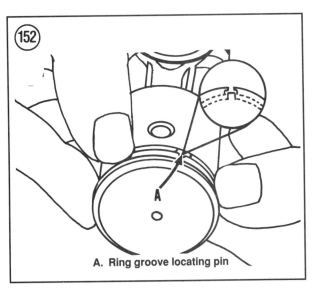

(152)

A. Ring groove locating pin

head. Install the 11 mounting screws and tighten to 60 in.-lb. (6.8 N·m) following the sequence shown in **Figure 150**.

15. Install the cylinder block cover with a new gasket. Tighten the 6 mounting screws to 60 in.-lb. (6.8 N·m) following the sequence shown in **Figure 151**.

**Power Head Assembly
(20 and 25 hp)**

Refer to **Figure 21** for this procedure.

NOTE
Use Quicksilver Premium Blend or Premium Plus Blend 2-Cycle Outboard Oil whenever the procedure specifies lubrication with a light oil. A torque wrench is essential for proper fastener tightening. Do not use any grease inside the power head that is not gasoline soluble. Replace all gaskets and seals during reassembly.

1. Lubricate the cylinder bores, pistons and piston rings with light oil. Make sure the piston ring end gaps are properly aligned with the locating pins in the grooves. See **Figure 152**.

2. With the crankshaft positioned horizontally above the cylinder block, guide the pistons into the cylinders.

3. Insert a thin screwdriver through the transfer and exhaust ports of each cylinder. Gently depress each piston ring with the screwdriver (**Figure 153**). The ring should spring back when the pressure is released. If not, the ring was probably broken during installation. Remove the crankshaft and pistons and replace any broken or damaged rings.

4. Carefully seat the crankshaft into the cylinder block. Rotate the center main bearing race until the hole in the race aligns with the locating pin in the block. Rotate each main roller bearing until its alignment boss engages with the notch in the block. Make sure the oil seals are flush with the outer edge of the block.

8

NOTE
The crankcase cover and cylinder block mating surfaces must be clean, dry and completely free of oil or other contamination before applying sealant in Step 5.

5. Clean the cylinder block and crankcase cover mating surfaces with Locquic Primer T and allow to air dry.

6. Apply a continuous 1/16 in. (1.6 mm) bead of Loctite Master Gasket Sealant (part No. 92-12564-1) to the crankcase cover as shown in **Figure 154**. Make sure the sealant bead is run along the inside of all mounting screw holes.

7. Install the crankcase cover to the cylinder block. Install the 6 crankcase cover screws and tighten evenly to 30 ft.-lb. (40.7 N.m) in the sequence shown in **Figure 155**.

8. Rotate the crankshaft several revolutions to check for binding or unusual noise. If binding or noise is noted, the power head must be disassembled and repaired before proceeding with reassembly.

9. Place a new rubber seal and gasket on the reed block assembly. Lubricate the rubber seal with Quicksilver 2-4-C Marine Lubricant.

10. Install the reed block assembly onto the power head. Install the carburetor adapter plate (with new gasket) onto the power head. Tighten the 3 mounting screws to 30 in.-lb. (3.4 N.m).

11. Install the exhaust manifold and exhaust cover using new gaskets. Apply Loctite 242 to the mounting screws and tighten to 80 in.-lb. (9.0 N.m).

12. Install the transfer port covers using new gaskets. Long edge of the deflector must face upward. Tighten the cover screws to 30 in.-lb. (6.8 N.m).

13. Install the cylinder block cover using a new gasket. Apply Loctite 242 to the threads of the cover mounting screws. Tighten the screws to 80 in.-lb. (9.0 N.m) following the sequence shown in **Figure 156**.

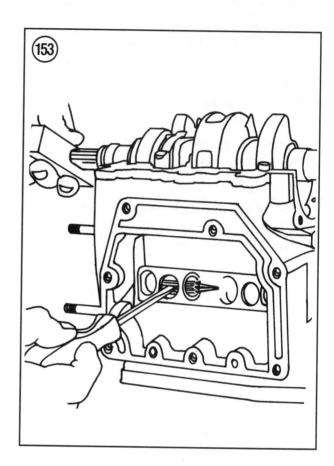

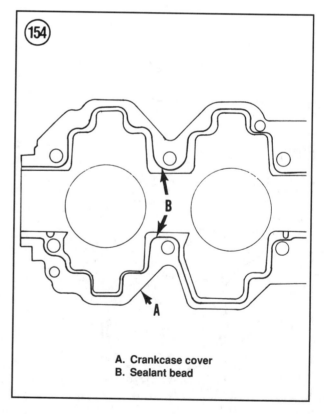

A. Crankcase cover
B. Sealant bead

**Power Head Assembly
(40 hp)**

> *NOTE*
> *Use Quicksilver Premium Blend or Premium Plus Blend 2-Cycle Outboard Oil whenever the procedure specifies lubrication with a light oil. A torque wrench is essential for proper fastener tightening. Do not use any grease inside the power head that is not gasoline soluble. Replace all gaskets and seals during reassembly.*

1. Place the crankshaft assembly on a power head stand clamped tightly in vise.

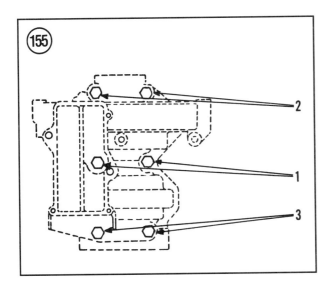

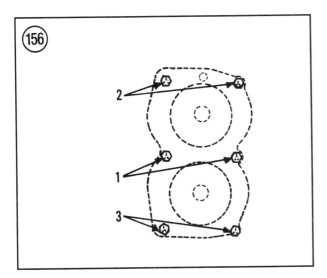

2. Lubricate the cylinder bores, pistons and rings with light oil.

> *NOTE*
> *Before tightening the piston ring compressors in the following steps, be sure that all piston ring end gaps are aligned with the locating pins in the ring grooves. Two piston ring compressor sets (part No. 91-31461A-2) are required to install the crankshaft assembly.*

3. Install the piston ring compressors as follows (**Figure 157**):

   a. Position the No. 1 piston straight away from the crankpin throw at the bottom of its stroke. Install a straight ring compressor.

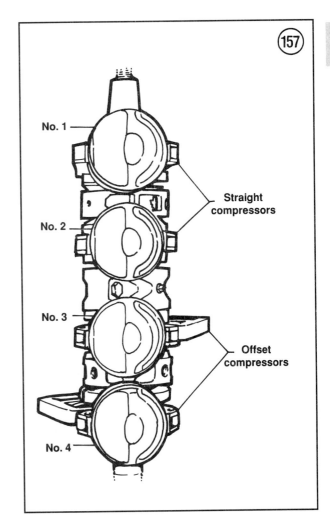

8

b. Position the No. 2 piston straight away from the crankpin throw at the top of its stroke. Install a straight ring compressor.

c. Position the No. 3 and No. 4 pistons in direct alignment with the No. 1 and No. 2 pistons. Install the offset ring compressors.

4. If removed, install the reed block locating pins into the cylinder block reed block bores.

5. With the crankshaft assembly positioned horizontally above the cylinder block, guide the pistons into their respective cylinders. See **Figure 158**. Remove the ring compressors as each piston enters its cylinder.

6. Rotate the center main bearing support and the reed blocks to align with the locating pins. Push downward on the reed blocks and center main bearing until the crankshaft assembly is fully seated in the cylinder block.

7. Insert a thin screwdriver through the exhaust ports and gently depress each piston ring. The ring should spring back when the pressure is released. If not, the ring was probably broken during installation. Remove the crankshaft and pistons and replace broken or damaged rings.

8. Install the oil pump drive gear key into its slot in the crankshaft. Install the drive gear with the chamfered side facing inward. Make sure the key slot in the gear properly aligns with the key.

9. Rotate the crankshaft several turns to check for binding or unusual noise. If binding or noise is noted, the power head must be disassembled and repaired before proceeding with reassembly.

10. Temporarily install the upper and lower end caps with their original shim packs. Install and securely tighten the end cap screws.

11. Using a soft-face mallet, tap the flywheel end of the crankshaft toward the bottom of the cylinder block.

12. Hold the crankshaft firmly against the lower end cap, then using a feeler gauge, measure the clearance between the inner race of the upper ball bearing and the thrust face of the crankshaft. This clearance (end play) should be within 0.008-0.012 in. (0.20-0.30 mm).

13. Add or subtract equally to the upper and lower shim packs to adjust the end play clearance. The thickness of the upper and lower shim packs should be equal to within 0.005 in. 0.13 mm) to ensure the crankshaft is centered in the cylinder block.

14. Loosen the upper and lower end cap screws. Slide the end caps away from the cylinder block to allow the crankcase cover to be installed.

NOTE
The crankcase cover and cylinder block mating surfaces must be clean, dry and

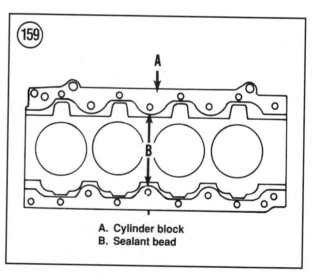

A. Cylinder block
B. Sealant bead

completely free of oil or other contamination before applying sealant.

15. Using Locquic Primer T or clean solvent, thoroughly clean the cylinder block and crankcase cover mating surfaces.

16. Apply a continuous 1/16 in. (1.6 mm) bead of Loctite Master Gasket Sealant (part No. 92-12564-1) on the cylinder block mating surface. Make sure the sealant bead is run along the inside of all mounting screw holes as shown in **Figure 159**.

17. Install the crankcase cover onto the cylinder block. Install the cover mounting screws and tighten to 210 in.-lb. (23.7 N•m) in the sequence shown in **Figure 160**.

18. Install the center main bearing support bolt (A, **Figure 160**) with a new locking tab washer. Install the reed block bolts (B, **Figure 160**) with

new locking tab washers. Note that reed block bolts are 5/8 in. (16 mm) long and center main bearing bolt is 1 in. (25.4 mm) long.

19. Tighten the center main bearing support bolt and reed block bolts to 75 in.-lb. (8.5 N•m). Bend the locking tab washer up against a flat on each bolt head.

20. Install the upper and lower end caps with their respective shim packs (determined in Steps 11-13). Tighten the end cap screws evenly, in a crossing pattern to 200 in.-lb. (22.6 N•m). After tightening the end cap screws, rotate the crankshaft several turns to ensure that the crankshaft turns freely.

21. Place a new gasket on each side of the exhaust divider plate. Install the divider plate and exhaust cover. Apply Loctite 271 to the threads of the cover screws, then install the screws and tighten to 200 in.-lb. (22.6 N•m) in the sequence shown in **Figure 161**.

8

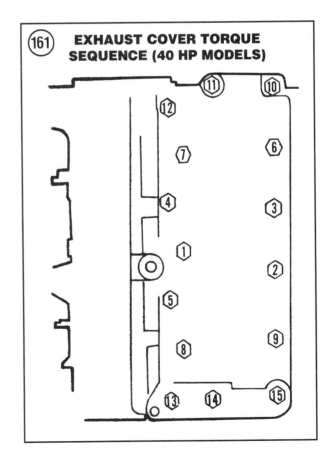

A. Center main bearing support mounting bolt
B. Reed block mounting bolts

22. Apply a suitable pipe sealant to the threads of the balance tube fittings. Install the fittings and balance tube.

23. Install the transfer port cover using new gaskets. Apply Loctite 242 to the threads of the cover screws, then install and tighten the screws to 65 in.-lb. (7.3 N·m).

24. Install the cylinder block cover using a new gasket. Apply Loctite 242 to the threads of the cover mounting screws. Install the screws and tighten to 100 in.-lb. (11.3 N·m), in 3 progressive steps, in the sequence shown in **Figure 162**.

25. Install the temperature sensor into the cylinder block cover next to the No. 1 spark plug hole.

26. Install the throttle/spark arm assembly and secure the assembly with the mounting bolt (**Figure 163**).

27. Install the throttle actuator assembly to the crankcase cover. Install and tighten the 3 mounting screws to 150 in.-lb. 17.0 N·m). See **Figure 164**.

28. Install the oil injection pump. See Chapter Eleven.

29. Install the carburetors, fuel pump and fuel enrichment valve as described in Chapter Six.

30. Install the starter motor as described in Chapter Seven.

31. Install the trigger plate, stator assembly and flywheel as described in Chapter Seven.

32. Install the rewind starter as described in Chapter Twelve.

Power Head Assembly
(50 and 60 hp Prior to Serial No. D000750)

NOTE
Use Quicksilver Premium Blend or Premium Plus Blend 2-Cycle Outboard Oil whenever the procedure specifies lubrication with a light oil. A torque wrench is essential for proper fastener tightening. Do not use any grease inside the power head that is not gasoline soluble. Replace all gaskets and seals during reassembly.

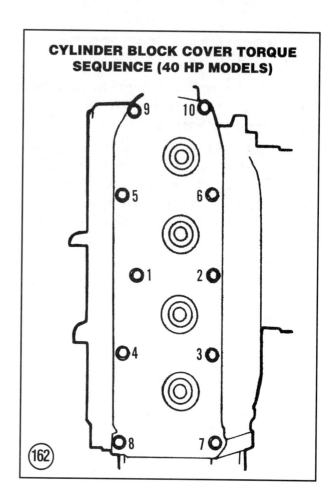

CYLINDER BLOCK COVER TORQUE
SEQUENCE (40 HP MODELS)

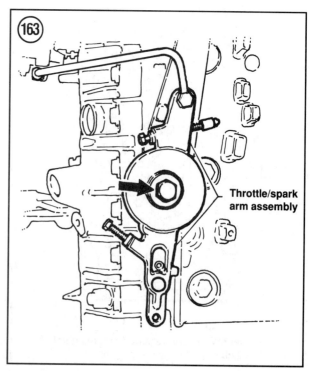

Throttle/spark
arm assembly

1. Place the crankshaft on a power head stand clamped tightly in a vise.

NOTE
Before tightening the ring compressors in Step 2 and Step 3, make sure that all piston ring end gaps are aligned with the locating pins in the ring grooves. See **Figure 165**.

2. Position the No. 1 and No. 2 pistons straight out from their crankpin throw and at the bottom (No. 1) and top (No. 2) of their stroke. Install a

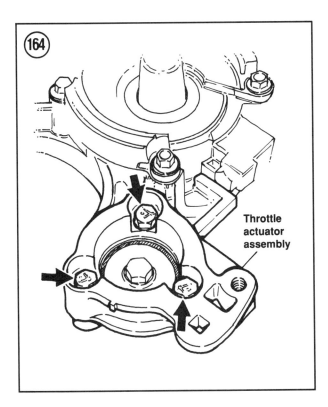

Throttle actuator assembly

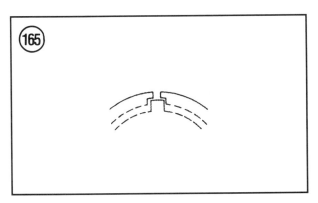

straight ring compressor on the No. 1 piston and an offset compressor on No. 2.

3. Position the No. 3 piston directly in line with the No. 1 and No 2. pistons. Install an offset ring compressor.

4. Install the reed block locating pins into the cylinder block.

5. Lubricate the cylinder bores, pistons and rings with light oil.

6. Position the crankshaft horizontally over the cylinder block and guide the pistons into their cylinders. Make sure the drive shaft end of the crankshaft is facing the power head mounting studs. Remove the ring compressors as the pistons enter their cylinders.

7. Align the holes in the reed blocks with the locating pins in the cylinder block. Push down on the reed blocks to seat the reed blocks and crankshaft into the cylinder block.

8. Insert a screwdriver through the exhaust or intake ports and depress each piston ring. The ring should spring back when the pressure is released. If not, the ring was probably broken during installation. Remove the crankshaft and pistons and replace broken or damaged rings.

9. Rotate the crankshaft several turns to check for binding or unusual noise. If binding or noise is noted, the power head must be disassembled and repaired before proceeding with reassembly.

10. Check crankshaft end play as follows:

    a. Install new O-rings on the upper and lower end caps. Lubricate the O-rings with light oil. Temporarily install the upper and lower end caps with their original shim(s) installed. See **Figure 166**.

    b. Without installing the crankcase cover, install and securely tighten the end cap screws.

    c. Using a soft-face mallet, tap the crankshaft toward the drive shaft end of the cylinder block.

    d. Hold the crankshaft firmly against the lower end cap and measure the clearance between the inner race of the upper ball

8

bearing and the crankshaft thrust face using a feeler gauge. The clearance (end play) should be 0.004-0.012 in. 0.10-0.30 mm).

   e. Add shims to increase end play or subtract shims to decrease end play. Upper and lower shim thickness should be equal to within 0.005 in. 0.13 mm) to ensure that crankshaft is centered inside the cylinder block.

11. Loosen the end cap screws and slide the end caps away from the block to provide clearance for crankcase cover installation.

12. Make sure the cylinder block and crankcase cover mating surfaces are clean, dry and free of oil or other contamination. If necessary, clean the mating surfaces with Locquic Primer or clean solvent.

13. Apply a continuous 1/16 in. (1.6 mm) bead of Loctite Master Gasket Sealant (part No. 92-12564-1) to the cylinder block mating surface. Make sure the sealant bead is continuous, but avoid excess application, especially near the bleed system holes. Lower the crankcase cover onto the cylinder block and install the attaching screws and lockwashers. Tighten the screws to 200 in.-lb. (22.6 N•m) following the sequence shown in **Figure 167**.

14. Install the thermostat and pressure relief valve.

15. Install the exhaust baffle using a new gasket, then install the exhaust cover using a new gasket. Tighten the exhaust cover screws to 200 in.-lb.

22.6 N•m) following the sequence shown in **Figure 168**.

16. Install the cylinder block cover using a new gasket. Tighten the screws to 70 in.-lb. (7.9 N•m) following the sequence shown in **Figure 169**.

17. Install the throttle actuator and linkage.

18. Install the ignition coils and switchbox. See Chapter Seven. Install the air box, carburetors, fuel filter and fuel pump. See Chapter Six.

19. Install the starter motor as described in Chapter Seven.

20. Install the trigger and stator assemblies. See Chapter Seven.

21. Connect the throttle lever linkage. Install the manual choke cable. Install the flywheel as described in Chapter Seven.

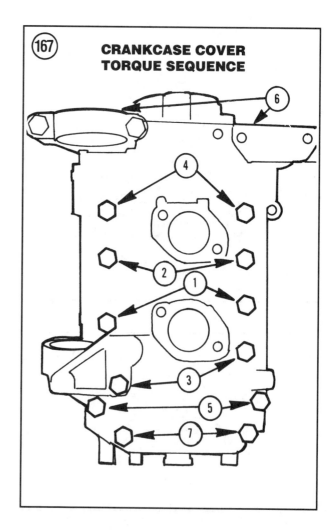

CRANKCASE COVER TORQUE SEQUENCE

Power Head Assembly
(50 and 60 hp [Serial No. D000750-on])

NOTE
Use Quicksilver Premium Blend or Premium Plus Blend 2-Cycle Outboard Oil whenever the procedure specifies lubrication with a light oil. A torque wrench is essential for proper fastener tightening. Do not use any grease inside the power head that is not gasoline soluble. Replace all gaskets and seals during reassembly.

1. Lubricate the upper crankshaft seal lip with light oil. Install the seal onto the crankshaft and seat it against the upper bearing. The seal lip should face toward the center of the engine.

NOTE
The crankcase cover and cylinder block mating surfaces must be clean, dry and free of oil or other contamination when applying sealant.

2. Clean the cylinder block and crankcase cover mating surfaces with Locquic Primer T. Allow the primer to air dry.

NOTE
When applying sealant in Step 3, make sure the bead extends up against each side of the center main bearings to prevent blow-by between cylinders.

3. Apply a continuous 1/16 in. (1.6 mm) bead of Loctite Master Gasket Sealant (part No. 92-12564-1) to the cylinder block mating surface.

8

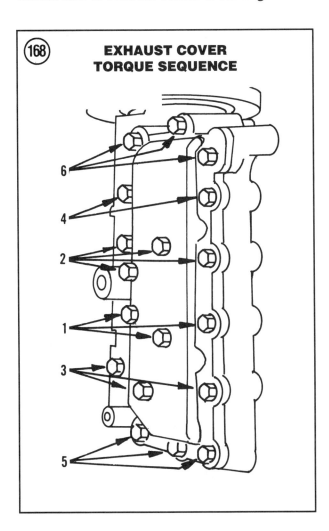

168 EXHAUST COVER
TORQUE SEQUENCE

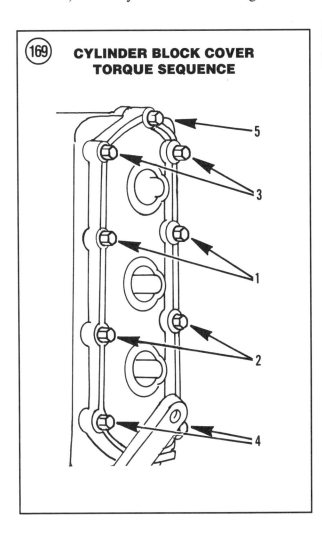

169 CYLINDER BLOCK COVER
TORQUE SEQUENCE

Run the sealant bead along the inside of all mounting screw holes and to each end of the cylinder block.

4. Install the crankcase cover and attaching screws. Lubricate the lower end cap seals and O-ring with light oil. Apply Quicksilver Perfect Seal to the end cap mating flange and install the end cap.

5. Tighten the crankcase cover screws to 18 ft.-lb. (24.4 N•m) in the sequence shown in **Figure 170**, then tighten the end cap screws evenly to 18 ft.-lb. (24.4 N•m).

6. Install the 2 check valve and holder assemblies into the crankcase cover.

7. Place new gaskets on each side of the reed block assembly. Place the intake manifold into position on the reed block, then install the manifold and reed block as an assembly. Install the manifold/reed block attaching screws and tighten to 18 ft.-lb. (24.4 N•m) in the sequence shown in **Figure 171**.

8. Install the thermostat, poppet valve and spring into the cylinder block. Install the thermostat cover using a new gasket. See **Figure 172**. Tighten the cover screws to 18 ft.-lb. (24.4 N•m).

9. Install the remote control cable anchor bracket and shift cable latch assembly.

10. Install the oil injection pump assembly. See Chapter Eleven.

11. Install the fuel pump and fuel enrichment valve. Install the carburetors and throttle linkage. See Chapter Six.

12. Install the starter motor and relay. See Chapter Seven.

13. Install the trigger coil and stator assembly, switchbox, ignition coils and flywheel. See Chapter Seven.

Power Head Assembly (75 and 90 hp)

NOTE
Use Quicksilver Premium Blend or Premium Plus Blend 2-Cycle Outboard Oil

whenever the procedure specifies lubrication with a light oil. A torque wrench is essential for proper fastener tightening. Do not use any grease inside the power head that is not gasoline soluble. Replace all gaskets and seals during reassembly.

1. Apply a coat of Quicksilver Perfect Seal on the lower crankcase end cap surface where the end cap and crankcase surfaces mate. Install the end cap and finger tighten the 2 end cap-to-cylinder block attaching screws.

NOTE
When applying sealant in Step 2, make sure the bead extends up against each side of the center main bearings to prevent blow-by between cylinders.

2. Apply a continuous 1/16 in. (1.6 mm) bead of Loctite Master Gasket Sealant (part No. 92-

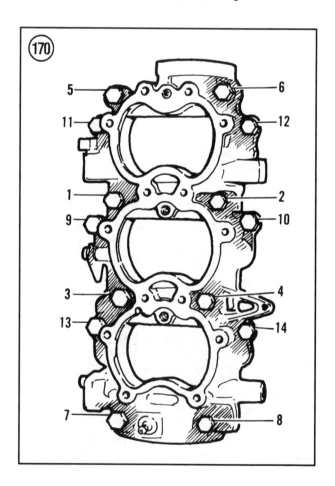

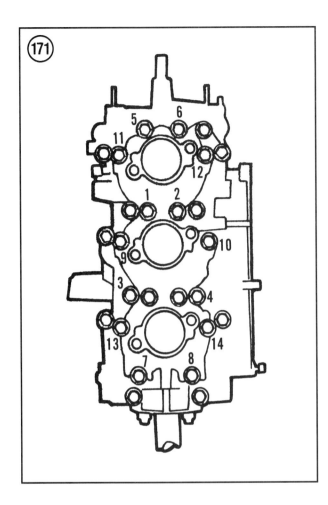

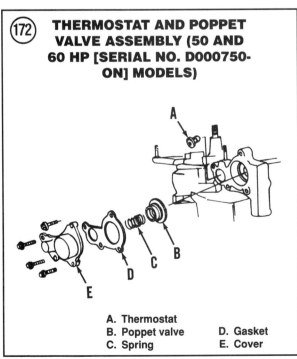

THERMOSTAT AND POPPET VALVE ASSEMBLY (50 AND 60 HP [SERIAL NO. D000750-ON] MODELS)

A. Thermostat
B. Poppet valve
C. Spring
D. Gasket
E. Cover

12564-1) to the cylinder block mating surface. Run the sealant bead along the inside of all mounting screw holes and to each end of the cylinder block. See **Figure 173**. Make sure the sealant bead extends to the edge of the center main bearings to prevent blow-by between cylinders.

3. Install the crankcase cover onto the cylinder block and install the attaching screws. Install the remaining crankcase end cap screw. Tighten the screws in the sequence shown in **Figure 174** as follows:

   a. Tighten the large screws (1-8, **Figure 174**) to 25 ft.-lb. (34 N·m).

   b. Tighten the small screws (1-12, **Figure 174**) to 220 in.-lb. (25 N·m).

   c. Tighten lower end cap screws to 220 in.-lb. (25 N·m).

4. Install the exhaust cover with divider plate and new gaskets. Tighten the cover fasteners to 220 in.-lb. (25 N·m) following the sequence shown in **Figure 175**.

5. Install the cylinder block cover with a new gasket. Finger tighten the cover fasteners.

6. Install the thermostat and poppet valve into the cylinder block cover.

7. Install thermostat housing and gasket. Finger tighten the cover fasteners.

8. Tighten the cylinder block cover fasteners to 220 in.-lb. (25 N·m) in the sequence shown in **Figure 176**.

8

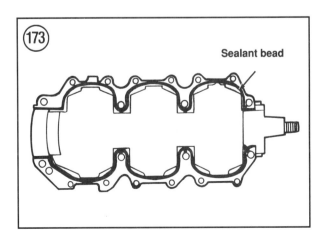

Sealant bead

9. Install the oil injection pump driven gear and pump. See Chapter Eleven.

10. Install the fuel pump assembly. See Chapter Six.

11. Install the starter motor and solenoid. Install the electrical components mounting plate, spark plug leads and temperature sensor.

12. Install the trigger plate and stator assembly. Install the flywheel. See Chapter Seven.

13. Install the reed block assemblies and intake manifolds using new gaskets. Tighten the fasteners to 220 in.-lb. (25 N.m).

Power Head Assembly
(100 and 115 hp)

NOTE
Use Quicksilver Premium Blend or Premium Plus Blend 2-Cycle Outboard Oil whenever the procedure specifies lubrication with a light oil. A torque wrench is essential for proper fastener tightening. Do not use any grease inside the power head that is not gasoline soluble. Replace all gaskets and seals during reassembly.

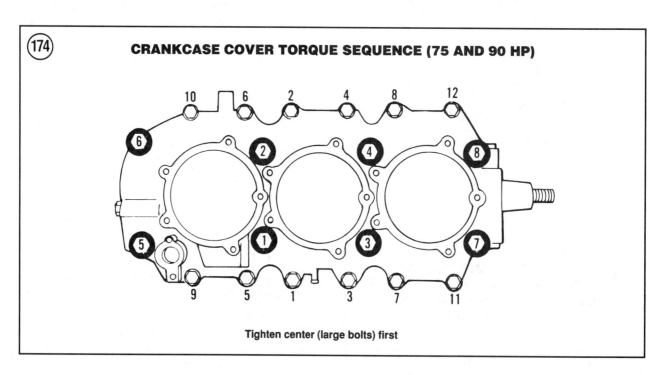

CRANKCASE COVER TORQUE SEQUENCE (75 AND 90 HP)

Tighten center (large bolts) first

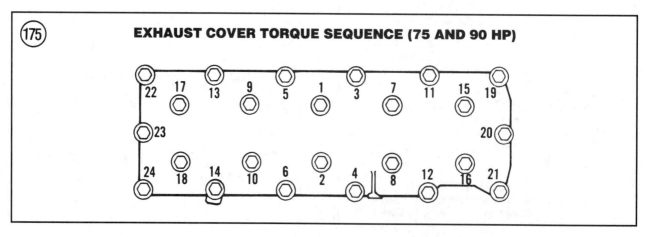

EXHAUST COVER TORQUE SEQUENCE (75 AND 90 HP)

1. Apply a coat of Quicksilver Perfect Seal on the lower crankcase end cap surface where the end cap and crankcase surfaces mate. Install the end cap and finger tighten the 2 end cap-to-cylinder block attaching screws.

NOTE
When applying sealant in Step 2, make sure the bead extends up against each side of the center main bearings to prevent blow-by between cylinders.

2. Apply a continuous 1/16 in. (1.6 mm) bead of Loctite Master Gasket Sealant (part No. 92-12564-1) to the cylinder block mating surface. Run the sealant bead along the inside of all mounting screw holes and to each end of the cylinder block. See **Figure 173**, typical. Make sure the sealant bead extends to the edge of the center main bearings to prevent blow-by between cylinders.

3. Install the crankcase cover onto the cylinder block and install the attaching screws. Install the remaining crankcase end cap screw. Tighten the screws in the sequence shown in **Figure 177** as follows:

  a. Tighten the large screws (1-8, **Figure 177**) to 25 ft.-lb. (34 N·m).

  b. Tighten the small screws (1-12, **Figure 177**) to 220 in.-lb. (25 N·m).

  c. Tighten lower end cap screws to 220 in.-lb. (25 N·m).

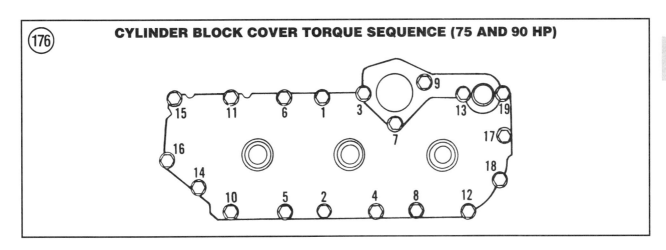

CYLINDER BLOCK COVER TORQUE SEQUENCE (75 AND 90 HP)

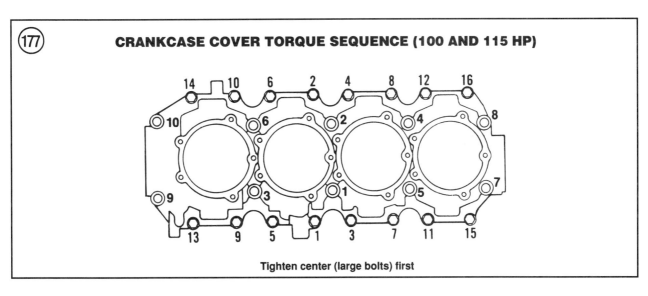

CRANKCASE COVER TORQUE SEQUENCE (100 AND 115 HP)

Tighten center (large bolts) first

4. Install the exhaust cover and divider plate using new gaskets. tighten the fasteners to 220 in.-lb. (25 N.m) following the sequence shown in **Figure 178**.

5. Install the cylinder block cover using a new gasket. Finger tighten the cover screws.

6. Install the thermostat and poppet valve assembly into the cylinder block.

7. Install the thermostat cover using a new gasket. Finger tighten the cover screws.

8. Tighten the cylinder block cover and thermostat cover screws to 220 in.-lb. (25 N.m) following the sequence shown in **Figure 179**.

9. Install the fuel pump assembly. See Chapter Six.

10. Install the oil injection pump driven gear and pump assembly. See Chapter Eleven.

NOTE
Some 100 and 115 hp models may have more than 1 gasket installed between the reed blocks and crankcase cover. However, when reassembling the power head on models so equipped, install only 1 gasket between the reed blocks and crankcase cover.

11. Install the reed blocks and intake manifolds using new gaskets. Tighten the fasteners to 220 in.-lb. (25 N.m).

12. If removed, install the accelerator pump check valves into the cylinder block (bottom cylinders). Install the accelerator pump. Tighten

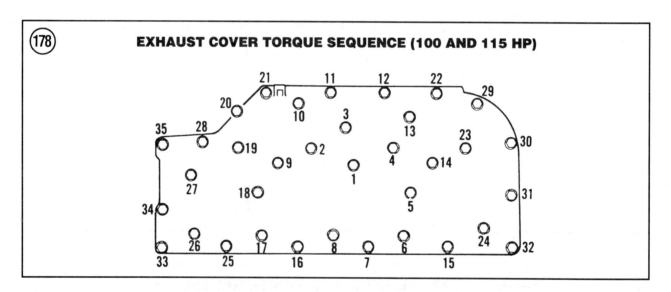

EXHAUST COVER TORQUE SEQUENCE (100 AND 115 HP)

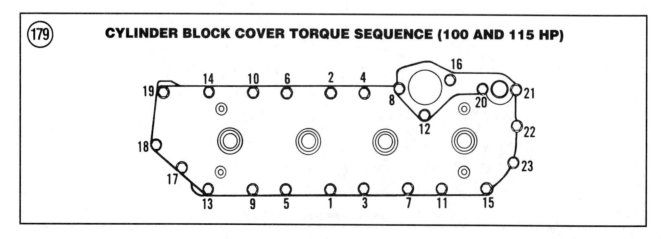

CYLINDER BLOCK COVER TORQUE SEQUENCE (100 AND 115 HP)

the pump mounting screws to 130 in.-lb. (14.7 N•m).

13. Install the bleed hoses between the upper and lower end caps.

14. Install the ignition plate assembly. Apply Loctite 242 to the threads of the low-oil warning module screws, then install the module and tighten the screws to 80 in.-lb. (9.0 N•m).

15. Install the trigger plate assembly. See Chapter Seven.

16. Install the stator assembly. See Chapter Seven.

17. Connect the fuel enrichment valve to the intake manifolds. Install the fuel enrichment valve to the power head.

18. Install the throttle/shift cable support bracket. Install new locking tab washers on each bracket mounting screw. Install and tighten the screws to 180 in.-lb. (20.3 N•m). Secure the screws by bending the locking tab washer against a flat area on the screw heads.

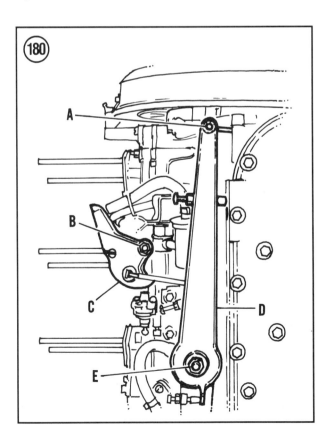

19. Install the throttle/spark arm assembly (D, **Figure 180**) and secure with the nut (E). Attach the trigger link arm (A, **Figure 180**) to the spark arm. Mount the throttle cam (C, **Figure 180**) on its stud and secure with a flat washer and self-locking nut (B).

20. Install the temperature sensor, sensor retainer and screw.

21. Install the starter motor. See Chapter Seven. Note that the battery ground cable (black) should be installed under the front lower starter mounting bolt.

22. Install the carburetors as described in Chapter Six.

23. Install the oil reservoir. See Chapter Eleven. Tighten the bottom aft oil reservoir bracket bolt to 180 in.-lb. (20.3 N•m).

24. Connect the oil pump control rod.

25. Install the attenuator plate and 8 mounting screws. Tighten the screws to 100 in.-lb. (11.3 N•m).

26. Install the 2 oil reservoir upper support bracket bolts. Install the bolts to 50 in.-lb. (5.6 N•m). Install the front lower oil reservoir mounting bolt. Tighten the bolt to 180 in.-lb. (20.3 N•m).

27. Install the attenuator cover and secure with 10 screws.

28. Install the lower cowl support bracket. Secure the bracket with 2 flat washers and screws. Tighten the screws to 150 in.-lb. (5.6 N•m).

29. Install the fuel hoses to the fuel pump and accelerator pump. Clamp the hoses with new Sta-straps.

30. Install the flywheel as described in Chapter Seven.

Power Head Assembly (135-200 hp)

NOTE
Use Quicksilver Premium Blend or Premium Plus Blend 2-Cycle Outboard Oil whenever the procedure specifies lubrication with a light oil. A torque wrench

is essential for proper fastener tightening. Do not use any grease inside the power head that is not gasoline soluble. Replace all gaskets and seals during reassembly.

When installing a new crankshaft into a previously-used cylinder block, inspect the crankshaft seal ring mating surfaces in the block and cover. If the old crankshaft sealing rings created wear grooves in the block and/or cover, the rings on the new crankshaft must fit into the grooves without binding the crankshaft, or the cylinder block/crankcase cover assembly must be replaced. To check for crankshaft binding, proceed as follows:

a. Check the seal ring grooves in the cylinder block and crankcase cover for burrs. Remove any burrs that are present.

b. Lubricate the crankshaft seal rings with light oil. Install the crankshaft into the cylinder block.

c. Temporarily install the upper and lower end caps and crankcase cover.

d. Rotate the crankshaft several turns while checking for binding or excessive drag. If drag is noted, recheck the seal ring grooves for burrs and remove any that are noted. If excessive drag is still evident, the seal rings are binding the crankshaft and the cylinder block/crankcase cover assembly should be replaced. Proceed as follows to assemble the power head.

1. Lubricate the crankshaft seal rings with light oil.

2. Make sure the 2 center main bearing locating pins in the cylinder block are properly installed. If not, install new locating pins into the center main bearing bores in the cylinder block.

3. Align the crankshaft seal rings so their gaps will face upward when the crankshaft is placed into the block.

4. Position the center main bearing races so the locating holes in the bearing outer races are aligned with the locating pins in the cylinder block.

5. Carefully lower the crankshaft into place in the cylinder block (**Figure 181**). Rotate the center main bearing outer races as necessary to align the cylinder block locating pins with the holes in the center main bearings. Push downward on the crankshaft until properly seated in the block.

6. Lubricate the oil seal areas on the crankshaft upper and lower end with light oil.

7. Install the upper and lower end caps (**Figure 182**, typical). Install and finger tighten the end cap-to-cylinder block screws.

8. Lubricate the pistons, rings and cylinder bores using light oil.

9. Match each piston with the cylinder from which it was removed. Position the pistons as shown in **Figure 183**: Pistons marked "P" must be installed into the port cylinder bank; pistons marked "S" must be installed into the starboard

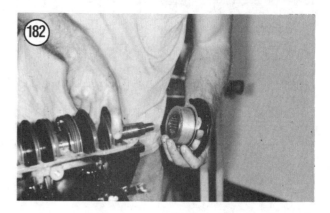

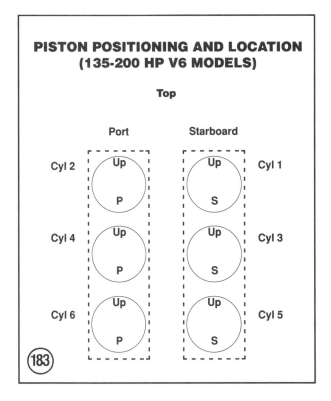

PISTON POSITIONING AND LOCATION (135-200 HP V6 MODELS)

Top

Port	Starboard
Cyl 2 — Up / P	Up / S — Cyl 1
Cyl 4 — Up / P	Up / S — Cyl 3
Cyl 6 — Up / P	Up / S — Cyl 5

(183)

(184)

(185)

cylinder bank; the "UP" mark must face the flywheel end of the power head.

10. Rotate each piston ring so the end gaps are properly aligned with the ring locating pins in the ring grooves.

11. Install a suitable piston ring compressor on one piston, making sure the ring groove locating pins are centered between the ring end gaps as the compressor is tightened.

12. If installed on the connecting rod, remove the rod cap and discard the rod cap screws.

13. Position the piston/connecting rod assembly as shown in **Figure 183** and fit it into the proper cylinder (**Figure 184**). Push the piston into the cylinder bore.

14. Coat the bearing surface of the connecting rod with Quicksilver Needle Bearing Assembly Grease (part No. 92-42649A-1). Install the rod bearing cage and rollers into the connecting rod, then bring the rod up to the crankshaft journal.

15. Coat the rod cap bearing surface with Quicksilver Needle Bearing Assembly Grease (part No. 92-42649A-1), then install the remaining rod bearing cage and rollers. Install the connecting rod cap, making sure the rod and cap match marks are aligned. See **Figure 185**.

16A. Prior to serial No. D082000:

    a. Clean the new connecting rod cap screws with Locquic Primer T (part No. 92-59327-1), then dry with compressed air.

    b. Apply Loctite 271 to the threads of the new rod cap screws. Install the screws finger-tight, then check connecting rod-to-cap alignment. See **Figure 186**.

    c. If alignment is acceptable, tighten the rod cap screws in 3 progressive steps to a final torque of 30 ft.-lb. (40.7 N•m).

16B. Serial No. D082000-on:

    a. Apply light oil to the threads of the new rod cap screws.

    b. Install the rod cap screws finger-tight, then check connecting rod-to-cap alignment.

    c. If alignment is acceptable, tighten the rod cap screws evenly to 15 ft.-lb. (20.3 N•m),

8

then to 30 ft.-lb. (40.7 N•m). After tightening to 30 ft.-lb. (40.7 N•m), tighten the screws an additional 90°.

17. Recheck rod and cap alignment (**Figure 186**). If necessary, loosen the rod cap screws and realign the cap. If perfect alignment can not be obtained, the rod and cap assembly must be replaced.

18. Repeat Steps 10-17 to install each remaining piston assembly.

19. Rotate the crankshaft several turns to check for binding or unusual noise. If binding or noise is noted, the power head must be disassembled and repaired before proceeding with reassembly.

20. Insert a thin screwdriver through the exhaust ports and gently depress each piston ring. The ring should spring back when the pressure is released. If not, the ring was probably broken during installation. Remove the piston and replace any broken or damaged rings.

NOTE
The cylinder block and crankcase cover mating surfaces must be clean, dry and free of oil or other contamination before applying sealant.

21. Clean the cylinder block and crankcase cover mating surfaces using Locquic Primer T, lacquer thinner or acetone. Do not use solvents with an oil or petroleum base.

22. Install new gasket strips into the crankcase cover grooves, then trim each end of the gasket strip flush with the ends of the cover.

23. Apply a thin even coat of Permatex #2 Form-a-Gasket (part No. 92-72592) to the cylinder block mating surface. Make sure the entire surface is coated.

24. Place the crankcase cover onto the cylinder block and install the 3/8 in. diameter (inner) crankcase cover screws. Following the tightening sequence shown in **Figure 187**, tighten the inner screws a few turns at a time to compress the crankshaft seal rings slowly and draw the

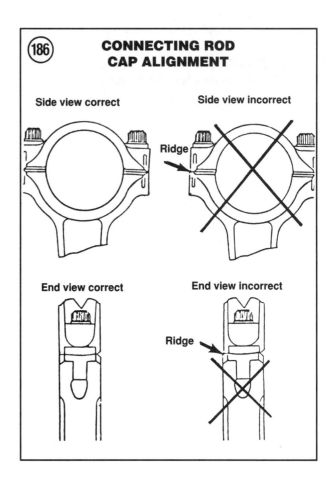

(186)   CONNECTING ROD CAP ALIGNMENT

Side view correct

Side view incorrect

Ridge

End view correct

End view incorrect

Ridge

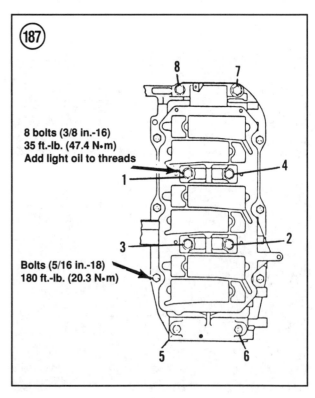

(187)

8

7

8 bolts (3/8 in.-16)
35 ft.-lb. (47.4 N•m)
Add light oil to threads

1

4

3

2

Bolts (5/16 in.-18)
180 ft.-lb. (20.3 N•m)

5

6

cover down to the block. Once the cover is tight against the block, tighten the screws to 35 ft.-lb. (47.4 N•m) in 3 progressive steps, following the sequence shown in **Figure 187**.

25. Install the 5/16 in. diameter (outer) crankcase cover screws and tighten to 180 in.-lb. (20.3 N•m) following the sequence shown in **Figure 187**.

26. Install the remaining end cap screws. Tighten the upper end cap screws to 150 in.-lb. (16.9 N•m) and the lower end cap screws to 80 in.-lb. (9.0 N•m).

27. Wipe off any excess sealant from the block/cover split line.

28. Rotate the crankshaft several turns to check for binding or unusual noise. If binding or noise is noted, the power head must be disassembled and repaired before proceeding with reassembly.

29. Install and connect the bleed hoses. See **Figure 188** (carbureted models) or **Figure 189** (EFI models).

30. Install a new gasket on the intake manifold assembly, then install reed blocks onto the manifold. See **Figure 190**. Finger tighten the reed block mounting screws.

31. Install the intake manifold onto the crankcase cover. Tighten the manifold mounting screws to 105 in.-lb. (11.9 N•m).

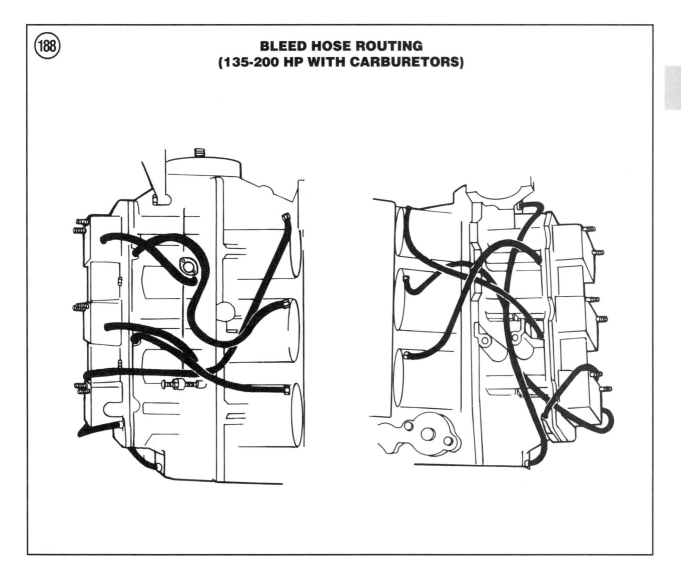

(188)

BLEED HOSE ROUTING
(135-200 HP WITH CARBURETORS)

8

32. Tighten the reed block mounting screws to 80 in.-lb. (9.0 N•m).

33. Assemble and install the exhaust cover components as follows:

a. Install the divider seal (3, **Figure 191**) into the slot in the cylinder block (between exhaust ports).

b. Position a new gasket on each side of the exhaust divider plate (2, **Figure 191**). Align all holes, then position divider plate and gaskets onto the cylinder block.

c. Place the exhaust cover (4, **Figure 191**) onto the divider plate.

d. Apply Loctite 271 to the threads of the exhaust cover attaching screws. Install and tighten the screws to 200 in.-lb. (22.6 N•m)

following the sequence shown in **Figure 192**.

34. Install the cooling system pressure relief valve as shown in **Figure 193**.

NOTE
The cylinder head screws must be retightened to specification after engine has been run 1/2 to 1 hour. Loosen each head screw 1/4 turn, then retighten to specification in the sequence shown in **Figure 194.**

35. Install the cylinder heads using new gaskets. The thermostat opening in each head should be up. Apply light oil to the threads of the head screws and tighten to 40 ft.-lb. (54.2 N•m) in the sequence shown in **Figure 194**.

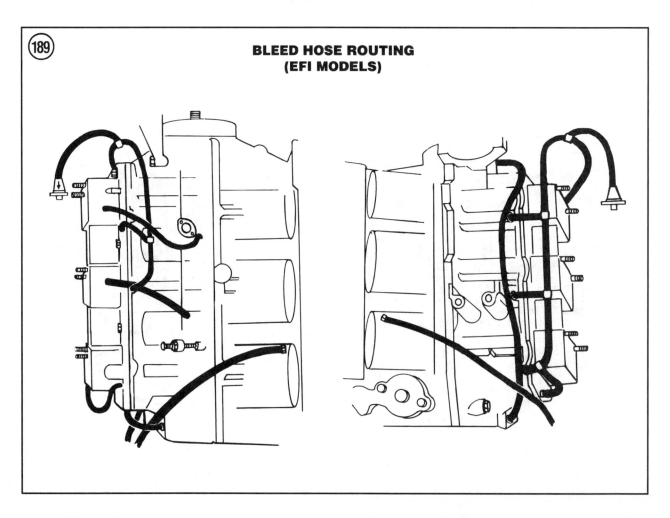

(189)

**BLEED HOSE ROUTING
(EFI MODELS)**

36. Install the thermostat assembly into each cylinder head. Install the thermostat covers using new gaskets. See **Figure 195**.

37. Install temperature sensor (**Figure 195**) into the starboard cylinder head, under the No. 1 spark plug hole.

38. EFI models—Install the fuel injection induction manifold assembly. See Chapter Six.

39. Install the oil injection pump, engine mounted oil reservoir and injection warning module. See Chapter Eleven.

40. Install the remote control cable anchor bracket and shift cable latch assembly.

41. Install the carburetor linkage and fuel pump. See Chapter Six.

42. Install the air silencer. Install the idle stabilizer or low speed-high speed spark advance module onto the top of the air silencer.

43. Install the starter motor, starter solenoid, switchboxes, ignition coils, voltage regulator/rectifier, trigger plate and stator assembly. See Chapter Seven.

44. Install the flywheel (Chapter Seven).

45. Connect all electrical and ignition wire connections on the power head. Install the electrical and ignition components mounting plate to the power head. Refer to the diagrams or instant pictures made during disassembly.

Power Head Assembly
(250 and 275 hp)

NOTE
Use Quicksilver Premium Blend or Premium Plus Blend 2-Cycle Outboard Oil whenever the procedure specifies lubrication with a light oil. A torque wrench is essential for proper fastener tighten-

8

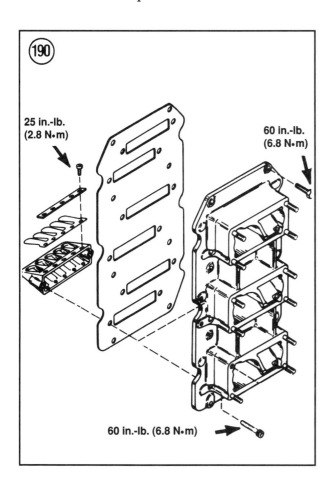

25 in.-lb.
(2.8 N•m)

60 in.-lb.
(6.8 N•m)

60 in.-lb. (6.8 N•m)

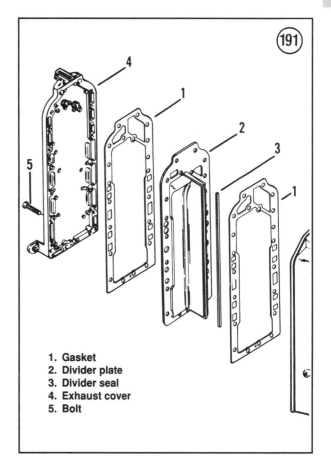

1. Gasket
2. Divider plate
3. Divider seal
4. Exhaust cover
5. Bolt

ing. Do not use any grease inside the power head that is not gasoline soluble. Replace all gaskets and seals during reassembly.

1. Lubricate the crankshaft seal rings with light oil.

2. Make sure the 2 center main bearing locating pins in the cylinder block are properly installed. If not, install new locating pins into the block center main bearing bores.

3. Align the crankshaft seal rings so their end gaps will face upward when the crankshaft is placed into the block.

4. Position the center main bearing races so the locating holes in the outer races are aligned with the locating pins in the cylinder block.

5. Carefully lower the crankshaft into place in the cylinder block (**Figure 181**). Rotate the center main bearing outer races as necessary to align the cylinder block locating pins with the holes in the bearings. Push downward on the crankshaft until properly seated in the block.

6. Lubricate the oil seal areas on the crankshaft upper and lower ends with light oil.

7. Install the oil pump drive gear onto the crankshaft lower end. Position the gear with the chamfered side facing the crankshaft ball bearing.

8. Apply Quicksilver Perfect Seal (part No. 92-34227-1) to the mating flange of the lower end cap, then install the end cap. Install the 2 end cap-to-cylinder block screws finger tight. Do not tighten at this time.

9. Lubricate the cylinder bores, pistons and rings with light oil.

10. Position the piston rings on one piston so the end gaps are aligned with the locating pins in the ring grooves.

11. If the rod cap is installed on the connecting rod, remove the cap and discard the rod cap screws.

12. Install a suitable piston ring compressor on the piston. Make sure the locating pins are cen-

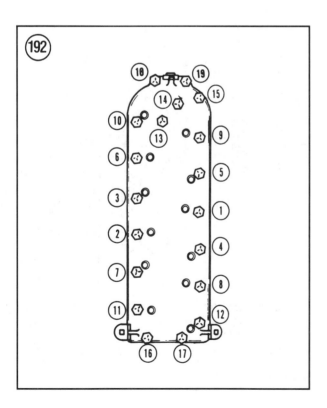

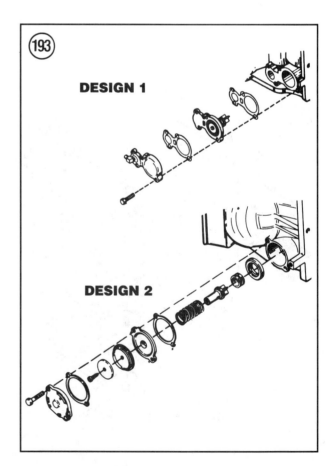

tered in the ring end gaps as the compressor is tightened.

13. Position the piston/connecting rod assembly into the cylinder from which it was removed. Pistons marked "P" on the crown must be installed into the port side cylinder bank; pistons marked "S" must be installed into the starboard cylinder bank; the "P" or "S" mark must face the flywheel end of the power head. See **Figure 196**.

14. Push on the piston crown until the piston slides into the cylinder and the ring compressor is pushed off the piston.

15. Coat the crankpin bearing surface of the connecting rod with Quicksilver Needle Bearing Assembly Grease (part No. 92-42649A-1), then install the appropriate bearing rollers and cage into the rod. Pull the rod up against the crankpin.

16. Coat the bearing surface of the connecting rod cap with Quicksilver Needle Bearing Assembly Grease (part No. 92-42649A-1), then install the appropriate bearing rollers and cage. Install the rod cap (**Figure 185**) making sure the rod and cap match marks are aligned. See **Figure 186**.

17. Clean new rod cap screws with Locquic Primer T and dry with compressed air. Apply Loctite 271 to the threads of the rod screws. Install the screws finger tight, then check the rod-to-cap alignment as shown in **Figure 186**. Loosen the screws and realign the rod and cap if necessary.

8

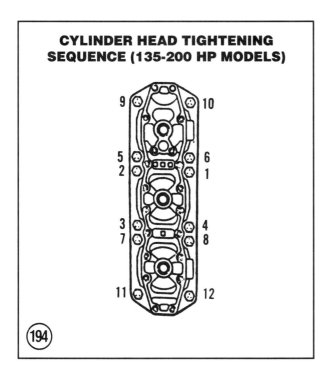

CYLINDER HEAD TIGHTENING SEQUENCE (135-200 HP MODELS)

194

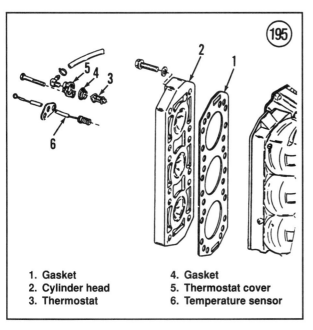

195

1. Gasket
2. Cylinder head
3. Thermostat
4. Gasket
5. Thermostat cover
6. Temperature sensor

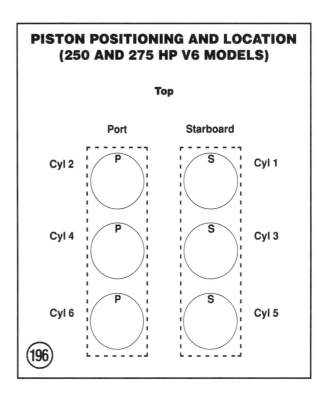

PISTON POSITIONING AND LOCATION (250 AND 275 HP V6 MODELS)

Top

Port   Starboard

Cyl 2   P   S   Cyl 1

Cyl 4   P   S   Cyl 3

Cyl 6   P   S   Cyl 5

196

18. If rod and cap alignment is acceptable, continue tightening the rod cap screws, equally in 3 progressive steps, to 360 in.-lb. (40.7 N·m). After the specified torque is obtained, tighten each rod cap screw an additional 1/4 turn.

19. Recheck rod-to-cap alignment (**Figure 186**). If necessary, loosen the rod cap screws and re-align. If perfect alignment cannot be obtained, the rod and cap assembly should be replaced.

20. Repeat Steps 10-19 to install the remaining piston/connecting rod assemblies.

21. Rotate the crankshaft several turns to check for binding or unusual noise. If binding or noise is noted, the power head must be disassembled and repaired before proceeding with reassembly.

NOTE
The cylinder block and crankcase cover mating surfaces must be clean, dry and

free of oil or other contamination before applying sealant.

22. Thoroughly clean the cylinder block and crankcase cover mating surfaces with Locquic Primer T, lacquer thinner or acetone. Do not use oil or petroleum base solvent.

23. Install the gasket strips into the crankcase cover grooves. Trim each gasket strip flush with the edges of the cover.

24. Apply a thin even coat of Permatex #2 Form-a-Gasket (part No. 92-72592) to the cylinder block mating surface. Make sure the entire surface is coated, but avoid excess application.

25. Install the crankcase cover onto the cylinder block. Lubricate the crankcase cover mounting screws with light oil, then install the screws.

26. Tighten screws (1-4, **Figure 197**) first, in 3 progressive steps, to 30 ft.-lb. (40.7 N·m) following sequence shown. Then tighten screws (5-14),

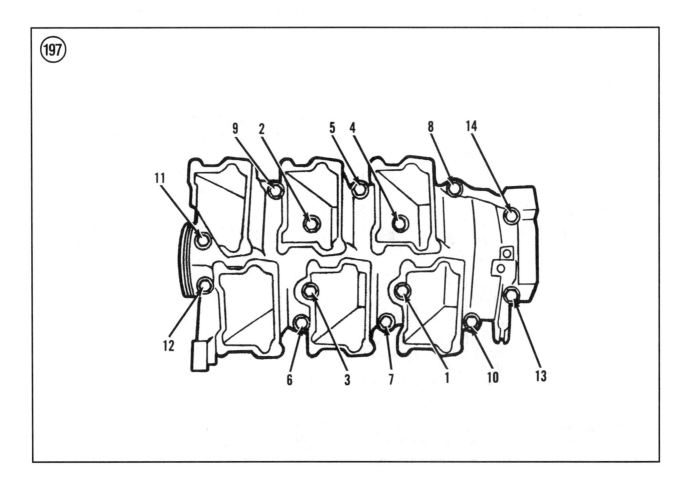

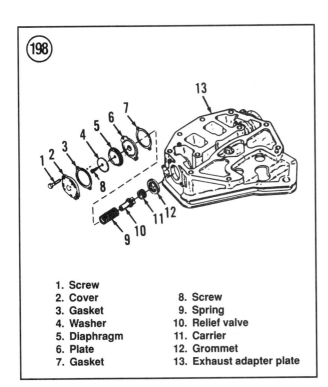

(198)

1. Screw
2. Cover
3. Gasket
4. Washer
5. Diaphragm
6. Plate
7. Gasket
8. Screw
9. Spring
10. Relief valve
11. Carrier
12. Grommet
13. Exhaust adapter plate

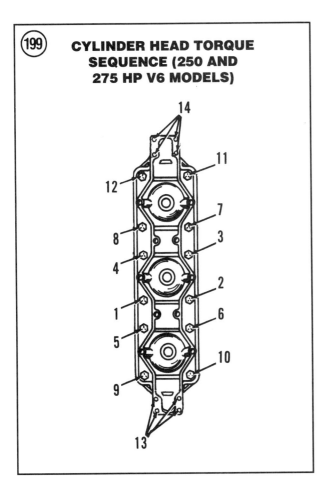

(199)

CYLINDER HEAD TORQUE SEQUENCE (250 AND 275 HP V6 MODELS)

in 3 steps, to 30 ft.-lb. (40.7 N.m) following the sequence shown.

27. Rotate the crankshaft to check for binding or excessive drag. If binding or drag is noted, remove the crankcase cover and check the crankshaft seal rings for correct alignment. Repair as necessary before reassembling the power head.

28. Remove the 2 end cap screws installed finger tight in Step 8. Clean all end cap screws with Locquic Primer T and dry with compressed air. Apply Loctite 271 to the threads of the screws. Install and tighten the screws to 150 in.-lb. (16.9 N.m).

29. If removed, install the water pressure relief valve assembly into the exhaust adapter plate using new gaskets. See **Figure 198**. Tighten screw (8) to 40 in.-lb. (4.5 N.m). Clean the screws (1) with Locquic Primer T and dry with compressed air. Apply Loctite 271 to the threads of the screws (1) and tighten to 150 in.-lb. (16.9 N.m).

30. Install the exhaust adapter plate to the power head using a new gasket. Install the lockwashers and nuts and tighten to 30 ft.-lb. (40.7 N.m).

31. Install new cylinder head O-ring seals into the grooves in the cylinder heads. The O-ring seals may be held in place with Quicksilver Needle Bearing Assembly Grease.

32. Lubricate the threads of the cylinder head screws with light oil.

33. Install the cylinder heads to the cylinder block. Make sure the O-ring seals remain in position when installing the heads.

34. Install and tighten the cylinder head screws in 3 progressive steps, to 180 in.-lb. (20.3 N.m) following the sequence shown in **Figure 199**.

35. Install the thermostats using new gaskets. Clean the thermostat housing screws with Locquic Primer T. Apply Loctite 242 to the threads of the screws and tighten securely.

36. Install the exhaust cover using a new gasket. Clean the exhaust cover attaching screws with Locquic Primer T. Apply Loctite 271 to the threads of the screws. Starting with the center

8

screws, tighten the screws in a crossing pattern to 150 in.-lb. (16.9 N·m).

37. Install the oil injection pump as described in Chapter Eleven.

38. Clean the reed block attaching screws (4, **Figure 200**) with Locquic Primer T, then apply Loctite 242 to the threads. Apply a light coat of GE Silicone Sealer to the reed block gaskets (2), then attach the reed blocks (1) to the reed block adapters (3). Tighten the attaching screws to 60 in.-lb. (6.8 N·m). Allow the sealer to cure for 24 hours before starting the engine.

39. Clean the carburetor adapter plate-to-reed block adapter plate screws with Locquic Primer T, then apply Loctite 242 to the threads. Attach the reed block and adapter assembly to the carburetor adapter plate using a new gasket. Tighten the screws to 60 in.-lb. (6.8 N·m).

40. Repeat Steps 38 and Step 39 to assemble the remaining reed block and carburetor adapter plate assemblies.

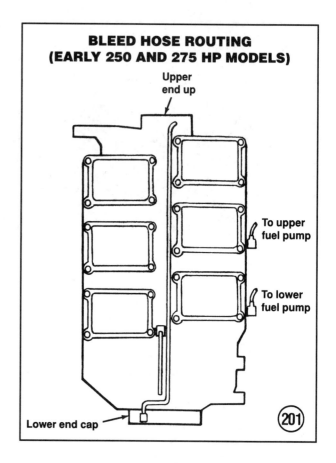

BLEED HOSE ROUTING (EARLY 250 AND 275 HP MODELS)

Upper end up

To upper fuel pump

To lower fuel pump

Lower end cap

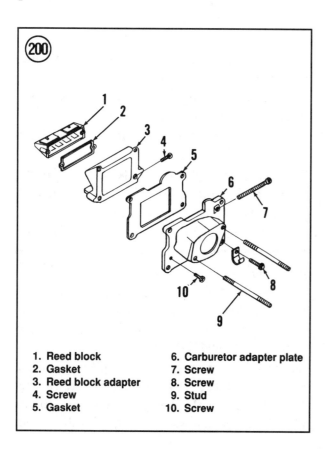

1. Reed block
2. Gasket
3. Reed block adapter
4. Screw
5. Gasket
6. Carburetor adapter plate
7. Screw
8. Screw
9. Stud
10. Screw

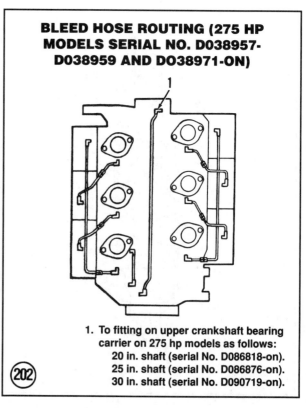

BLEED HOSE ROUTING (275 HP MODELS SERIAL NO. D038957-D038959 AND DO38971-ON)

1. To fitting on upper crankshaft bearing carrier on 275 hp models as follows:
    20 in. shaft (serial No. D086818-on).
    25 in. shaft (serial No. D086876-on).
    30 in. shaft (serial No. D090719-on).

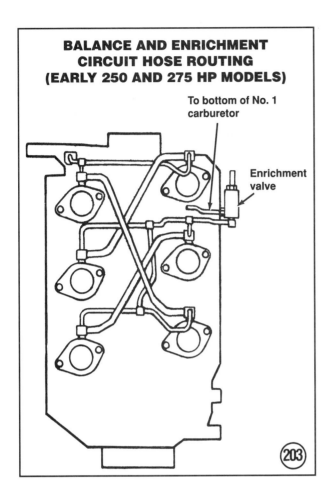
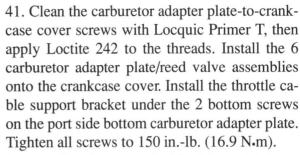

BALANCE AND ENRICHMENT CIRCUIT HOSE ROUTING (EARLY 250 AND 275 HP MODELS)

To bottom of No. 1 carburetor

Enrichment valve

203

41. Clean the carburetor adapter plate-to-crankcase cover screws with Locquic Primer T, then apply Loctite 242 to the threads. Install the 6 carburetor adapter plate/reed valve assemblies onto the crankcase cover. Install the throttle cable support bracket under the 2 bottom screws on the port side bottom carburetor adapter plate. Tighten all screws to 150 in.-lb. (16.9 N·m).

42. Install and connect the bleed hoses. Refer to **Figure 201** and **Figure 202** for correct bleed hose routing.

43. Install and connect the balance and enrichment system hoses. Refer to **Figures 203-205**.

CAUTION
*The following 275 hp models are equipped with a new design upper bearing carrier which uses a bleed fitting. The bleed hose should be clamped to the bleed fitting with a sta-strap. To prevent the sta-strap from interfering with movement of the trigger assembly, the locking tab on the sta-strap **must** face the cylinder head side of the block.*

8

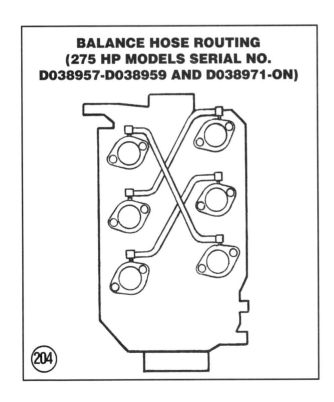

BALANCE HOSE ROUTING (275 HP MODELS SERIAL NO. D038957-D038959 AND D038971-ON)

204

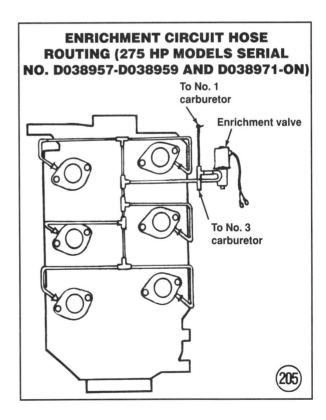

ENRICHMENT CIRCUIT HOSE ROUTING (275 HP MODELS SERIAL NO. D038957-D038959 AND D038971-ON)

To No. 1 carburetor

Enrichment valve

To No. 3 carburetor

205

20 in. shaft—serial No. D086818-on.

25 in. shaft—serial No. D086876-on.

30 in. shaft—serial No. D090719-on.

44. Install the trigger plate and stator assembly. See Chapter Seven.

45. Install the ignition plate assembly to the power head. Install the ignition coils (Chapter Seven).

46. Install the voltage regulator (Chapter Seven).

47. Install the engine temperature sensor and overheat warning sensor.

48. Install the fuel enrichment valve and bracket assembly to the power head. Connect the yellow/black wire and the black wires to the terminal block.

49. Install the starter motor as described in Chapter Seven.

50. Install the fuel pump assemblies. See Chapter Six.

51. Install the throttle/spark advance arm assembly to the power head. Connect the trigger linkage to the spark advance arm (Chapter Seven). Install the throttle cam. Attach the oil injection pump control rod to the throttle cam and pump.

52. Install the carburetors and attenuator cover as described in Chapter Six. Install the fuel delivery hoses to the fuel pumps.

53. Install the engine mounted oil reservoir as described in Chapter Eleven.

54. Install the flywheel as described in Chapter Seven.

Table 1 TIGHTENING TORQUES (3, 3.3, 4, 5, 8, 9.9, 15, 20 AND 25 HP MODELS)

Fastener	in.-lb.	ft.-lb.	N.m
Capacitor charging coil			
3-5 hp	14		1.6
Carburetor adapter plate			
20 & 25 hp			
Screws	30		3.4
Nut	180		20.3
Connecting rod screw			
8, 9.9 & 15 hp	100		11.3
20 & 25 hp	150		16.9
Crankcase cover screws			
3 & 3.3 hp	50		5.6
4 & 5 hp	90		10.2
8, 9.9 & 15	200		22.6
20 & 25 hp		30	40.7
Cylinder block cover screws			
8, 9.9 & 15 hp	60		6.8
20 & 25 hp	80		9.0
Cylinder head screws			
3 & 3.3 hp	85		9.6
4 & 5 hp	215		24.3
Exhaust cover screws			
8, 9.9 & 15 hp	60		6.8
20 and 25 hp	80		9.0
Flywheel			
3 & 3.3 hp (nut)		30	40.7

(continued)

Table 1 TIGHTENING TORQUES (3, 3.3, 4, 5, 8, 9.9, 15, 20 AND 25 HP MODELS) (continued)

Fastener	in.-lb.	ft.-lb.	N·m
Flywheel (continued)			
4 & 5 hp (nut		40	54.2
8, 9.9 & 15 hp (nut)		50	67.8
20 & 25 hp (bolt)		50	67.8
Lower end cap			
3 & 3.3 hp	50		5.6
4 & 5 hp	70		7.9
Power head-to-drive shaft housing			
3 & 3.3 hp	50		5.6
4 & 5 hp	70		7.9
8, 9.9 & 15 hp	120		13.5
20 & 25	200		22.6
Reed block-to-crankcase cover screws			
8, 9.9 & 15 hp	60		6.8
Reed valve/Stop screws			
3-5 hp	9		1.0
8, 9.9 & 15 hp	20		2.3
20 & 25 hp	25		2.8
Spark plug			
4 & 5 hp	168		19.0
All others		20	27.0
Stator mounting screws			
8-25 hp	30		3.4
Thermostat cover screws			
8, 9.9 & 15 hp	30		3.4
Transfer port cover screws			
8, 9.9 & 15 hp	60		6.8
20 & 25 hp	30		3.4

8

Table 2 TIGHTENING TORQUES (40-115 HP MODELS)

Fastener	in.-lb.	ft.-lb.	N·m
Connecting rod cap			
40 hp	200		22.6
50 & 60 hp (prior to serial No. D000750)	180		20.3
50 & 50 hp (serial No. D000750-on)			
Step 1	15		1.7
Step 2			
1/4 in. screw	180		20.3
5/16 in. screw		27	36.6
75 & 90 hp			
Step 1	15		1.7
Step 2		30	40.7
100 & 115 hp			
Step 1	15		1.7
Step 2		30[1]	40.71

(continued)

Table 2 TIGHTENING TORQUES (40-115 HP MODELS) (continued)

Fastener	in.-lb.	ft.-lb.	N·m
Crankcase cover screws			
40 hp	210		23.7
50 & 60 (prior to serial No. D000750)	200		22.6
50 & 60 (serial No. D000750-on)		18	24.4
75-115 hp			
Large screws		25	33.9
Small screws	220		24.9
Cylinder block cover screws			
40 hp	100		11.3
50 & 60 (prior to serial No. D000750)	70		7.9
75-115 hp	220		24.9
End cap screws			
40 hp			
Upper and lower	200		22.6
50 & 60 (prior to serial No. D000750)			
Upper and lower	150		16.9
50 & 60 (serial No. D000750-on)			
Lower		18	24.4
75-115 hp			
Lower	220		24.9
Exhaust cover screws			
40 hp	200		22.6
50 & 60 (prior to serial No. D000750)			
1/4 in. screws	115		13.0
5/16 in. screws	200		22.6
75-115 hp	220		24.9
Flywheel nut			
40 hp		75	101.7
50 & 60 hp (prior to serial No. D000750)		85	115.2
50 & 60 hp (serial No. D000750-on), 75-115 hp		120	162.7
Fuel pump screws			
40 hp	60		6.8
50 & 60 hp (prior to serial No. D000750)	70		7.9
50 & 60 hp (serial No. D000750-on)	40		4.5
75-115 hp	40		4.5
Intake mainfold screws			
50 & 60 (serial No. D000750-on)		18	24.4
75-115 hp	220		24.9
Main bearing/reed block support bolts			
40 hp	75		8.5

(continued)

Table 2 TIGHTENING TORQUES (40-115 HP MODELS) (continued)

Fastener	in.-lb.	ft.-lb.	N·m
Oil injection pump screws			
40 hp	45		5.1
50 & 60 (serial No. D000750-on)	45		5.1
75-115 hp	60		6.8
Power head-to-drive shaft housing			
40 hp	160		18.0
50 & 60 (prior to serial No. D000750)	180		20.3
50 & 60 (serial No. D000750-on)		28	38.0
75 & 90 hp	165		18.6
100 & 115 hp		44	59.6
Reed valve/stop screws			
40 hp	40		4.5
50 & 60 hp (prior to serial No. D000750)	30		3.4
50 & 60 hp (serial No. D000750-on)	60		5.1
75-115 hp	80		9.0
Reed block halves			
40 hp, 50 & 60 hp (prior to serial No. D000750)	55		6.2
Spark plug			
All models		20	27.1
Starter motor mounting screws			
40 hp	180		20.3
50 & 60 hp (prior to serial No. D000750)	180		20.3
50 & 60 hp (serial No. D000750-on)		18	24.4
75-115 hp	175		19.8
Stator screws[2]			
40 hp	35		4.0
50-115 hp	60		5.1
Transfer port cover screws			
40 hp	65		7.3
50 & 60 hp (prior to serial No. D000750)	160		18.1

1. Tighten fasteners an additional 90° after obtaining 30 ft.-lb. (40.7 N·m).
2. If patch screws are not used, apply a suitable thread locking compound to the threads of fasteners.

Table 3 TIGHTENING TORQUES (V6 MODELS)

Fastener	in.-lb.	ft.-lb.	N·m
Carburetor adapter plate-to-crankcase cover screws			
250 & 275 hp	150		16.9
(continued)			

8

Table 3 TIGHTENING TORQUES (V6 MODELS) (continued)

Fastener	in.-lb.	ft.-lb.	N·m
Connecting rod screws			
Step 1		15	19.0
Step 2[1]		30	40.7
Crankcase cover screws			
135-200 hp			
5/16 in. screws	180		20.3
3/8 in. screws		35	47.4
250 & 275 hp		30	40.7
Cylinder head screws			
135-200 hp		40	54.2
250 & 275 hp	180		20.3
End cap screws			
135-200 hp			
Upper	150		16.9
Lower	80		9.0
250 & 275 hp			
Lower	150		16.9
Exhaust cover screws			
135-200 hp	200		22.6
250 & 275 hp	150		16.9
Exhaust plate adapter			
250 & 275 hp		30	40.7
Flywheel nut			
135-200 hp		120	162.7
250 & 275 hp		100	135.6
Fuel pump screws			
All models	50-60		5.6-6.8
Fuel rail-to-induction manifold screws (EFI)	35		3.9
Induction manifold-to-crankcase cover screws (EFI)	80-100		9.0-11.3
Oil injection pump screws			
135-200 hp	25		2.8
250 & 275 hp	60		6.8
Power head-to-drive shaft housing			
All models		30	40.7
Pressure relief valve cover screws			
All Models	150		16.9
Reed block-to-housing screws			
135-200 hp	80		9.0
250 & 275 hp	60		6.8
Reed block housing-to-crankcase cover			
135-200 hp	105		11.9
Reed valves/stops-to-reed block screws			
All models	25		2.8
Stator screws			
135-200 hp	60		6.8
250 & 275 hp	150		16.9

(continued)

Table 3 TIGHTENING TORQUES (V6 MODELS) (continued)

Fastener	in.-lb.	ft.-lb.	N·m
Thermostat cover screws			
135-200 hp	200		22.6
250 & 275 hp	150		16.9

1. On 250 & 275 hp models and 135-200 hp models (serial No. D082000-on), tighten connecting rod screws an additional 90° after 30 ft.-lb. (40.7 N·m) is obtained.

Table 4 PISTON DIAMETER AND CYLINDER BLOCK FINISH HONE (40-275 HP MODELS)

Models	Piston diameter (above rings)	Piston diameter (bottom of skirt)	Cylinder block finish hone
40 hp			
Standard piston		2.558 in.	2.565 in.
0.015 in. oversize		2.573 in.	2.580 in.
0.030 in. oversize		2.588 in.	2.595 in.
50 & 60 hp (prior to serial No. D000750)			
Standard piston	2.863 in.	2.872 in.	2.875 in.
0.015 in. oversize	2.878 in.	2.887 in.	2.890 in.
0.030 in. oversize	2.893 in.	2.902 in.	2.905 in.
50 & 60 hp (serial No. D000750-on)			
Standard piston		2.950 in.	2.954 in.
0.015 in. oversize		2.965 in.	2.969 in.
75-115 hp			
Standard piston		3.371 in.	3.375 in.
0.015 in. oversize		3.386 in.	3.390 in.
0.030 in. oversize		3.401 in.	3.405 in.
V6 (121.9 cu. in.)[1]			
Standard piston		3.115 in.	3.125 in
0.015 in. oversize		3.130 in.	3.140 in.
0.030 in. oversize		3.145 in.	3.155 in.
V6 (142.2 cu. in.)[2]			
Standard piston		3.3710 in.	3.377 in.
0.015 in. oversize		3.3860 in.	3.392 in.
V6 (153 cu. in.)[2]			
Standard piston		3.4939 in.	3.501 in.
0.015 in. oversize		3.5089 in.	3.516 in.
V6 (207 cu. in.)[3]			

1. Piston diameters are all ± 0.002 in. Measure piston diameter 29/32 in. up from bottom of skirt at 90° to piston pin bore.
2. Piston diameters are all ± 0.0005 in. Measure piston diameter 1/2 in. up from bottom of skirt at 90° to piston pin bore.
3. Cylinder bores are chrome plated. No oversize pistons and rings available.

8

Table 5 ENGINE SPECIFICATIONS (3-25 HP)

Cylinder bore diameter	
3 & 3.3 hp	
Standard bore	1.850 in.
Wear limit	1.852 in.
Oversize bore	1.869 in.
Wear limit	1.871 in.
4 & 5 hp	
Standard bore	2.165 in.
Oversize bore	2.185 in.
Max. allowable taper	0.003 in.
Max. allowable out-of-round	0.003 in.
8 & 9.9 hp	
Standard bore	2.125 in.
Max. allowable taper/out-of-round	0.002 in.
15 hp	
Standard bore	2.375 in.
Max. allowable taper/out-of-round	0.002 in.
20 & 25 hp	2.560 in.
Max. allowable taper/out-of-round	0.003 in.
Crankshaft runout (max.)	
3 & 3.3 hp	0.001 in.
4 & 5 hp	0.002 in.
Connecting rod deflection	
3 & 3.3 hp	0.022-0.056 in.
Connecting rod side clearance	
4 & 5 hp	0.005-0.015 in.
Piston clearance	
3 & 3.3 hp	0.002-0.005 in.
4 & 5 hp	0.0012-0.0024 in.
8-15 hp	0.002-0.005 in.
Piston diameter	
4 & 5 hp	
Standard piston	2.164 in.
Oversize piston	2.184 in.
8 & 9.9 hp	
Standard piston	2.123 in.
15 hp	
Standard piston	2.373 in.
20 & 25 hp	
Standard piston	2.559 in.
Piston rings	
End gap	
3 & 3.3 hp	0.006-0.012 in.
4 & 5 hp	0.008-0.016 in.
Side clearance	
3 & 3.3 hp	0.0003-0.0010 in.
4 & 5 hp	
Top ring	0.0012-0.0028 in.
Bottom ring	0.0008-0.0024 in.
Reed stop opening	
3 & 3.3 hp	0.236-0.244 in.
4 & 5 hp	0.240-0.248 in.
8 & 9.9 hp	7/32 in.
15 hp	19/64 in.

Table 6 ENGINE SPECIFICATIONS (40-275 HP MODELS)

Connecting rod side clearance	
40 hp	0.091-0.092 in.
250 & 275 hp	0.003-0.009 in.
Crankshaft runout (max.)	0.002 in.
Cylinder bore	
40 hp	
Standard diameter	2.565 in.
0.015 in. oversize	2.580 in.
0.030 in. oversize	2.595 in.
Max. taper/out-of-round	0.004 in.
50 & 60 hp (prior to serial No. D000750)	
Standard diameter	2.875 in.
0.015 in. oversize	2.890 in.
0.030 in. oversize	2.905 in.
Max. taper/out-of-round	0.004 in.
50 & 60 hp (serial No. D000750-D047798)	
Standard diameter	2.954 in.
0.015 in. oversize	2.969 in.
Max. taper/out-of-round	0.003 in.
50 & 60 hp (serial No. D047799-on)	
Standard diameter	2.955 in.
0.015 in. oversize	2.970 in.
Max. taper/out of round	0.003 in.
75-115 hp	
Standard diameter	3.375 in.
0.015 in. oversize	3.390 in.
0.030 in. oversize	3.405 in.
Max. taper/out-of-round	0.003 in.
V6 (121.9 cu. in.)	
Standard diameter	3.125 in.
0.015 in. oversize	3.140 in.
0.030 in. oversize	3.155 in.
Max. taper/out-of-round	0.006 in.
V6 (142.2 cu. in.)	
Standard diameter	3.377 in.
0.015 in. oversize	3.392 in.
Max. taper/out-of-round	0.006 in.
V6 (153 cu. in.)	
Standard diameter	3.501 in.
0.015 in. oversize	3.516 in.
Max. taper/out-of-round	0.006 in.
V6 (207 cu. in.)	
Standard diameter	3.740 in.
Max. taper/out-of-round	0.006 in.
Piston diameter	See *Cleaning and Inspection* in this chapter
Piston ring end gap	
40 hp	0.0015-0.014 in.
50 & 60 hp (serial No. D000750-on)	0.10-0.18 in.
V6 (except 250 & 275 hp)	0.18-0.25 in.
V6 (250 & 275 hp)	0.012-0.024 in.
Reed stop opening	
40 hp	5/32 in.
50 & 60 hp (prior to serial No. D000750)	0.180 in.
250 & 275 hp	0.130 in.

8

Chapter Nine

Lower Unit Gear Housing

A drive shaft transfers engine torque from the engine crankshaft through the drive shaft housing to the lower unit gear housing. A pinion gear on the drive shaft meshes with a drive gear in the lower unit gear housing to change the vertical power flow into a horizontal flow through the propeller shaft.

On outboard motors which have a shift capability, a sliding clutch engages a forward or reverse gear in the lower unit gear housing. This creates a direct coupling that transfers the power flow from the pinion to the propeller shaft.

The lower unit gear housing can be removed from the drive shaft housing without removing the entire outboard from the boat. This chapter contains removal, overhaul and installation procedures for the lower unit gear housing, water pump and propeller. **Tables 1-5** are located at the end of the chapter.

The gear housings covered in this chapter differ somewhat in construction and require slightly different service procedures. The chapter is arranged in a normal disassembly/assembly sequence. When only a partial repair is required, follow the procedure(s) to the point where the faulty parts can be replaced, then reassemble the unit.

Figure 1 shows a cross-sectional view of a typical gear housing, showing the component relationship. Since this chapter covers a large range of models, the lower units shown in the accompanying pictures are the most common models. While it is possible that the components shown in the pictures may not be identical with those being serviced, the step-by-step procedures may be used with all models covered in this manual.

SERVICE PRECAUTIONS

When working on a Mercury outboard motor, there are several good procedures to keep in mind that will make your work easier, faster and more accurate.

1. Never use elastic stop nuts more than twice. It is good practice to replace such nuts each time they are removed. Never use worn out stop nuts or nonlocking nuts.

2. Use special tools where noted. In some cases, it may be possible to perform a procedure with makeshift tools, however, it is not recommended.

The use of makeshift tools can damage the components and may cause serious personal injury.

3. Use a vise with protective jaws to hold housings or parts. If protective jaws are not available, insert blocks of wood or similar padding on each side of the part before clamping in the vise.

4. Remove and install pressed-on parts with an appropriate mandrel, support and hydraulic press. Do not attempt to pry or hammer press-fit components on or off.

5. Refer to the appropriate table at the end of the chapter for torque values, if not given in the text. Proper torque is essential to ensure long life and satisfactory service from outboard components.

6. Apply Quicksilver Perfect Seal (part No.92-34277-1) to the outer surfaces of all bearing carrier, retainer and housing mating surfaces during reassembly. Do *not* allow Perfect Seal to enter bearings or gears.

7. Discard all O-rings, seals and gaskets during disassembly. Apply Quicksilver 2-4-C Marine Lubricant to new O-rings and seal lips to provide initial lubrication.

8. Apply Loctite 242 to the outside diameter of all metal-case oil seals.

9. Record the location and thickness of all shims removed from the gear housing. As soon as the shims are removed, inspect them for damage and

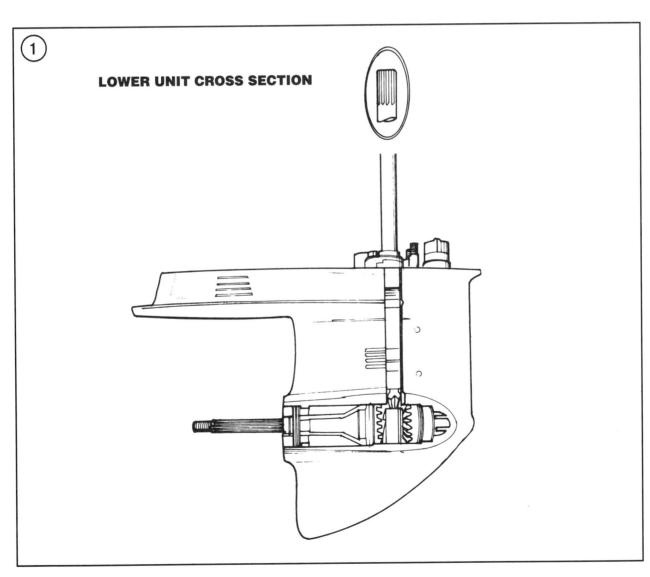

(1)

LOWER UNIT CROSS SECTION

9

write down their thickness and location. Wire the shims together for reassembly and place them in a safe place. Follow shimming instructions closely. If gear backlash is not properly adjusted, the unit will be noisy and suffer premature gear failure. Incorrect bearing preload will result in premature bearing failure.

10. Work in an area where there is good lighting and sufficient space for component storage. Keep an ample number of clean containers available for storing small parts. When not being worked on, cover parts and assemblies with clean shop towels.

GEAR HOUSING

Removal
(3 hp)

> *NOTE*
> *The water pump can be serviced without gear housing removal on 3 hp models.*

1. Disconnect and ground the spark plug lead to prevent accidental starting.
2. Close the fuel shut-off valve.
3. Tilt the outboard to the fully UP position.
4. Remove 2 mounting bolts and pull the gear housing off the drive shaft housing.

Removal
(3.3 hp)

1. Close the fuel shut-off valve.
2. Disconnect and ground the spark plug lead to prevent accidental starting.
3. Tilt the outboard to the fully UP position and engage the tilt lock lever.
4. Shift the outboard into the NEUTRAL gear position.
5. Remove the rubber plug on the port side of the drive shaft housing. Insert an appropriate size socket into the hole and loosen (but do not remove) the shift rod clamp bolt enough to allow the shift rods to separate.

6. Remove the 2 gear housing mounting bolts, then pull the gear housing straight down from the drive shaft housing.
7. Mount the gear housing in a suitable holding fixture. If necessary, drain the lubricant from the unit as described in Chapter Four.

Removal
(4 and 5 hp)

1. Disconnect and ground the spark plug lead to prevent accidental starting.
2. Shift the outboard into REVERSE gear.
3. Tilt the outboard to the fully UP position and engage the tilt lock lever.
4. Remove the propeller as described in this chapter.
5. Remove the rubber plug on the starboard side of the drive shaft housing. Insert an appropriate size socket into the hole and loosen the shift shaft clamp bolt enough to allow the shift rods to separate from the clamp.
6. Remove the two bolts and flat washers from below the front and rear of the antiventilation plate.

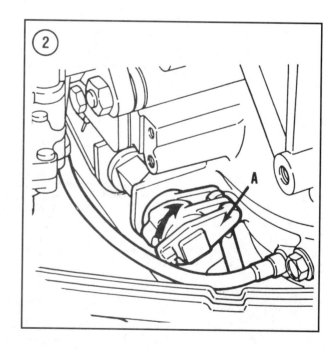

7. Carefully pull the gear housing from the drive shaft housing.

8. Mount the gear housing into a suitable holding fixture. If necessary, drain the lubricant from the unit.

Removal
(8, 9.9 and 15 hp)

1. Disconnect and ground the spark plug leads to prevent accidental starting.

2. Shift the outboard into FORWARD gear.

3. Tilt the outboard to the fully UP position, then engage the tilt lock lever.

4. Remove the shift shaft retainer (A, **Figure 2**) located under the cowl. Disconnect the shift shaft from the coupling yoke.

5. Remove the reverse lock actuator (A, **Figure 3**).

NOTE
It is not necessary to drain the gear housing if only water pump service is to be performed.

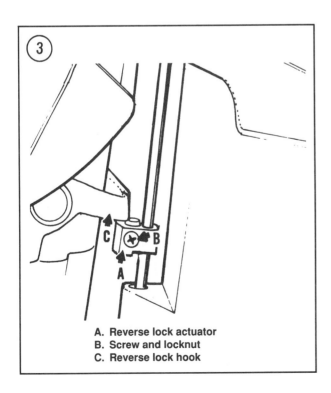

A. Reverse lock actuator
B. Screw and locknut
C. Reverse lock hook

6. Place a container under the gear housing. Remove the fill and vent plugs and allow the lubricant to drain into the container.

NOTE
If the lubricant is white or creamy in color, or if metal particles are found in Step 7, the gear housing should be disassembled to determine and repair the cause of the problem.

7. Rub a small amount of lubricant between a finger and thumb to check for the presence of metal particles or chips. A small amount of fine particles (powder-like) indicates normal wear. Note the color of the lubricant. A white or creamy appearance indicates water contamination in the lubricant. Check the drain container for water separation from the lubricant.

8. Remove the propeller as described in this chapter.

9. Remove the attaching bolt on each side of the gear housing. Remove the bolt at the front of the gear housing. Separate and remove the gear housing from the drive shaft housing.

10. Place the gear housing into a suitable holding fixture.

Removal
(20 and 25 hp)

1. Disconnect and ground the spark plug leads to prevent accidental starting.

NOTE
On electric start models, pull the bottom of the port side cowl away from the motor to provide access for Step 2.

2. Remove the screw holding the shift shaft coupler to the shift shaft actuator rod. Slide the coupler off the rod. See **Figure 4**.

3. Tilt the outboard to the fully UP position and engage the tilt lock lever.

9

NOTE
It is not necessary to drain the gear housing if only water pump service is to be performed.

4. Place a container under the gear housing. Remove the fill plug (**Figure 5**). Remove the vent plug (**Figure 6**) and allow the lubricant to drain into the container.

NOTE
If the lubricant is white or cream colored, or if metal particles are found in Step 5, the gear housing should be disassembled to determine and correct the problem.

5. Rub a small amount of lubricant between a thumb and finger to check for the presence of metal particles or chips. A small amount of fine particles (powder-like) indicates normal wear. Note the color of the lubricant. A white or cream color indicates water contamination in the lubricant. Check the drain container for water separation from the lubricant.

6. Remove the propeller as described in this chapter.

NOTE
A flat washer is installed near the top of the shift shaft. When gear and drive shaft housings are separated in Step 7, the washer may slide off shift shaft. Do not lose washer, as it must be reinstalled in the same location.

7. Remove the 2 attaching bolts on each side of the gear housing. Separate and remove the gear housing from the drive shaft housing. If the water tube pulls out of the drive shaft housing and remains attached to the water pump, remove the tube from the pump and reinstall into the drive shaft housing.

8. Place the unit into a suitable holding fixture.

9. Check reverse gear backlash as described in this chapter before disassembling the gear housing. Record the backlash for reference during the shim selection procedure during reassembly.

Removal
(40 hp and 50-60 hp Prior to Serial No. D000750)

1. Disconnect and ground the spark plug leads to prevent accidental starting.

NOTE
It is not necessary to drain the gear housing if only water pump service is to be performed.

2. Place the outboard in the normal running position.

3. Place a container under the gear housing, then remove the drain/fill plug (**Figure 7**) and the vent plug (**Figure 8**). Allow the lubricant to drain into the container.

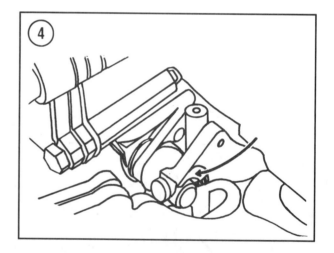

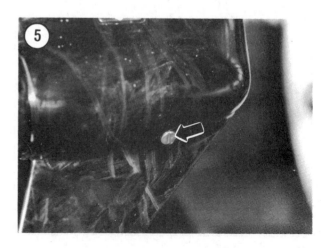

NOTE
If the lubricant is white or cream color, or if metal particles are found in Step 4, the gear housing should be disassembled to determine and repair the cause of the problem.

4. Rub a small amount of lubricant between a thumb and finger to check for the presence of metal particles or chips. A small amount of fine (powder-like) particles indicates normal wear.

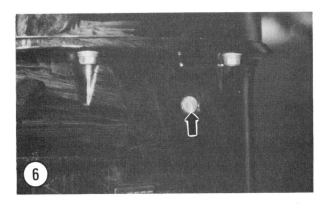

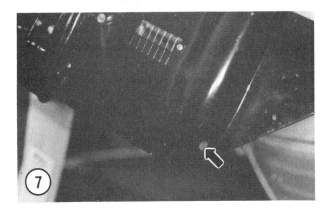

Note the color of the lubricant. A white or creamy appearance indicates water contamination. Check the drain container for water separation from the lubricant.

5. Remove the propeller as described in this chapter.

6. Place match marks on the antiventilation plate and trim tab for reference during reassembly. The trim tab should be reinstalled in the same position. Pry the plastic plug from the rear of the drive shaft housing (**Figure 9**), then insert an appropriate size socket into the hole and remove the bolt securing the trim tab.

7. Shift the outboard into FORWARD gear. Tilt the outboard to the fully UP position.

8. Remove the locknut from inside the trim tab cavity. Remove the locknut located at the center bottom of the antiventilation plate, then remove the 2 locknuts at the front of the gear housing (1 on each side).

9. Separate and remove the gear housing from the drive shaft housing. Place the housing into a suitable holding fixture.

Removal
(50-60 hp [Serial No. D000750-on]; and 75-115 hp)

1. Disconnect and ground the spark plug leads to prevent accidental starting.

2. Place the outboard in the normal operating position.

NOTE
It is not necessary to drain the gear housing if only water pump service is to be performed.

3. Place a container under the gear housing. Remove the fill/drain plug and the 2 vent plugs. Note on 75-115 hp models (serial No. D027991-on), the forward plug is the oil level plug and the rear plug is the vent plug. Allow the lubricant to drain into the container.

NOTE
If the lubricant is white or cream color, or if metal particles are found in Step 4, the gear housing should be disassembled to determine and repair the problem.

4. Rub a small amount of lubricant between a thumb and finger to check for the presence of metal particles or chips. A small amount of fine (powder-like) particles indicates normal wear. Note the color of the lubricant. A white or cream color indicates water contamination of the lubricant. Check the container for water separation from the lubricant.

5. Remove the propeller as described in this chapter.

6. Shift the outboard into FORWARD gear. Tilt the outboard to the fully UP position.

7. Remove 4 gear housing mounting bolts and washers (2 on each side).

8A. 50-60 hp—Place match marks on the antiventilation plate and trim tab for reference during reassembly. The trim tab should be reinstalled in the same position. Remove the locknut and washer located inside the trim tab cavity.

8B. 75-115 hp—Remove the locknut and washer located at the bottom center of the antiventilation plate.

9. Separate and remove the gear housing from the drive shaft housing. Place the housing into a suitable holding fixture.

Removal
(135-275 hp [V6])

1. Disconnect and ground the spark plug leads. Remove the spark plugs from the engine.

2. Shift the outboard into NEUTRAL, then tilt to the fully UP position.

3. Remove the propeller as described in this chapter.

4. Place match marks on the antiventilation plate and trim tab for reference during reassembly. The

trim tab should be reinstalled in the same position.

5A. 250 and 275 hp—Remove the bolt securing the trim tab to the gear housing. Remove the trim tab (**Figure 10**).

5B. 135-200 hp—Pry the plastic access plug from the rear of the drive shaft housing. See **Figure 9**. Insert a suitable socket into the hole

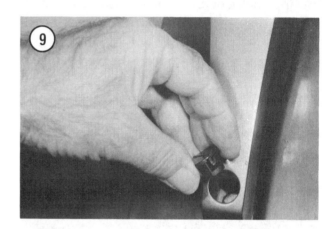

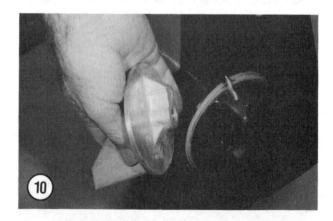

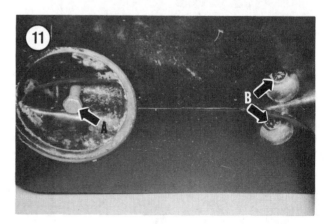

and remove the bolt securing the trim tab. Remove the trim tab (**Figure 10**).

6. Remove the nut or bolt and washer located inside the trim tab cavity. See A, **Figure 11**.

7. Remove the 2 locknuts from the bottom center of the antiventilation plate. See B, **Figure 11**.

8. Remove the locknut from the front gear housing mounting stud. See **Figure 12**.

9. Loosen the side mounting locknuts (**Figure 13**) on each side equally and drop the gear housing slightly. On badly corroded units, the water tubes and drive shaft may be frozen in the gear housing, making it necessary to pry the gear housing loose from the drive shaft housing.

10. Holding the gear housing firmly, remove the loosened nuts and separate the gear housing from the drive shaft housing.

11. Mount the gear housing into a suitable holding fixture.

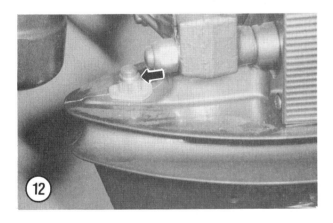

NOTE
It is not necessary to drain the gear housing if only water pump service is to be performed.

12. Place a container under the gear housing.

13. Remove the fill/drain plug and the vent plug(s). Note that 250 and 275 hp models are equipped with an upper and lower vent plug. Remove both plugs. Allow the lubricant to drain into the container.

NOTE
If the lubricant is white or cream color, or if metal particles are found in Step 4, the gear housing should be disassembled to determine and repair the problem.

14. Rub a small amount of lubricant between a thumb and finger to check for the presence of metal particles or chips. A small amount of fine (powder-like) particles indicates normal wear. Note the color of the lubricant. A white or cream color indicates water contamination of the lubricant. Check the container for water separation from the lubricant.

Installation
(3 hp)

1. Tilt the outboard to the fully UP position.

2. Apply Quicksilver Perfect Seal to the threads of the 2 gear housing mounting bolts. Apply Quicksilver 2-4-C Marine Lubricant to the outside diameter of the tube (**Figure 14**), then insert the tube into the drive shaft housing until seated as shown.

3. Apply Quicksilver 2-4-C Marine Lubricant to the inside diameter (both ends) of the upper drive shaft. Insert the shaft into the tube (**Figure 14**), then onto the engine crankshaft.

4. Apply Quicksilver 2-4-C Marine Lubricant to the water tube seals.

5. Install the gear housing while aligning the water tube and upper and lower drive shafts. Rotate the propeller shaft clockwise to engage

9

the drive shafts. Install the 2 gear housing mounting bolts and lockwashers. Tighten the bolts to 25 in.-lb. (2.8 N•m).

6. Reconnect the spark plug lead.

7. Refill the gear housing with the correct lubricant as described in Chapter Four.

Installation
(3.3 hp)

1. Place the gear housing and the outboard shift lever in the NEUTRAL gear position.

2. Apply a light coat of Quicksilver 2-4-C Marine Lubricant to the drive shaft splines. Do not apply lubricant to the top of the shaft.

3. Apply Quicksilver 2-4-C Marine Lubricant to the water tube seals.

4. Mate the gear housing to the drive shaft housing, guiding the water tube into place. The end of the lower shift rod must be properly positioned in the shift rod clamp. If necessary, rotate the engine clockwise to align the crankshaft and drive shaft splines.

5. Install the 2 mounting bolts and tighten to 50 in.-lb. (5.6 N•m).

6. Securely tighten shift rod clamp bolt.

7. To check shift rod adjustment, place the shift lever in NEUTRAL. The propeller shaft should turn freely in both directions. Place the shift lever in FORWARD. The propeller shaft should turn approximately 90° in either direction, then stop. If not, loosen the shift rod clamp and adjust the rods as necessary.

8. If drained, fill the gear housing with the correct lubricant (Chapter Four).

9. Reconnect the spark plug lead.

Installation
(4 and 5 hp)

1. Place the outboard shift lever into the REVERSE position. While rotating the propeller shaft clockwise, push downward on the gear housing shift shaft to engage REVERSE gear.

2. Make sure the plastic water tube guide is positioned over the tube seal in the water pump cover.

3. Apply a light coat of Quicksilver 2-4-C Marine Lubricant to the drive shaft splines.

4. Mate the gear housing to the drive shaft housing, guiding the water tube into place. The shift shaft end must also pass through the hole in the end of the upper shift shaft clamp. If necessary, rotate the propeller shaft to align the drive shaft and crankshaft splines.

5. Install the 2 mounting bolts with flat washers. Tighten the bolts to 70 in.-lb. (8.0 N•m).

6. Insert a suitable socket wrench through the shift clamp plug hole in the starboard side of the gear housing and tighten the shift rod clamp bolt securely, then reinstall the plug.

7. Release the tilt stop/lock and return the outboard to the normal operating position.

8. Reinstall the propeller as described in this chapter.

9. Reconnect the spark plug lead.

10. Fill the gear housing with the correct lubricant. See Chapter Four.

Installation
(8, 9.9 and 15 hp)

1. Place the outboard shift linkage into the FORWARD gear position. Place the gear housing in NEUTRAL gear.

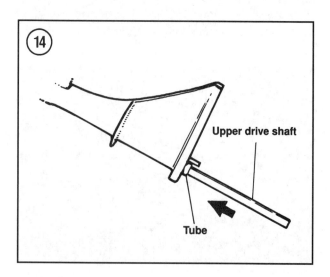

2. Measure the distance between the top of the water pump base and the center of the hole in the top of the shift shaft. The distance should be:

 a. Short shaft models—16-1/2 in. (419.1 mm).

 b. Long shaft models—22 in. (558.9 mm).

 c. Extra long shaft models—27-1/2 in. (698.5 mm).

Rotate the shift shaft as necessary to obtain the specified distance (clockwise to decrease distance).

3. Shift the gear housing into FORWARD gear.

4. Run a 1/4 in. (6.4 mm) diameter bead of RTV sealant along the rear of the water pump base.

5. Insert the drive and shift shafts into the drive shaft housing and move the gear housing upward, keeping the mating surfaces parallel.

6. Guide the shift shaft through the mid-section hole, the water tube into the water tube guide and the drive shaft into the crankshaft. If necessary, rotate the flywheel to align the drive shaft and crankshaft splines.

7. Guide the shift shaft end into the coupling yoke under the cowl. See **Figure 15**.

8. Install and tighten attaching bolts to 180 in.-lb. (20.3 N•m).

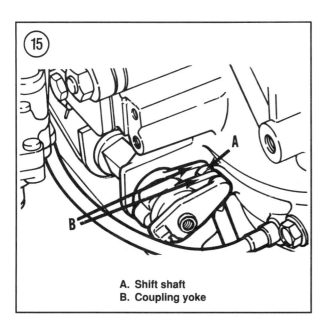

A. Shift shaft
B. Coupling yoke

9. Install the shift shaft retainer under the cowl. Rotate the retainer until it locks into place.

NOTE
If the gear housing does not shift as described in Step 10, remove the gear housing and readjust the shift shaft length as described in Step 2.

10. With the engine in FORWARD gear, the propeller shaft should not turn counterclockwise. Shift the outboard into NEUTRAL. The propeller shaft should rotate freely in either direction. Shift the outboard into REVERSE gear. The propeller shaft should not turn clockwise.

11. Place the shift lever into NEUTRAL and loosely install the reverse lock actuator. Position the actuator so it just touches the reverse lock hook and tighten the screw. See **Figure 3**.

12. Release the tilt stop/lock and return the outboard to the normal operation position.

13. Reinstall the propeller as described in this chapter.

14. Refill the gear housing with the correct lubricant as described in Chapter Four.

9

**Installation
(20 and 25 hp)**

1. Rotate the drive shaft clockwise while pulling up on the shift shaft until the gear housing is in FORWARD gear.

2. Tilt the outboard to the fully UP position and secure with the tilt lock lever.

3. Install the flat washer onto the shift shaft. Install a new O-ring seal onto the drive shaft.

4. Check the drive shaft housing to make sure the water tube is connected properly to the adaptor plate tube seal.

5. Place the outboard shift lever into the FORWARD gear position.

NOTE
Do not lubricate drive shaft splines. Lubrication is provided by normal engine operation.

6. Insert the drive and shift shafts into the drive shaft housing. Move the gear housing upward, keeping the mating surfaces parallel.

7. Guide the shift shaft through the reverse lock rod loop, the water tube into the pump cover seal and the drive shaft into the crankshaft. If necessary, rotate the flywheel to align the drive shaft and crankshaft splines.

8. Apply Loctite 271 to the threads of the gear housing mounting bolts. Install and tighten the bolts evenly and securely.

NOTE
It may be necessary to push actuator rod from starboard to port side of power head before performing Step 9.

9. Reconnect the shift shaft coupler to the actuator rod with the coupler pin inserted through the shift shaft. Install and tighten the coupler attaching screw securely.

10. Lower the outboard to the normal operating position.

11. Reconnect the spark plug leads.

12. Fill the gear housing with the correct lubricant. See Chapter Four.

Installation
(40 hp and 50-60 hp
[Prior to Serial No. D000750])

1. Tilt the outboard to the fully UP position and engage the tilt lock lever.

2. Install the exhaust tube support plate and tube seal into the gear housing. The ribbed side of the support plate must face down.

3. Install the rubber seal and seat assembly onto the top of the drive shaft.

4. Shift the gear housing into FORWARD gear while rotating the propeller shaft clockwise to ensure full gear engagement.

5. Install the shift shaft guide onto the shift shaft.

6. Apply Quicksilver 2-4-C Marine Lubricant to the drive shaft splines, shift shaft splines and the

inside diameter of the water tube. Do not apply lubricant to the top of the drive shaft.

7. Insert the water tube into the drive shaft housing and into the seal at the bottom of the exhaust plate.

8. Align the gear housing with the drive shaft housing studs. Insert the gear housing drive shaft into the drive shaft housing, aligning the water tube with the water pump cover.

9. Join the lower unit to the drive shaft housing, rotating the flywheel clockwise to align the crankshaft and drive shaft splines.

10. Install new elastic stop nuts finger tight onto the drive shaft housing studs.

NOTE
If gear housing and drive shaft housing do not mate in Step 9, the 2 shift shafts may not be aligned. Separate the units and realign the shift shafts. Make sure the outboard shift linkage and the gear housing are in the FORWARD gear position.

11. Push the upper shift shaft onto the lower shift shaft with a punch or drift and seat the gear housing against the drive shaft housing.

NOTE
If the gear housing does not shift as described in Step 12, remove the housing and repeat Steps 4-11.

12. Shift the outboard into FORWARD gear. Propeller shaft should not turn counterclock-

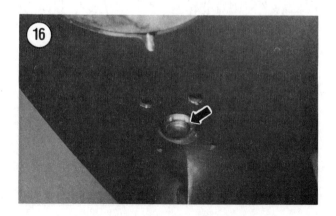

wise. Shift the outboard into NEUTRAL. Propeller shaft should rotate freely in either direction.

13. Install the nut onto the stud inside the trim tab cavity finger tight.

14. Install the nut onto the stud at the bottom center of the antiventilation plate (**Figure 16**) finger tight.

15. Tighten all nuts snugly, beginning with those on the side of the drive shaft housing. When all nuts are snug, tighten all nuts to 40 ft.-lb. (54.2 N•m).

16. Install the trim tab, align the match marks made during removal, then tighten the trim tab bolt to 20 ft.-lb. (27 N•m). Reinstall the plastic access plug into the hole.

17. Install the propeller as described in this chapter.

18. Reconnect the spark plug leads.

19. Fill the gear housing with the correct lubricant as described Chapter Four.

Installation
(50 and 60 hp Serial No. D000750-on)

1. Place the outboard shift linkage into the FORWARD gear position.

2. Tilt the outboard to the fully UP position and engage the tilt lock lever.

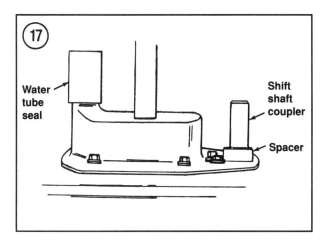

3. Shift the gear housing into NEUTRAL. The propeller shaft should turn freely in both directions.

4. Apply Quicksilver 2-4-C Marine Lubricant to the inside diameter of the water tube seal and to the shift shaft splines. Install the water tube seal onto the water pump housing. Install the shift shaft spacer and coupler onto the shift shaft. See **Figure 17**.

> *CAUTION*
> *Do not apply lubricant to the top of the drive shaft in Step 5. Excess lubricant between the top of the drive shaft and the engine crankshaft can create a hydraulic lock, preventing the drive shaft from fully engaging the crankshaft.*

5. Apply a light coat of Quicksilver 2-4-C Marine Lubricant to the drive shaft splines. Wipe any lubricant off the top of the drive shaft.

6. Shift the gear housing into FORWARD gear.

7. Place the drive shaft into the drive shaft housing. Lift the gear housing toward the drive shaft housing while aligning the shift shaft coupler, water tube seal and drive shaft splines. If necessary, rotate the propeller shaft counterclockwise to align the crankshaft and drive shaft splines. In addition, move the shift block on the power head if necessary to align the shift shaft splines.

8. Apply Loctite 271 to the threads of the gear housing mounting bolts. Install the 4 mounting bolts and washers (2 on each side) and 1 nut and washer onto the stud in the trim tab cavity.

9. Tighten the 4 bolts and 1 nut evenly to 40 ft.-lb. (54.2 N•m).

10. Shift the outboard into FORWARD gear. The propeller shaft should ratchet when turned clockwise. Shift into NEUTRAL. The propeller shaft should turn freely in both directions. Shift into REVERSE gear. The propeller shaft should not turn in either direction. If shift operation is not as specified, remove the gear housing from the drive shaft housing and realign the upper shift shaft with the lower shift shaft coupler.

9

11. Install the propeller as described in this chapter.

12. Install the trim tab, aligning the match marks made during removal. Tighten the trim tab bolt to 22 ft.-lb. (29.8 N.m).

13. Reconnect the spark plug leads to the spark plugs.

14. Lower the outboard to the normal operating position. Refill the gear housing with the correct lubricant. See Chapter Four.

Installation
(75-115 hp)

1. Place the outboard shift block in the FORWARD gear position. When in the proper position, the shift block will extend 1/8 in. (3.2 mm) past the front of the shift rail. See **Figure 18**.

2. Tilt the outboard to the fully UP position and engage the tilt lock lever.

3. Shift the gear housing into NEUTRAL. Make sure the propeller shaft turns freely in both directions.

4. Apply Quicksilver 2-4-C Marine Lubricant to the inside diameter of the water tube seal. Install the water tube seal onto the water pump housing.

5. Run a 1/4 in. (6.4 mm) bead of RTV sealant along the back side of the water pump base.

CAUTION
Do not apply lubricant to the top of the drive shaft in Step 5. Excess lubricant between the top of the drive shaft and the engine crankshaft can create a hydraulic lock, preventing the drive shaft from fully engaging the crankshaft.

6. Lightly lubricate the drive shaft splines with Quicksilver 2-4-C Marine Lubricant. Wipe any grease from the top of the shaft. Lightly lubricate the upper shift shaft and gear housing shift shaft splines with 2-4-C Marine Lubricant.

7. Install the nylon spacer over the shift shaft. Install the shift shaft coupler as shown in **Figure**

19 (models equipped with power trim) or **Figure 20** (models without power trim).

8. Shift the gear housing into FORWARD gear. With forward gear properly engaged, resistance should be felt when turning the propeller shaft counterclockwise and the propeller shaft should ratchet when turned clockwise.

9. Apply Loctite 271 to the threads of the gear housing mounting bolts. Lift the gear housing into position on the drive shaft housing, aligning the upper shift shaft with the shift coupler, the water tube with the water tube seal and the drive shaft splines with the crankshaft.

10. If necessary, rotate the propeller shaft clockwise to align the drive shaft and crankshaft splines. It may also be necessary to move the shift block (**Figure 18**) slightly to align the shift shaft and coupler splines.

11. With the gear housing fully mated to the drive shaft housing, install the 4 mounting bolts (2 on each side) and washers and 1 nut and washer (bottom of antiventilation plate). Tighten all mounting fasteners evenly to 40 ft.-lb. (54.2 N.m)

12. Shift the outboard into FORWARD gear. The propeller shaft should ratchet when turned clockwise, but not turn in the counterclockwise direction. The propeller shaft should turn freely in

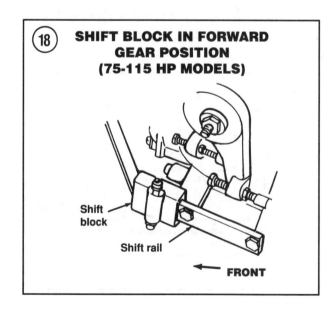

(18) **SHIFT BLOCK IN FORWARD GEAR POSITION (75-115 HP MODELS)**

Shift block

Shift rail

← FRONT

both directions when shifted into NEUTRAL and not turn in either direction when shifted into REVERSE. If shift operation is not as specified, remove the gear housing and realign the upper shift shaft and shift shaft coupler as necessary.

13. Install the propeller as described in this chapter.

14. Reconnect the spark plug leads to the spark plugs.

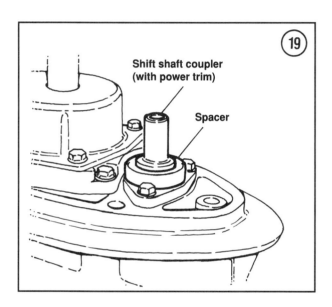

Shift shaft coupler
(with power trim)

Spacer

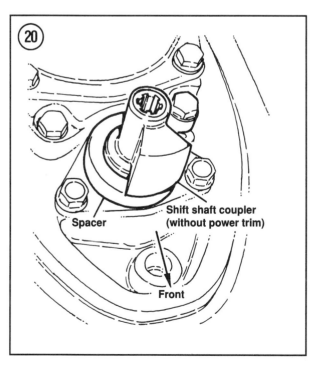

Spacer

Shift shaft coupler
(without power trim)

Front

15. Refill the gear housing with the correct lubricant. See Chapter Four.

Installation
(135-200 hp [V6])

1. Tilt the engine to the fully UP position and engage the tilt lock lever.

CAUTION
Do not apply lubricant to the top of the drive shaft in Step 2. Excess lubricant between the top of the drive shaft and the engine crankshaft can create a hydraulic lock, preventing the drive shaft from fully engaging the crankshaft.

2. Lightly lubricate the shift shaft and drive shaft splines with 2-4-C Marine Lubricant. Wipe any grease off the top of the shafts.

3. Run a thin bead of GM Silicone Sealer (part No. 92-91600-1 across the top of the exhaust divider plate.

4. Install the trim tab retaining bolt into the rear hole at the rear of the gear housing.

5. Shift the gear housing into FORWARD gear.

6. Make sure the guide block anchor pin is positioned as shown in **Figure 21**.

9

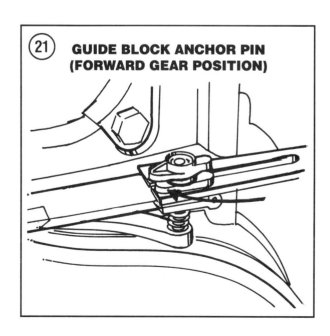

**GUIDE BLOCK ANCHOR PIN
(FORWARD GEAR POSITION)**

7. Position the gear housing with the drive shaft inserted into the drive shaft housing. Align the shift shaft splines and fit the water tube into the water tube guide as the gear housing is lifted into position.

8. Mate the gear housing with the drive shaft housing. If necessary, turn the propeller shaft counterclockwise to align the drive shaft and crankshaft splines.

9. Install flat washers onto the studs on each side of the drive shaft housing, then install nuts onto the studs and tighten finger tight.

10. Install, but do not tighten the bolt located inside the trim tab cavity.

11. Make sure the shift shaft splines are properly aligned, then tighten the nuts installed in Step 9 to 55 ft.-lb. (74.6 N•m) on 3/8 in. nuts or 65 ft.-lb. (88.1 N•m) on 7/16 in. nuts.

12. Check shift operation after tightening the 2 nuts. Move the guide block anchor pin into FORWARD gear. When rotating the flywheel clockwise (as viewed from top), the propeller shaft should turn clockwise. Move the anchor pin into the NEUTRAL position. The propeller shaft should rotate freely in both directions. Move the anchor pin into the REVERSE position. When the flywheel is rotated clockwise (as viewed from top), the propeller shaft should turn counterclockwise. If shift operation is not as specified, remove the gear housing and correct the problem.

13. Install the washers and nuts onto the studs in the antiventilation plate cavity and tighten to specification (**Table 2**).

14. Install the special flat washer and nut onto the stud at the leading edge of the drive shaft housing and tighten to specification (**Table 2**).

15. Tighten the bolt in the trim tab cavity (started in Step 10) to specification (**Table 2**).

16. Install the trim tab, align the match marks made during removal, then tighten the bolt to 25 ft.-lb. (33.9 N•m). Install the plastic cap into the trim tab fastener hole.

17. Install the propeller as described in this chapter.

18. Reconnect the spark plug leads to the spark plugs.

19. Fill the gear housing with the correct lubricant. See Chapter Four.

Installation
(250-275 hp [V6])

1. Tilt the outboard to its fully UP position and engage the tilt lock lever.

2. Slide the splined nylon tube (**Figure 22**), then the rubber seal onto the drive shaft. Make sure the splined side of the rubber seal is facing the nylon tube.

> *CAUTION*
> *Do not apply lubricant to the top of the drive shaft in Step 3. Excess lubricant between the top of the drive shaft and the engine crankshaft can create a hydraulic lock, preventing the drive shaft from fully engaging the crankshaft.*

3. Lightly lubricate the drive shaft and shift shaft splines with Quicksilver 2-4-C Marine Lubricant. Wipe any lubricant off the top of the shafts.

4. Shift the gear housing into FORWARD gear. The gear housing shift shaft should be turned to its fully clockwise position.

5. Place the power head shift lever in the FORWARD gear position.

6. Clean the threads of all gear housing mounting fasteners with Locquic Primer T. Allow to dry, then apply Loctite 271 to the threads of the fasteners.

7. Position the gear housing with the drive shaft inserted into the drive shaft housing. Align the shift shaft splines and fit the water tube into the water tube guide as the gear housing is lifted into position. Insert the speedometer hose through the shift shaft hole in the mid-section.

8. Place a flat washer onto the gear housing mounting studs (2 on each side), then install the nuts and tighten finger tight.

9. Install the remaining mounting nuts or bolts and washers and tighten finger tight.

10. Make sure the shift shaft splines are properly aligned, then tighten the 4 nuts (installed in Step 8) to 40 ft.-lb. (54.2 N·m).

11. Check shift operation as follows:

a. Shift into FORWARD gear and rotate the engine flywheel clockwise. The propeller shaft should turn clockwise.

b. Shift into NEUTRAL. The propeller shaft should turn freely in both directions.

c. Remove the gear housing, then determine and correct the problem if shift operation is not as specified.

12. If shift operation is acceptable, tighten the remaining gear housing mounting fasteners to 40 ft.-lb. (54.2 N·m).

13. Apply Loctite 271 to the threads of the trim tab fastener. Install the trim tab, align the match

marks made during removal, then tighten the bolt to 180 in.-lb. (20.3 N·m).

14. Install the propeller as described in this chapter.

15. Reconnect the spark plug leads to the spark plugs.

16. Fill the gear housing with the correct lubricant. See Chapter Four.

WATER PUMP

Removal and Disassembly

The manufacturer recommends replacing all seals and gaskets whenever the water pump is removed. The manufacturer also recommends replacing the water pump impeller anytime the pump is disassembled. **Figure 23** (pressure type) and **Figure 24** (volume type) are exploded views of water pump assemblies typical of the outboards (except 3 hp) covered in this manual.

3 hp

A rubber impeller water pump is located inside the gear housing. The impeller is mounted on and driven by the propeller shaft. The water pump can be serviced without gear housing removal on 3 hp models.

1. Remove the propeller and shear pin as described in this chapter. Drain the gear housing lubricant. See Chapter Four.

2. Remove the 2 screws securing the pump gear housing cover (12, **Figure 25**). Separate the cover from the gear housing and slide it off the propeller shaft.

3. Inspect the impeller wear surface of the cover. Replace the cover if excessively worn.

4. Pry the impeller off the propeller shaft using a screwdriver or similar tool.

5. Inspect the impeller for cracked, worn or glazed blades. Inspect the impeller hub for separation from the rubber. Replace the impeller if any defects are found.

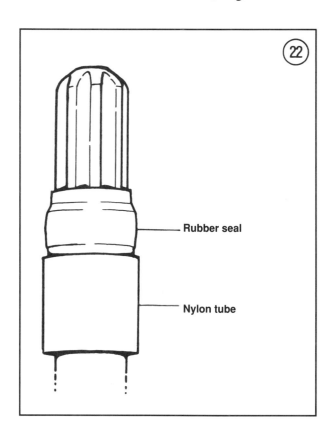

(22)

Rubber seal

Nylon tube

9

6. Remove the impeller drive pin from the propeller shaft.

7. Remove the pump housing (10, **Figure 25**) from the gear housing. Inspect the impeller wear surface on the housing. Replace the housing if necessary.

8. Inspect the bearing inside the pump housing. Replace the bearing if it does not roll smoothly or if rust or other damage is noted. Remove the bearing from the housing using a suitable puller.

9. Place the pump housing on a bench and drive out the seal (2, **Figure 25**) from the housing using a suitable punch and hammer. Discard the seal. Remove and discard the O-ring seal around the housing.

3.3, 4 and 5 hp

1. Remove the gear housing as described in this chapter. Place the gear housing in a suitable holding fixture or a vise with protective jaws. If protective jaws are not available, position the unit upright in the vise with the skeg between wooden blocks.

2. Remove the 4 screws and flat washers from the water pump housing. Carefully pry the pump housing up enough to grasp it, then slide the housing up and off the drive shaft.

3. If the impeller remained on the drive shaft, slide it up and off the shaft.

4. Remove the impeller drive pin or key from the drive shaft or impeller.

5. Remove the pump housing gasket, plate and plate gasket. Discard the gaskets.

6. Except 3.3 hp–Remove the screw, washer and retainer plate (located at front of the pump base) securing the shift shaft and bushing assembly in place. Remove the shift shaft and bushing assembly.

7A. 3.3 hp—Remove the lower shift rod bushing and O-ring from the shift rod bore in the pump housing. Remove and discard the O-ring.

7B. 4 and 5 hp—Remove and discard the O-ring from the shift rod bore in the pump base. Then,

carefully pry the pump base upward and slide it off the drive shaft. Remove and discard the pump base gasket.

NOTE
If the drive shaft is pulled loose from the pinion gear in Step 8, the propeller shaft and bearing carrier must be removed

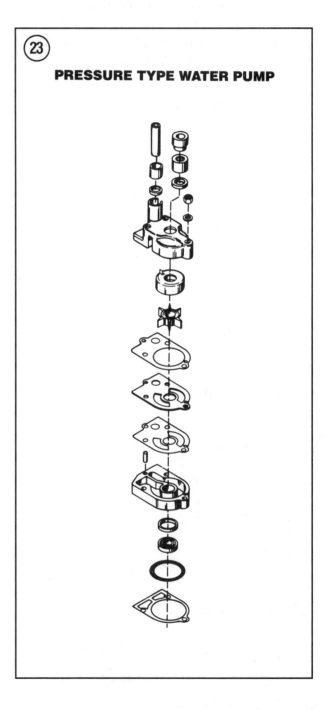

㉓

PRESSURE TYPE WATER PUMP

from the gear housing to properly reinstall the drive shaft.

8. 3.3 hp—If water pump base removal is necessary, hold down securely on the drive shaft and dislodge the base by carefully prying on both sides of the base using screwdrivers or similar tools. Pry at the bosses located on each side of the base. Do not allow the drive shaft to move upward and disengage the pinion gear or complete gear housing disassembly will be necessary. Remove and discard the lower shift rod O-ring from the pump base.

9. If necessary, remove the insert from the pump housing. Tap the insert from the housing with a small punch and hammer.

10. Support the pump base in a vise with protective jaws and remove the drive shaft oil seal with a suitable puller and appropriate jaws.

8, 9.9 and 15 hp

Refer to **Figure 26** for this procedure.

1. Remove the gear housing as described in this chapter. Secure the housing in a vise with protective jaws. If protective jaws are not available, position the unit upright in a vise with the skeg between wooden blocks.

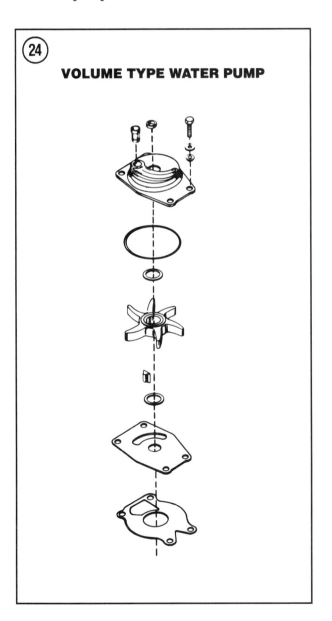

VOLUME TYPE WATER PUMP ㉔

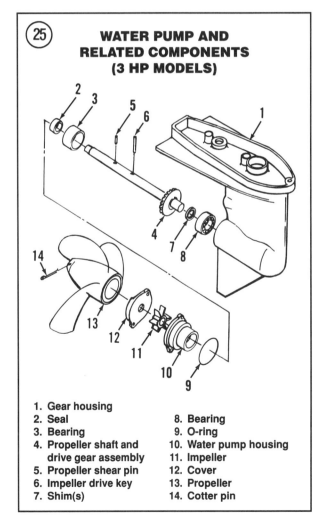

㉕ **WATER PUMP AND RELATED COMPONENTS (3 HP MODELS)**

1. Gear housing
2. Seal
3. Bearing
4. Propeller shaft and drive gear assembly
5. Propeller shear pin
6. Impeller drive key
7. Shim(s)
8. Bearing
9. O-ring
10. Water pump housing
11. Impeller
12. Cover
13. Propeller
14. Cotter pin

9

2. Unbolt the water pump cover. Carefully pry the cover up enough to grasp it, then slide the cover up and off the drive shaft.

3. If the impeller remained on the drive shaft, slide the impeller up and off the shaft.

4. Remove the impeller drive pin from the slot in the drive shaft.

5. Remove the pump base plate and plate gasket. Discard the gasket.

6. Remove the screw and washer at the front of the water pump base. Lift the pump base and shift shaft assembly from the gear housing, disengaging the water tube from its seal.

7. Remove and discard the pump base gasket.

8. Remove the screw and retainer holding the water tube to the pump base, then pull the water tube from the pump base. Check the water tube seal and replace as required.

9. Remove and discard the 2 pump base seals.

10. Remove and discard the pump cover seal. Inspect the inside of the cover for excessive grooves and replace as required.

20 and 25 hp

1. Remove the gear housing as described in this chapter. Secure the housing in a suitable holding fixture or a vise with protective jaws. If protective jaws are not available, position the unit upright in a vise with the skeg between wooden blocks.

2. Slide the rubber centrifugal slinger (A, **Figure 27**) up and off the drive shaft.

> *NOTE*
> *Plastic isolators installed under pump cover screws may come out with screws in Step 3. If not, they can be removed from the cover once it is off the gear housing.*

3. Remove the screws and flat washers (B, **Figure 27**) holding the pump cover to the gear housing.

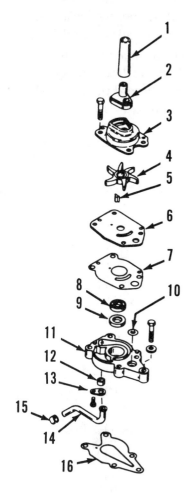

(26) WATER PUMP (8, 9.9 AND 15 HP MODELS)

1. Water tube guide	9. Seal
2. Seal	10. Shift shaft O-ring
3. Cover	11. Pump base
4. Impeller	12. Pickup tube seal
5. Drive key	13. Pickup tube retainer
6. Plate	14. Pickup tube
7. Gasket	15. Pickup tube seal
8. Seal	16. Gasket

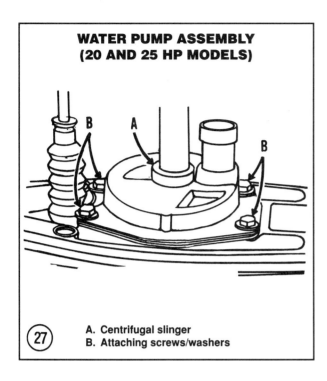

**WATER PUMP ASSEMBLY
(20 AND 25 HP MODELS)**

(27)
A. Centrifugal slinger
B. Attaching screws/washers

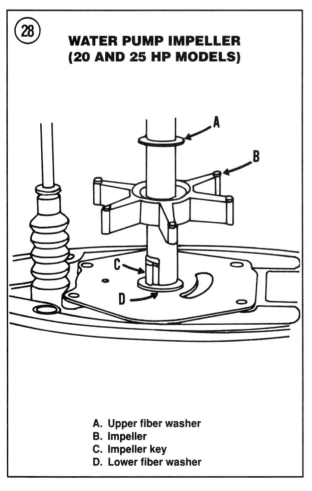

(28)
**WATER PUMP IMPELLER
(20 AND 25 HP MODELS)**

A. Upper fiber washer
B. Impeller
C. Impeller key
D. Lower fiber washer

4. Press downward on the drive shaft and slide the pump cover up and off the shaft.

NOTE
Pump impeller and upper washer may come off with the pump cover.

5. Remove the upper washer, impeller, impeller key and lower washer from the gear housing. See **Figure 28**.

6. Carefully loosen the face plate from the gear housing using a putty knife. Slide the face plate and gasket up and off the drive shaft. Discard the gasket.

40 hp, 50-60 hp (prior to serial No. D000750) and 135-200 hp

1. Remove the gear housing as described in this chapter. Secure the gear housing in a suitable

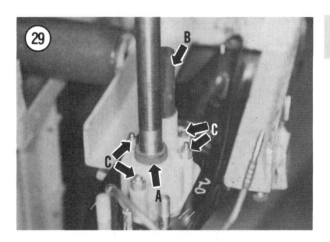

(29)

9

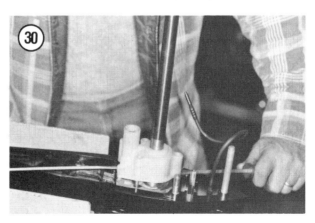

(30)

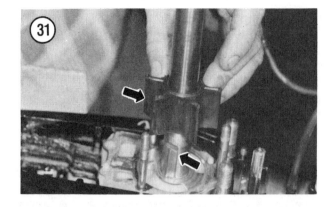

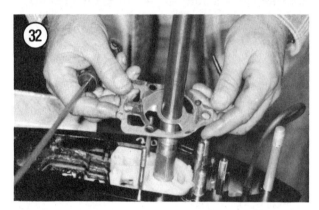

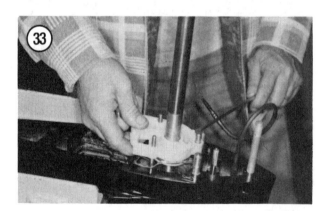

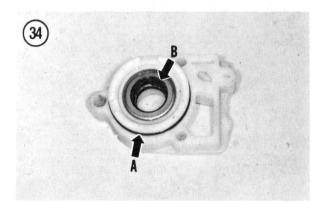

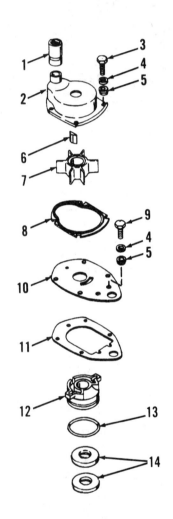

WATER PUMP (50 AND 60 [SERIAL NO. D000750-ON] HP MODELS)

1. Water tube seal
2. Pump cover
3. Screw
4. Washer
5. Insulator
6. Drive key
7. Impeller
8. Gasket
9. Screw
10. Plate
11. Gasket
12. Pump base
13. O-ring
14. Seals

holding fixture or a vise with protective jaws. If protective jaws are not available, position the unit upright in a vise with the skeg between wooden blocks.

2. Remove the drive shaft seal from the top of the shaft. Remove the rubber centrifugal slinger (A, **Figure 29**) from the drive shaft.

3. If so equipped, remove the water tube guide (B, **Figure 29**) and seal from the pump cover. Discard the seal.

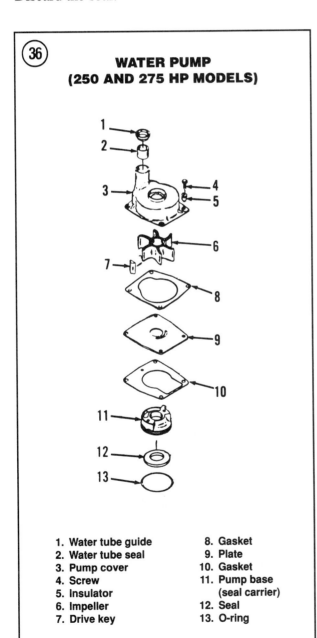

(36)

**WATER PUMP
(250 AND 275 HP MODELS)**

1. Water tube guide
2. Water tube seal
3. Pump cover
4. Screw
5. Insulator
6. Impeller
7. Drive key
8. Gasket
9. Plate
10. Gasket
11. Pump base (seal carrier)
12. Seal
13. O-ring

4. Remove the fasteners (C, **Figure 29**) holding the water pump cover to the gear housing.

5. Insert screwdrivers at the fore and aft ends of the pump cover and pry the cover upward. See **Figure 30**. Lift the cover up and off the drive shaft.

NOTE
In extreme cases, it may be necessary to split the impeller hub with a hammer and chisel to remove it from the drive shaft in Step 6.

6. Remove the impeller and drive key from the drive shaft. If necessary, drive the impeller upward on the shaft with a punch and hammer. See **Figure 31**.

7. Remove the pump face plate with top and bottom gaskets (**Figure 32**). Discard the gaskets.

8. Insert screwdrivers at the fore and aft ends of the pump base. Pad the pry areas under each screwdriver with clean shop towels and pry the pump base loose. Remove the base from the shaft (**Figure 33**).

9. Remove and discard the pump base-to-gear housing O-ring (A, **Figure 34**).

10. Pry the drive shaft seals (B, **Figure 34**) from the pump base from the gear housing side of the base.

11. If the water pump insert must be replaced, drive the insert from the pump cover with a punch and hammer. If the insert refuses to come out, carefully drill a 3/16 in. (4.8 mm) hole through the top (but not through the insert) on each side of the cover and drive the insert out with a hammer and punch.

9

50-60 hp (serial No. D000750-on); 75-115 hp, 250 and 275 hp

Refer to **Figure 35** (50 and 60 hp), **Figure 36** (250 and 275 hp) or **Figure 37** (75-115 hp) for this procedure.

1. Remove the gear housing as described in this chapter. Secure the gear housing in a suitable

holding fixture or a vise with protective jaws. If protective jaws are not available, position the unit upright in a vise with the skeg between wooden blocks.

2. Remove the water tube guide (250-275 hp) and water tube seal from the pump cover.

NOTE
The isolators installed on the front 2 cover screws on 50-60 hp models are a different design than the remaining isolators. Note the location of the front isolators for reference during reassembly.

3. Remove 6 pump cover retaining screws and isolators on 50 and 60 hp models or 4 retaining screws and isolators on 75-115, 250 and 275 hp models. Lift the pump cover up and off the drive shaft. If necessary, dislodge the cover from the gear housing by carefully prying at each end using suitable tools.

NOTE
In extreme cases, it may be necessary to split the impeller hub with a hammer and chisel to remove it in Step 4.

4. Remove the impeller from the drive shaft. If the impeller is frozen to the shaft, it may be necessary to drive the impeller off the shaft using a punch and hammer. See **Figure 31**.

5. Remove the impeller drive key from its slot in the drive shaft (**Figure 31**).

6. Remove the pump face plate with the upper and lower gaskets. Discard the gaskets.

7A. 75-115 hp—Remove the 6 screws and washers securing the pump base to the gear housing. Dislodge the base from the gear housing by carefully prying at each end using 2 screwdrivers. Lift the base up and off the drive shaft. Remove and discard the base-to-gear housing gasket. Carefully pry the drive shaft seal from the pump base.

NOTE
A plastic water pump base is used on some 75-115 hp models. The base uses silicone impregnated seals and does not

require gaskets. The pump base may be reused if the silicone seals are in acceptable condition. If, however, the seals become damaged, the pump base must be replaced. The plastic water pump base can NOT be used on gear housings which require the aluminum base and gaskets.

7B. All others—Remove the pump base by carefully prying on each side of the base using 2 screwdrivers. On 250 and 275 hp models, 2 water pump cover screws can be threaded into

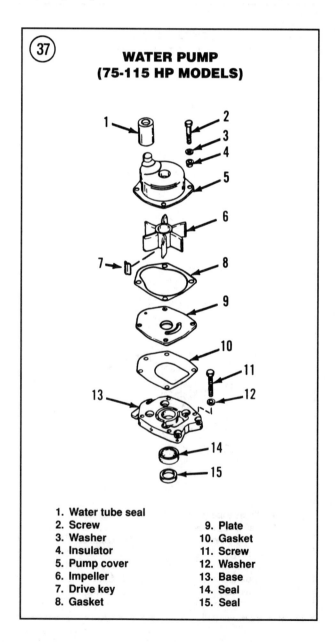

③⑦ **WATER PUMP
(75-115 HP MODELS)**

1. Water tube seal	
2. Screw	
3. Washer	9. Plate
4. Insulator	10. Gasket
5. Pump cover	11. Screw
6. Impeller	12. Washer
7. Drive key	13. Base
8. Gasket	14. Seal
	15. Seal

the base to ease removal from the gear housing. Remove and discard the pump base O-ring and seal(s).

Cleaning and Inspection

1. Clean all metal parts in solvent and dry with compressed air.
2. Clean all gasket material from all mating surfaces.
3. Check the pump cover and base for cracks or distortion from overheating.
4. Check face plate and water pump insert for grooves or rough surfaces. Replace the insert (or cover) or face plate if necessary.

NOTE
The water pump impeller must be able to float on the drive shaft. Clean the impeller area of the drive shaft thoroughly using crocus cloth. Be certain the impeller slides onto the drive shaft easily.

5. Check the bonding of the rubber to the impeller hub for separation. Check the side seal surfaces and blade ends for cracks, tears, excessive wear or a glazed or melted appearance. If any of these defects are noted, do *not* reuse the original impeller.

NOTE
On 50 and 60 (serial No. D000750-on) hp, 75, 90, 100 and 115 hp models, the impeller sealing ring may wear a circular groove in the water pump cover and face plate. This groove will not affect water pump performance and should be disregarded.

6. 50-60 (serial No. D000750-on), 75, 90, 100 and 115 hp:
   a. Measure the thickness of the pump cover at the discharge slots. Replace the cover if the metal thickness is 0.060 in. (1.52 mm) or less.
   b. Inspect the pump cover and face plate for grooves or excessive wear. Replace the

cover and/or plate if grooves (except the impeller seal ring grooves) exceed 0.030 in. (0.76 mm) deep.

Assembly and Installation

Replace all gaskets, seals and O-rings during reassembly. The manufacturer recommends replacing the impeller anytime the pump is disassembled, regardless of its appearance. If the original impeller must be reused, be certain it is installed in the same rotational direction as removed to prevent premature failure. The curl of the impeller blades must be positioned in a counterclockwise direction, as seen from the top of the pump unit. See **Figure 38**. Impeller rotation is clockwise on all models.

3 hp

Refer to **Figure 25** for this procedure.

1. Press a new seal into the water pump housing using a suitable mandrel and driver. The seal lip should face away from the propeller end of the housing.
2. If removed, press a new ball bearing into the pump housing. Press the bearing from the numbered side, until seated in the housing.
3. Install a new O-ring onto the pump housing.
4. Lubricate the ball bearing, O-ring and seal lip with Quicksilver 2-4-C Marine Lubricant.
5. Install the pump housing into the gear housing.
6. Insert the impeller drive pin into the propeller shaft.
7. Slide the impeller onto the propeller shaft. Install the impeller into the pump housing while rotating the impeller in a clockwise direction. Make sure the impeller properly engages the drive pin.
8. Apply Quicksilver Perfect Seal to the threads of the pump housing retaining screws. Install the screws and tighten to 25 in.-lb. (2.8 N•m).

9

3.3, 4 and 5 hp

1. Place the water pump base on a flat work surface and press a new oil seal into the bore with a suitable mandrel and driver. Press the seal into the bore until it is flush with the bore surface.

2. Lubricate the seal lips with Quicksilver 2-4-C Marine Lubricant.

3. 3.3 hp—Install a new O-ring onto the shift rod bushing. Lubricate the O-ring and bushing with Quicksilver 2-4-C Marine Lubricant. Install the bushing/O-ring assembly into the shift rod bore in the pump base.

4. Install a new water pump base gasket, then install the base over the drive shaft and onto the gear housing.

5A. 3.3 hp—Install a new shift rod O-ring into the pump housing. Lubricate the O-ring with Quicksilver 2-4-C Marine Lubricant.

5B. 4 and 5 hp—Lubricate the shift rod bushing O-ring with Quicksilver 2-4-C Marine Lubricant, then install the O-ring into the pump base.

Install the shift rod and bushing assembly into the water pump base. Install the retainer plate, washer and screw. Tighten the screw to 70 in.-lb. (8.0 N·m).

6. Place new upper and lower gaskets onto the water pump plate. Install the plate and gaskets over the drive shaft and shift rod, then seat the plate/gaskets on the pump base.

7. If the pump insert was removed from the housing, align the insert tab with its respective hole in the housing. Press the insert into the housing.

8. Install the water pickup tube seal and water tube seal into the pump housing. Lubricate the inside diameter of the seals with Quicksilver 2-4-C Marine Lubricant.

9. Install the pump pickup tube into the pump housing seal.

10. Lubricate the impeller drive pin with 2-4-C Marine Lubricant. Fit the key into the slot in the drive shaft, then slide the impeller over the drive

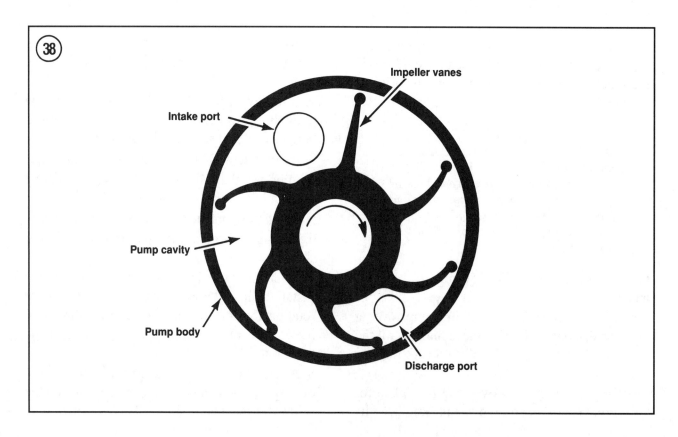

shaft and drive key. Lubricate the impeller blades with 2-4-C Marine Lubricant.

11. Slide the pump housing over the drive shaft and down to the impeller. Align the water tube with the housing seal. Rotate the drive shaft clockwise while pushing downward on the pump housing, until the housing is seated.

12. Install the housing screws and washers. Tighten the screws to 70 in.-lb. (8.0 N•m).

8, 9.9 and 15 hp

Refer to **Figure 26** for this procedure.

1. Install a new seal into the base (lip facing up) with tool part No. 91-13655, or equivalent. Repeat this step to install the second seal (lip facing down).

2. Install the water tube seal onto the water tube, if removed. Insert the seal end of the tube into the water pump base. Install the tube retainer and screw. Securely tighten the screw.

3. Insert the shift shaft through the pump base and install the retainer clip into the groove on the shift shaft.

4. Install a new water pump base gasket. Make sure the lone screw hole in the gasket is positioned on the starboard side of the housing.

5. Install the water pump base and shift shaft assembly into the housing, guiding the end of the water tube into the housing seal.

6. Apply Loctite 242 to the threads of the pump base screws. Install the pump base and tighten the screws to 40 in.-lb. (4.5 N•m).

7. Install a new O-ring over the shift shaft and fit it into the pump base bore.

8. Install the water pump plate. Fit a new gasket over the shift shaft and onto the plate.

9. Lubricate the outside diameter of a new water tube seal with Quicksilver 2-4-C Marine Lubricant. Press the seal onto the pump cover. Install the water tube guide onto the water tube seal.

10. Install the impeller drive key into the slot in the drive shaft. Hold the key in position with Quicksilver 2-4-C Marine Lubricant. Slide the impeller onto the drive shaft. Align the impeller key slot with the drive key, then install the impeller.

11. Lubricate the inside of the pump cover with Quicksilver 2-4-C Marine Lubricant. Slide the pump cover over the drive shaft and down to the impeller. Rotate the drive shaft clockwise while pushing downward on the cover, until the cover is seated.

12. Apply Loctite 242 to the threads of the pump cover screws. Install the screws and tighten in a crossing pattern to 40 in.-lb. (4.5 N•m).

20 and 25 hp

1. Press down and rotate the drive shaft to seat the shaft and pinion gear splines.

2. Install a new face plate gasket and the stainless steel face plate onto the gear housing.

3. Install a fiber washer flat against the face plate.

4. Install the impeller drive key into its slot in the drive shaft. Hold the key in position with Quicksilver 2-4-C Marine Lubricant.

5. Align the impeller key slot with the drive key and seat the impeller against the face plate.

6. Install a fiber washer flat against the impeller.

7. Install a new pump cover O-ring, using 2-4-C Marine Lubricant to hold it in place. Install the pump cover against the impeller.

8. Depress the pump cover assembly and rotate the drive shaft clockwise until the cover is seated on the face plate.

> *CAUTION*
> *If holes are not properly aligned in Step 9, the plastic isolators may crack or crush when the cover screws are tightened.*

9. Align the mounting holes in the gear housing, gasket, face plate and cover. Install a plastic isolator into each cover mounting hole.

10. Install flat washers and attaching screws into the cover. Tighten the screws evenly and securely. Do *not* overtighten.

11. Install the rubber centrifugal slinger over the drive shaft and against the water pump cover.

40 hp, 50-60 hp (prior to serial No. D000750) and 135-200 hp

1. If the pump housing insert was removed, coat the insert area in the cover with Quicksilver Perfect Seal and press the new insert into the cover. Align the insert tab with its respective recess in the cover.

> *NOTE*
> *If insert removal required drilling holes into the pump cover, fill the holes with a suitable RTV sealant.*

2. Position the pump base on a press. Apply Loctite 271 to the outside diameter of each pump base seal. Press the smaller diameter seal (lip facing impeller) into the pump base until seated. Press the larger diameter seal into the pump base with the seal lip facing the gear housing.

3. Install a new O-ring into its groove in the pump base.

4. Lubricate the O-ring and oil seal lips with Quicksilver 2-4-C Marine Lubricant.

5. Install a new pump base gasket over the pump mounting studs. Wrap a suitable tape around the drive shaft O-ring groove to prevent the groove from cutting the pump base seals. Install the pump base over the drive shaft and into position in the housing. See **Figure 39**.

6. Install new lower and upper gaskets on the pump face plate. Install the plate and gaskets onto the pump base. See **Figure 40**. Make sure the dowel pins on the base properly engage the face plate and gaskets.

7. Place the impeller drive key into its slot in the drive shaft. Hold the key in position with 2-4-C Marine Lubricant. Slide the impeller over the drive shaft and onto the drive key. See **Figure 41**. Make sure the impeller properly engages the drive key.

8. Install a new water tube seal into the pump cover with the plastic side of the seal facing downward.

9. Install the water tube guide into the pump cover.

10. Apply a light coat of Quicksilver 2-4-C Marine Lubricant to the inside diameter of the pump cover.

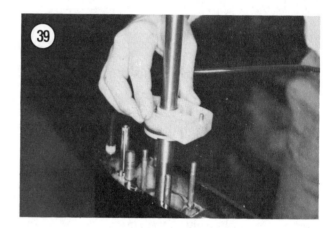

11. Slide the pump cover over the drive shaft. Align the pump cover holes with the pump base studs. Push downward on the cover while rotating the drive shaft clockwise, until the cover is seated.

CAUTION
Do not overtighten the fasteners in Step 12 or pump cover may crack during operation.

12. Install the cover washers and nuts (and screw on V6 models). On V6 models, tighten the nuts evenly to 50 in.-lb. (5.6 N•m) and the screw to 35 in.-lb. (3.9 N•m). On all other models, tighten the nuts evenly to 30 in.-lb. (3.4 N•m).

13. Install the rubber centrifugal slinger over the drive shaft and against the pump cover.

14. Remove the tape from the drive shaft O-ring groove. Clean any tape residue from the drive shaft.

50-60 hp (serial No. D000750-on); 75-115 hp, 250 and 275 hp

Refer to **Figure 35** (50-60 hp), **Figure 36** (250 and 275 hp) or **Figure 37** (75-115 hp) for this procedure.

1A. 50-60 hp—Lubricate the outer diameter of the water pump base seals with Quicksilver Gear

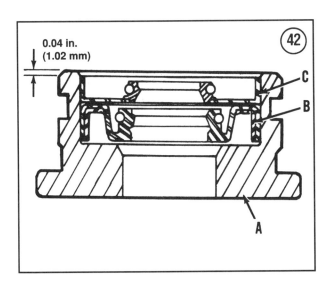

Lubricant (or equivalent). Using a suitable mandrel, press seal (B, **Figure 42**) into the pump base (A) with its seal lip facing down, until fully seated. Next press seal (C, **Figure 42**) into the pump base (lip facing up) until the top of the seal is 0.04 in. (1.02 mm) below the surface of the base as shown (**Figure 42**). Install a new pump base O-ring into its groove. Lubricate the O-ring with Quicksilver Special Lubricant 101.

1B. 250-275 hp—Apply Loctite 271 to the outer diameter of the pump base seal. Using a suitable mandrel, press the seal into the bottom of the base until the seal is flush with the bottom surface of the base. Note the seal lip must face down when the base is installed. Install a new pump base O-ring into its groove. Lubricate the O-ring with Quicksilver Needle Bearing Assembly Grease.

1C. 75-115 hp—Apply Loctite 271 to the outer diameter of the water pump base seals. Place the upper seal onto the long end of seal installer (part No. 92-13949). The seal lip should face away from the shoulder of the tool. Press the seal into the bottom of the pump base until the shoulder of the seal installer tool bottoms on the base. Next, place the lower seal onto the short end of seal installer part No. 91-13949. The seal lip should be facing the tool shoulder. Press the seal into the bottom of the base until the seal installer bottoms on the base. Lubricate the seal lips with Quicksilver Needle Bearing Assembly Grease.

2A. 75-115 hp:

  a. Install a new pump base-to-gear housing gasket.

  b. Install the pump base. Apply Loctite 271 to the threads of the pump base retaining screws, install the screws and tighten to 60 in.-lb. (6.8 N•m).

2B. All others—Install the water pump base into the gear housing. Make sure the base is fully seated. If removed, install the divider plate (behind pump base). Run a bead of RTV sealant on each end of the plate.

NOTE
On 75-115 hp models equipped with a plastic water pump base, the base-to-face plate gasket is not required.

3. Install a new face plate gasket, then install the face plate. Install a new pump cover gasket on top of the face plate. The seal ring on the gasket (if so equipped) should face up.

4. Place the impeller drive key into its slot in the drive shaft. Hold the key in place with Quicksilver 2-4-C Marine Lubricant.

5. Install the impeller, making sure the drive key properly engages the impeller slot.

6. Apply a light coat of Quicksilver Needle Bearing Assembly Grease to the inside diameter of the pump cover.

7. Slide the pump cover over the drive shaft. Align the pump cover holes with the screw holes in the gear housing. Push downward on the cover while rotating the drive shaft clockwise, until the cover is seated.

8. On 250 and 275 hp models, apply Quicksilver Perfect Seal to the threads of the pump cover screws. On all other models, apply Loctite 271 to the cover screws. Install the pump cover screws and isolators. On 50-60 hp models, the front 2 isolators are not the same as the remaining isolators. Be sure the isolators are installed in their proper locations (as noted during removal).

9. Tighten the cover screws in a crossing pattern to 60 in.-lb. (6.8 N·m).

10. Lubricate the inside diameter of the water tube seal with Quicksilver 2-4-C Marine Lubricant. Install the seal onto the pump cover. On models so equipped, install the water tube guide.

BEARING CARRIER AND PROPELLER SHAFT

Removal
(3 hp)

Refer to **Figure 43** for this procedure.

1. Remove the water pump and pump housing as described in this chapter.

2. Using a screwdriver or similar tool, reach into the gear cavity and remove the clip securing the pinion gear to the lower drive shaft. Lift the drive shaft out the top of the gear housing, then remove the pinion gear from the gear cavity.

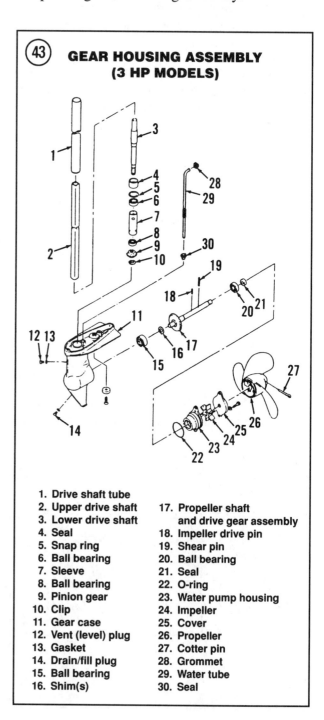

43 GEAR HOUSING ASSEMBLY (3 HP MODELS)

1. Drive shaft tube
2. Upper drive shaft
3. Lower drive shaft
4. Seal
5. Snap ring
6. Ball bearing
7. Sleeve
8. Ball bearing
9. Pinion gear
10. Clip
11. Gear case
12. Vent (level) plug
13. Gasket
14. Drain/fill plug
15. Ball bearing
16. Shim(s)
17. Propeller shaft and drive gear assembly
18. Impeller drive pin
19. Shear pin
20. Ball bearing
21. Seal
22. O-ring
23. Water pump housing
24. Impeller
25. Cover
26. Propeller
27. Cotter pin
28. Grommet
29. Water tube
30. Seal

3. Pull the propeller shaft and drive gear assembly from the gear housing. Be sure to retrieve the shim(s) located on the end of the shaft. See 16, **Figure 43**.

Removal
(3.3 hp)

Refer to **Figure 44** for this procedure. The bearing carrier and propeller shaft can be removed without removing the gear housing from the drive shaft housing. Some 3.3 hp models (serial No. 901217-on) may be equipped with a nonshiftable gear housing. On models so equipped, refer to *3 Hp Models* for gear housing service.

1. Drain the gear housing lubricant as described in Chapter Four.
2. Remove the propeller and shear pin as described in this chapter.
3. Remove the 2 propeller shaft bearing housing mounting screws and washers.
4. Tap on either side of the bearing carrier and attempt to rotate it in the gear housing to break the seal.
5. When the bearing carrier is loose, pull it, along with the propeller shaft assembly, out of the gear housing.

Removal
(4 and 5 hp)

Refer to **Figure 45** for this procedure.
1. Remove the gear housing as described in this chapter.
2. Remove the 2 bolts holding the bearing carrier in the gear housing.
3. Clamp the propeller shaft into a vise with protective jaws or between wooden blocks.
4. Tap the gear housing at a point mid-way between the antiventilation plate and the propeller shaft with a soft-face mallet while pulling the housing off the propeller shaft assembly.

5. Remove the propeller shaft from the vise. Make sure the cam follower came out of the housing with the propeller shaft. If it did not, retrieve it from the gear cavity and reinstall it onto the front of the propeller shaft.
6. Remove the propeller shaft and reverse gear from the bearing carrier.

Removal
(8, 9.9 and 15 hp)

Refer to **Figure 46** and **Figure 47** for this procedure.
1. Remove the gear housing as described in this chapter.
2. Unthread the bearing carrier from the gear housing using Bearing Carrier Tool part No. 91-13664. If the tool is not available, separate the cap from the thrust hub with a hammer. Install the thrust hub onto the shaft and tighten it with a suitable box-end wrench to unthread the carrier.
3. Remove the propeller shaft and bearing carrier from the gear housing. Make sure the cam follower came out of the housing with the propeller shaft. If it did not, retrieve it from the housing gear cavity and reinstall it into the front of the propeller shaft.
4. Remove the propeller shaft and reverse gear from the bearing carrier.

Removal
(20 and 25 hp)

Refer to **Figure 48** for this procedure.
1. Remove the gear housing as described in this chapter.
2. Remove the 3 screws securing the anode ring, O-ring retainer plate and O-ring. Remove the assembly from the gear cavity.
3A. Models equipped with a 2-piece thrust hub (1990 and 1991 models):
   a. Remove the thrust hub from the propeller, then separate the cap from the thrust hub by

9

tapping gently with a small hammer. Once the cap is removed, install the hub onto the propeller shaft and align its ears with the recesses in the bearing carrier.

    b. Temporarily reinstall the propeller onto the propeller shaft. Slide the propeller up against the thrust hub.

    c. Thread the propeller nut onto the propeller shaft to provide pressure against the thrust hub.

    d. Place a wrench on the propeller hex-head hub and turn the hub clockwise to unthread the bearing carrier. Remove the nut, propeller and thrust hub from the propeller shaft.

3B. Models equipped with a 1-piece thrust hub (1992-on models):

    a. Slide bearing carrier tool part No. 91-93843 onto the propeller shaft and engage it with the bearing carrier.

    b. Unthread the bearing carrier by turning the tool clockwise with an appropriate size wrench.

4. Withdraw the propeller shaft and bearing carrier assembly from the gear housing.

5. Remove the cam follower from the propeller shaft. If the cam follower is not on the end of the shaft, retrieve it from the gear cavity.

6. Remove the bearing carrier from the propeller shaft.

Removal
(40 hp and 50-60 hp
[Prior to Serial No. D000750])

Refer to **Figure 49** for this procedure.

1. Remove the gear housing as described in this chapter.

2. Bend the locking tab on the tab washer back away from the cover nut recess with a screwdriver or punch and hammer. See **Figure 50**.

NOTE
If the cover nut is frozen in place and cannot be moved in Step 3, even with the assistance of heat and tapping on the tool, use an electric drill to drill out one

---

GEAR HOUSING COMPONENTS
(1993 3.3 HP MODELS)

1. Screw
2. Washer
3. Water pump housing
4. Grommet
5. Water tube
6. Water tube guide
7. Grommet
8. Water pump insert
9. Impeller
10. Gasket
11. Plate
12. Gasket
13. Water pump base
14. Seal
15. Gasket
16. Drive shaft
17. Impeller drive key
18. Bearing
19. Spacer
20. Bearing
21. Gear housing
22. Gasket
23. Vent (level) plug
24. Drain/fill plug
25. Pinion gear
26. Screw
27. Anode
28. Bearing
29. Shim(s)
30. Drive gear
31. Cam follower
32. Spring
33. Clutch
34. Propeller shaft
35. Bearing
36. Seal
37. O-ring
38. Propeller shaft bearing carrier
39. Propeller shear pin
40. Propeller
41. Cotter pin
42. Pin
43. Shift cam
44. Pin
45. Lower shift rod
46. O-ring
47. Shift rod bushing
48. O-ring
49. Screw
50. Washer
51. Clamp
52. Upper shift rod
53. Shift rod lever
54. Screw
55. Washer
56. O-rings
57. Spring
58. Detent ball
59. Shift lever

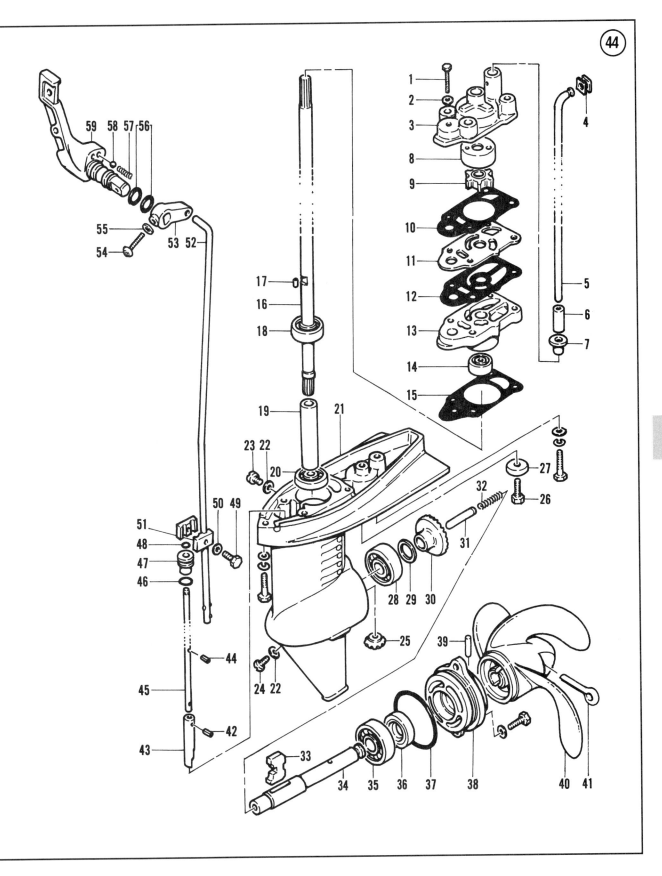

side of the nut. This will permit removal of the nut without damage to the housing.

3. Unscrew the cover nut using cover nut tool part No. 91-91947. See **Figure 51**. Remove the cover nut from the housing.

4. Remove the locking tab washer from the housing.

5. Install puller jaws part No. 91-46086A-1 and puller bolt part No. 91-85716 (or equivalent) and dislodge the bearing carrier from the gear housing. If necessary, use the propeller thrust hub (**Figure 52**) to prevent the puller jaws from sliding inward. Remove the bearing carrier from the gear housing (**Figure 53**).

6. Pull the propeller shaft assembly from the gear housing.

Removal
(50-60 hp [Serial No. D000750-on]; 75, 90, 100 and 115 hp)

Refer to **Figure 54** (50-60 hp) or **Figure 55** (75-115 hp) for this procedure.

1. Remove the gear housing as described in this chapter.

2. Remove the 2 bolts and washers, or self-locking nuts (if so equipped) securing the bearing carrier to the gear housing.

3. Install puller jaws part No. 91-46086A-1 and puller bolt part No. 91-85716 (or equivalent) and dislodge the bearing carrier from the gear housing. If necessary, use the propeller thrust hub (**Figure 56**) to prevent the puller jaws from sliding inward.

4. Remove the bearing carrier and propeller shaft components (**Figure 57**), then the propeller shaft (**Figure 58**) from the gear housing. Make sure the shift cam follower (and steel balls on 75-115 hp) is removed with the propeller shaft. If not, reach into the gear housing and withdraw the follower (and balls).

**GEAR HOUSING COMPONENTS
(4 AND 5 HP MODELS)**

1. Bolt
2. Washer
3. Water pump housing
4. Seal
5. Water pickup tube
6. Seal
7. Water tube
8. Seal
9. Cartridge insert
10. Impeller
11. Gasket
12. Plate
13. Gasket
14. Bolt
15. Washer
16. Retainer
17. Water pump base
18. Oil seal
19. Shim
20. Gasket
21. Gear housing
22. Washer
23. Bolt
24. Water pickup
25. Screw
26. Cotter pin
27. Nut
28. Washer
29. Propeller
30. Bolt
31. Washer
32. Thrust hub
33. Bearing carrier
34. O-ring
35. Oil seal
36. Bearing
37. Reverse gear
38. Washer
39. Propeller shaft
40. Spring
41. Sliding clutch
42. Cross pin
43. Guide
44. Cam follower
45. Forward gear
46. Shim
47. Bearing
48. Oil fill plug
49. Gasket
50. Bolt
51. Washer
52. Gasket
53. Oil level plug
54. Bearing
55. Anode
56. Bolt
57. Pinion gear
58. Drive shaft assembly
59. Drive pin

45

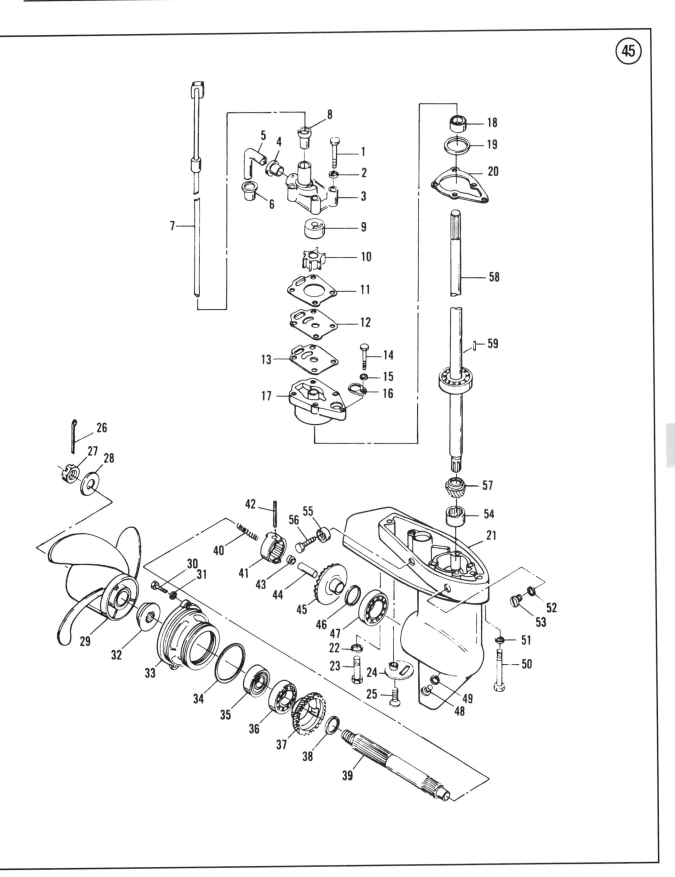

9

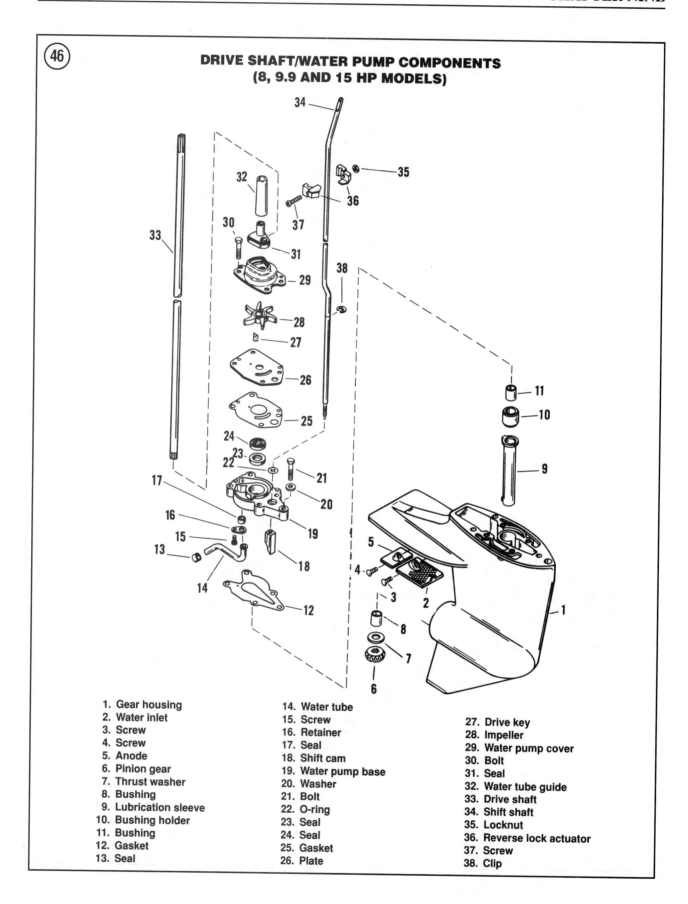

**DRIVE SHAFT/WATER PUMP COMPONENTS
(8, 9.9 AND 15 HP MODELS)**

1. Gear housing
2. Water inlet
3. Screw
4. Screw
5. Anode
6. Pinion gear
7. Thrust washer
8. Bushing
9. Lubrication sleeve
10. Bushing holder
11. Bushing
12. Gasket
13. Seal
14. Water tube
15. Screw
16. Retainer
17. Seal
18. Shift cam
19. Water pump base
20. Washer
21. Bolt
22. O-ring
23. Seal
24. Seal
25. Gasket
26. Plate
27. Drive key
28. Impeller
29. Water pump cover
30. Bolt
31. Seal
32. Water tube guide
33. Drive shaft
34. Shift shaft
35. Locknut
36. Reverse lock actuator
37. Screw
38. Clip

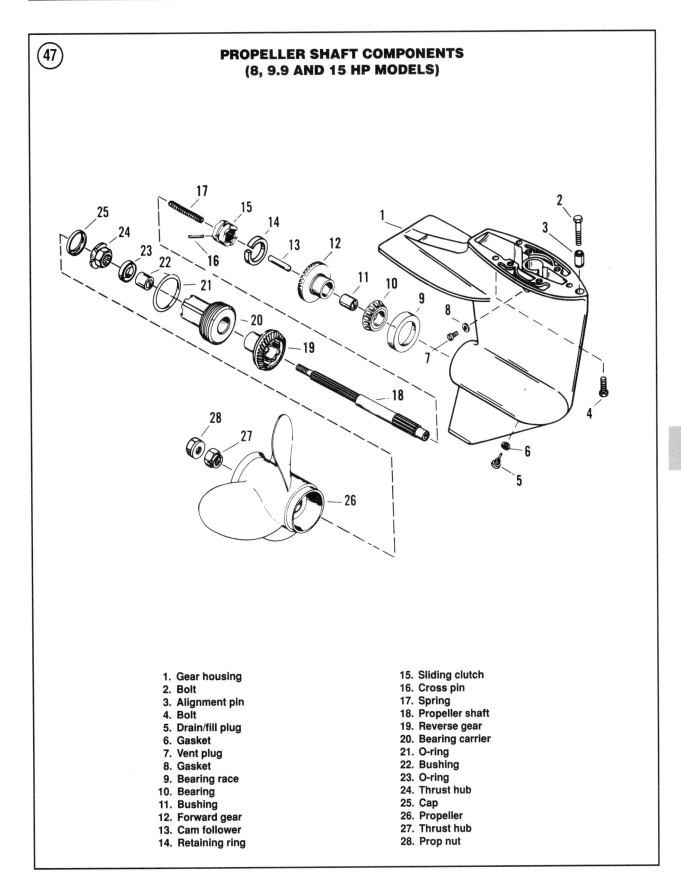

PROPELLER SHAFT COMPONENTS
(8, 9.9 AND 15 HP MODELS)

1. Gear housing
2. Bolt
3. Alignment pin
4. Bolt
5. Drain/fill plug
6. Gasket
7. Vent plug
8. Gasket
9. Bearing race
10. Bearing
11. Bushing
12. Forward gear
13. Cam follower
14. Retaining ring
15. Sliding clutch
16. Cross pin
17. Spring
18. Propeller shaft
19. Reverse gear
20. Bearing carrier
21. O-ring
22. Bushing
23. O-ring
24. Thrust hub
25. Cap
26. Propeller
27. Thrust hub
28. Prop nut

9

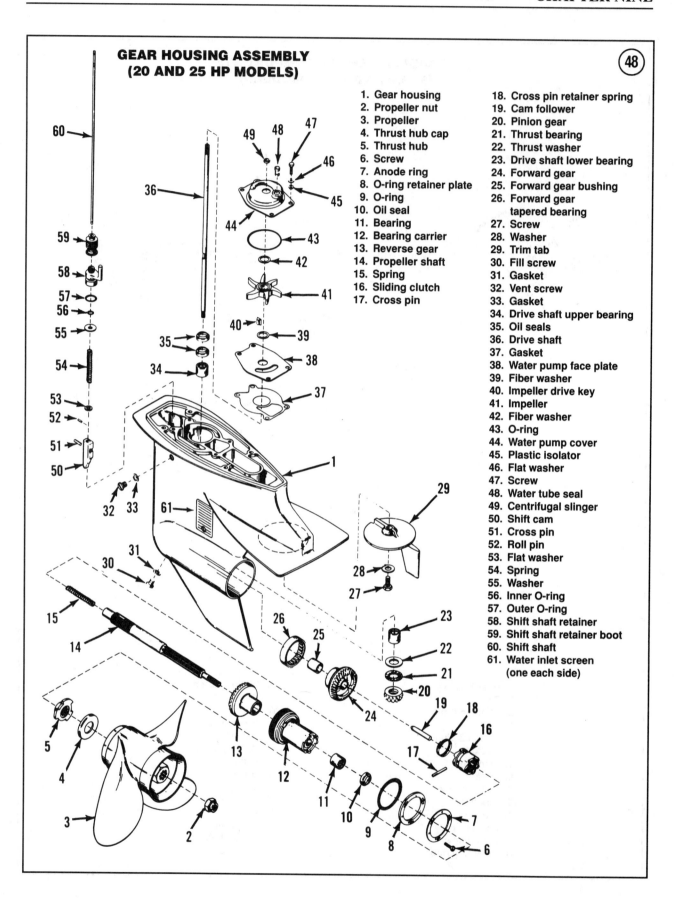

**GEAR HOUSING ASSEMBLY
(20 AND 25 HP MODELS)**

48

1. Gear housing
2. Propeller nut
3. Propeller
4. Thrust hub cap
5. Thrust hub
6. Screw
7. Anode ring
8. O-ring retainer plate
9. O-ring
10. Oil seal
11. Bearing
12. Bearing carrier
13. Reverse gear
14. Propeller shaft
15. Spring
16. Sliding clutch
17. Cross pin
18. Cross pin retainer spring
19. Cam follower
20. Pinion gear
21. Thrust bearing
22. Thrust washer
23. Drive shaft lower bearing
24. Forward gear
25. Forward gear bushing
26. Forward gear
   tapered bearing
27. Screw
28. Washer
29. Trim tab
30. Fill screw
31. Gasket
32. Vent screw
33. Gasket
34. Drive shaft upper bearing
35. Oil seals
36. Drive shaft
37. Gasket
38. Water pump face plate
39. Fiber washer
40. Impeller drive key
41. Impeller
42. Fiber washer
43. O-ring
44. Water pump cover
45. Plastic isolator
46. Flat washer
47. Screw
48. Water tube seal
49. Centrifugal slinger
50. Shift cam
51. Cross pin
52. Roll pin
53. Flat washer
54. Spring
55. Washer
56. Inner O-ring
57. Outer O-ring
58. Shift shaft retainer
59. Shift shaft retainer boot
60. Shift shaft
61. Water inlet screen
   (one each side)

Removal
(V6 Models)

V6 models may be equipped with a Cam-Shift (150XR4 and 150XR6) or E-Z Shift gear housing (all other models). Externally, the 2 housings appear identical but the internal components are different. For this reason, disassembly procedures differ according to type. Refer to **Figure 59** (Cam-Shift) and **Figure 60** and **Figure 61** (**E-Z** Shift). If it is not known which type is being serviced, shift the gear housing into neutral and turn the shift shaft to either side of the neutral position. The shift shaft on a Cam-Shift housing will rotate 360° counterclockwise, while the shift shaft on an E-Z Shift housing will only turn 30° to either side of the neutral position.

Cam-shift models

1. Remove the gear housing as described in this chapter.
2. Bend the locking tab on the tab washer back away from the cover nut recess with a screwdriver or punch and hammer. See **Figure 50**.

> *NOTE*
> *If the cover nut is frozen in place and cannot be moved in Step 3, even with the assistance of heat and tapping on the tool, drill out one side of the nut. This will permit removal of the nut without damage to the housing.*

3. Unscrew the housing cover nut using Cover Nut Tool part No. 91-73688. See **Figure 51**.
4. Remove the cover nut and tab washer.
5. Install puller jaws part No. 91-46086A-1 and puller bolt part No. 91-85716 (or equivalent) and dislodge the bearing carrier from the gear housing. If necessary, use the propeller thrust hub (**Figure 52**) to prevent the puller jaws from sliding inward.
6. Remove the bearing carrier and propeller shaft components (**Figure 57**), then the propeller shaft (**Figure 58**) from the gear housing. Be sure to

retrieve the bearing carrier locating key when the carrier is removed from the gear housing.

E-Z shift models

1. Remove the gear housing as described in this chapter.
2. Shift the gear housing into NEUTRAL.
3. Unthread (but do not remove from the shift shaft) the shift shaft bushing with bushing tool part No. 91-31107.

> *NOTE*
> *Do not rotate shift shaft either direction during removal in Step 4. Make sure the gear housing is in NEUTRAL before removing the shift shaft.*

4. Pull the shift shaft from the gear housing (**Figure 62**). If necessary to use pliers to remove the shaft; protect the shift shaft splines by wrapping a strip of aluminum or other soft metal, around the splines.
5. Bend the tab on the cover nut lock out of the cover nut recess with a screwdriver or punch and hammer. See **Figure 50**.

> *NOTE*
> *If the cover nut is frozen in place and cannot be moved in Step 6, even with the assistance of heat and tapping on the tool, drill out one side of the nut. This will permit removal of the nut without damage to the housing.*

6. Install cover nut tool part No. 91-61069 and unthread the cover nut. See **Figure 63**.
7. Remove the cover nut and tab washer from the gear housing.
8. Install puller jaws part No. 91-46086A-1 and puller bolt part No. 91-85716 (or equivalent) and remove the bearing carrier from the gear housing (**Figure 64**). If necessary, use propeller thrust hub to prevent the puller jaws from sliding inward. When the carrier is removed, be sure to retrieve the carrier locating key.

9

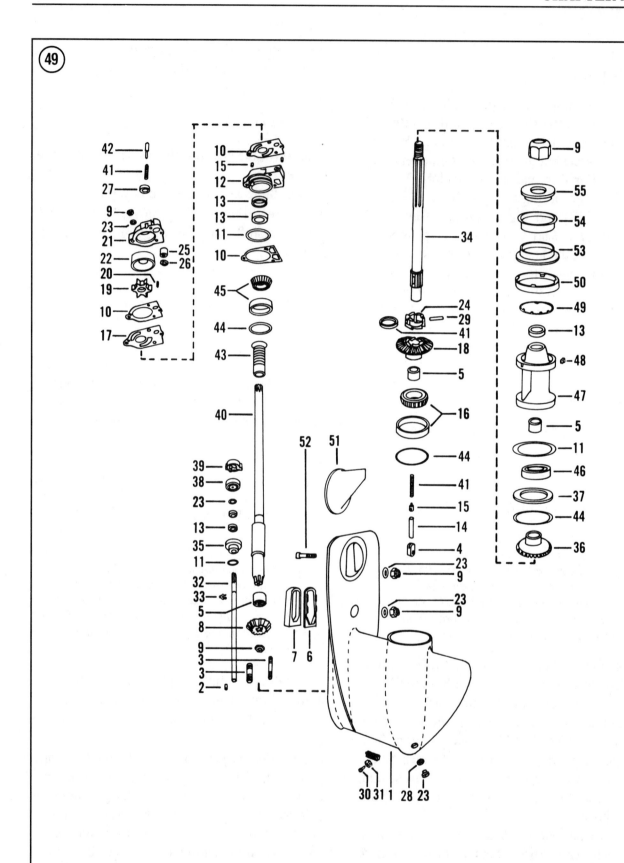

GEAR HOUSING ASSEMBLY (40 AND 50-60 HP [PRIOR TO SERIAL NO. D000750] MODELS

1. Gear housing
2. Dowel pin
3. Stud
4. Shift cam
5. Roller bearing
6. Support plate
7. Exhaust tube seal
8. Pinion gear
9. Nut
10. Gasket
11. O-ring
12. Water pump base
13. Oil seal
14. Cam follower
15. Guide block
16. Tapered roller bearing assembly
17. Face plate
18. Forward gear
19. Impeller
20. Impeller drive pin
21. Water pump cover
22. Water pump insert
23. Washer
24. Sliding clutch
25. Water tube seal
26. Nylon washer
27. Centrifugal slinger
28. Drain/fill plug
29. Cross pin
30. Flush plug
31. Flush plug washer
32. Shaft assembly
33. E-clip
34. Propeller shaft
35. Shift shaft bushing
36. Reverse gear
37. Thrust waher
38. Drain/fill plug
39. Reverse lock cam
40. Drive shaft
41. Spring
42. Pin
43. Lubrication sleeve
44. Shim
45. Tapered bearing assembly
46. Ball bearing
47. Bearing carrier
48. Alignment key
49. Tab washer
50. Cover nut
51. Trim tab
52. Screw
53. Thrust hub
54. Thrust hub washer
55. Splined washer

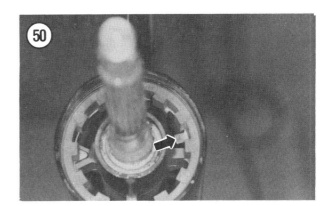

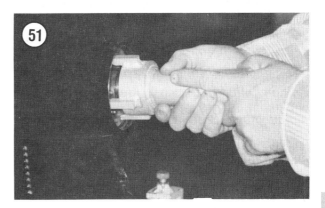

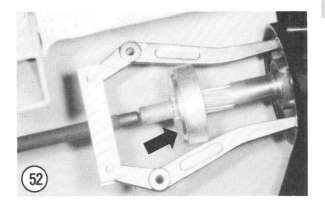

9

CAUTION
*At this point, side force must **not** be applied to the propeller shaft or it may break the clutch actuator rod neck.*

9. Pull the propeller shaft, cam follower and shift cam straight out of the gear housing with single smooth movement. See **Figure 65**. If the shaft can not be removed easily, proceed as follows:

a. Push the propeller shaft back into place against the forward gear. Look into the shift shaft hole with a flashlight. If the splined hole in the shift cam is visible, reinstall the shift shaft and rotate it to the neutral position. Remove the shift shaft and remove the propeller shaft, cam follower and shift cam.

b. If propeller shaft still cannot be removed, push the shaft back into place against the forward gear. Reinstall the bearing carrier sufficiently to support the propeller shaft. Remove the gear housing from the holding fixture and lay it on its port side. Strike the upper leading edge of the housing with a rubber mallet to dislodge the shift cam from the cam follower. Remove the bearing carrier and pull the propeller shaft from the housing. To remove the shift cam and follower, remove the forward gear as described in this chapter.

Cleaning and Inspection

1. Clean all parts in clean solvent and dry with compressed air.

2. On 3 hp models, replace the drive gear/propeller shaft assembly if the impeller drive pin hole, or the propeller shear pin hole is elongated or excessively worn. Inspect the propeller shaft bearing (inside gear housing). Replace the bearing if rusted, discolored or if it does not roll smoothly and freely. On 3.3 hp models, replace the propeller shaft if the propeller shear pin hole is elongated or excessively worn.

GEAR HOUSING ASSEMBLY (50 AND 60 [SERIAL NO. D000750-ON] HP MODELS)

1. Water tube seal	33. Vent plug
2. Screw	34. Vent plug
3. Washer	35. Shift cam
4. Insulator	36. Pinion gear
5. Water pump cover	37. Pinion gear nut
6. Impeller drive key	38. Shim pack
7. Impeller	39. Bearing race
8. Gasket	40. Tapered roller bearing
9. Face plate	41. Roller bearing
10. Gasket	42. Forward gear
11. Water pump base	43. Shift cam follower
12. O-ring	44. Guide
13. Seals	45. Spring
14. Drive shaft cover nut	46. Sliding clutch
15. Bearing race	47. Cross pin
16. Tapered roller bearing	48. Cross pin retainer
17. Shim pack	49. Propeller shaft
18. Drive shaft	50. Trim tab
19. Seal and plate	51. Washer
20. Plug	52. Screw
21. Roller bearing	53. Reverse gear
22. Dowel pin	54. Ball bearing
23. Shift shaft coupler	55. O-ring
24. Spacer	56. Bearing carrier
25. Seal	57. Screw
26. Bushing	58. Roller bearing
27. O-ring	59. Seals
28. Retaining ring	60. Thrust hub
29. Shift shaft	61. Propeller
30. Gear housing	62. Tab washer
31. Drain/fill plug	63. Propeller nut
32. Gasket	

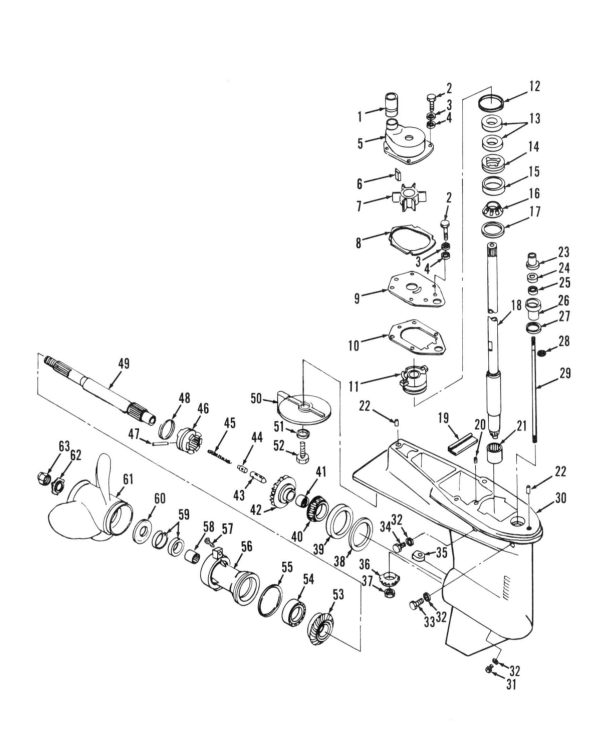

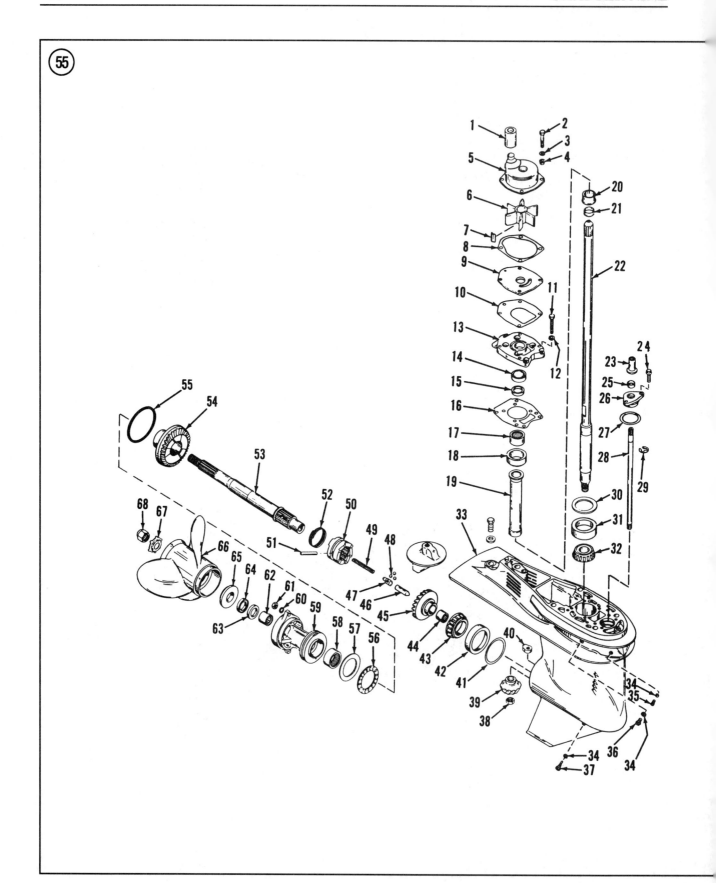

GEAR HOUSING ASSEMBLY
(75-115 HP MODELS)

1. Water tube seal
2. Screw
3. Washer
4. Insulator
5. Water pump cover
6. Impeller
7. Impeller drive key
8. Gasket
9. Face plate
10. Gasket
11. Screw
12. Washer
13. Water pump base
14. Seal
15. Seal
16. Gasket
17. Roller bearing
18. Carrier
19. Sleeve
20. Wear sleeve
21. Seal ring
22. Drive shaft
23. Shift shaft coupler
24. Screw
25. Seal
26. Shift shaft retainer
27. O-ring
28. Shift shaft
29. Retaining ring
30. Shim pack
31. Bearing race
32. Tapered roller bearing
33. Gear housing
34. Gasket
35. Plug
36. Plug
37. Plug
38. Pinion gear nut
39. Pinion gear
40. Shift cam
41. Shim pack
42. Bearing race
43. Tapered roller bearing
44. Roller bearing
45. Forward gear
46. Shift cam follower
47. Guide
48. Balls
49. Spring
50. Sliding clutch
51. Cross pin
52. Cross pin retainer
53. Propeller shaft
54. Reverse gear
55. O-ring
56. Thrust bearing
57. Thrust washer
58. Roller bearing
59. Bearing carrier
60. Washer
61. Nut
62. Roller bearing
63. Seal
64. Seal
65. Thrust hub
66. Propeller
67. Tab washer
68. Propeller nut

NOTE
Do not remove the bearings from the bearing carrier unless replacement is necessary.

3. Inspect the bearing carrier casting for cracks or other damage.

4. Check bearing carrier roller/needle bearing contact points on the propeller shaft. If pits, grooves, scoring, heat discoloration or embed-

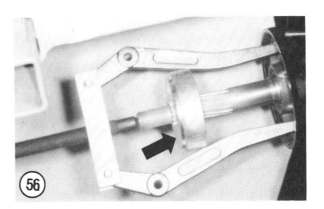

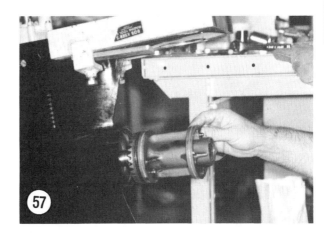

9

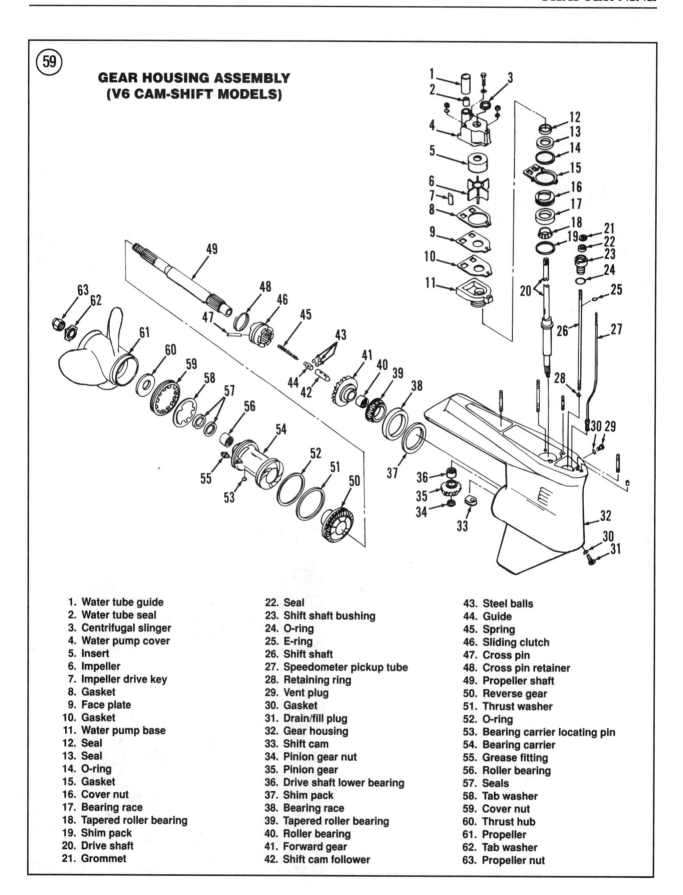

**GEAR HOUSING ASSEMBLY
(V6 CAM-SHIFT MODELS)**

1. Water tube guide
2. Water tube seal
3. Centrifugal slinger
4. Water pump cover
5. Insert
6. Impeller
7. Impeller drive key
8. Gasket
9. Face plate
10. Gasket
11. Water pump base
12. Seal
13. Seal
14. O-ring
15. Gasket
16. Cover nut
17. Bearing race
18. Tapered roller bearing
19. Shim pack
20. Drive shaft
21. Grommet

22. Seal
23. Shift shaft bushing
24. O-ring
25. E-ring
26. Shift shaft
27. Speedometer pickup tube
28. Retaining ring
29. Vent plug
30. Gasket
31. Drain/fill plug
32. Gear housing
33. Shift cam
34. Pinion gear nut
35. Pinion gear
36. Drive shaft lower bearing
37. Shim pack
38. Bearing race
39. Tapered roller bearing
40. Roller bearing
41. Forward gear
42. Shift cam follower

43. Steel balls
44. Guide
45. Spring
46. Sliding clutch
47. Cross pin
48. Cross pin retainer
49. Propeller shaft
50. Reverse gear
51. Thrust washer
52. O-ring
53. Bearing carrier locating pin
54. Bearing carrier
55. Grease fitting
56. Roller bearing
57. Seals
58. Tab washer
59. Cover nut
60. Thrust hub
61. Propeller
62. Tab washer
63. Propeller nut

ded metallic material is present, replace the propeller shaft and bearing carrier bearings.

5. Check oil seal contact areas of the propeller shaft. Replace the shaft and seals if deep grooves are noted.

6. Check the propeller shaft for twisted, rusty or excessively worn splines. Replace the shaft if necessary. Support the propeller shaft (except 3 hp) at its bearing surfaces on V-blocks. Mount a dial indicator just forward of the shear pin hole (3.3 hp) or the propeller splines (4-275 hp). Rotate the propeller shaft while observing the dial indicator. A reading of more than 0.006 in. (0.15 mm) indicates excessive shaft runout and the propeller shaft should be replaced.

7. Apply a light oil to the rear propeller shaft bearing (3.3 hp) or the reverse gear ball bearing (4-275 hp). Rotate the bearing to check for rough spots. Push and pull on the reverse gear to check for bearing side play. If movement is excessive, replace the bearing.

8A. 3.3 hp—Check the teeth and clutch engagement area of the drive gear. Replace the drive gear if the teeth are pitted, chipped, broken or excessively worn. Replace the gear if the clutch engagement surfaces are chipped, cracked, rounded or excessively worn.

8B. 4-275 hp—Check the forward and reverse gear teeth and clutch engagement dogs (**Figure 66**). If the teeth are pitted, chipped, broken or excessively worn, replace the gear(s). If the clutch engagement surfaces are chipped or rounded, replace the gear(s) and check for improper shift cable adjustment, excessive rpm during idle speed or poor operator shift habits (shifting too slowly into gear).

9A. 3.3 hp—Check the engagement surfaces of the clutch for chips, cracks or excessive wear. Replace the clutch as required.

9B. 4-275 hp—Check forward and reverse gear clutch engagement dogs on the sliding clutch (**Figure 67**). Replace the clutch if the dogs are chipped, broken, cracked or excessively worn.

Replace the clutch if its internal splines are twisted, damaged, corroded or excessively worn.

10. Check the drive gear-to-pinion gear wear surfaces. If it is not smooth and even, replace the drive gear(s) and the pinion gear.

11. Check the cam follower for wear, pitting, scoring or a rough contact surface. If any defects are noted, replace the cam follower and shift cam.

12. Inspect the cover nut (models so equipped) for cracks and damaged or corroded threads. Replace the nut as necessary.

Propeller Shaft Bearing Removal/Installation (3 hp)

1. Remove the propeller shaft bearing from the gear housing using a suitable puller.

2. Apply a light oil to the outside diameter of the new bearing.

3. Using a suitable mandrel and driver rod, drive the new bearing into the gear housing until fully seated. The numbered side of the bearing should face the propeller end of the gear housing. Make sure the mandrel contacts only the outer race of the bearing during installation.

Bearing Carrier Disassembly/Assembly (3.3 hp)

The propeller shaft seal (36, **Figure 44**) can not be removed from the bearing carrier without first removing the propeller shaft bearing (35). The bearing, however, is often damaged or destroyed during removal. Therefore, closely inspect the seal and bearing and remove only if necessary. Proceed as follows if inspection determines that bearing or seal (or both) replacement is required.

1. Remove and discard the bearing carrier O-ring.

2. Support the bearing carrier in a vise with protective jaws. Then, use a suitable slide ham-

9

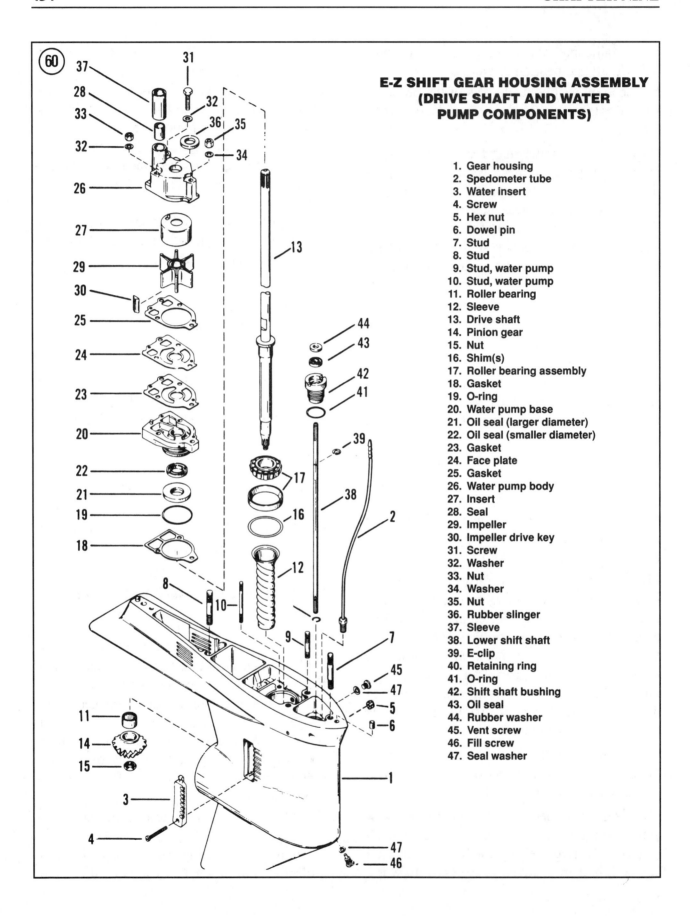

60

E-Z SHIFT GEAR HOUSING ASSEMBLY (DRIVE SHAFT AND WATER PUMP COMPONENTS)

1. Gear housing
2. Spedometer tube
3. Water insert
4. Screw
5. Hex nut
6. Dowel pin
7. Stud
8. Stud
9. Stud, water pump
10. Stud, water pump
11. Roller bearing
12. Sleeve
13. Drive shaft
14. Pinion gear
15. Nut
16. Shim(s)
17. Roller bearing assembly
18. Gasket
19. O-ring
20. Water pump base
21. Oil seal (larger diameter)
22. Oil seal (smaller diameter)
23. Gasket
24. Face plate
25. Gasket
26. Water pump body
27. Insert
28. Seal
29. Impeller
30. Impeller drive key
31. Screw
32. Washer
33. Nut
34. Washer
35. Nut
36. Rubber slinger
37. Sleeve
38. Lower shift shaft
39. E-clip
40. Retaining ring
41. O-ring
42. Shift shaft bushing
43. Oil seal
44. Rubber washer
45. Vent screw
46. Fill screw
47. Seal washer

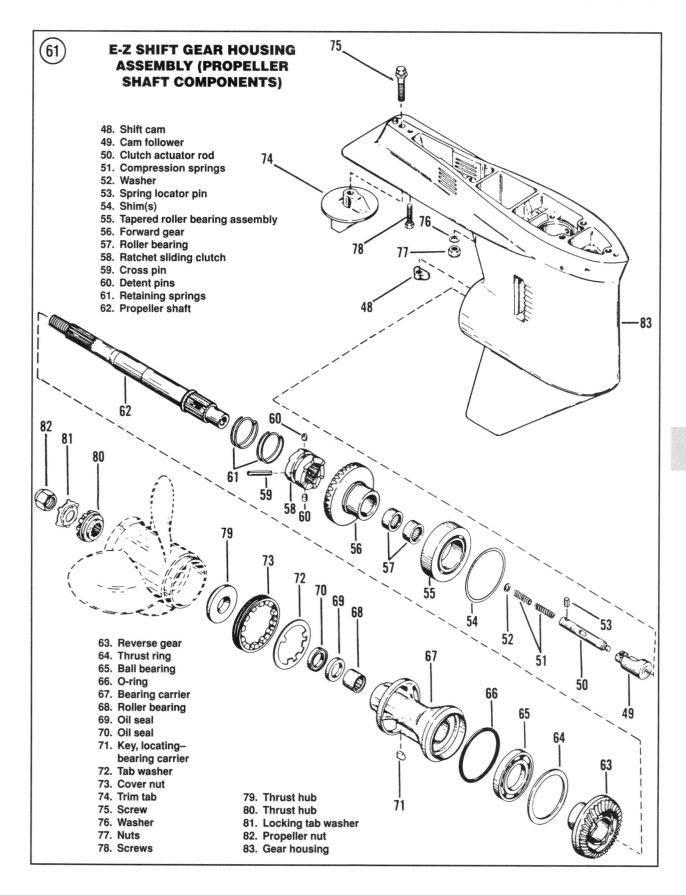

61

E-Z SHIFT GEAR HOUSING ASSEMBLY (PROPELLER SHAFT COMPONENTS)

48. Shift cam
49. Cam follower
50. Clutch actuator rod
51. Compression springs
52. Washer
53. Spring locator pin
54. Shim(s)
55. Tapered roller bearing assembly
56. Forward gear
57. Roller bearing
58. Ratchet sliding clutch
59. Cross pin
60. Detent pins
61. Retaining springs
62. Propeller shaft

63. Reverse gear
64. Thrust ring
65. Ball bearing
66. O-ring
67. Bearing carrier
68. Roller bearing
69. Oil seal
70. Oil seal
71. Key, locating–bearing carrier
72. Tab washer
73. Cover nut
74. Trim tab
75. Screw
76. Washer
77. Nuts
78. Screws
79. Thrust hub
80. Thrust hub
81. Locking tab washer
82. Propeller nut
83. Gear housing

9

mer type puller with internally expanding jaws to remove the bearing.

3. After the bearing is removed, lay the carrier on a flat work (propeller side up) surface and tap the seal out using a punch and hammer.

4. To reassemble, lay the bearing carrier (propeller side down) on a press plate.

5. Position the propeller shaft seal with its flat side facing upward. Using a suitable driver (13/16 in. socket), press the seal into the carrier until it is fully seated. Lubricate the seal lip with Quicksilver 2-4-C Marine Lubricant.

6. Install the bearing using driver part No. 91-37323 (or equivalent). Press on the bearing outer race, from the numbered side, until fully seated in the carrier. Lubricate the bearing with Quicksilver Needle Bearing Assembly Grease.

7. Install a new O-ring around the bearing carrier. Lubricate the O-ring with Quicksilver 2-4-C Marine Lubricant.

Bearing Carrier Disassembly/Assembly (4 and 5 hp)

The propeller shaft bearing inside the bearing carrier is damaged during removal. Inspect the bearing carefully, but do not remove it unless replacement is necessary.

NOTE
The propeller shaft bearing must be removed from the carrier before the propeller shaft seal can be removed.

1. If inspection determines that the propeller shaft bearing or seal requires replacement, clamp the carrier into a vise with protective jaws or between wooden blocks.

2. Remove the propeller shaft bearing using puller part No. 91-83165M, or equivalent.

3. After bearing removal, use the same tool to remove the oil seal from the carrier.

4. Remove and discard the carrier O-ring.

5. Place the bearing carrier on a flat work bench surface and install a new oil seal into the carrier

using mandrel part No. 91-83174M and driver part No. 91-84529M (or equivalent). Install the seal until fully seated in the carrier. Lubricate the seal lips with Quicksilver 2-4-C Marine Lubricant.

CAUTION
Press only on the bearing outer race (from numbered side) during installation in Step 6.

6. Press a new propeller shaft bearing into the carrier using mandrel part No. 91-84536M (or equivalent). Make sure the bearing is fully seated in the carrier.

7. Install a new O-ring onto the carrier. Lubricate the O-ring with Quicksilver 2-4-C Marine Lubricant.

Bearing Carrier Disassembly/Assembly (8, 9.9 and 15 hp)

1. Remove and discard the bearing carrier O-ring.

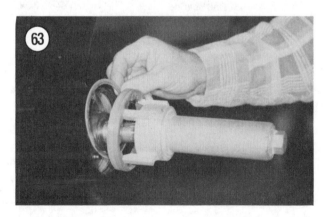

2. If inspection indicates that the bearing carrier bushing requires replacement, place the carrier into a suitable holding fixture or clamp the carrier into a vise with protective jaws, or between wooden blocks. Be careful not to damage the carrier threads.

3. Drive the carrier bushing and seal from the carrier using mandrel part No. 91-13656.

4. Press the bushing into the propeller end of the carrier using mandrel part No. 91-13658.

5. Apply Loctite 271 to the outer diameter of the bearing carrier seal. Place the seal into the propeller end of the carrier (seal lip facing away from the propeller end) and press into position using mandrel part No. 91-13655.

6. Install a new O-ring around the carrier. Lubricate the O-ring with Quicksilver 2-4-C Marine Lubricant.

7. Lubricate the reverse gear with Quicksilver Gear Lube and insert the gear into the bearing carrier.

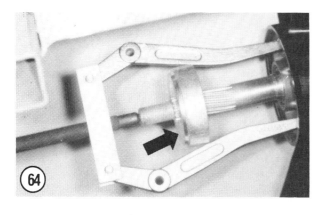

Bearing Carrier Disassembly/Assembly (20 and 25 hp)

1. Remove the reverse gear from the carrier.

NOTE
The carrier roller bearing is damaged during removal. Closely inspect the bearing, but do not remove unless replacement is necessary.

2. Clamp the bearing carrier into a vise with protective jaws, or between wooden blocks. Do *not* clamp on the bearing carrier threads.

3. Using a suitable punch and hammer, tap the 2 seals out the aft end of the carrier.

4. If bearing replacement is necessary, drive the bearing from the aft end of the carrier using a suitable punch and hammer.

5. To reassemble the carrier, lubricate the carrier roller bearing bore with Quicksilver Gear Lube. Press the roller bearing into aft end of the carrier until the end is flush with the bearing bore (**Figure 68**). Press only from the lettered end of the bearing.

6. Apply Loctite 271 to the outer diameter of the bearing carrier inner seal. Press the seal into the aft end of the carrier (lip facing in) until fully seated. Wipe off any excess Loctite. See **Figure 68**.

7. Apply Loctite 271 to the outer diameter of the carrier outer seal. Press the seal into the aft end of the carrier (lip facing out) until fully seated. See **Figure 68**. Wipe off any excess Loctite.

8. Lubricate the seal lips and the bearing rollers with Quicksilver 2-4-C Marine Lubricant.

9. Lubricate the bearing surface of the reverse gear with Quicksilver Gear Lube and insert the gear into the bearing carrier.

Bearing Carrier Disassembly/Assembly (40, 50 60, 135-200 hp [Except 150XR4 and 150XR6]; 250 and 275 hp)

1. Clamp the carrier assembly into a vise with protective jaws, or between wooden blocks.

9

2. Remove the reverse gear from the bearing carrier using a suitable slide hammer puller.

3. If the reverse gear ball bearing remains in the carrier, remove it with a slide hammer puller. If the bearing remained on the reverse gear, remove it using a universal puller plate and arbor press.

4. Remove and discard the carrier O-ring (A, **Figure 69**).

5. If the carrier roller bearing is in acceptable condition, pry the propeller shaft seals (B, **Figure 69**) from the carrier using a screwdriver or similar tool.

6. If the roller bearing requires replacement, press the bearing and the seals from the carrier with a suitable mandrel and arbor press.

7. To reassemble, place the reverse gear (teeth down) on a wooden block. Install the thrust washer onto the gear with its beveled side facing the gear.

8. Lubricate the inner diameter of the reverse gear ball bearing with Quicksilver Gear Lube. Position the bearing on the gear with its numbered side facing up.

9. Press the bearing onto the reverse gear until fully seated using a mandrel which applies pressure only on the inner bearing race. Be certain the bearing is fully seated on the gear.

10. Lubricate the outside diameter of the roller bearing with Quicksilver Gear Lube. Press the bearing into the aft end of the carrier until the upper surface of the bearing is just below the inner propeller shaft seal bore. Press the bearing from the numbered side only.

11. Apply Loctite 271 to the outer diameter of the propeller shaft seals.

12A. 40 hp and 50-60 (prior to serial No. D000750) hp—Using a suitable mandrel, press the inner seal into the aft end of the bearing carrier (lip facing forward end of carrier) until fully seated. Press the outer seal (lip facing aft end of carrier) into the aft end of the carrier until fully seated. If the outer seal is a fish line cutter, be certain the sharp cutting edge is facing the propeller. Wipe off any excess Loctite.

12B. 50-60 (serial No. D000750-on) hp—Using a suitable mandrel, press the inner propeller shaft seal (lip facing forward end of carrier) into the aft end of the carrier to a depth of 0.44 in. (11 mm) from the aft end of the carrier as shown in **Figure 70**. Next, press the outer seal (lip facing aft end of carrier) into the carrier to a depth of 0.04 in. (1.0 mm) as shown. Wipe off any excess Loctite.

12C. V6 (except 150XR4 and 150XR6)—Place the inner propeller shaft seal onto the long shoulder of oil seal driver part No. 91-31108. The seal lip should be facing away from the shoulder of the tool. Press the seal into the aft end of carrier until the tool bottoms against the carrier. Next, place the outer seal onto the short shoulder of the seal driver (part No. 91-31108) with the lip facing the shoulder of the tool. Press the seal into the aft end of the carrier until the tool bottoms against the carrier. Wipe off any excess Loctite.

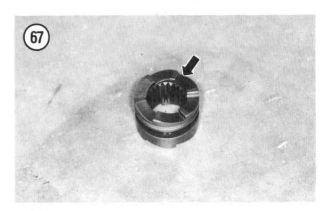

13. Lubricate the seal lips and roller bearing with Quicksilver Needle Bearing Assembly Grease.

14. Lubricate the outer diameter of the reverse gear ball bearing with Quicksilver Gear Lube. Place the reverse gear, teeth down, on a wooden block. Press the bearing carrier assembly onto the reverse gear ball bearing until fully seated using a suitable mandrel or plate and arbor press.

15. Install a new O-ring around the bearing carrier. Lubricate the O-ring with Quicksilver Special Lube 101 or 2-4-C Marine Lubricant.

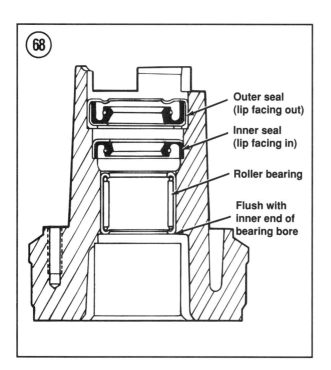

Outer seal
(lip facing out)

Inner seal
(lip facing in)

Roller bearing

Flush with
inner end of
bearing bore

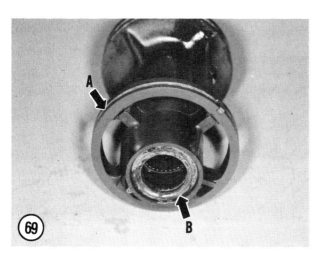

Bearing Carrier Disassembly/Assembly (75-115 hp, 150XR4 and 150XR6)

1. Lift the reverse gear out of the bearing carrier. Remove the thrust washer on XR4 and XR6 models and the thrust bearing and washer on 75-115 hp models. Remove and discard the bearing carrier O-ring.

NOTE
The propeller shaft roller bearing(s) is damaged during removal from the bearing carrier. Carefully inspect the bearing(s), but do not remove unless replacement is necessary.

2. If the propeller shaft roller bearings require replacement, clamp the carrier into a vise with protective jaws, or between wooden blocks.

3A. 75-115 hp:

  a. Remove the forward roller bearing using puller part No. 91-34569A-1 (or a suitable equivalent slide hammer puller).

  b. Next, place the bearing carrier (aft end down) onto an arbor press. Press the aft roller bearing and propeller shaft seals from the carrier using mandrel part No. 91-36569 (or equivalent) and driver rod part No. 91-37323 (or equivalent).

3B. 150XR4 and 150XR6—If the propeller shaft roller bearing in the carrier is in acceptable condition, pry the propeller shaft seals from the carrier using a screwdriver or similar tool. If the bearing requires replacement, proceed as follows:

  a. Place the bearing carrier (aft end down) onto an arbor press.

  b. Press the propeller shaft roller bearing and seals out the aft end of the carrier using the appropriate mandrel and driver rod from the bearing removal and installation tool kit part No. 91-31229A-1 (or equivalent).

4A. 75-115—Reassemble the bearing carrier as follows:

  a. Place the forward end of the bearing carrier onto bearing installation tool part No. 91-

9

13945 to protect the lip on the forward side of the carrier.

b. Place the carrier and tool into an arbor press (aft end up). Lubricate the outer diameter of the rear propeller shaft roller bearing with Quicksilver Needle Bearing Assembly Grease.

c. Using mandrel part No. 91-37263 and a suitable driver rod, press the rear roller bearing into the carrier (numbered side facing mandrel) until fully seated.

d. Place the inner propeller shaft seal onto the long shoulder of seal driver part No. 91-31108. The seal lip should face away from the tool shoulder. Press the seal into the aft end of the carrier until the installation tool bottoms on the carrier.

e. Place the outer propeller shaft seal onto the short shoulder of seal driver part No. 91-31108. The seal lip should face the shoulder of the tool. Apply Loctite 271 to the outer diameter of the seal, then press the seal into the aft end of the carrier until the tool bottoms on the carrier.

f. Remove the bearing installation tool part No. 91-13945 from the front end of the carrier, then place the carrier onto the arbor press with the aft end facing down.

g. Place the front propeller shaft roller bearing onto bearing installation tool part No. 91-13949. The numbered side of the bearing should face the tool shoulder.

h. Lubricate the outer diameter of the bearing with Quicksilver Needle Bearing Assembly Grease. Press the bearing into the front end of the bearing carrier until the installation tool bottoms on the carrier.

i. Coat the reverse gear thrust washer and bearing with Quicksilver Gear Lube. Install the washer and bearing onto the carrier, then install the reverse gear into the carrier.

j. Install a new O-ring onto the bearing carrier. Lubricate the seal lips and roller bearings with Quicksilver Needle Bearing Assembly Grease. Lubricate the O-ring with Quicksilver Special Lube 101 or 2-4-C Marine Lubricant.

4B. 150XR4 and 150XR6—Assemble the bearing carrier as follows:

a. Lubricate the outer diameter of the propeller shaft roller bearing with Quicksilver Needle Bearing Assembly Grease.

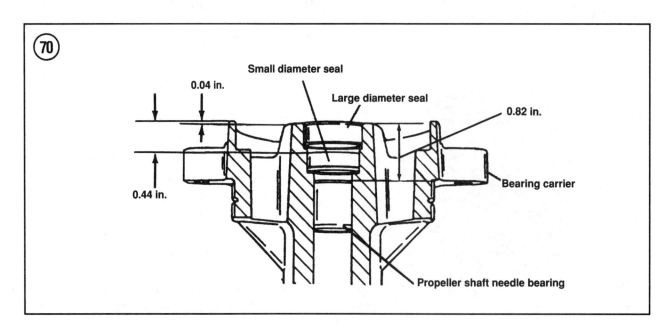

70

Small diameter seal

0.04 in.

Large diameter seal

0.82 in.

0.44 in.

Bearing carrier

Propeller shaft needle bearing

b. Place the bearing into the aft end of the bearing carrier. Press the bearing into the carrier using a suitable mandrel and driver rod.

c. Apply Loctite 271 to the outer diameter of the propeller shaft seals.

d. Place the inner propeller shaft seal onto the long shoulder of seal driver part No. 91-31108. The seal lip should face away from the tool shoulder. Press the seal into the aft end of the carrier until the installation tool bottoms on the carrier.

e. Place the outer propeller shaft seal onto the short shoulder of seal driver part No. 91-31108. The seal lip should face the shoulder of the tool. Apply Loctite 271 to the outer diameter of the seal, then press the seal into the aft end of the carrier until the tool bottoms on the carrier.

f. Install a new O-ring onto the bearing carrier.

g. Place the thrust washer onto the bearing carrier. The side of the washer with the smaller diameter must face the carrier.

h. Lubricate the thrust washer and reverse gear bearing journal with Quicksilver Gear Lube, then install the reverse gear into the carrier. Lubricate the propeller shaft seal lips with Quicksilver Needle Bearing Assembly Grease. Lubricate the bearing carrier O-ring with Quicksilver Special Lube 101 or 2-4-C Marine Lubricant.

Propeller Shaft Disassembly/Assembly (3.3 hp)

Refer to **Figure 44** for this procedure.

1. Slide the shift cam follower out of the propeller shaft.

2. Using a small screwdriver, awl or similar tool, compress the clutch spring, toward the aft end of the propeller shaft, sufficiently to slide the clutch out of the propeller shaft.

3. After the clutch is removed, the spring can be removed from the front of the shaft.

4. To reassemble, insert the clutch spring into the front of the propeller shaft.

5. Using a screwdriver, awl or similar tool, compress the spring toward the aft end of the shaft. When the spring is sufficiently compressed, insert the clutch in the propeller shaft slot. Release the spring securing the clutch in the shaft.

6. Coat the shift cam follower with Quicksilver Super Duty Gear Lube and insert it into the front of the propeller shaft.

Propeller Shaft Disassembly/Assembly (4 and 5 hp)

1. Slide the reverse gear and washer off the propeller shaft.

2. Remove the shift cam follower and guide from the front end of the shaft.

3. Place the shaft on a flat work bench and carefully drive the cross pin from the sliding clutch with a suitable pin punch and hammer. Do not remove the pin punch from the clutch hole at this time.

4. Position the shaft upright with the cam follower end resting on a solid surface. Slowly withdraw the punch from the clutch and carefully release the spring compression. Remove the spring from the end of the shaft, then slide the clutch off the propeller shaft.

5. To reassemble, install the sliding clutch onto the propeller shaft aligning the cross pin hole in the clutch with the slot in the shaft.

6. Reinstall the spring into the shift cam follower end of the shaft.

7. Clamp a suitable pin punch horizontally in a vise. Position the shaft so the punch will fit inside and compress the spring installed in Step 6. Once the spring is compressed beyond the cross pin hole, insert a suitable pin punch through the hole in the clutch to hold the spring and to align the hole in the clutch with the propeller shaft slot.

8. Install the cross pin into the clutch from the opposite side of the pin punch. Tap the cross pin into the clutch until it contacts the pin punch,

9

then carefully drive the cross pin into the clutch, pushing out the pin punch. When properly installed, the cross pin should be centered in the sliding clutch.

9. Lubricate the shift cam follower and guide with Quicksilver 2-4-C Marine Lubricant. Install the cam follower guide and cam follower into the propeller shaft.

10. Reinstall the washer and reverse gear onto the propeller shaft.

Propeller Shaft Disassembly/Assembly (8-25 hp)

1. Carefully pry the cross pin retainer off the clutch using a suitable screwdriver or similar tool. See **Figure 71**. Be careful not to stretch or distort the retainer spring.

2. If the shift cam follower is removed from the propeller shaft, reinstall it into the end of the shaft. Position the propeller shaft assembly with the cam follower against a solid surface. Push the propeller shaft against the cam follower to compress the spring, then push out the clutch cross pin using a suitable punch.

3. Relieve the spring tension, then remove the cam follower, spring and sliding clutch from the propeller shaft.

> *NOTE*
> *The short end of the sliding clutch must face forward when installed on the propeller shaft.*

4. To reassemble, install the sliding clutch onto the propeller shaft aligning the cross pin hole in the clutch with the slot in the propeller shaft.

5. Install the spring into the cam follower end of the shaft.

6. Clamp a suitable pin punch horizontally in a vise. Position the propeller shaft so the punch will fit inside and compress the spring installed in Step 5. Once the spring is compressed beyond the cross pin hole, insert the cross pin and center it in the sliding clutch.

7. Carefully install the cross pin retainer around the clutch and into its groove. On 20 and 25 hp models, make sure the retainer spring windings are flat and not overlapped.

8. Lubricate the shift cam follower with Quicksilver 2-4-C Marine Lubricant, then install it into the propeller shaft.

Propeller Shaft Disassembly/Assembly (40-115 hp, 150XR4 and 150XR6)

1. Carefully pry the cross pin retainer off the clutch using a suitable screwdriver or similar tool. See **Figure 71**. Be careful not to stretch or distort the retainer spring.

2. If the shift cam follower is removed from the propeller shaft, reinstall it (and 3 steel balls on 75-115 hp, XR4 and XR6) into the end of the shaft. Position the propeller shaft assembly with the cam follower against a solid surface. Push the propeller shaft against the cam follower to compress the spring, then push out the clutch cross pin using a suitable punch.

3. Relieve the spring tension, then remove the cam follower, steel balls (75-115 hp, XR4 and XR6 models), cam follower guide, spring and sliding clutch from the propeller shaft.

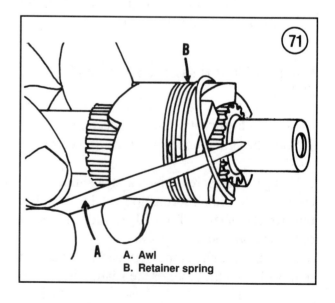

A. Awl
B. Retainer spring

NOTE
On 40-60 hp models, the short end of the sliding clutch must face forward when installed on the propeller shaft. On 75-115 hp, 150XR4 and 150XR6 models, the grooved end of the sliding clutch must face rearward when installed on the propeller shaft.

4. To reassemble, install the sliding clutch onto the propeller shaft aligning the cross pin hole in the clutch with the slot in the propeller shaft. Make sure the short end of the clutch is facing forward on 40-60 hp models, or the grooved end is facing rearward on 75-115 hp, 150XR4 and 150XR6 models.

5. Install the spring into the cam follower end of the shaft. Install the cam follower guide into the propeller shaft making sure the cross pin hole in the guide is aligned with the cross pin hole in the shaft and clutch.

6. On 75-115 hp, 150XR4 and 150XR6 models, install the 3 steel balls into the propeller shaft. Install the cam follower on all models.

7. Position the cam follower against a solid surface and push the propeller shaft to compress the

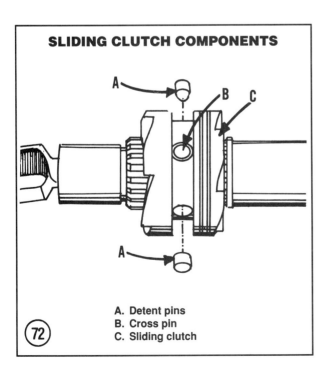

SLIDING CLUTCH COMPONENTS

A. Detent pins
B. Cross pin
C. Sliding clutch

⑦②

spring. When the spring is sufficiently compressed and the cross pin holes are aligned, insert the cross pin into the clutch. If necessary, use a drift punch to align the holes.

8. Carefully install the cross pin retainer around the clutch and into its groove. Make sure the retainer spring windings are flat and not over-lapped.

Propeller Shaft Disassembly/Assembly (135-200 hp [Except XR4 and XR6]; 250 and 275 hp)

1. Remove the shift cam from the cam follower.

2. Insert a thin-blade screwdriver or similar tool under the front coil of the cross pin retainer. Lift the coil up and rotate the propeller shaft to un-wind the spring from the sliding clutch. Be care-ful not to stretch or distort the spring.

3. Repeat Step 2 to remove the remaining cross pin retainer. Remove the detent pins from the sliding clutch. See **Figure 72**.

4. Push the cross pin through the clutch and propeller shaft using a suitable punch. Slide the clutch off the shaft.

5. Pull the cam follower and clutch actuator rod straight out of the propeller shaft. Do not move the cam follower up and down or side-to-side during removal.

6. Separate the clutch actuator rod from the cam follower.

NOTE
Record the location and thickness of any shim(s) removed from the clutch actua-tor rod for reference during reassembly.

7. Push the locating pin (E, **Figure 73**) out of the actuator rod using a suitable punch. Remove the spring(s) and shim(s) from the rod.

NOTE
The clutch actuator rod on 135-200 hp models prior to serial No. D044293 and 250 and 275 hp models prior to serial No. D038988 is equipped with 2 springs

9

and 1 or more shims. On later models, only 1 spring is used; the front actuator spring and shim(s) are no longer used.

8. Measure the free length of the clutch actuator rod spring(s). Spring free length should be 1-17/32 to 1-9/16 in. (38.9-39.7 mm). Replace the spring(s) if not as specified.

9. To reassemble, insert the actuator spring(s) into the actuator rod, then install the shim washer.

10. Lubricate the spring locating pin with Quicksilver Needle Bearing Assembly Grease. Install the locating pin, with its flat side facing the shim washer, into the actuator rod.

NOTE
A suitable cross pin tool (Step 11a) can be fabricated by grinding a point on one end of an appropriate size pin.

11. 135-200 hp prior to serial No. D044293, 250 and 275 hp prior to serial No. D038988:

   a. Insert cross pin tool part No. 91-86642 into the actuator rod between the 2 springs. See **Figure 73**. Force the cross pin tool back and forth, compressing and releasing the springs to remove any initial set in the springs.

   b. Measure from one side of the cross pin tool to the edge of the slot in the rod (F, **Figure 73**). Repeat the measurement on the other side of the cross pin tool (G, **Figure 73**).

   c. The 2 measurements must be equal to within 1/64 in. (0.4 mm) of each other. If not, disassemble the actuator rod and install additional shim(s) as necessary to provide the specified measurement.

12. Partially install the clutch actuator rod assembly into the propeller shaft (approximately 1/2 way). Install the cam follower onto the end of the actuator rod, then push the rod fully into the propeller shaft. Align the propeller shaft and actuator rod cross pin slots.

13. Install the sliding clutch onto the propeller shaft. The grooves on the clutch must the face

the propeller end of the shaft. Align the cross pin and detent holes in the clutch with the slot and notches on the propeller shaft. See **Figure 74**.

14. Install the cross pin tool (part No. 91-86642) into the sliding clutch, through the propeller shaft and actuator rod. Be certain the cross pin tool is located between the 2 actuator rod springs on models so equipped.

15. Install the cross pin into the sliding clutch, pushing out the cross pin tool. Make sure the flat side(s) of the cross pin is facing the actuator rod spring(s). Center the pin in the clutch.

16. Apply a small quantity of Quicksilver 2-4-C Marine Lubricant on the detent pins. Install the detent pins into the sliding clutch. Make sure the rounded ends of the pins are facing the propeller shaft. See **Figure 72**.

17. Insert the tang end (hook) of the first cross pin retainer spring into the detent pin. Wind the retainer spring into the sliding clutch groove. The straight end of the retainer spring should be against the side of the clutch groove.

18. Insert the tang end of the remaining cross pin retainer spring into the other detent pin. Wind the retainer spring into the sliding clutch groove in the opposite direction of the first retainer. Posi-

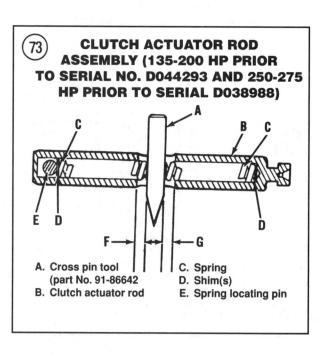

CLUTCH ACTUATOR ROD ASSEMBLY (135-200 HP PRIOR TO SERIAL NO. D044293 AND 250-275 HP PRIOR TO SERIAL D038988)

A. Cross pin tool (part No. 91-86642)
B. Clutch actuator rod
C. Spring
D. Shim(s)
E. Spring locating pin

tion the straight end of the retainer spring against the side of the clutch groove. Make sure the retainer springs lay flat and are not overlapped.

Installation
(3 hp)

1. Install the original shim(s) onto the front of the drive gear and propeller shaft assembly.

2. Install the drive gear and propeller shaft assembly into the gear housing.

3. Install the water pump housing. The slots in the housing should be facing toward the port side of the gear housing.

4. Install the impeller drive pin into the propeller shaft. Install the water pump impeller onto the shaft. Rotate the propeller shaft clockwise while pushing the impeller into the housing.

5. Install the water pump cover over the propeller shaft and against the pump housing.

6. Apply Quicksilver Perfect Seal to the threads of the water pump cover screws. Install the screws and tighten to 25 in.-lb. (2.8 N•m).

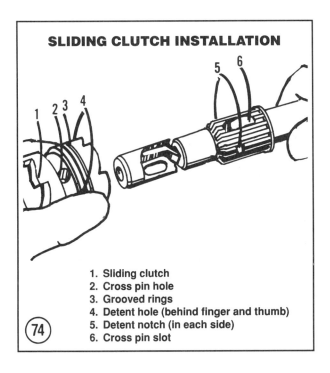

SLIDING CLUTCH INSTALLATION

1. Sliding clutch
2. Cross pin hole
3. Grooved rings
4. Detent hole (behind finger and thumb)
5. Detent notch (in each side)
6. Cross pin slot

(74)

Installation
(3.3, 4 and 5 hp)

1. Install the bearing carrier onto the propeller shaft. Apply Quicksilver 2-4-C Marine Lubricant to the bearing carrier O-ring.

2. Insert the bearing carrier/propeller shaft assembly into the gear housing.

3. Align the bearing carrier bolt holes with the gear housing holes, then install the bolts and washer. Tighten the bolts to 50 in.-lb. (5.6 N•m) on 3.3 hp models or 70 in.-lb. (7.9 N•m) on 4 and 5 hp models.

Installation
(8, 9.9 and 15 hp)

1. Lubricate the reverse gear bearing journal with Quicksilver Gear Lube. Insert the gear into the bearing carrier.

2. Lubricate the bearing carrier O-ring with Quicksilver 2-4-C Marine Lubricant. Lubricate the bearing carrier threads with Quicksilver Special Lube 101 or 2-4-C Marine Lubricant.

3. Insert the propeller shaft assembly into the bearing carrier. Install the shaft and carrier assembly into the gear housing.

4. Install the bearing carrier tool (part No. 91-13664) over the propeller shaft and tighten the bearing carrier to 60 ft.-lb. (81.3 N•m).

Installation
(20 and 25 hp)

1. Insert the propeller shaft assembly into the gear housing and center in the forward gear.

2. Install the reverse gear onto the propeller shaft and into position inside the gear housing.

3. Make sure the bearing carrier seal lips are lubricated with 2-4-C Marine Lubricant, or equivalent.

NOTE
Bearing carrier has left-hand threads.

9

4. Install the bearing carrier onto the propeller shaft. Screw the carrier into the housing as far as possible by hand.

5A. Models equipped with a 2-piece thrust hub (1990 and 1991 models):

   a. Install the thrust hub with the cap onto the propeller shaft. The ears on the hub should align with the recesses in the carrier.

   b. Temporarily install the propeller against the thrust hub. Thread the propeller nut onto the shaft and tighten against the propeller to maintain pressure on the thrust hub.

   c. Install an appropriate size wrench onto the propeller hex head hub and turn it counterclockwise to tighten the bearing carrier securely in place.

   d. Remove the propeller nut, propeller and thrust hub.

5B. Models equipped with a 1-piece thrust hub (1992 and 1993 models):

   a. Slide bearing carrier tool part No. 91-93843 over the propeller shaft and engage it with the bearing carrier.

   b. Tighten the bearing carrier, by turning the tool counterclockwise, to 80 ft.-lb. (108.5 N•m).

NOTE
For identification purposes, the zinc anode ring is thinner than the O-ring retainer plate in Step 9.

6. Install a new O-ring, retainer plate and the zinc anode ring on the bearing carrier.

7. Install the retaining screws and tighten securely.

Installation
(40 hp and 50-60 hp
[Prior to Serial No. D000750])

1. Lubricate the propeller shaft seal lips and the bearing carrier O-ring with Quicksilver Needle Bearing Assembly Grease.

2. Lubricate all other areas of the bearing carrier outside diameter that contact the gear housing.

3. Carefully slide the bearing carrier over the propeller shaft to prevent seal damage.

4. Install the bearing carrier/propeller shaft assembly into the gear housing making sure the key slots in the carrier and gear housing are aligned. Rotate the drive shaft to ensure the pinion and reverse gears are properly meshed.

5. Install the alignment key (**Figure 75**).

NOTE
The manufacturer does not recommend reusing plastic cover nuts. If the original cover nut is plastic, it should be discarded and replaced with a new nut.

6. Lubricate the threaded area of the gear housing with Quicksilver Special Lube 101.

7. Install the locking tab washer. Install the cover nut with "OFF" marking facing outward. Using cover nut tool part No. 91-91947, tighten the cover nut to 100 ft.-lb. (135.6 N•m).

8. Determine which locking tab on the washer will properly align with a cover nut slot, then bend the tab into the slot. Bend the remaining tabs down flat, toward the front of the gear housing.

Installation
(50 and 60 hp Serial No. D000750-on)

1. Slide the bearing carrier over the propeller shaft. Use care not to damage the propeller shaft seals.

2. Lubricate the bearing carrier outer diameter and O-ring with Quicksilver Special Lube 101.

3. Install the bearing carrier/propeller shaft assembly into the gear housing, aligning the carrier bolt holes with the gear housing holes. Be careful not to damage the carrier O-ring during installation.

4. Apply Loctite 271 to the threads of the bearing carrier bolts. Install the bolts and tighten to 150 in.-lb. (16.9 N•m).

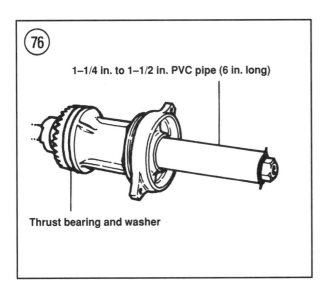

1–1/4 in. to 1–1/2 in. PVC pipe (6 in. long)

Thrust bearing and washer

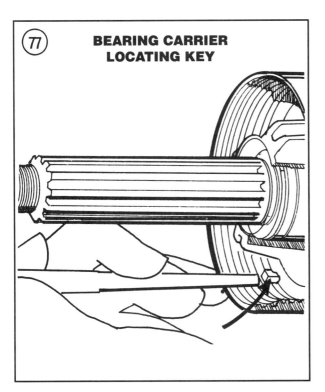

BEARING CARRIER LOCATING KEY

Installation (75, 90, 100 and 115 hp)

1. Install the bearing carrier over the propeller shaft. Be careful not to damage the propeller shaft seals.

NOTE
The reverse gear thrust bearing and washer can easily fall out of position during bearing carrier installation. Be sure to secure the reverse gear against the thrust bearing as described in Step 2 prior to installing the carrier assembly.

2. Obtain a piece of 1-1/4 or 1-1/2 in. diameter PVC pipe 6 in. long. Install the PVC pipe over the propeller shaft, then install the propeller nut and locking tab washer. See **Figure 76**. Tighten the propeller nut snugly to hold the reverse gear securely against the thrust bearing and washer to prevent the bearing and washer from being dislodged during carrier installation.

3. Lubricate the bearing carrier outer diameter (both ends) and O-ring with Quicksilver Special Lube 101.

4. Position the bearing carrier with the "TOP" marking facing upward. Install the carrier/propeller shaft assembly into the gear housing.

5. Apply Loctite 271 to the threads of the carrier mounting fasteners. If bolts are used, tighten to 150 in.-lb. (16.9 N•m). If nuts are used, tighten to 275 in.-lb. (31.0 N•m).

Installation (V6 Cam-Shift [150XR4 and 150XR6])

1. Install the propeller shaft assembly into the gear case and insert it into the forward gear.

2. Lubricate the bearing carrier O-ring and outer diameter with Quicksilver Special Lube 101.

3. Align the alignment key slots in the bearing carrier and gear housing, then install the carrier over the propeller shaft. Use care not to damage the propeller shaft seals. Rotate the drive shaft to

9

ensure the pinion and reverse gears are properly meshed.

4. Push the bearing carrier into the gear housing as far as possible by hand, then install the alignment key using a small punch (**Figure 77**).

5. Install a new tab washer against the bearing carrier.

6. Apply Quicksilver Perfect Seal to the cover nut threads.

7. Install the cover nut with the "OFF" marking facing outward. Screw the nut into the gear housing as far as possible by hand.

8. Install cover nut tool part No. 91-73688 and tighten the cover nut to 210 ft.-lb. (284.7 N•m).

9. Determine which locking tab on the washer is aligned with a cover nut slot. Bend the tab over firmly into the cover nut slot to lock the nut in place. Bend the remaining tabs over flat toward the front of the gear housing.

Installation
(V6 E-Z Shift)

1. Coat the cam follower pocket with Quicksilver 2-4-C Marine Lubricant. See **Figure 78**.

2. Place the shift cam into the cam follower pocket (**Figure 78**). Be sure the numbered side of the cam is facing up.

3. With the shift cam positioned as shown in **Figure 78**, install the propeller shaft assembly into the gear housing, inserting the shift cam follower into the forward gear, until the shaft is fully seated. Make sure the shift cam did not fall out of the follower.

> *CAUTION*
> *At this time, use extreme caution not to apply any side load to the propeller shaft. Until the bearing carrier is installed, the neck of the clutch actuator rod can be easily broken by side-to-side or up-and-down propeller shaft movement.*

4. Make sure the retaining ring and E-ring are properly positioned on the shift shaft (**Figure**

79). Install the shift shaft into the gear housing and through the shift cam. If necessary, rotate the shift shaft back and forth slightly to engage the shift cam splines.

> *NOTE*
> *Do not allow Perfect Seal or Special Lube 101 to contact shift shaft bushing seals or O-ring in Step 5.*

5. Apply Quicksilver Perfect Seal or Special Lube 101 to the threads of the shift shaft bushing. Thread the bushing in place, but do not tighten.

6. Lubricate the bearing carrier O-ring with Quicksilver 2-4-C Marine Lubricant.

7. Apply a light coat of Quicksilver Perfect Seal or Special Lube 101 to the outer diameter of the bearing carrier, at all areas of the carrier that contact the gear housing. Do not allow the Perfect Seal or Special Lube 101 to enter the carrier bearings or seals.

8. Align the bearing carrier and gear housing alignment key slots, then install the bearing carrier over the propeller shaft. Use care not to damage the propeller shaft seals. While installing the carrier, rotate the drive shaft clockwise

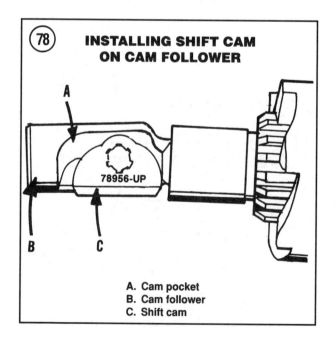

(78) **INSTALLING SHIFT CAM ON CAM FOLLOWER**

A. Cam pocket
B. Cam follower
C. Shift cam

(viewed from top) to ensure the pinion and reverse gears properly mesh.

9. Push the bearing carrier into the gear housing as far as possible by hand, then install the alignment key using a small punch. See **Figure 77**.

10. Install a new locking tab washer against the bearing carrier.

11. Apply Quicksilver Perfect Seal or Special Lube 101 to the threads of the cover nut. Thread the cover nut into the gear housing as far as possible by hand. Make sure the "OFF" marking on the nut is facing outward.

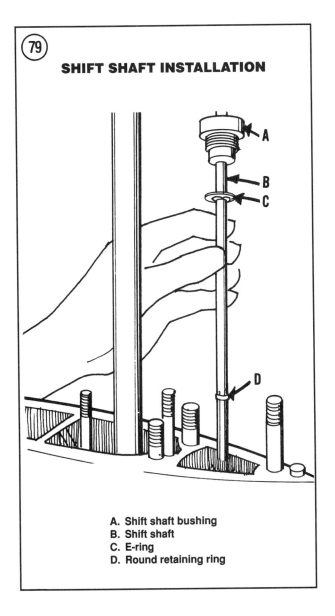

(79)

SHIFT SHAFT INSTALLATION

A. Shift shaft bushing
B. Shift shaft
C. E-ring
D. Round retaining ring

12. Using cover nut tool part No. 91-61069, tighten the cover nut to 210 ft.-lb. (284.7 N•m).

13. Determine which locking tab is aligned with a cover nut slot. Bend the tab over firmly into the slot. Bend the remaining tabs over flat toward the front of the gear housing.

14. Using bushing tool part No. 91-31107, tighten the shift shaft bushing to 50 ft.-lb. (67.8 N•m).

PINION GEAR, DRIVE SHAFT AND FORWARD GEAR

Removal
(3 hp)

1. Remove the water pump as described in this chapter.

2. Using a screwdriver or similar tool, reach into the gear housing and remove the E-ring securing the pinion gear to the drive shaft.

3. Lift the drive shaft out the top of the gear housing.

4. Reach into the gear cavity and withdraw the pinion gear.

NOTE
Do not remove the drive shaft forward bearing from the gear housing unless bearing replacement is necessary.

5. If necessary, use a suitable slide hammer puller to extract the forward bearing from the gear housing.

Removal
(3.3 hp)

Refer to **Figure 44** for this procedure.

1. Remove the water pump assembly, including the pump base, as described in this chapter.

2. Remove the propeller shaft and bearing carrier as described in this chapter.

3. Lift the drive shaft and spacer out the top of the gear housing.

9

4. Reach into the gear cavity and remove the pinion gear, then slide the drive gear (30, **Figure 44**) out of the ball bearing (28). Be sure to retrieve the drive gear shim(s) (29).

NOTE
*The front propeller shaft bearing (28, **Figure 44**), is often damaged or destroyed during removal. Do not remove the bearing unless inspection determines that replacement is necessary.*

5. To remove the front propeller shaft ball bearing, use bearing puller part No. 91-27780, or slide-hammer puller. Insert the puller jaws into the inside diameter of the bearing. Remove and discard the bearing.

Removal
(4 and 5 hp)

1. Remove the water pump and bearing carrier/propeller shaft assembly as described in this chapter.
2. Remove and save the shims on top of the drive shaft bearing.
3. Reach inside the gear cavity with one hand and push upward on the pinion gear while pulling the drive shaft out the top of the housing with the other hand. Remove the drive shaft and pinion gear.

NOTE
Drive shaft bearing, sleeve and bushing are not serviceable. If one or more of these components require replacement, the entire drive shaft assembly must be replaced.

4. Grasp the gear housing and strike the open end of the housing against a wooden block to dislodge the forward gear from the bearing. Remove and retain the shims located behind the forward gear.

CAUTION
The forward gear bearing is damaged during removal from the gear housing.

Do not remove the bearing unless replacement is necessary.

5. If necessary, remove the forward gear bearing from the gear housing using puller part No. 91-27780, or a suitable slide hammer puller.

Removal
(8, 9.9 and 15 hp)

1. Remove the water pump cover as described in this chapter.
2. Remove the bearing carrier/propeller shaft assembly as described in this chapter.
3. Lift the drive shaft out the top of the gear housing.
4. Reach inside the gear cavity and withdraw the pinion gear, pinion gear thrust washer and forward gear and bearing assembly.

NOTE
Do not remove the forward gear bearing race from the gear housing unless the race or the bearing requires replacement.

5. If the forward gear roller bearing or bearing race requires replacement, remove the race from the gear housing using puller assembly part No. 91-83165M and puller plate part No. 91-29310 (or equivalent).

Removal
(20, 25 and 40 hp and 50-60 hp
[Prior to Serial No. D000750])

1. Remove the bearing carrier, propeller shaft and water pump assemblies as described in this chapter.
2. Clamp the drive shaft into a vise with protective jaws, or between wooden blocks.
3. Using an appropriate size wrench or socket, remove the pinion gear bolt (20 and 25 hp) or nut (all others). See **Figure 80**.
4. Pull the gear housing off the drive shaft. If the drive shaft is stuck in the housing, place a

wooden block against the gear housing mating surface and tap the block with a mallet until the drive shaft is free. Use caution not to damage the drive shaft or gear housing.

5. Remove the pinion gear, nut and forward gear from the gear housing. See **Figure 81**.

6. 40-60 hp—Remove the drive shaft upper bearing race from the gear housing using slide hammer puller part No. 91-34569A-1- (or equivalent). See **Figure 82**. Remove and save any shims located under the bearing race.

7. If so equipped, remove the gear housing lubrication sleeve with puller part No. 91-27780 as shown in **Figure 83**.

NOTE
The forward gear tapered roller bearing is damaged during removal from the gear. Do not attempt to remove the bearing unless replacement is necessary. Always replace the bearing and race as a set.

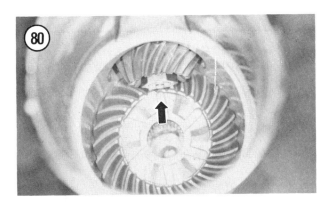

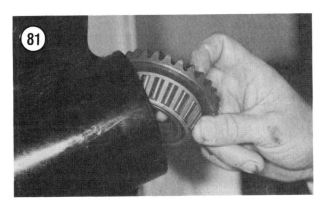

8. To remove the tapered roller bearing from the forward gear, install a universal bearing plate between the bearing and gear. Using a suitable arbor press and mandrel, press the bearing off the gear.

9. Remove the forward gear bearing race from the gear housing using slide hammer puller part No. 91-34569A-1- (or equivalent). Retrieve and save any shims located behind the bearing race.

10. If the forward gear contact area on the propeller shaft is pitted, scored, grooved or discolored, replace the propeller shaft and remove the bushing or needle bearing from the inner diameter of the forward gear for replacement:

   a. Clamp the forward gear into a vise with protective jaws.

   b. Using a suitable punch and hammer, drive the bushing or bearing from the gear. The bushing/bearing should be driven out from the tooth side of the gear.

Removal
(50-60 hp [Serial No. D000750-on])

1. Remove the bearing carrier and propeller shaft assemblies as described in this chapter.

2. Remove the water pump and pump base as described in this chapter.

3. Place drive shaft holding tool part No. 91-817070 onto the drive shaft upper spline.

4. Hold the drive shaft by placing an appropriate size wrench onto the drive shaft holding tool, then remove the pinion gear nut using a wrench or socket.

5. Unscrew the drive shaft upper bearing retainer using bearing retainer tool part No. 91-43506. Remove the bearing retainer.

6. Lift the drive shaft out the top of the gear housing along with the upper bearing and race. Remove and save the shim(s) located under the upper bearing.

7. Remove the pinion gear, nut and forward gear from the gear cavity.

9

8. If the forward gear contact area on the propeller shaft is pitted, scored, grooved or discolored, replace the propeller shaft and the needle bearing inside the forward gear. Remove the forward gear needle bearing as follows:

a. Clamp the forward gear into a vise with protective jaws.

b. Using a suitable punch and hammer, drive the bearing from the gear. The bushing/bearing should be driven out from the tooth side of the gear.

> *NOTE*
> *The forward gear tapered roller bearing is damaged during removal from the gear. Do not attempt to remove the bearing unless replacement is necessary. Always replace the bearing and race as a set.*

9. To remove the tapered roller bearing from the foward gear, install a universal bearing plate between the bearing and forward gear. Using an arbor press and a suitable mandrel, press the bearing from the gear.

10. Remove the forward gear bearing race from the gear housing using puller part No. 91-27780, or a suitable equivalent slide hammer puller. Retrieve and save the shim(s) located behind the bearing race.

Removal
(75-115 hp)

1. Remove the bearing carrier and propeller shaft assemblies as described in this chapter.

2. Remove the water pump and pump base as described in this chapter.

3. Install drive shaft holding tool part No. 91-56775 onto the drive shaft upper spline.

4. Place an appropriate size wrench onto the pinion gear nut (**Figure 80**). Loosen and remove the nut by turning the drive shaft counterclockwise while holding the pinion nut from turning.

5. Lift the drive shaft out the top of the gear housing.

6. Remove the pinion gear, pinion gear nut, pinion bearing and forward gear from the gear cavity.

7. To remove the needle bearing from the forward gear, clamp the gear into a vise (teeth side up) with protective jaws, or between wooden blocks.

8. Using a suitable punch and hammer, drive the bearing from the gear.

> *NOTE*
> *The forward gear tapered roller bearing is damaged during removal from the forward gear. Do not remove the bearing unless replacement is necessary. Always replace the bearing and race as a set.*

9. To remove the tapered roller bearing from the forward gear, install a universal bearing plate between the bearing and gear. Using an arbor press and a suitable mandrel, press the bearing from the gear.

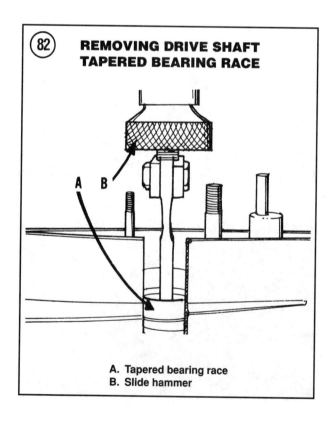

(82) **REMOVING DRIVE SHAFT TAPERED BEARING RACE**

A. Tapered bearing race
B. Slide hammer

10. If the forward gear tapered bearing requires replacement, remove the forward gear bearing race using slide hammer part No. 91-34569A-1- (or equivalent). Remove and save the shim(s) located behind the race. See **Figure 84**.

11. Inspect the drive shaft wear sleeve for grooves or other damage that could allow water to enter the gear housing. If deep grooves or damage are noted, install universal bearing plate (part No. 91-37241, or equivalent) around the drive shaft. Do not clamp the drive shaft tightly with the bearing plate. Place the bearing plate onto a vise as shown in **Figure 85** and tap the top of the shaft downward with a soft-face mallet to remove the sleeve from the shaft. Remove the rubber seal ring located under the sleeve.

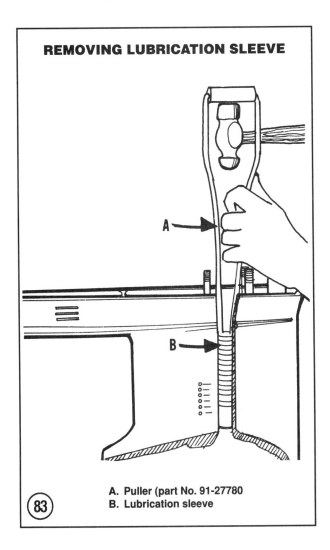

REMOVING LUBRICATION SLEEVE

A. Puller (part No. 91-27780
B. Lubrication sleeve

(83)

Removal
(V6 Cam-Shift [150XR4 and 150XR6])

1. Remove the bearing carrier and propeller shaft assemblies as described in this chapter.
2. Remove the water pump and pump base as described in this chapter.
3. Loosen and unscrew the drive shaft upper bearing retainer using retainer tool part No. 91-43506. Remove the bearing retainer from the drive shaft.
4. Install drive shaft holding tool part No. 91-34377A-1 onto the drive shaft upper spline.
5. Hold the pinion nut using a socket and flex handle. Pad the area around the flex handle with shop towels to prevent housing damage.
6. Loosen and remove the pinion nut by turning the drive shaft counterclockwise. Remove the pinion nut from the housing.
7. Clamp the drive shaft into a vise with protective jaws, or between wooden blocks. Clamp as close to the water pump studs as possible.

NOTE
On 150XR4 and 150XR6 models, the lower drive shaft bearing contains 18 loose bearing rollers that may fall out during drive shaft removal. Be sure to retrieve all rollers from the housing.

8. Place a wooden block against the gear housing mating surface. Hold the housing securely and tap the wooden block with a mallet until the drive shaft separates from the pinion gear. Pull the housing off the drive shaft. Remove 18 loose bearing rollers from the drive shaft lower bearing race.
9. Remove and save the shim(s) located under the drive shaft upper bearing.
10. Remove the pinion and forward gears from the gear cavity.

NOTE
The forward gear tapered roller bearing is damaged during removal from the gear. Do not remove the bearing unless

9

replacement is necessary. Always re-place the bearing and race as a set.

11. To remove the tapered bearing from the forward gear, install a universal bearing plate between the bearing and gear. Then using an arbor press and a suitable mandrel, press the bearing from the gear.

12. If the forward gear bearing requires replacement, remove the bearing race from the gear housing using slide hammer part No. 91-34569A-1, or equivalent. See **Figure 84**. Remove and save the shim(s) behind the bearing race.

Removal
(V6 E-Z Shift)

1. Remove bearing carrier and propeller shaft assemblies as described in this chapter.

2. Remove the water pump and pump base as described in this chapter.

3. Loosen and remove the drive shaft upper bearing retainer using bearing retainer tool part No. 91-43506 (except 250-275 hp) or 91-93227 (250-275 hp).

4. Install drive shaft holding tool part No. 91-34377A-1 onto the drive shaft upper spline.

5. Hold the pinion nut with a socket and flex handle. Pad the area around the flex handle to prevent housing damage.

6. While holding the pinion nut securely, loosen and remove the nut by turning the drive shaft counterclockwise. Remove the nut from the housing.

7. Clamp the drive shaft into a vise with protective jaws, or between wooden blocks. Do not damage the shaft.

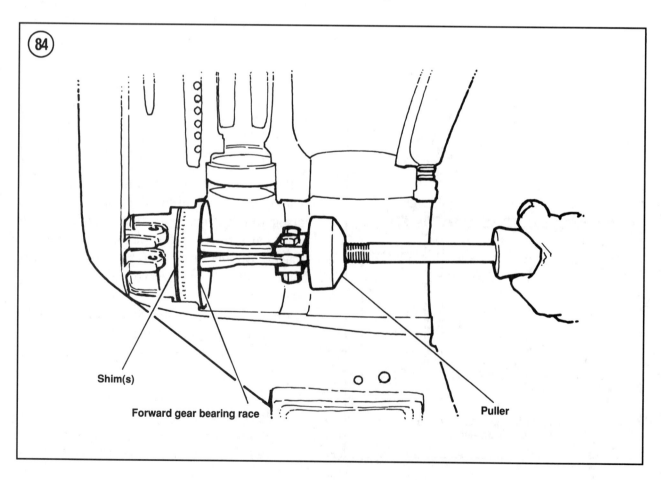

84

Shim(s)

Forward gear bearing race

Puller

NOTE
The lower drive shaft bearing contains 18 loose bearing rollers that may fall out during drive shaft removal. Be sure to retrieve all rollers from the gear housing.

8. Place a wooden block against the gear housing mating surface. Hold the housing securely and tap the wooden block with a mallet until the drive shaft separates from the pinion gear. Pull the housing off the drive shaft. Remove the 18 loose bearing rollers from the drive shaft lower bearing

race. Remove and save the shim(s) located under the drive shaft upper tapered roller bearing.
9. Remove the pinion and forward gears from the gear cavity.
10. If necessary, carefully remove the lubrication sleeve using puller part No. 91-27780, or equivalent (**Figure 83**).

NOTE
The forward gear tapered roller bearing and needle roller bearings are damaged during removal from the gear. Do not remove unless the bearings require replacement. Always replace tapered roller bearings and races as a set.

11. To remove the tapered roller bearing from the forward gear, install a universal bearing plate between the bearing and gear. Using an arbor press and a suitable mandrel, press the gear from the bearing.
12. If the forward gear bearing requires replacement, remove the bearing race from the gear housing using slide hammer part No. 91-34569A-1 as shown in **Figure 84**. Remove and save the shim(s) located behind the bearing race.
13. If the needle roller bearings inside the forward gear require replacement, clamp the gear (teeth side up) into a vise with protective jaws, or between wooden blocks. Using a suitable punch and hammer drive the bearings from the gear.

Cleaning and Inspection

1. Clean all components with solvent, then dry with compressed air.
2. Check forward and pinion gears for pitting, grooving, scoring, uneven or excessive wear, discoloration, chipped or broken teeth. Replace gear(s) as necessary.

NOTE
The needle roller bearing contact area on the propeller shaft and drive shaft is a good indicator of needle bearing condition. Inspect these areas closely for

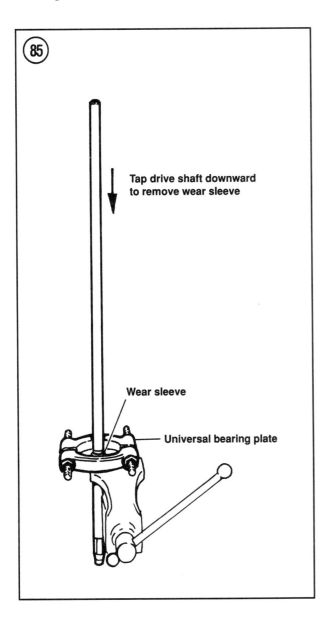

(85)

Tap drive shaft downward to remove wear sleeve

Wear sleeve

Universal bearing plate

9

scoring, galling, uneven or excessive wear, heat discoloration or other damage. If any defects are noted, replace the shaft and bearing(s) involved.

3. Check the drive shaft needle roller bearing contacts surfaces for pitting, scoring, discoloration or excessive wear. If any defects are noted, replace the needle bearing(s) and drive shaft.

4. Inspect the propeller shaft at the forward gear needle roller bearing contact area. Replace the shaft and bearings if rusted, pitted, scored, discolored or excessively worn.

5. Replace the drive shaft if the splines are excessively worn or twisted.

6. Check the drive shaft oil seal contact areas for deep grooves or excessive wear. Replace the shaft as necessary.

NOTE
Do not remove tapered roller bearings from the drive shaft or forward gear, or needle roller bearings from the gear housing unless replacement is necessary. If bearing failure has occurred, causing the bearing outer race to spin in the gear housing, the housing must be replaced.

7. Inspect all bearings for rust, corrosion, pitting, galling, excessive wear, roughness or other damage. Replace bearings as required. Always replace tapered roller bearings and races as a set.

Drive Shaft Bearing Replacement (3 hp)

1. Pry the water tube seal and drive shaft oil seal from the top of the gear housing. Discard the seals.

2. Remove the snap ring securing the drive shaft upper bearing in the gear housing.

3. Remove the drive shaft upper ball bearing using a suitable puller.

4. Lift the drive shaft sleeve from the gear housing.

5. Using a suitable driver rod, drive the lower bearing downward into the gear cavity.

6. Lubricate the outer diameter of the lower bearing with Quicksilver Gear Lube.

7. Assemble a 3/8 in. threaded rod with a plate and washers as shown in **Figure 86**. The outside diameter of the lower washer (5) must be 1 in. (25.4 mm). Place the drive shaft lower bearing onto the rod (numbered side facing up) as shown. Tighten the top nut (2) until the bearing is seated in the gear housing.

8. Lubricate the upper bearing with Quicksilver Gear Lube.

9. Using a suitable mandrel, drive the bearing into the housing until fully seated. Drive only on the bearing outer race.

10. Install the bearing snap ring.

11. Apply Quicksilver Bellows Adhesive (part No. 92-86166) to the outer diameter of the water tube seal. Install the water tube seal and drive shaft oil seal into the gear housing. Lubricate the inner diameter of both seals with Quicksilver 2-4-C Marine Lubricant.

Drive Shaft Bearing Replacement (3.3 hp)

1. Remove the drive shaft, propeller shaft and bearing carrier as described in this chapter.

2. Slide the drive shaft sleeve off the shaft.

3. Place the drive shaft (crankshaft end down) in an arbor press. Place shaft protector part No. 91-24161 (or equivalent) over the drive shaft pinion gear splines.

4. Situate a universal bearing plate under the drive shaft upper bearing then press the bearing from the shaft.

5. Insert a suitable driver (3/4 in. socket) into the drive shaft lower bearing bore. Remove the bearing from the gear housing by driving it downward into the gear cavity.

6. Lubricate a new drive shaft lower bearing with Quicksilver Needle Bearing Assembly Grease.

7. Insert the bearing (numbered side up) into its bore in the gear housing.

8. Using a suitable driver (3/4 in. socket), carefully drive the bearing into the gear housing until the bearing is 1/8 in. (3.2 mm) from the bottom of the bearing bore as shown in **Figure 87**.

NOTE
The drive shaft upper bearing must be installed at a point 3-5/8 in. (92.1 mm) from the pinion gear end of the drive

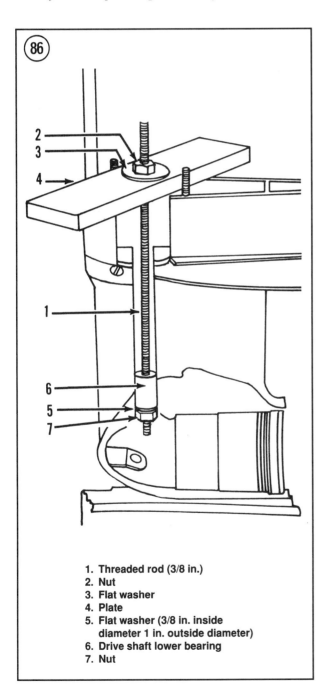

1. Threaded rod (3/8 in.)
2. Nut
3. Flat washer
4. Plate
5. Flat washer (3/8 in. inside diameter 1 in. outside diameter)
6. Drive shaft lower bearing
7. Nut

*shaft as shown in **Figure 88**. To ease installation, fabricate an installer tool from a piece of pipe with a 13/32 in. (10.3 mm) inside diameter, 3-5/8 in. (92.1 mm) long.*

9. Place the drive shaft (crankshaft end down) on a padded surface. Place the upper bearing on the pinion gear end of the drive shaft. The numbered side of the bearing should face up.

10. Obtain a piece of pipe with a 13/32 in. (10.3 mm) inside diameter. The pipe must be exactly 3-5/8 in. (92.1 mm) long.

11. Place the pipe over the end of the drive shaft and install the bearing by tapping the pipe until it is even with the end of the drive shaft. When installed, the bearing must be 3-5/8 in. (92.1 mm) from the pinion gear end of the drive shaft as shown in **Figure 88**.

Drive Shaft Bearing Replacement (4 and 5 hp)

Upper (ball) bearing

The drive shaft upper ball bearing is not serviceable. If the drive shaft bearing, sleeve or bushing requires replacement, the entire drive shaft assembly must be replaced.

Lower needle roller bearing

1. Drive the bearing from the housing using bearing tool part No. 91-17351, or a suitable equivalent driver. Drive the bearing downward into the gear cavity, then remove and discard the bearing. See **Figure 89**.

2. Lubricate the outer diameter of a new bearing with Quicksilver Gear Lube.

3. Place the bearing onto the end of the removal/installation tool (part No. 91-17351). The numbered side of the bearing should face the tool.

9

4. Insert the tool and bearing into the gear housing. Drive the bearing into the housing until the tool bottoms out on the housing.

Drive Shaft Bushing Replacement (8, 9.9 and 15 hp)

1. Remove the drive shaft upper bushing using Snap-On Expanding Rod (part No. CG40-4), Snap-On Collet (part No. CG40-15) and a suitable slide hammer puller. See **Figure 90**. Pull the bushing out the top of the gear housing.

NOTE
Snap-On tools can be purchased by contacting Snap-On Tools Corporation, 2801 80th Street, Kenosha, Wisconsin, 53141-1410.

2. Lift the lubrication sleeve out the top of the gear housing.

3. Insert drive shaft bushing removal tool part No. 91-13657A-1 into the gear housing and drive shaft lower bushing.

4. Drive the bushing downward into the gear cavity. Reach into the gear cavity and remove the bushing.

5. Use bushing installation tool part No. 91-13654A-1 to install the drive shaft bushings. Tighten the nut on the installation tool to draw the lower bushing into position.

6. Insert the lubrication sleeve into the gear housing.

7. Place the upper bushing onto the installation tool. Tighten the nut on the tool to draw the upper bushing into the gear housing.

Drive Shaft Bearing Replacement (20 and 25 hp)

1. Using puller part No. 91-27780, remove the 2 drive shaft oil seals from the gear housing.

2. Using a suitable mandrel and driver rod, drive the drive shaft upper bearing downward into the gear cavity.

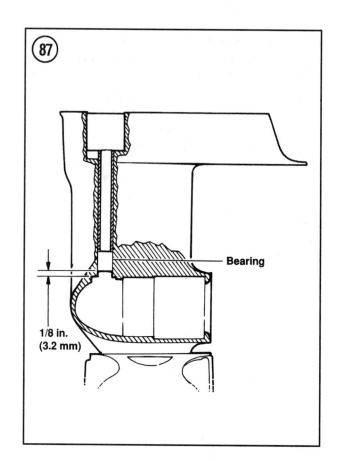

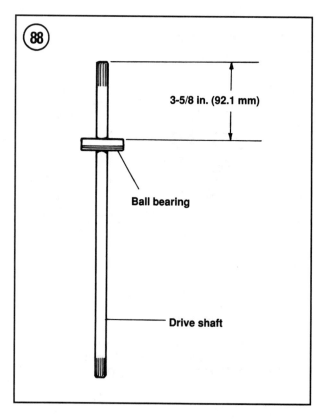

3. Drive the lower tapered bearing race downward into the gear cavity using a long punch and hammer. Remove the race from the gear cavity.

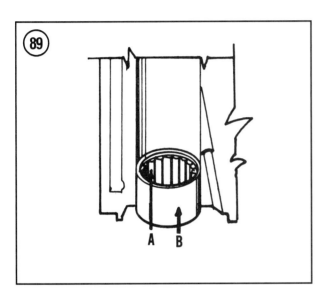

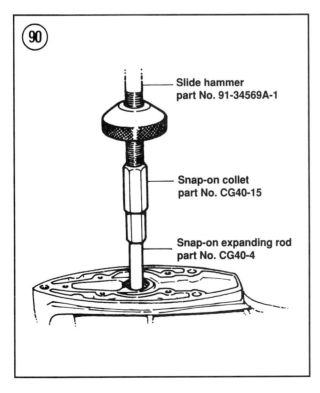

4. Place the upper bearing into the gear housing. The numbered side of the bearing should face up.

5. Using a suitable mandrel, carefully drive the bearing into its bore, until the bearing is just below the oil hole in the bearing bore.

6. Lubricate the outer diameter of a new lower bearing race with gear lube.

7. Arrange a suitable threaded rod, plate and washers as shown in **Figure 91**. Install the bearing race (cupped side facing down) on the rod, then install the washer (6, **Figure 91**) and lower nut.

8. Tighten the upper nut to draw the race into the gear housing, until fully seated.

9. Apply Loctite 271 to the outer diameter of the drive shaft oil seals.

10. Install the lower seal into the gear housing bore with its lip facing down. Using a suitable mandrel, drive the seal into the housing until the seal is just below the top of the drive shaft bore.

11. Place the upper seal directly on top of the lower seal. The upper seal lip should be facing up. Using the mandrel, drive both seals into the bore, until the upper seal is 3/16 in. (4.8 mm) below the top of the drive shaft bore. See **Figure 92**. Wipe off any excess Loctite. Lubricate the seal lips and upper bearing with Quicksilver 2-4-C Marine Lubricant.

Drive Shaft Bearing Replacement (40-60 hp)

1. If the drive shaft tapered roller bearing requires replacement, press the bearing from the shaft using a universal bearing plate and arbor press.

2. 40 hp and 50-60 hp (prior to serial No. D000750):

   a. If not removed during drive shaft removal, remove the tapered bearing race from the gear case as described in this chapter under *Pinion Gear, Drive Shaft And Forward Gear*.

9

b. Remove the lubrication sleeve from the gear housing, if not previously removed. See **Figure 83**.

3A. 40 hp and 50-60 hp (prior to serial No. D000750)—Remove the drive shaft needle roller bearing by driving it downward into the gear cavity using mandrel part No. 91-37312, or a suitable equivalent. See **Figure 93**.

3B. 50-60 hp (serial No. D000750-on)—Remove the drive shaft needle roller bearing by driving it downward into the gear cavity using bearing tool part No. 91-817058A-1 (or a suitable equivalent).

4. Lubricate outer and inner diameters of a new drive shaft needle roller bearing with Quicksilver Needle Bearing Assembly Grease. Install the new bearing (numbered side facing up) into the gear housing.

5A. 40 hp and 50-60 hp (prior to serial No. D000750)—Using mandrel part No. 91-37312 (or equivalent), drive the bearing into the housing until the bearing is approximately centered in its bore.

5B. 50-60 hp (serial No. D000750-on)—Using bearing tool part No. 91-817058A-1, drive the bearing into the housing until the tool bottoms on the top of the gear housing. If the bearing tool is not available, the bearing should be driven into the housing to a depth of 7.05-7.07 in. (179.1-179.6 mm) from the top of the gear housing as shown in **Figure 94**.

6. Press the new drive shaft tapered roller bearing onto the shaft until fully seated.

Drive Shaft Bearing Replacement (75-115 hp)

1. Using puller assembly part No. 91-83165M (or equivalent), pull the drive shaft upper bearing, then the bearing sleeve. See **Figure 95**.

2. After removing the bearing and bearing sleeve, remove the lubrication sleeve from the gear housing using puller part No. 91-83165M (or equivalent).

NOTE
The drive shaft tapered roller bearing race (lower bearing) can be removed without removing the upper bearing assembly and lubrication sleeve, providing the proper tool (part No. 91-14308A1) is used.

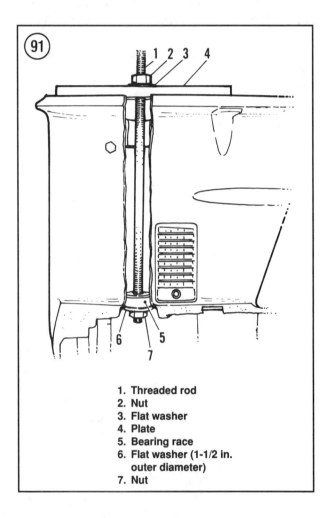

1. Threaded rod
2. Nut
3. Flat washer
4. Plate
5. Bearing race
6. Flat washer (1-1/2 in. outer diameter)
7. Nut

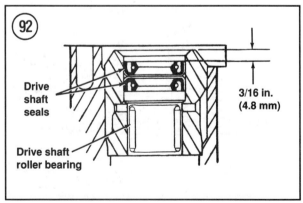

Drive shaft seals

Drive shaft roller bearing

3/16 in. (4.8 mm)

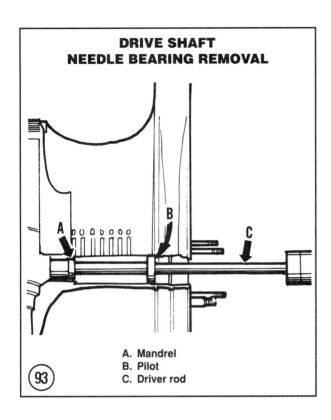

DRIVE SHAFT NEEDLE BEARING REMOVAL

A. Mandrel
B. Pilot
C. Driver rod

93

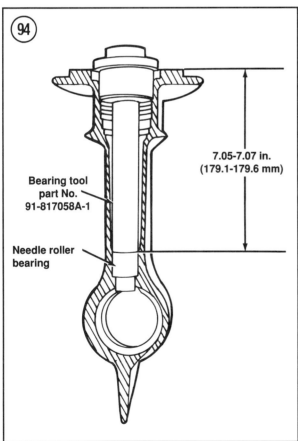

94

Bearing tool part No. 91-817058A-1

Needle roller bearing

7.05-7.07 in. (179.1-179.6 mm)

3. Remove the mandrel from the driver rod of bearing race tool part No. 91-14308A1. See **Figure 96**. Squeeze the mandrel together and insert it (spring end down) into the gear cavity and into the drive shaft lower bearing race. Make sure the lip on the mandrel securely engages the bearing race.

4. Insert the driver rod into the drive shaft bore, and into the driver mandrel, then drive the bearing race downward into the gear cavity.

5. Remove and save the shim(s) located between the race and gear housing.

6. Lubricate the outer diameter of the new lower bearing race with gear lube.

NOTE
If the original shim(s) between the lower bearing race and housing is lost or damaged, install an initial shim pack 0.025 in. (0.635 mm) thick in Step 7.

7. Install the original shim(s) and the bearing race into the gear housing.

8. Using threaded rod (part No. 91-31229) and bearing installation kit (part No. 91-14309A1), draw the bearing race into the gear housing until fully seated.

9. Install the lubrication sleeve into the drive shaft bore.

10. Lubricate the inside diameter of the upper bearing sleeve with Quicksilver Needle Bearing Assembly Grease.

11. Place the upper bearing sleeve in an arbor press with its beveled side facing down. With the numbered side facing up, press the upper bearing into the sleeve using a suitable mandrel.

12. With the beveled side facing down, insert the sleeve and bearing assembly into the gear housing. Using threaded rod (part No. 91-31299) and bearing installation kit (part No. 91-31229A5), draw the bearing into the gear housing.

9

Drive Shaft Bearing Replacement
(V6 Models)

1A. 250-275 hp—Remove the drive shaft lower tapered bearing using a universal bearing plate and arbor press. Thread the pinion gear nut onto the drive shaft to protect the threads. To remove the upper bearing from the drive shaft, place the shaft into a vise (pinion end down) with the jaws contacting the bearing inner race. Do not tighten the vise on the drive shaft. Using a lead hammer, tap the drive shaft downward, driving the bearing off toward the top of the shaft. Do not damage the drive shaft-to-crankshaft splines.

1B. 135-200 hp—Place the drive shaft (pinion end down) into a vise with the jaws contacting the bearing inner race. Do not tighten the vise on the shaft. Using a lead hammer, tap the drive shaft downward, driving the bearing off toward the top of the shaft. Do not damage the drive shaft-to-crankshaft splines.

NOTE
Two different size drive shaft needle bearings have been used on 150XR4 and 150XR6 models. Each design requires different special tools and service procedures to remove and install the lower drive shaft bearing. Early and late model gear housings can be identified by the shape of the leading edge as shown in ***Figure 97***.

NOTE
*On 135-200 hp models, late 150XR4 (***Figure 97***) and 150 XR6 models, the drive shaft lower bearing contains 18 loose bearing rollers that may fall out of the race during drive shaft removal. The loose bearing rollers must be reinstalled into the outer race to provide a contact surface for the removal tool to drive against.*

2A. Early style 150XR4 and XR6—Using driver rod (part No. 91-37323), pilot (part No. 91-37571) and a suitable size mandrel assembled as shown in **Figure 93**, drive the lower bearing

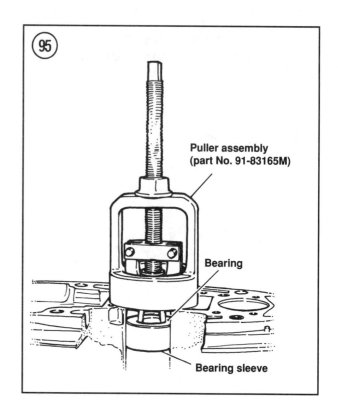

(95)

Puller assembly (part No. 91-83165M)

Bearing

Bearing sleeve

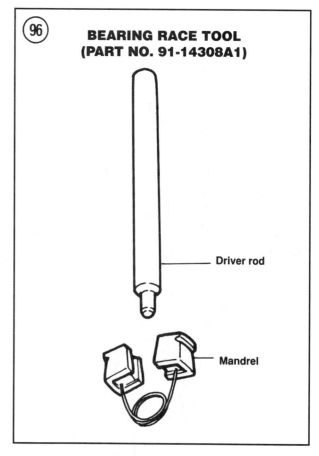

(96)

BEARING RACE TOOL (PART NO. 91-14308A1)

Driver rod

Mandrel

assembly into the gear cavity. Remove and discard the bearing.

2B. 135-200 hp and late 150XR4 and XR6:

a. Install the 18 loose bearing rollers into the lower bearing race. Use a suitable grease to hold the rollers in place.

b. Using mandrel (part No. 91-37263), pilot (part No. 91-36571) and driver rod (part No. 91-37323) assembled as shown in **Figure 93**, drive the lower bearing into the gear cavity. Remove and discard the bearing making sure all loose bearing rollers are retrieved.

2C. 250 and 275 hp—Using a heat lamp, heat both sides of the gear housing in the area of the drive shaft lower bearing. Using mandrel (part No. 91-092789), pilot (part No. 91-92790) and driver rod (part No. 91-37323), drive the bearing into the gear cavity. See **Figure 93**. Remove and discard the bearing.

CAUTION
If drive shaft lower bearing failure has occurred, causing the bearing outer race to spin inside the housing, the housing must be replaced. A new bearing installed into a worn bearing bore will result in premature bearing/gear housing failure.

3. Lubricate the new drive shaft lower bearing with Quicksilver Needle Bearing Assembly Grease.

4A. Early style 150XR4 and XR6:

a. Place the gear housing into its holding fixture with the drive shaft bore in a horizontal position.

b. Insert the new bearing (numbered side facing mandrel) into the drive shaft bore.

c. Using mandrel (part No. 91-37263), pilot (part No. 91-36571) and driver rod (part No. 91-37323), drive the bearing into its bore until the bearing is approximately 1/16 in. (1.6 mm) above the bottom of the bearing bore.

4B. 135-200 hp, late 150XR4 and XR6, 250 and 275 hp:

a. Make sure all 18 bearing rollers are properly installed in the bearing outer race. Reaching through the propeller shaft gear cavity, insert the bearing (numbered side facing up) into its bore. Assembly the following installation tools as shown in **Figure 98**.

b. 135-200 hp and late 150XR4 and XR6—Mandrel part No. 91-92788 (standard drive shaft) or 91-38628 (preloaded drive shaft), pilot part No. 91-36571, plate part No. 91-29310 and threaded rod part No. 91-31229.

c. 250 and 275 hp—Mandrel part No. 91-92788, pilot part No. 91-92790, plate part

9

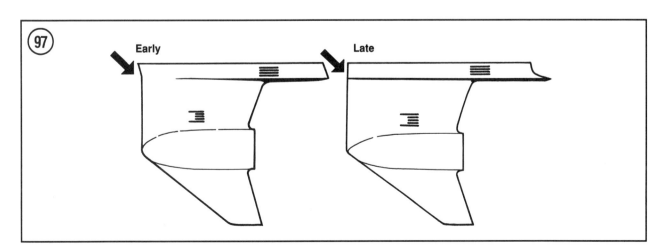

No. 91-29310 and threaded rod part No. 91-31229.

   d. Turning the top nut (**Figure 98**), draw the bearing into the gear housing until fully seated. Do not apply excessive force to the bearing.

5. Lubricate the drive shaft tapered roller bearing(s) with Quicksilver Needle Bearing Assembly Grease.

6. Press the bearing(s) onto the drive shaft using a suitable bearing plate and an arbor press.

Installation
(3 hp)

1. Install the drive gear propeller shaft assembly as described in this chapter.

2. Insert the drive shaft into the gear housing.

3. Install the pinion gear onto the drive shaft and secure with the E-ring.

4. Install the water pump assembly as described in this chapter.

Installation
(3.3 hp)

Refer to **Figure 44** for this procedure.

1. If removed, lubricate a new propeller shaft ball bearing with Quicksilver Needle Bearing Assembly Grease. Place the bearing into the gear housing. Using bearing driver part No. 91-37323, drive the bearing into its bore until full seated.

2. Place the original drive gear shim(s) on the drive gear. Lubricate the gear with gear lube, then install the gear into the gear housing. Make sure the gear properly enters, and is fully seated in, the ball bearing.

3. Install the drive shaft sleeve on the drive shaft.

4. Insert the pinion gear into the gear cavity. While holding the pinion gear in place under the drive shaft bore, install the drive shaft into the gear housing. Rotate the shaft as necessary to engage the pinion gear, then seat it fully in the housing bore.

5. Install the bearing carrier, propeller shaft and the water pump assemblies as described in this chapter.

Installation
(4 and 5 hp)

1. Install the original shims onto the forward gear. Position the forward gear and shim pack on the end of the propeller shaft and insert into the gear cavity to engage the forward gear bearing. Remove the propeller shaft.

2. Insert the pinion gear into the gear cavity. Engage the pinion gear with the forward gear and position the pinion gear under the drive shaft bore.

3. Insert the drive shaft while holding the pinion gear with one hand. Rotate the drive shaft to engage the pinion gear, then seat it fully in the housing bore.

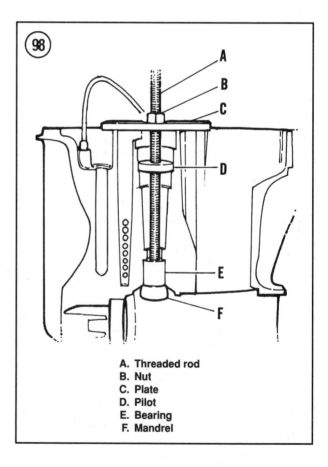

A. Threaded rod
B. Nut
C. Plate
D. Pilot
E. Bearing
F. Mandrel

4. Reinstall the original shims on top of the drive shaft ball bearing.

5. Reinstall the bearing carrier and propeller shaft assemblies and the water pump as described in this chapter.

Installation
(8, 9.9 and 15 hp)

1. If removed, lubricate a new forward gear bearing race with gear lube.

2. Insert the race into the gear housing. Place mandrel part No. 91-13658 (or equivalent) onto the end of bearing carrier tool part No. 91-13664.

3. Insert the bearing carrier tool and mandrel into the gear housing and against the bearing race. Drive the race into position by tapping on the end of the bearing carrier tool.

4. If removed, press a new bearing onto the forward gear using a suitable mandrel.

5. If removed, press a new bushing into the forward gear using mandrel part No. 91-13658 (or equivalent).

6. Install the forward gear into the gear cavity and into the forward gear bearing.

7. Lubricate the top of the pinion gear with Quicksilver 2-4-C Marine Lubricant to hold the thrust washer in place. Grooved side of the thrust washer should face the pinion gear.

8. Insert the pinion gear and thrust washer into the gear cavity. Engage the pinion and forward gear teeth, placing the pinion gear directly under the drive shaft bore.

9. Insert the drive shaft while holding the pinion gear and thrust washer with one hand. Rotate the drive shaft to align the pinion gear and drive shaft splines, then seat the shaft fully in the housing bore.

10. Reinstall the water pump cover, bearing carrier and propeller shaft assemblies as described in this chapter.

Installation
(20, 25 and 40 hp and 50-60 hp
[Prior to Serial No. D000750])

1. If removed, install a new bushing (20 and 25 hp) or needle bearing (40-60 hp) into the forward gear as follows:

   a. Place the gear (teeth down) on an arbor press.

   b. Lubricate the outer diameter of a new bushing or bearing with gear lube. Place the bushing or bearing (numbered side up) into the forward gear bore.

   c. Press the bushing or bearing into the gear until the bearing is flush with the top of the gear to 0.020 in. (0.51 mm) recessed.

2. If removed, press a new forward gear tapered roller bearing onto the gear using a suitable mandrel. Press only on the bearing inner race.

3. If removed, install a new forward gear bearing race as follows:

   a. Install the original forward gear shims (except 20 and 25 hp) into the gear housing.

   b. Lubricate the outer diameter of the race with gear lube.

   c. Place mandrel part No. 91-36571 (20 and 25 hp) or 91-31361 (40-60 hp) onto the forward end of the propeller shaft.

   d. Insert the propeller shaft and mandrel into the gear cavity and against the bearing race. Install the bearing carrier over the propeller shaft and into the gear housing to serve as a guide. See **Figure 99**. On 20 and 25 hp models, thread the bearing carrier into the housing a few turns.

   e. Using a soft-face mallet, tap on the propeller end of the shaft to drive the race into the gear housing until fully seated.

   f. Remove the propeller shaft, bearing carrier and mandrel.

4. 40-60 hp—Install the lubrication sleeve into the drive shaft bore. The tab on the sleeve must face forward. Install the original shims into the gear housing, then press the drive shaft upper

9

bearing race into the gear housing until fully seated.

5. Lubricate the forward gear bearing with gear lube. Install the gear into the gear cavity and properly seat into its bearing.

6A. 20 and 25 hp:

a. Lubricate the pinion gear bearing with gear lube, then place the bearing into position inside the gear cavity. Place the pinion gear into position in the gear cavity with the teeth engaged with the forward gear teeth.

b. Install the drive shaft into the gear housing while holding the pinion gear in place. Rotate the drive shaft to align the drive shaft and pinion gear splines.

c. Install the pinion gear retaining bolt. Clamp the drive shaft into a vise with protective jaws or wooden blocks. Tighten the pinion gear bolt to 100 in.-lb. (11.3 N•m).

6B. 40-60 hp:

a. Install the pinion gear into position in the gear housing, with its teeth engaged with the forward gear teeth.

b. Install the drive shaft into the gear housing while holding the pinion gear in place. Rotate the drive shaft to align the pinion gear and drive shaft splines.

NOTE
Always install a new pinion gear nut during reassembly. However, the old nut should be used to secure the pinion gear to the drive shaft during the shim selection process. After the proper shim adjustments have been performed, remove the old nut and install the new one.

c. Install the original pinion gear nut. Clamp the drive shaft into a vise with protective jaws or between wooden blocks, then tighten the pinion gear nut to 50 ft.-lb. (67.8 N•m).

d. Check the pinion gear depth and backlash as described in this chapter.

e. After the pinion gear depth and gear backlash is properly adjusted, remove the old

pinion gear nut. Apply Loctite 271 to the threads of a new pinion gear nut, then install the nut and tighten to 50 ft.-lb. (67.8 N•m).

7. Install the bearing carrier, propeller shaft and water pump assemblies as described in this chapter.

Installation
(50-60 hp Serial No. D000750-on)

1. If removed, install the original forward gear shim(s) into the gear housing. If the original shim pack is lost, damaged or if a new gear housing is being used, use an initial shim thickness of 0.010 in. (0.25 mm).

2. Lubricate the outer diameter of the forward gear bearing race with gear lube and insert the race into the gear housing.

3. Place mandrel part No. 91-817009 onto the forward end of the fully assembled propeller shaft. Insert the shaft and mandrel into the gear housing and against the race. Install the bearing carrier (fully assembled) over the propeller shaft and into the gear housing. See **Figure 99**, typical.

4. Thread a propeller nut onto the propeller shaft to prevent damage to the threads. Using a soft-face mallet, tap on the propeller shaft to drive the

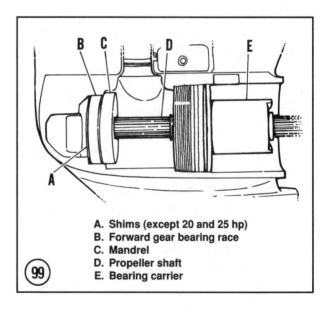

A. Shims (except 20 and 25 hp)
B. Forward gear bearing race
C. Mandrel
D. Propeller shaft
E. Bearing carrier

99

forward gear bearing race into the housing until fully seated. Remove the propeller shaft, bearing carrier and mandrel.

5. If removed, press a new propeller shaft needle bearing into the forward gear using mandrel part No. 91-817005 (or equivalent). Press the bearing from the numbered side only.

6. If removed, press a new tapered roller bearing onto the forward gear until fully seated, using mandrel part No. 91-817007.

7. Lubricate the forward gear bearing with gear lube. Install the gear into the gear housing.

8. Install the pinion gear into position with its teeth engaged with the forward gear teeth.

9. Install the original shims into the drive shaft bore.

10. Lubricate the drive shaft upper bearing with gear lube. Place the bearing race onto the drive shaft and seat it on the upper bearing.

11. Install the drive shaft into the gear housing while holding the pinion gear in place. Rotate the drive shaft slightly to align the pinion gear and drive shaft splines.

12. Install the drive shaft upper bearing retainer. Using retainer tool part No. 91-43506, tighten the retainer to 75 ft.-lb. (101.7 N.m).

NOTE
Always install a new pinion gear nut during reassembly. However, the old nut should be used to secure the pinion gear to the drive shaft during the shim selection process. After the proper shim adjustments have been performed, remove the old nut and install the new one.

13. Install the old pinion gear nut. Make sure the recessed side of the nut is facing the pinion gear. Place drive shaft holding tool part No. 91-817070 onto the drive shaft upper splines. Hold the pinion nut using an appropriate size socket and flex handle and turn the drive shaft to tighten the pinion nut to 50 ft.-lb. (67.8 N.m). See **Figure 100**.

14. Perform pinion gear depth and forward gear backlash adjustments as described in this chap-

ter. After the pinion depth and backlash have been correctly established, remove the old pinion gear nut. Apply Loctite 271 to the threads of a new nut, then install and tighten the nut to 50 ft.-lb. (67.8 N.m). See **Figure 100**.

15. Install the propeller shaft, bearing carrier and water pump assemblies as described in this chapter.

Installation (75-115 hp)

1. If removed, install a new rubber wear sleeve seal onto the drive shaft. Apply Loctite 271 to the outer diameter of the seal.

2. Using wear sleeve installation tool (part No. 91-14310A1), press a new wear sleeve onto the drive shaft until fully seated. Wipe off any excess Loctite.

3. Place the forward gear (teeth down) on an arbor press. Lubricate the inner diameter of the gear with Quicksilver Needle Bearing Assembly Grease.

4. Place a new propeller shaft bearing (numbered side up) into the forward gear. Press the bearing into the gear until fully seated, using a suitable mandrel.

5. Press a new tapered roller bearing onto the forward gear, using mandrel part No. 91-37350. Press on the bearing inner race only.

6. If removed, reinstall the original forward gear shim(s) into the gear housing. If the original shim pack is lost, damaged or if a new gear housing is being used, use an initial shim thickness of 0.010 in. (0.25 mm).

7. Lubricate the outer diameter of the forward gear bearing race with gear lube and insert the race into the gear housing.

8. Place mandrel part No. 91-31106 onto the forward end of the fully disassembled propeller shaft. Insert the shaft and mandrel into the gear housing and against the race. Install the bearing carrier (fully assembled) over the propeller shaft and into the gear housing. See **Figure 99**, typical.

9. Thread a propeller nut onto the propeller shaft to prevent damage to the threads. Using a soft-face mallet, tap on the propeller shaft to drive the forward gear bearing race into the housing until fully seated. Remove the propeller shaft, bearing carrier and mandrel.

10. Lubricate the forward gear bearing with gear lube. Install the bearing into the gear housing.

11. Lubricate the drive shaft lower bearing with gear lube. Install the bearing and pinion gear into the gear housing.

12. While holding the pinion gear firmly in place, install the drive shaft into the gear housing. Rotate the shaft slightly to align the pinion gear and drive shaft splines.

NOTE
Always install a new pinion gear nut during reassembly. However, the old nut should be used to secure the pinion gear to the drive shaft during the shim selection process. After the proper shim adjustments have been performed, remove the old nut and install the new one.

13. Install the old pinion gear nut. Make sure the recessed side of the nut is facing the pinion gear. Place drive shaft holding tool part No. 91-56775 onto the drive shaft upper splines. Place an appropriate size socket and flex handle on the pinion nut. While holding the pinion nut securely, turn the drive shaft to tighten the pinion to 70 ft.-lb. (95 N.m). See **Figure 100**.

14. Perform pinion gear depth and forward gear backlash adjustments as described in this chapter. After the pinion depth and backlash have been correctly established, removed the old pinion gear nut. Apply Loctite 271 to the threads of a new nut, then install (recessed side facing gear) and tighten the nut to 70 ft.-lb. (95 N.m). See **Figure 100**.

15. Install the propeller shaft, bearing carrier and water pump assemblies as described in this chapter.

Installation (V6 Cam-Shift [150XR4 and 150XR6])

1. If removed, reinstall the original forward gear shim(s) into the gear housing. If the original shim pack is lost, damaged or if a new gear housing is being used, use an initial shim thickness of 0.010 in. (0.25 mm).

2. Lubricate the outer diameter of the forward gear bearing race with gear lube and insert the race into the gear housing.

3. Place mandrel part No. 91-31106 onto the forward end of the fully disassembled propeller shaft. Insert the shaft and mandrel into the gear housing and against the race. Install the bearing

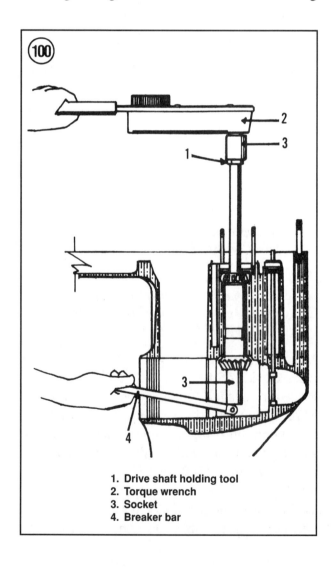

1. Drive shaft holding tool
2. Torque wrench
3. Socket
4. Breaker bar

carrier (fully assembled) over the propeller shaft and into the gear housing. See **Figure 99**, typical.

4. Install a propeller nut onto the propeller shaft to prevent damage to the threads. Using a soft-face mallet, tap on the propeller shaft to drive the forward gear bearing race into the housing until fully seated. Remove the propeller shaft, bearing carrier and mandrel.

5. Place the forward gear (teeth down) on an arbor press. Place a new propeller shaft needle bearing (numbered side up) into the gear. Press the bearing into the gear using mandrel part No. 91-818149.

6. Press a new tapered roller bearing onto the forward gear using a suitable mandrel. Make sure the bearing is fully seated.

7. Late models—If removed, install 18 loose bearing rollers into the drive shaft lower bearing race. Use Quicksilver Needle Bearing Assembly Grease to hold the rollers in place.

8. Lubricate the forward gear bearing with gear lube and install the gear into the gear housing.

9. Place the pinion gear into position in the gear housing. Install the drive shaft into the housing while holding the pinion gear in place. Apply Loctite 271 to the threads of a *new* pinion gear nut. Install the nut (recessed side facing gear) and tighten by hand.

10. Install the original shim(s) into the drive shaft bore. If the shims are lost or damaged, use an initial shim pack thickness of 0.010 in. (0.25 mm).

11. Lubricate the upper bearing with gear lube. Install the upper race and bearing retainer. The "OFF" marking on the retainer must be facing up.

12. Tighten the bearing retainer to 100 ft.-lb. (135.6 N·m) using retainer tool part No. 91-43506.

13. Place drive shaft holder tool part No. 91-34377A1 onto the drive shaft upper splines.

14. Hold the pinion nut using an appropriate size socket and flex handle. Pad the area around the flex handle to prevent damage to the gear hous-

ing. While securely holding the pinion nut, turn the drive shaft to tighten the pinion nut to 80 ft.-lb. (108.5 N·m). See **Figure 100**.

15. Perform pinion gear depth and forward gear backlash adjustments as described in this chapter.

16. Install the propeller shaft, bearing carrier and water pump assemblies as described in this chapter.

Installation
(V6 E-Z Shift)

1. If removed, reinstall the original forward gear shim(s) into the gear housing. If the original shim pack is lost, damaged or if a new gear housing is being used, use an initial shim thickness of 0.010 in. (0.25 mm) on 135-200 hp models, or 0.020 in. (0.51 mm) on 250-275 hp models.

2. Lubricate the outer diameter of the forward gear bearing race with gear lube and insert the race into the gear housing.

3. Place mandrel part No. 91-87120 onto the forward end of the fully disassembled propeller shaft. Insert the shaft and mandrel into the gear housing and against the race. Install the bearing carrier (fully assembled) over the propeller shaft and into the gear housing. See **Figure 99**, typical.

4. Install a propeller nut onto the propeller shaft to prevent damage to the threads. Using a soft-face mallet, tap on the propeller shaft to drive the forward gear bearing race into the housing until fully seated. Remove the propeller shaft, bearing carrier and mandrel.

5. If removed, press new propeller shaft bearing(s) into the forward gear using a suitable mandrel.

6. If removed, press a new tapered roller bearing onto the forward gear. Make sure the bearing is fully seated on the gear.

7. Lubricate the forward gear bearings with gear lube. Install the gear into the gear housing.

8. Except 250-275 hp—Insert the lubrication sleeve into the drive shaft bore, aligning the flats

9

in the bore with the flats on the sleeve. The notch in the top of the sleeve should face the leading edge of the gear housing. Tap the sleeve into the housing using a suitable wooden block until the sleeve is just below the tapered bearing shim surface.

9. Install the original shim(s) into the drive shaft bore. If the original shim(s) are lost or damaged, use an initial shim pack thickness of 0.010 in. (except 250-275 hp) or 0.020 in. (250-275 hp).

10. Place the pinion gear into position in the gear housing.

11. While firmly holding the pinion gear in place, install the drive shaft into the gear housing. Rotate the drive shaft to align the pinion gear and drive shaft splines. Apply Loctite 271 to the threads of a *new* pinion gear nut. Install the pinion gear washer and nut hand tight.

12. Install the drive shaft upper bearing race. Lubricate the threads of the upper bearing retainer with Quicksilver Special Lube 101, then install the retainer as follows:

   a. Except 250-275 hp—The "OFF" marking on the retainer must face up.

   b. 250 and 275 hp—The side of the retainer without threads should be facing down.

13. Using retainer tool part No. 91-43506 (135-200 hp) or 91-93227 (250-275 hp), tighten the upper bearing retainer to 100 ft.-lb. (135.6 N•m).

14. Install the drive shaft holding tool part No. 91-34377A1 (except 250-275 hp) or 91-12362 (250-275 hp) onto the drive shaft upper splines.

15. Hold the pinion gear using an appropriate size socket and flex handle. Pad the area around the flex handle to prevent damage to the gear housing.

16. While holding the pinion nut securely, turn the drive shaft and tighten the pinion nut to 75 ft.-lb. (101.7 N•m) on 135-200 hp models or 70 ft.-lb. (95 N•m) on 250 and 275 hp models. See **Figure 100**.

17. Perform pinion gear depth and forward gear backlash measurements as described in this chapter.

18. Install the propeller shaft, bearing carrier and water pump assemblies as described in this chapter.

LOWER SHIFT SHAFT, BUSHING AND CAM

Removal and Disassembly (3.3 hp)

Refer to **Figure 44** for this procedure.

1. Remove the water pump and pump base as described in this chapter.

2. Remove the shift rod bushing from the pump cover. Remove and discard the bushing O-ring. Remove and discard the shift rod O-ring in the water pump base.

3. Grasp the lower shift rod and pull it up and out of the gear housing.

4. Further disassembly should not be necessary for cleaning and inspection. However, if the shift cam requires replacement, drive out the roll pin holding it to the shift rod and remove the cam.

Removal and Disassembly (4 and 5 hp)

1. Remove the bolt, washer and retainer plate at the front of the water pump assembly.

2. Grasp the shift shaft and pull it straight up and out of the gear housing/water pump assembly. Remove the O-ring from the shift shaft bore.

3. Slide the bushing off the shift shaft.

4. Further disassembly should not be necessary for cleaning and inspection purposes. However, if the shift cam requires replacement, drive out the roll pin holding it to the shaft and remove the cam. The center pin can also be removed from the shaft, if necessary.

Removal and Disassembly
(8, 9.9 and 15 hp)

1. Remove the water pump as described in this chapter. The shift shaft is removed with the pump assembly.
2. Remove the E-ring from the shift shaft.
3. Pull the shift shaft from the water pump base.
4. Unthread the shift cam from the shift shaft.

Removal and Disassembly
(20 and 25 hp)

Refer to **Figure 101** for this procedure.

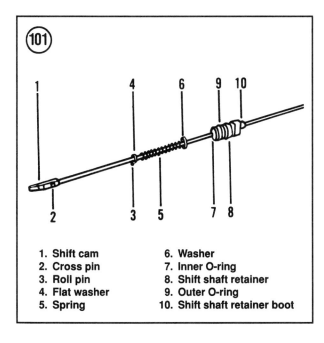

1. Shift cam
2. Cross pin
3. Roll pin
4. Flat washer
5. Spring
6. Washer
7. Inner O-ring
8. Shift shaft retainer
9. Outer O-ring
10. Shift shaft retainer boot

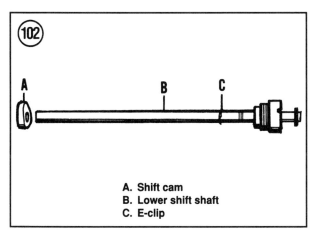

A. Shift cam
B. Lower shift shaft
C. E-clip

1. Remove the propeller shaft, bearing retainer, drive shaft and forward gear as described in this chapter.
2. Pull the shift shaft from the gear housing.
3. Remove the outer O-ring from the shift shaft. Do *not* remove the inner O-ring unless it must be replaced.
4. Check the shift shaft retainer condition. Replace the shaft if cracked.
5. Check shift cam condition. If pitted or grooved, replace the cam.

Removal and Disassembly
(40 hp; 50-60 hp [Prior to Serial No. D000750]; and V6 [Cam-Shift])

1. Remove the bearing carrier, propeller shaft, drive shaft and forward gear as described in this chapter.
2. Loosen and unscrew the shift shaft bushing from the gear housing using shift shaft bushing tool part No. 91-23033 (40-60 hp) or 91-31107 (all other models).
3. Lift the shift shaft up and out of the gear housing. Reach into the gear cavity and remove the shift cam. See **Figure 102**.
4. Slide the bushing off the shift shaft.
5. Remove and discard the shift shaft bushing O-ring.

NOTE
The seals are not serviceable on shift shaft bushings equipped with 2 seals. If the seals require replacement, replace the bushing assembly.

6. Remove the shift shaft bushing seal by prying with a screwdriver. Discard the seal.

Removal and Disassembly
(V6 [EZ-Shift])

NOTE
On V6 EZ-Shift models, the gear housing must be in NEUTRAL and the shift shaft

9

must be removed before the propeller shaft can be removed.

1. Shift the gear housing into NEUTRAL.

2. Remove the shift shaft, bearing carrier and propeller shaft as described in this chapter.

3. Slide the shift shaft bushing off the shift shaft. Remove the rubber washer from the bushing.

4. Pry the shift shaft oil seal from the bushing using a screwdriver or similar tool. Discard the seal.

5. If necessary, remove the E-ring and retaining ring from the shift shaft.

Removal and Disassembly (50-60 hp Serial No. D000750-on)

1. Remove the bearing carrier, propeller shaft, drive shaft and forward gear as described in this chapter.

2. Remove the shift shaft coupler and spacer from the shaft.

3. Using suitable pliers, pull the shift shaft and bushing from the gear housing. Use caution not to damage the shaft splines.

4. Remove the shift cam from the gear cavity.

5. Slide the bushing off the shaft.

6. Remove and discard the shift shaft bushing O-ring and seal.

Removal and Disassembly (75-115 hp)

1. Remove the bearing carrier, propeller shaft, drive shaft and forward gear as described in this chapter.

2. Remove the shift shaft coupler and nylon spacer from the shaft.

3. Remove the 2 screws securing the shift shaft bushing to the gear housing.

4. Using screwdrivers on each side of the bushing, carefully pry the shift shaft bushing out of the housing. Lift the shaft and bushing assembly out of the gear housing.

5. Remove the shift cam from the gear cavity.

6. Slide the bushing off the shaft. Remove and discard the bushing O-ring. Pry the shift shaft seal from the bushing. Discard the seal.

Cleaning and Inspection

3.3-25 hp

1. Thoroughly clean all parts in solvent and dry with compressed air.

2. Check the shift shaft splines and seal surfaces for excessive or uneven wear or corrosion. Replace the shaft as necessary.

3. Replace the E-ring if bent or damaged.

4. Inspect the shift cam for excessive wear. Replace the cam if chipped, cracked or excessively worn.

40-275 hp

1. Clean all parts with solvent and dry with compressed air.

2. Inspect the shift shaft splines and seal surface. Replace the shaft if the splines are twisted or excessively worn, or if the seal surface is excessively or unevenly worn or corroded.

3. Replace the shaft E-ring if bent or damaged. See **Figure 102**.

4. Replace the shift cam if chipped, cracked or excessively worn.

Assembly and Installation (3.3 hp)

1. If removed, install the shift cam on the lower shift rod. Secure the cam with a new roll pin.

2. Install the shift rod assembly into the gear housing.

3. Install new O-ring seals on the shift rod bushing and water pump base. Lubricate the seals with Quicksilver 2-4-C Marine Lubricant.

4. Install the shift rod bushing into the water pump cover. Reinstall the water pump assembly as described in this chapter.

Assembly and Installation
(4 and 5 hp)

1. If the shift cam is removed, reinstall it on the shift shaft and insert and install the roll pin. Make sure the taper on the cam is facing away from the bend in the shift shaft. Reinstall the center pin, if removed.

2. Slide the bushing onto the shift shaft.

3. Lubricate a new O-ring with Quicksilver 2-4-C Marine Lubricant and install it into the shift shaft bore.

4. With the taper on the shift cam facing the drive shaft, carefully insert it through the water pump base and into the gear housing.

5. Install the shift shaft retainer plate, washer and screw. Tighten the retainer screw to 70 in.-lb. (7.9 N.m).

Assembly and Installation
(8, 9.9 and 15 hp)

1. Slide the water pump base onto the shift shaft.

2. Install the E-ring into the shift shaft groove.

3. Thread the shift cam onto the shaft.

4. Hold the shift shaft vertically and position the water pump base on the gear housing. Shift cam taper must face the drive shaft.

5. Insert the shift shaft into the gear housing and seat the water pump base.

6. Reinstall the water pump as described in this chapter.

Assembly and Installation
(20 and 25 hp)

1. Lubricate the O-rings with gear lube.

2. Install the shift shaft components onto the shaft (**Figure 101**).

3. Install the shift shaft assembly into the gear housing. The shift cam taper must face the drive shaft.

4. Install the forward gear, drive shaft, bearing carrier and propeller shaft as described in this chapter.

Assembly and Installation
(40-275 hp)

1A. 40 hp and 50-60 (prior to serial No. D000750):

  a. Using a suitable mandrel, press a new seal (lip facing up) into the shift shaft bushing.

  b. Install a new O-ring onto the bushing.

  c. Lubricate the seal lip and O-ring with Quicksilver 2-4-C Marine Lubricant.

  d. If removed, install the E-clip (**Figure 102**) into its groove on the shift shaft. Slide the bushing assembly, then the rubber washer onto the shift shaft.

1B. 50-60 hp (serial No. D000750-on):

  a. Apply Quicksilver Perfect Seal to the outer diameter of a new shift shaft bushing seal.

  b. Using a suitable mandrel, press the seal (lip facing up) into the bushing until fully seated.

  c. Install a new O-ring onto the shift shaft bushing. Lubricate the seal lip and O-ring with Quicksilver Needle Bearing Assembly Grease.

  d. If removed, install the E-clip (**Figure 102**) into its groove in the shift shaft. Slide the bushing assembly onto the shaft.

NOTE
Replacement shift shaft bushing equipped with 2 shaft seals is provided with both seals installed.

1C. 75-115 hp and V6 models:

  a. Apply Loctite 271 to the outer diameter of a new shift shaft bushing seal.

9

b. Using a suitable mandrel, press the seal (lip facing up) into the shift shaft bushing. Wipe off any excess Loctite.

c. Install a new O-ring onto the shift shaft bushing. Lubricate the seal lip and O-ring with Quicksilver 2-4-C Marine Lubricant.

d. If removed, install the E-clip (**Figure 102**) into its groove in the shaft.

e. Slide the bushing onto the shift shaft. If so equipped, install the rubber washer onto the shaft and position it against the bushing seal.

2A. 40-115 hp models—Install the shift cam into the gear housing, aligning the hole in the cam with the holes in the gear housing. Position the cam facing rearward (numbered side up) as shown in **Figure 103**. Install the shift shaft assembly (**Figure 104**, typical) making sure the shaft properly engages the cam. Rotate the shaft as necessary to align the shaft and cam splines.

2B. 150XR4 and XR6 models—Install the shift cam into the gear housing. The longer side of the cam must be facing the port side and the ramps on the cam must be visible from the rear of the gear housing. See **Figure 105**. Install the shift shaft assembly (**Figure 104**), making sure the shaft properly engages the cam. Rotate the shaft as necessary to align the shaft and cam splines.

2C. V6 E-Z Shift models:

a. Coat the shift cam pocket in the cam follower with Quicksilver 2-4-C Marine Lubricant.

b. With the numbered side facing up, place the shift cam into the follower pocket as shown in **Figure 106**. The flat side of the cam should be parallel with the shift cam follower.

c. Install the propeller shaft into the gear housing, then install the shift shaft (**Figure 104**), making sure the shaft properly engages the shift cam. Rotate the shaft as necessary to align the cam and shaft splines.

3A. 50-60 (serial No. D000750-on)—Push downward on the shift shaft bushing, making

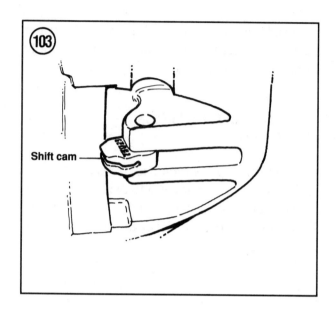

Shift cam

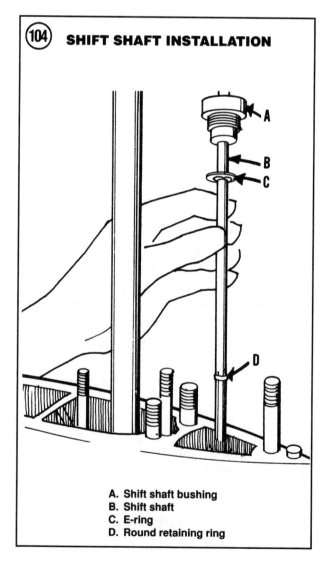

SHIFT SHAFT INSTALLATION

A. Shift shaft bushing
B. Shift shaft
C. E-ring
D. Round retaining ring

sure it's fully seated in the gear housing. Install the nylon spacer and shift shaft coupler onto the shaft.

3B. 75-115 hp—Seat the shift shaft bushing in the gear housing. Apply Loctite 271 to the threads of the bushing retaining screws, then install and tighten to 60 in.-lb. (6.8 N·m). Install the nylon spacer and shift shaft coupler onto the shaft.

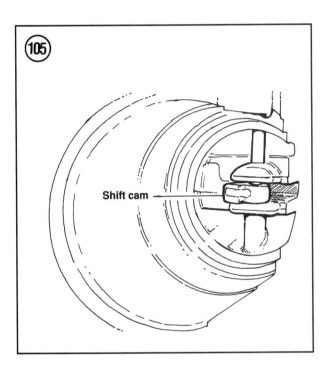

3C. All others—Apply a light coat of Quicksilver Perfect Seal to the threads of the shift shaft bushing. Do not allow Perfect Seal onto the bushing seal or O-ring. Thread the bushing into the gear housing, then tighten to 50 ft.-lb. (67.8 N·m) using shift shaft bushing tool part No. 91-23033 (40 hp and 50-60 [prior to serial No. D000750 hp] or 91-31107 (all others).

4. Install the forward gear, propeller shaft and bearing carrier as described in this chapter.

PINION DEPTH/GEAR BACKLASH

Proper pinion gear engagement and forward/reverse gear backlash are crucial for smooth, quiet operation and long service life. Two or three shimming procedures must be performed to set up the lower unit gear housing properly. The pinion gear must be shimmed to the correct depth and the forward gear must be shimmed to the pinion gear for the proper backlash. Reverse gear backlash is not adjustable, but should be checked on most models to ensure the gear housing is properly assembled.

3.3 hp

Drive gear backlash

The amount of backlash between the pinion and drive gears is not critical as long some lash is present. If no backlash is present between the gears, premature gear and gear housing failure will result.

1. To check gear backlash, firmly press downward on the drive shaft while pushing upward on the pinion gear. Note that the pinion gear must float on the drive shaft.

2. While holding the drive shaft and pinion gear in this position, have an assistant rock the propeller shaft back and forth. Approximately 0.002-0.006 in. (0.05-0.15 mm) lash should be present between the drive and pinion gears.

3. If excessive backlash is noted over 0.012 in. (0.30 mm), check the pinion gear, drive gear and related components for excessive wear.

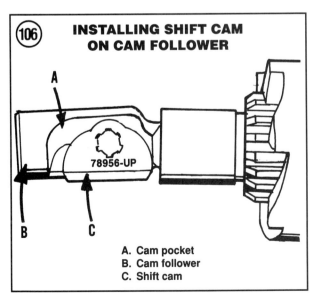

INSTALLING SHIFT CAM ON CAM FOLLOWER

78956-UP

A. Cam pocket
B. Cam follower
C. Shift cam

4. If no backlash is noted, one or more of the following problems exists:

a. The front ball bearing is not fully seated in the gear housing.

b. The drive gear is not fully seated in the front ball bearing.

c. The drive shaft lower bearing is positioned too low in the bearing bore.

40 hp and 50-60 hp (Prior to Serial No. D000750)

Pinion gear depth

1. Thoroughly wipe the gear cavity clean using clean shop towels.

2. Insert shim tool part No. 91-89670 into the gear cavity. Align the access hole in the tool with the pinion gear. Make sure the tool is fully seated in the gear cavity.

3. While applying downward pressure on the drive shaft, rotate the shaft several turns to seat the tapered bearing.

4. While maintaining firm downward pressure on the drive shaft, insert a 0.025 in. (0.64 mm) flat feeler gauge into the shim tool access hole. The feeler gauge should just fit between the pinion gear and the gauging surface of the shim tool. See **Figure 107**.

5. If the clearance is not 0.025 in. (0.64 mm), remove the drive shaft, pinion gear and drive shaft upper bearing race as described in this chapter. Add or subtract shims under the race as necessary to obtain the specified clearance. Increasing shim thickness increases clearance while decreasing shim thickness decreases clearance.

6. Reassemble the drive shaft and pinion gear as described in this chapter, then recheck pinion gear depth. After the correct pinion gear depth is established, remove and discard the old pinion nut. Apply Loctite 271 to the threads of a new nut, then install and tighten as described in this chapter.

Forward gear backlash

1. Establish the correct the pinion gear depth as described in this chapter before attempting to adjust forward gear backlash.

2. Install the propeller shaft and bearing carrier as described in this chapter.

3. Install bearing carrier puller assembly part No. 91-46086A1 (jaws) and part No. 91-85716 (bolt) as shown in **Figure 108**.

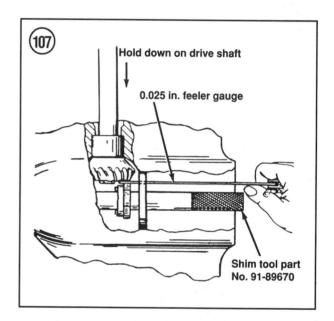

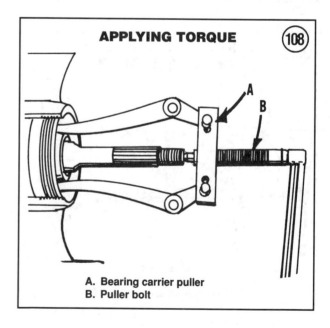

A. Bearing carrier puller
B. Puller bolt

4. Tighten the puller bolt to 45 in.-lb. (5.1 N•m), then turn the drive shaft 5-10 revolutions to seat the forward gear bearing and race.

5. Install dial indicator adapter (part No. 91-83155) onto one water pump stud, then install

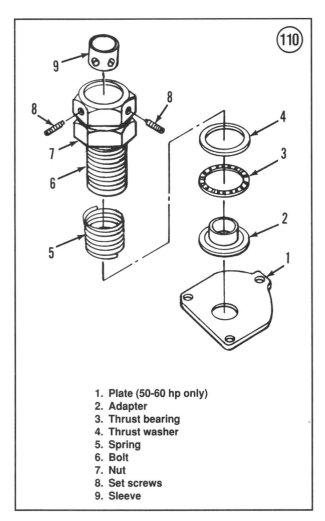

1. Plate (50-60 hp only)
2. Adapter
3. Thrust bearing
4. Thrust washer
5. Spring
6. Bolt
7. Nut
8. Set screws
9. Sleeve

dial indicator (part No 91-58222A1) onto the adapter. Place backlash indicator tool (part No. 91-78473) onto the drive shaft, align the indicator tool with the dial indicator plunger, then tighten the tool securely on the drive shaft. See **Figure 109**. Adjust the dial indicator mounting so the plunger is aligned with line "4" on the backlash indicator tool. Zero the indicator gauge.

6. Apply firm downward pressure on the drive shaft and lightly turn the shaft back and forth (propeller shaft should not move) while noting the dial indicator reading. The reading is forward gear-to-pinion gear backlash and should be within 0.007-0.010 (0.18-0.25 mm).

NOTE
A 0.001 in. (0.0.025 mm) change in forward gear bearing shim thickness will change forward gear backlash by approximately 0.00125 in. (0.032 mm).

7. If backlash is excessive, add shim(s) to the forward gear bearing race. If backlash is insufficient, subtract shim(s) from the forward gear bearing race.

50-60 hp (Serial No. D000750-on) and 75-275 hp

Pinion gear depth

1. Install the forward gear assembly into the gear housing as described in this chapter.

2. Using a clean shop towel, thoroughly clean the gear cavity, especially the area around the bearing carrier shoulder.

3. Position the gear housing with the drive shaft facing upward.

NOTE
*Drive shaft bearing preload tool part No. 91-14311A2 (50-60 hp) or 91-14311A1 (all others) is necessary to check/adjust pinion gear depth and gear backlash properly. Plate (1, **Figure 110**) is used on 50-60 hp models only.*

9

4. Install the bearing preload tool part No. 91-14311A2 (50-60 hp) or 91-14311A1 (all others) onto the drive shaft in the order shown in **Figure 110**.

   a. Make sure the thrust bearing and washer are clean and lightly oiled.

   b. Screw the nut (7) completely onto the bolt (6), then securely tighten the set screws (8) making sure the holes in the sleeve (9) are aligned with the set screws.

   c. Measure the distance (D, **Figure 111**) between the top of the nut and the bottom of the bolt head. Then screw the nut downward increasing the distance (D) by 1 in. (25.4 mm).

   d. Rotate the drive shaft 10-12 turns to seat the drive shaft bearing(s).

5A. 50-60 hp—Insert pinion locating tool (part No. 91-817008A2) into the gear housing. Make sure the tool engages the forward gear, with its access hole facing the pinion gear.

5B. All others:

   a. Assemble the pinion gear locating tool as shown in **Figure 112**. Install the gauging block with the numbered side facing away from the split collar. Do not tighten the collar screws at this time.

   b. Insert the tool into the forward gear with the gauging block under the pinion gear. Without disturbing the position of the gauging block, remove the tool and tighten the collar screws securely.

   c. Reinsert the pinion gear locating tool into the forward gear. Position the specified gauging block flat under the pinion gear, then install the specified locating disc (**Figure 113**). Make sure the locating disc is fully seated against the bearing carrier shoulder inside the gear cavity and the disc access hole is aligned with the pinion gear. Set up the pinion gear locating tool as follows:

75-90 hp—Flat No. 8 and locating disc No. 3.

100-115 hp—Flat No. 2 and locating disc No. 3.

135-200 hp (except XR4 and XR6)—Flat No. 7 and locating disc No. 2.

150XR4 and XR6—Flat No. 1 and locating disc No. 1.

250-275 hp—Flat No. 4 and locating disc No. 2.

6. Insert a 0.025 in. (0.64 mm) flat feeler gauge between the gauging block and pinion gear. See

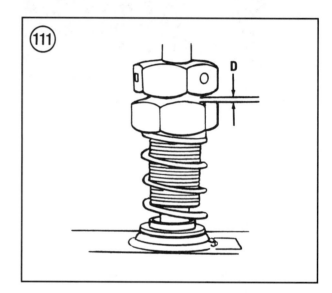

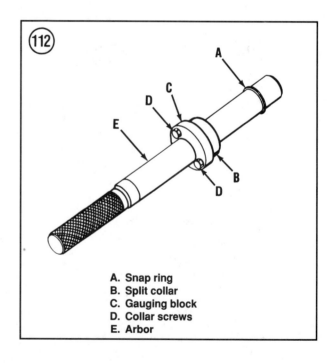

A. Snap ring
B. Split collar
C. Gauging block
D. Collar screws
E. Arbor

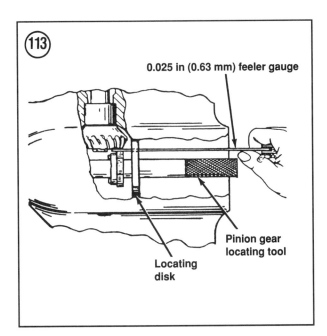

0.025 in (0.63 mm) feeler gauge

Pinion gear
locating tool

Locating
disk

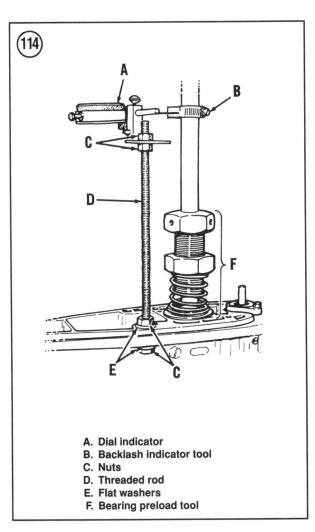

A. Dial indicator
B. Backlash indicator tool
C. Nuts
D. Threaded rod
E. Flat washers
F. Bearing preload tool

Figure 113. The clearance between the gear and gauging block should be 0.025 in. (0.64 mm).

7. If the clearance (Step 6) is not 0.025 in. (0.64 mm), proceed as follows:

   a. 75-115 hp—Add shim(s) behind the drive shaft lower bearing race to decrease pinion gear clearance or subtract shim(s) to increase clearance.

   b. All others—Add shim(s) under the drive shaft upper bearing race to increase pinion gear clearance or subtract shim(s) to decrease clearance.

8. If the clearance (Step 6) is correct, leave the drive shaft bearing preload tool installed and continue at *Forward Gear Backlash*.

Forward gear backlash

1. Establish the correct pinion gear depth as described in this chapter.

2. Make sure drive shaft bearing preload tool is correctly installed as described in this chapter.

3. Install the propeller shaft (without shift cam on E-Z Shift models) and fully assembled bearing carrier into the gear housing. Install bearing carrier puller jaws (part No. 91-46086A1) and puller bolt (part No. 91-85716) as shown in **Figure 108**. Tighten the puller bolt to 80 in.-lb. (9.0 N.m) on 250-275 hp models and 45 in.-lb. (5.1 N.m) on all other models. Rotate the propeller shaft 10-12 revolutions to seat the bearings. Retighten the puller bolt to the previously specified torque.

4. On 135-200 hp models, screw stud adapter (part No. 91-14311A1) onto 1 rear water pump stud, then install a dial indicator to the stud adapter. On all other models, fasten a suitable threaded rod (**Figure 114**) to the gear housing using flat washers and nuts. Install a dial indicator to the threaded rod (**Figure 114**).

5A. 50-60 hp—Install backlash indicator tool part No. 91-19660-1 onto the drive shaft and tighten securely. Adjust the dial indicator as nec-

9

essary to align its plunger with line No. 1 on the backlash indicator tool.

5B. 75-90 hp—Install backlash indicator tool part No. 91-78473 onto the drive shaft and tighten securely. Adjust the dial indicator as necessary to align its plunger with line No. 4 on the backlash indicator tool.

5C. 100-115 hp—Install backlash indicator tool part No. 91-19660 onto the drive shaft and tighten securely. Adjust the dial indicator as necessary to align its plunger with line No. 1 on the backlash indicator tool.

NOTE
On 135-200 hp models (except 150XR4 and XR6), count the teeth on the pinion gear to determine lower unit gear ratio. If the pinion gear has 15 teeth, the gear ratio is 1.87:1. If the gear has 14 teeth, the gear ratio is 2:1.

5D. 135-200 hp (except 150XR4 and XR6)—Install backlash indicator tool part No. 91-78473 onto the drive shaft and tighten securely. Adjust the dial indicator as necessary to align its plunger with the line No. 1 (1.87:1 gear ratio) or line No. 2 (2:1 gear ratio).

5E. 150XR4 and XR6—Install backlash indicator tool part No. 91-19660 onto the drive shaft and tighten securely. Adjust the dial indicator as necessary to align its plunger with line No. 2 on the backlash indicator tool.

5F. 250-275 hp—Install backlash indicator tool part No. 91-53459 onto the drive shaft and tighten securely. Adjust the dial indicator as necessary to align its plunger with line No. 1 on the backlash indicator tool.

6. Zero the dial indicator needle. Lightly turn the drive shaft back and forth (propeller shaft should not move) while noting the dial indicator. The amount of travel in the drive shaft without moving the propeller shaft is forward gear backlash. The forward gear backlash should be as follows:

   a. 50-60 hp—0.013-0.019 in. (0.33-0.48 mm).

   b. 75-90 hp—0.012-0.019 in. (0.30-0.48 mm).

   c. 100-115 hp—0.015-0.022 in. (0.38-0.56 mm).

NOTE
On 135-200 hp models (except 150XR4 and XR6), count the teeth on the pinion gear to determine lower unit gear ratio. If the pinion gear has 15 teeth, the gear ratio is 1.87:1. If the gear has 14 teeth, the gear ratio is 2:1.

   d. 135-200 hp (except 150XR4 and XR6)—0.018-0.027 in. (0.46-0.69 mm) on models with 1.87:1 gear ratio; 0.015-0.022 in. (0.38-0.56 mm) on models with 2:1 gear ratio.

   e. 150XR4 and XR6—0.016-0.019 in. (0.41-0.48 mm).

   f. 250-275 hp—0.019-0.027 in. (0.48-0.69 mm).

7. All models—If forward gear backlash is not as specified, remove the forward gear bearing race as described in this chapter. Subtract shim(s) behind the race to increase backlash or add shim(s) behind the race to decrease backlash.

8. After establishing the correct pinion gear depth and forward gear backlash, remove the bearing carrier and propeller shaft. Apply Loctite 271 to the threads of a *new* pinion gear nut and install as described in this chapter. On V6 models, leave the drive shaft bearing preload tool, dial indicator and backlash indicator tool installed and continue at *Reverse Gear Backlash*.

On all other models, remove the special tools and complete gear housing reassembly as described in this chapter.

Reverse gear backlash (V6 models)

Reverse gear backlash is not adjustable, however it may be checked as follows to ensure the gear housing is properly assembled.

1. Install the fully assembled propeller shaft and bearing carrier into the gear housing.

2. Install the shift shaft into the gear housing. Shift the gear housing into REVERSE gear.

3. Install a piece of PVC pipe 6 in. (152.4 mm) long and 1-1/2 in. (38.1 mm) in diameter over the propeller shaft and against the bearing carrier. Tighten the pipe against the bearing carrier using the propeller nut and tap washer. Do not overtighten.

4. Gently turn the drive shaft back and forth (propeller shaft should not move) while noting the dial indicator. The amount of drive shaft travel indicates reverse gear backlash, which should be within 0.030-0.050 in. (0.76-1.27 mm).

5. If the backlash is not within specification, the gear housing is incorrectly assembled, or contains excessively worn components. Disassemble the gear housing, determine and repair the problem before returning the gear housing to service.

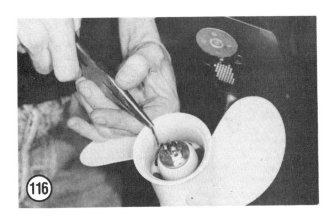

PROPELLER

Removal/Installation

> *WARNING*
> *To prevent accidental engine starting during propeller service, disconnect all spark plug leads from the plugs and shift into forward gear. Remove the key from the ignition switch on models so equipped.*

3 and 3.3 hp

1. Remove and discard the cotter pin securing the propeller to the propeller shaft. Slide the propeller off the shaft.

2. Remove the shear pin (**Figure 115**) from the propeller shaft.

3. Coat the propeller shaft with Quicksilver Special Lubricant 101, 2-4-C Marine Lubricant or Perfect Seal, to ease future propeller removal.

4. Install the shear pin into the shaft, install the propeller, then install a new propeller cotter pin. Bend the cotter pin ends over to secure the pin.

4-25 hp

1. 4 and 5 hp—Remove and discard the cotter pin from the propeller nut (**Figure 116**).

2. Place a block of wood between the propeller blades and antiventilation plate to prevent the propeller from turning. See **Figure 117**.

3. Remove the propeller nut and washer. Remove the reverse thrust hub, if so equipped. Remove the propeller.

4. Remove the forward thrust hub (**Figure 118**).

5. Installation is the reverse of removal. Coat the propeller shaft splines with Quicksilver Special Lubricant 101, 2-4-C Marine Lubricant or Perfect Seal. Tighten the propeller nut to specification (**Table 1**) and install a new cotter pin to secure the nut.

40-275 hp

Refer to **Figure 119** for this procedure.

1. Using a suitable punch and hammer, bend the tabs of the locking tab washer back away from the propeller nut.

2. Place a block of wood between the propeller blades and antiventilation plate to prevent the propeller from turning.

3. On V6 models, remove the nut, locking tab washer, splined washer and continuity washer. On all other models, remove the nut and locking tab washer.

4. Remove the propeller and forward thrust hub.

5. Check the propeller shaft splines for wear and corrosion. Replace the propeller shaft if excessively worn. Clean corrosion from the propeller.

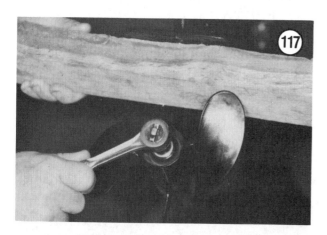

6. Coat the propeller shaft splines with Quicksilver Special Lubricant 101, 2-4-C Marine Lubricant or Perfect Seal.

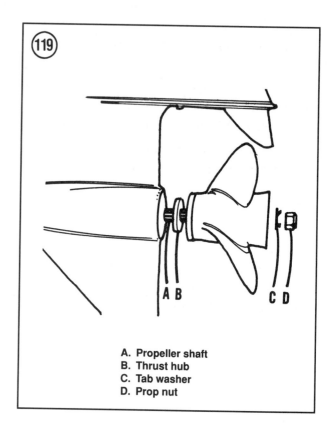

A. Propeller shaft
B. Thrust hub
C. Tab washer
D. Prop nut

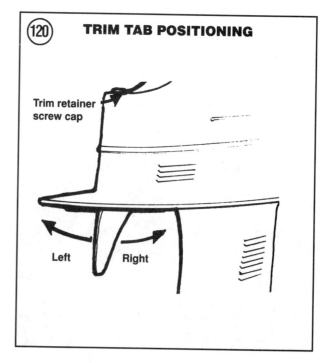

TRIM TAB POSITIONING

Trim retainer screw cap

Left   Right

7. Install the thrust hub, propeller, continuity washer and splined washer (if so equipped), locking tab washer and propeller nut.

8. Place the block of wood between the propeller blades and antiventilation plate. Tighten the propeller nut to specification (**Table 2** or **Table 3**).

9. Bend one tab on the locking tab washer over against the propeller nut to lock the nut in place.

TRIM TAB ADJUSTMENT

The trim tab should be positioned so the steering wheel will turn with equal ease in each direction at cruising speed. If the boat turns more easily to the right than the left, loosen the trim tab retaining screw and move the tab trailing edge to the right. If the boat turns more easily to the left, move the tab to the left. See **Figure 120**.

Table 1 TIGHTENING TORQUES (3-25 HP MODELS)

Fastener	in.-lb.	ft.-lb.	N·m
Bearing carrier screws			
3.3 hp	50		5.6
4 and 5 hp	70		7.9
Bearing carrier			
8-15 hp		60	81.3
20 and 25 hp		80	108.5
Gear housing-to-drive			
shaft housing screws			
3 and 3.3 hp	25		2.8
4 and 5 hp	70		7.9
8-15 hp	180		20.3
20 and 25 hp		25	33.9
Pinion gear screw			
20 and 25 hp	100		11.3
Propeller nut			
4 and 5 hp	150		16.9
8-15 hp	70		7.9
20 and 25 hp	120		13.6
Water pump base screws			
4 and 5 hp	70		7.9
8-15 hp	40		4.5
20 and 25 hp	25		2.8
Water pump cover			
3 hp	25		2.8
3.3, 4 and 5 hp	70		7.9
8-15 hp	40		4.5
20 and 25	25		2.8
Standard screws			
4 mm	10		1.1
5 mm	25		2.8
6 mm	50		5.6
8 mm	120		13.6
1/4-20	20		2.2
1/4-28	30		3.4
5/16-24	40		4.5

9

Table 2 TIGHTENING TORQUES (40-115 HP MODELS)

Fastener	in.-lb.	ft.-lb.	N·m
Bearing carrier screws[1]			
50-60 hp (serial No. D000750-on) & 75-115 hp	150		16.9
Bearing carrier cover nut			
40 hp & 50-60 (prior to serial No. D000750)		100	135.6
Drive shaft upper bearing retainer			
50-60 hp (serial No. D000750-on)		75	101.7
Gear housing-to-drive shaft housing nuts/screws			
40 hp & 50-60 (prior to serial No. D000750) hp		60	81.3
50-60 hp (serial No. D000750-on) & 75-115 hp		40	54.2
Pinion nut			
40-60 hp		50	67.8
75-115 hp		70	94.9
Propeller nut		55	74.6
Shift shaft bushing			
40 hp & 50-60 hp (prior to serial No. D000750)		50	67.8
Shift shaft bushing screws			
75-115 hp	60		6.8
Trim tab screw		22	29.8
Water pump base screws			
75-115 hp	60		6.8
Water pump cover nuts			
40 hp & 50-60 (prior to serial No. D000750)	30		3.4
Water pump cover screws			
50-60 hp (serial No. D000750-on) & 75-115 hp	60		6.8

1. If bearing carrier is secured with nuts on 75-115 hp models, tighten nuts to 275 in.-lb. (31.1 N·m).

Table 3 TIGHTENING TORQUES (V6 MODELS)

Fasteners	in.-lb.	ft.-lb.	N·m
Bearing carrier cover nut		210	284.7
Drive shaft upper bearing retainer		100	135.6
Gear housing-to-drive shaft housing nuts/bolts			
135-200 hp			
3/8-16 nuts		55	74.6
7/16-20 bolts		65	88.1
250-275 hp		40	54.2

(continued)

Table 3 TIGHTENING TORQUES (V6 MODELS) (continued)

Fasteners	in.-lb.	ft.-lb.	N·m
Pinion nut			
135-200 hp (except 150XR4 and XR6)		75	101.7
150 XR4, XR6		80	108.5
250-275 hp		70	94.9
Propeller nut		55	74.6
Shift shaft bushing		50	67.8
Trim tab screw			
135-200 hp		25	33.9
250-275		15	20.3
Water pump nuts			
135-200 hp	50		5.6
Water pump screws			
250-275 hp	30		3.4
135-200 hp	35		3.9

Table 4 GEAR HOUSING LUBRICANT CAPACITY

Model	Capacity
3 hp	3 oz. (88.7 mL)
3.3 hp	2.5 oz. (74 mL)
4-5 hp	6.6 oz. (195 mL)
8-15 hp	6.5 oz. (192 mL)
20-25 hp	7.6 oz. (225 mL)
40 hp	12.5 oz. (370 mL)
50-60 hp (prior to serial No. D000750)	12.5 oz. (370 mL)
50-60 hp (serial No. D000750-on)	11.5 oz. (340 mL)
75-115 hp	22.5 oz. (665 mL)
135-200 hp (except 150 XR4 & XR6)	24.25 oz. (717 mL)
150 XR4 & XR6	21 oz. (621 mL)
250-275 hp	29 oz. (857 mL)

Table 5 RECOMMENDED LUBRICANTS, ADHESIVES AND SEALANT

Material	Part No.
Quicksilver Needle Bearing Assembly Grease	92-42649A1
Quicksilver 2-4-C Marine Lubricant	92-90018A12
Quicksilver Special Lubricant 101	92-13872A1
Quicksilver Perfect Seal	92-34277-1
Loctite 271 (grade A)	92-32609-1
Loctite Primer T	92-59327-1
RTV Sealant	92-91601-1

9

Chapter Ten

Power Trim and Tilt System

The usual method of raising and lowering the outboard motor is a mechanical one, consisting of a series of holes in the transom mounting bracket. To trim the engine, an adjustment stud is removed from the bracket, the outboard is repositioned and the stud reinserted in the proper holes to hold the unit in place. With power trim, low-effort control of the outboard position is provided whether the boat is underway or at rest.

Five different trim systems are used on outboard motors covered in this manual:

 a. Manual tilt assist system.
 b. One-ram integral system.
 c. Three-ram integral, design I (side fill) system.
 d. Three-ram integral, design II (aft fill) system.
 e. One-ram Oildyne system.

The manual tilt assist and 1-ram integral systems are used on 40-60 hp models), the 3-ram integral (designs I and II) systems are used on 75-200 hp models and the 1-ram Oildyne system is used on 250 and 275 hp models.

This chapter includes maintenance, trim cylinder replacement and troubleshooting procedures for the manual tilt assist, 1-ram integral, 3-ram integral and the 1-ram Oildyne trim systems.

MANUAL TILT ASSIST SYSTEM

The manual tilt consists of a tilt/shock cylinder, valve body, control rod, manual release lever and a nitrogen-filled accumulator. See **Figure 1**. When the manual release lever is opened, the pressurized, nitrogen-filled accumulator eases the effort required to tilt the outboard manually for shallow water operation or trailering the boat. The system is contained between the outboard transom brackets (**Figure 1**).

If the outboard will not hold in the tilted position, lowers during acceleration or trails out during reverse operation or during high speed deceleration, check for external fluid leakage and repair as necessary. Make sure the manual release lever and control rod open and close freely. Adjust the control rod as necessary.

To check for a discharged accumulator, place the manual release lever in the open position. Affix a suitable spring weight scale to the outboard as shown in **Figure 2**, then raise the outboard with the scale. If it requires more than 50 lb.-ft. (68 N•m) of force to raise the outboard from the fully down position to fully up, the accumulator is probably discharged

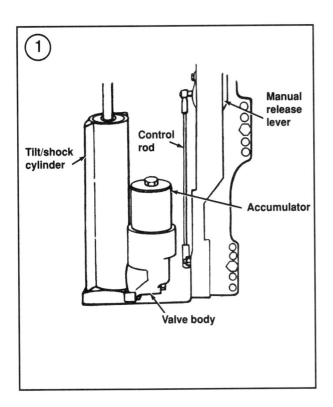

①

Tilt/shock cylinder

Control rod

Manual release lever

Accumulator

Valve body

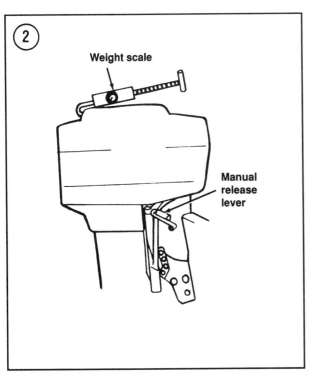

②

Weight scale

Manual release lever

Manual Tilt System Removal/Installation

1. Remove the engine cowling. Disconnect the spark plug leads from the spark plugs.

> *WARNING*
> *Be certain the tilt lock lever is properly engaged during all tilt system service. If a sudden loss of pressure in the shock cylinder should occur, the outboard will fall to the fully down position resulting in personal injury if the tilt lock lever is not engaged.*

2. Raise the outboard to the fully up position and engage the tilt lock lever.

3. Disconnect the release valve control rod (**Figure 1**).

4. Using a suitable chisel or similar tool, drive the dowel pin securing the upper pivot shaft downward. Remove and save the dowel pin. See **Figure 3**. Drive the upper pivot shaft from the bracket using a punch and hammer.

5. Using a suitable punch, drive the dowel pin securing the lower pivot shaft upward. Remove and save the dowel pin. See **Figure 4**. Drive the

10

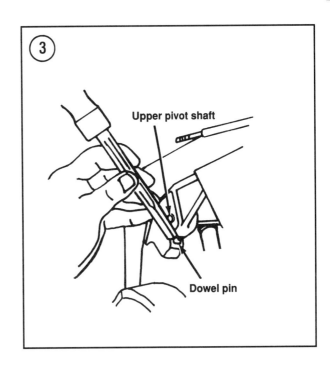

③

Upper pivot shaft

Dowel pin

lower pivot shaft from the bracket using a punch and hammer.

6. Tilt the top of the tilt assembly out away from the transom bracket and remove the unit.

NOTE
The tilt system is under high pressure. Tilt system service other than removal and installation should be referred to a dealer or qualified marine service facility.

7. Apply Quicksilver 2-4-C Marine Lubricant to the upper and lower pivot shafts and shaft bores.

8. Install the tilt unit, inserting the bottom into the bracket first. Install the lower pivot shaft flush with the outer surfaces and secure with the dowel. Drive the dowel in until fully seated.

9. Install the upper pivot shaft into the swivel bracket and through the shock rod. The shaft should be flush with the swivel bracket outer surfaces. Drive the dowel into its hole until fully seated.

10. Connect the manual release valve. The cam should open and close freely. If not, adjust the rod as necessary.

ONE-RAM INTEGRAL POWER TRIM SYSTEM (40-60 HP MODELS)

Components

The power trim system consists of an electric motor, pressurized fluid reservoir (not externally vented), pump assembly, 1 trim cylinder and the necessary wiring, switches and hydraulic lines. The switches that operate the system are located within the remote control or control panel.

Operation

Depressing the UP trim switch energizes the UP solenoid under the engine cowl, closing the circuit to the pump motor. The motor drives the hydraulic pump, forcing the fluid into the up side of the trim cylinder. The trim cylinder positions the outboard motor at the desired angle (trim out) within the maximum 20° trim out range. The outboard can be trimmed beyond the 20° maximum providing the engine speed is below 2000 rpm. When engine speed exceeds 2000 rpm, the forward thrust from the propeller limits maximum trim out to 20° or less.

Depressing the DOWN trim switch energizes the DOWN solenoid and closes the circuit to the pump motor. The motor runs in the opposite direction, driving the fluid into the down side of the trim cylinder, which moves the outboard downward (trim in) to the desired angle.

To trailer the boat, depress and hold the UP trim switch. The trim cylinder will extend fully, raising the outboard to the fully up position.

Manual Trim

WARNING
The outboard will drop to the fully down position when the manual release valve is loosened. Be certain all persons are clear of the outboard before loosening the valve.

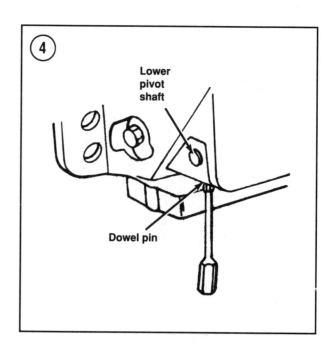

The trim system allows the outboard motor to be manually tilted up or down by opening the manual release valve. Insert a suitable screwdriver through the port side transom bracket

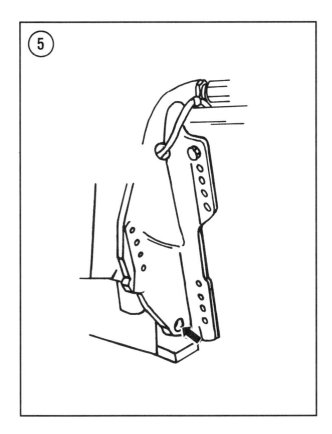

(**Figure 5**) and turn the manual release valve 3-4 turns counterclockwise, then lift or lower the outboard as required. Close the manual release valve to continue normal operation.

Hydraulic Pump

Fluid check

1. Tilt the outboard motor to the fully UP position and engage the tilt lock lever.

> *NOTE*
> *The hydraulic system is under pressure. Do not remove the reservoir fill plug unless the outboard is tilted to the fully UP position.*

2. Clean the area around the fill plug (**Figure 6**). Slowly remove the screw and visually check the fluid level in the fill plug hole. The fluid should be even with the bottom threads in the fill plug hole.

3. If low, add Quicksilver Power Trim & Steering Fluid, Type F, Type FA or Dexron II automatic transmission fluid as necessary.

4. Reinstall the fill plug securely.

10

Bleeding hydraulic system

The hydraulic system should be bled whenever air enters it. Air in the power trim system will compress, rather than transmit pressure to the trim cylinders. To determine if bleeding is necessary, trim the outboard up until the trim cylinder is slightly extended. Apply downward pressure on the outboard gear housing. If the trim rod retracts into the cylinder more than 1/8 in. (0.7 mm), air is present in the system and should be purged out. Bleeding is also necessary whenever a hydraulic line is disconnected. The trim system is essentially self bleeding and will purge air from the system during operation.

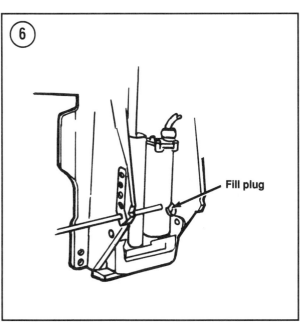

Fill plug

NOTE
The hydraulic system is under pressure. Do not remove the reservoir fill plug unless the outboard is tilted to the fully UP position.

1. Check the fluid level and add fluid as necessary as described in this chapter.

2. Reinstall the fill plug securely.

3. Disengage the tilt lock lever and trim the outboard through its entire range.

4. Repeat Steps 1-3 as necessary to purge air from the system.

Troubleshooting

Should a problem develop in the power trim system, the initial step is to determine if the malfunction is in the electrical or hydraulic system. Electrical tests are given in this chapter. If the problem appears to be in the hydraulic system and cannot be corrected by bleeding the system, refer it to a dealer or qualified specialist for the necessary service. Make sure the manual release valve is closed.

Before attempting to troubleshoot any electrical circuit:

1. Make sure the connectors are properly engaged and that all terminals and wires are free of corrosion. Clean and tighten all connections as required.

2. Make sure the battery is fully charged. Charge or replace the battery as required.

All Circuits Inoperative

Refer to **Figure 7** (40 hp), **Figure 8** (50-60 [prior to serial No. D000750] hp), **Figure 9** (50-60 [serial No. D000750-on] hp) and **Figure 10** (side mount remote control) for this procedure.

1. Remove the engine cover and check the condition of 20 amp fuse(s). Replace the fuse(s) if blown.

2. If the fuse(s) is good, connect a suitable voltmeter between a good engine ground and the battery side of the starter solenoid (test point 3). Battery voltage should be indicated. If not, check for loose or corroded battery cable connections or an open circuit in the battery cables.

3. If normal battery voltage is noted in Step 2, connect the voltmeter between engine ground and test point 8. Depress the UP trim button while noting the voltmeter.

4. If normal battery voltage is noted in Step 3, check the black ground leads for loose or corroded connections. Repair as necessary.

5. If ground connections are in acceptable condition (Step 4), the power trim motor is defective and should be repaired or replaced.

6. If no voltage is noted in Step 3, connect the voltmeter between engine ground and test point 5.

7. If normal battery voltage is noted in Step 6, the trim switch is defective or an open circuit is present between the trim buttons and pump assembly.

   a. Check the trim switch.

   b. Check all power trim harness connectors for loose or corroded connections.

   c. Inspect harness for broken wires.

8. If no voltage is noted in Step 6, proceed as follows, place the ignition switch in the ON position (engine not running). Connect the voltmeter between ground and any instrument and note the voltmeter.

   a. If normal battery voltage is noted in Step 8, an open circuit is present between test point 5 and the red wire terminal at back of the ignition switch. Repair or replace the circuit as necessary.

   b. If no voltage is noted (Step 8), an open circuit is present between the ignition switch red wire terminal and test point 3. Check for loose or corroded connections, or broken wire. Repair or replace the wire as necessary.

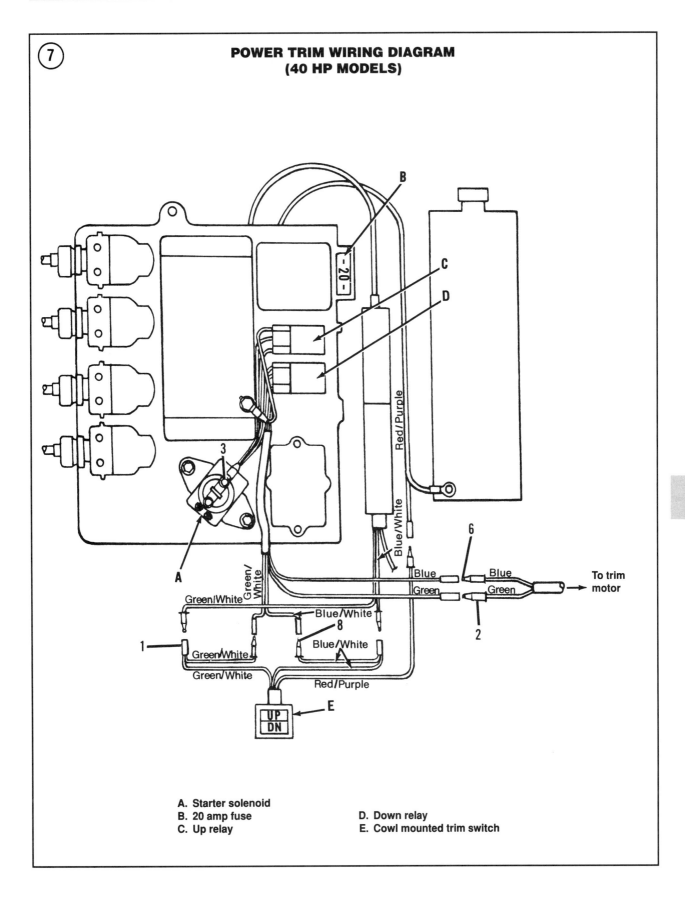

⑦ **POWER TRIM WIRING DIAGRAM**
(40 HP MODELS)

A. Starter solenoid
B. 20 amp fuse
C. Up relay

D. Down relay
E. Cowl mounted trim switch

10

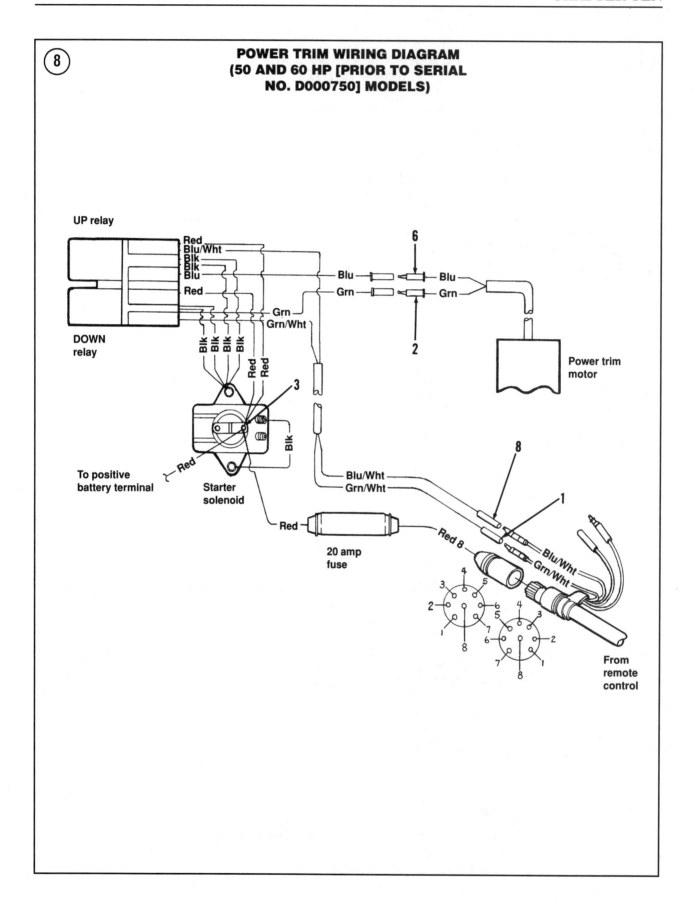

**POWER TRIM WIRING DIAGRAM
(50 AND 60 HP [PRIOR TO SERIAL
NO. D000750] MODELS)**

UP relay

Red
Blu/Wht
Blk
Blk
Blu
Red

DOWN
relay

Blk Blk Blk Blk

Grn
Grn/Wht

Blu
Grn

Blu
Grn

6

2

Power trim
motor

Red Red

3

Blk

To positive
battery terminal

Red

Starter
solenoid

Red

20 amp
fuse

Blu/Wht
Grn/Wht

8

1

Red 8

Blu/Wht
Grn/Wht

From
remote
control

DOWN Circuit Inoperative— UP Circuit Good

Refer to **Figure 7** (40 hp), **Figure 8** (50-60 [prior to serial No. D000750] hp), **Figure 9** (50-60 [serial No. D000750-on] hp) and **Figure 10** (side mount remote control) for this procedure.

1. Connect the voltmeter between engine ground and test point 1. Depress the DOWN trim button and note the voltage.

2. If no voltage is noted in Step 1, connect the voltmeter between ground and test point 4. Depress the DOWN trim button and note voltmeter.

   a. If normal voltage is noted in Step 2, an open circuit is present between test points 1 and 4. Repair or replace the circuit as required.

   b. If no voltage is noted in Step 2, connect the voltmeter between ground and test point 5. If normal battery voltage is noted, the trim switch is defective and should be replaced. If no voltage is noted, check for loose or

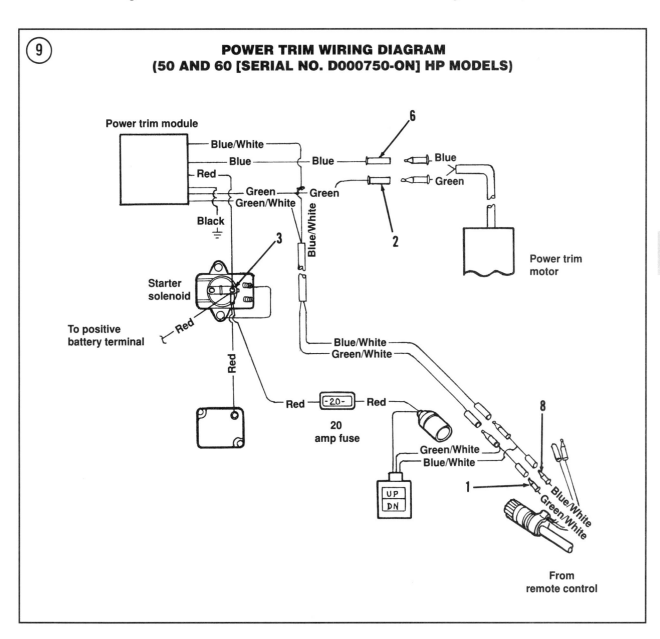

POWER TRIM WIRING DIAGRAM (50 AND 60 [SERIAL NO. D000750-ON] HP MODELS)

10

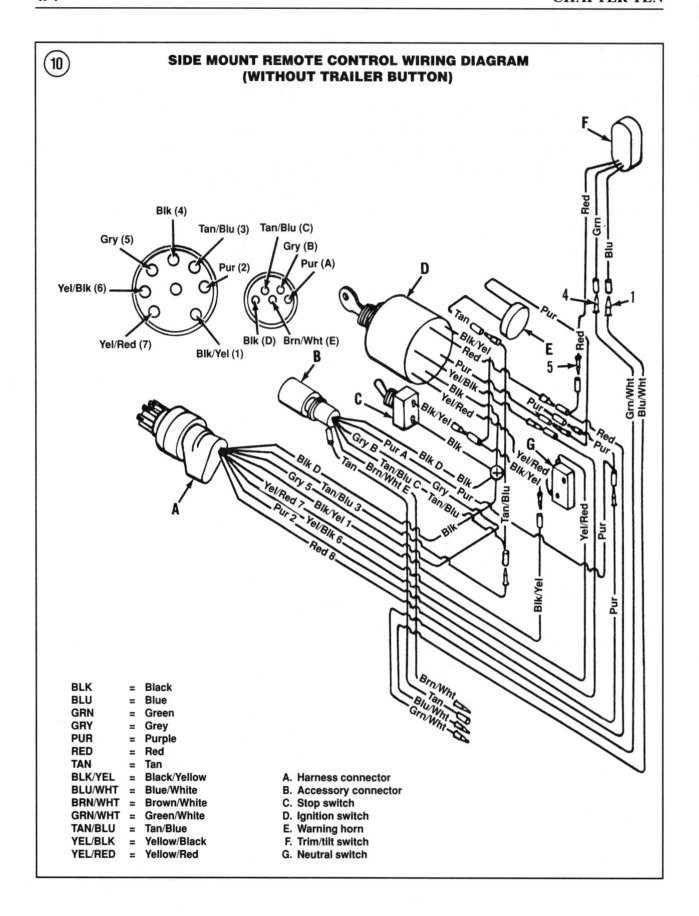

10

SIDE MOUNT REMOTE CONTROL WIRING DIAGRAM
(WITHOUT TRAILER BUTTON)

Blk (4)
Tan/Blu (3)
Tan/Blu (C)
Gry (5)
Gry (B)
Pur (2)
Pur (A)
Yel/Blk (6)
Yel/Red (7)
Blk (D)
Brn/Wht (E)
Blk/Yel (1)

D

F

Red
Grn
Blu

4
1
Pur
Red
5

Tan
Blk/Yel
Red
Pur
Yel/Blk
Blk
Yel/Red
E

Grn/Wht
Blu/Wht
Red
Pur

B

C

Blk/Yel

Gry B — Pur A — Blk D — Blk
Tan — Tan/Blu C — Gry — Pur
Tan — Brn/Wht E — Tan/Blu

G
Yel/Red
Blk/Yel

Pur

Blk D
Gry 5 — Tan/Blu 3
Yel/Red 7 — Blk/Yel 1
Pur 2 — Yel/Blk 6
Red 8

Blk

Tan/Blu

A

Blk/Yel

Yel/Red

Pur

Brn/Wht
Tan
Blu/Wht
Grn/Wht

BLK	= Black
BLU	= Blue
GRN	= Green
GRY	= Grey
PUR	= Purple
RED	= Red
TAN	= Tan
BLK/YEL	= Black/Yellow
BLU/WHT	= Blue/White
BRN/WHT	= Brown/White
GRN/WHT	= Green/White
TAN/BLU	= Tan/Blue
YEL/BLK	= Yellow/Black
YEL/RED	= Yellow/Red

A. Harness connector
B. Accessory connector
C. Stop switch
D. Ignition switch
E. Warning horn
F. Trim/tilt switch
G. Neutral switch

corroded connections at test point 5 or an open circuit in the wire leading to test point 5.

3. If normal battery voltage is noted in Step 1, connect the voltmeter between ground and test point 3. If no voltage is noted, an open circuit is present between the positive battery terminal and test point 3.

4. If normal battery voltage is noted in Step 3, connect the voltmeter between engine ground and test point 2. Depress the DOWN trim button and note voltmeter.

   a. If no voltage is noted in Step 4, the DOWN solenoid is defective.

   b. If voltage is noted, the trim pump or the trim pump wiring is defective. Repair or replace as required.

UP Circuit Inoperative— Down Circuit Good

Refer to **Figure 7** (40 hp), **Figure 8** (50-60 [prior to serial No. D000750] hp) and **Figure 9** (50-60 [serial No. D000750-on] hp) and **Figure 10** (side mount remote control) for this procedure.

1. Connect the voltmeter between engine ground and test point 8. Depress the UP trim button and note the voltmeter.

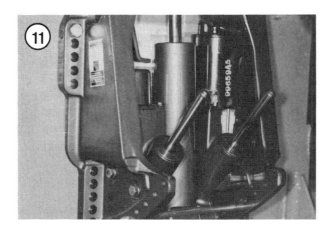

2. If no voltage is noted in Step 1, connect the voltmeter between ground and test point 7. Depress the UP trim button and note the voltmeter.

   a. If battery voltage is noted (Step 2), an open circuit is present between test points 7 and 8. Repair or replace the circuit as necessary.

   b. If no voltage is noted (Step 2), connect the voltmeter between ground and test point 5. If battery voltage is present at test point 5, the trim switch is defective. If no battery voltage is noted, check for a loose or corroded connection at test point 5 or an open circuit in the wire leading to test point 5.

3. If normal voltage is noted in Step 1, connect the voltmeter between ground and test point 3.

4. If no voltage is noted in Step 3, an open circuit is present between the positive battery terminal and test point 3.

5. If voltage is noted in Step 3, connect the voltmeter between ground and test point 6. Depress the UP trim buton and note the voltmeter.

   a. If no voltage is noted, the UP solenoid is defective and must be replaced.

   b. If voltage is noted the pump motor or pump motor wiring is defective and must be repaired or replaced as required.

10

THREE-RAM INTEGRAL POWER TRIM SYSTEM (75-200 HP MODELS)

Components

An integral power trim assembly mounted between the engine transom brackets (**Figure 11**) is used. V6 models may be equipped with a Design I unit (side fill) or a Design II unit (aft fill).

The integral power trim assembly consists of an electric motor, 2 trim cylinders, 1 tilt cylinder, and the related electrical circuits and hydraulic lines. The switches which operate the system are contained within the remote control or control panel. An anode plate is installed on the underside of the transom/power trim assembly and should be replaced when reduced to approximately 50 percent of its original size.

Operation

Depressing the UP trim switch energizes the UP solenoid under the engine cowl, closing the circuit to the pump motor. The motor drives the hydraulic pump, forcing the fluid into the up side of the trim cylinder. The trim cylinder positions the outboard motor at the desired angle (trim out) within the maximum 20° trim range. The outboard can be trimmed beyond the 20° maximum providing the engine speed is below 2000 rpm. When engine speed exceeds 2000 rpm, the forward thrust from the propeller limits maximum trim out to 20° or less.

Depressing the DOWN trim switch energizes the DOWN solenoid and closes the circuit to the pump motor. The motor runs in the opposite direction, driving the fluid into the down side of the trim cylinder, which moves the outboard downward (trim in) to the desired angle.

To trailer the boat, depress and hold the UP trim switch. The trim cylinder will extend fully, raising the outboard to the fully up position.

Manual Trim

> *WARNING*
> *If in the up position, the outboard motor will fall to the fully down position when the manual release valve is opened. Be certain that all persons are clear of the outboard when the valve is opened.*

The integral power trim system allows the outboard motor to be manually tilted up or down by opening the manual release valve (**Figure 12**) 3-4 turns counterclockwise, then lifting up or allowing the outboard to drop slowly as necessary. Close the manual release valve (clockwise) to resume normal operation.

Hydraulic Pump

Fluid check

1. Tilt the outboard motor to the fully UP position and engage the tilt lock lever.

> *WARNING*
> *The hydraulic system is under pressure. Never loosen or remove the fill plug unless the outboard motor is tilted to the fully up position with the tilt lock lever engaged.*

2. Clean the area around the fill plug. See **Figure 13** (side fill) or **Figure 14** (aft fill). Slowly remove the plug and visually check the fluid level. The fluid should be visible in the fill plug hole.

3. If fluid is not visible, add Quicksilver Power Trim and Steering Fluid, or Type F, Type FA or Dexron II automatic transmission fluid.

4. Reinstall and securely tighten the fill plug. Wipe off any spilled fluid.

5. Disengage the tilt lock lever and lower the outboard to its normal running position.

Bleeding hydraulic system

If air should enter the hydraulic system, it should be purged (bled) out. Air in the system will compress, rather than transmit pressure to the trim cylinders. To determine if bleeding is necessary, trim the outboard up until both trim rods are slightly extended. The tilt ram must not be extended. Apply downward pressure on the gear housing. If the trim rods retract into the cylinder more than 1/8 in. (3.2 mm), air is present in the system. Bleeding is also necessary whenever a hydraulic line is disconnected.

1. Tilt the outboard to its fully UP position and engage the tilt lock lever.

WARNING
The hydraulic system is under pressure. Never loosen or remove the fill plug unless the outboard motor is tilted to the fully up position with the tilt lock lever engaged.

2. Check the hydraulic fluid level as previously described. Add fluid as required.

3. Reinstall and securely tighten the fill plug. Disengage the tilt lock lever.

4. Operate the trim system through 3-4 fully up-to-fully down cycles. Check the fluid level after each up cycle and add as required.

5. Repeat the process until all air is purged from the system.

Troubleshooting

Should a problem develop in the power trim system, the initial step is to determine if the malfunction is in the electrical or hydraulic system. Electrical tests are given in this chapter. If the problem appears to be in the hydraulic system and cannot be corrected by bleeding the system, refer it to a dealer or qualified specialist for the necessary service. Make sure the manual release valve is closed.

Before attempting to troubleshoot any electrical circuit:

1. Make sure the connectors are properly engaged and that all terminals and wires are free of corrosion. Clean and tighten all connections as required.

2. Make sure the battery is fully charged. Charge or replace the battery as required.

All Circuits Inoperative (Remote Control With Trailer Button)

Refer to **Figures 15-19** as necessary for this procedure.

10

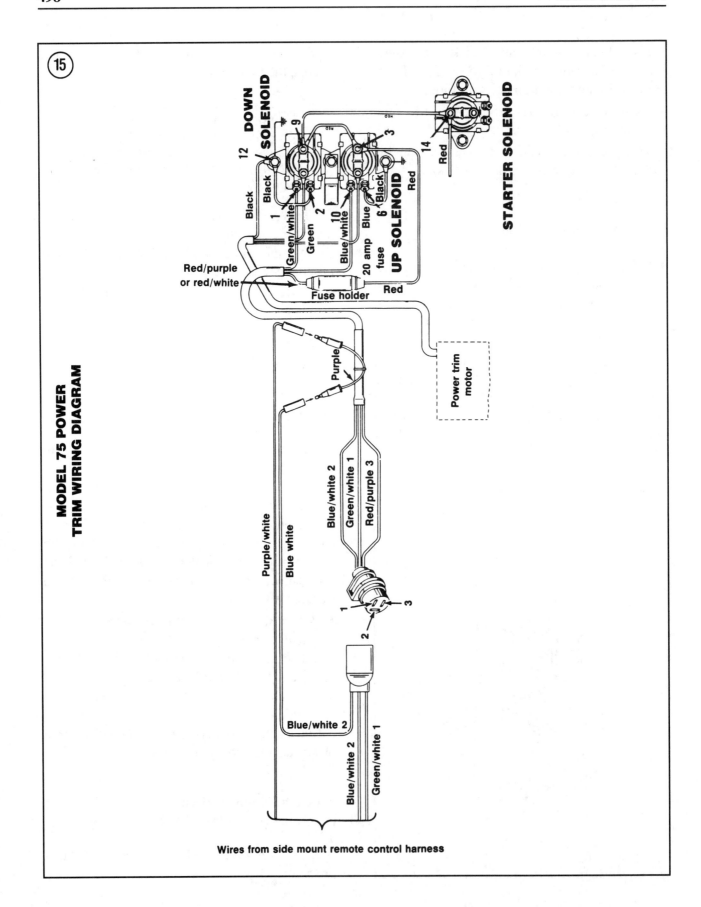

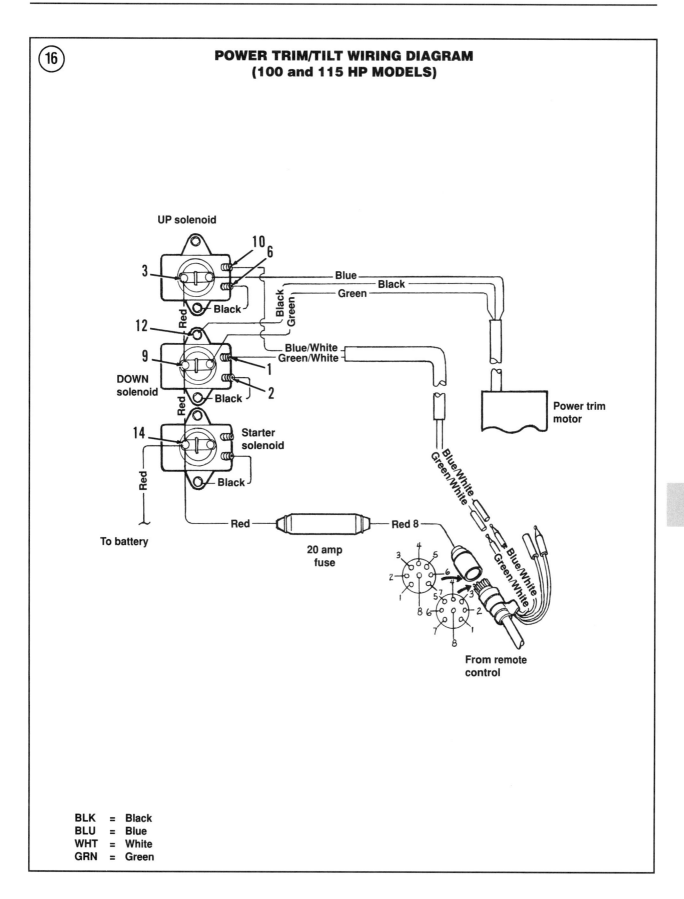

POWER TRIM/TILT WIRING DIAGRAM
(100 and 115 HP MODELS)

16

UP solenoid

10
6
3
Blue
Black
Green
Red
Black
Black
Green

12
Blue/White
9
Green/White
1
DOWN
solenoid
Red
Black
2

14
Starter
solenoid
Red
Black

To battery

Red

20 amp
fuse

Red 8

Power trim
motor

Blue/White
Green/White

Blue/White
Green/White

From remote
control

10

BLK = Black
BLU = Blue
WHT = White
GRN = Green

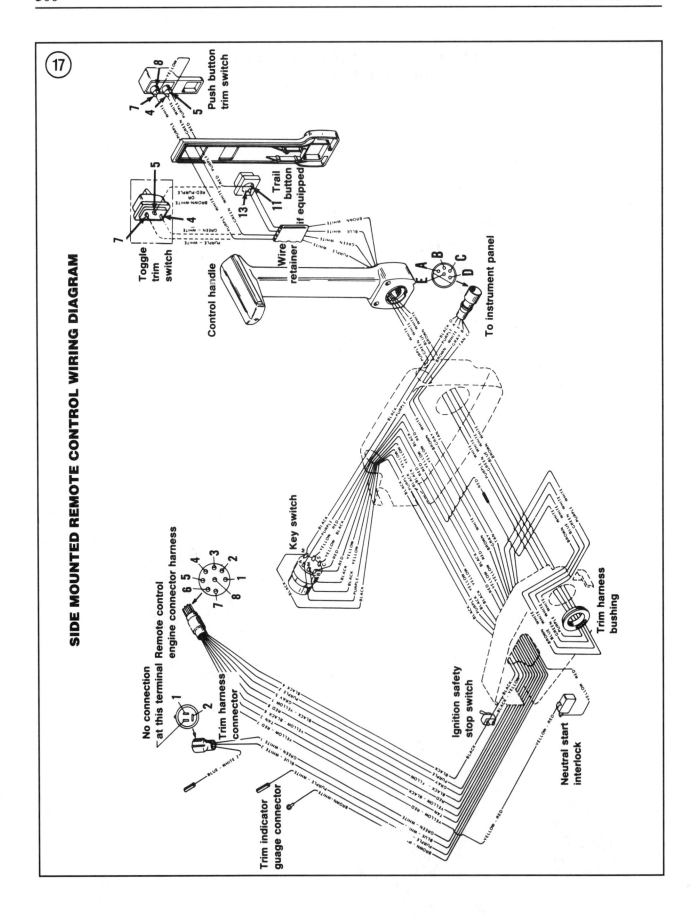

SIDE MOUNTED REMOTE CONTROL WIRING DIAGRAM

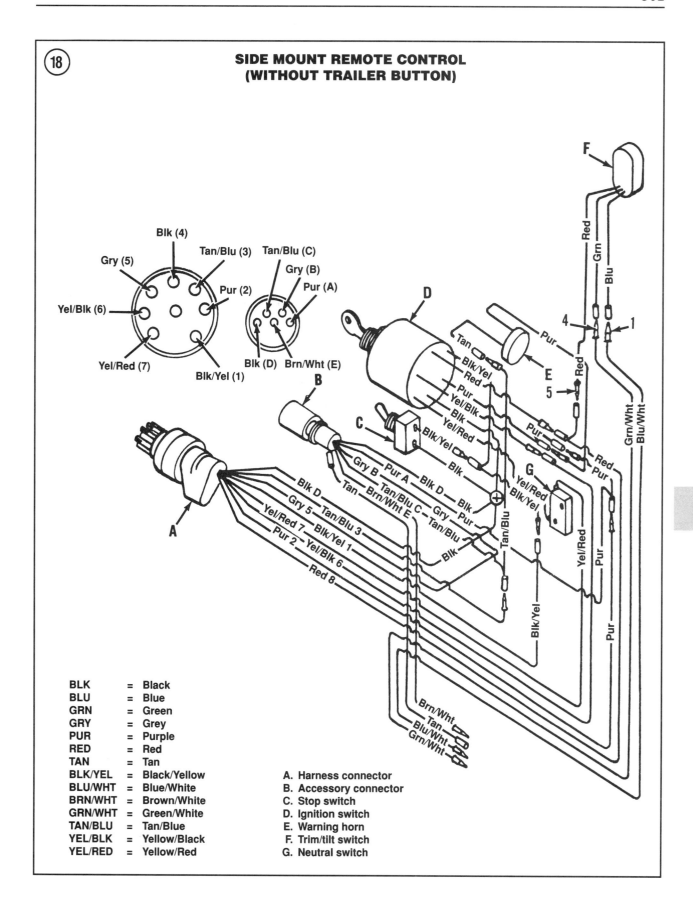

SIDE MOUNT REMOTE CONTROL (WITHOUT TRAILER BUTTON)

BLK	=	Black
BLU	=	Blue
GRN	=	Green
GRY	=	Grey
PUR	=	Purple
RED	=	Red
TAN	=	Tan
BLK/YEL	=	Black/Yellow
BLU/WHT	=	Blue/White
BRN/WHT	=	Brown/White
GRN/WHT	=	Green/White
TAN/BLU	=	Tan/Blue
YEL/BLK	=	Yellow/Black
YEL/RED	=	Yellow/Red

A. Harness connector
B. Accessory connector
C. Stop switch
D. Ignition switch
E. Warning horn
F. Trim/tilt switch
G. Neutral switch

10

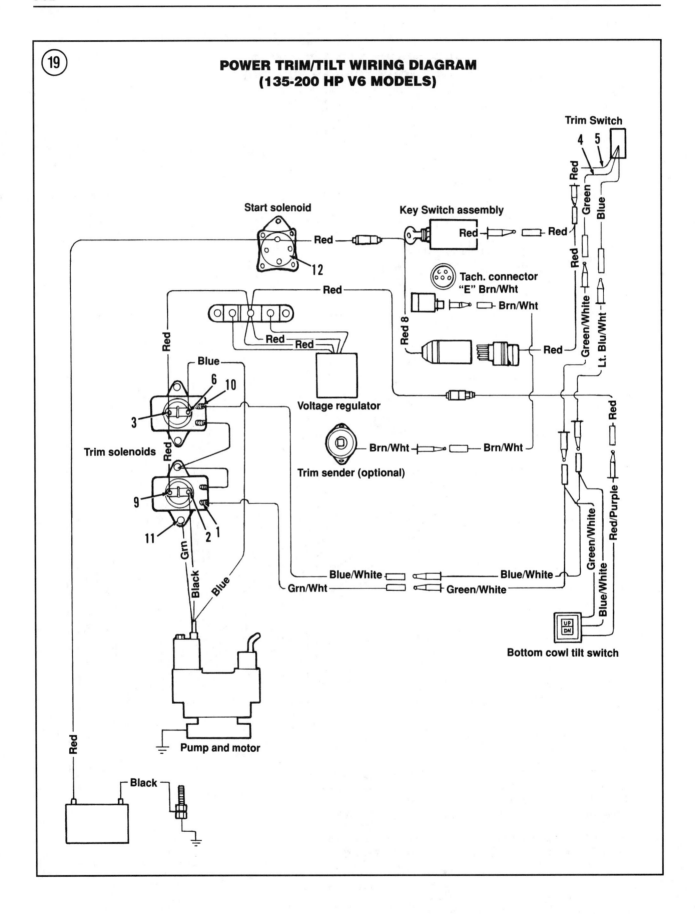

**POWER TRIM/TILT WIRING DIAGRAM
(135-200 HP V6 MODELS)**

Trim Switch

Start solenoid

Key Switch assembly

Tach. connector
"E" Brn/Wht

Voltage regulator

Trim solenoids

Trim sender (optional)

Bottom cowl tilt switch

Pump and motor

1. Remove the engine cover and check the condition of the power trim fuses. Replace the fuses if blown then determine and repair the cause of the blown fuses.

2. If the fuses are good, connect a voltmeter between engine ground and test point 3. If battery voltage is not shown, check for loose or corroded connections or an open circuit in the red and black wires to the battery or the red wires between the starter motor solenoid and test point 3.

3. If battery voltage is noted in Step 2, connect the voltmeter between test point 10 and engine ground. Depress the TRAILER or UP button and note the voltmeter reading.

4. If battery voltage is noted in Step 3, check the black ground wires for loose or corroded connections at the power trim solenoids. If the ground connections are good, check the trim motor black ground wire at test point 12 for a poor connection. If this ground is good, the pump motor is defective.

5. If battery voltage is not shown in Step 3, connect the voltmeter between test point 11 and engine ground. If battery voltage is indicated, an open circuit is present in the wires between the trim buttons and UP solenoid. Check for pinched/broken wires or for loose or corroded connections.

6. If no voltage is noted in Step 5, place the ignition switch in the ON position (engine not running). Connect the voltmeter between engine ground and any other instrument to check for voltage. If no voltage is indicated, check for a loose or corroded connection or an open circuit in the wire between test point 14 and terminal B on the back of the ignition switch.

7. If battery voltage is noted in Step 6, check for an open circuit in the wire between test point 11 and terminal B on the back of the ignition switch.

TRAILER Circuit Inoperative—UP Circuit Good (Remote Control With Trailer Button)

Refer to **Figures 15-19** as necessary for this procedure.

1. Disconnect the wire between the UP solenoid at test point 10 and trailer button at test point 13. Check the wire for continuity using an ohmmeter.

2. If no continuity is indicated, repair or replace the wire.

3. If continuity is noted in Step 1, disconnect all battery leads from the battery. Check for continuity between the trailer button terminals with the trailer button depressed. If no continuity is indicated, replace the trailer button.

UP And Trailer Circuit Inoperative— DOWN Circuit Good (Remote Control With Trailer Button)

Refer to **Figures 15-19** as necessary for this procedure.

1. Connect the voltmeter between engine ground and test point 10. Depress the TRAILER button while noting the voltmeter.

2. If no voltage is noted in Step 1, an open circuit is present in the wires between the UP solenoid and the trim buttons.

3. If battery voltage is noted in Step 1, connect the voltmeter between ground and test point 3.

4. If no voltage is noted in Step 3, check for loose or corroded connections at test points 3 and 9, or an open circuit in the red wire between test points 3 and 9.

5. If battery voltage is noted in Step 3, connect the voltmeter between ground and test point 6. Depress the TRAILER button and note the voltmeter.

6. If no voltage is noted in Step 5, the UP solenoid is defective and must be replaced.

7. If battery voltage is noted in Step 5, check for loose or corroded connections at the UP solenoid. Check the UP solenoid ground (black) wires for loose or corroded connections or open circuits. Repair connections and/or replace wires as necessary. If malfunction remains, replace the UP solenoid.

UP Circuit Inoperative—
TRAILER Circuit Good
(Remote Control With Trailer Button)

Refer to **Figure 15-19** as necessary for this procedure.

1. Check for continuity between test point 7 and test point 10 using an ohmmeter.

2. If no continuity is noted in Step 1, an open circuit is present in the wire between test points 7 and 10.

3. If continuity is noted in Step 1, connect a voltmeter between engine ground and test point 5 (toggle-type trim switch) or test point 8 (push-button trim switch).

4. If no voltage is noted in Step 3, an open circuit is present in the circuit between the TRAILER button and the trim switch.

5. If voltage is noted in Step 3, connect the voltmeter between test point 7 and engine ground. Depress the UP trim button and note the voltmeter.

6. If no voltage is noted in Step 5, the trim switch is defective.

7. If voltage is noted in Step 5, check for a loose or corroded connection at test point 7.

All Circuits Inoperative
(Remote Control Without Trailer Button)

Refer to **Figures 15-19** as necessary for this procedure.

1. Remove the engine cowl and check the condition of the 2 inline fuses. Replace the fuses if blown and determine and repair the cause of the blown fuses.

2. If the fuses are good, connect the voltmeter between engine ground and test point 3. Note the voltmeter reading.

3. If no voltage is noted in Step 2, check for loose or corroded battery cable connections, check red wires between the starter solenoid and test point 3 for poor connections or open circuits. Repair connections or wires as necessary.

4. If battery voltage is noted in Step 2, connect the voltmeter between engine ground and test point 10. Depress the UP trim switch and note the voltmeter reading.

5. If battery voltage is noted in Step 4, check the black ground wires at the trim solenoids for loose or corroded connections. If the ground connections are good, check the trim motor ground wire connection at test point 12 (75-115 hp) or test point 11 (V6). If the ground wire and connection are acceptable, the trim motor is defective and must be repaired or replaced.

6. If no voltage is noted in Step 4, connect the voltmeter between ground and test point 5 and note the voltage reading.

7. If battery voltage is noted in Step 6, the trim switch is defective or an open circuit is present in the wires between the trim switch and trim pump assembly. Check the trim harness connectors for loose or corroded connections. Check for pinched or broken wires. Replace the trim switch as necessary.

8. If no voltage is noted in Step 6, place the ignition switch in the ON position (engine not running). Connect the voltmeter between ground and any other instrument to check for voltage.

9. If battery voltage is indicated in Step 8, an open circuit is present in the wire between ignition switch red wire terminal and test point 5. Repair or replace the wire as necessary.

10. If no voltage is noted in Step 8, an open circuit is present in the red wire between the ignition switch red wire terminal and test point 14 (75-115 hp) or test point 12 (V6). Check for loose or corroded connections or a pinched or broken wire. Repair or replace the wire as necessary.

DOWN Circuit Inoperative—
UP Circuit Good (Remote Control
Without Trailer Button)

Refer to **Figures 15-19** as necessary for this procedure.

1. Connect a voltmeter between engine ground and test point 1. Depress the DOWN trim button and note voltmeter.

2. If no voltage is noted in Step 1, connect the voltmeter between ground and test point 4. Depress the DOWN trim button and note voltmeter.

   a. If battery voltage is noted, an open circuit is present in the wire between test points 1 and 4.

   b. If no voltage is noted, connect the voltmeter between ground and test point 5. If normal voltage is now noted, the trim switch is defective. If no voltage is present at test point 5, check for an open circuit in the wire supplying current to test point 5, or loose or corroded connection at test point 5.

3. If battery voltage is noted in Step 2, connect the voltmeter between ground and test point 9.

4. If no voltage is noted in Step 3, an open circuit is present between the positive battery terminal and test point 9. Check for loose or corroded connections or pinched or broken wire.

5. If battery voltage is noted in Step 3, connect the voltmeter between ground and test point 2. Depress the DOWN trim button and note voltmeter.

6. If no voltage is noted in Step 5, the DOWN solenoid is defective and should be replaced.

7. If battery voltage is noted in Step 5:

   a. Check the DOWN solenoid for loose or corroded connections.

   b. Check the solenoid ground wire (black) for loose or corroded connections.

   c. Replace the DOWN solenoid.

UP Circuit Inoperative—
DOWN Circuit Good (Remote Control Without Trailer Button)

Refer to **Figures 15-19** as necessary for this procedure.

1. Connect voltmeter between engine ground and test point 10. Depress the UP trim button and note voltmeter.

2. If no voltage is noted in Step 1, an open circuit is present in the wires between the UP solenoid and the trim switch.

   a. Check all trim system harness connectors for loose or corroded connections.

   b. Check for pinched or broken wires.

   c. Replace the trim switch.

3. If battery voltage is noted in Step 1, connect the voltmeter between ground and test point 3.

4. If no voltage is noted in Step 3, check for loose or corroded connections at test points 3 and 9, or an open circuit in the red wire between test points 3 and 9.

5. If battery voltage is noted in Step 3, connect the voltmeter between ground and test point 6. Depress the UP trim button and note the voltmeter.

6. If no voltage is noted in Step 5, the UP solenoid is defective and must be replaced.

7. If battery voltage is noted in Step 5:

   a. Check UP solenoid for loose or corroded connections and repair as necessary.

   b. Check UP solenoid ground wire (black) for a loose or corroded connection.

   c. Replace the UP solenoid.

Solenoid Test

1. Disconnect all solenoid terminal wires.

2. Connect an ohmmeter between the 2 large terminals.

3. Connect a 12-volt battery between the 2 small solenoid terminals.

4. If the solenoid does not click and the ohmmeter indicates zero ohms, the solenoid is defective.

Trim Sender Test

The trim sender is an optional accessory. If so equipped, check trim sender operation as follows (**Figure 20**):

10

1. Make sure the black trim sender wire has a good ground connection.

2. Trim the outboard to its fully DOWN position and turn the ignition switch to the OFF position.

3. Connect an ohmmeter (calibrated to R × 1) between a good engine ground and test point 1, **Figure 20**.

4. Depress the UP trim button. If the meter needle does not move as the outboard trims out/up, replace the trim sender.

Trim Sender Replacement

Refer to **Figure 21** for this procedure.

1. Tilt the outboard to its fully UP position and engage the tilt lock lever.

2. Disconnect the trim sender wires.

3. Remove the sender attaching screws. Remove the sender.

4. Installation is the reverse of removal. Check the trim indicator gauge needle position and adjust as described under *Trim Indicator Gauge Needle Adjustment* if necessary.

Trim Indicator Gauge Needle Adjustment

Refer to **Figure 21** for this procedure.

1. With the outboard in the fully DOWN position, the trim indicator needle should rest at the bottom of the green area on the gauge. If not, trim the engine to its fully UP position and engage the tilt lock lever.

2. Loosen the trim sender attaching screws. Rotate the sender unit counterclockwise to raise or clockwise to lower the trim indicator needle.

3. When the correct needle position is obtained, securely tighten the trim sender attaching screws.

ONE-RAM OILDYNE POWER TRIM SYSTEM (250-275 HP MODELS)

Components

The 1-Ram Oildyne power trim system consists of a hydraulic pump (containing an electric motor, oil reservoir, oil pump and valve body), a single engine mounted trim cylinder and the related electrical wiring and hydraulic lines. The

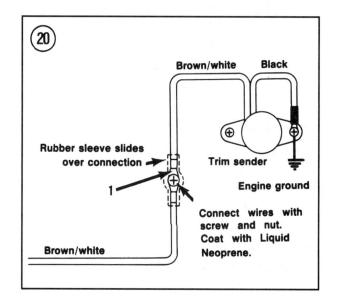

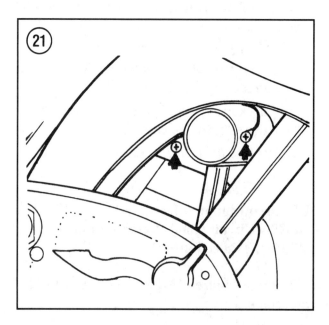

switches which operate the system are contained in the remote control or control panel.

Operation

Depressing the UP trim switch closes the pump motor circuit, causing the motor to drive the oil pump, forcing oil into the up side of the trim cylinder. The engine will trim out/up until the switch is released or the trim limit cutout switch opens the circuit to keep the swivel bracket within the supporting flanges of the clamp bracket.

Depressing the IN or DOWN trim switch also closes the pump motor circuit. The motor runs in the opposite direction, driving the oil pump to force oil into the down side of the trim cylinders and trimming the outboard to the desired position. If the switch is not released when the outboard reaches the limit of its downward travel, an overload cutout switch opens to shut the pump motor off and prevent system damage.

Depressing the TRAILERING button or UP/OUT switch tilts the outboard upward and bypasses the trim limit switch to permit the outboard to be tilted up for trailering, docking or shallow water operation.

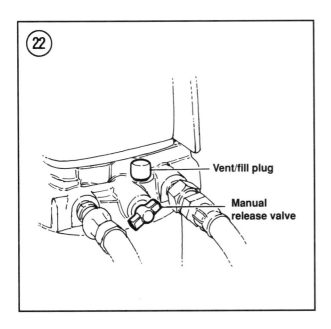

22

Vent/fill plug

Manual release valve

Manual Trim

The power trim system allows the outboard motor to be manually tilted up or down should power trim system failure occur.

WARNING
If in the up position, the outboard will drop when the manual release valve is opened. Be certain all persons are clear of the outboard motor.

To raise or lower the outboard manually, turn the manual release valve (**Figure 22**) fully counterclockwise (open). If the outboard is in the up position, it will drop to the fully down position, or if the outboard is down, it can now be raised. When the outboard is in the desired position, turn the manual release valve fully clockwise. The manual release valve must be fully closed (clockwise) for normal trim system operation.

Hydraulic Pump

Fluid check

1. Tilt the outboard to its fully DOWN position.

2. Clean the area around the pump vent/fill plug (**Figure 22**). Remove the plug and check the oil level on the dipstick portion of the plug. The oil level should be at the full mark (**Figure 23**) on the dipstick.

3. If necessary, add SAE 10W-30 or 10W-40 engine oil as required to bring oil level to the full mark. Do not overfill the system.

NOTE
The vent/fill plug must be backed out 1-1/2 turns from a seated position to allow the reservoir to vent properly.

4. Reinstall the vent/fill plug. Tighten the plug lightly, then back out 1-1/2 turns.

10

Bleeding the hydraulic system

If air should enter the hydraulic system, it should be purged (bled) out. Air in the system will compress, rather than transmit pressure to the trim cylinders. To determine if bleeding is necessary, trim the outboard up to the trim limit position. Apply downward pressure on the gear housing. If the trim rods retract into the cylinder more than 1/8 in. (3.2 mm), air is present in the system. Bleeding is also necessary whenever a hydraulic line is disconnected.

The 1-Ram Oildyne trim system has a self-bleeding feature. To bleed air from the system:

1. Make sure the manual release valve (**Figure 22**) is fully closed (clockwise).

2. Make sure the vent/fill plug (**Figure 22**) is backed out 1-1/2 turns from a seated position.

3. Operate the TRAILER circuit to tilt the outboard to the fully UP position. If the outboard will not reach full UP due to an insufficient oil level, lower the outboard and add oil as described in this chapter.

4. Trim the outboard through several fully UP/fully DOWN cycles, adding oil to the reservoir, if necessary, when the outboard is in the down position. Repeat as necessary until all air is purged from the system.

Troubleshooting

Should a problem develop in the power trim system, the initial step is to determine if the malfunction is in the electrical or hydraulic system. Electrical tests are given in this chapter. If the problem appears to be in the hydraulic system and cannot be corrected by bleeding the system, refer it to a dealer or qualified specialist for the necessary service. Make sure the manual release valve is closed.

Before attempting to troubleshoot any electrical circuit:

1. Make sure the connectors are properly engaged and that all terminals and wires are free of corrosion. Clean and tighten all connections as required.

2. Make sure the battery is fully charged. Charge or replace the battery as required.

All Circuits Inoperative

Refer to **Figures 24-26** for this procedure.

1. Connect a voltmeter red lead to test point 8 and black lead to test point 3. Note the voltmeter.

2. If no voltage is noted in Step 1:

   a. Inspect the battery terminals for loose or corroded connections.

   b. Make sure the battery is in acceptable condition and fully charged.

   c. Check the fuse (if so equipped) at the trim pump assembly, or trim solenoids. Replace the fuse if blown, then determine and repair the cause of the blown fuse.

3. If battery voltage is noted in Step 1, connect the voltmeter between engine ground and test point 9. Depress the TRAILER button and note the voltmeter.

4. If battery voltage is noted in Step 3, the trim pump is defective. Repair or replace the motor.

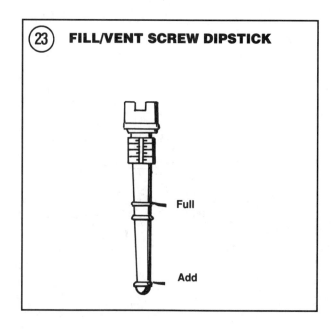

23 **FILL/VENT SCREW DIPSTICK**

Full

Add

5. If no voltage is noted in Step 3, connect the voltmeter between ground and test point 10. Note the voltmeter reading.

6. If battery voltage is noted in Step 5, an open circuit is present in the wires between the trim switch and trim pump.

   a. Check all power trim harness connectors for loose or corroded connections.

   b. Check for pinched or broken wires.

   c. Repair or replace wires as required.

7. If no voltage is noted in Step 5, place the ignition switch in the RUN position (engine not running). Connect the voltmeter between ground and any instrument.

8. If battery voltage is noted in Step 7, an open circuit is present in the wire between the ignition switch terminal B and test point 10.

9. If no voltage is noted in Step 7, connect the voltmeter between ground and the red wire terminal at the starter solenoid.

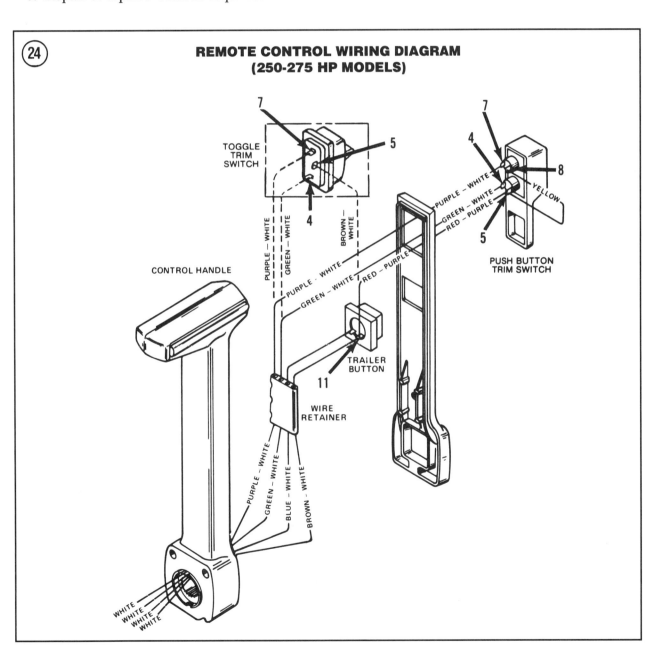

**REMOTE CONTROL WIRING DIAGRAM
(250-275 HP MODELS)**

10

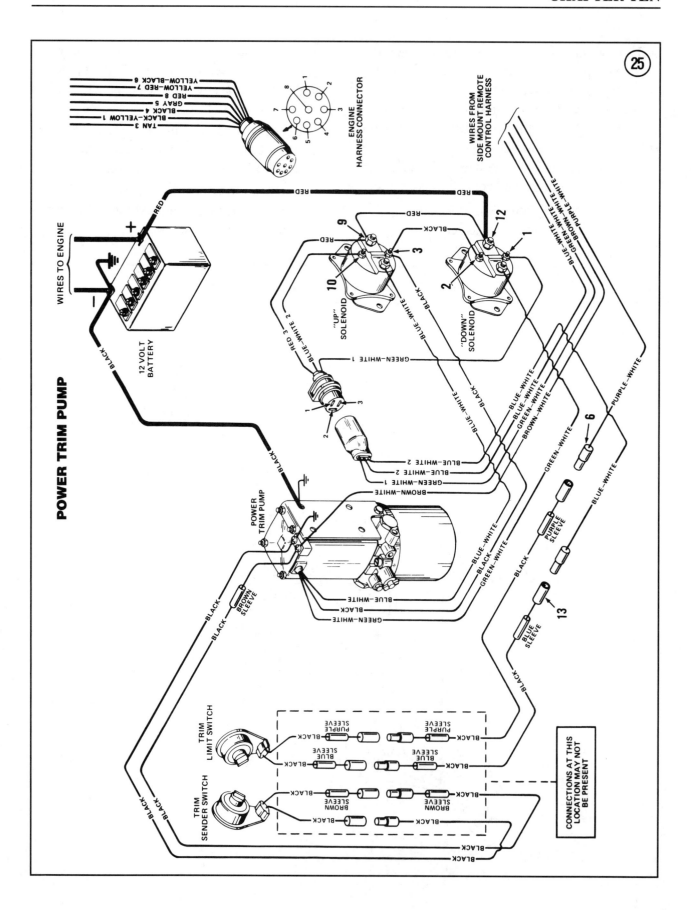

POWER TRIM PUMP

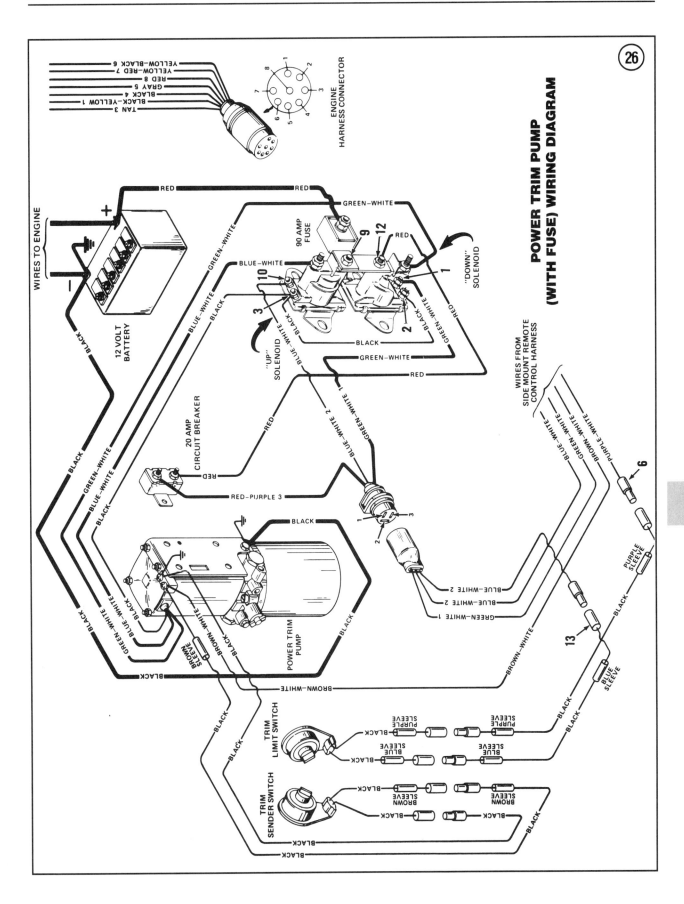

POWER TRIM PUMP
(WITH FUSE) WIRING DIAGRAM

10. If battery voltage is noted in Step 9, the red wire is open between the starter solenoid red wire terminal at the starter solenoid and terminal B at the rear of the ignition switch. Check for loose or corroded connections and pinched or broken wires.

11. If no voltage is noted in Step 9, the battery positive cable is open between the battery and the red wire terminal on the starter solenoid. Check for loose or corroded connections and pinched or broken wire.

TRAILER Circuit Inoperative— UP Circuit Good

Refer to **Figures 24-26** for this procedure.

1. Using an ohmmeter, check for continuity of the wire between the UP solenoid at test point 9 and the trailer button.

2. If no continuity is present, repair or replace the wire between test point 9 and the trailer button.

3. If continuity is present, replace the trailer button.

UP and TRAILER Circuits Inoperative—DOWN Circuit Good

Refer to **Figures 24-26** for this procedure.

1. Connect the voltmeter red lead to test point 9 and the black lead to test point 3. Depress the trailer button and note the voltmeter.

2. If no voltage is noted in Step 1, an open circuit is present in the blue/white and purple/white wires between the UP solenoid and the trim switch.

3. If battery voltage is noted in Step 1, check the UP solenoid terminals for loose or corroded connections. If the connections are acceptable, replace the UP solenoid.

DOWN Circuit Inoperative— UP Circuit Good

Refer to **Figures 24-26** for this procedure.

1. Connect the red voltmeter lead to test point 1 and the black voltmeter lead to test point 2. Depress the DOWN trim button and note the voltmeter. Battery voltage should be indicated.

2. If no voltage is noted in Step 1, move the black voltmeter lead to test point 3. Depress the DOWN trim button and note the voltmeter.

  a. If battery voltage is indicated (Step 3), an open circuit is present in the black jumper wire between the trim solenoids. Repair or replace the jumper wire as necessary.

  b. If no voltage is noted (Step 3), move the red voltmeter lead to test point 4. Depress the DOWN trim button and note the voltmeter. If battery voltage is noted, an open circuit is present in the green/white wire between test points 4 and 1. If no voltage is noted, move the red voltmeter lead to test point 5. If battery voltage is now indicated, the trim switch is defective. If no voltage is present, check for a loose or corroded connection at test point 5, or an open circuit in the wire leading to test point 5.

3. If battery voltage is noted in Step 1, connect the red voltmeter lead to test point 11 and the black voltmeter lead to test point 1.

4. If battery voltage is noted in Step 3, check for loose or corroded connections at the DOWN solenoid terminals. If all terminal connections are acceptable, replace the DOWN solenoid.

5. If no voltage is noted in Step 3, an open circuit is present between the positive battery terminal and test point 11.

  a. Check for loose or corroded connections.

  b. Check the condition of the fuse (if so equipped) at the trim pump. Replace the fuse if blown, then determine and repair the cause of the blown fuse.

UP Circuit Inoperative— TRAILER Circuit Good

Refer to **Figures 24-26** for this procedure.

1. Trim the outboard to the fully DOWN position, then disconnect the purple/white wire from the black wire with the purple sleeve at test point 6. Connect the black voltmeter lead to test point 3 and the red voltmeter lead to the purple/white wire at test point 6. Depress the UP trim switch while noting the voltmeter.

2. If battery voltage is noted in Step 1, reconnect the purple/white and black wire (with purple sleeve) at test point 6. Then, disconnect the blue/white wire from the black wire with the blue sleeve at test point 12. Move the red voltmeter lead to the black wire with blue sleeve. Keep the black voltmeter lead connected to test point 3. Depress the UP trim switch and note the voltmeter.

   a. If battery voltage is indicated, an open circuit is present in the blue/white wire between test point 12 and the 3-pin harness connector at the trim pump.

   b. If no voltage is noted, check for loose or corroded connections between test points 6 and 12, or a defective or maladjusted trim limit switch. See *Trim Limit Switch Test* and *Trim Angle Adjustment* in this chapter.

3. If no voltage is noted in Step 1, move the red voltmeter lead to test point 5.

4. If no voltage is noted in Step 3, an open circuit is present in the wire between the trim switch at test point 5 and the trailer button.

5. If battery voltage is noted in Step 3, move the red voltmeter lead to test point 7, depress the UP trim switch and note the voltmeter.

   a. If no voltage is noted, the trim switch is defective.

   b. If voltage is noted, an open circuit is present in the white/purple wire between test points 6 and 7. Repair or replace the wire as necessary.

Solenoid Test

1. Disconnect all solenoid terminal wires.
2. Connect an ohmmeter (calibrated at R × 1) between the 2 larger solenoid terminals.
3. Connect a 12-volt battery between the 2 small threaded solenoid terminals.
4. The solenoid should click when the battery is connected and the meter should indicate zero ohm resistance. If not, the solenoid is defective.

Trim Limit Switch Test

1. Trim the outboard to the fully DOWN position.
2. Disconnect the trim limit switch wires (**Figure 25** and **Figure 26**):
   a. Black wire with purple sleeve from the purple/white wire.
   b. Black wire with the blue sleeve from the blue/white wire.
3. Calibrate an ohmmeter on the R × 1 scale. Connect the ohmmeter between the trim limit switch wires. Continuity should be indicated.
4. If continuity is not indicated, perform OUT angle adjustment as described under *Trim Angle Adjustments* in this chapter. Repeat Step 3. If continuity is still not present, replace the trim limit switch. If continuity is now noted, continue at Step 5.
5. Reconnect the trim limit switch wires. Depress the UP trim button. The outboard should trim out to the trim limit.
6. If the outboard fails to trim out to the trim limit, or trims past the trim limit, the OUT angle is not properly adjusted or the trim limit switch is defective. Perform OUT angle adjustment as described under *Trim Angle Adjustments* or replace the switch.

Trim Sender Switch Test

1. Trim the outboard to the fully DOWN position.

10

2. Disconnect the black and black with brown sleeve trim sender wires from the junction block on the power trim pump assembly. See **Figures 25 and 26.**

3. Connect an ohmmeter (calibrated at R × 1) between the trim sender wires. Depress the TRAILER button while noting the ohmmeter.

4. The resistance should increase as the outboard trims out/up. If not, the trim sender is defective.

Trim Angle Adjustment

Trim OUT angle

Always water test the boat after making a trim angle adjusting. If handling characteristics are undesirable, readjust the trim angle to reduce the OUT trim limit.

> *WARNING*
> *NEVER adjust the OUT angle so that less than 1-1/2 in. (38 mm) of the swivel bracket is engaged inside the transom bracket with the outboard trimmed out to the trim limit. See **Figure 27**. Readjust the OUT angle as necessary to obtain at least 1-1/2 in. (38 mm) engagement.*

1. To adjust the OUT angle, loosen the clamp (A, **Figure 28**). Rotate the trim limit switch clockwise to reduce trim out angle or counterclockwise to increase trim out angle.

2. Tighten the trim limit switch clamp screws securely.

3. Water test the boat with the outboard trimmed out to the trim limit. If undesirable handling characteristics are noted, reduce the trim out angle.

Trim IN angle

Always water test the boat after performing trim IN angle adjustments. Some boat hull configurations may experience undesirable handling characteristics when operated at planing speeds with the outboard trimmed fully in. The

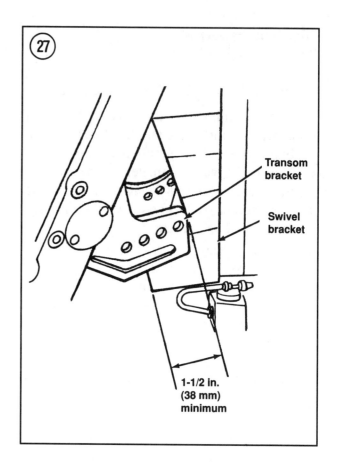

Transom bracket

Swivel bracket

1-1/2 in. (38 mm) minimum

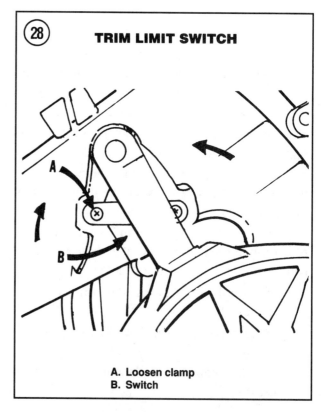

TRIM LIMIT SWITCH

A. Loosen clamp
B. Switch

trim IN adjustment bolt (**Figure 29**) is installed at the factory and is used to limit the trim IN angle. Remove the bolt and water test the boat with the outboard trimmed fully in. If unsafe handling or steering conditions are noted, install the trim adjustment bolt into the proper holes and secure with a locknut. Tighten the locknut sufficiently to remove any play but *do not* overtighten or the transom brackets will be pulled inward and interfere with swivel bracket movement.

Trim Indicator Gauge Needle Adjustment

1. With the outboard in the fully DOWN position, the trim indicator needle should rest at the bottom of the green area on the gauge. If not, trim

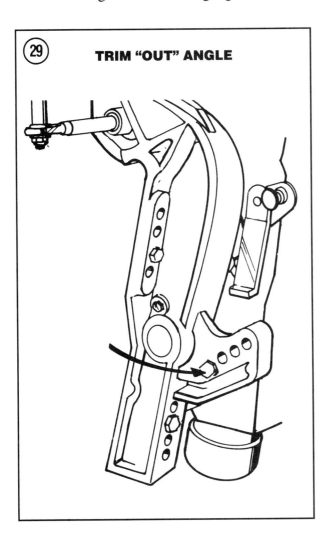

(29) TRIM "OUT" ANGLE

the engine to its fully UP position and engage the tilt lock lever.

2. Loosen the trim sender clamp screws. Rotate the sender unit counterclockwise to raise or clockwise to lower the trim indicator needle.

3. When the correct needle position is obtained, securely tighten the trim sender attaching screws.

Trim Limit Switch Replacement

1. Disconnect the trim limit switch wires. See **Figure 25** or **Figure 26.**

2. Remove the 2 screws securing the trim switch clamp. Remove the clamp and trim limit switch. See **Figure 28**.

3. To install the switch, reverse the removal procedure. Make sure the switch wires are properly routed. Adjust the trim OUT angle as described in this chapter.

POWER TRIM ASSEMBLY REMOVAL/INSTALLATION

One-Ram Integral (40-60 hp)

1. Tilt the outboard to the fully up position and engage the tilt lock lever.

2. Disconnect the battery cables from the battery.

3. Disconnect the power trim harness from the outboard harness.

4. Remove any clamps or clips securing the power trim wiring harness to the clamp bracket.

5. Using a suitable chisel, remove the upper pivot shaft dowel pin by driving it downward as shown in **Figure 30**.

6. Using a suitable punch and hammer, drive out the upper pivot shaft.

7. Using a suitable punch, remove the lower pivot shaft dowel pin by driving it upward as shown in **Figure 31**.

8. Remove the lower pivot shaft from the clamp bracket by driving it out with a suitable punch and hammer.

10

9. Tilt the top of the trim unit outward, then lift the assembly from the clamp bracket.

10. To install the power trim assembly, lubricate the upper and lower pivot shaft bores and shafts with Quicksilver 2-4-C Marine Lubricant.

11. Start the lower pivot shaft into its bore. Install the power trim assembly (bottom first) between the clamp brackets. Route the power trim wiring harness through the hole in the starboard clamp bracket. Drive the lower pivot shaft into the clamp bracket and through the trim assembly, until the shaft is flush with the outer surfaces of the clamp brackets.

12. Using a suitable punch, drive the lower shaft dowel pin into its bore until fully seated.

13. Align the tilt ram bore with the upper pivot shaft bore in the swivel bracket, then install the upper pivot shaft. Using a suitable mallet, drive the upper shaft into the swivel shaft and through the tilt ram, until the shaft is flush with the outer surfaces of the swivel shaft. Install the upper pivot shaft dowel pin into its bore, until fully seated.

14. Connect the power trim wiring harness to the outboard motor harness. Connect the battery ca-

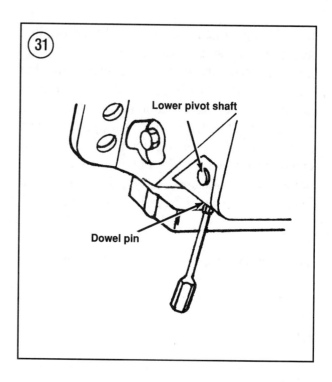

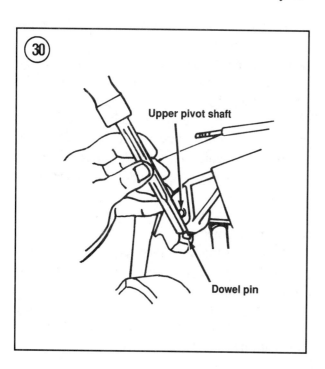

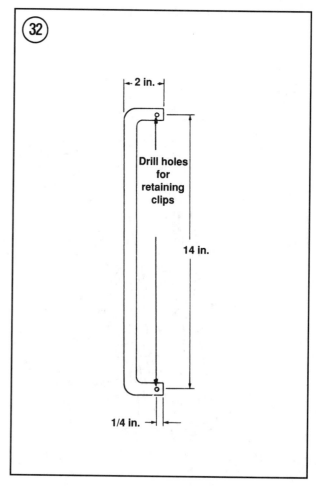

bles to the battery. Check the power trim fluid level and bleed the system as necessary.

Three-Ram Integral (75-200 hp)

WARNING
Failure to support the outboard motor properly during power trim assembly removal/installation can result in severe personal injury and/or damage to the boat or motor.

This procedure requires the use of a suitable hoist, or the fabrication of a support tool made from a used shift shaft or other 3/8 in. (7.5 mm) diameter rod material as shown in **Figure 32**. Use the hoist or the support tool to prevent the outboard motor from falling during power trim assembly removal/installation procedures.

1. Remove the engine cover.

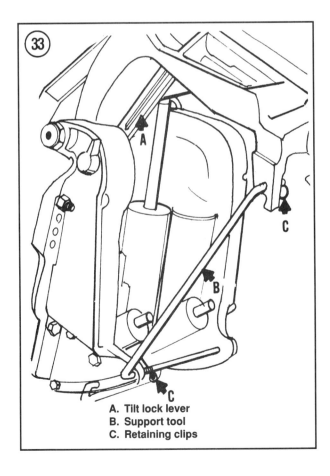

A. Tilt lock lever
B. Support tool
C. Retaining clips

2. Disconnect the battery cables from the battery.

3. Open the manual release valve and tilt the outboard to the fully up position, then engage the tilt lock lever, or support the outboard with a hoist.

4. Support the outboard using the fabricated tool as shown in **Figure 33**.

5. Disconnect the power trim wiring harness from the outboard harness. Remove the trim system wiring harness clamps and sta-straps.

6. If so equipped, disconnect the cowl mounted trim switch. If necessary, remove the ignition plate cover to gain access to the switch connector.

7. On V6 models, remove the 4 screws securing the lower engine cowl on the starboard side. Remove the lower cowl.

8. Disconnect the blue, green and black trim motor wires from the trim solenoids.

9. Attach a suitable wooden block under the engine swivel bracket with a large C-clamp to support the starboard side of the outboard. See **Figure 34**.

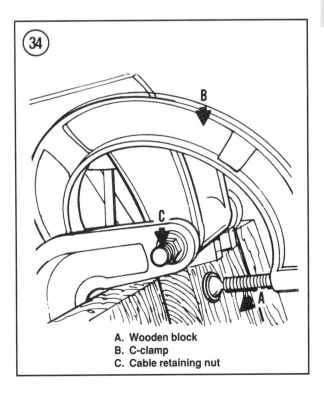

A. Wooden block
B. C-clamp
C. Cable retaining nut

10

10. If equipped with through-the-tilt tube steering, remove the cable retaining nut from the end of the tilt tube. See C, **Figure 34**.

11. On the starboard side of the outboard, remove the 2 transom bracket mounting bolts. Remove the tilt tube nut and the 3 bolts holding the transom bracket to the power trim assembly.

12. Move the starboard transom bracket away from the power trim assembly far enough to allow the manual release valve to clear the bracket when the assembly is removed.

NOTE
*Do not reuse the cross pin that secures the cylinder retaining pin (**Figure 35**) once it is removed.*

13. Drive out the cross pin holding the tilt cylinder retaining pin with a suitable punch. Discard the cross pin. Remove the retaining pin. See **Figure 35**.

14. Remove the 3 bolts holding the power trim assembly to the port transom bracket. Remove the power trim assembly.

15. To reinstall the power trim assembly, apply Loctite 271 to the threads of the 3 port side power trim assembly mounting bolts. Install the trim assembly to the port transom bracket. Install the 3 bolts with lockwashers, and tighten finger tight.

16. Install the wave washer onto the tilt tube.

17. Route the power trim wiring harness through the hole in the top of the starboard transom bracket.

18. Apply Loctite 271 to the threads of the starboard transom bracket-to-power trim assembly bolts. Install the starboard transom bracket, then fasten the bracket to the trim assembly with the 3 bolts and lockwashers. Use caution not to damage the power trim manual release valve. Tighten the port and starboard bolts to 30 ft.-lb. (41 N•m).

19. Coat the shanks (not threads) of the outboard mounting bolts with a suitable marine sealer, then reattach the starboard transom bracket to the

boat transom with the bolts, flat washers and locknuts. The installation *must* be water tight.

20. Install the tilt tube nut and tighten securely.

21. Remove the C-clamp and wooden block (**Figure 34**).

22. If equipped with through-the-tilt tube steering, reinstall the cable retaining nut onto the tilt tube and tighten it securely.

NOTE
If the tilt ram overextends in Step 23, retract it by connecting the green wire to the positive battery terminal.

23. Connect the trim motor to a 12-volt battery to extend the tilt ram enough to install the retaining pin. Use a pair of jumper cables and connect the trim motor blue wire to the positive battery terminal and the black wire to the negative battery cable. When the end of the tilt ram is aligned with the retaining pin hole, disconnect the jumper cables.

24. Align the cross pin hole in the retaining pin with the hole in the end of the tilt ram (**Figure 36**) and install the retaining pin. The slot in the

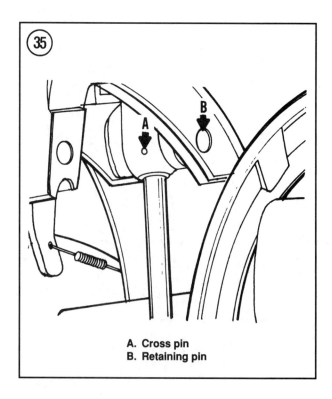

A. Cross pin
B. Retaining pin

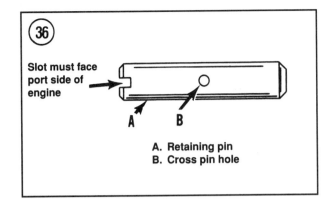

36

Slot must face
port side of
engine

A
B

A. Retaining pin
B. Cross pin hole

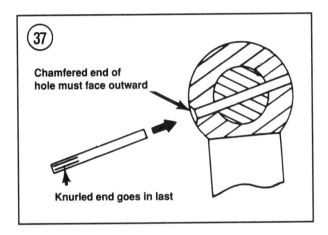

37

Chamfered end of
hole must face outward

Knurled end goes in last

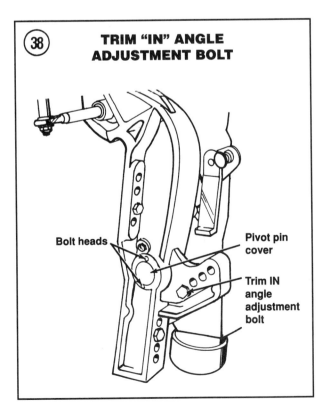

38

**TRIM "IN" ANGLE
ADJUSTMENT BOLT**

Bolt heads

Pivot pin
cover

Trim IN
angle
adjustment
bolt

end of the pin can be used to move it back and forth. A suitable punch installed in the tilt ram cross pin hole will engage the retaining pin as it is moved. Once the holes are aligned, remove the punch and install a new cross pin as shown in **Figure 37**. Tap the cross pin in until flush with the tilt ram surface.

25. Route and connect the trim motor wires to the trim system solenoids. Install all retainers, clamps and sta-straps. Coat all electrical connections with Quicksilver Liquid Neoprene.

One-Ram Oildyne
(250 and 275 hp)

Trim cylinder removal/installation

1. Disconnect the battery cables from the battery.

WARNING
If the outboard is in the UP position, it will drop when the manual release valve is opened in Step 2. Be certain all personnel are clear of the motor to prevent personal injury.

2. Open the manual release valve to its fully counterclockwise position.

3. Manually raise the outboard to the fully UP position. Block the motor up with a suitable solid metal bar. As an added precaution, use a rope and hoist to support the motor.

4. Remove the trim IN angle adjustment bolt from the clamp bracket. See **Figure 38**.

WARNING
Considerable pressure may be present in the hydraulic hoses. Use caution when disconnecting the hoses from the trim cylinder in Step 5.

5. Place a suitable container under the trim cylinder, then remove the hydraulic hoses from the cylinder. Plug the hoses to prevent leakage or contamination.

6. Remove the pivot pin cover plates (**Figure 38**) from each side of the clamp bracket.

10

7. Thread a 5/16 × 18 bolt into the pivot pin on each side of the clamp bracket. Using the bolts, remove the pivot pins, washers and springs from the clamp bracket.

8. Remove the trim sender and trim OUT limit switch as described in this chapter.

9. Using a suitable punch and hammer, drive out the retaining pin that secures the trim cylinder cross pin in the swivel bracket. See **Figure 35**.

10. While supporting the trim cylinder, drive out the trim cylinder cross pin (**Figure 35**) using a blunt punch. Remove the trim cylinder assembly.

11. To install the trim cylinder, lubricate the trim cylinder cross pin with Quicksilver 2-4-C Marine Lubricant. Support the trim cylinder in position, then install the cross pin.

12. Align the cross pin hole with the retaining pin hole in the upper end of the trim cylinder. Install the retaining pin until flush with the outer surface of the trim cylinder.

13. Lubricate the pivot pins with Quicksilver 2-4-C Marine Lubricant. Align the trim cylinder and clamp bracket pivot pin holes, then install the springs into the holes. Install the washers between the trim cylinder and clamp bracket, then install the pivot pins into the clamp bracket and trim cylinder.

14. Install the pivot pin cover plates.

15. Install the trim sender and trim limit switch as described in this chapter.

16. Connect the hydraulic hoses to the trim cylinder.

17. Install the trim IN angle adjustment bolt and locknut. Do not over-tighten the nut.

18. Remove the hoist and/or support bar holding the outboard in the up position.

19. Close the manual release valve (clockwise).

20. Reconnect the battery cables to the battery.

21. Fill the hydraulic reservoir with the recommended fluid and bleed the air from the system as described in this chapter.

Trim pump assembly removal/installation

1. Disconnect the battery cables from the battery.

2. Disconnect the 3-pin trim harness connector from the trim pump.

3. Open the manual release valve (counterclockwise).

4. Remove the hydraulic hoses from the pump assembly. Plug the hoses to prevent leakage or contamination.

5. Remove the pump assembly fastener and remove the pump from its mounting bracket.

6. To install the trim pump assembly, place the pump into its bracket and secure with the fastener and lockwasher.

7. Connect the hydraulic hoses to the pump.

8. Reconnect the 3-pin trim harness connector to the pump.

9. Close the manual release valve (clockwise).

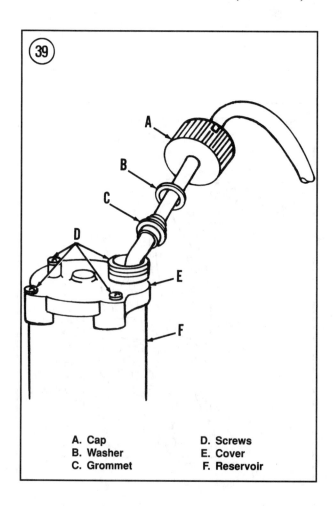

A. Cap
B. Washer
C. Grommet
D. Screws
E. Cover
F. Reservoir

10. Connect the battery cables to the battery.

11. If necessary, fill the reservoir with the recommended fluid, then bleed air from the system as described in this chapter.

POWER TRIM MOTOR AND PUMP ASSEMBLY REMOVAL/INSTALLATION

One-Ram Integral Trim System (40-60 hp)

1. Remove the power trim assembly as described in this chapter. Drain the pump reservoir, then

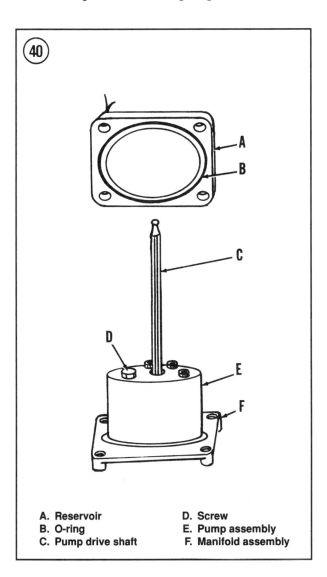

A. Reservoir
B. O-ring
C. Pump drive shaft
D. Screw
E. Pump assembly
F. Manifold assembly

clamp the trim assembly into a vise with protective jaws.

2. Unscrew the wiring harness cap and remove the washer and grommet from the pump reservoir. See **Figure 39**.

3. Remove the 4 screws securing the cover (E, **Figure 39**) to the reservoir (F). Remove the cover.

4. Lift the pump motor out of the reservoir, disconnect the pump wires at the bullet connectors and remove the motor.

CAUTION
Do not mistake the reverse thrust valve for the manual release valve. The reverse thrust valve must not be removed, adjusted or tampered with. The manual release valve can be identified by its larger size and the E-ring attached to it.

5. Remove the manual release valve from the trim manifold.

6. Remove the 4 screws securing the reservoir (F, **Figure 39**) to the trim manifold. Lift the reservoir off the manifold. Remove the oil pump drive shaft from the pump assembly. See **Figure 40**.

7. Remove the screw (D, **Figure 40**), then lift the pump assembly (E) off the manifold. Remove the pump O-rings, check ball and check ball spring from the manifold.

8. To install the pump assembly, install new pump O-rings onto the manifold. Install the check valve assembly (spring and ball) into the manifold, place the pump assembly onto the manifold and secure with the screw (D, **Figure 40**). Tighten the screw to 90 in.-lb. (10.2 N•m).

9. Insert the pump drive shaft into the pump (**Figure 40**).

10. Connect the pump wires at their respective bullet connectors and install the motor into the reservoir. Make sure the motor wires are properly positioned in the reservoir cavity, or the motor will not seat properly inside the reservoir.

11. Install the foam pad onto the motor. Install a new O-ring onto the reservoir cover.

10

12. Install the reservoir cover and secure with 4 screws (**Figure 39**). Tighten the screws to 13 ft.-lb. (17.6 N•m).

13. Install the grommet and washer into the reservoir, then screw on the cap (**Figure 39**).

14. Carefully install the reservoir and motor assembly, making sure the pump drive shaft is properly aligned with the motor. Mate the reservoir onto the manifold, install the 4 reservoir screws and tighten to 70 in.-lb. (7.9 N•m).

15. Inspect the O-rings on the manual release valve and replace as necessary. Lubricate the O-rings with Quicksilver Power Trim and Steering Fluid or automatic transmission fluid, then install the manual release valve into the manifold.

16. Reinstall the power trim assembly as described in this chapter.

Three-Ram Integral Power Trim System (75-200 hp with Side Fill Reservoir)

The hydraulic pump is not repairable. It must be replaced if defective.

> *NOTE*
> *The pump and electric motor can be removed and installed without removing the power trim assembly from the outboard motor.*

1. Tilt the outboard to the fully UP position. If necessary, open the manual release valve and raise the outboard manually as described in this chapter. Engage the tilt lock lever.

2. Disconnect the battery cables from the battery.

3. Disconnect the trim motor wires from the trim solenoids.

4. Remove the starboard transom bracket as described under *Power Trim Assembly Removal/installation*.

5. Carefully remove the reservoir fill plug to allow pressure within the system to bleed.

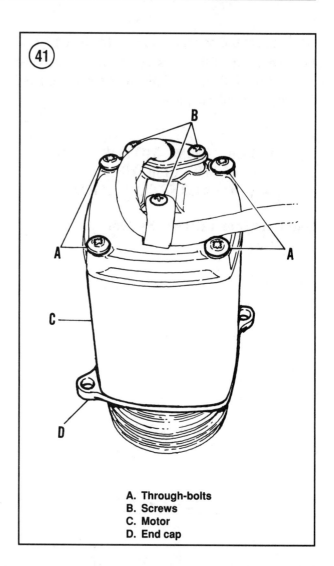

A. Through-bolts
B. Screws
C. Motor
D. End cap

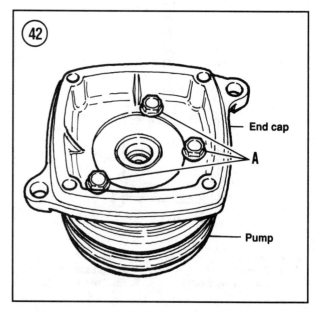

End cap

A

Pump

6. Slowly open the manual release valve (counterclockwise) 4 full turns to bleed any remaining pressure.

7. Remove the 2 Allen screws and lockwashers securing the motor and pump assembly to the manifold. Dislodge the motor and pump assembly from the manifold by carefully prying at the slots provided. Lift the motor and pump assembly from the manifold.

8. Remove the screws (B, **Figure 41**) and the wire harness clamp. Remove the 4 through-bolts (A, **Figure 41**), then lift the motor assembly (C) from the end cap (D). Be careful not to drop the motor armature when separating the motor from the end cap.

9. Remove the 3 bolts (A, **Figure 42**) securing the pump assembly to the end cap. Separate the pump from the end cap.

CAUTION
Absolute cleanliness is essential during pump installation. Be certain all components are free of dirt, lint or other debris.

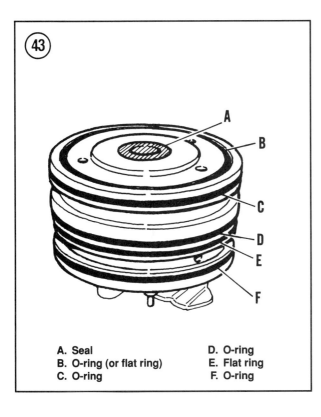

43

A. Seal
B. O-ring (or flat ring)
C. O-ring
D. O-ring
E. Flat ring
F. O-ring

10. Lubricate the pump O-rings, flat ring and seal with Quicksilver Power Trim & Steering Fluid or automatic transmission fluid. Make sure all seals are properly installed. See **Figure 43**.

11. Apply Loctite 271 to the threads of the 3 screws (A, **Figure 42**). Install the end cap to the pump, install the 3 screws and tighten securely.

12. Install the motor assembly to the end cap. Tighten the 4 through-bolts securely.

13. Install the pump and motor assembly to the trim manifold. Apply Quicksilver Perfect Seal to the threads of the Allen screws that secure the pump/motor assembly to the manifold. Install the screws and tighten securely.

14. Apply Quicksilver Liquid Neoprene to the pump and motor assembly-to-manifold seam to waterproof the trim system.

15. Install the starboard transom bracket as described in this chapter.

16. Connect the trim motor wires to the trim solenoids. Connect the battery cables to the battery.

17. Fill the pump reservoir with a recommended fluid. Close the manual release valve and bleed the system as described in this chapter.

10

Three-Ram Integral Power Trim System (135-200 hp with Aft Fill Reservoir)

The pump assembly is not repairable and must be replaced if defective.

NOTE
The pump and electric motor can be removed and installed without removing the power trim assembly from the outboard motor.

1. Tilt the outboard to the fully UP position and engage the tilt lock lever.

2. Disconnect the battery cables from the battery. Disconnect the trim motor wires at the solenoids.

3. Make certain the outboard is securely supported in the UP position, then open the manual release valve (counterclockwise) and loosen the

reservoir fill plug to release any pressure within the hydraulic system.

4. Remove the starboard transom bracket as described in this chapter.

5. Remove the 2 motor attaching screws (1, **Figure 44**), then remove the motor. The pump drive shaft is loose in the motor and may fall out when the motor is removed. Be sure to retrieve the shaft.

6. Remove the 2 Allen screws securing the pump assembly (5, **Figure 44**). Lift the pump off the manifold.

CAUTION
Absolute cleanliness is essential during pump installation. Be certain all components are free of dirt, lint or other debris.

7. To reassemble, install new O-rings (6, 7, 8, **Figure 44**) onto the manifold. Install the pump assembly onto the manifold. Make sure the flat area (F, **Figure 44**) is facing the starboard transom bracket.

8. Install the pump mounting screws and tighten securely. Fill the pump with Quicksilver Power Trim & Steering Fluid or automatic transmission fluid.

9. Insert the pump drive shaft into the pump.

10. Install a new motor-to-pump O-ring. Install the motor, making sure the motor and drive shaft are properly aligned. Install the 2 motor attaching screws and tighten securely. Connect the motor wires to the appropriate terminals on the trim solenoids.

11. Complete installation by reversing the removal procedure. Fill the reservoir with a recommended oil and bleed air from the system as described in this chapter.

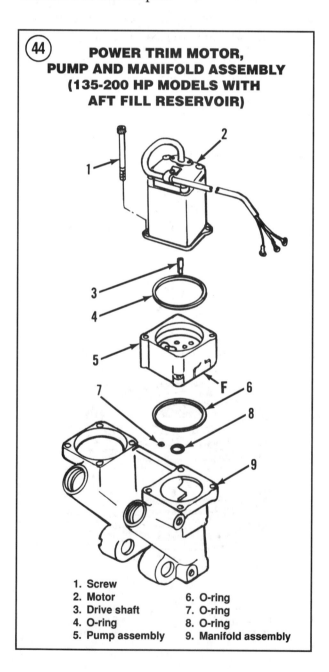

(44) POWER TRIM MOTOR, PUMP AND MANIFOLD ASSEMBLY (135-200 HP MODELS WITH AFT FILL RESERVOIR)

1. Screw
2. Motor
3. Drive shaft
4. O-ring
5. Pump assembly
6. O-ring
7. O-ring
8. O-ring
9. Manifold assembly

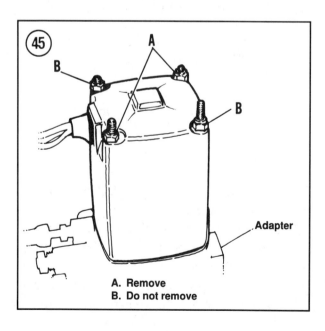

(45)

A. Remove
B. Do not remove

Adapter

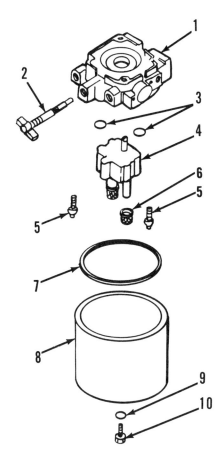

POWER TRIM PUMP, ADAPTER AND RESERVOIR (ONE-RAM OILDYNE [250-275 HP MODELS])

1. Adapter assembly
2. Manual release valve
3. O-rings
4. Pump assembly
5. Screws
6. Filter
7. O-ring
8. Reservoir
9. O-ring
10. Screw

One-Ram Oildyne Trim System (250-275 hp)

Motor removal/installation

1. If necessary, remove the power trim pump assembly from the outboard motor as described in this chapter.

2. Disconnect the trim motor wires from the trim solenoids. Remove the solenoid mounting plate along with the solenoids from the pump assembly.

> *NOTE*
> *Do not loosen or remove the nuts (B, **Figure 45**) in Step 3.*

3. Remove the 2 locknuts (A, **Figure 45**) from the motor mounting studs. If the studs turn with the nuts, remove the studs along with the nuts.

4. Lift the motor off the mounting studs. Remove and discard the O-ring from the motor mounting base.

5. To install the motor, install a new O-ring onto the motor mounting base.

6. Install the motor onto the mounting studs, making sure the motor shaft is aligned with the pump coupling. The motor will sit flush on the adapter when the shaft and coupling are properly aligned.

7. Install the 2 locknuts removed in Step 3. Tighten the nuts securely.

8. Install the solenoid mounting plate and attach the motor wires to their respective solenoids.

9. If removed, install the power trim pump assembly onto the outboard motor as described in this chapter.

Pump assembly removal/installation

The pump is not repairable and must be replaced if defective.

1. If necessary, remove the power trim assembly from the outboard motor as described in this chapter.

2. Remove the screw (10, **Figure 46**) and pump reservoir (8).

10

3. Discard the power trim fluid in the reservoir. Remove and discard the O-rings (9 and 7).

NOTE
*Do not loosen or remove the screws (B, **Figure 47**) in Step 4.*

4. Using an appropriate TORX socket, remove the pump mounting screws (A, **Figure 47**). Do not loosen or remove screws (B, **Figure 47**). Remove the pump from the adapter. Be sure to retrieve the pump-to-motor coupling. Remove and discard the pump O-rings (3, **Figure 46**).

5. Replace all O-rings and seals. Lubricate the O-rings and seals with Quicksilver Power Trim & Steering Fluid or automatic transmission fluid.

6. Install the pump, making sure the pump-to-motor coupling is in place. Tighten the pump mounting screws (A, **Figure 47**) to 75 in.-lb. (8.5 N.m) using an appropriate TORX socket.

7. Install the reservoir. Install the pump assembly onto the outboard motor, if removed. Fill the reservoir with a recommended fluid, then bleed air from the system as described in this chapter.

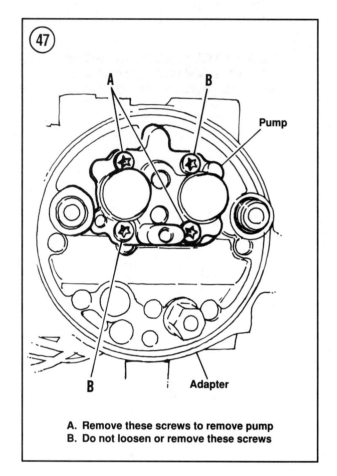

A. Remove these screws to remove pump
B. Do not loosen or remove these screws

Chapter Eleven

Oil Injection System

Two-stroke engines are lubricated by mixing oil with the gasoline. The various engine components are lubricated as the fuel and oil mixture passes through the crankcase and cylinders. The optimum fuel:oil ratio required by outboard motors depends on engine demand. Without oil injection, the oil must be hand mixed with the gasoline at a predetermined ratio to ensure sufficient lubrication is provided at all engine speeds and load conditions. While this predetermined ratio is adequate for high-speed operation, it may contain more oil than necessary during idle and slow-speed operation. This often results in excessive smoking and fouled spark plugs when operated at slow engine speeds.

Oil injection eliminates the need to hand mix oil and gasoline together in the fuel tank. On models equipped with variable-ratio oil injection, the amount of oil delivered to the engine can be varied instantly and accurately to supply the optimum fuel:oil ratio for all engine speeds and load conditions.

Four different oil injection systems are used on models covered in this manual:

a. AutoBlend II gasoline and oil mixing system—50 and 60 hp models prior to serial No. D000750.
b. Constant-ratio injection—40 hp and 50-60 (serial No. D000750-on) hp models.
c. Variable-ratio injection—75-115 hp models.
d. Variable-ratio injection—V6 models.

AUTOBLEND II (50 AND 60 HP PRIOR TO SERIAL NO. D000750)

Operation

Models 50 and 60 hp (prior to serial No. D000750), are equipped with AutoBlend II fuel and oil mixing system. The AutoBlend system is a self-contained unit and is designed to deliver a constant 50:1 fuel and oil mixture to the power head at all engine speeds.

The AutoBlend II unit is installed into the fuel line between the fuel tank and the outboard motor. See **Figure 1**. The AutoBlend unit is bracket mounted and should be located as close to the fuel tank as possible and at a level at or near the bottom of the fuel tank.

A battery powered warning system activates a warning horn should the oil level in the AutoBlend unit drop to approximately 1/2 pt. (0.23 L), or if the AutoBlend shuttle valve should stick or discontinue functioning. The low-oil warning horn can be easily tested by filling the AutoBlend reservoir with a recommended oil, removing the unit from its mounting bracket, then inverting it allowing the low-oil sensor to trigger the warning horn. A battery test button (G, **Figure 2**) is provided to test the condition of the battery and low-oil warning system. If the warning horn does not sound when the battery test button is depressed, remove the cover from the battery box and remove the battery. Check the battery voltage using a suitable voltmeter. Replace the battery if the voltage is not 5.85 volts or more. When installing the battery, make sure the terminals are free of corrosion or water.

> *CAUTION*
> *Certain two-stroke oils have a tendency to gel due to the use of additives containing calcium sulfonate and can plug the AutoBlend filter screens. A strainer kit (part No. 91-15387A1), should be installed on units sold without it.*

Break-In Procedure

During the break-in period (first 30 gallons of fuel) of a new or rebuilt power head, a 50:1 fuel and oil mixture should be used in the fuel tank and consumed in combination with the AutoBlend unit. After using the first 30 gallons of fuel, switch to straight gasoline in the fuel tank.

Draining and Cleaning

A drain plug (D, **Figure 2**) allows fuel to be drained from the unit before storage or during extended periods of nonuse. To drain and clean the unit reservoir, proceed as follows:

1. Remove the AutoBlend unit from the boat.

2. Remove the drain plug and allow the contents to drain into a suitable container.

3. Thoroughly rinse out the reservoir using clean solvent.

4. Inspect seals, O-rings and gaskets for deterioration, swelling, cracking or other damage.

5. Inspect the side cover plates for cracks, scratches, warpage or other damage.

6. Inspect the reservoir for holes, cracks or other damage.

7. Check the drain plug O-ring for swelling, cracking or deterioration. Replace the O-ring as required.

8. Lubricate the drain plug O-ring with 2-stroke engine oil. Install the drain plug and tighten to 30 in.-lb. (3.4 N•m).

Fuel Filter Replacement

Periodically remove the AutoBlend cover and inspect the translucent fuel filter (C, **Figure 2**) for sediment. The filter should be replaced each

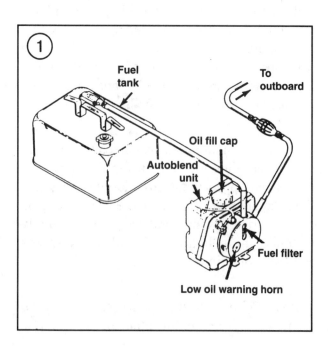

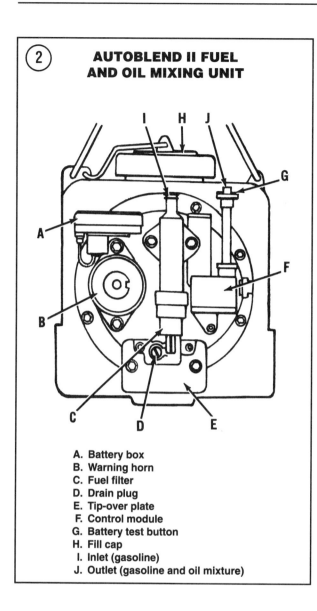

AUTOBLEND II FUEL AND OIL MIXING UNIT

A. Battery box
B. Warning horn
C. Fuel filter
D. Drain plug
E. Tip-over plate
F. Control module
G. Battery test button
H. Fill cap
I. Inlet (gasoline)
J. Outlet (gasoline and oil mixture)

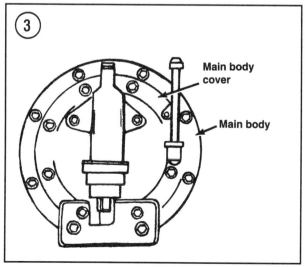

Main body cover

Main body

season, or as required whenever excessive sediment is noted.

1. Disconnect the inlet and outlet hoses from the AutoBlend unit. Remove the unit from the boat.

2. Remove the cover from the AutoBlend unit.

3. Remove the 2 screws securing the tip-over plate (E, **Figure 2**). Remove the tip-over plate.

4. Remove the 2 screws securing the top of the fuel filter. Remove the filter by pulling straight out from the AutoBlend unit.

5. Inspect the filter O-rings and replace if swelling, cracking or deterioration is noted.

6. To install the filter, lubricate the filter O-rings with 2-stroke engine oil. Install the filter into position, then install the 2 screws and washers at the top of the filter. Tighten the screws to 30 in.-lb. (3.4 N·m).

7. Install the tip-over plate. Secure the plate with 2 screws and washers. Tighten the screws to 30 in.-lb. (3.4 N·m).

Diaphragm Removal/Installation

The AutoBlend diaphragm should be removed and inspected once per year. To remove the diaphragm, proceed as follows:

1. Disconnect the inlet and outlet hoses from the AutoBlend unit. Remove the unit from the boat.

2. Remove the battery box from the unit, but do not disconnect the wires.

3. Remove the warning horn from the unit, but do not disconnect the horn wires.

4. Remove the fuel filter as described in this chapter.

5. Remove the electronic control module, but do not disconnect the module wires.

6. Drain the reservoir as described in this chapter.

7. Remove the 8 screws securing the main body cover to the main body. See **Figure 3**. Note the location of all brackets for reference during reassembly. Remove the main body cover from the main body.

11

8. Remove the clip securing the diaphragm to the actuating shaft, then remove the diaphragm from the main body. See **Figure 4**.

9. Inspect the diaphragm for deterioration, swelling, cracking or other damage. Replace the diaphragm if any defects are noted.

10. To install the diaphragm, install the diaphragm into the main body making sure the diaphragm outer rib is properly seated in the main body groove.

11. Install the clip onto the shaft (**Figure 4**). Be certain the clip properly engages the groove in the shaft.

12. Install the main body cover onto the main body. Make sure the drain screw is facing the bottom of the unit.

13. Install the cover brackets in their original locations. Install, but do not tighten the bracket retaining screws.

14. Install the battery box bracket and secure with the screw and washer. Do not tighten the screw.

15. Install the fuel filter and tip-over plate. Do not tighten the tip-over plate screws.

16. Using a crossing pattern, tighten all screws evenly to 30 in.-lb. (3.4 N•m).

17. Complete the remaining reassembly by reversing the disassembly procedure.

CONSTANT RATIO OIL INJECTION (40 HP AND 50-60 [SERIAL NO. D000750-ON] HP MODELS)

A constant-ratio oil injection system is standard on 40 hp models equipped with electric start and all 50-60 hp models (serial No. D000750-on). Oil injection is optional on 1990 40 hp models with manual start. The injection system delivers a constant 50:1 fuel and oil mixture at all engine speeds and load conditions.

Operation

Oil is delivered to the oil pump from an engine mounted oil reservoir (**Figure 5**). Reservoir capacity is 0.935 gal. (3.54 L) on 40 hp models and 3 qts. (2.8 L) on 50 and 60 hp models. The reservoir is equipped with a low-oil sensor which activates a warning horn should the oil level drop to 7.5 fl. oz. (225 mL) on 40 hp models or 14.5 fl. oz. (435 mL) on 50-60 hp models. A full oil reservoir should provide approximately 7 hours of operation at wide open throttle on 40 hp models or 10.5 hours of operation at wide-open throttle on 50-60 hp models. After the low-oil warning system is activated, the remaining oil should provide approximately 30 minutes of wide-open throttle operation on 40 hp models and 1-1/2 hours of wide-open throttle operation on 50 and 60 hp models. The reservoir is equipped with a sight gauge to determine the oil level visually without removing the engine cover. A check-valve vent is provided for atmospheric venting of the reservoir and to prevent oil leakage when the outboard motor is tilted up.

The system is equipped with an electronic warning module which briefly activates the warning horn as a self test each time the ignition switch is turned on. The module will activate the warning horn if a low oil signal is received from

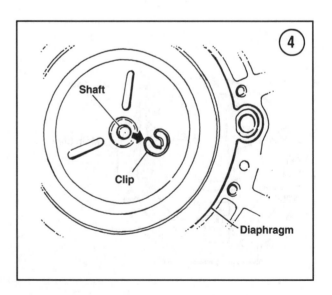
Shaft
Clip
Diaphragm

the low-oil sensor, or if the engine temperature exceeds 300°F (65°C).

The oil injection pump is driven by a gear on the crankshaft and delivers a constant 50:1 fuel and oil mixture to the power head. The pump injects oil into the fuel stream ahead of the fuel pump. See **Figure 5**.

A 2 psi (13.8 kPa) check valve is installed in the fuel line between the fuel line connector and the oil pump discharge line. See **Figure 5**. The check valve is used to prevent gasoline from entering the pump discharge line.

CAUTION
Fuel pressure must not exceed 2 psi (13.8 kPa). If using an electric fuel pump, install a pressure regulator between the pump and power head and adjust the regulator at 2 psi (13.8 kPa) maximum.

Break-In Procedure

To provide the additional lubrication required during the power head break-in period (initial 15 gallons of fuel), a 50:1 fuel and oil mixture

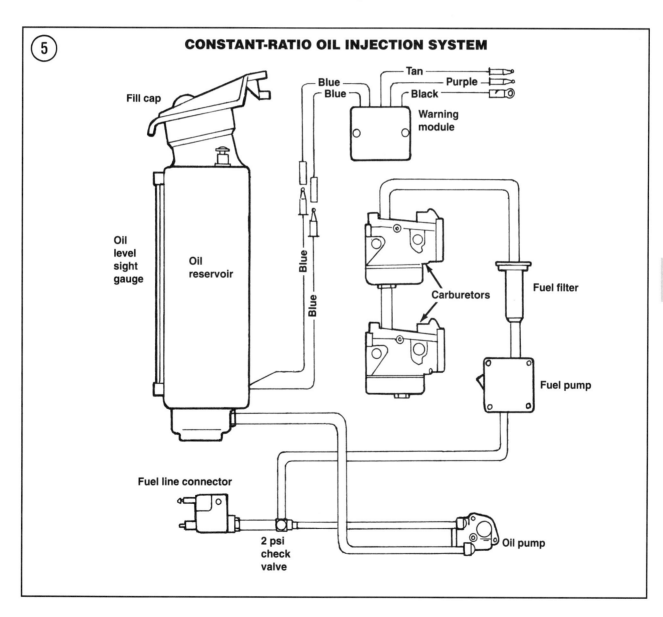

5 **CONSTANT-RATIO OIL INJECTION SYSTEM**

Fill cap

Oil level sight gauge

Oil reservoir

Blue
Blue

Blue

Blue

Tan
Purple
Black

Warning module

Carburetors

Fuel filter

Fuel pump

Fuel line connector

2 psi check valve

Oil pump

11

should be added to the fuel tank and consumed in combination with the lubricant supplied by the oil injection system. After the break-in period, ensure the injection system is functioning properly (oil level in reservoir diminishing), then switch to straight gasoline in the fuel tank. This break-in procedure applies to new or rebuilt power heads.

Low-Oil Warning System Troubleshooting

If a malfunction is suspected in the oil injection system (warning horn sounds), immediately stop the engine and check the oil level in the engine mounted reservoir. If the oil is low, fill the reservoir with a recommended oil.

> *CAUTION*
> *If an oil injection system malfunction is suspected, do not operate the outboard on straight gasoline. Connect the power head to a remote fuel tank containing a 50:1 fuel and oil mixture.*

If warning horn does not activate briefly when the ignition switch is turned ON

1. Disconnect the warning module tan/blue wire from the overheat sensor located in the cylinder head.
2. Ground the warning module wire to the engine using a suitable jumper wire. The warning horn should activate when the wire is grounded (ignition switch ON).
   a. If the warning horn does not activate, check the tan/blue wire between the warning horn and power head for an open circuit. If the tan/blue wire is good, replace the horn.
   b. Check all warning module wires for clean tight connections.

If warning horn remains on after the ignition switch is ON

1. Turn the ignition key to the ON position.

2. Disconnect the engine overheat sensor tan/blue wire at the bullet connector. If the warning horn stops when the wire is disconnected, the engine overheat sensor is defective and should be replaced.

If the warning horn activates intermediately when the engine is running and the oil reservoir is full:
1. Disconnect the 2 blue low-oil sensor wires at the bullet connectors.
2. Connect an ohmmeter between the 2 blue wires.
   a. No continuity should be present with the reservoir full.
   b. If continuity is noted, the low-oil sensor is defective and should be replaced.

If all previous tests are acceptable, replace the warning module and repeat the test procedure.

INJECTION SYSTEM SERVICE

Bleeding Injection Pump

If air is present in the oil pump inlet hose, proceed as follows to bleed air:
1. Place a shop towel below the oil pump to absorb oil.

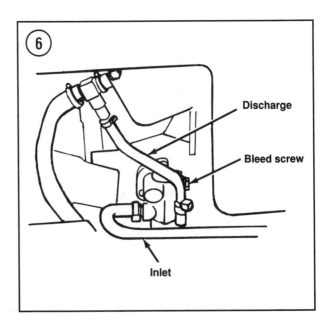

2. Loosen the oil pump bleed screw 3-4 turns (**Figure 6**).

3. Allow oil to flow from the bleed screw until no air bubbles are noted in the inlet hose.

4. Tighten the bleed screw to 25 in.-lb. (2.8 N•m).

If air is present in the pump discharge hose, pour a 50:1 fuel:oil mixture into the fuel tank. Start the engine and run at idle until no air bubbles are noted in the discharge hose.

Warning Module Removal/Installation

1. Disconnect the battery cables from the battery. Place the ignition switch in the OFF position.

2. Remove the engine cover.

3. 40 hp—Remove the 6 screws securing the electrical access cover and remove the cover.

4. Disconnect the warning module purple, tan and blue wires at their bullet connectors.

NOTE
The warning module is located adjacent to the switchbox on 40 hp models and in

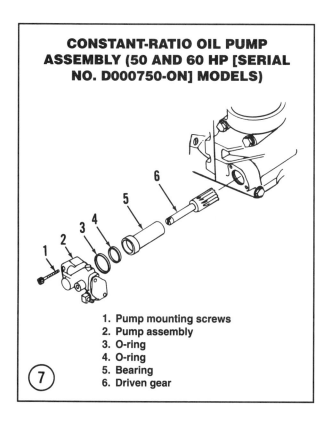

CONSTANT-RATIO OIL PUMP ASSEMBLY (50 AND 60 HP [SERIAL NO. D000750-ON] MODELS)

⑦

1. **Pump mounting screws**
2. **Pump assembly**
3. **O-ring**
4. **O-ring**
5. **Bearing**
6. **Driven gear**

the lower cowl adjacent to the cowl mounted trim switch on 50-60 hp models.

5. Remove the warning module mounting screws. Disconnect the black module ground wire (under mounting screw) and remove the module.

6. Installation is the reverse of removal. Make sure the black module ground wire is secured to 1 mounting screw.

Oil Reservoir Removal/Installation

1. Disconnect the battery cables from the battery.

2. Remove the engine upper cowl.

3. Remove the flywheel cover.

4. 50-60 hp—Remove the starter motor upper mounting bracket.

5A. 40 hp—Tilt the oil reservoir sufficiently to access the bottom of the reservoir.

    a. Remove the screw securing the low-oil sensor to the bottom of the reservoir. Remove the sensor.

    b. Disconnect the oil outlet hose from the reservoir, then remove the reservoir from the outboard.

5B. 50-60 hp—Disconnect the blue low-oil sensor wires at their bullet connectors. Disconnect the oil outlet hose, then remove the reservoir from the outboard. If necessary, remove the low-oil sensor from the reservoir.

6. Installation is the reverse of removal. Clamp the oil hose to the reservoir outlet using a new sta-strap.

7. Bleed the injection system as described in this chapter.

Oil Pump Removal/Installation

Refer to Chapter Eight for oil pump drive gear removal/installation procedures. Refer to **Figure 7** for this procedure.

11

1. Disconnect the oil inlet and discharge hoses from the pump.

2. Remove the pump mounting screws.

3. Remove the pump assembly from the power head. If the pump driven gear remains in the engine block, retrieve it using needlenose pliers.

4. To install the pump, thoroughly lubricate the driven gear shaft with Quicksilver Needle Bearing Assembly Grease (part No. 92-42649A-1). Insert the driven gear into the bearing assembly, making sure the gear properly engages the pump shaft.

5. Install new O-rings onto the pump. Lubricate the O-rings with Quicksilver Needle Bearing Assembly Grease.

6. Install the pump assembly onto the power head. Apply Loctite 271 to the threads of the pump mounting screws. Install the screws and tighten to 45 in.-lb. (5.1 N·m).

7. Reconnect the oil inlet and discharge hoses to the pump. Securely clamp the hoses to the pump using new sta-straps.

8. Perform oil pump bleeding procedure as described in this chapter.

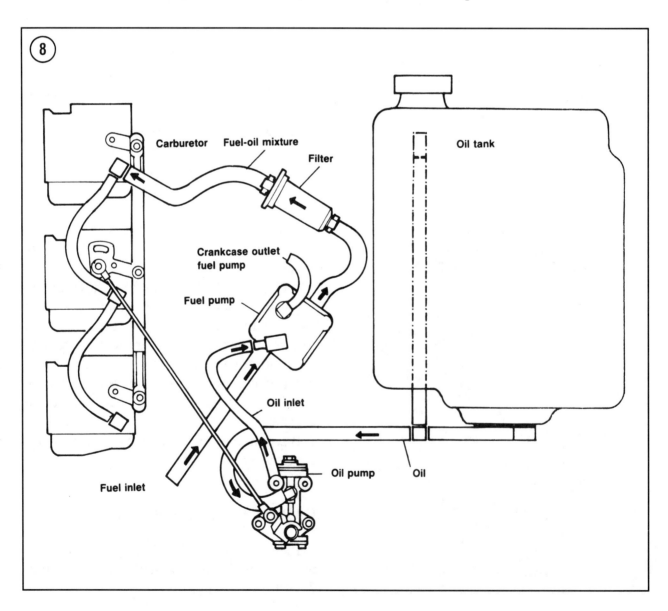

VARIABLE-RATIO OIL INJECTION (75-115 HP MODELS)

A variable-ratio oil injection system is used on 75-115 hp models. The injection system delivers oil to the power head relative to engine and speed and throttle position. A linkage rod connects the oil pump control lever to the throttle linkage and varies the oil pump stroke according to throttle

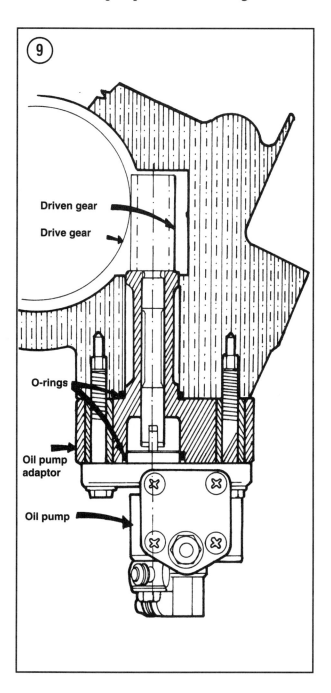

opening. The fuel:oil ratio is varied from approximately 80:1 at idle to approximately 50:1 at wide-open throttle.

Operation

Refer to **Figure 8**. An engine-mounted oil reservoir gravity feeds oil to the oil pump. Oil reservoir capacity is 1 gal. (3.8 L) on 75 and 90 hp models and 1.4 gal. (5.3 L) on 100 and 115 hp models. A full reservoir should provide approximately 6 hours (75-90 hp) or 5 hours (100-115 hp) of operation at wide-open throttle. The reservoir is equipped with a low-oil sensor that activates a warning horn should the oil level in the reservoir drop to 1 qt. (0.95 L). After the warning horn activates, the remaining oil should provide approximately 1 hour (75-90 hp) or 50 minutes (100-115 hp) of wide-open throttle operation. A reservoir sight gauge is provided to check the oil level visually without removing the engine cowl.

A crankshaft-driven oil injection pump injects oil directly into the fuel pump. See **Figure 8** for injection system flow circuit, **Figure 9** for a cross-sectional view of the oil pump assembly and **Figure 10** for an exploded view of the pump assembly. The variable-ratio oil pump delivers oil to the power head relative to crankshaft speed and throttle position. A linkage rod connects the oil pump control lever to the throttle linkage (**Figure 8**).

Should the oil level in the reservoir drop to approximately 1 qt. (0.95 L), a magnetic float (low-oil sensor) completes the circuit between the sensor leads, causing the warning horn to activate. The warning horn also is connected to the power head temperature sensor. If the warning horn sounds, the oil level in the engine mounted reservoir is low or the power head is overheated. A warning horn test button (some 75-90 hp models) is located adjacent to the reservoir fill cap. With the ignition switch in the ON position, the warning horn should sound when

11

the button is depressed. On models without a warning horn test button (some 75-90 hp models and all 100-115 hp models), an electronic warning module (located on starboard side of engine block) monitors oil condition and engine temperature and activates the warning system if necessary.

Break-In Procedure

To provide the additional lubrication required during the power head break-in period (initial 15 gallons of fuel), a 50:1 fuel and oil mixture should be added to the fuel tank and consumed in combination with the lubricant supplied by the oil injection system. After the break-in period, ensure the injection system is functioning properly (oil level in reservoir diminishing), then switch to straight gasoline in the fuel tank. This break-in procedure applies to new or rebuilt power heads.

WARNING HORN SYSTEM

The warning horn system consists of the ignition switch, warning horn, low-oil sensor, engine temperature sensor and warning horn test button. On models not equipped with a test button, a warning module is used to monitor oil level and engine temperature.

To test the warning system on models equipped with a test button, place the ignition switch in the ON position (engine not running). Depress the test button located adjacent to the oil reservoir fill cap. If the system is operating properly, the warning horn will sound. On models without a test button, the warning horn should activate briefly each time the ignition switch is turned to the ON position.

Warning System Troubleshooting (Models Without Test Button)

If a malfunction is suspected in the oil injection system (warning horn sounds), immediately stop the engine and check the oil level in the engine mounted reservoir. If the oil is low, fill the reservoir with a recommended oil.

> *CAUTION*
> *If an oil injection system malfunction is suspected, do not operate the outboard on straight gasoline. Connect the power head to a remote fuel tank containing a 50:1 fuel and oil mixture.*

Warning horn does not activate briefly when ignition switch is turned ON

1. Disconnect the tan wire from the main engine harness at the terminal block.

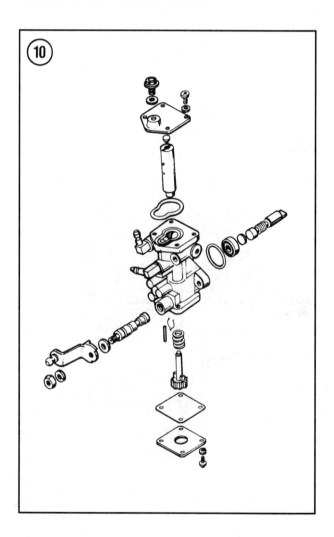

2. Ground the tan lead to a good engine ground. The warning horn should activate. If not, proceed as follows:

   a. Check the tan wire for an open circuit between the warning horn and the engine.

   b. Check all warning module connections for looseness or corrosion. Repair as necessary.

   c. If the tan wire and all connections are acceptable, replace the warning horn or warning module.

Warning horn remains on after ignition switch is turned ON

1. Disconnect the black temperature sensor wire from the terminal block.

2. Place the ignition switch in the ON position (engine not running).

   a. If the warning horn stops, replace the power head temperature sensor.

   b. If the warning horn continues to sound, replace the warning module as described in this chapter.

Warning horn activates with engine running/reservoir oil level full

1. Disconnect the 2 light blue low-oil sensor wires from their bullet connectors.

2. Connect an ohmmeter between the sensor wires.

3. With the oil reservoir full, no continuity should be present between the sensor wires. If continuity is noted, replace the low-oil sensor.

4. If no continuity is noted in Step 3, perform oil pump output test as described in this chapter.

5. If oil pump output is as specified, the warning module is defective and must be replaced as described in this chapter.

Low-Oil Sensor Test (Models Equipped with Warning System Test Button)

Refer to **Figure 11** for this procedure.

1. Disconnect the low-oil sensor tan and black wires from the terminal block.

2. Connect an ohmmeter between the sensor wires (black and tan).

3. With the reservoir 1/2 full to full, no continuity should be noted between the tan and black wires. If continuity is noted, check the sensor float for sticking. Make sure the sensor magnet is not loose. If the float is not sticking and the magnet is not loose, replace the sensor.

4. With the reservoir empty, continuity should be present between the tan and black wires. If no continuity is noted, check the sensor float for sticking. If the float is not sticking, replace the low-oil sensor.

INJECTION SYSTEM SERVICE

Carburetor and Oil Pump Synchronization

Refer to Chapter Five for synchronizing and adjusting procedures.

Bleeding Injection System

If air enters the oil injection system, or if any injection system components are replaced, the air must be purged (bled) from the pump and oil lines before operating the outboard motor.

To bleed air from the injection pump inlet line, proceed as follows:

1. Place a shop towel under the oil pump to absorb spilled oil.

2. Loosen the pump bleed screw (**Figure 8**) 3-4 turns and allow oil to drain from around the screw threads.

3. Continue bleeding until no air bubbles are noted in the oil pump inlet line.

4. Tighten the bleed screw to 25 in.-lb. (2.8 N•m).

11

To bleed air from the pump discharge line, connect a remote fuel tank containing a 50:1 fuel and oil mixture to the power head. Start the engine and run at idle speed until no air bubbles are present in the pump discharge line.

Injection Pump Output Test

Obtain an accurate graduated container to perform the following test.

1. Connect a remote fuel tank containing a 50:1 fuel and oil mixture to the power head. If during the power head break-in period, the tank should contain a 25:1 mixture.

2. Place the outboard motor into a test tank or attach a suitable flushing device to the motor.

3. Remove the engine cowl.

4. Disconnect the oil pump discharge line (**Figure 8**) from the fuel pump fitting. Plug the fuel pump fitting.

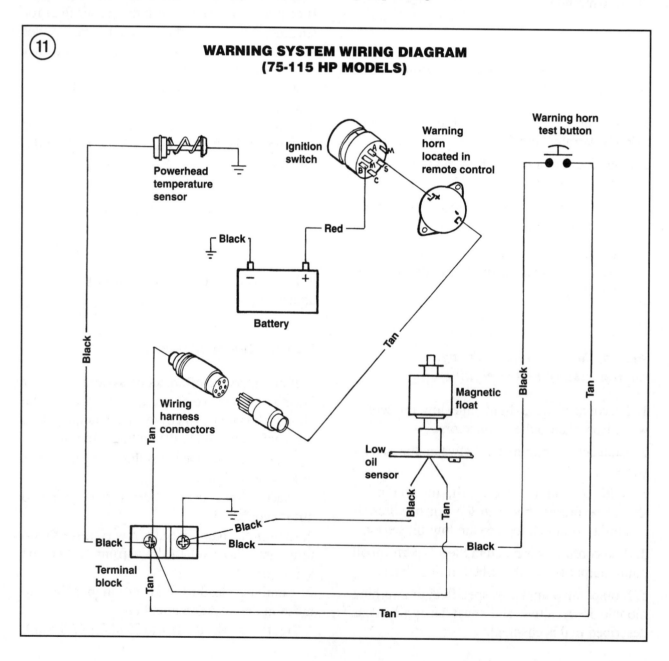

WARNING SYSTEM WIRING DIAGRAM
(75-115 HP MODELS)

5. Remove the oil pump linkage rod from the pump control lever.

6. Rotate the pump control lever to the wide-open throttle position (fully counterclockwise).

7. Connect an accurate shop tachometer to the power head as described in the tachometer instructions.

8. Insert the disconnected end of the pump discharge line into the graduated container.

9. Start the outboard motor and run at 700 rpm for exactly 15 minutes.

NOTE
Injection pump output specifications are based on tests performed at 70°F (21°C). If ambient temperature is more or less, actual pump output may vary from that specified.

10. Stop the engine and check the graduated container. On 75-90 hp models, pump output should be 18.7 cc minimum. On 100-115 hp models, pump output should be 25.5 cc minimum.

11. If injection pump output is less than specified, replace the pump assembly as described in this chapter.

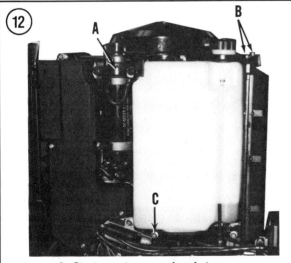

A. Starter motor upper bracket
B. Upper support bracket screws
C. Aft support bracket screw

12. Reconnect the injection pump control linkage. Reconnect the pump discharge line to the fuel pump. Bleed the injection system as described in this chapter.

Warning Module Removal/Installation

The warning module (on models so equipped) is located on the starboard side of the engine block.

1. Disconnect the 2 warning module blue wires from the low-oil sensor at the bullet connectors.

2. Disconnect the module purple wire at its bullet connector.

3. Disconnect the module tan and black wires from the terminal block.

4. Remove the 2 module mounting screws and remove the module.

5. Installation is the reverse of removal. Tighten the module mounting screws securely.

Engine Mounted Oil Reservoir Removal/Installation

Refer to **Figure 12** for this procedure.

1. Remove the engine cowl.

2. Disconnect the reservoir outlet line from the "T" fitting and drain the reservoir into a suitable container.

3. Disconnect the low-oil sensor wires at the bullet connectors located at the bottom of the reservoir.

4. Remove the starter motor upper mounting bracket.

5. Remove the 2 screws securing the reservoir upper support bracket.

6. Remove the reservoir lower support screw and remove the reservoir.

7. Reverse the removal procedure to install the reservoir. Tighten the support bracket screws to 180 in.-lb. (20.3 N•m). Tighten the starter motor bracket bolts to 175 in.-lb. (19.8 N•m). Securely clamp the reservoir outlet line to the fitting using a new sta-strap.

11

Oil Injection Pump Removal/Installation

1. Remove the engine cowl.

2. Disconnect the pump inlet and outlet lines from the pump. See **Figure 8**.

3. Remove 2 screws securing the pump assembly to the power head. Remove the pump, pump adapter and pump driven gear as an assembly. See **Figure 9**.

4. Remove and discard the O-rings from the pump and pump adapter.

5. Install new O-rings onto the oil pump and pump adapter.

6. Lubricate the driven gear shaft with Quicksilver Needle Bearing Assembly Grease (part No. 92-42649A-1), then insert the gear into the pump adapter.

7. Install the oil pump onto the adapter making sure the pump shaft properly engages the driven gear.

8. Install the pump, adapter and driven gear to the power head as an assembly. Tighten the pump mounting screws to 60 in.-lb. (6.8 N•m).

9. Connect the oil lines to the pump. Securely clamp the lines using new sta-straps.

10. Bleed the oil injection system as described in this chapter.

VARIABLE-RATIO OIL INJECTION (V6 MODELS)

CAUTION
Fuel pressure at the power head must not exceed 2 psi (13.8 kPa). If an electric fuel pump is used on oil injected models, install a pressure regulator between the pump and power head. Adjust the regulator to 2 psi (13.8 kPa) maximum.

All V6 models are equipped with a variable-ratio oil injection system. The crankshaft-driven oil injection pump delivers oil to the power head relative to engine speed and throttle opening. A linkage rod connects the pump control lever to the throttle linkage. The fuel:oil ratio is varied from approximately 100:1 (80:1 on 250-275 hp) at idle speeds to approximately 50:1 at wide-open throttle.

Operation

Refer to **Figure 13** (135-200 hp) and **Figure 14** (250-275 hp). A 3 gallon (11.4 L) remote oil tank supplies oil to the engine-mounted oil reservoir. The remote oil tank is pressurized by crankcase pressure through a one-way check valve, feeding oil from the remote tank into the engine-mounted reservoir. The oil pickup tube in the remote tank is equipped with a filter screen to prevent dirt or other contamination from entering the injection system. Should the remote tank become empty, the engine-mounted reservoir contains sufficient oil for approximately 30 minutes of wide-open throttle operation on 135-200 hp models or 60 minutes of wide-open throttle operation on 250 and 275 hp models.

A 2 psi (13.8 kPa) check valve (5, **Figure 13** or **Figure 14**) is installed in the oil line between the remote tank and engine-mounted reservoir. If an obstruction should occur in the oil line between the tank and reservoir, the check valve (5) will unseat, allowing air to enter the system. This will prevent the oil injection pump from creating a vacuum within the reservoir and oil lines.

The crankshaft-driven oil injection pump injects oil into the fuel stream just ahead of the fuel pump (lower pump on 250-275 hp models). Refer to **Figure 9** for a cross-sectional view of the oil pump and drive assembly. Refer to **Figure 10** for an exploded view of the oil pump assembly, typical. A linkage rod connects the oil pump control lever to the throttle linkage to meter the oil flow according to throttle opening and engine speed.

A 2 psi (13.8 kPa) check valve (6, **Figure 13** or **Figure 14**) is used to prevent gasoline from being forced into the oil lines.

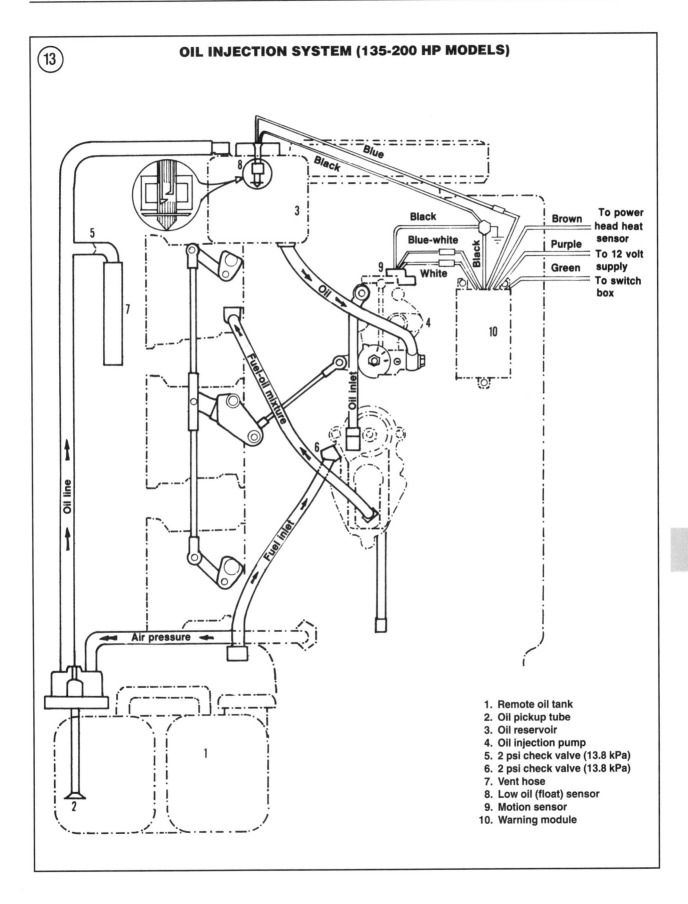

⑬ **OIL INJECTION SYSTEM (135-200 HP MODELS)**

Blue

Black

3

5

7

Black

Blue-white

White

Black

8

9

4

10

Brown — To power head heat sensor

Purple — To 12 volt supply

Green — To switch box

Oil

Oil inlet

Fuel-oil mixture

6

Fuel inlet

Oil line

Air pressure

1

2

1. Remote oil tank
2. Oil pickup tube
3. Oil reservoir
4. Oil injection pump
5. 2 psi check valve (13.8 kPa)
6. 2 psi check valve (13.8 kPa)
7. Vent hose
8. Low oil (float) sensor
9. Motion sensor
10. Warning module

11

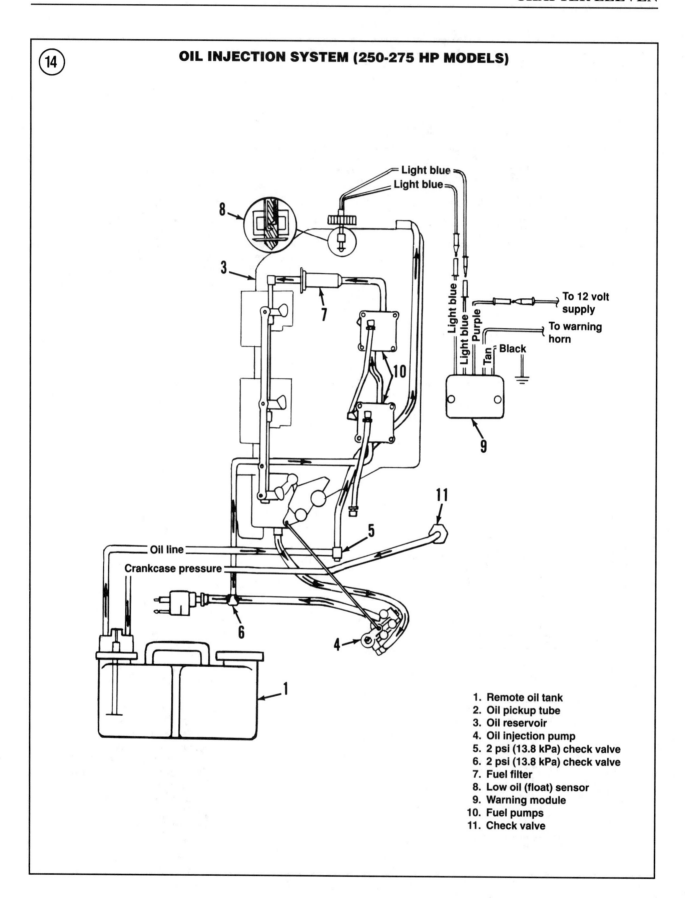

OIL INJECTION SYSTEM (250-275 HP MODELS)

(14)

Light blue
Light blue

8

3

7

10

Light blue

Light blue
Purple
Tan
Black

To 12 volt
supply

To warning
horn

9

11

5

Oil line

Crankcase pressure

6

4

1

1. Remote oil tank
2. Oil pickup tube
3. Oil reservoir
4. Oil injection pump
5. 2 psi (13.8 kPa) check valve
6. 2 psi (13.8 kPa) check valve
7. Fuel filter
8. Low oil (float) sensor
9. Warning module
10. Fuel pumps
11. Check valve

The engine-mounted reservoir is equipped with a float-type low-oil sensor built into the reservoir fill cap. If the oil level in the reservoir becomes low, the sensor signals the warning module to activate the warning horn.

Models 135-200 hp are equipped with an injection pump motion sensor (9, **Figure 13**) that detects the rotation of the pump drive system. If the pump drive should become inoperative, the motion sensor will signal the warning module to activate the warning horn. As a self-test feature, the warning module briefly activates the warning horn each time the ignition switch is turned from OFF to ON (engine not running), indicating the warning system is functioning.

Break-In Procedure

To provide the additional lubrication required during the power head break-in period (first 30 gallons of fuel), a 50:1 fuel and oil mixture should be added to the fuel tank and consumed in combination with the lubricant supplied by the oil injection system. After the break-in period, ensure the injection system is functioning properly (oil level diminishing), then switch to straight gasoline in the fuel tank. This break-in procedure applies to new or rebuilt power heads.

WARNING HORN SYSTEM

The warning horn system consists of the ignition switch, low-oil sensor, power head temperature sensor, oil pump motion sensor (135-200 hp models), warning module and related circuitry.

Each time the ignition switch is turned to ON (engine not running) from the OFF position, the warning module should briefly activate the warning horn to indicate the warning system is functioning. If an oil injection malfunction occurs, the warning module will trigger an intermittent tone from the warning horn. If the power head overheats, the module will trigger a continuous tone from the horn.

Warning System Troubleshooting

If the warning horn should activate during operation, immediately shut down the engine and check the oil level in the engine-mounted reservoir. If necessary, fill the remote tank with a recommended oil. If the reservoir oil level is low, but the remote tank is full, proceed as follows:

1. Check the O-rings or gaskets in the reservoir fill cap for cracking, deterioration or other damage. Replace the O-rings or gaskets as necessary. Make sure the fill caps are screwed tightly on the reservoir and remote tank. Air leakage at the remote tank will prevent the movement of oil from the tank to the reservoir. Leakage at the reservoir will result in oil spillage.

2. Check the oil line between the remote tank and reservoir for kinks, restrictions or leakage. Repair or replace the line as required.

3. Check the crankcase pressure line between the crankcase check valve and remote tank for kinks, restrictions or leakage. Make sure the crankcase one-way check valve is functioning properly.

4. Check the oil pickup tube and filter for restrictions. Clean or replace the tube or filter as necessary.

5. Check all oil lines for kinks, cracks, deterioration, leakage or other damage. Make sure all connections are tightly clamped.

Warning horn does not sound when ignition switch turned to ON position

1. Place the ignition switch in the ON position (engine not running).

2. Using a jumper wire, connect the tan (135-200 hp) or tan/blue (250-275 hp) wire at the terminal block to a good engine ground.

   a. The warning horn should sound. If not, check the tan or tan/blue wire for an open circuit between the horn and engine. If the wire is good, the horn may be defective.

11

b. Make sure all warning module connections are clean and tight.

c. If the horn and all wiring and connections are in acceptable condition, replace the warning module.

Warning horn continues to sound after the ignition switch is turned to ON position

1. Disconnect the black temperature sensor wire at the terminal block.

2. Place the ignition switch in the ON position.

a. If the horn sounds a continuous tone, the warning module is defective.

b. If the horn does not sound, the temperature sensor is defective. Replace the module or temperature sensor and retest.

Warning horn activates during operation—engine-mounted reservoir is full

1. Disconnect both low-oil sensor wires (blue and black [135-200 hp] or light blue [250-275 hp]).

2. Do not remove the reservoir fill cap.

3. Connect an ohmmeter between the disconnected sensor wires.

4. With the reservoir full, no continuity should be present between the sensor wires. If continuity is present, the low-oil sensor is defective.

WARNING
Prior to testing the motion sensor, disconnect all spark plug leads, ground the leads to the engine and remove the spark plugs.

5A. 135-200 hp (motion sensor):

a. Disconnect the white warning module wire at its bullet connector between the module and motion sensor. Connect a voltmeter between a good engine ground and the white wire from the module. Turn the ignition switch to the ON position and note the

voltmeter. The voltage should be 11-13 volts.

NOTE
Motion sensor wires must be connected during the remaining sensor tests.

b. Reconnect the white wire to the module. Insert a suitable probe into the blue/white wire bullet connection between the motion sensor and warning module. A paper clip or piece of wire is sufficient.

c. Connect a voltmeter between engine ground and the blue/white wire. Place the ignition switch in the ON position.

d. Using the emergency starting rope, rotate the flywheel while noting the voltmeter. The voltage should peak at 4-6 volts, then drop to less than 1.0 volt during every 2 revolutions of the flywheel.

e. If no voltage is noted, the motion sensor is defective or the oil pump drive is not turning. Check oil pump output as described in this chapter. If pump output is acceptable, replace the motion sensor as described in this chapter, then recheck the voltage.

5B. 250-275 hp—Check oil pump output as described in this chapter. If output is not as specified, check the pump drive system (drive and driven gears). If the drive system is good, replace the oil pump assembly.

INJECTION SYSTEM SERVICE

Carburetor and Injection Pump Synchronizing

Refer to Chapter Five for synchronizing and adjusting procedures.

Bleeding Injection System

If air enters the oil injection system from leakage or component replacement, it must be purged (bled) from the system before operating the outboard motor.

Bleeding injection pump

1. Place a shop towel under the oil pump to absorb spilled oil.

2. With the engine not running, loosen the bleed screw (**Figure 15**, typical) 3-4 turns.

3. Allow oil to drain from the bleed screw hole until no air bubbles are present in the oil.

Bleeding pump discharge line

In most cases, small amounts of air in the injection pump discharge line will be purged from the system during operation. If necessary, bleed the discharge line as follows:

1. Disconnect the linkage rod from the pump control lever. See **Figure 15**, typical.

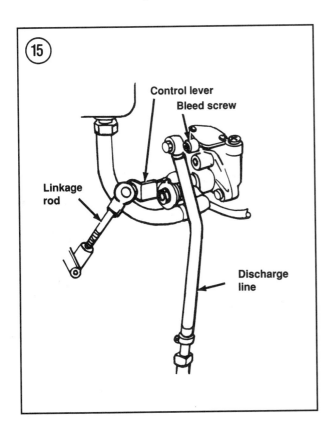

Control lever
Bleed screw
Linkage rod
Discharge line

2. Place the outboard into a test tank or attach a flushing device to the lower unit.

3. Start the outboard and allow to run at 1000-1500 rpm. Rotate the injection pump control lever to the fully clockwise position.

4. If necessary, gently pinch the fuel hose between the injection pump "T" fitting and remote fuel tank connector, causing the fuel pump to create a slight vacuum in the hose. This will quicken the purging process.

5. Continue running the outboard until all air is purged, then stop the engine and reconnect the linkage rod to the control lever.

Injection Pump Output Test (135-200 hp)

Obtain an accurate graduated container to perform the following test.

1. Connect a remote fuel tank containing a 50:1 fuel and oil mixture to the power head. If during the power head break-in period, the tank should contain a 25:1 mixture.

2. Place the outboard motor into a test tank or attach a suitable flushing device to the motor.

3. Remove the engine cowl.

4. Disconnect the oil pump (clear) discharge line from the fuel pump fitting. Plug the fuel pump fitting to prevent fuel leakage.

5. Connect an accurate shop tachometer to the power head as described in the tachometer instructions.

6. Insert the disconnected end of the pump discharge line into the graduated container.

7. Start the outboard motor and run at 1500 rpm for exactly 3 minutes. Stop the engine and note the pump output in the graduated container.

8. Empty the container. Disconnect the linkage rod from the injection pump control lever. See **Figure 15**. Rotate the control lever to the wide-open throttle position (fully counterclockwise), then repeat Step 6 and Step 7.

11

NOTE
Injection pump output specifications are based on tests performed at 70°F (21°C). If ambient temperature is more or less, actual pump output will vary from that specified.

9A. 135-175 hp—Injection pump output should be as follows:

   a. Linkage rod connected—6.1-7.5 cc.

   b. Linkage rod disconnected—15.3-18.7 cc.

9B. 200 hp—Injection pump output should be as follows:

   a. Linkage rod connected—7.4-9.0 cc.

   b. Linkage rod disconnected—17.3-21.1 cc.

10. If injection pump output is less than specified, replace the pump assembly as described in this chapter.

11. Reconnect the injection pump control linkage. Reconnect the pump discharge line to the fuel pump. Securely clamp all lines using new sta-straps. Bleed the injection system as described in this chapter.

Injection Pump Output Test (250 and 275 hp)

Obtain an accurate graduated container to perform the following test.

1. Connect a remote fuel tank containing a 50:1 fuel and oil mixture to the power head. If during the power head break-in period, the tank should contain a 25:1 mixture.

2. Place the outboard motor into a test tank or attach a suitable flushing device to the motor.

3. Remove the engine cowl.

4. Disconnect the oil pump discharge line (**Figure 15**) from the fuel pump fitting. Plug the fuel pump fitting.

5. Remove the oil pump linkage rod from the pump control lever. See **Figure 15**.

6. Rotate the pump control lever to the wide-open throttle position (fully counterclockwise).

7. Connect an accurate shop tachometer to the power head as described in the tachometer instructions.

8. Insert the disconnected end of the pump discharge line into the graduated container.

9. Start the outboard motor and run at 700 rpm for exactly 15 minutes.

NOTE
Injection pump output specifications are based on tests performed at 70°F (21°C). If ambient temperature is more or less, actual pump output will vary from that specified.

10. Stop the engine and check the graduated container. The minimum injection pump output is 61.25 cc.

11. If injection pump output is less than specified, replace the pump assembly as described in this chapter.

12. Reconnect the injection pump control linkage. Reconnect the pump discharge line to the fuel pump. Securely clamp the oil line with a new sta-strap. Bleed the injection system as described in this chapter.

Warning Module Removal/Installation (135-200 hp)

1. Disconnect the battery cables from the battery.

NOTE
Note the warning module wire routing for reference during installation.

2. Disconnect the warning module purple and tan wires from the terminal block located on the starboard side of the power head (above ignition plate).

3. Disconnect the module blue, blue/white and white wires at their bullet connectors.

NOTE
The green wire from the warning module may be connected to either switchbox. If connected to the inner switchbox, separate the switchboxes as described in Chapter Seven.

4. Disconnect the green module wire from the switchbox.

5. Disconnect the black module ground wire.

6. Remove the 3 module mounting screws and remove the module (**Figure 16**).

7. To install the module, apply Loctite 222 to the threads of the mounting screws. Install the module and tighten the 3 screws to 25 in.-lb. (2.8 N•m).

8. Connect the module wires at their respective locations. Route the module wires as noted during removal. Reconnect the battery cables to the battery.

Warning Module Removal/Installation (250 and 275 hp)

1. Disconnect the battery cables from the battery.

NOTE
Note the routing of the warning module wires for reference during installation.

2. Disconnect the light blue module wires from the engine mounted reservoir fill cap.

3. Disconnect the tan and black module wires from the terminal block located adjacent to the starter motor solenoid.

4. Disconnect the module purple wire at its bullet connector.

5. Remove the module mounting screws and remove the module.

6. To install the module, apply Loctite 222 to the threads of the mounting screws. Install the module and tighten the screws to 25 in.-lb. (2.8 N•m).

7. Connect the module wires. Route the wires as noted during removal. Reconnect the battery cables to the battery.

Engine Mounted Reservoir Removal/Installation

1. Disconnect the clear reservoir oil line at the oil pump. If the reservoir contains oil, plug the line to prevent leakage.

2. Disconnect the oil input line from the reservoir.

3. Disconnect the low-oil sensor wires or remove the fill cap from the reservoir.

4. Remove the reservoir mounting screws and remove the reservoir.

5. Install the reservoir by reversing the removal procedure. Apply Loctite 222 to the threads of the mounting screws. Tighten the screws to 25 in.-lb. (2.8 N•m) on 135-200 hp models or 150 in.-lb. (16.9 N•m) on 250 and 275 hp models. Install the reservoir inlet and outlet lines. Securely clamp the oil lines using new sta-straps. Bleed the injection system as described in this chapter.

Oil Injection Pump Removal/Installation

1. Disconnect the inlet and outlet oil lines from the injection pump. Plug the lines to prevent leakage or contamination.

2. Disconnect the linkage rod from the pump control lever.

3. Remove the 2 screws securing the pump to the cylinder block, then remove the pump assembly.

4A. 135-200 hp models—remove the bushing and seal assembly (**Figure 17**) from the pump.

11

If the worm gear is removed with the bushing, be sure to retrieve the thrust washer located between the pump and worm gear. Remove and discard the O-rings from the bushing. If the seal inside the bushing is defective, the bushing assembly must be replaced.

4B. 250 and 275 hp—If necessary, remove the pump adapter and driven gear from engine cylinder block. See **Figure 18**. Remove and discard the O-rings (2 and 5, **Figure 18**).

5. Inspect all components for excessive wear or other damage. If the teeth on the driven gear are damaged, the pump drive gear on the crankshaft must be replaced. See Chapter Eight.

6. Install new O-rings prior to installing the pump. Lubricate the O-rings with 2-stroke engine oil.

7A. 135-200 hp—Install the worm gear into the pump assembly. Be certain the thrust washer is properly positioned between the pump body and worm gear.

7B. 250 and 275 hp—If removed, install the pump driven gear and adapter into the cylinder block.

8. Apply Loctite 271 to the threads of the pump mounting screws. Install the pump and tighten the screws to 25 in.-lb. (2.8 N•m) on 135-200 hp models and 50 in.-lb. (5.6 N•m).

9. Reconnect the oil inlet and outlet lines to the pump. Securely clamp the lines using new sta-straps.

10. Reconnect the linkage rod to the pump control lever.

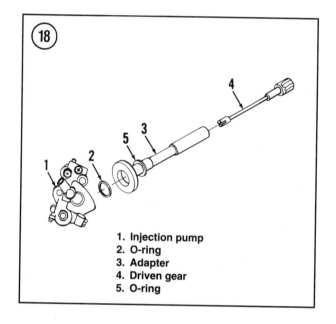

18

1. Injection pump
2. O-ring
3. Adapter
4. Driven gear
5. O-ring

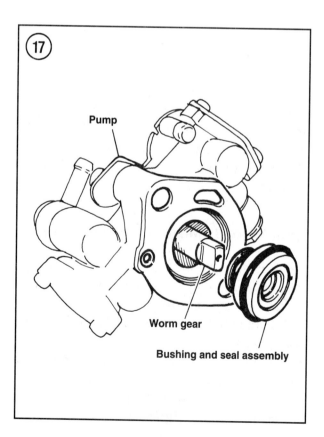

17

Pump

Worm gear

Bushing and seal assembly

19

11. Bleed the injection system as described in this chapter. Check carburetor and oil pump synchronization as described in Chapter Five.

Motion Sensor Removal/Installation

1. Remove the screw securing the motion sensor (**Figure 19**) to the injection pump.

2. Disconnect the sensor white and blue/white wires from the warning module. Remove the sensor black ground wire from the engine ground.

3. Remove the motion sensor.

4. Install the motion sensor by reversing the removal procedure. Tighten the sensor mounting screw to 30 in.-lb. (3.4 N•m).

11

Chapter Twelve

Manual Rewind Starters

Manual start models are equipped with a rope-operated rewind starter assembly. The starter assembly is mounted above the flywheel on all models. Pulling the rope handle causes the starter rope pulley to rotate, engage the flywheel and turn the engine.

Rewind starters are relatively trouble free; a broken or frayed rope is the most common failure. This chapter covers starter removal, disassembly, cleaning and inspection, reassembly and installation.

3 AND 3.3 HP MODELS

Starter Removal/Installation

Refer to **Figure 1** for this procedure.

1. Remove 3 screws securing the rewind starter assembly to the power head. Lift the starter off the power head.
2. To install the starter, place the starter onto the power head. If necessary, extend the starter rope slightly to engage the ratchet with the starter cup.

3. Install the starter mounting screws. Tighten the screws securely.

Starter Disassembly/Reassembly

Refer to **Figure 1** for this procedure.

1. Remove the starter as described in this chapter. Untie the knot securing the rope handle to the rope. While securely holding the rope pulley from turning, remove the handle from the rope.
2. Slowly, allow the rope pulley to unwind (clockwise), releasing the tension on the rewind spring.
3. Invert the starter and remove the clip (10, **Figure 1**), thrust washer (9) and friction plate (8).
4. Remove the return spring (7, **Figure 1**), cover (6) and friction spring (5).
5. Carefully lift the rope pulley approximately 1/2 in. (13 mm) out of the housing, then turn the pulley back and forth to disengage the rewind spring from the pulley.

6. Remove the pulley from the housing. Remove the rope from the pulley.

NOTE
Do not remove the rewind spring from the starter housing unless replacement is necessary. Wear suitable hand and eye protection when removing or installing rewind spring.

7. If rewind spring replacement is necessary, place the starter housing upright (rewind spring facing down) on a suitable bench. Tap the top of

the housing until the rewind spring falls out and unwinds inside the housing.

8. To reassemble the starter, lubricate the rewind spring area of the starter housing with Quicksilver 2-4-C Marine Lubricant.

9. The rewind spring must be installed into the starter housing in a counterclockwise direction, starting from the outer coil as shown in **Figure 2**. Make sure the hook in the outer coil of the spring is properly engaged with the catch in the housing as shown.

10. Cut the new starter rope to the same length as the old rope.

11. Insert the rope through the hole in the pulley. Tie a suitable knot in the rope, then push the knot into the recess of the pulley.

12. Wind the starter rope onto the pulley in a clockwise direction as viewed from the rewind spring side of the pulley.

13. Install the pulley and rope assembly into the housing. Make sure the hook on the inner coil of the rewind spring properly engages the slot in the pulley.

14. Install the ratchet (4, **Figure 1**), friction spring (5) and cover (6) onto the starter housing center shaft.

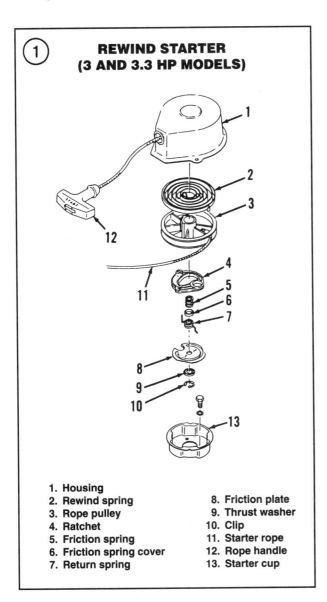

**REWIND STARTER
(3 AND 3.3 HP MODELS)**

1. Housing
2. Rewind spring
3. Rope pulley
4. Ratchet
5. Friction spring
6. Friction spring cover
7. Return spring
8. Friction plate
9. Thrust washer
10. Clip
11. Starter rope
12. Rope handle
13. Starter cup

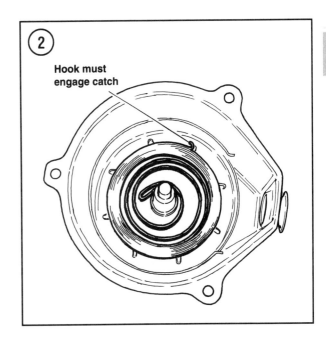

Hook must engage catch

12

15. Hook one end of the return spring into the friction plate and the other end of the spring into the ratchet. See **Figure 3**. Install the friction plate and return spring onto the center shaft. Install the spacer (9, **Figure 1**) and the clip (10).

16. Place the rope into the notch (**Figure 4**) in the pulley. While holding the rope in the notch, rotate the rope pulley 3 turns counterclockwise to apply tension on the rewind spring.

17. Hold the rope securely, then pass the rope through the rope guide in the housing and into the rope handle. Fix the handle to the rope with a knot (**Figure 5**).

18. Install the starter assembly onto the power head as described in this chapter.

4 AND 5 HP MODELS

Starter Removal/Installation

Refer to **Figure 6** for this procedure.

1. Remove the engine cowl.

2. Disconnect the interlock rod from the lever (21, **Figure 6**).

3. Remove the 3 screws holding the starter assembly to the power head. Lift the starter off the power head.

4. Installation is the reverse of removal. Tighten the 3 starter mounting screws to 70 in.-lb. (7.9 N.m).

Disassembly

Refer to **Figure 6** for this procedure.

NOTE
*The starter rope cap be replaced without complete starter disassembly. Refer to **Reassembly**.*

1. Remove the starter assembly as described in this chapter.

2. Fully extend the starter rope, then securely hold the rope pulley from turning.

3. While holding the pulley from turning, lift the knot in the rope from the recess in the pulley. Untie or cut off the knot, then allow the rope pulley to unwind slowly, relieving the tension on the rewind spring.

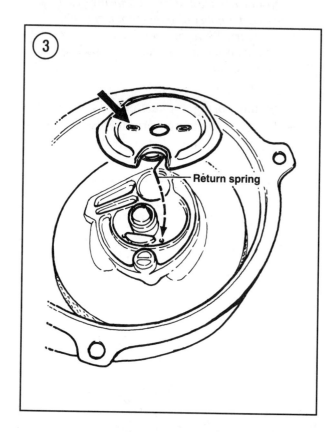

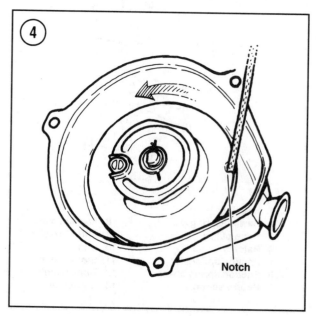

4. If necessary, untie or cut off the knot securing the rope to the handle and retainer. See **Figure 7**.

5. While holding nut (27, **Figure 6**), remove the bolt (11). Remove the friction plate (10) and friction spring (7). Remove the pawls and pawl return springs from the rope pulley. Carefully remove the rope pulley from the starter housing. Use caution not to dislodge the rewind spring.

WARNING
Do not remove rewind spring from its case unless replacement is necessary. Wear hand and eye protection when servicing the rewind spring.

6. If necessary, lift the rewind spring and spring case out of the rope pulley.

7. Further disassembly is not necessary to replace the rewind spring or rope. If necessary, remove the rope guide (12, **Figure 6**) and neutral start interlock components (21-26, **Figure 6**) from the housing.

Cleaning and Inspection

1. Clean all components in solvent, then dry with compressed air.

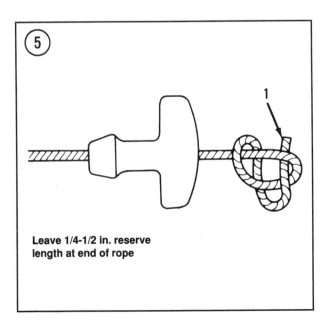

Leave 1/4-1/2 in. reserve
length at end of rope

WARNING
It is not necessary to remove the rewind spring from its case for inspection. Do not remove the spring from the case unless replacement is necessary. Wear hand and eye protection when handling the rewind spring.

2. If replacement is necessary, remove the rewind spring from its case by carefully unwinding the spring (inner coil first).

3. Inspect the rewind spring for kinks, burrs, corrosion, cracks or other damage.

4. Inspect the starter pulley and housing for nicks, cracks, excessive wear or other damage.

5. Inspect the neutral start interlock components for excessive wear or other damage.

6. Inspect the starter rope for excessive wear, cuts, fraying or other damage.

Reassembly

Refer to **Figure 6** for this procedure.

1. Lubricate the spring cavity of the rewind spring case with a thin coat of water-resistant grease.

2. Insert the hook in the outer coil of the rewind spring into the slot in the outer rim of the spring case. Wind the rewind spring into the case in a clockwise direction.

3. If removed, reinstall the rope guide and neutral start interlock components. Apply Loctite 242 to the threads of screw (22, **Figure 6**) and tighten securely.

4. Lubricate the inner hub of the starter housing with a small amount of Quicksilver 2-4-C Marine Lubricant.

5. Install the starter pawls and returns springs into the rope pulley.

6. Install the rewind spring and case assembly into the rope pulley. Install the rope pulley into the starter housing.

7. Lubricate the friction plate with a small amount of Quicksilver 2-4-C Marine Lubricant, then install the friction spring and plate. Apply

12

REWIND STARTER (4 AND 5 HP MODELS)

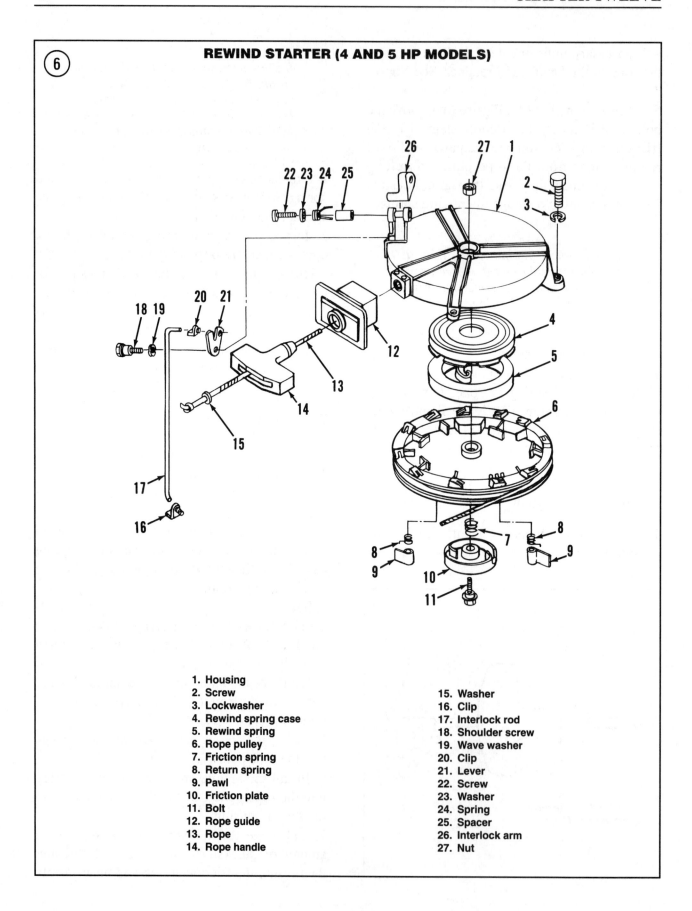

1. Housing
2. Screw
3. Lockwasher
4. Rewind spring case
5. Rewind spring
6. Rope pulley
7. Friction spring
8. Return spring
9. Pawl
10. Friction plate
11. Bolt
12. Rope guide
13. Rope
14. Rope handle
15. Washer
16. Clip
17. Interlock rod
18. Shoulder screw
19. Wave washer
20. Clip
21. Lever
22. Screw
23. Washer
24. Spring
25. Spacer
26. Interlock arm
27. Nut

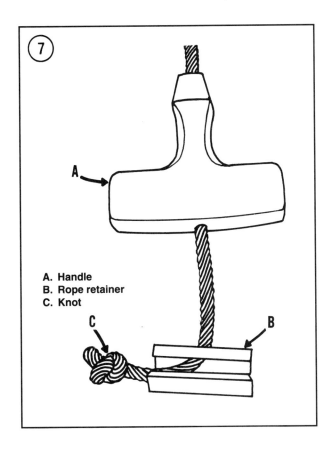

A. Handle
B. Rope retainer
C. Knot

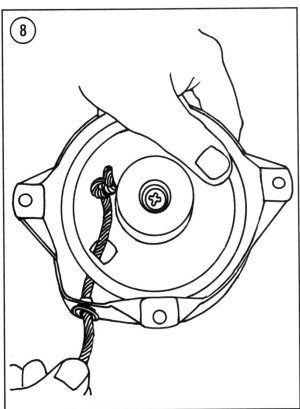

Loctite 242 to the threads of bolt (11, **Figure 6**), install the bolt and tighten to 70 in.-lb. (7.9 N·m).

8. Attach the rope to the rope handle and retainer as shown in **Figure 7**. Insert the rope into the rope guide and through the hole in the rope pulley. See **Figure 8**. Tie a suitable knot in the rope, then push the knot into the recess in the pulley.

9. Wind the rope onto the pulley by turning the pulley 2-1/2 turns clockwise. Then, place the rope into the notch in the outer rim of the pulley and turn the pulley 3 turns counterclockwise. Slowly release the pulley, allowing it to rewind the remaining rope. Make sure the rope rewinds completely.

10. Install the starter assembly onto the power head as described in this chapter.

8, 9.9, 15, 20 AND 25 HP MODELS

The starter rope can be replaced without removing the starter assembly from the power head.

Rope Replacement

1. Remove the engine cowl.

2. Disconnect the spark plug wires. Remove the spark plugs.

3. Pry the top retainer from the starter handle. Cut the rope or untie the knot and remove the retainer and handle.

4. Install the handle and retainer onto the new rope (**Figure 7**). Tie a suitable knot into the end of the rope and push the retainer into the handle.

5. Pry the plastic cover from the rewind starter housing window with a small screwdriver (**Figure 9**).

6. Position the gear selector into neutral to disengage the shift interlock and rope pulley.

7. Slowly rotate the flywheel/rope pulley clockwise until the knotted end of the rope appears in the housing window.

12

8. Remove the knot from the recess in the pulley. Untie the knot or cut the rope and remove the remainder of the old rope from the pulley.

9. Rotate the flywheel/pulley clockwise to tension the rewind spring. As the flywheel is rotated, depress the pulley through the housing window to prevent it from unwinding.

10. Once the spring is wound tightly, release pressure on the pulley slightly and allow it to turn counterclockwise slowly until the rope knot recess appears in the window. Stop the pulley and hold it in this position.

11. Thread the end of the new rope through the starter housing guide and pulley (**Figure 10**). Pull the rope from the recess and tie a slip knot in it to prevent the pulley from unwinding.

12. Tie a knot in the end of the rope. Untie the slip knot and place the knot in the pulley recess (**Figure 11**). Slowly allow the pulley to wind up the remaining rope.

13. Install the plastic cover onto the housing window.

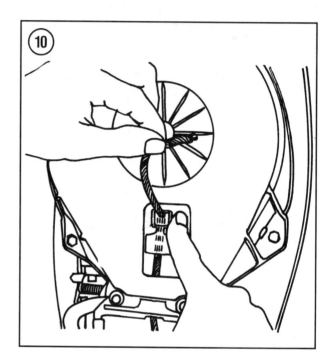

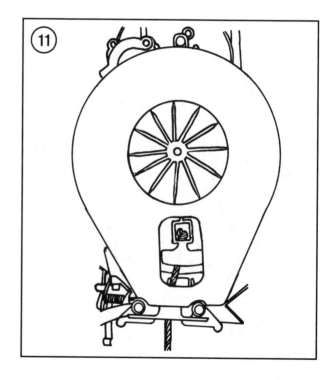

14. Reinstall the spark plugs and connect the spark plug leads.

15. Reinstall the engine cowl.

Starter Removal/Installation (8-25 hp)

Refer to **Figure 12** (8-15 hp) or **Figure 13** (20 and 25 hp) for this procedure.

1. Remove the engine cowl.

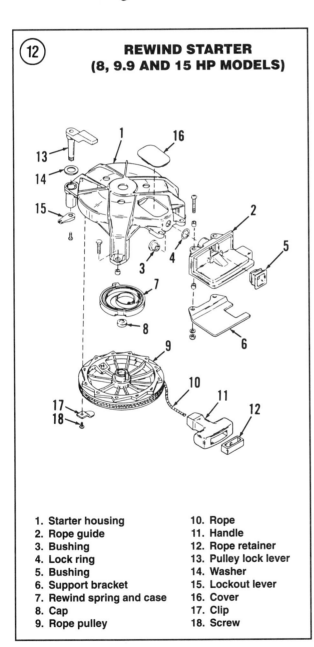

1. Starter housing	10. Rope
2. Rope guide	11. Handle
3. Bushing	12. Rope retainer
4. Lock ring	13. Pulley lock lever
5. Bushing	14. Washer
6. Support bracket	15. Lockout lever
7. Rewind spring and case	16. Cover
8. Cap	17. Clip
9. Rope pulley	18. Screw

2. Pry the fuel filter assembly straight downward away from the rope guide. Do not disconnect the fuel hoses.

3. 8-15 hp—Disconnect the interlock rod from the lower lock lever (15, **Figure 12**).

4. Remove the 3 starter mounting screws, then lift the starter assembly from the power head.

5. To reinstall, place the starter into position on the power head. Install the 3 mounting fasteners and tighten securely.

6. 8-15 hp—Reconnect the interlock rod to the lower lock lever.

7. Reinstall the fuel filter assembly into place. Push the filter straight upward to prevent breaking the fuel hose connections on the filter.

Disassembly (8-15 hp)

Refer to **Figure 12** for this procedure.

WARNING
Wear hand and eye protection when servicing the rewind starter.

1. Remove the starter rope as described under *Rope Replacement* in this chapter. Remove the starter assembly from the power head as described in this chapter.

2. Invert the starter housing and loosen the 3 screws (18, **Figure 12**), then swing the clips (17) away from the rope pulley.

3. Carefully lift the rope pulley out of the housing.

NOTE
Do not remove the rewind spring from its case.

4. Place the starter housing upright on a bench. Insert an awl or similar tool through the holes in the top of the housing and push out the rewind spring and case assembly.

5. Using a suitable punch, tap the plastic cap from the center hole of the rope pulley. Pry the oil seal from the starter pulley.

12

Cleaning and Inspection
(8-15 hp)

1. Clean all components in solvent and dry with compressed air.

NOTE
It is not necessary to remove the rewind spring from its case for inspection. If the spring requires replacement, the spring and case are replaced as an assembly.

2. Inspect the rewind spring in its case for cracks, burrs, breakage or other damage. Replace the spring and case as an assembly if necessary.

3. Inspect the rope pulley and starter housing for cracks, breakage, nicks, grooves, distortion or other damage.

4. Check the starter clutch for excessive wear, lack of lubrication or other damage. The starter clutch and rope pulley are replaced as an assembly.

5. Inspect the starter rope for excessive wear. Replace the rope as necessary.

Reassembly
(8-15 hp)

Refer to **Figure 12** for this procedure.

1. Install a new seal into the rope pulley. The seal lip should face the starter clutch.

2. Tap the plastic cap into the rope pulley center hole.

3. Lubricate the rewind spring with a suitable water-resistant grease. Install the spring and case assembly into the housing.

4. Install the rope pulley into the housing. Position the pulley retaining clips over the pulley, then securely tighten the screws.

5. Install the starter rope as described under *Rope Replacement*. Install the starter assembly onto the power head as described in this chapter.

Disassembly
(20 and 25 hp)

Refer to **Figure 13** for this procedure.

WARNING
Wear hand and eye protection when servicing the starter.

1. Remove the starter assembly from the power head as described in this chapter.

2. Invert the starter. Fully extend the starter rope and hold the rope pulley from turning. Pull the knot in the rope from the recess in the pulley, then untie or cut the knot from the rope. Allow the pulley to unwind slowly, relieving the rewind spring tension.

3. Remove the pulley bolt (19, **Figure 13**). Remove the cam (18) and spring (17).

4. Lift the rope pulley off the housing center shaft.

5. Lift the rewind spring and case assembly from the housing.

6. Remove the felt pad (9).

7. If necessary, remove the E-rings securing the starter pawls (13). Remove the pawls and pawl return springs from the rope pulley.

Cleaning and Inspection
(20 and 25 hp)

1. Clean all components in solvent and dry with compressed air.

NOTE
It is not necessary to remove the rewind spring from its case for inspection. If the spring requires replacement, the spring and case are replaced as an assembly.

2. Inspect the rewind spring in its case for cracks, burrs, breakage or other damage. Replace the spring and case as an assembly if necessary.

3. Inspect the rope pulley and starter housing for cracks, breakage, nicks, grooves, distortion or other damage. Inspect the pawl pivot pins on the

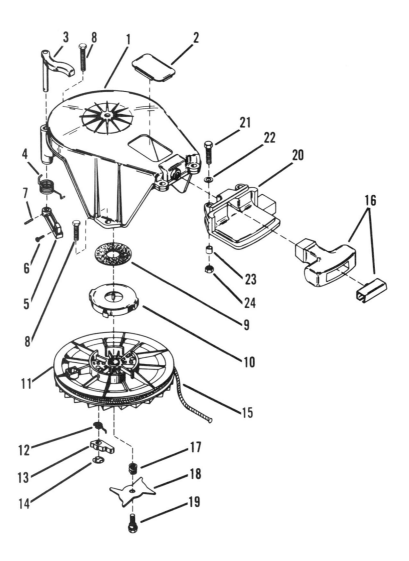

**REWIND STARTER
(20 AND 25 HP MODELS)**

1. Starter housing
2. Starter housing cover
3. Upper lock lever
4. Upper lock lever spring
5. Lower lock lever
6. Lower lock lever screw
7. Lock lever roll pin
8. Screw
9. Felt pad
10. Rewind spring
11. Rope pulley
12. Spring
13. Pawl
14. Cam retaining ring
15. Starter rope
16. Starter rope handle assembly
17. Cam spring
18. Cam
19. Screw
20. Starter handle support
21. Screw
22. Washer
23. Spacer
24. Nut

12

pulley for excessive wear. Replace the rope pulley as necessary.

4. Check the starter pawls and pawl springs for excessive wear or breakage and replace as necessary. Check the starter cam for excessive wear and replace as necessary.

5. Inspect the starter rope for excessive wear. Replace the rope as necessary.

Reassembly
(20 and 25 hp)

Refer to **Figure 13** for this procedure.

1. If removed, install the starter pawls and springs onto the rope pulley pivot pins. Secure the pawls with the E-rings.

2. Place the felt pad into place over the housing center shaft. The felt pad may be held in place with a small amount of grease.

3. Lubricate the outer side of the rewind spring with a suitable water-resistant grease. Install the spring and case assembly into the rope pulley.

4. Install the rope pulley and rewind spring assembly onto the housing center shaft. Turn the pulley to engage the rewind spring and housing shaft. If the rope pulley and rewind spring are properly seated, the housing center shaft and the pawl side of the rope pulley will be flush.

5. Install the cam spring and cam. Install the shoulder bolt and tighten securely.

6. Install the starter assembly as described in this chapter.

40 HP MODELS

Removal/Installation

Refer to **Figure 14** for this procedure.

WARNING
Wear hand and eye protection when servicing rewind starter.

1. Remove the engine cowl.

2. Remove the cotter pin and screw securing the neutral interlock cable to the starter housing.

3. Remove the starter mounting screws and lift the starter off the power head.

4. To install the starter, place the starter assembly onto the power head and install the mounting fasteners. Tighten the fasteners to 100 in.-lb. (11.3 N•m).

5. Reconnect the neutral start interlock cable to the housing with the screw and new cotter pin.

6. Adjust the neutral start interlock cable as described in this chapter.

Disassembly

WARNING
Wear hand and eye protection when servicing the rewind starter.

Refer to **Figure 14** for this procedure.

1. Remove the starter as described in this chapter.

2. Remove the rope handle and retainer, then allow the rope pulley to unwind, relieving the tension on the rewind spring.

NOTE
*Nut (37, **Figure 14**) has left-hand threads.*

3. Bend the locking tabs of tab washer (38, **Figure 14**) away from the nut (37). Remove the nut (37). Turn the nut clockwise (left-hand threads).

4. Remove the rope pulley from the housing.

5. Remove the rewind spring retaining plate (5, **Figure 14**) from the rope pulley.

6. Remove the rope pulley shaft (16, **Figure 14**), along with wave washer (15), lever (14) and washer (13). Remove the spacer (8) and bushing (7), if necessary.

7. Place the rope pulley onto 2 wooden blocks (rewind spring facing down). Tap on the top of the pulley dislodging the rewind spring from the pulley, allowing it to uncoil between the wooden blocks.

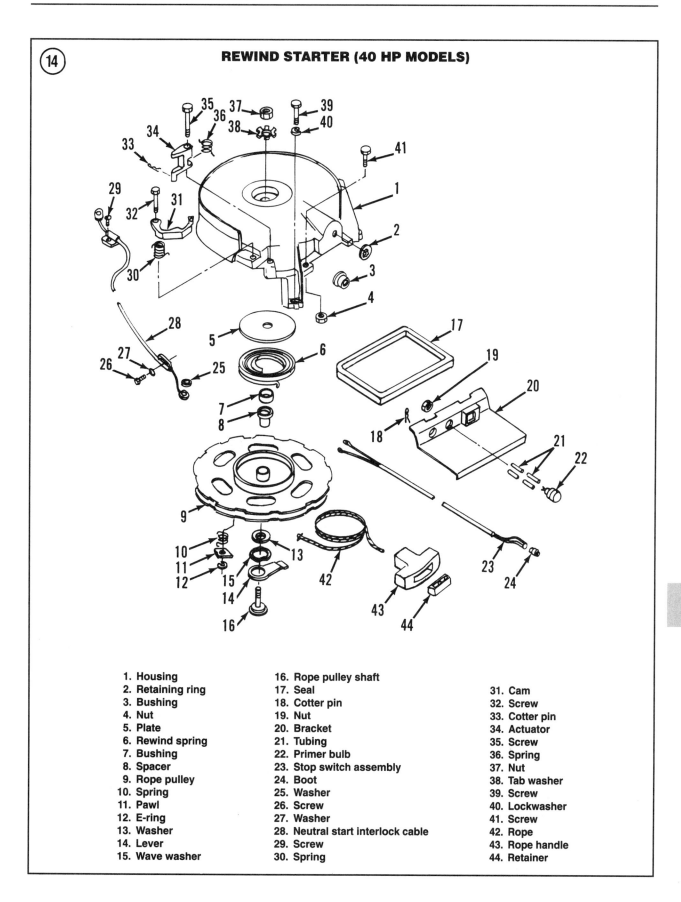

REWIND STARTER (40 HP MODELS)

1. Housing	16. Rope pulley shaft
2. Retaining ring	17. Seal
3. Bushing	18. Cotter pin
4. Nut	19. Nut
5. Plate	20. Bracket
6. Rewind spring	21. Tubing
7. Bushing	22. Primer bulb
8. Spacer	23. Stop switch assembly
9. Rope pulley	24. Boot
10. Spring	25. Washer
11. Pawl	26. Screw
12. E-ring	27. Washer
13. Washer	28. Neutral start interlock cable
14. Lever	29. Screw
15. Wave washer	30. Spring

31. Cam
32. Screw
33. Cotter pin
34. Actuator
35. Screw
36. Spring
37. Nut
38. Tab washer
39. Screw
40. Lockwasher
41. Screw
42. Rope
43. Rope handle
44. Retainer

12

Cleaning and Inspection

1. Clean all starter components in solvent and dry with compressed air.

2. Inspect the rewind spring for cracks, burrs, corrosion, breakage or other damage. Replace the spring as necessary.

3. Inspect the rope pulley and starter housing for cracks, distortion, grooves, excessive wear or other damage.

4. Inspect bushings, starter drive pawl, and spring for excessive wear, breakage or other damage.

5. Inspect the starter rope for excessive wear, cuts or other damage. Replace the rope if necessary.

Rewind Spring Installation

Installing original rewind spring

> WARNING
> Wear hand and eye protection during starter service. The rewind spring can cause personal injury if it uncoils rapidly.

1. Lubricate the rewind spring with a suitable water-resistant grease.

2. Insert the hook in the outer coil of the rewind spring into the notch in the rope pulley. Wind the spring into the pulley in a counterclockwise direction starting with the outer coil.

Installing new rewind spring

> WARNING
> Wear hand and eye protection during starter service. The rewind spring can cause personal injury if it uncoils rapidly.

1. Remove the retainers securing the rewind spring in its shipping container.

2. Insert the hook on the end of the rewind spring into the rope pulley anchor. Allow the support tabs on the spring container to rest on the rope

pulley as shown in **Figure 15**. Push the rewind spring into position by inserting wide-blade screwdrivers into the holes (**Figure 15**) in the spring container.

Reassembly

Refer to **Figure 14** for this procedure.

1. Insert the starter rope into the hole in the pulley. Secure the rope to the pulley using a suitable knot.

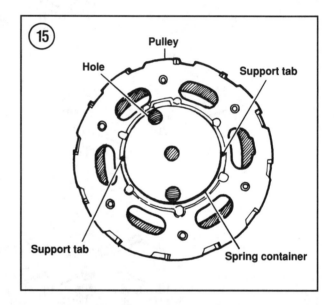

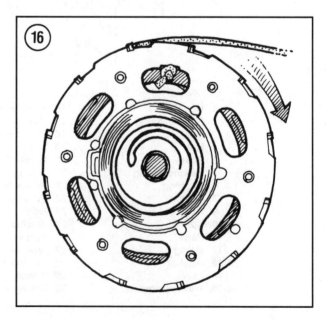

2. Wind the rope onto the pulley in a clockwise direction as viewed from the rewind spring side of the pulley. See **Figure 16**.

3. Lubricate the shoulder of the rope pulley shaft (16, **Figure 14**) with a suitable water-resistant grease. Install the lever (14) and wave washer (15) onto the shaft.

4. Lubricate all components with a suitable water-resistant grease.

5. If removed, install the pawl and spring onto the rope pulley. Secure the pawl and spring with the E-ring.

6. Install the pulley shaft assembly (13-16, **Figure 14**) into the rope pulley. Install the spacer (9) and bushing (7), if removed.

7. Install the rewind spring retainer plate over the pulley shaft. Make sure the tab on the plate properly engages the inner hook of the rewind spring.

8. Insert the starter rope through the rope guide in the housing, then install the pulley assembly into the housing.

9. Install a new tab washer (38, **Figure 14**) onto the shaft. The cupped side of the washer should be facing downward. Install the nut (40) onto the shaft and tighten hand tight. Note the nut has left-hand threads.

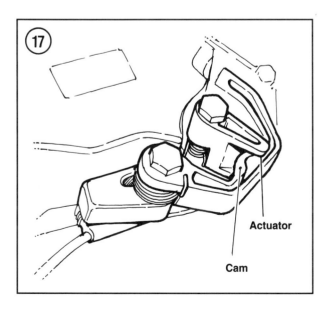

10. To adjust the rewind spring tension, tie a slip knot in the starter rope approximately 12 in. (305 mm) from the end of the rope.

11. While holding the nut (37, **Figure 14**), turn the shaft (16) counterclockwise with a screwdriver until the slip knot contacts the rope guide. After the knot contacts the rope guide, turn the shaft an additional 2 full turns to apply the proper tension on the rewind spring. Tighten the nut (37) and secure with the locking tab washer. Bend 2 tabs over the nut and the 2 remaining tabs downward into the housing.

12. Untie the slip knot in the starter rope and install the rope handle. Do not allow the rope to wind into the housing before the handle is installed.

13. Check starter operation by slowly extending the rope.

   a. The starter pawl should extend to the engaged position as the lever starts to turn.

   b. Pull the rope to the fully extended position, then allow to rewind slowly. Operation should be smooth without catching.

   c. If operation is not as specified, disassemble the starter and repair the reason. Make sure the pulley shaft is properly aligned with the washers.

14. Install the starter assembly and adjust neutral start interlock cables as described in this chapter.

Neutral Start Adjustment

CAUTION
Do not attempt to shift into REVERSE gear while the engine is not running, or shift mechanism could be damaged.

1. Shift the outboard motor into NEUTRAL.

2. Loosen the interlock cable attaching screw (29, **Figure 14**) sufficiently to allow cable movement.

3. With the outboard in NEUTRAL, the interlock actuator must be aligned with the interlock cam as shown in **Figure 17**. Move the interlock cable as necessary, then securely tighten the screw (29, **Figure 14**).

INDEX

13

IGNITION SYSTEM
3 HP MODELS

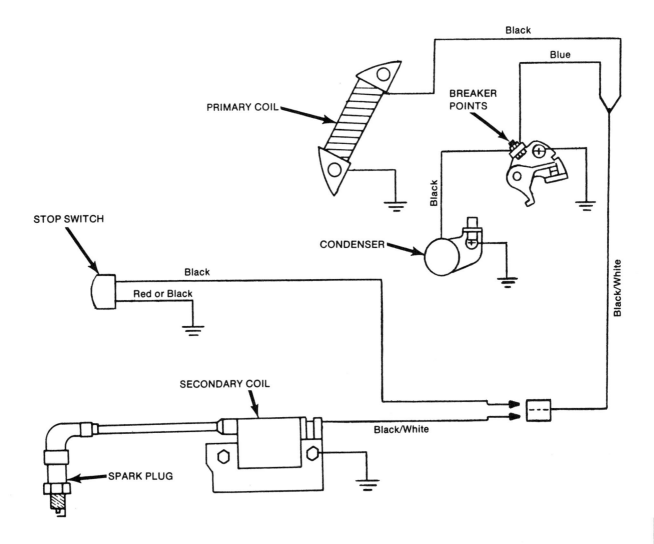

Black

Blue

BREAKER
POINTS

PRIMARY COIL

Black

STOP SWITCH

CONDENSER

Black

Red or Black

Black/White

SECONDARY COIL

Black/White

SPARK PLUG

14

IGNITION SYSTEM
3.3 HP MODELS

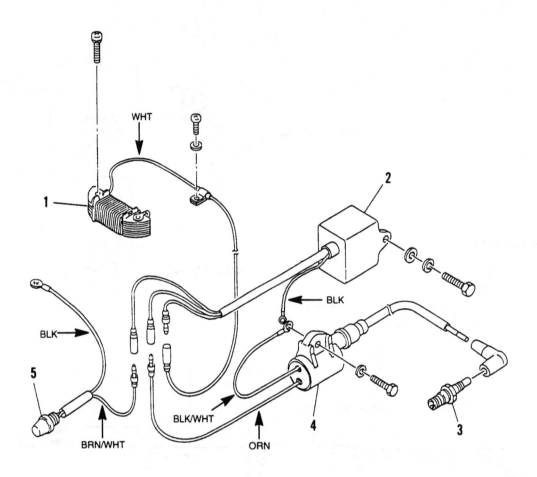

WHT

BLK

BLK

BLK/WHT

ORN

BRN/WHT

1. **Capacitor charging coil/trigger coil**
2. **CDI unit**
3. **Ignition coil**
4. **Spark plug**
5. **Stop switch**

BLK = BLACK
BRN = BROWN
ORN = ORANGE
WHT = WHITE

IGNITION SYSTEM
4 AND 5 HP MODELS

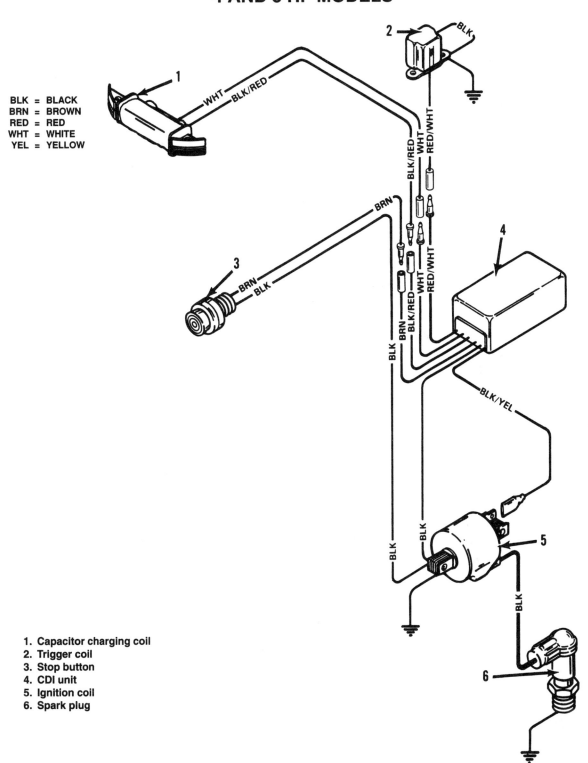

BLK = BLACK
BRN = BROWN
RED = RED
WHT = WHITE
YEL = YELLOW

1. Capacitor charging coil
2. Trigger coil
3. Stop button
4. CDI unit
5. Ignition coil
6. Spark plug

14

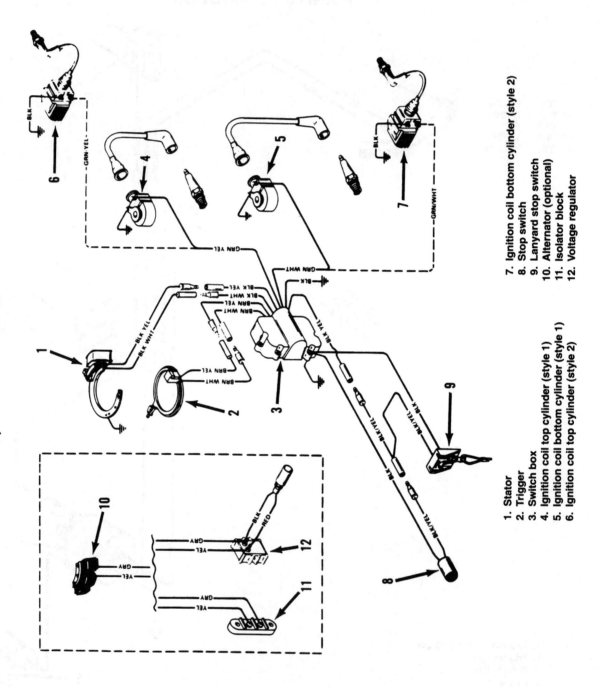

MANUAL START
8, 9.9 AND 15 HP

1. Stator
2. Trigger
3. Switch box
4. Ignition coil top cylinder (style 1)
5. Ignition coil bottom cylinder (style 1)
6. Ignition coil top cylinder (style 2)
7. Ignition coil bottom cylinder (style 2)
8. Stop switch
9. Lanyard stop switch
10. Alternator (optional)
11. Isolator block
12. Voltage regulator

BLK = BLACK
BRN = BROWN
GRY = GRAY
GRN = GREEN
RED = RED
WHT = WHITE
YEL = YELLOW

8, 9.9 AND 15 HP ELECTRIC START (TILLER HAND START)

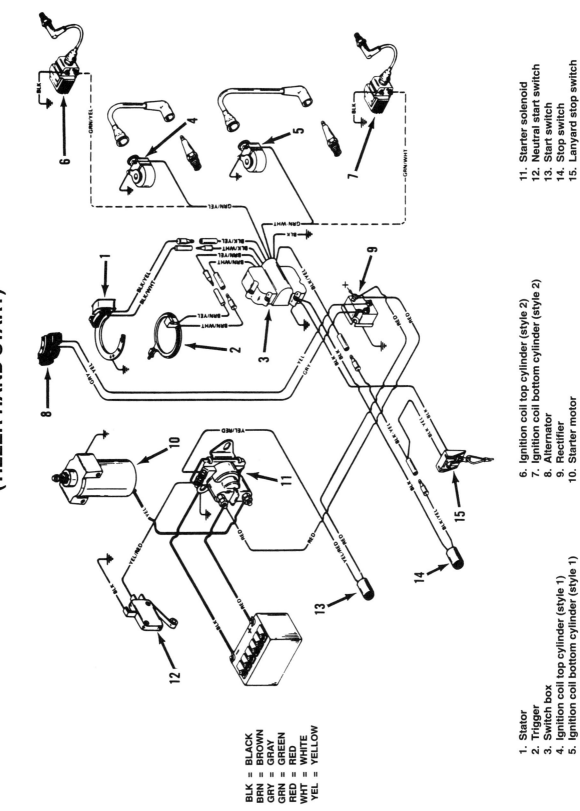

BLK = BLACK
BRN = BROWN
GRY = GRAY
GRN = GREEN
RED = RED
WHT = WHITE
YEL = YELLOW

1. Stator
2. Trigger
3. Switch box
4. Ignition coil top cylinder (style 1)
5. Ignition coil bottom cylinder (style 1)
6. Ignition coil top cylinder (style 2)
7. Ignition coil bottom cylinder (style 2)
8. Alternator
9. Rectifier
10. Starter motor
11. Starter solenoid
12. Neutral start switch
13. Start switch
14. Stop switch
15. Lanyard stop switch

14

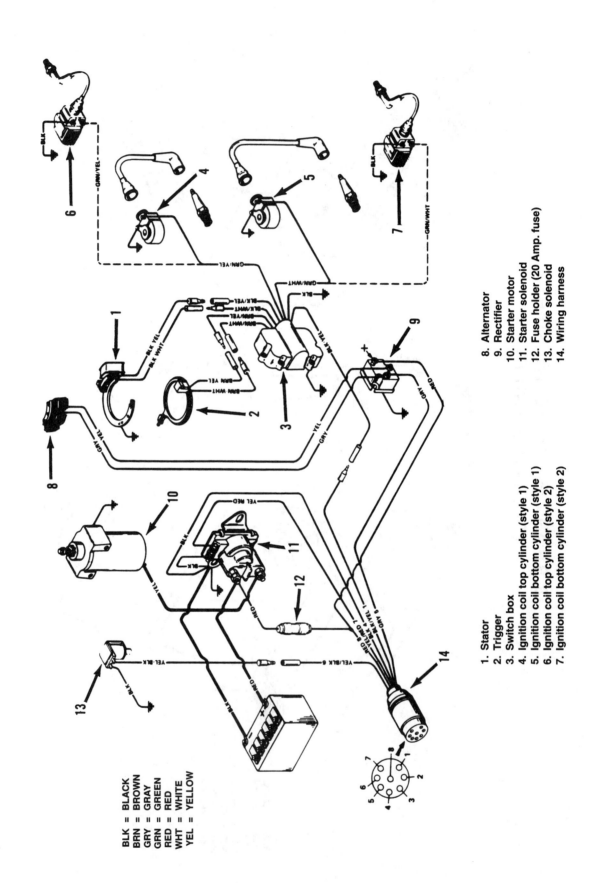

8, 9.9 AND 15 HP (REMOTE CONTROL)

1. Stator
2. Trigger
3. Switch box
4. Ignition coil top cylinder (style 1)
5. Ignition coil bottom cylinder (style 1)
6. Ignition coil top cylinder (style 2)
7. Ignition coil bottom cylinder (style 2)

8. Alternator
9. Rectifier
10. Starter motor
11. Starter solenoid
12. Fuse holder (20 Amp. fuse)
13. Choke solenoid
14. Wiring harness

BLK = BLACK
BRN = BROWN
GRY = GRAY
GRN = GREEN
RED = RED
WHT = WHITE
YEL = YELLOW

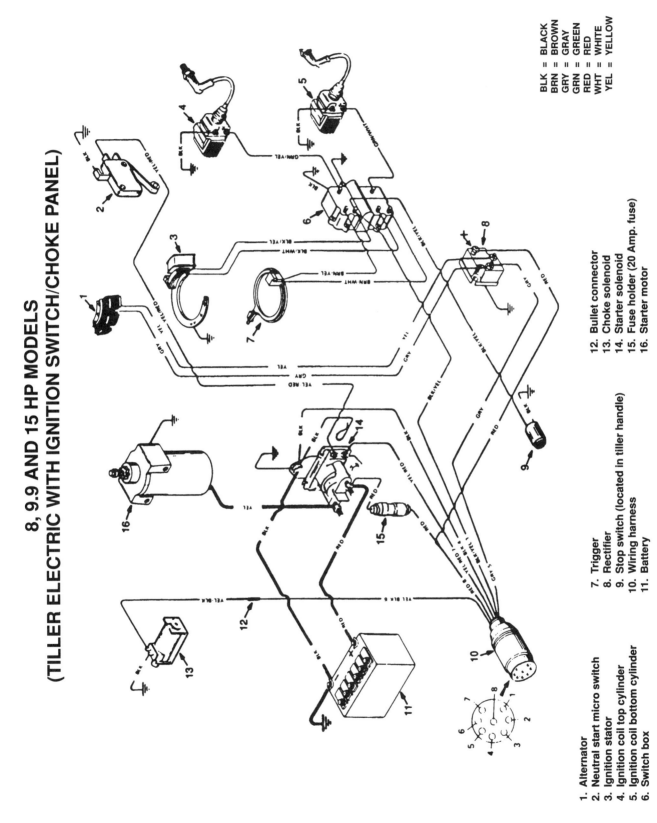

8, 9.9 AND 15 HP MODELS
(TILLER ELECTRIC WITH IGNITION SWITCH/CHOKE PANEL)

BLK = BLACK
BRN = BROWN
GRY = GRAY
GRN = GREEN
RED = RED
WHT = WHITE
YEL = YELLOW

1. Alternator
2. Neutral start micro switch
3. Ignition stator
4. Ignition coil top cylinder
5. Ignition coil bottom cylinder
6. Switch box
7. Trigger
8. Rectifier
9. Stop switch (located in tiller handle)
10. Wiring harness
11. Battery
12. Bullet connector
13. Choke solenoid
14. Starter solenoid
15. Fuse holder (20 Amp. fuse)
16. Starter motor

14

COMMANDER 2000 SIDE MOUNT REMOTE CONTROL (MANUAL)
8, 9.9 AND 15 HP MODELS

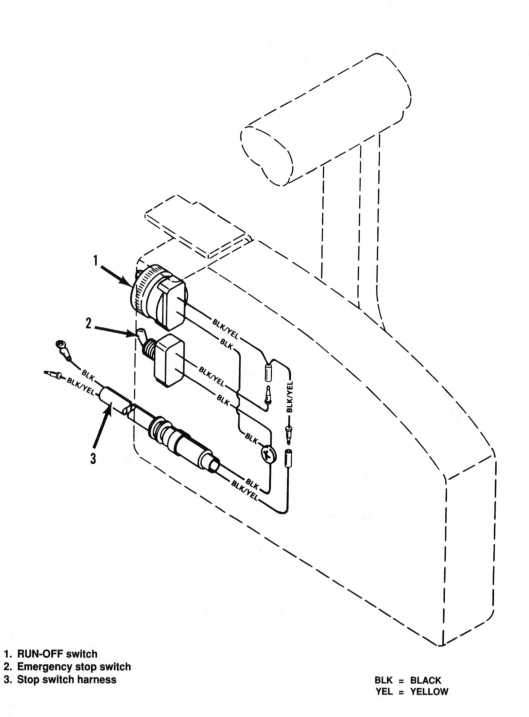

1. **RUN-OFF switch**
2. **Emergency stop switch**
3. **Stop switch harness**

BLK = BLACK
YEL = YELLOW

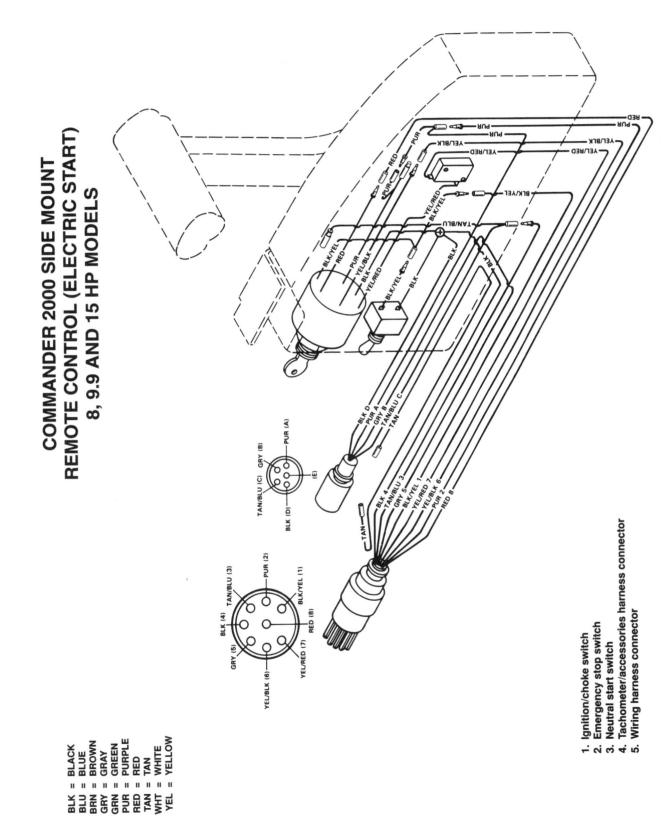

COMMANDER 2000 SIDE MOUNT
REMOTE CONTROL (ELECTRIC START)
8, 9.9 AND 15 HP MODELS

BLK = BLACK
BLU = BLUE
BRN = BROWN
GRY = GRAY
GRN = GREEN
PUR = PURPLE
RED = RED
TAN = TAN
WHT = WHITE
YEL = YELLOW

1. Ignition/choke switch
2. Emergency stop switch
3. Neutral start switch
4. Tachometer/accessories harness connector
5. Wiring harness connector

14

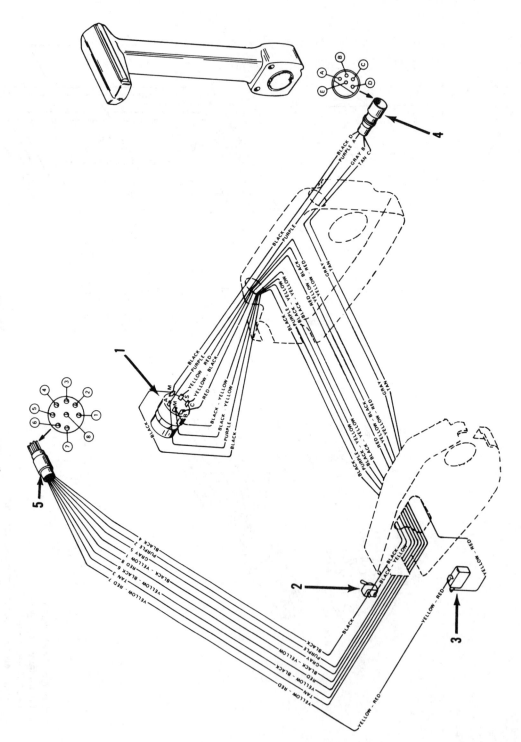

COMMANDER SIDE MOUNT REMOTE CONTROL (ELECTRIC START) 8, 9.9 AND 15 HP MODELS

1. Ignition/choke switch
2. Emergency stop switch
3. Neutral start switch
4. Tachometer/accessories harness connector
5. Wiring harness connector

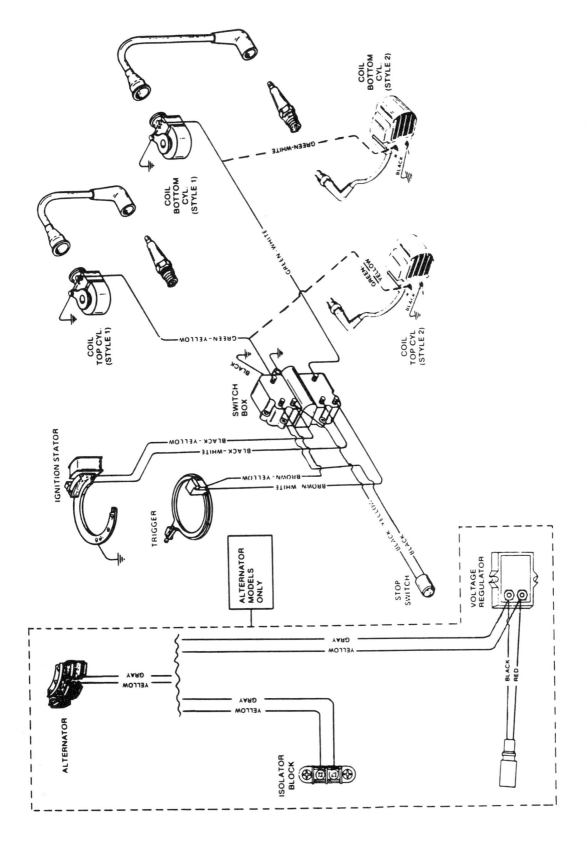

20 AND 25 HP MANUAL START

14

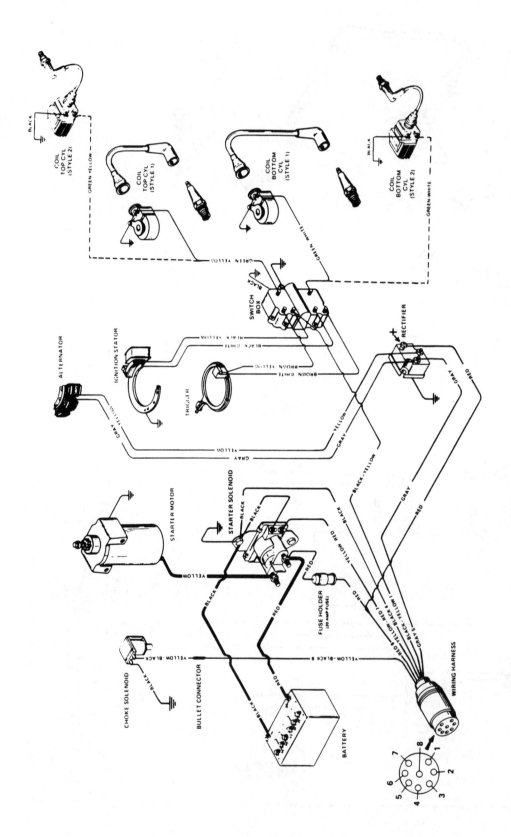

20 AND 25 HP ELECTRIC START (REMOTE CONTROL)

20 AND 25 HP ELECTRIC START (TILLER HANDLE START BUTTON)

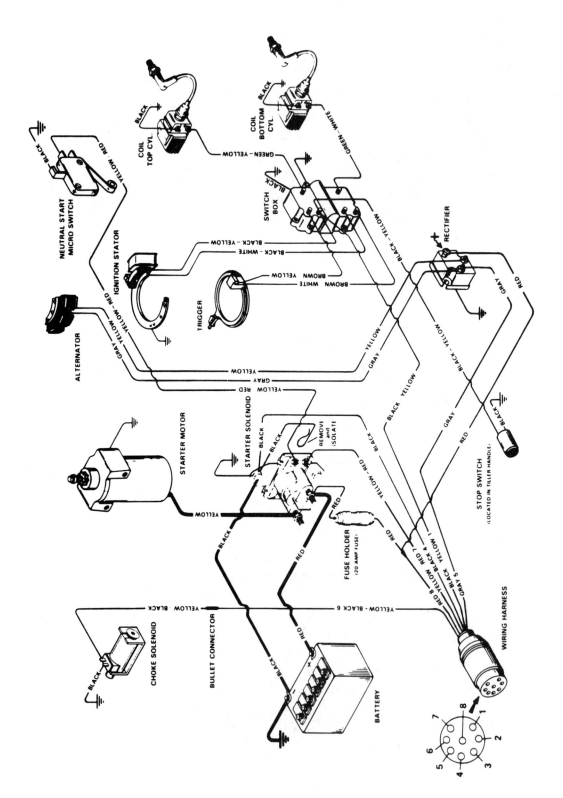

**20 AND 25 HP ELECTRIC START
(TILLER HANDLE AND IGNITION KEY/CHOKE PANEL)**

IGNITION KEY/CHOKE PANEL
20 AND 25 HP MODELS

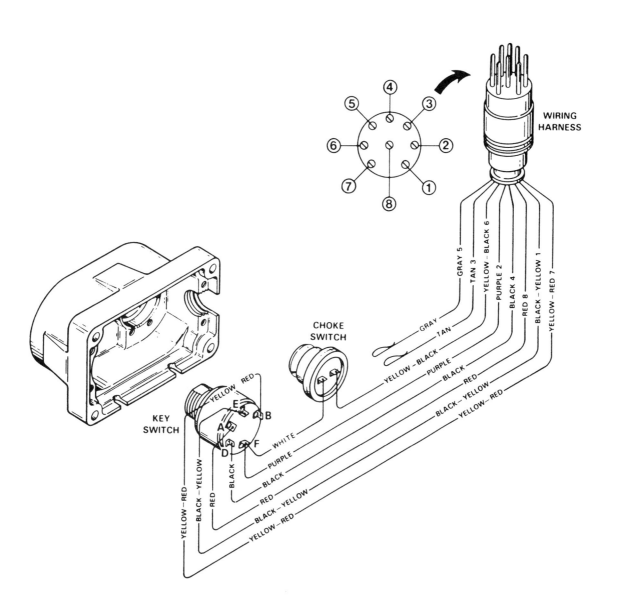

14

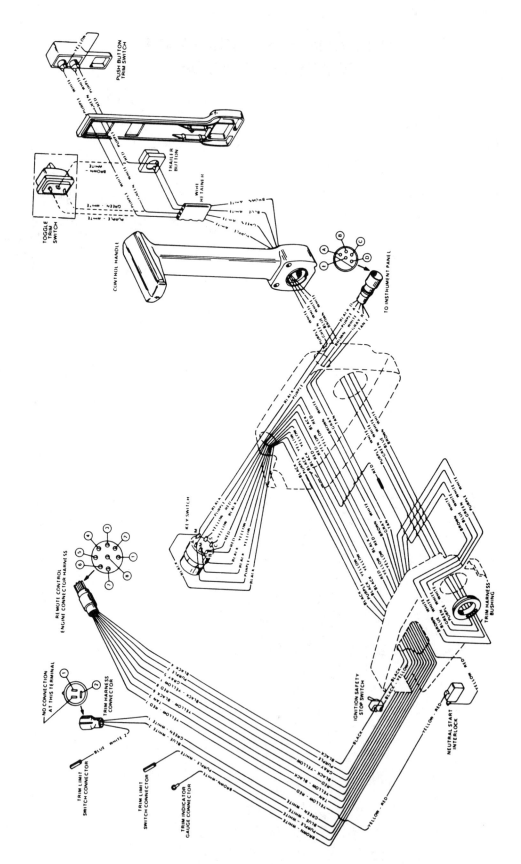

SIDE MOUNT REMOTE CONTROL
(WITHOUT POWER TRIM)
10 AND 25 HP MODELS

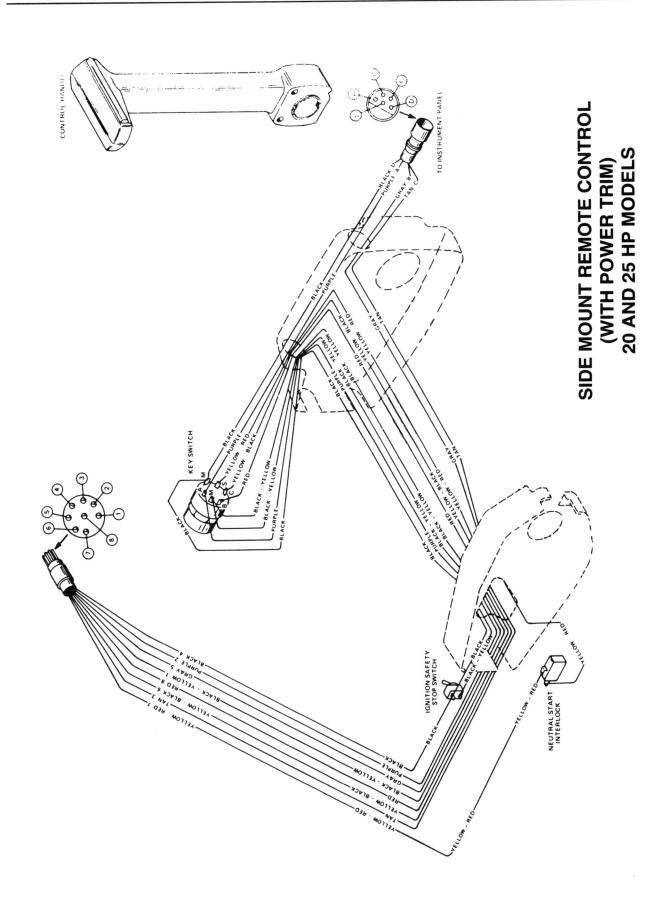

**SIDE MOUNT REMOTE CONTROL
(WITH POWER TRIM)
20 AND 25 HP MODELS**

14

40 HP MODELS (MANUAL START)

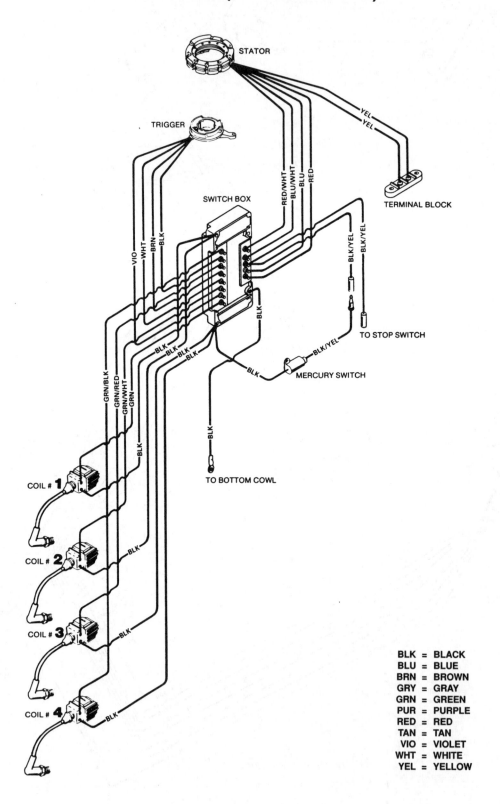

STATOR

TRIGGER

SWITCH BOX

TERMINAL BLOCK

RED/WHT
BLU/WHT
BLU
RED

YEL
YEL

VIO
WHT
BRN
BLK

BLK/YEL
BLK/YEL

TO STOP SWITCH

BLK

BLK/YEL

MERCURY SWITCH

BLK
BLK
BLK

GRN/BLK
GRN/RED
GRN/WHT
GRN

BLK

BLK

TO BOTTOM COWL

COIL # 1

BLK

COIL # 2

BLK

COIL # 3

BLK

COIL # 4

BLK

BLK = BLACK
BLU = BLUE
BRN = BROWN
GRY = GRAY
GRN = GREEN
PUR = PURPLE
RED = RED
TAN = TAN
VIO = VIOLET
WHT = WHITE
YEL = YELLOW

40 HP MODELS ELECTRIC START
(SERIAL NO. 221500–D082000)

BLK = BLACK
BLU = BLUE
BRN = BROWN
GRY = GRAY
GRN = GREEN
LIT BLU = LIGHT BLUE
PUR = PURPLE
RED = RED
TAN = TAN
VIO = VIOLET
WHT = WHITE
YEL = YELLOW

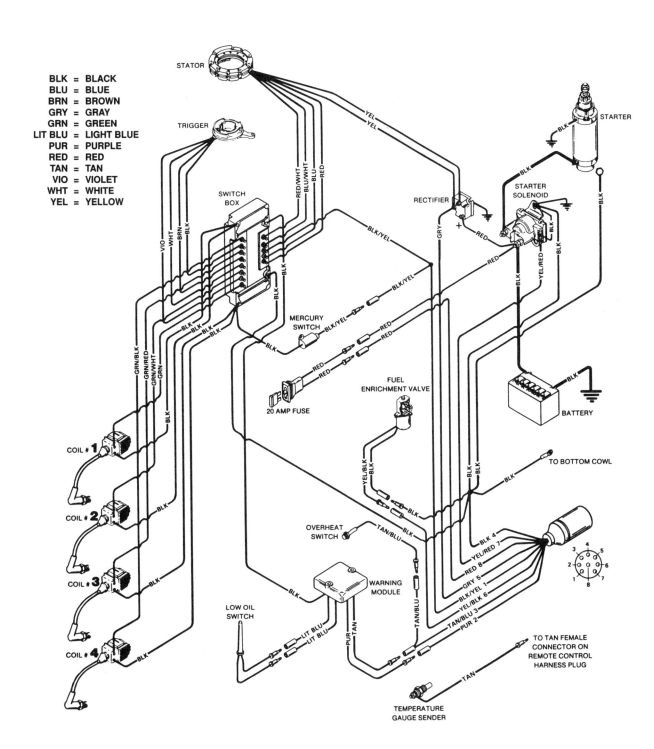

14

40 HP MODELS ELECTRIC START WITH VOLTAGE REGULATOR (SERIAL NO. D182000–ON)

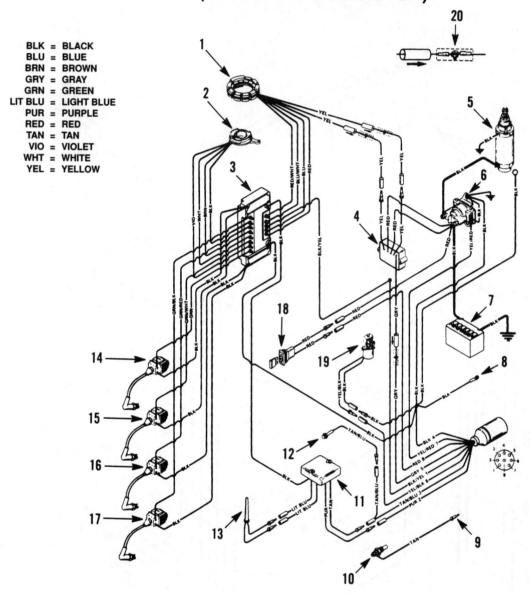

BLK = BLACK
BLU = BLUE
BRN = BROWN
GRY = GRAY
GRN = GREEN
LIT BLU = LIGHT BLUE
PUR = PURPLE
RED = RED
TAN = TAN
VIO = VIOLET
WHT = WHITE
YEL = YELLOW

1. Stator
2. Trigger
3. Switch box
4. Voltage regulator
5. Starter
6. Starter solenoid
7. Battery
8. To bottom cowl
9. To tan female connector on remote control harness plug
10. Temperature gauge sender
11. Warning module
12. Overheat module
13. Low oil switch
14. Coil No. 1
15. Coil No. 2
16. Coil No. 3
17. Coil No. 4
18. 20 Ampere fuse
19. Fuel enrichment valve
20. Nut and screw covered with sleeve

40 HP MODELS POWER TRIM

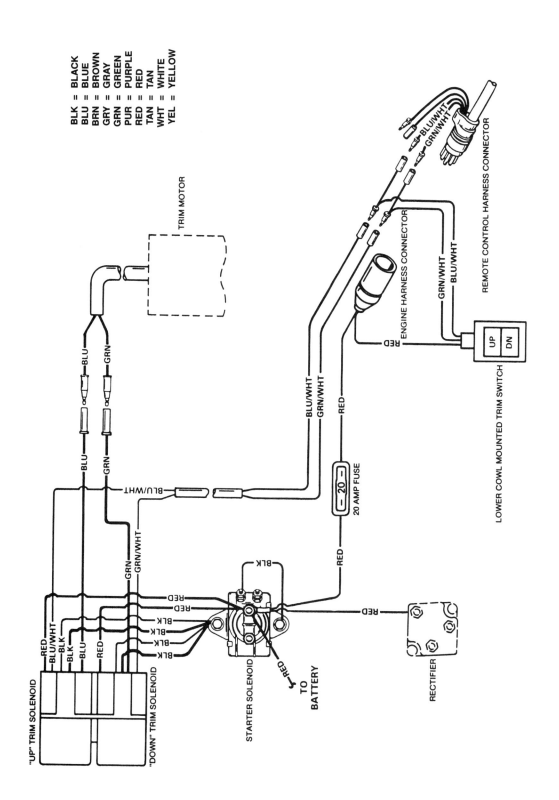

BLK = BLACK
BLU = BLUE
BRN = BROWN
GRY = GRAY
GRN = GREEN
PUR = PURPLE
RED = RED
TAN = TAN
WHT = WHITE
YEL = YELLOW

TRIM MOTOR

REMOTE CONTROL HARNESS CONNECTOR

BLU/WHT
GRN/WHT

ENGINE HARNESS CONNECTOR

GRN/WHT
BLU/WHT
RED

LOWER COWL MOUNTED TRIM SWITCH

UP
DN

BLU
GRN

BLU/WHT
GRN/WHT
RED

20 AMP FUSE

RED

BLK

"UP" TRIM SOLENOID

RED
BLU/WHT
BLK
BLU
RED
GRN
GRN/WHT

"DOWN" TRIM SOLENOID

RED
RED
BLK
BLK
BLK

STARTER SOLENOID

RED
TO
BATTERY

RED

RECTIFIER

14

50 AND 60 HP MODELS
(PRIOR TO SERIAL NO. D000750)

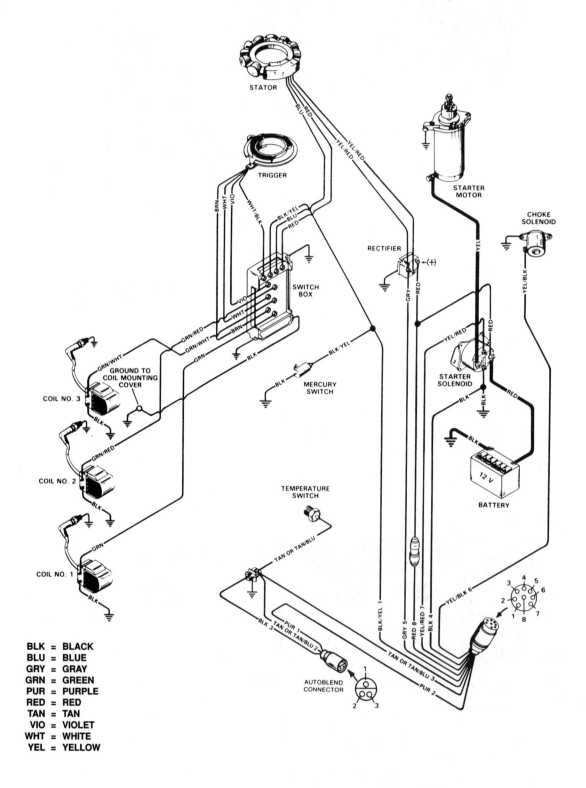

BLK = BLACK
BLU = BLUE
GRY = GRAY
GRN = GREEN
PUR = PURPLE
RED = RED
TAN = TAN
VIO = VIOLET
WHT = WHITE
YEL = YELLOW

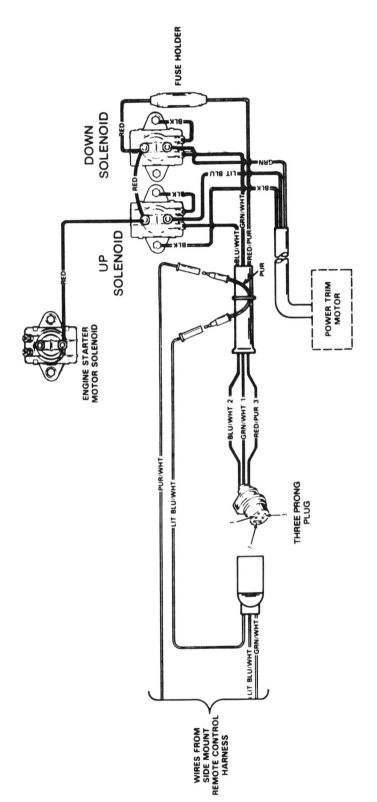

POWER TRIM 50 AND 60 HP MODELS
(PRIOR TO SERIAL NO. D000750)

BLK = BLACK
BLU = BLUE
GRN = GREEN
LIT BLU = LIGHT BLUE
PUR = PURPLE
RED = RED
WHT = WHITE

14

MANUAL START 50 AND 60 HP MODELS
(SERIAL NO. D000750-ON)

1. Stator
2. Trigger
3. Switch box
4. Ignition coil cylinder No. 1
5. Ignition coil cylinder No. 2
6. Ignition coil cylinder No. 3
7. Temperature switch
8. Overheat/overev warning module
9. Warning horn
10. Stop button
11. Lanyard stop switch

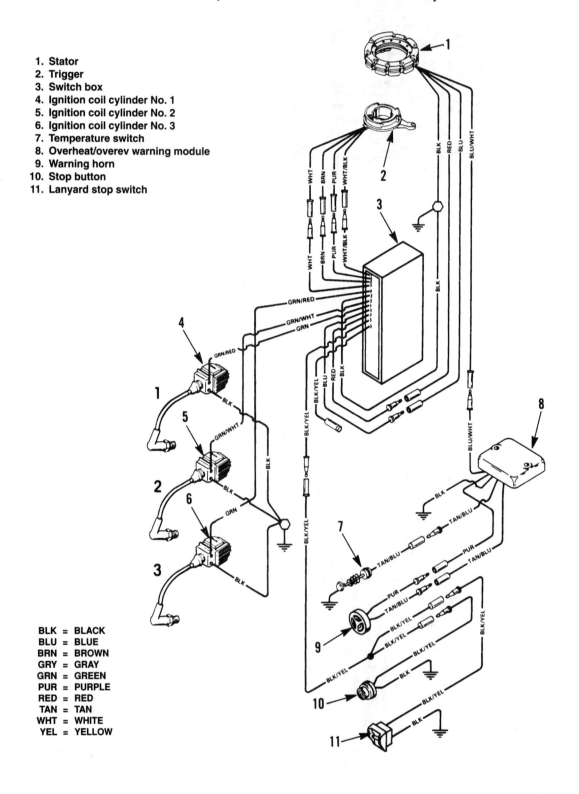

BLK = BLACK
BLU = BLUE
BRN = BROWN
GRY = GRAY
GRN = GREEN
PUR = PURPLE
RED = RED
TAN = TAN
WHT = WHITE
YEL = YELLOW

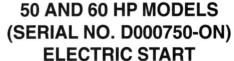

50 AND 60 HP MODELS
(SERIAL NO. D000750-ON)
ELECTRIC START

1. Stator
2. Trigger
3. Switch box
4. Ignition coil cylinder No. 1
5. Ignition coil cylinder No. 2
6. Ignition coil cylinder No. 3
7. Starter motor
8. Starter solenoid
9. Rectifier
10. Fuse holder (20 Amp. fuse)
11. Battery
12. Wiring harness connector
13. Enrichment valve
14. Temperature switch
15. Low oil warning module
16. Low oil sensor

BLK = BLACK
BLU = BLUE
BRN = BROWN
GRY = GRAY
GRN = GREEN
LIT BLU = LIGHT BLUE
PUR = PURPLE
RED = RED
TAN = TAN
WHT = WHITE
YEL = YELLOW

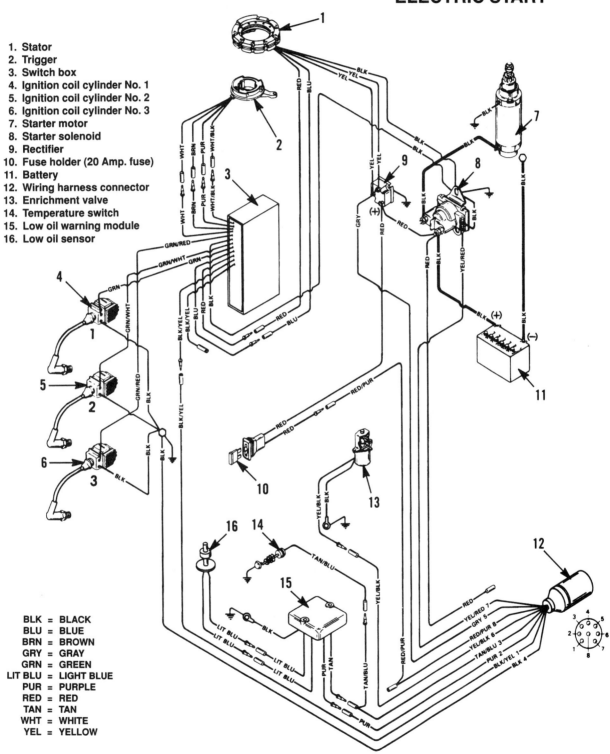

14

POWER TRIM
50 AND 60 HP MODELS
(SERIAL NO. D000750-ON)

1. Power trim
2. Power trim relay
3. Engine starter motor solenoid
4. Rectifier
5. Cowl mounted trim switch
6. Red (+) battery cable
7. Fuse holder (20 Amp. fuse)
8. Engine wiring harness connector
9. Remove control wiring harness connector

BLK = BLACK
BLU = BLUE
BRN = BROWN
GRY = GRAY
GRN = GREEN
LIT BLU = LIGHT BLUE
PUR = PURPLE
RED = RED
TAN = TAN
WHT = WHITE
YEL = YELLOW

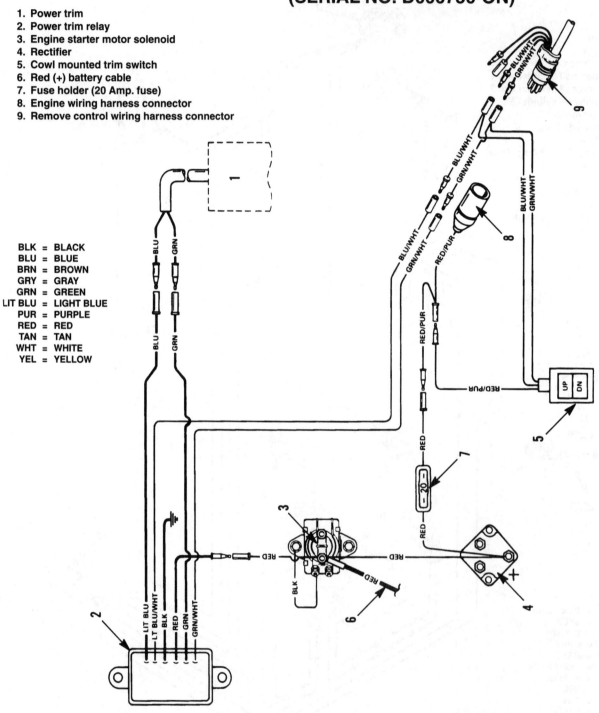

75 AND 90 HP MODELS SERIAL NO. C221500–D081999
(WITH LOW-OIL WARNING MODULE)

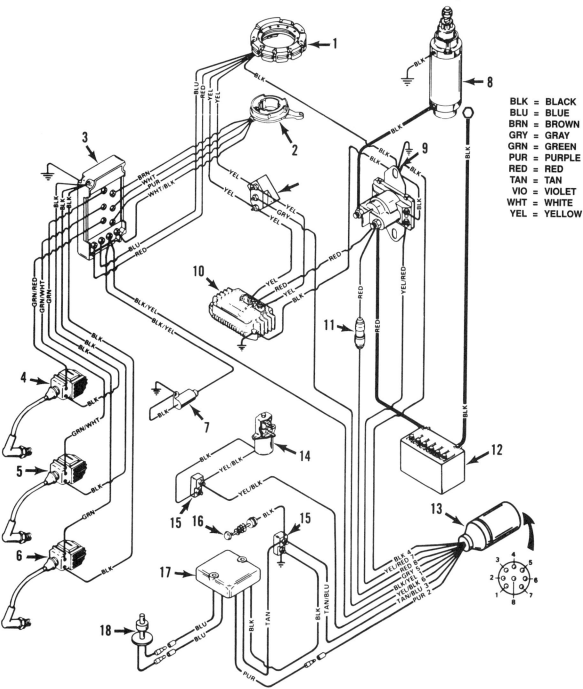

BLK = BLACK
BLU = BLUE
BRN = BROWN
GRY = GRAY
GRN = GREEN
PUR = PURPLE
RED = RED
TAN = TAN
VIO = VIOLET
WHT = WHITE
YEL = YELLOW

1. Stator
2. Trigger
3. Switch box
4. Ignition coil cylinder No. 1
5. Ignition coil cylinder No. 2
6. Ignition coil cylinder No. 3
7. Mercury (tilt) stop switch
8. Starter motor
9. Starter solenoid
10. Voltage regulator/rectifier
11. Fuse holder (20 Amp. fuse)
12. Battery
13. Wiring harness connector
14. Enrichment valve
15. Terminal block
16. Temperature switch
    Opens [170° F ± 8° (77° C ± 8°)]
    Closes [190° F ± 8° (88° C ± 8°)]
17. Low oil warning module
18. Low oil sensor

14

75 AND 90 HP MODELS SERIAL NO. C221500–D081999
(WITHOUT LOW-OIL WARNING MODULE)

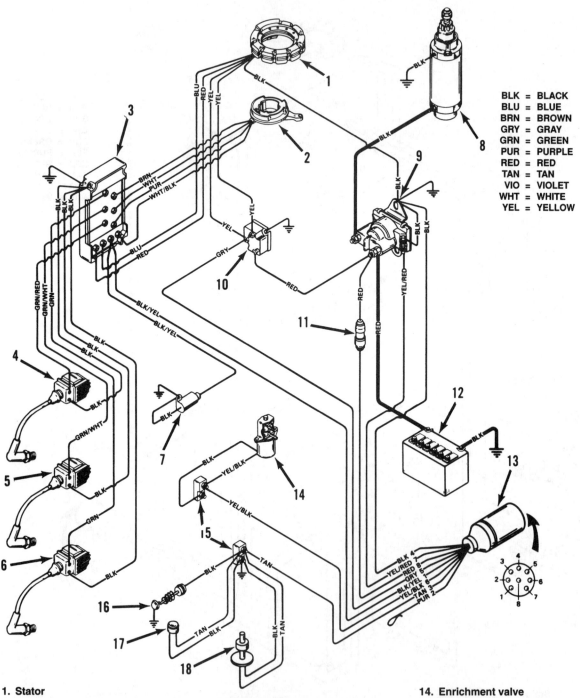

BLK = BLACK
BLU = BLUE
BRN = BROWN
GRY = GRAY
GRN = GREEN
PUR = PURPLE
RED = RED
TAN = TAN
VIO = VIOLET
WHT = WHITE
YEL = YELLOW

1. Stator
2. Trigger
3. Switch box
4. Ignition coil cylinder No. 1
5. Ignition coil cylinder No. 2
6. Ignition coil cylinder No. 3
7. Mercury (tilt) stop switch
8. Starter motor
9. Starter solenoid
10. Rectifier
11. Fuse holder (20 Amp. fuse)
12. Battery
13. Wiring harness connector
14. Enrichment valve
15. Terminal block
16. Temperature switch
    Opens [170° F ± 8° (77° C ± 8°)]
    Closes [190° F ± 8° (88° C ± 8°)]
17. Test button
18. Low oil sensor

75 AND 90 HP MODELS SERIAL NO. D082000–ON (WITH LOW OIL WARNING MODULE AND VOLTAGE REGULATOR/RECTIFIER)

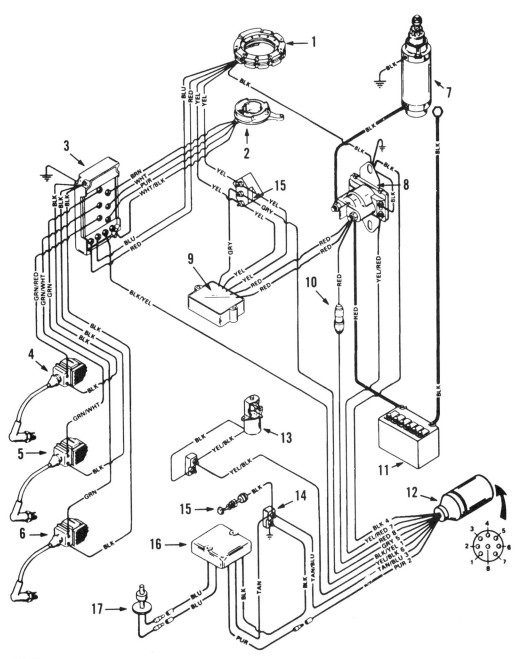

BLK = BLACK
BLU = BLUE
BRN = BROWN
GRY = GRAY
GRN = GREEN
PUR = PURPLE
RED = RED
TAN = TAN
VIO = VIOLET
WHT = WHITE
YEL = YELLOW

1. Stator
2. Trigger
3. Switch box
4. Ignition coil cylinder No. 1
5. Ignition coil cylinder No. 2
6. Ignition coil cylinder No. 3
7. Starter motor
8. Starter solenoid
9. Voltage regulator/rectifier

10. Fuse holder (20 Amp. fuse)
11. Battery
12. Wiring harness connector
13. Enrichment valve
14. Terminal block
15. Temperature switch
16. Low oil warning module
17. Low oil sensor

14

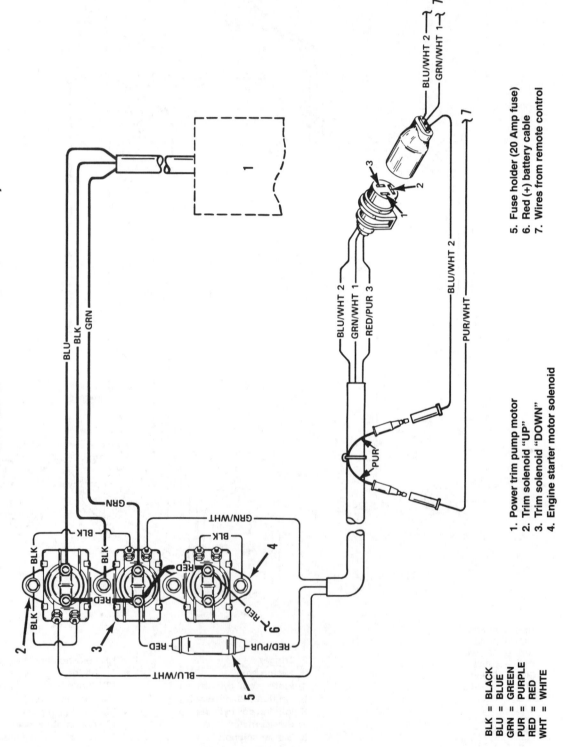

POWER TRIM SYSTEM 75 AND 90 HP MODELS (WITH COMMANDER SIDE-MOUNT REMOTE CONTROL)

1. Power trim pump motor
2. Trim solenoid "UP"
3. Trim solenoid "DOWN"
4. Engine starter motor solenoid
5. Fuse holder (20 Amp fuse)
6. Red (+) battery cable
7. Wires from remote control

BLK = BLACK
BLU = BLUE
GRN = GREEN
PUR = PURPLE
RED = RED
WHT = WHITE

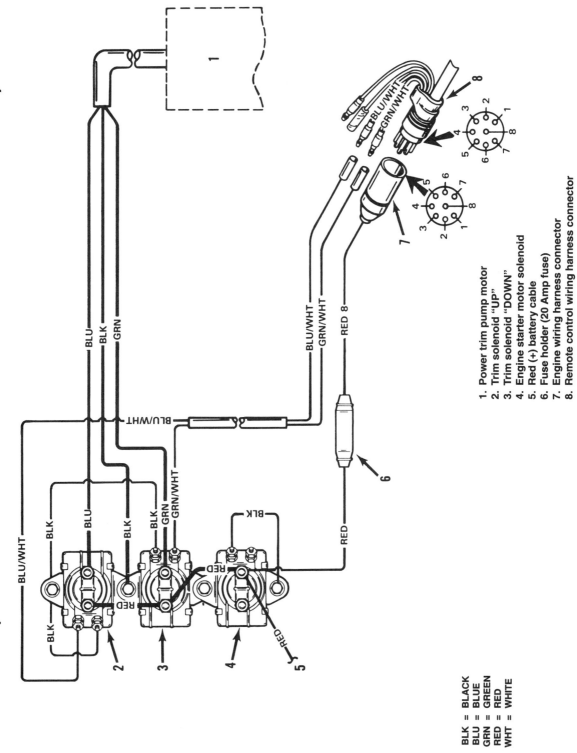

POWER TRIM SYSTEM 75 AND 90 HP MODELS (WITH COMMANDER 2000 SIDE-MOUNT REMOTE CONTROL)

1. Power trim pump motor
2. Trim solenoid "UP"
3. Trim solenoid "DOWN"
4. Engine starter motor solenoid
5. Red (+) battery cable
6. Fuse holder (20 Amp fuse)
7. Engine wiring harness connector
8. Remote control wiring harness connector

BLK = BLACK
BLU = BLUE
GRN = GREEN
RED = RED
WHT = WHITE

14

75 AND 90 HP MODELS SERIAL NO. D082000–ON
(WITHOUT OIL INJECTION)

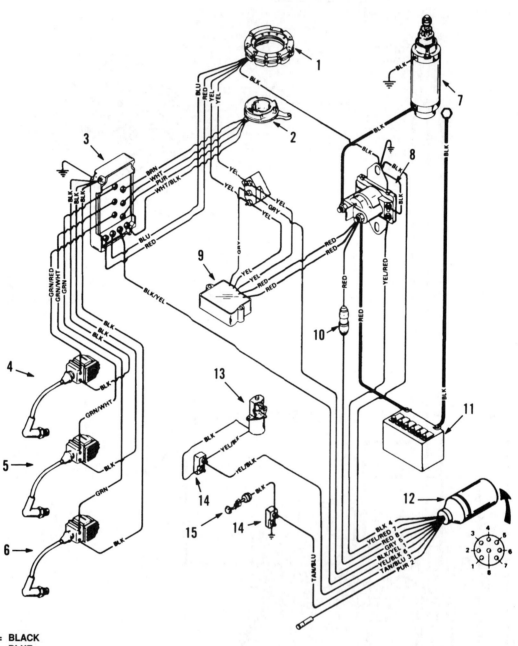

BLK = BLACK
BLU = BLUE
BRN = BROWN
GRY = GRAY
GRN = GREEN
PUR = PURPLE
RED = RED
TAN = TAN
VIO = VIOLET
WHT = WHITE
YEL = YELLOW

1. Stator
2. Trigger
3. Switch box
4. Ignition coil cylinder No. 1
5. Ignition coil cylinder No. 2
6. Ignition coil cylinder No. 3
7. Starter motor
8. Starter solenoid

9. Rectifier
10. Fuse holder (20 Amp. fuse)
11. Battery
12. Wiring harness connector
13. Enrichment valve
14. Terminal block
15. Temperature sensor

100 AND 115 HP MODELS
PRIOR TO SERIAL NO. D082000

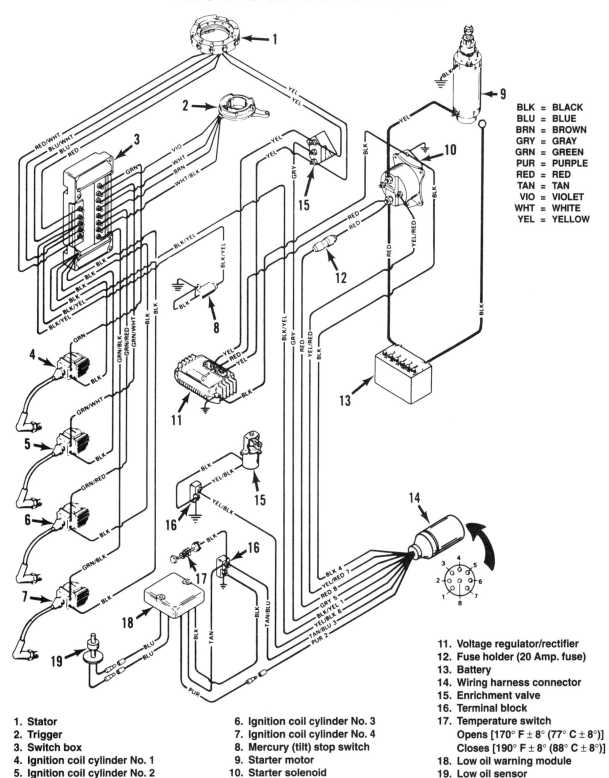

BLK = BLACK
BLU = BLUE
BRN = BROWN
GRY = GRAY
GRN = GREEN
PUR = PURPLE
RED = RED
TAN = TAN
VIO = VIOLET
WHT = WHITE
YEL = YELLOW

1. Stator
2. Trigger
3. Switch box
4. Ignition coil cylinder No. 1
5. Ignition coil cylinder No. 2
6. Ignition coil cylinder No. 3
7. Ignition coil cylinder No. 4
8. Mercury (tilt) stop switch
9. Starter motor
10. Starter solenoid
11. Voltage regulator/rectifier
12. Fuse holder (20 Amp. fuse)
13. Battery
14. Wiring harness connector
15. Enrichment valve
16. Terminal block
17. Temperature switch
   Opens [170° F ± 8° (77° C ± 8°)]
   Closes [190° F ± 8° (88° C ± 8°)]
18. Low oil warning module
19. Low oil sensor

14

100 AND 115 HP MODELS
SERIAL NO. D082000–ON

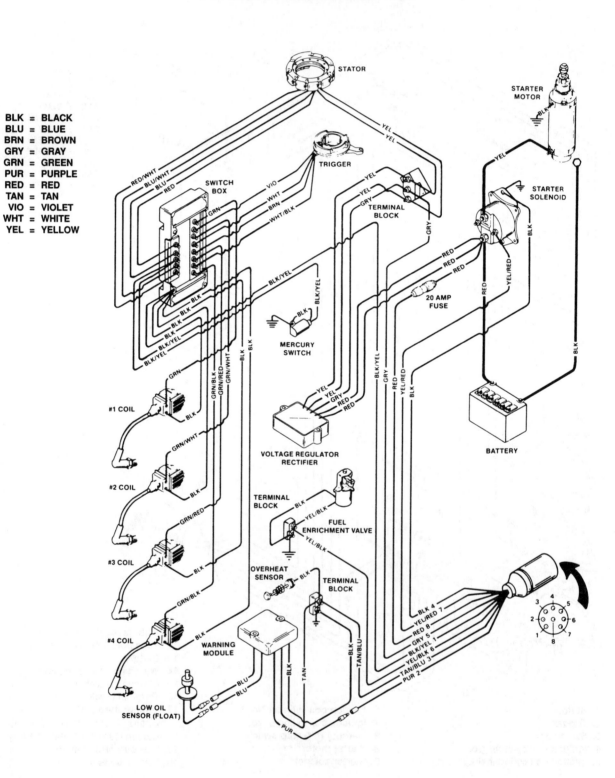

BLK = BLACK
BLU = BLUE
BRN = BROWN
GRY = GRAY
GRN = GREEN
PUR = PURPLE
RED = RED
TAN = TAN
VIO = VIOLET
WHT = WHITE
YEL = YELLOW

STATOR

STARTER MOTOR

STARTER SOLENOID

TRIGGER

SWITCH BOX

TERMINAL BLOCK

20 AMP FUSE

MERCURY SWITCH

BATTERY

VOLTAGE REGULATOR RECTIFIER

#1 COIL

#2 COIL

#3 COIL

#4 COIL

TERMINAL BLOCK

FUEL ENRICHMENT VALVE

OVERHEAT SENSOR

TERMINAL BLOCK

WARNING MODULE

LOW OIL SENSOR (FLOAT)

BLK 4
YEL/RED 7
RED 8
GRY 5
BLK/YEL 1
YEL/BLK 6
TAN/BLU 3
PUR 2

POWER TRIM SYSTEM 100 AND 115 HP MODELS
(WITH COMMANDER 2000 SIDE MOUNT REMOTE CONTROL)

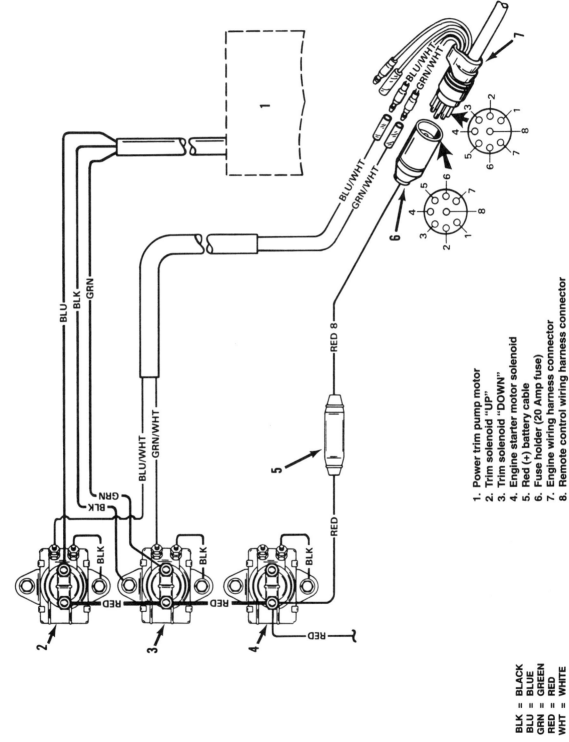

1. Power trim pump motor
2. Trim solenoid "UP"
3. Trim solenoid "DOWN"
4. Engine starter motor solenoid
5. Red (+) battery cable
6. Fuse holder (20 Amp fuse)
7. Engine wiring harness connector
8. Remote control wiring harness connector

BLK = BLACK
BLU = BLUE
GRN = GREEN
RED = RED
WHT = WHITE

14

135, 150 AND 175 HP MODELS
(WITH 16 AMP STATOR)

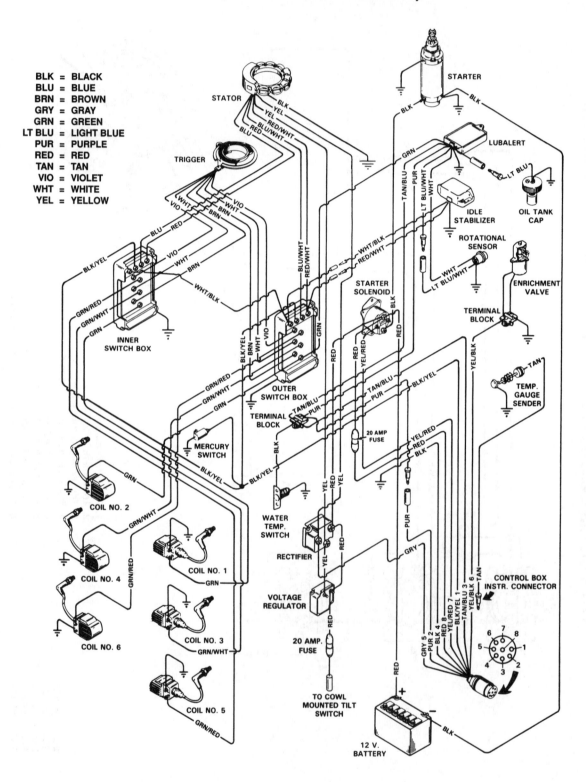

BLK = BLACK
BLU = BLUE
BRN = BROWN
GRY = GRAY
GRN = GREEN
LT BLU = LIGHT BLUE
PUR = PURPLE
RED = RED
TAN = TAN
VIO = VIOLET
WHT = WHITE
YEL = YELLOW

135, 150 AND 175 HP; 200 HP SERIAL NO. C291560-D077246 (WITH 40 AMP STATOR)

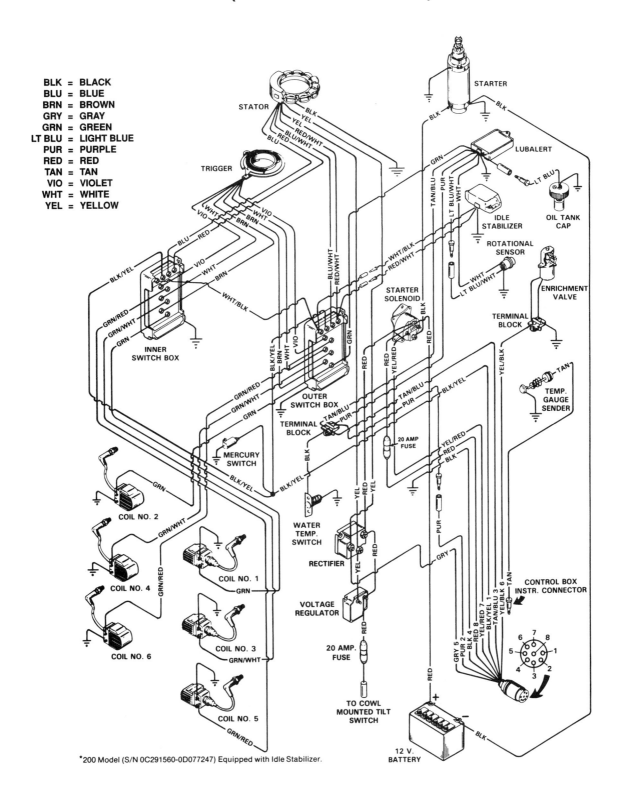

BLK = BLACK
BLU = BLUE
BRN = BROWN
GRY = GRAY
GRN = GREEN
LT BLU = LIGHT BLUE
PUR = PURPLE
RED = RED
TAN = TAN
VIO = VIOLET
WHT = WHITE
YEL = YELLOW

STATOR

TRIGGER

INNER SWITCH BOX

MERCURY SWITCH

COIL NO. 2

COIL NO. 4

COIL NO. 6

COIL NO. 1

COIL NO. 3

COIL NO. 5

OUTER SWITCH BOX

TERMINAL BLOCK

WATER TEMP. SWITCH

RECTIFIER

VOLTAGE REGULATOR

20 AMP. FUSE

TO COWL MOUNTED TILT SWITCH

STARTER

LUBALERT

IDLE STABILIZER

OIL TANK CAP

ROTATIONAL SENSOR

ENRICHMENT VALVE

TERMINAL BLOCK

STARTER SOLENOID

20 AMP FUSE

TEMP. GAUGE SENDER

LT BLU

CONTROL BOX INSTR. CONNECTOR

12 V. BATTERY

*200 Model (S/N 0C291560-0D077247) Equipped with Idle Stabilizer.

14

200 HP MODELS (SERIAL NO. D077247–ON WITH IDLE STABILIZER/SPARK ADVANCE MODULE)

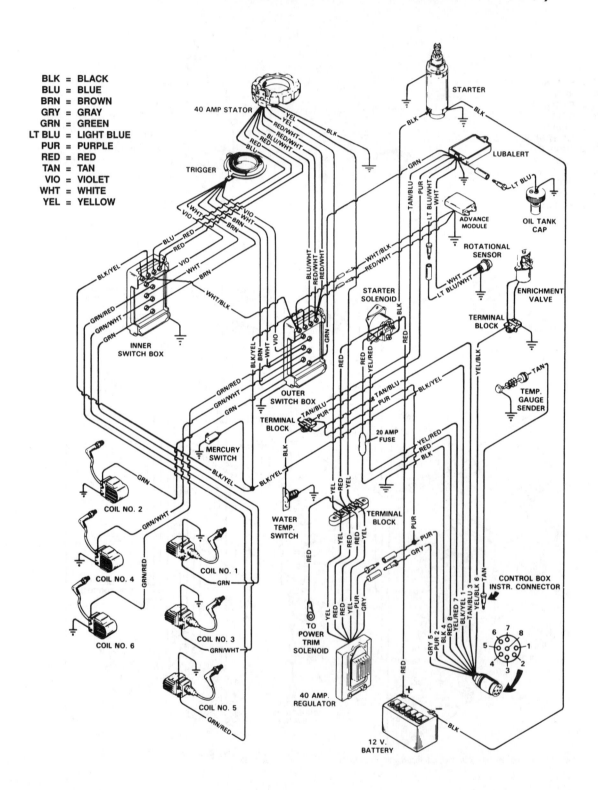

BLK = BLACK
BLU = BLUE
BRN = BROWN
GRY = GRAY
GRN = GREEN
LT BLU = LIGHT BLUE
PUR = PURPLE
RED = RED
TAN = TAN
VIO = VIOLET
WHT = WHITE
YEL = YELLOW

40 AMP STATOR

STARTER

LUBALERT

OIL TANK CAP

TRIGGER

TAN/BLU
PUR
LT BLU/WHT
WHT

ADVANCE MODULE

LT BLU

ROTATIONAL SENSOR

WHT
LT BLU/WHT

ENRICHMENT VALVE

BLK/YEL

INNER SWITCH BOX

GRN/RED
GRN/WHT
GRN

WHT/BLK

BLU/WHT
RED/WHT
RED/WHT

STARTER SOLENOID

TERMINAL BLOCK

YEL/BLK

TAN

TEMP. GAUGE SENDER

GRN/RED
GRN/WHT
GRN

OUTER SWITCH BOX

TERMINAL BLOCK

TAN/BLU
PUR

TAN/BLU
PUR

BLK/YEL

20 AMP FUSE

YEL/RED
RED
BLK

MERCURY SWITCH

BLK/YEL
BLK/YEL

COIL NO. 2

GRN

WATER TEMP. SWITCH

TERMINAL BLOCK

PUR

CONTROL BOX INSTR. CONNECTOR

GRN/WHT

COIL NO. 4

GRN/RED

COIL NO. 1

GRN

RED

PUR
GRY

YEL
RED
YEL
PUR
GRY

COIL NO. 6

COIL NO. 3

GRN/WHT

TO POWER TRIM SOLENOID

GRY 5
PUR 2
BLK 8
RED 4
YEL/RED 7
BLK/YEL 1
TAN/BLU 3
YEL/BLK 6
TAN

6 7 8
5   1
4 3 2

COIL NO. 5

GRN/RED

40 AMP. REGULATOR

RED

12 V. BATTERY

BLK

150XR4 MODELS (SERIAL NO. C248591–C254931)
WITH IDLE STABILIZER/SPARK ADVANCE MODULE

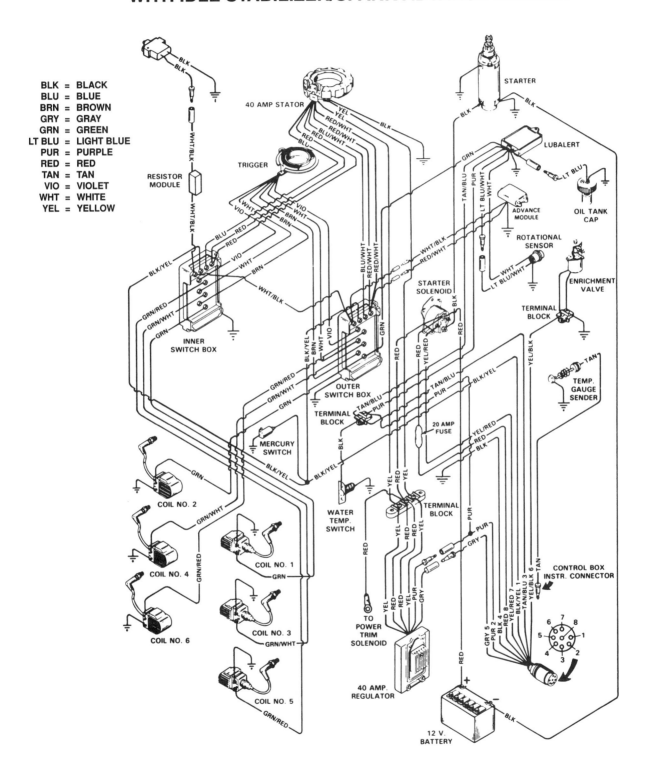

BLK = BLACK
BLU = BLUE
BRN = BROWN
GRY = GRAY
GRN = GREEN
LT BLU = LIGHT BLUE
PUR = PURPLE
RED = RED
TAN = TAN
VIO = VIOLET
WHT = WHITE
YEL = YELLOW

150XR4 MODELS (SERIAL NO. C254932–D081999) WITH IDLE STABILIZER MODULE

BLK = BLACK
BLU = BLUE
BRN = BROWN
GRY = GRAY
GRN = GREEN
LT BLU = LIGHT BLUE
PUR = PURPLE
RED = RED
TAN = TAN
VIO = VIOLET
WHT = WHITE
YEL = YELLOW

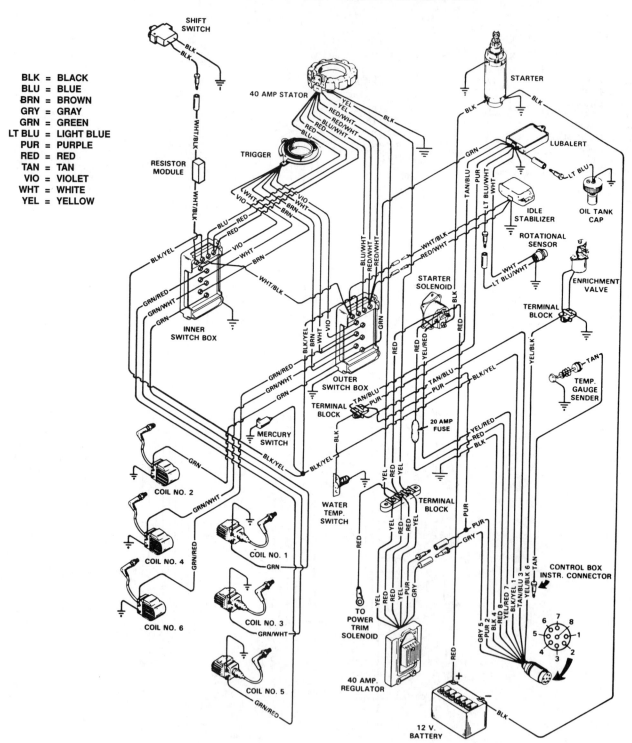

150XR6 MODELS

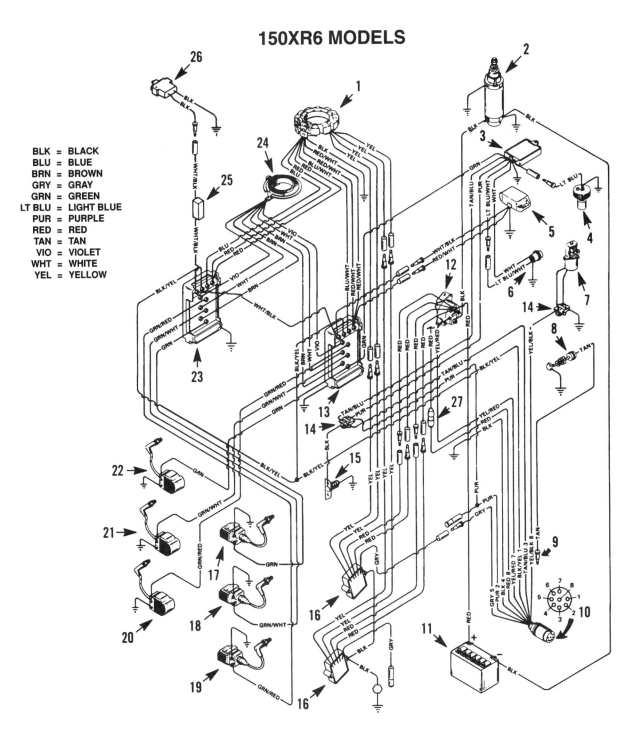

BLK = BLACK
BLU = BLUE
BRN = BROWN
GRY = GRAY
GRN = GREEN
LT BLU = LIGHT BLUE
PUR = PURPLE
RED = RED
TAN = TAN
VIO = VIOLET
WHT = WHITE
YEL = YELLOW

1. 40 ampere stator
2. Starter
3. Lubalert
4. Oil tank cap
5. Idle stabilizer
6. Rotational sensor
7. Enrichment valve
8. Temperature gauge sender
9. Control box instrument connector
10. Engine harness
11. 12V battery
12. Starter solenoid
13. Outer switch box
14. Terminal block
15. Water temperature switch
16. Voltage regulator
17. Coil #1
18. Coil #3
19. Coil #5
20. Coil #6
21. Coil #4
22. Coil #2
23. Inner switch box
24. Trigger
25. Resistor
26. Shift switch
27. 20 ampere fuse

14

135-200 HP MODELS WITH 40 AMP
STATOR AND DUAL VOLTAGE REGULATORS

BLK = BLACK
BLU = BLUE
BRN = BROWN
GRY = GRAY
GRN = GREEN
LT BLU = LIGHT BLUE
PUR = PURPLE
RED = RED
TAN = TAN
VIO = VIOLET
WHT = WHITE
YEL = YELLOW

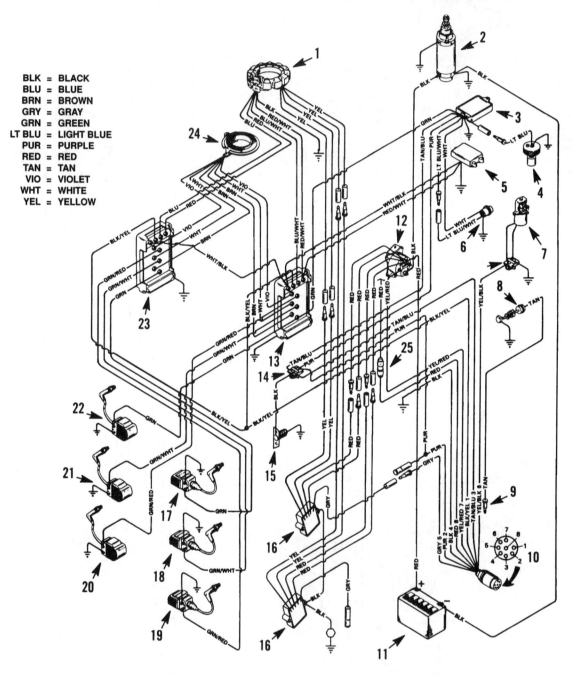

1. 40 ampere stator
2. Starter
3. Lubealert
4. Oil tank cap
5. Advance module
6. Rotational sensor
7. Enrichment valve

8. Temperature gauge sender
9. Control box instrument connector
10. Engine harness
11. 12V battery
12. Starter solenoid
13. Outer switch box

14. Terminal block
15. Water temperature switch
16. Voltage regulator
17. Coil #1
18. Coil #3
19. Coil #5

20. Coil #6
21. Coil #4
22. Coil #2
23. Inner switch box
24. Trigger
25. 20 ampere fuse

175XRi (EFI) MODELS

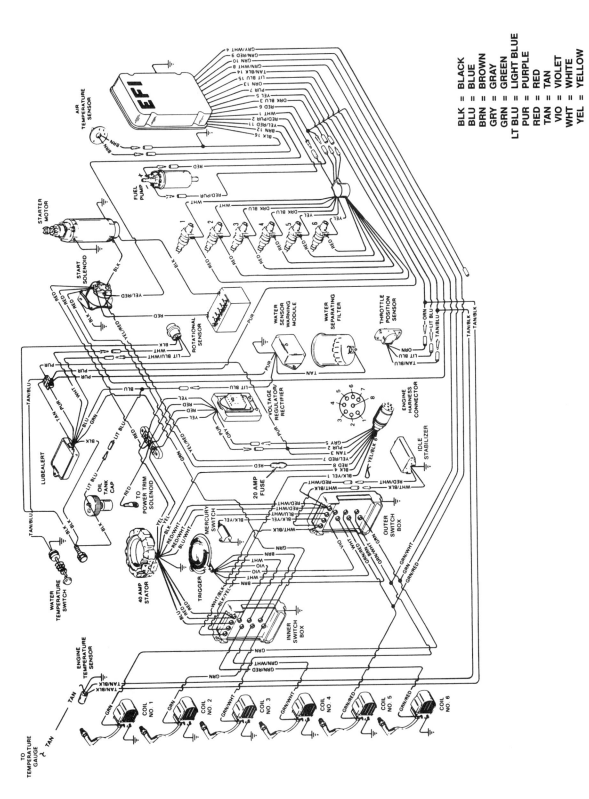

BLK = BLACK
BLU = BLUE
BRN = BROWN
GRY = GRAY
GRN = GREEN
LT BLU = LIGHT BLUE
PUR = PURPLE
RED = RED
TAN = TAN
VIO = VIOLET
WHT = WHITE
YEL = YELLOW

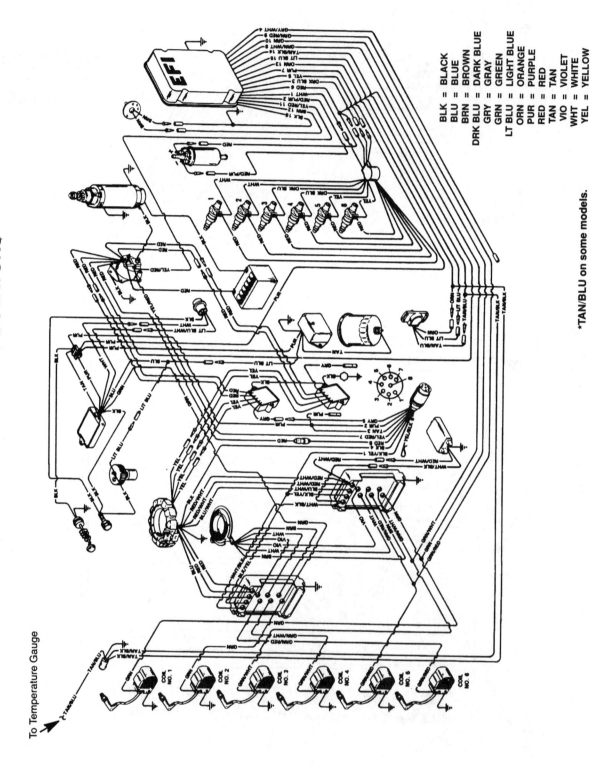

150XRi AND 175XRi MODELS WITH DUAL VOLTAGE REGULATORS

BLK = BLACK
BLU = BLUE
BRN = BROWN
DRK BLU = DARK BLUE
GRY = GRAY
GRN = GREEN
LT BLU = LIGHT BLUE
ORN = ORANGE
PUR = PURPLE
RED = RED
TAN = TAN
VIO = VIOLET
WHT = WHITE
YEL = YELLOW

*TAN/BLU on some models.

To Temperature Gauge

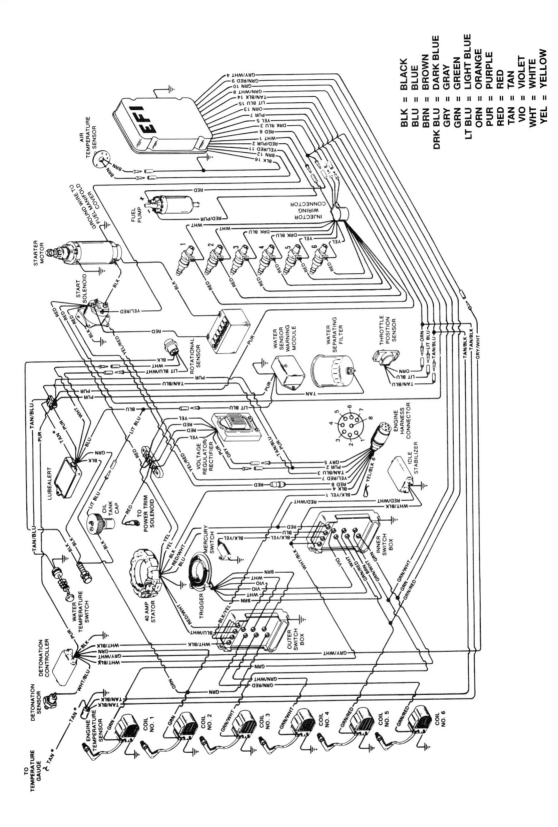

200XRi (EFI) MODELS

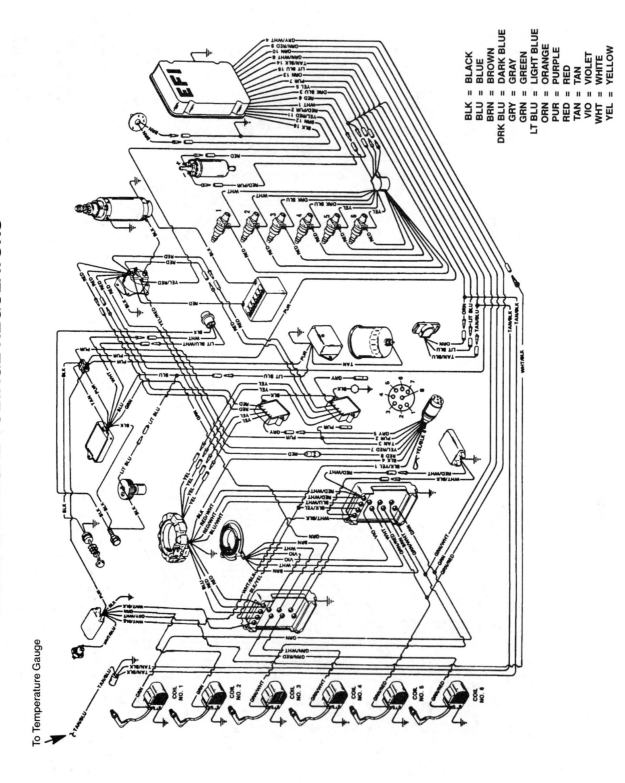

200XRi WITH DUAL VOLTAGE REGULATORS

To Temperature Gauge

BLK = BLACK
BLU = BLUE
BRN = BROWN
DRK BLU = DARK BLUE
GRY = GRAY
GRN = GREEN
LT BLU = LIGHT BLUE
ORN = ORANGE
PUR = PURPLE
RED = RED
TAN = TAN
VIO = VIOLET
WHT = WHITE
YEL = YELLOW

POWER TRIM SYSTEM
135-200 HP MODELS

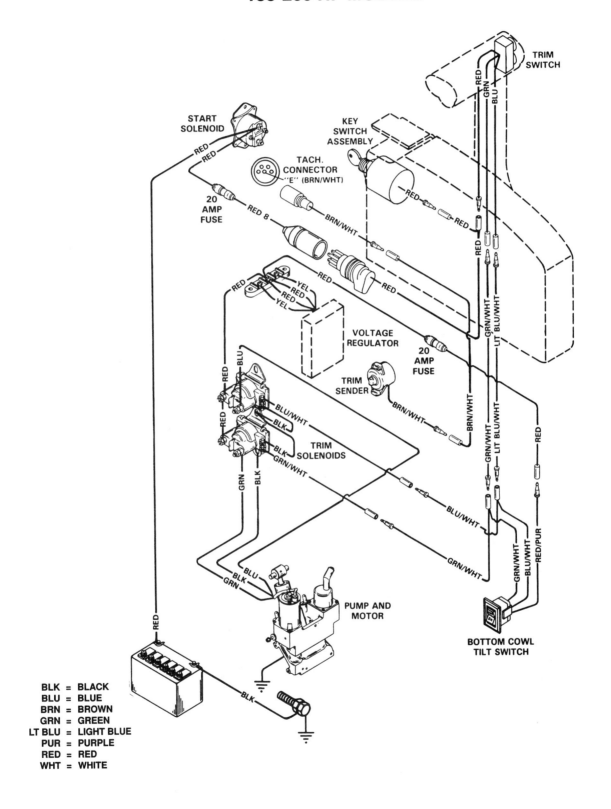

BLK = BLACK
BLU = BLUE
BRN = BROWN
GRN = GREEN
LT BLU = LIGHT BLUE
PUR = PURPLE
RED = RED
WHT = WHITE

14

250 AND 275 HP MODELS
(WITH 16 AMP STATOR)

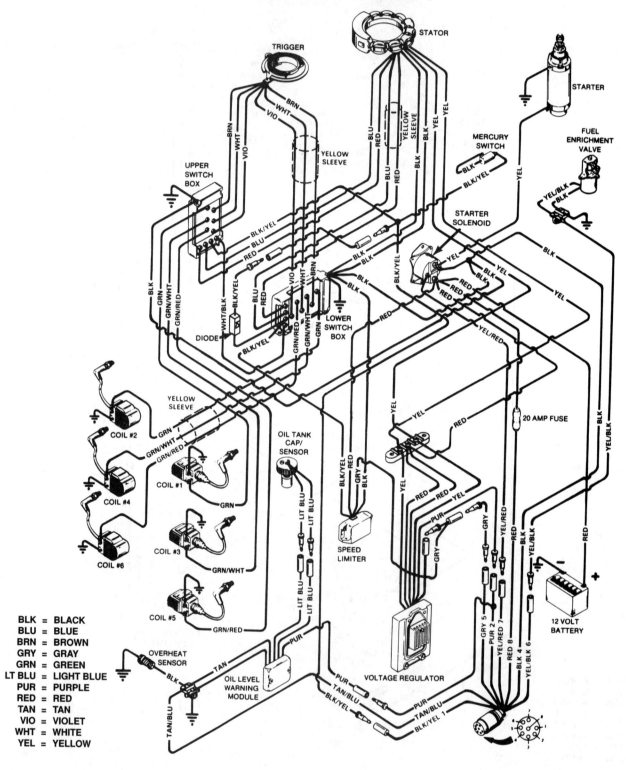

BLK = BLACK
BLU = BLUE
BRN = BROWN
GRY = GRAY
GRN = GREEN
LT BLU = LIGHT BLUE
PUR = PURPLE
RED = RED
TAN = TAN
VIO = VIOLET
WHT = WHITE
YEL = YELLOW

250 AND 275 HP MODELS
(WITH 40 AMP STATOR)

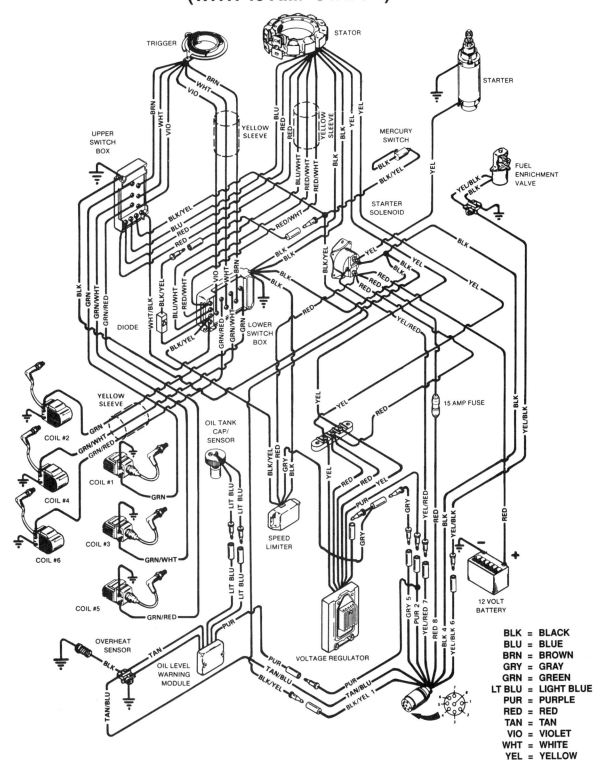

BLK = BLACK
BLU = BLUE
BRN = BROWN
GRY = GRAY
GRN = GREEN
LT BLU = LIGHT BLUE
PUR = PURPLE
RED = RED
TAN = TAN
VIO = VIOLET
WHT = WHITE
YEL = YELLOW

14

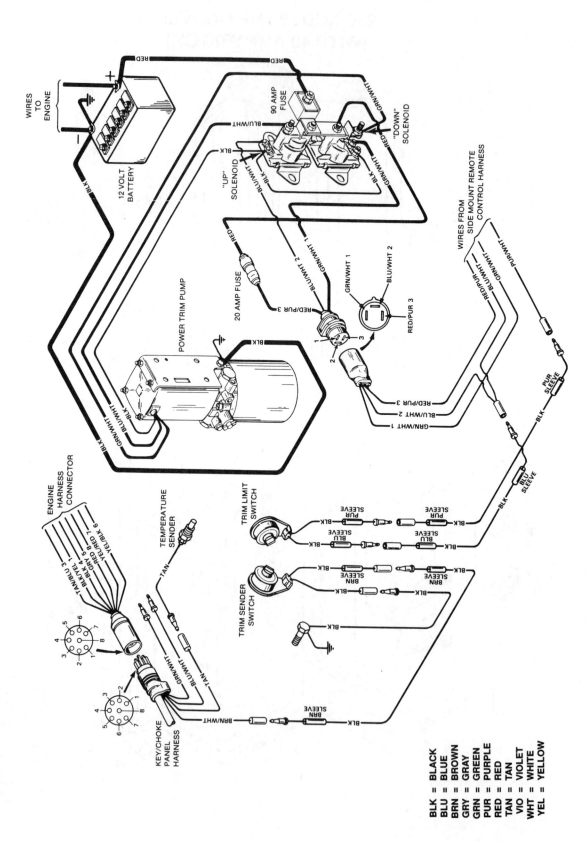

POWER TRIM SYSTEM
250 AND 275 HP MODELS

WIRES TO ENGINE

12 VOLT BATTERY

90 AMP FUSE

"DOWN" SOLENOID

"UP" SOLENOID

WIRES FROM SIDE MOUNT REMOTE CONTROL HARNESS

POWER TRIM PUMP

20 AMP FUSE

ENGINE HARNESS CONNECTOR

TEMPERATURE SENDER

TRIM LIMIT SWITCH

TRIM SENDER SWITCH

KEY/CHOKE PANEL HARNESS

BLK = BLACK
BLU = BLUE
BRN = BROWN
GRY = GRAY
GRN = GREEN
PUR = PURPLE
RED = RED
TAN = TAN
VIO = VIOLET
WHT = WHITE
YEL = YELLOW

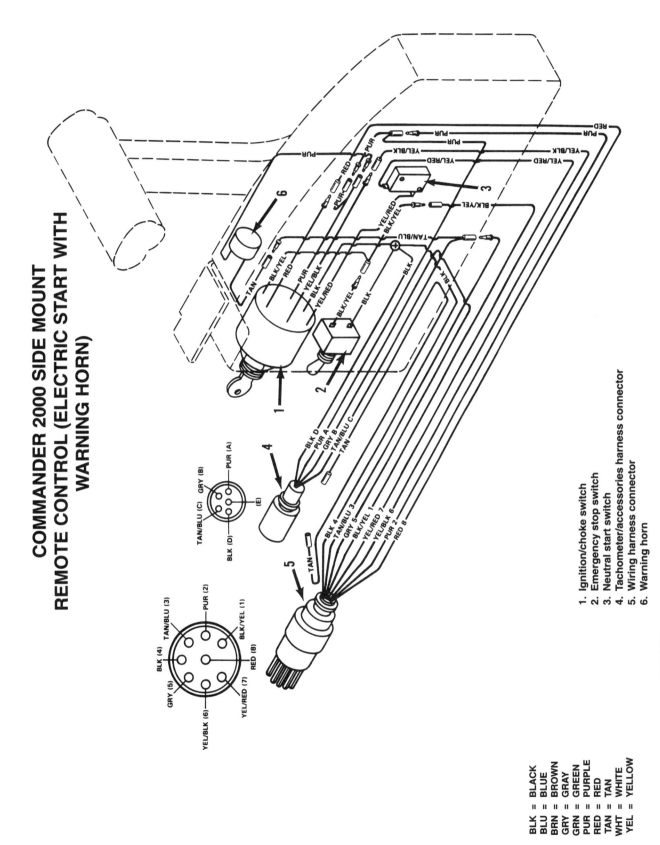

COMMANDER 2000 SIDE MOUNT
REMOTE CONTROL (ELECTRIC START WITH
WARNING HORN)

1. Ignition/choke switch
2. Emergency stop switch
3. Neutral start switch
4. Tachometer/accessories harness connector
5. Wiring harness connector
6. Warning horn

BLK = BLACK
BLU = BLUE
BRN = BROWN
GRY = GRAY
GRN = GREEN
PUR = PURPLE
RED = RED
TAN = TAN
WHT = WHITE
YEL = YELLOW

14

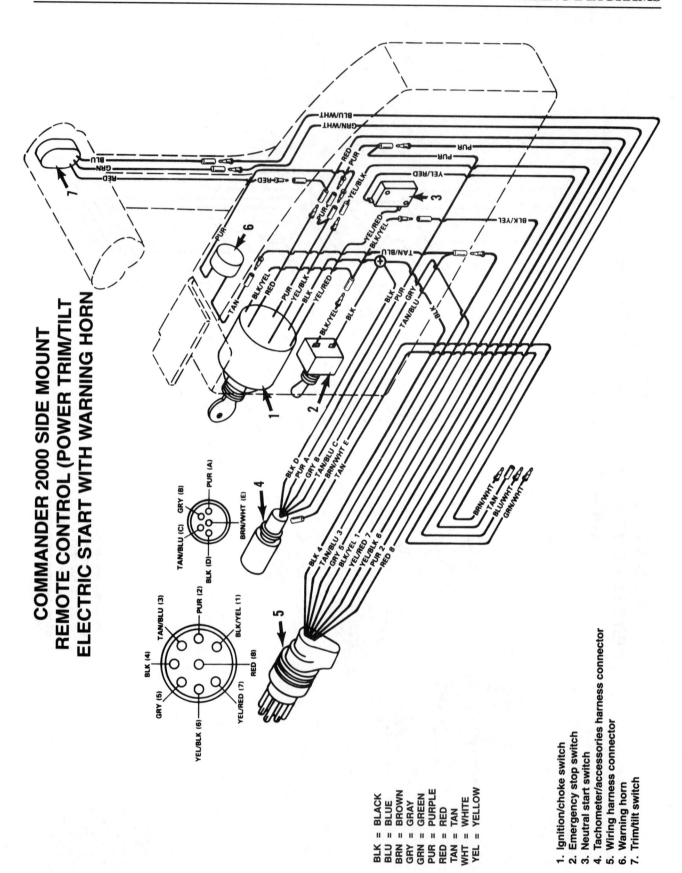

**COMMANDER 2000 SIDE MOUNT
REMOTE CONTROL (POWER TRIM/TILT
ELECTRIC START WITH WARNING HORN**

BLK = BLACK
BLU = BLUE
BRN = BROWN
GRY = GRAY
GRN = GREEN
PUR = PURPLE
RED = RED
TAN = TAN
WHT = WHITE
YEL = YELLOW

1. Ignition/choke switch
2. Emergency stop switch
3. Neutral start switch
4. Tachometer/accessories harness connector
5. Wiring harness connector
6. Warning horn
7. Trim/tilt switch

COMMANDER SIDE MOUNT
REMOTE CONTROL (POWER TRIM/TILT
ELECTRIC START WITH WARNING HORN)

1. Ignition/choke switch
2. Emergency stop switch
3. Neutral start switch
4. Tachometer/accessories harness connector
5. Wiring harness connector
6. Warning horn
7. Trim/tilt switch
8. Wire retainer
9. Control handle
10. Trim harness bushing
11. Trim harness connector
12. Lead to trim indicator gauge

BLK = BLACK
BLU = BLUE
BRN = BROWN
GRY = GRAY
GRN = GREEN
LT BLU = LIGHT BLUE
PUR = PURPLE
RED = RED
TAN = TAN
WHT = WHITE
YEL = YELLOW

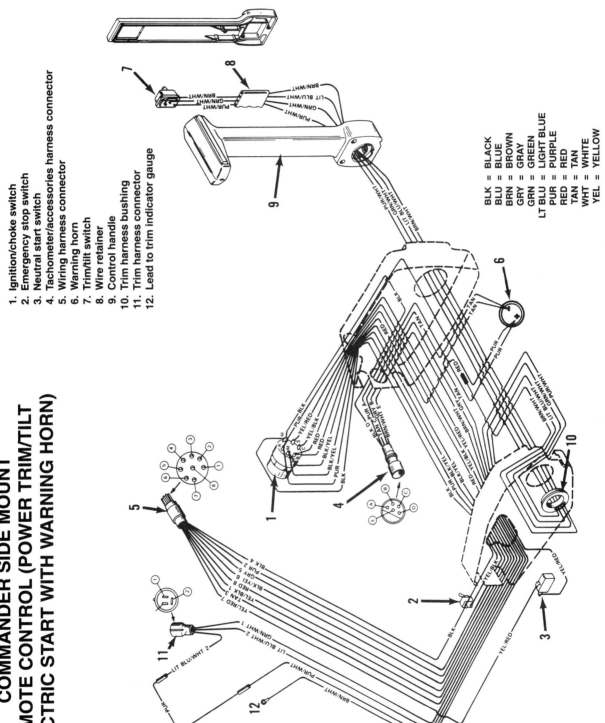

14

NOTES

NOTES

NOTES

MAINTENANCE LOG

Service Performed	Mileage Reading				
Oil change (example)	2,836	5,782	8,601		